Dun & Bradstreet's Guide to

$YOUR

INVESTMENTS$℠

1982

Twenty-Seventh Edition

C. COLBURN HARDY, R.I.A.

HARPER & ROW, PUBLISHERS, New York
Cambridge, Philadelphia, San Francisco, London,
Mexico City, São Paulo, Sydney

1817

Every attempt has been made to assure the accuracy of the statistics that appear throughout *Your Investments*. In some cases, data may vary from your reports because of interpretations or accounting changes made after the original publication. In others, there may be errors—for which we apologize. Please remember that *Your Investments* is a *guide,* not a definitive source of financial information. When you have a question, check with your broker's Research Department.

The title *$Your Investments$* is a registered trademark of Harper & Row, Publishers, Inc.

DUN & BRADSTREET'S GUIDE TO $YOUR INVESTMENTS$ 1982. Copyright © 1982, 1981, 1980, 1979, 1978, 1977, 1976, 1975, 1974, 1973 by Harper & Row, Publishers, Inc. All rights reserved. Printed in the United States of America. No part of this book may be used or reproduced in any manner whatsoever without written permission except in the case of brief quotations embodied in critical articles and reviews. For information address Harper & Row. Publishers, Inc., 10 East 53rd Street, New York, N.Y. 10022. Published simultaneously in Canada by Fitzhenry & Whiteside Limited, Toronto.

ISBN 0–06–014935–3   82 83 84 85 86 10 9 8 7 6 5 4 3 2 1
ISBN 0–06–090928–5   82 83 84 85 86 10 9 8 7 6 5 4 3 2 1

LIBRARY OF CONGRESS CATALOG CARD NUMBER 73–18050

Contents

EDITOR:

C. Colburn Hardy

SENIOR EDITORS:

Ruth E. Hart
Hart Munn

EDITORIAL ASSOCIATES:

Jonas Blake
Clark Hunt
Dorcas R. Hardy

FOUNDING AUTHOR:

Leo D. Barnes, Ph.D.

About the Editor

C. Colburn Hardy, who has edited *Your Investments* since 1974, is the author of over 1,300 articles on investments, money management, estate/financial planning and retirement. He has written eight books, five under his own name: *Funk & Wagnall's Personal Money Management, ABCs of Investing Your Retirement Funds, Investor's Guide to Technical Analysis, Your Money & Your Life* and *Safe in Retirement;* three others for or with nationally known authorities; and is currently completing two new publications: *Inflation-Proof Retirement* and *Q-V-T (Quality-Value-Timing): The Three Keys to Successful Investing* (with John Winthrop Wright).

Mr. Hardy is financial editor of *Physician's Management* and a frequent contributor to business publications. He is registered as an investment adviser with the Securities and Exchange Commission and has appeared as a feature speaker at financial seminars, has taught at colleges, and is a regular guest on both local and national radio and TV programs.

A Phi Beta Kappa graduate of Yale, Mr. Hardy worked as a public relations executive with major agencies and corporations before taking early retirement to start a second career as a writer. He now lives in West Palm Beach, Florida, in, as described on one book jacket, "a manner that suggests the potential benefits from his advice."

With Professional Assistance From:

Victor D. Aldeheff, *ENI Corp.*
Alph C. Beane, Sr., *Dean Witter Reynolds*
Alph C. Beane, Jr., *Dean Witter Reynolds*
Richard Blackman, *Richard Blackman & Co.*
Garrett Cole, *Oppenheimer Industries*
Richard D. Donchian, *Shearson Loeb Rhoades*
Leroy Gross, *Dean Witter Reynolds*
John B. Halper, *Real Estate Consultant*
Hans Jacobsen, *Herzog, Heine & Geduld*
Glenn Johnson, *Federated Funds*
James A. Lebenthal, *Lebenthal & Co.*
Jack Maurer, *Indicator Digest*
Robert W. Ross, *Shearson Loeb Rhoades*
Robert W. Stovall, *Dean Witter Reynolds*
D. Bruce Trainor, *Omni-Exploration*
John Winthrop Wright, *Wright Investors' Service*

Advanced Investment Strategies
American Birthright Trust
Bache Halsey Stuart Shields
Barron's
Boardroom Reports
Bottom Line
Business Week
Canadian Business Service
Chicago Board of Options
Chicago Board of Trade
Comex Exchange
Federal Reserve Bank of New York
Financial Weekly
Financial World
Forbes
Fortune
International Monetary Exchange
Investment Company Institute
Merrill Lynch, Pierce, Fenner & Smith
Money
The Money Reporter
Moody's Investors Service
Municipal Bond Insurance Association
New York Times
Physician's Management
Research Institute of America
Securities Research Company
Standard & Poor's
Stock Research Corp.
T. Rowe Price, Inc.
United Business Service
Vanguard Group
Wall Street Journal
Zweig Advisory Service

And special credit for assistance from:
American Stock Exchange
National Association of Securities Dealers
New York Stock Exchange

Introduction

If it were possible, this book would carry a guarantee of investment success—that everyone who reads *Your Investments* carefully, heeds the advice and uses common sense will make a *lot of money* over a period of time. And, better yet, losses will be few and small.

There are no tricks, no real risks. All you need is consistent savings, carefully selected investments and prompt reinvestment of all income.

The basis for these "guaranteed profits" is the record of the "Sample Portfolios for Times of Your Life." Since they were first suggested in the edition that went on sale in January 1976, these securities have shown an average annual rate of return of well over 16%: income plus appreciation. Last year, the four portfolios averaged +43%! And those selections were made in May—seven months prior to publication—and could not be changed. Surely, if a writer can achieve such a consistent record of profits, the serious investor who can control timing should do even better. (N.B. It is impossible to set exact rates of return over the years because some stocks were sold, or bought, for illustration; dividends were estimated; and there were no deductions for commissions and fees.)

That *lot of money* depends on how much and how long you save, but, as detailed later, with compounding and with investments in personal pension plans where taxes are deferred until withdrawal, almost everyone under age 25 can retire a millionaire. Annual savings of $1,000, invested at 15%, will grow to over $2 million in 40 years, the average working lifetime. Or if you're older, that magic million will require less than $5,000 annually for 25 years.

Or to put it another way, a $10,000 trust fund, set up at the birth of a child or grandchild, invested in a 15% bond with interest reinvested, will grow to $180,442 when the youngster is 20 years old and to $3,225,594 in 40 years. Granted, that million won't buy as much in the future as it would today but it still will be nice to have.

These huge sums are the result of the Magic of Compounding: earning income on income. The tables below point up the wisdom and profitability of setting up and maintaining a regular savings program or of making an early-in-life gift to someone you love. Pension plans, with their almost mandated deposits, make such savings easier; but if you have extra assets, you should start your program now.

ANOTHER VIEW OF COMPOUNDING

Rate of Return	Average Annual Return on Original Investment				
	5 yrs.	10 yrs.	15 yrs.	20 yrs.	25 yrs.
6%	6.8%	7.9%	9.3%	11.0%	13.2%
7	8.1	9.7	11.7	14.3	17.7
8	9.4	11.6	14.5	18.3	23.4
9	10.8	13.7	17.6	23.0	30.5
10	12.2	15.9	21.1	28.6	39.3
11	13.7	18.4	25.2	35.3	50.3
12	15.2	21.0	29.8	43.2	64.0

Or if you want to know how long it takes for your savings to double, at various rates of return, use the rule of 72: divide 72 by the yield: i.e. at 12%, 6 years; at 15%, 4.8 years.

THE POWER OF COMPOUND INTEREST

A regular investment of $100 per year, invested at:	Will, compounded annually, grow to this sum after this number of years							
	5	10	15	20	25	30	35	40
6%	$598	$1,397	$2,467	$3,899	$5,816	$8,380	$11,812	$16,404
8	634	1,565	2,932	4,942	7,895	12,234	18,610	27,978
9	652	1,656	3,200	5,576	9,232	14,857	23,512	35,820
10	671	1,753	3,496	6,300	10,818	18,094	29,812	48,685
12	712	1,965	4,175	8,070	14,933	27,029	48,346	85,914
13	732	2,081	4,567	9,347	17,585	33,132	61,775	114,549
14	754	2,204	4,998	10,377	20,733	40,674	79,067	152,991
15	775	2,335	5,472	11,781	24,471	49,957	101,335	204,595

To get the corresponding total for any other annually invested amount (A), multiply the dollar total given above for the interest rate and number of years by $\frac{A}{100}$. Example: You plan to invest $75 per month, $900 per year. What capital sum will that provide after 35 years, at 10% compounded annually? Check where the lines cross for 10% and 35 years.

Answer: $29,812 \times \frac{900}{100} = $268,308.

Like most worthwhile concepts, the basic principles are simple: Quality, Value and Timing plus Compounding. To make the most money, buy stocks of strong companies that continue to make high profits and reinvest all income promptly.

This logical approach is far different from the alarms sounded by the gloomsayers and financial "wizards." These prophets denigrate American business and their "advice" is destructive for the investor. They tell you to buy gold at $800 an ounce; yet its recent price was under $500. They let you in on the secret of making millions in real estate by using other people's money: $1 down and a big, long-term mortgage. That approach may have had some merit with a 10% interest rate and a 15% annual appreciation, but not these days when you have to pay 15% for a short-term loan and property values are declining. Most of these "advisers" make more money from their books and lectures than they do by following their own investment counsel.

Once in a while, a few people (I won't call them investors) will be lucky enough to score by following temporary trends, but for most of us investing is a long-term process that requires study, review and patience.

This is the 27th edition of *Your Investments.* Any publication that has maintained interest for over a quarter of a century must be doing something right. The format may appear formidable but the text is easy to understand, the examples are clear and basic and the charts/tables are handy and relevant. As one reviewer, David R. Francis of the *Christian Science Monitor,* wrote last year, "Mr. Hardy has a solid, common-sense attitude. This is no get-rich-quick book advocating high risk, speculative investments that can also lose buckets of money.

"In fact, the book is so comprehensive in its consideration of investment theories, possibilities, and facts that the new would-be investor may find his head spinning. Hardy does not offer a specific buy-this, buy-that formula. Rather, he gives good advice on the mechanics of investment in various markets and on how to acquire the detailed knowledge needed for wise investment."

Your Investments is not an advisory service and has no products or services to sell. It is designed as a guide to the intelligent use of savings; through tables, charts and words, it shows you how to make more money with the money you have made or inherited.

Forget about fancy formulas, ratios, curves, square roots, the length of a dress hem, sunspots and such client-impressing terms as *alpha* and *beta.* All anyone has to do to accumulate wealth is to view the stock market as an investment device, not as a game or a gamble.

When you invest in shares of *quality* corporations (generally, companies that are financially strong, are leaders in their fields and have fairly consistent records of high profitability and growth), you will ALWAYS make money over a period of time.

Here's why:

If a company earned 15% on stockholders' equity (the money invested by shareholders), it ends the year with 15¢ per dollar more. Generally, the dividend payout is about 5¢ per share. That leaves 10¢ to be reinvested for future growth. Thus the underlying value of the corpora-

tion doubles in about 7.5 years. The same 15¢ rate of return will produce double the earnings and, often, double the dividends. Eventually these extra values will be reflected in the price of the common stock. That's why the best investments are shares of companies which keep on making a lot of money.

With *value* (the ratio of tomorrow's price to today's market quotation), the profits will come by buying when the stock is underpriced and selling when it becomes fully valued. Even if you buy too soon, you will profit as long as the company prospers.

Timing purchases and sales enhances profits and reduces losses. As is explained by many examples, the key points of timing can be determined by technical analysis—primarily charts, but often by other indices.

But, always, there must be common sense!

Keep in mind that when an *investor* buys any stock, he is acquiring a share in a business enterprise because he feels it is worthwhile holding regardless of any short- or intermediate-term action. When a *speculator* buys a security, he assumes that someone else will pay more; the sooner, the better.

Successful investing takes time and patience. Spectacular moves, up or down, are exciting, but they seldom last and they are usually followed by equally sharp reactions. The slow, steady advance is best because it builds a strong base and, when the upmove continues, protects capital and provides opportunities for big profits. The long view is hard to find in the financial press, but you can rely on your own research and common sense in making investments. You will be right 80% of the time, which is a much better record than that of most so-called professional money managers. The sample portfolios prove this. *To repeat:* Anyone with common sense can make money with investments in securities. This Guide will help you to do this.

I am still bullish on the stock market. Over many years of business and community activity, I have learned that, in America, the optimists are right more often than the pessimists.

There may be more rewarding opportunities in some areas abroad but when you invest in securities of established American corporations, you are buying proven performance. You can logically project the future values of their stocks and, as long as management is competent, you can count on substantial income and appreciation. That's *true* investing.

Inflation

No book on investments can ignore inflation. Actually, inflation is not as bad as the headlines (and politicians) proclaim. Some major expenditures, such as mortgage payments and straight life insurance premiums, remain the same over the years. And the basic data, projected from the Consumer Price Index, does not reflect actual costs—i.e., they assume that every family takes out a new mortgage every month and that people are eating more beef than chicken (as they were in the base years of 1972–73).

Still, inflation does erode purchasing power, as shown by this table:

FUTURE VALUE OF DOLLAR WITH INFLATION

Years Hence	At This Rate of Inflation			
	8%	10%	12%	15%
5	0.681	0.621	0.567	0.497
10	0.558	0.386	0.322	0.247
15	0.417	0.239	0.183	0.123
20	0.312	0.149	0.104	0.061
25	0.233	0.092	0.059	0.030
30	0.174	0.057	0.033	0.015

SOURCE: Stolper & Co., San Diego, Calif.

On the other hand, remember that inflation can work both ways. It raises the value of real property and boosts salaries/wages. In theory, property worth $70,000 today will cost $151,200 in 10 years with 8% inflation. And a $25,000 salary will grow to $54,000. Realistically, of course, there will probably be adjustments.

HOW TO CALCULATE THE EFFECT OF INFLATION

Years From Now	8%	10%	12%	15%
5	1.46	1.61	1.76	2.01
6	1.59	1.77	1.97	2.31
7	1.71	1.94	2.21	2.66
8	1.85	2.14	2.47	3.06
9	1.99	2.36	2.77	3.52
10	2.16	2.59	3.10	4.04
15	3.17	4.18	5.47	8.14
20	4.66	6.73	9.65	16.37
25	6.85	10.83	17.00	32.92
30	10.06	17.45	29.96	66.21

SOURCE: David Thorndike, ed. *The Thorndike Encyclopedia of Banking & Financial Tables* (Boston: Warren, Gorham & Lamont, 1977)

Common Stocks Can Beat Inflation

Common stocks can serve as an inflation hedge in two ways: rising market prices and increasing dividends. High interest rates hurt stocks over the short term but benefit them over the years of true investments. Throughout *Your Investments,* you will find examples of profitable corporations that keep on making 15%, 20%, even 25% on invested capital. Most of these companies share these gains with their stockholders with higher dividends. When their stock prices reflect these returns, their prices rise and the shareholders benefit.

Currently, many stocks are priced so low that you can buy assets at less than replacement value. This is discouraging. But keep the faith. Stock prices are like pendulums that swing back and forth from the middle line of rationality, which represents what a company is really worth. The stock market spends 90% of its time on one side or the other of that line. Lately, the pendulum, for most stocks, has been close to a nadir.

After you've gone through a few of these market cycles, you accept the fact that there is no way to assess how illogical major investors can be. Eventually, of course, the real world wins out and patient investors profit handsomely.

I have no idea when the market will start a real uptrend, or how long this will last, but analysts whom I respect are optimistic about the 1980s. John Winthrop Wright, whose firm manages over a billion dollars of fiduciary funds of some of the nation's largest corporations, projects the Dow Jones Industrial Average to over 1500 by 1986; and Edson Gould, who has been forecasting with considerable accuracy for 50 years, sees the Dow topping 3400 in 1990.

Already there are bullish signs. Major investors are more confident and are moving out of fixed-income holdings into equities. Once the yields of money market funds drop two or three points, more individual investors will shift to stocks. With this demand, stock prices will rise. And, at all times, smart investors can make money in the stock market when they are flexible, rely on facts and pay attention to what's happening.

Profits Ahead

To repeat and expand last year's comment: "Investors should be of good cheer. More than at any time in modern history, they have highly profitable investment opportunities." They can count on:

• *High yields of 15%* or more with short-term liquid assets such as Treasury bills, certificates of deposit and shares of money market funds; or, long-term, from well-rated corporate and government agency bonds.

• *Total returns of 16%* or more from quality common stocks.

And there is little indication that there will be significant changes in these returns in the near future.

But always stay flexible. Interest rates can move swiftly and even the best of companies can get into trouble or be adversely affected by temporary conditions outside management's control. These shifts will push down the prices of stocks for a while but if the value is there, it will be recognized, usually in 24 to 36 months, or, if there's a takeover move, more quickly.

The trend of the stock market has always been up and, I believe, will continue in the years ahead. See the full-page chart.

About This Edition

This year, the changes are extensive: almost all tables, charts and information have been edited, updated and revised to meet the astounding shifts that have occurred in the past year. In the chapters on real estate and tax shelters, the examples have been simplified and the caveats expanded so that readers can relate their holdings to those of more complicated deals.

Some chapters on general advice have been combined and others refocused to emphasize what appear to be future opportunities. And there are two new chapters: Money Market Funds and Financial Futures, both spinoffs from previous commentaries.

Throughout *Your Investments,* all material is designed and presented to help the individual investor with his or her personal savings: directly or through a pension/profit-sharing plan portfolio. The securities mentioned are *suggestions,* not recommendations. They are the type of

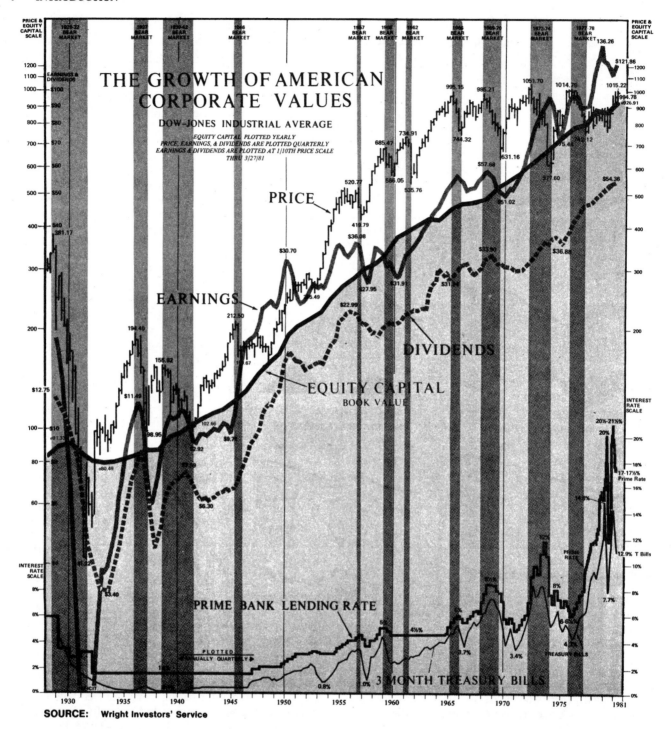

SOURCE: Wright Investors' Service

holdings to consider when they can help you meet your investment goals. But take nothing for granted and always check the latest data before committing any money. Investigate *before* you invest; *while* you invest; and, to improve your skill, *after* you have made the sale.

None of the counsel or techniques are applicable to all stocks at all times. They should be used only when common sense tells you that they are likely to be effective.

If you have any doubts, do not spend your money. It's just as important to sleep well as to make money.

The goals of *Your Investments* are the same as they

have been since the first edition: to provide information to help thoughtful investors understand securities and commodities, the operation of their markets and the standards and methods that have proven successful. In investing, there is no substitute for knowledge which, in turn, depends on information. Add a little luck and you can make your savings grow rapidly.

As you will learn from reading this book, the stock market is not as mysterious nor as complex as many people would have you believe. Wall Street is often puzzling, usually frustrating and frequently foolish . . . for a short while. This is understandable because the stock market is the end result of the fears, hopes, prejudices and pride of millions of people and billions of dollars. Their actions and reactions are influenced by rumors and headlines; too few are the result of facts and common sense. Yet, over the long-term, the stock market is logical, and facts and fundamentals will always prove rewarding.

In the stock market, there are profit-making opportunities regardless of the trend. There are certain industry groups or types of stocks which perform better than the averages. In this book you will find rules, concepts, facts and techniques to help you select those securities when they are undervalued and sell them when they become fully priced. Or, in erratic markets, to use leverage, sell short, use options or warrants, or cash in with bonds and convertibles. That's what money management is all about.

Unlike most books on the stock market, *Your Investments* seeks to show you how to avoid and minimize losses. *In successful investing, it is just as important NOT to lose money as to make a profit.*

Throughout the book, there are many warnings. They are important because, as Charles H. Dow wrote at the turn of the century, "The man who is prudent and careful in carrying on a store, factory or real estate business seems to think that totally different methods should be employed in dealing with stocks. Nothing is further from the truth."

The two most important elements in successful investing are *accurate information* and *common sense*. By stressing dangers and pitfalls, *Your Investments* hopes to persuade you to use your intelligence and business or professional experience to make wise decisions.

Your Investments is edited for the intelligent investor, whether new or sophisticated. The information is as accurate as its source, and whenever possible, it has been double-checked by authorities. But before you buy any specific security, review all of the facts with your broker.

The techniques and recommendations are not gospel. They should be used only when common sense tells you that they will enhance your profits or reduce your losses. *They have three goals: to preserve your capital, to build your assets, and to boost your income.*

DOW JONES INDUSTRIAL AVERAGE

YEARLY PERFORMANCE AND RATES OF RETURN

Year	Closing Price	% Change in Year	% Dividend*	Total Change
1950	235.41	+17.6%	8.1%	+25.7%
1951	269.23	+14.4	6.9	+21.3
1952	291.90	+ 8.4	5.7	+14.1
1953	280.90	− 3.8	5.5	+ 1.7
1954	404.39	+44.0	6.2	+50.2
1955	488.44	+20.8	5.3	+26.1
1956	499.47	+ 2.3	4.7	+ 7.0
1957	435.69	−12.8	4.3	− 8.5
1958	583.65	+34.0	4.6	+38.6
1959	679.36	+16.4	3.6	+20.0
1960	615.89	− 9.3	3.1	− 6.2
1961	731.14	+18.7	3.7	+22.4
1962	652.10	−10.8	3.2	− 7.6
1963	762.95	+17.0	3.6	+20.6
1964	874.13	+14.6	4.1	+18.7
1965	969.26	+10.9	3.3	+14.2
1966	785.69	−18.9	3.3	−15.6
1967	905.11	+15.2	3.8	+19.0
1968	943.75	+ 4.3	3.5	+ 7.8
1969	800.36	−15.2	3.6	−11.6
1970	838.92	+ 4.8	3.9	+ 8.7
1971	890.20	+ 6.1	3.7	+ 9.8
1972	1020.02	+14.6	3.6	+18.2
1973	850.86	−16.6	3.5	−12.7
1974	616.24	−28.0	5.4	−22.6
1975	852.41	+38.0	5.1	+43.1
1976	1005.00	+18.0	4.4	+22.4
1977	831.00	−17.0	5.1	−11.9
1978	805.00	− 3.0	6.1	+ 3.1
1979	838.74	+ 4.2	6.3	+10.5
1980	965.99	+14.9	5.7	+20.6

* On prior year-end price

PROJECTED

	High	Low	Earnings
1981	1050	835	$121.22
1982	1250	1000	133.60
1985	1650	1350	163.21

SOURCE: Wright Investors' Service

STOCK PRICES IN PAST FIVE RECESSIONS

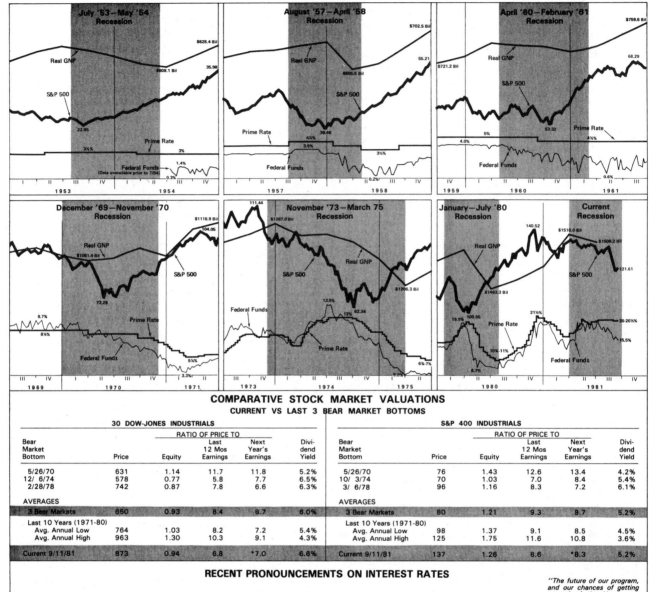

COMPARATIVE STOCK MARKET VALUATIONS
CURRENT VS LAST 3 BEAR MARKET BOTTOMS

30 DOW-JONES INDUSTRIALS						S&P 400 INDUSTRIALS					
		RATIO OF PRICE TO						RATIO OF PRICE TO			
Bear Market Bottom	Price	Equity	Last 12 Mos Earnings	Next Year's Earnings	Dividend Yield	Bear Market Bottom	Price	Equity	Last 12 Mos Earnings	Next Year's Earnings	Dividend Yield
5/26/70	631	1.14	11.7	11.8	5.2%	5/26/70	76	1.43	12.6	13.4	4.2%
12/ 6/74	578	0.77	5.8	7.7	6.5%	10/ 3/74	70	1.03	7.0	8.4	5.4%
2/28/78	742	0.87	7.8	6.6	6.3%	3/ 6/78	96	1.16	8.3	7.2	6.1%
AVERAGES						AVERAGES					
3 Bear Markets	650	0.93	8.4	8.7	6.0%	3 Bear Markets	80	1.21	9.3	9.7	5.2%
Last 10 Years (1971-80) Avg. Annual Low	764	1.03	8.2	7.2	5.4%	Last 10 Years (1971-80) Avg. Annual Low	98	1.37	9.1	8.5	4.5%
Avg. Annual High	963	1.30	10.3	9.1	4.3%	Avg. Annual High	125	1.75	11.6	10.8	3.6%
Current 9/11/81	873	0.94	6.8	*7.0	6.6%	Current 9/11/81	137	1.26	8.6	*8.3	5.2%

RECENT PRONOUNCEMENTS ON INTEREST RATES

"No question, we have to keep restraining the growth of money and credit. Yes, we intend to stick with it."

FRB Chairman Paul Volcker
8/30/81

"The FRB is independent, and they're hurting us in what we're trying to do as much as they're hurting everyone else."

President Reagan
8/81

"We can have and should have some loosening of interest rates because they're now contributing to the inflation we are trying to cure."

President Reagan
8/81

"The time is now to address the high interest rates and get them down."

Senate Majority Leader
Senator Howard Baker
9/8/81

"We can't live with a 20 percent prime rate and expect to see any economic recovery."

House Minority Leader
Representative Robert Michel
9/8/81

"The future of our program, and our chances of getting control of the House, are right now tied to interest rates. We've got to see improvement, we've got to be headed in the right direction."

Head of the Republican
Congressional Campaign Committee
Representative Guy Vander Jagt
9/8/81

(*): Based on *WIS* projected earnings.

SOURCE: Wright Investor's Service

CHAPTER 1

How to Be a Successful Investor

Everyone can be a successful investor if he/she sets goals, follows proven-profitable rules, exercises self-discipline and uses common sense.

With all types of investment, the degree of success depends largely on the type of person you are: conservative, aggressive, or speculative. With most people, their personality/philosophy determines their sleep-well level. If any investment causes you, or your spouse, to worry, do not make it, or if you have already done so, sell it. Money, by itself, is never as important as peace of mind which, usually, is a synonym for happiness.

The conservative investor stresses safety and income. He aims, first, to preserve his capital and, second, to earn a moderate, sure, stable return on his money. He usually buys a security and holds it until maturity, which may be 20 years or more.

That's great for peace of mind but it's poor protection against inflation. At the current rate, the purchasing power of his savings will be cut in half every decade.

Traditionally, the conservative investor has put his money into long-term bonds or certificates of deposit. He felt secure with an 8% return on an eight-year savings certificate or a long-term bond. He knew that he could always get back his full investment at maturity.

But such inflexibility has been disastrous in recent years. The thrift institutions now pay 15% (or more) on 6 month Treasury-bill-related CDs and that "stable" 8% coupon bond has been selling at 60 or less.

There are still occasions when it may pay to lock in high yields of 13% or 14% with newly issued quality bonds but, as we'll see later, greater rewards can be achieved by buying debt securities at a discount to profit from the sure appreciation or, at this time, investing in liquid assets such as Treasury bills, CDs or money market funds. They are safe and, currently, provide high yields. Even though their income is taxed at the highest rate, for most investors, that's a tough combination to beat.

The enterprising investor takes slightly more risks. He looks for total returns—income plus capital gains—averaging at least 15% a year: roughly 5% in dividends and 10% in appreciation. With some stocks, he buys and sells, usually after holding for 12 months; with others, he holds for substantial profits: e.g. Houston Natural Gas. Between 1969 and 1980, its dividends, adjusted for three stock splits that gave investors 500 shares for each original 100, rose from 16¢ to $1.30 per share and its stock price, also adjusted, soared from 14 to 63. These are welcome returns, especially when the realized appreciation will be taxed at the low, long-term capital gains rate.

The speculator takes the most risks. He buys and sells frequently in an effort to achieve the largest gains in the shortest time. But he always faces the probability of losses on the majority of his holdings. He must look for high gains from his winning selections.

Investment Mistakes

Now that we've suggested steps to success, let's take a look at the most frequent investment mistakes:

Overcaution. Fixed assets/fixed income investments are usually safe but do not grow. Quality stocks and real estate will always be worth more over the years.

Guessing instead of thinking. There is nothing complex about most securities investments. All you have to do is to review readily available statistics, look at the record of the corporation and use common sense.

Overinfluence by opinions of others. Forget about that shibboleth that other people know more than you do about investments. This will be true with details, but, in most cases, you are just as smart as the so-called experts. According to one survey, 75% of all investment advisory services are wrong more often than they are right.

Neglecting the erosion of inflation. For every dollar you invest, you must get a return large enough to pay the tax on the income and gain enough to make up the loss of purchasing power. To project the rate of return you will need to beat inflation, divide the inflation rate by the difference between 100 and the rate at which you are taxed.

In the 40% tax bracket, with inflation at 10%, you will be getting poorer unless you get income of over 16.6%:

$$\frac{10}{100-40} = 16.6\%$$

With long-term capital gains, where the tax applies to only 40% of the profit, the return needed will be 11.9%:

$$\frac{10}{100-20} = 11.9\%$$

With a combination of one-third dividends and two-thirds capital gains, you'll need to get 12.84%.

Inflexibility. Too many people are slow to shift with changing economic, industry or corporate conditions. They are reluctant to admit a mistake or to switch from a traditional stance. They hold bonds and utility stocks when their prices fall as interest rates rise. They justify their delay on the grounds that they are getting the originally anticipated interest or dividends. They refuse to sell the General Motors stock which they inherited despite the reduced dividend and plummeting stock price.

These days, the money world is so erratic that only a handful of high-quality investments, of any type, can be regarded as sacrosanct.

Lack of planning. Only 1 of 20 investors has a systematic, sensible, long-range plan for his or her family finances, investments and estate. This is foolish and often tragic because it makes it impossible for the individual to fulfill goals for personal retirement or the family's future.

Yet wise financial planning is easy, enjoyable and rewarding. *Not* planning will take more time and far more money. And regret over financial mistakes is always more harrowing than the temporary irritations from the extra time spent in understanding and implementing the fundamentals of successful investing.

For those responsible for pension plans, this failure to plan can be even more disastrous. They hold fiduciary roles that, legally and morally, require intelligent decisions in making and monitoring prudent investments. For many people, their pension plan *is* their investment program.

There are many different ways to make and keep money by investing in stocks, bonds, real estate, annuities, commodities and other types of financial assets. *Your Investments* explains and evaluates many of these and provides proven guidelines and easy-to-follow examples. Throughout this guide you will find *DO's that should enhance your profits* and *DON'Ts that can minimize, if not eliminate, your losses.* At all times, it assumes that the reader is intelligent, concerned and anxious to increase his/her wealth.

Factors to Check

How conservative, enterprising or speculative you should be depends on how you evaluate such factors as:

Age and family status. A family man cannot afford to take the same risks as a bachelor, spinster or childless widow. If you are young and have small children, you should set more conservative goals than would an older person whose children are grown up. Ironically, the psychological tendency is to do just the opposite.

Every young person with 30 or 40 income-producing years ahead should concentrate on long-term capital appreciation rather than current income, no matter how generous.

Emergency funds: for illness, accidents and natural calamities. Always keep reserves in savings and/or insurance. The exact amount will depend on your probable need and available resources. Under no circumstances should you consider investing in securities or real estate until you have provided for these "rainy days."

Future responsibilities: a new home, college for the kids, your own business and so forth. These expenses require clearly defined plans for savings and investments.

Current and anticipated income, savings and wealth. A worker earning $18,000 a year has quite different investment objectives than does an executive of a major corporation or a professional. An individual with a career post in government or a job with a large, stable company does not have the same goals as one in a less secure enterprise (advertising, public relations, a defense-oriented contrac-

tor, etc.). So, too, with anyone who expects to change jobs frequently in his drive to reach the top.

Pension and profit-sharing plans are becoming an ever more important consideration. If you are an employee in a corporate pension plan, be sure that you do not count these savings until you become vested: usually 50% after 10 years, 100% after 15 years, with benefits after age 65.

You should also consider your spouse's income and wealth and any assured inheritances. (Be cautious: your parents' estate can be dissipated should there be severe illness or long years of nursing-home care.)

Insurance coverage. This means adequate life, health and disability protection for both present and future needs. In most cases, it is wise to plan these for the full family until your children are self-supporting.

If you need $200,000 to protect your spouse and heirs and, presently, have a net worth of only $75,000, buy $125,000 life insurance, mostly term because it costs far less than straight life. As you add to your savings and possessions and your investments grow in value, you can reduce the coverage. Once you've paid for college costs you can drop some policies unless you have raised your financial sights substantially. Life insurance is the single least expensive way to provide income that will be lost at your death.

Tax position. If your income or wealth puts you in a high tax bracket, your investments should be selected with an eye to saving or postponing taxes. Your income holdings, for example, might be tax-exempt municipals or real estate where the income is tax-sheltered. Your capital investments might be capital shares of dual funds (which pay no dividends) or stocks of fast-growing companies which reinvest most of their profits and pay small or no dividends. *But never make the mistake of letting tax benefits override investment value. The name of the game is PROFITS, not tax savings.*

If you are in a lower tax bracket and need the extra income, consider common stocks with good yields and prospects of slow but steady growth: utilities, banks and finance companies. These types of dividend-paying securities are excellent investments for retired people who need income and receive favored tax treatment.

Whether to invest for income or for capital gains depends partly on your tax bracket.

Retirement for you and your spouse. Statistically, after reaching age 65, a male will live about 16 more years and a female, 19. Think back to prove to yourself how long a time this is. To assure a comfortable, worry-free old age, you should integrate your savings, Social Security and pension to provide income equal to 75% of your last working year's earnings for a couple; 60% for a single individual.

Time. Generally, the more time you can devote to your investments, the more aggressive your selections can be. If you are unwilling or unable to check business news and financial reports, put your money in certificates of deposit or shares of investment companies.

If you can spend only 30 minutes a week on research/review, choose solid blue chip stocks. They are likely to trade within a narrow range but, over the years, will *always* be worth more.

If you are interested enough to read books, attend lectures, subscribe to magazines and investment advisory reports and study statistics, you can make use of many of the suggestions in this guide and, as a result, make more money.

The magic of compounding: earning income on income. As stressed earlier, this is the single most important factor in successful investing. Consistent savings and prompt reinvestment of all earnings can swell your assets at an amazing rate.

Coordinate Your Investments with Your Financial Planning

No matter which approach you choose, all of your investments should be considered as part of your total financial and estate planning. Savings are essential to help you reach your goals of economic security and money-carefree retirement but it is not enough to set aside money regularly. You must make every saved dollar work as hard after you have earned it as you worked to gain it in the first place. Too many people have too many of their assets in holdings that fail to meet this basic criterion.

After you have finished this book, review all of your investments and rate them according to their actual and potential income and appreciation each year for the next three years. Then, unless you have no financial worries, start developing a program that you feel can be carried out. Keep it flexible so that shifts can be made as resources and goals change.

At all times, your spouse and your children (when old enough) should participate or, at least, be adequately informed. Once you have agreed upon a viable plan, make it a point to set aside a long evening every six months to explain what, why, and how you are investing. This is the way to teach your spouse to carry on the program and to show your sons and daughters how to be adults in handling their financial affairs.

The results are up to you. As an investor you are responsible for: (1) setting goals in terms of your personal, family or fiduciary obligations; (2) selecting techniques best suited to those investment goals, your own abilities and resources; (3) deciding to what extent you should handle your own investments or let others do it for you; (4) in terms of these basic decisions, developing your own set of personal operating rules that you can use promptly, readily and comfortably when you select, buy and/or sell securities or other investments; (5) using your own common sense and the experience of your business or profession to make financial decisions. *The rules for success in investing are the same as those in any successful enterprise:* Get the facts, make logical, realistic assumptions and projections, act decisively and stick to your plan until and unless circumstances change.

Choose Rules YOU Can Live With

Your Investments is written for individuals and families who are skillful or fortunate enough to have more money than is required for immediate living expenses and, thus, have savings to invest. From personal and business experience, they understand the importance of rules. This chapter summarizes some guidelines that have proven effective over the years. They are simple, logical and generally easy to follow.

In developing your own investment program, choose rules and techniques that you can live with throughout your working years. Specific investment decisions will change with shifts in economic and stock market conditions, but your basic money-making plan should be followed until you are ready to retire or there are drastic changes in your income or lifestyle. The approach you select should be broad and flexible enough to cover almost all anticipated contingencies. *Nothing is more harmful to successful investing than frequent shifts of basic policy. Making money requires persistence and patience.*

Few rules will last forever in exactly the same form, but the principles hold. Times change and so do investors, but there needs to be some continuing concept. *Only when you are fully convinced that your previous guidelines are no longer suitable should you make a planned and orderly shift to more appropriate new rules.* Make this decision slowly and carefully.

Because of the wide scope of investment targets, approaches, techniques and opportunities covered in *Your Investments,* some of the rules may seem contradictory. In practice, they seldom are because most of them are intended to apply to different types of investors or different investment situations. Similarly, where rules seem obvious or platitudinous, remember: basic truths stand repeating.

As you read this book, make a checklist of rules which you feel apply to your financial situation and your personal and family plans. At the end, review your notes and select those ideas which you want to follow. Consult them whenever you consider buying or selling any security. To make it easy, type them on an 8½-by-11 sheet of paper and slip them into a plastic holder. Then use it as a placemark whenever you consult *Your Investments.*

Do's & Don'ts for All Investors

There is no rule book or mysterious key to success in the stock market. Whether investment or speculation, it's a business of common sense, faith, courage, knowledge and patience—with a reasonable amount of luck.

The stock market is people, with all their fears, enthusiasms, prejudices, stupidity and, occasionally, wisdom. That's why it's well to keep in mind the basic rules that will apply tomorrow as well as today.

In Selecting and Holding Investments

1. Investigate BEFORE you invest. Do not buy or sell on impulse, hunch or rumor. Make all investments according to your specific plan of action, preferably one which shows approximate buying and selling zones. Write down the facts you know. If there are gaps, get the information from your broker or your library. *Never buy or sell a security except as an integral part of your overall plan.*

Not only will a poor stock lose your money but it will also cause unnecessary mental anguish. *Take nothing for granted. Get the facts lest the lack of facts gets you.*

2. Equate the rewards with the risks. Never buy any stock that does not have twice as much potential of rising as probability of falling. Base this decision on past performance and future prospects, not hopes. To a large extent, the difference between investment and speculation is the rate, and probability, of change. The price of the investment may move more slowly but it's also more predictable.

The prices of securities/contracts are always affected, to varying degrees, by psychology and prospects. Neither can be measured precisely, but it is possible to calculate the potential rewards (if all goes well) and the degree of risk (if things turn sour).

This reward-to-risk ratio is the basis for all successful speculations and most swinging investments. With securities, an amateur can develop his own ratios but will probably do better to rely on professional advisory reports and recommendations. With commodities, currency, etc., expert assistance is imperative until you can become knowledgeable and are able to devote time to research and analysis that can project those reward-to-risk ratios.

You should always make your own decisions. You should never act until conditions are favorable in the economy, in the trading market and in your own investment strategy. *Remember: "favorable" may mean BUY in a bull market, SELL or HEDGE in a bear market.*

Here's how to project reward-to-risk ratios. You feel that a stock (or any other type of easily traded property), now at 40, has the potential of moving up to 60. Or there's a risk of a decline to 35. The reward-to-risk ratio is 20 points up vs. 5 points down: a healthy 4:1 ratio.

You buy and the stock goes to 55. The potential gain is now only 5 points, but the risk is still 20 points down. That's a dangerous 1:4 ratio and a signal to sell or, possibly, to enter a stop order.

Be careful not to sell too soon when the ratio shifts from, say, 5:1 to 4:2.5. You will limit your profit potential and end up with relatively small gains.

3. Investigate AFTER you invest. For anyone with sufficient resources to justify buying this book, there is no such thing as a permanent investment to be locked away in a strong box. As veteran investment adviser John Magee says, "I have 100,000 shares of various stocks I inherited from my grandfather. All showed great promise when he bought them. But there was nothing to guarantee that the investment conditions that prevailed when he put his money in them would continue. Today, those stocks are worth nothing."

Review all your securities every six months to determine which you should hold or sell. On the average, a successful portfolio will mean an annual turnover of 20%: One of every five holdings should be sold each year.

4. Be patient. Avoid flitting from one stock to another. This will make your broker rich, but it will cut your potential profits and, unless you are very wise and very lucky, will not increase your capital. Few *investments* achieve substantial appreciation in less than 12 months!

One of the major faults of amateurs is to try too hard to make too much money too soon. As with most business decisions, do not be in a hurry to spend your money.

5. Look for total returns: income plus appreciation. With all securities, all income, from interest or dividends, is taxable at your highest rate. With capital gains, attained after 12 months, only 40% of the profits are taxed.

Thus, for an investor in the 40% tax bracket, 12% interest nets 7.2%; a 12% long-term capital gain nets 10.08%, and a combined 12% return—5% dividends plus 7% long-term capital gain—nets 8.08%. There's one important exception: pension funds where all interest/income/realized appreciation is tax-free until withdrawn.

6. Watch developing trends. When you read newspapers or magazines, ask yourself, "What are the investment implications of new developments in science, technology, interest rates, domestic and international politics? Which firms will benefit?"

The news-facts should be background for further study. Only rarely does news have an immediate, *effective* impact on an industry or a corporation (unless there's a near disaster). Such factors can be important for the long-term outlook, especially with the real professional money managers whose funds either have or will acquire large holdings in a company's stock.

7. Be ready for the unexpected. Even when you are bullish about an industry or a company, do not let your enthusiasm overcome your judgment. *ALWAYS be prepared for the unexpected in the stock market.* Adjust your plans promptly and review the situation objectively. Unless you have the capital and stamina to hold out for a long time, never "fight the tape." *You cannot win!*

On the other hand, do not be panicked (as so many nervous Nellies are) when there are temporary, irrational actions in the stock market: e.g. in January 1981 when technician Joseph E. Granville's "Sell" wire set off a 24-point drop in the Dow Jones Industrial Average. Some of the stocks were overvalued and, probably, would have fallen anyway. But most of the worthwhile issues moved back in the next few months. *Successful investing is a long-term commitment.* If you choose wisely, such aberrations, however annoying, are meaningless.

8. Specialize and concentrate. Do not try to cover the waterfront and handle a score of stocks in varied industries. Keep your eligible list selective and small: not over 20, preferably no more than 10 to own and 10 to study. When you spread too far, you lessen your opportunities for profit. It's just like the corporation whose stock you want to own. In most cases the majority of its profits come from a few products or services.

You will always do better with a 20-point gain in one stock than a one-point rise in 20 holdings—if only because of the commissions.

9. Act promptly. Once you have made your decision to buy or sell, give the order to your broker. If you are shooting for a 50% gain over the next two years, a quarter of a point makes little difference. Do not let a well-thought-out decision drop because of inertia, laziness or greed.

10. Stand by your investment rules. There are few occasions when the opportunity is so great and so certain that it is worthwhile to break your own rules. There will be another similar opportunity along soon; there are some 10,000 readily available common stocks and hundreds of thousands of bonds from which to choose!

In Buying and Selling Securities

1. Set targets. Even the best professionals seldom buy at the bottom or sell at the top. Target prices provide a frame of reference to restrain overenthusiasm and temper excessive gloom. And properly determined, they reflect the real value of the security.

Goals for investments should be average annual total returns of 13% to 15%: 13% readily available from interest on quality bonds and dividends of preferred stocks and common stocks of utilities; 14% from money market funds and certificates of deposit: and 15% from common stocks: 4% to 5% dividends plus 10% to 11% appreciation.

These will shift with the cost of money and investors' attitudes but provide a solid frame of reference. When you heed the counsel in *Your Investments,* you will attain such returns and, with experience and wise timing, will surpass them. These figures should be net, after commissions/fees, so set your sights slightly higher. With stocks, for example, project a 35% to 40% total gain in 24 months. You will not always hit your targets so you must shoot high and be patient. Some stocks will move up rapidly; others will lag for months and then edge ahead.

If you trade, you will suffer some losses and you will be out of the market some of the time so you must set higher goals and a shorter time frame: a 25% gain in three months or a 50% gain in a year or less.

When you write options, start with a projected gross profit, if the stock is called, of 20% in six months; and 25% in nine months. That's premium plus appreciation plus dividends.

2. Be sure the economic and stock market prospects are favorable for *(a)* the industry and *(b)* the company for at least the next year. Never buy any stock *solely* because it is a bargain. You are investing to make money, not to break even or lose. Keep the odds in your favor by buying UP stocks in UP markets.

It seldom matters how many winners you do NOT buy. What hurts is the number of losers you DO buy.

3. Be sure this is the most profitable use of your money at this time. Always stay flexible and be ready to take advantage of ever-changing opportunities. When liquid asset investments—Treasury bills, CDs and money market funds—pay 15% or more, sell laggard, low-yielding stocks and buy these temporarily rewarding holdings. When these returns drop a point or two, move back to popular stocks in popular industries.

At all times, keep a "future" list of worthwhile investments. Review them frequently and do your homework to determine which ones offer the best prospects of profit on the basis of your goals, available funds and time targets. *And never be in a hurry to spend your money.*

Do not limit your selections to standard securities. There are times when it pays to consider convertibles, warrants, rights, options, tax-exempts and, once in a while, tax shelters.

4. Check the timing. If there's active trading, buy a market. If you are dealing with a stock that is beginning to attract attention, you may save a point or so by waiting for a temporary dip. Usually, such stocks flex their values before they take off.

5. Pay heed to Technical Analysis. Use it to deter-

mine if there have been unusual movements, to check the trendlines, to watch for breakouts and to locate areas of resistance. T.A. can be a valuable tool in improving timing and in visualizing the stock's trend. Use charts and moving averages as *part of,* but not the final factor in, your decision.

6. Take your losses fast. The cheapest loss is the first one. Do not let pride or stubbornness stop you from accepting and correcting an error. Sell if conditions change or if you discover that your facts were inadequate or your decision faulty. *Unless it is an unusual situation, do not average down.* Take your beating and put the proceeds into a situation where there is a profit potential. If you are convinced that your original choice was sound, you will have to be patient until other investors agree with you—and that may be a long time.

On the downside, use stop orders (at fractions of a point) 10% to 15% below the cost or recent high.

Do not become overly concerned with tax losses. You'll get enough of these without trying. Unless you are a sophisticated investor in a high tax bracket, tax losses are seldom worthwhile—despite what your broker may tell you.

7. Let your profits ride—but not too far. If the rise is rapid, review the situation when your stock hits its target price. If the prospects are so promising that you can logically (and objectively) set a new profit range, let your profits ride. Otherwise, *sell. It is always better to sell "too soon" than "too late."* When an overvalued stock starts to decline, the descent can be fast and steep. Again, this is a time to consider a stop order.

8. Don't be a stock switcher. Four trades a year, at a percentage cost of 1% to 1½% of stock value, equal the annual 4% to 6% income on the average stock. Commissions are a significant cost for speculators.

N.B.: If you have a sizable portfolio and trade frequently, consider using a discount broker. The savings can amount to as much as a full point on a round-trip transaction.

9. Upgrade your portfolio periodically. Every six months or so, review your holdings and consider selling at least one of your securities. Replace your weakest stock with one of greater potential. If the stock is lagging behind the industry and the market, you may have made a poor choice. *The only reason to hold any stock is the prospect of substantial future gain or, if you are primarily interested in income, a better-than-average return.*

10. Watch the ex-dividend date, especially if you (or your spouse) want income. When a company declares a dividend, it designates a *record date* ("ex-div." column). All shareholders on the corporate books on that date will receive the dividend. At that time, the price of the stock will be reduced by approximately the amount of the payout. In a normal market, the price of the stock will move up in a day or two.

That means that if you buy the stock on that date, you will not receive that dividend check. But if you tell your broker to buy the stock for cash and call for same-day delivery, you qualify for the dividend. In such a case, the seller charges a premium for his trouble and for losing the extra payment.

When a stock goes ex-dividend, there will be an *x*

after its name in the stock tables. If the record date is Friday, the stock is declared ex-dividend the preceding Monday, since it takes five days to deliver the shares in a regular trade.

RETURN FROM INVESTMENT DOLLAR

If you put your money in:

	1981*	1980	1979	1978	1977
U.S. Treasury Bills (90 day)	14.15%	14.77%	9.93%	9.56%	5.20%
U.S. Treasury Bills (180 days)	14.37	14.82	10.11	10.03	5.50
CDs (90 days)	14.45	16.50	10.00	9.13	5.50
U.S. Government Notes	13.59	13.29	9.17	9.24	5.80
U.S. Bonds (long-term)	13.24	12.06	9.02	8.94	7.40
Municipals (long-term)	10.10	9.20	5.85	6.20	5.71
Corporate Bonds (AA)	13.60	12.60	9.00	9.00	8.47
Dow Jones Industrial Stocks	5.50	5.63	5.65	6.03	4.90
Dow Jones Untilities Stocks	9.72	8.77	9.55	9.08	7.30

* Spring   Other prices as of year-end

SOURCE: Wright Investors' Service

In Managing Your Portfolio

1. Follow the market trends. Do not try to buck the tide. If it's a bear market, be cautious in buying. If it's a fluctuating market, think twice. If it's a bull market, take greater risks.

2. Limit your purchases until your forecast is confirmed. If you feel you have latched on to a "hot" one, cut your order in half even if it means buying less than a round lot. When the chart's trendline shows that you are right, buy more. You may lose a few points' profit by waiting, but you will minimize your losses. Always wait for confirmation before making major commitments.

3. Average up when you pick a winner. If you get into a really profitable situation where the stock moves up in active trading, buy more shares while the stock is still rising. *Be sure that there is a fairly solid basis for such optimism.* Hopes of a stock split will push a stock up, but if the split does not occur, the shares will drop sharply. If you do buy more shares, set a stop order, actually or mentally.

4. Be slow to average down. If the stock is slipping, there are probably good reasons why. More important, when the trend continues, it indicates that the market does not like the stock. Buy stock on its way down *only* if you are convinced of its worth and *know* that the reasons for the decline are transitory. The lower the stock drops, the higher it will have to go for you to make up losses on the shares you already own. And how do you know that the stock won't fall even more?

5. Use leverage. When prospects are bright, take advantage of margin, warrants and options. As long as you feel that your research is sound and the conditions promising, make your dollars work overtime. The cost of the interest will not be significant if your forecasts are correct.

6. Watch the 12-month date. This is the time when gains qualify for special tax treatment. When you buy any stock, mark the next year's calendar 12 months ahead of: (*a*) the date on which the stock rise started (this is when investors with profits will start selling) and (*b*)

your purchase date so that your profits can qualify for the lower tax levy.

Such a timetable can also be valuable if you have a loss. By waiting a few days, you may be able to shift that loss from short to long term, again with tax benefits. This can be risky with a volatile stock.

7. Be flexible. Be willing to change your thoughts and strategy to meet new conditions. The same goes for *types* of securities. Shift from stocks to bonds in a bear market; vice versa in a bull market. And always be ready to take advantage of warrants, convertibles, short sales, etc.

8. Be skeptical. This is a repeat of that all-important *Investigate* rule. As they used to say in the Old West, "I trust you, honey, but cut the cards." With all investments, be from Missouri.

Specific Guidelines

Here are some additional guidelines as set by John Winthrop Wright, a leading fundamentalist:

Review a stock when its price/earnings ratio goes to, or above, its average annual high P/E ratio for the last five years. The ratio is not always the last word in making a *sell* decision because the company's growth rate and earnings prospects may be getting better or worse. But it's a good checkpoint.

Buy a stock when it is selling well below its average P/E ratio of the past decade and there are good prospects for rising earnings and a strong stock market.

Sell a stock when it is fully priced in relation to past performance, future prospects and its historical price/earnings ratio. When any stock which, over the years, has sold at 8 to 10 times profits gets to a price/earnings ratio of over 12, watch it carefully. At a multiple of 14, get

STANDARD & POOR'S MARKET AVERAGE

Year	High	Low	Last
1930	20	11	12
1935	13	8	13
1940	12	9	10
1945	17	13	17
1950	21	16	21
1955	50	36	48
1960	65	55	61
1965	99	86	98
1970	103	76	101
1971	116	99	113
1972	133	112	132
1973	135	103	109
1974	112	70	76
1975	107	78	101
1976	121	102	119
1977	119	100	105
1978	119	86	107
1979	124	107	121
1980	161	111	154
PROJECTED			
1981	168	134	151
1982	187	149	168
1983	210	166	198
1984	233	185	209
1985	252	200	226

SOURCE: Wright Investors' Service

ready to sell unless there are strong reasons to anticipate unusually fast and sustained growth. Very few stocks trade at ratios well above those of their industry or their past averages.

It is better to make Baron Rothschild's famous mistake of always making a little less by selling too soon than to take the greater risk of overstaying the market in an overpriced stock.

To these can be added two other checkpoints used by other analysts for stock review:

• When the price of the stock rises to a price which is considerably more than double the shareholders' equity at corporate book value per common share. When buyers are willing to pay more than twice the tangible value of a company, they are adding a premium for future growth. Be sure that premium is well justified.

Example: Hobart Corp., when the price of its stock, as the result of a takeover bid, rose to 32. This was almost double the book value of $18.40 per share. The company's growth record was a good, but not exceptional, 11.6%. This sell decision was aided by the excellent profit: 20 points since it was bought a little more than a year before.

• When the dividend yield falls below 3%. If the company is utilizing its cash for research and expansion, that's good. But growth has to be substantial to justify accepting a current return of less than 3% for the use of your money.

CHAPTER 2

When and How to Choose Outside Advisers

From my experience, I believe that most individuals can become successful investors on their own. But there are times when outside counsel can be valuable. A competent lawyer is essential and an investment adviser can be useful if only to buttress your own decisions.

The attorney can show you how to set up your assets so that your program will protect your loved ones while you live and fulfill your wishes after you die. The investment counsellor can help you to increase your wealth safely and can teach you how to manage your money more effectively. Together, they can point out how to take advantage of the many tax-saving and tax-avoiding opportunities that are available to those in the middle and upper tax brackets. With the right advisers, the fees will be returned many times over, in dollars and peace of mind.

Choose any type of financial adviser slowly and carefully and do not be afraid to make changes if you feel his advice no longer meets your needs. Too often, the most convenient counsel comes from those with selfish interests: *for investments,* from a stockbroker or mutual fund representative who relies on commissions from buying and selling securities; *for insurance,* from a broker/agent whose livelihood depends on his ability to sell policies; *for retirement and estates,* from a banker whose institution provides savings and trust services.

Do not rely too heavily on others. It's your money. You worked hard to earn it. In most cases, you can plan more wisely and invest more profitably than they can. It's well to heed outside advice but the ultimate decision should be yours ... as you will realize as you read this book.

Investment Aid

Whether you retain a professional directly, purchase shares in a pooled portfolio or subscribe to a market letter, study all information and recommendations, check the character and reputation of the individual/sponsor and review the long-term record.

If you are interested enough in your investments to buy this book, you can probably learn enough to achieve better results than those of most outsiders. Of course, when there are other factors such as limited time or responsibility for substantial assets, investment counsel can be worthwhile. In such cases, it's more a matter of convenience than of making the most rewarding use of your savings. In every case, keep abreast of what's happening and do not hesitate to make a change. A wrong choice can be costly.

Broadly, you have these choices:

Investment companies. These are described in detail later. They are pools of funds, from a large number of investors, used to buy and sell a diversified list of securities (and, increasingly, other forms of property such as commodities, metals, options) selected for specific financial goals (growth, income or a combination).

In addition to professional management, you usually get prompt reinvestment of income, detailed reports for tax returns, the opportunity to switch to other funds under the same management and, if you so desire, extras such as regular checks, check-writing privileges, low-cost life insurance and loans against your holdings. In most cases, the initial investment is small, you can make additional purchases easily and can buy and sell quickly.

Commingled investment accounts. These are operated like investment companies and are available through banks, insurance companies and professional money-management organizations. Generally, they require minimum investments of $10,000.

Brokerage firms. These involve a minimum outlay of $100,000 and are managed on a discretionary basis. They are best for an aggressive portfolio seeking special situations or short-term trading profits.

There are also special arrangements for smaller accounts in special "managed" programs. In effect, your money is pooled with that of other customers through standard portfolios. These are a better sales tool than a customer benefit; most people want their investments to be made for their personal goals.

Remember: your broker is a salesman, not an investment adviser. A good registered representative will provide information but insist that you make your own decisions.

Professional money managers. These are individuals or groups; some operate independently, but most are associated with brokerage firms, bank holding companies or financial service organizations. To avoid conflict of interest under new pension-fund legislation, many firms have become independent.

Roughly, their fees are 1% of portfolio value with a minimum of $500 or $1,000 a year. Above $1 million, the fees are scaled down. Small savings, under $250,000, are handled through standard portfolios designed for various investment objectives. Larger holdings receive personal attention.

Generally, their performance will be mediocre but your money is safe, fees are relatively low, reports are detailed and all you have to do is write checks regularly.

Model portfolios. These are available from investment advisory services that publish weekly reports or letters. You have the option to follow their recommendations, but if you do so, you are, in effect, turning over control of the management of your money.

Checkpoints

Regardless of the type of investment adviser, find out about:

Experience. Look for individuals with at least five years of portfolio responsibility and firms whose principals have collective experience of 25 years or more.

Target goals. If they anticipate total returns of less than 10% a year, forget 'em. You can do better with unmanaged bonds. If they mention 20%, be wary. And never believe any *promises*.

Willingness to sell. Successful investing relies on two factors: how much you make and how little you lose. Check the composition of all portfolios for the past 10 years. If they are still holding glamour stocks bought at peaks and now near lows, move on! I am constantly amazed at how many so-called professionals ignore their losses. One of the major growth funds (with a good overall record) has owned a large block of Avon Products for many years. Yet, this stock sold at 140 in 1973, fell below 20 in 1974 and, recently, was in the mid-30s. Trading would have been wise but there are times when even the best of stocks should be sold: when they become overvalued and when they are unpopular because of poor prospects. A professional should know that it seldom pays to fight the market.

Source of profits. Review the annual reports to discover whether the gains came from a few big winners or from a number of wise selections. Look for consistency based on clearly stated procedures.

Types of clients. If you're 40 and still building an estate, do not select an adviser/manager specializing in trust accounts for wealthy retirees. Professionals can follow only a limited number of securities and, in this case, will concentrate on stable dividend payers, not the growth stocks you want.

Integrity. If the individual or firm has had a brush with the law, the SEC or the New York Stock Exchange, look elsewhere. You cannot afford to take any chances of this nature with your savings.

Performance. This is the single most important consideration. You want someone who has a solid, if not outstanding, record. Always get the complete results of ALL recommendations, not just the "sample" portfolio. Then study the movement of EVERY stock, year by year. (If this information is not shown in the annual report, get a 12-year chart book and see for yourself.) You want to know: How great were the gains? How long did they take? Were the stocks bought near their lows and sold close to their highs? or vice versa? Similarly, check the losses. Were they in line with the overall market or the results of poor choices?

If the predictions and recommendations were right 60% of the time, that's a good batting average. And always relate the results to your own experience. Why pay someone else to buy the same stocks you made money with?

Market Letters?

Some of these are listed at the back of the *Guide*. They are usually more interesting than profitable. The best way to check these printed commentaries is by trial subscription as offered in *Barron's* and other financial publications. Or take advantage of special sample offers: 20 services for $11.95 from Select Information Exchange, 2095 Broadway, New York, N.Y. 10023; or 25 for $25 from The Hirsch Organization, 6 Deer Trail, Old Tappan, N.J. 07675.

With these letters, in addition to the checkpoints listed above, study:

Audience. If the service goes to hundreds of thousands of people, its comments will be general and useful primarily as background. If it's directed to a small segment of investors, it's probably too expensive and too limited for your needs.

Investment philosophy. You want counsel with investment objectives that match yours. If you are looking for long-term growth, don't subscribe to a technically oriented chart-based service.

Clarity. Look for advice that's easy to understand and implement. Beware of obfuscations, complex language and generalities such as "buy on weakness, sell on strength," etc. You want background data to enable you to improve your investment returns: specific buy prices, target points and logical reasons why actions should be taken.

And, perhaps most important, heed the advice of one of Wall Street's oldest professionals: "Read all advisory reports with skepticism. If the authors were so wise, why aren't they rich enough to retire?"

Special Situations

One occasion when a financial adviser can be helpful is when you receive a large sum—from a legacy or sale of a small business or property. Now you face the problem of a bulk investment and must consider financial, tax and estate planning.

Finding competent counsel for such a one-shot situation is difficult for people with modest means. According to one knowledgeable friend of mine, "97% of all firms/ individuals offering personal financial and estate planning advice are not truly independent advisers because their remuneration is based primarily on the products/services they sell. They are connected with insurance companies, bank trust departments or brokerage houses."

There are three possibilities:

• *Certified Financial Planner (CFP)*. This is an individual who has been approved by the College for Financial Planning after meeting standards of character and education, completing correspondence courses and passing three five-hour exams.

Most CFPs are up-to-date on laws and taxes but,

until they become established (and even after), usually have to supplement their fees with commissions from packaged investment deals: limited partnerships for real estate, oil and gas tax shelters and so forth. But they can provide an organized approach and present you with alternatives.

• *Professional management firms* that aid physicians and dentists in organizing their practice, monitoring their operations and supervising their pension and profit-sharing plans. They also provide an organized approach but they are accustomed to dealing with high-income individuals who are anxious to take advantage of every tax-saving opportunity and who, usually, can make up losses.

• *Advisory firms retained by major corporations* to aid executives in reorienting financial plans or reducing or postponing tax liabilities. For suggestions, check a financial officer in your company or write to The Ayco Company, headquartered in Albany, N.Y.

But I still believe a conscientious individual can manage his savings more profitably than can most outsiders!

CHAPTER 3

Common Stocks for the Best Total Returns

In the past few years, many investors have been attracted to fixed-income investments, such as certificates of deposit and shares of money market funds, because of their high yields. It's hard to beat a safe 15% rate of return but all that income is taxed at the highest rate and the real values, at redemption, are almost always less than their cost because of the erosion of inflation. For those who really want to make money, fixed-income holdings are temporary parking places that help to keep savings flexible.

Over the long term of true investments, the best total returns—income plus appreciation—are achieved by common stocks of growing, profitable corporations. You gain by: (1) ever-increasing dividends; (2) constantly higher underlying values; (3) rising prices for corporate shares.

When a sound, well-managed company makes money, it usually pays out a fair share of these profits to its owners in the form of dividends. Even if the percentage of payout remains the same, dividend dollars will rise. For example, in one year a company earns $1.00 per common share and pays out 50¢ in dividends. Fifteen years later, it is earning $10.00 per share and still paying out half its profits—so the income, to the happy shareholder, is $5.00 per share.

Meantime, the net asset value of the corporation has been growing. For every dollar in dividends, the company

has been plowing back an equal amount for new plants, new products, new markets, etc. Your share of corporate assets will also be worth ten times your cost. And these profits will be tax free until you sell the shares.

There are hundreds of common stocks to meet the needs of both conservative and speculative investors. You must choose those most suitable for your financial goals and *reject all others. Repeat:* the greatest investment profits come from owning shares of companies that meet high standards of quality and value but speculative profits can be achieved by trading in shares of lower-grade issues, special securities, commodities, etc.

These are the same principles that are repeated on that long-running TV favorite, *Wall Street Week,* by host Louis Rukeyser, his knowledgeable panelists and most of his thoughtful guests.

There are, of course, periods when other securities should be considered but, at all times, a portion of savings should be invested in common stocks. Look at the record!

Over some 81 years, the cumulative return (with income reinvested) from common stocks was 113,986%. In one man's lifetime, an original $1,000 would have grown to $113 million. This is based on an average, so the astute investor would have done even better.

In more realistic terms, except in the Depression and the 1970–79 decade, common stocks always provided better returns than did either bonds or Treasury bills.

COMMON STOCKS FOR BEST TOTAL RETURNS

| | Stock Return Cumulative | Average Compound Annual Rates | | | |
Period	Total % Change	Stocks	Bonds	90 Day T-Bils	Inflation GNP Deflator
1900-09	+145.9%	+ 9.4%	+4.2%	+ 5.6%	+2.1%
1910-19	+167.5	+10.3	+2.6	+ 5.2	+7.2
1920-29	+282.8	+14.3	+6.4	+ 3.8	−1.4
1930-39	− 0.3	0	+3.1	+ 0.6	−1.5
1940-49	+125.5	+ 8.5	+3.8	+ 0.5	+6.4
1950-59	+464.5	+18.9	+1.1	+ 2.0	+2.5
1960-69	+ 67.2	+ 5.3	+2.8	+ 4.0	+2.5
1970-79	+ 65.8	+ 5.2	+7.5	+ 6.3	+6.5
1980	+ 29.0	+22.6	−2.7	+12.0	+9.7
81 years					
1900-80	+113,986%	+ 9.0%	+3.8%	+3.6%	+3.1%

SOURCE: Wright Investors' Service

And when the stock market was good, it was very, very good as in the booming 50s and, it seems likely, in the 80s.

Advantages of Common Stocks

1. Higher long-term yields. Historically, common stocks have shown a higher rate of return (dividends plus capital appreciation) than almost all other types of investments. Part of this has been due to the rising prices of the securities, but over the years the dividends grow so that they provide a far better return than is available from interest on fixed-income investments: bonds, mortgages, Treasury bills, savings accounts, etc. *Stocks are LIVE investments. The good ones GROW.* Bonds and savings are *DEAD* investments. Their basic value remains *static. Note:* As outlined later, there are times when common stocks are not as profitable as fixed-income securities. For maximum investment returns, be flexible and willing to shift holdings to areas of the greatest current and potential rewards.

The market value of a common stock grows as the corporation prospers. This growth keeps pace and, hopefully, exceeds the erosion of inflation. The face value of bonds remains the same so that, over the years, their real value, in terms of purchasing power, decreases.

Under normal conditions, investors, mindful of the debilitation of inflation, buy more common stocks. This tends to drive their prices up and their yields down. But these purchases are based on optimism which, usually, develops many months after the facts are available.

By contrast, the prices of bonds are almost completely controlled by interest rates and take effect immediately. When the cost of money rises, bond values drop to maintain competitive returns. Vice versa when interest rates decline. Bonds are traded by yields; stocks by what investors believe to be future corporate prospects.

In the late 1970s, the higher yields caused many investors to switch from stocks to bills, bonds, CDs and money market funds. With returns of 12% to 16%, they felt they were beating inflation. This was true for those in low-to-middle tax brackets but not for the well-to-do. For the 50% taxpayer, the net return was a low 8%!

In late 1979, smart investors began to switch part of their savings to equities. They acquired quality stocks at

HIGHER DIVIDENDS FOR THE LAST 10 YEARS

QUALITY COMPANIES
American Brands
American Express
American Home Products
American Hospital Supply
American Natural Resources
ARA Services
Avon Products
Beatrice Foods
Caterpillar Tractor
Central Telephone
Colgate-Palmolive
Combustion Engineering
Dr. Pepper
Dover Corp.
Dun & Bradstreet
Eagle-Picher
Echlin Mfg.
Emerson Electric
ENSERCH Corp.
Florida P&L
Fort Howard Paper
General Mills
Genuine Parts
Heinz (H.J)
Heublein, Inc.
Household Finance
Houston Industries
Interco, Inc.
Inter. Flavors
Johnson & Johnson
Jostens, Inc.
Kellogg Co.

K-Mart
Lilly (Eli)
Longs Drug Stores
Masco Corp.
Melville Corp.
Mobil Corp.
Nicor, Inc.
Peoples Energy
Procter & Gamble
Public Service, Indiana
Quaker Oats
Richardson-Merrell
Rochester Telephone
Rubbermaid, Inc.
Schering-Plough
Snap-On Tools
Southern Union
Southwestern P.S.
Sperry Corp.
Standard Brands
Tampa Electric
Texas Commerce Bank
Texas Eastern Corp.
Texas Gas Transmission
Texas Utilities
Thomas & Betts
United Telecommunications
Winn-Dixie Stores

GOOD BUT NOT TOP QUALITY COMPANIES
Allied Maintenance
Allright Auto Parks

Amer. Bldg. Maintenance
Amer. Business Products
Amer. Electric Power
Amer. Heritage Life
Atlantic City Electric
Bearings, Inc.
Block (H&R)
Brockway Glass
Cleveland Electric
Combined Inter.
Conn. General Ins.
Conn. Natural Gas
Consol. Natural Gas
Continental Illinois
Continental Telephone
Corroon & Black
Diebold, Inc.
Dillon Cos.
Dow Chemical
General Tire
Hall (Frank B.)
Hawaiian Electric
Holiday Inns
Inter. Multifoods
I.T. & T.
IU International
James (Fred S.)
Jefferson-Pilot
Jim Walter
Kansas G&E
Kansas P&L
Levi Strauss
Long Island Light

Louisville G&E
Malone & Hyde
Mapco, Inc.
Marsh & McLennan
Mid-Continent Tele.
Middle South Utilities
Minnesota Gas
Missouri P.S.
Nevada Power
Northwest Bancorp
Overnite Transportation
Papercraft Co.
Parker-Hannifin
Philip Morris
Pillsbury Co.
Rochester G&E
Seafirst Corp.
Sierra Pacific Power
So. Carolina E&G
Southland Corp.
Standex International
Sun Co.
Thomas Industries
Tidewater, Inc.
Trans Union
Unilever N.V.
Utah P&L
Weis Markets
Wisconsin Electric
Wisconsin P.S.
Wometco Enterprises

SOURCE: Standard & Poor's

bargain levels and, within a year, had profits of 25% to 50% as the S&P 400 zoomed from 112 to 167. If they held for the full 12 months, their profits may have been a bit less than those at the peaks, but their taxes were lower so that their *net,* on many holdings, was at least 30%: double the *gross* yield of fixed-income securities.

Certainly, the stock market fluctuates, but the long-term trend has *always* been up and there has been better than a 3–1 edge for the years of gains versus those of decline. *Buy quality common stocks when they are undervalued and sell them when they become fully priced.* With patience, experience and compounding, you can do far better than that target of an annual average return of +16%. That's what *Your Investments* is all about.

2. Bigger gains with real winners. The benefits are greatest with fast-growing, profitable, popular equities. In just 12 years, 1969 through 1980, 100 shares of Schlumberger, Ltd., after five stock splits, grew to 1,600 shares. Their dollar value per share (adjusted) rose from 3½ to 131: from $350 to $209,600; dividends from 9¢ to 97¢ per share.

Such a gain was exceptional, but the stock of Caterpillar, Inc.—not exactly a swinger nor so affected by external pressures—bought at 20 (adjusted for a split), soared to 64 and per share dividends rose from 80¢ to $2.33.

3. Effective tax shelter. The earnings which are *not* paid out to shareholders in dividends represent tax-deferred income. These profits are reinvested to make the corporation grow and prosper. As long as you continue to own stock in a profitable company, your money is growing in value. You will pay no taxes on these "gains" until you sell. Under present tax laws, you will pay tax on only 40% of the gains. For most people, that is an effective rate of no more than 16%.

4. Extraordinary gains from "special situations" and "glamour-growth" stocks. From time to time, investors in common stocks may hit a jackpot and multiply their capital manyfold in a relatively short time.

Engelhard Minerals, adjusted for stock splits and stock dividends, rose from 7 to a peak of 64. Thus, an original 100 shares, costing $700, became 421 shares with a value of $26,944.

Such opportunities sometimes occur with quality companies but are usually involved with less stable corporations where there are extra risks for the stockholder. You can avoid failures and losses by thorough research, avoiding all tips and using common sense instead of hunches.

Disadvantages of Common Stocks

There are two major disadvantages in owning common stocks. Both can be controlled, if not overcome, by setting strict rules and being sure to stick to them—over the long term.

1. The risk of permanent loss of capital. You may lose all your profits and some of your capital if you speculate in "poor" stocks (and, occasionally, if you do so with quality stocks). The problem is *you.* When you speculate in high-flying stocks which are temporarily popular, the odds are against success. Only a few strong-minded people have the courage to sell such stocks when they become overpriced. When such equities start down, too many people hang on in hopes of a comeback. This seldom happens.

Speculation in stocks should be limited to money which you can afford to lose.

2. Continual market-price fluctuations. Short-term fluctuations in common stocks are unavoidable. That is the price you pay for the liquidity of your investment. If you have bought a stock for steady capital growth and/or income, forget about the weekly or monthly dips and squiggles in its price. If the company's management has a proven record of financial success, the price of the stock will eventually move up and reflect the rising profits.

The careful investor can turn these price fluctuations to substantial advantage: buying quality stocks when they are at bargain prices and, as their prices rise, adding to holdings on temporary dips.

Common Stocks for Safety

Some folks shy away from common stocks because they feel they are risky. This is not necessarily true. Is there any real risk in shares of a company that has paid dividends for 40 years? or one that has increased its payout consistently for 25 years? or of an industry leader that, for two decades, has earned over 20% on shareholders' equity? *Properly selected common stocks are just as safe as an AAA-rated bond and a darn sight more rewarding . . .* as long as their companies meet standards of quality.

For investors who choose peace of mind over total returns, there are two criteria for safety:

Historical record: Assess the long-term ability of corporate management to make money enough to pay dividends as shown by the list of Consistent Dividend Payers for 50 Years. If that's not a long enough record to keep peace in the family, look for those firms that have paid an annual dividend for 75 years or more. You'll find some familiar names: American Express, A.T. & T., Bristol-Myers, Chesebrough-Pond's, IBM and Procter & Gamble.

Even then, be skeptical and check further. Some of the real old-timers, such as utilities, are monopolies. Their continuous profits may be the result of the market position rather than of management's ability. You want investments in organizations that continue to achieve an adequate return on invested capital. Consolidated Edison, for example, has paid a dividend every year since 1885, but in early 1974 it was forced to omit a quarterly payment because of meager profits, minimal growth, and a cash squeeze. The price of its stock fell from 21 to 7 but, with rising profits, moved back up to 28.

Important as it is, the corporation's past record is no guarantee of its future. Managements change, industries decline or become outmoded, governments regulate and consumers lose interest. Well-run firms keep improving their products and services, develop new areas, modernize their plant and equipment and so maintain industry leadership. If you select an heirloom stock, be sure to check its recent record of profitability and growth. You may find that your future income may be steady but is not

CONSISTENT DIVIDEND PAYERS FOR 50 YEARS OR MORE

These are industrial/service corporations which have paid at least one dividend annually for at least half a century. Most of them are listed on the New York Stock Exchange. Banks and investment/holding companies are not included.

With such long records of profitable operation, these companies can be expected to keep on rewarding shareholders but take nothing for granted, especially with utilities. One of the great claims of the Pennsylvania Railroad was its more-than-a century of dividend payments--before it went bankrupt.

COMPANY	Dividends Paid Since	COMPANY	Dividends Paid Since	COMPANY	Dividends Paid Since
Abbott Laboratories	1926	Cincinnati Gas & Electric	1853	Georgia-Pacific	1927
AFA Protective	1889	Cincinnati Milacron	1923	Gillette Co.	1906
Affiliated Publications	1882	Clark (J.L.)	1921	Gray Drug Stores	1928
Albany International	1922	Cleveland Electric	1901	Great Lakes International	1920
Alexander & Alexander	1922	Cluett, Peabody	1923	Great Northern Nekoosa	1910
Allied Chemical	1887	Colgate-Palmolive	1895	Guardsman Chemical	1918
Amerada Hess	1922	Coca-Cola	1893		
American Bakeries	1928	Columbus & Southern	1927	Hackensack Water	1886
American Brands	1905	Combustion Engineering	1911	Handy & Harman	1905
American Can	1923	Cominco, Ltd.	1924	Hanover Insurance	1853
American Dist. Telegraph	1903	Commonwealth Edison	1890	Harcourt, Brace & Jovanovich	1922
American Electric Power	1909	Cone Mills	1914	Hartford Steam Boiler	1871
American Express	1870	Conn. Energy	1850	Hawaiian Electric	1901
American General Insurance	1929	Conn. General Insurance	1867	Heinz (H.J.)	1911
American Home Products	1919	Conn. Natural Gas	1851	Heller International	1921
American Maize	1929	Consolidated Edison	1885	Hercules, Inc.	1913
American National Insurance	1923	Consumers Power	1913	Hershey Foods	1930
American Natural Resources	1905	Continental Corp.	1854	Hobart Corp.	1906
American Sterilizer	1914	Continental Group	1923	Hollinger-Argus	1912
A. T. & T.	1881	Conwood Corp.	1903	Home Beneficial	1906
AMF, Inc.	1927	Corning Glass	1881	Honeywell, Inc.	1920
Amfac, Inc.	1898	Courier Corp.	1919	Hormel (Geo. A.)	1928
Anchor-Hocking	1914	Courtlands, Ltd.	1913	Houghton Mifflin	1908
Archer-Daniels-Midland	1927	CPC International	1920	Household Finance	1917
Arizona Public Service	1920	CrownAmerica, Inc.	1888	Houston Industries	1922
Arvin Industries	1925	CSX Corp.	1922	Hydraulic Co.	1903
Atlantic City Electric	1919				
Atlantic-Richfield	1927	Dart & Kraft, Inc.	1924	Idaho Power	1917
Avon Products	1919	Dayton P&L	1919	Ideal Basic Industries	1911
Avondale Mills	1904	Delmarva P&L	1921	Imasco, Ltd.	1912
		DeLuxe Check Printing	1921	Imperial Chemical ADR	1927
Baker International	1929	Dentsply International	1900	Imperial Group	1928
Baltimore G&E	1910	Detroit Edison	1909	INA Corp.	1874
Bangor Hydro Electric	1925	Diamond International	1882	Indianapolis Water	1926
Bankers' Security Life	1923	Dillon Cos.	1922	Ingersoll-Rand	1910
Bay State Gas	1853	Dixico, Inc.	1925	Ingredient Technology	1927
Becton Dickinson	1926	Discount Corp. of N.Y.	1920	INTERCO, Inc.	1913
Bekins Corp.	1923	Dr. Pepper	1930	IBM	1916
Belknap, Inc.	1880	Dome Mines, Ltd.	1920	International Harvester	1910
Bell & Howell	1915	Donnelly (R.R.) & Sons	1911	International Multifoods	1923
Bell Telephone of Canada	1881	Dow Chemical	1911	Iowa Resources	1909
Bemis Co.	1922	Dow Jones & Co.	1906		
Beneficial Corp.	1929	Duckwall-Alco Stores	1917	Jefferson-Pilot	1913
Berkshire Gas	1858	Duke Power	1926	Jewel Companies	1928
Bird & Co.	1924	DuPont, E.I.	1904	Johnson Controls	1901
Blue Bell	1923	Duquesne Light	1913	Johnson & Johnson	1905
Borden, Inc.	1899	Durham Corp.	1918	Joy Manufacturing	1929
Borg-Warner	1928			JWT Corp.	1917
Boston Edison	1890	Eastern Utilities	1928		
Briggs & Stratton	1929	Eastman Kodak	1902	Kahler Corp.	1918
Bristol-Myers	1900	Eaton Corp.	1923	Kansas City Life	1907
British Petroleum	1917	El Paso Electric	1928	Kansas City P&L	1921
Brockway Glass	1927	Emhart Corp.	1902	Kansas G&E	1922
Brown Group	1923	ENSERCH Corp.	1926	Kansas P&L	1924
Burroughs Corp.	1895	Equifax, Inc.	1913	Kellogg Co.	1923
Business Men's Assurance	1924	Equimark, Inc.	1872	K-Mart, Inc.	1913
		Equitable of Iowa	1889	Kroger Co.	1902
Calif. Portland Cement	1909	Exxon Corp.	1882		
Campbell Soup	1902			Lane Co.	1922
Cannon Mills	1890	Federal Co.	1926	Lilly (Eli) & Co.	1885
Carpenter Technology	1907	Firestone Tire	1924	Louisville G&E	1913
Carter-Wallace	1883	Fisher Scientific	1907	Ludlow Corp.	1872
Castle & Cooke	1896	Fitchburg G&E	1859		
Caterpillar Tractor	1914	Flickinger (SM)	1920	Macy (R.H.)	1927
Ceco Corp.	1921	Fleming Cos.	1927	Madison G&E	1909
Central Hudson G & E	1903	Fort Howard Paper	1922	Mallinckrodt Corp.	1923
Central Illinois Light	1921	Foxboro Co.	1916	Manhattan Life	1851
Champion Spark Plug	1919	Freeport Minerals	1927	Marsh & McLennan	1923
Chattem, Inc.	1923			May Department Stores	1911
Chesebrough-Pond's	1883	Gannett Co.	1929	McCormick & Co.	1929
Chessie System	1922	GATX Corp.	1919	Means Service	1928
Chubb Corp.	1902	General Electric	1889	Media General	1923
Church & Dwight	1901	General Foods	1922	Melville Corp.	1916
C-I-L, Inc.	1912	General Mills	1898	Meredith Corp.	1930
Cincinnati Bell	1879	General Motors	1915	Middlesex Water	1912

COMPANY	Dividends Paid Since	COMPANY	Dividends Paid Since	COMPANY	Dividends Paid Since
Mine Safety Appliance	1918	Potomac Electric	1904	Sun Co.	1904
MMM	1916	PPG Industries	1899		
Mirro Corp.	1902	Pratt & Lambert	1905	Tampa Electric	1900
Mobil Corp.	1902	Procter & Gamble	1891	Tasty Baking	1915
Monarch Capital	1867	Providence Gas	1849	Texaco, Inc.	1903
Monarch Machine Tool	1913	Provident Life & Accident	1925	Texas Utilities	1917
Monsanto Co.	1925	Public Service (Colo)	1907	Texasgulf, Inc.	1921
Morton-Norwich	1925	Public Service E & G	1907	Time, Inc.	1930
Mountain States Telephone	1911			Times-Mirror	1892
Multimedia, Inc.	1921	Quaker Oats, Inc.	1906	Timken Co.	1921
Murphy (G.C.)	1913			Tokheim Corp.	1920
		Raybestos-Manhattan	1895	Toledo Edison	1922
Nabisco, Inc.	1899	Redpath Industries	1930	Towle Mfg.	1917
Nalco Chemical	1928	Reece Corp.	1882	Trans-Union Corp.	1914
Nashua Corp.	1926	Republic Financial	1920	Travelers Corp.	1864
National Fuel Gas	1903	Rexnord, Inc.	1894	Trico Corp.	1928
National-Standard	1916	Reynolds (R.J.) Industries	1900	Tucson Electric	1918
National Steel	1907	Richardson-Merrell	1922		
National Utilities	1923	Rockaway Corp.	1928	UGI Corp.	1885
New York State E&G	1910	Rochester Telephone	1926	Union Carbide	1918
NL Industries	1906	Rohm & Haas	1927	Union Electric	1906
NLT Corp.	1920	Rose's Stores	1928	Union Oil of Calif.	1916
Norfolk & Western	1901			Union Pacific	1900
Northeast Utilities	1927	Safeway Stores	1927	United Illuminating	1900
Northern States Power	1910	St. Paul Companies	1872	U.S. Gypsum	1919
Norton Co.	1922	San Diego G&E	1909	U.S. Tobacco	1912
Noxell Corp.	1925	Savannah Foods	1924	Universal Leaf Tobacco	1927
		SCOA Industries	1929	Upjohn Co.	1909
Ohio Art	1930	Scott Paper	1915		
Ohio Casualty	1923	Scovill Mfg.	1856	Virginia Electric	1925
Ohio Edison	1930	SFN Companies	1922		
Oklahoma G&E	1908	Shell Transport	1898	Walco National	1890
Olin Corp.	1926	Sierra Pacific Power	1916	Walker (Hiram) Consumers	1848
Orange & Rockland Utilities	1908	Singer Co.	1863	Warner-Lambert	1926
Outlet Co.	1926	SmithKline Corp.	1923	Washington Gas Light	1852
Owens-Illinois	1907	Sonoco Products	1925	Washington National	1923
		So. Calif. Edison	1909	Washington Water Power	1899
Pacific G&E	1919	So. N.E. Telephone	1891	Waverly Press	1925
Pacific Lighting	1909	Southland Royalty	1926	Weston (George)	1930
Pacific Resources	1912	Springs Mills	1898	West Point-Pepperell	1888
Pacific Telephone	1925	Squibb Corp.	1902	Westvaco Corp.	1892
Peavey Co.	1915	SRA Corp.	1930	Whirlpool Corp.	1929
Penney (J.C.)	1922	Stanadyne	1905	Wickes Co.	1895
Penn-Virginia	1916	Standard Brands	1899	Wiley (John)	1904
Pennwalt Corp.	1863	Standard-Coosa	1922	Woolworth (F.W.)	1912
Pennzoil Co.	1925	Standard Oil (Calif.)	1912	Wrigley (Wm.) Jr.	1912
Peoples Drug	1927	Standard Oil (Ind.)	1894	Wyman-Gordon	1916
Pfizer, Inc.	1901	Standard Register	1927		
Philadelphia Electric	1902	Stanley Works	1877	Xerox Corp.	1930
Philip Morris	1928	Stauffer Chemical	1915		
Pillsbury Co.	1927	Sterling Drug	1902	Zale Corp.	1925
Post Corp.	1921	Sun Chemical	1929		

SOURCE: Standard & Poor's

likely to increase much over the years—e.g., Ludlow Corporation, a diversified manufacturer of carpet yarn, home furnishings and specialty paper, has paid something to shareholders since 1872 but its earnings have faltered so that its stock price has fallen from a 1968 high of 45 to a 1975 low of 5 and, recently, was about 15—not exactly a rewarding investment.

Professional preference. These are stocks chosen by the "experts": managers of mutual funds, pension plans, endowments, etc. Usually, these are shares of large, well-known corporations traded on the New York Stock Exchange. But, increasingly, as professionals seek better performance, they include stocks listed on the American Stock Exchange or traded over the counter.

Institutional ownership does not always indicate "good" investments but it's an excellent place to start your search. Without such professional interest, few stocks will move up substantially.

In most cases, the companies whose shares are held in professionally managed portfolios must meet strict standards of financial strength, investment acceptance, profitability, growth and, to some extent, income. You know that someone has researched the corporation and feels that its prospects are good. Too many institutions still buy name and fame but, by and large, when any stock is owned by more than 50 institutions, it is worth checking further. Information is available in Standard & Poor's *Stock Guide,* Moody's *Handbook of Common Stocks, The Value Line* and analyses available from brokerage firms and investment advisory services.

And if you want to track portfolio changes, watch for reports on actions of investment companies in *Barron's,*

Monthly Stock Digest and the quarterly summaries published by *Lipper Analytical Services, Vickers Associates,* and *Wiesenberger Services.*

But be cautious. The public information comes months after decisions have been made. By the time you get the word, prices may have risen so much that your benefits will be comparatively small. Or you may be buying just before the Big Boys, realizing their mistakes, start selling.

It's also wise to check the type of fund. If it's designed for long-term holdings, following its action can be worthwhile if you are patient.

No matter how popular a stock may be, if it's volatile and has run up rapidly, be doubly cautious. The individual investor can get caught in a computer-triggered situation. What happens is that the money manager sets his computer so that when a stock reaches a certain price, there is an automatic sell order. When this large block of stock hits the market, especially at a lower price than the previous close, this triggers other computers and, in a few hours, the stock price is down, down, down.

Following the leaders can also be profitable when you speculate. By watching institutional portfolios keyed to growth, you can find the names of AMEX and OTC stocks that have passed some sort of review. Usually, these are companies that are "emerging" or "turnarounds" where there's hope of quick gains. Still, before you commit your savings, get a copy of the company's annual report, check advisory services for comments and wait until other major investors start buying. Such caution may cost a few points of profit but it will save a lot more in losses. And always remember that these are speculations, not investments.

INSTITUTIONAL FAVORITES

Owned by more than 500 institutions

American Home Products	Johnson & Johnson
A. T. & T.	MacDonald's
Atlantic-Richfield	Merck & Co.
Caterpillar Tractor	MMM
Citicorp.	Mobil Corp.
Coca-Cola	Phillips Petroleum
Conoco, Inc.	Procter & Gamble
Dow Chemical	Raytheon Co.
Eastman Kodak	Sears Roebuck
Exxon Corp.	Standard Oil (Cal.)
General Electric	Standard Oil (Ind.)
General Motors	Tenneco, Inc.
General Telephone	Texaco, Inc.
Gulf Oil	Union Carbide
Halliburton, Inc.	Union Oil
IBM	Union Pacific

By 400-500 major investors

Abbott Laboratories	K—Mart
Avon Products	Lilly (Eli)
Bristol-Myers	Revlon, Inc.
Burroughs Corp.	Reynolds (R.J.) Industries
Digital Equipment	Schlumberger, Ltd.
Dresser Industries	Standard Oil (Ohio)
DuPont (E.I.)	Texas Utilities
I. T. & T.	Union Carbide

By over 250 investment, Insurance companies, etc.

Aetna Life & Casualty	INA Corp.
Alcan Aluminum	Inco, Ltd.
Allied Chemical	International Paper
AMAX, Inc.	InterNorth, Inc.
Amerada-Hess	Kerr-McGee
American Cyanamid	Louisiana Land
American Electric Power	Marathon Oil
American Express	Middle South Utilities
American Hospital Supply	Monsanto Co.
AMP, Inc.	Morgan (J.P.)
Baker International	Motorola, Inc.
BankAmerica	NCR, Inc.
Baxter-Travenol	NL Industries
Beatrice Foods	Penney (J.C.)
Black & Decker	Pennzoil Co.
Boeing Co.	PepsiCo, Inc.
CBS, Inc.	Pfizer, Inc.
Central & Southwest	Philip Morris
Champion International	Public Service E&G
Chase-Manhattan	RCA Corp.
Cities Service	Royal Dutch
Colgate-Palmolive	Santa Fe Industries
Conn. General Insurance	Schering-Plough
Continental Corp.	Shell Oil
CPC International	SmithKline Corp.
Dart & Kraft, Inc.	Southern Calif. Edison
Disney (Walt)	Sperry Corp.
Emerson Electric	Squibb Corp.
Federated Dept. Stores	Sterling Drug
Florida P&L	Sun Co.
Ford Motor Co.	Superior Oil
General Foods	Texas Instruments
General Mills	Travelers Insurance
Georgia Pacific	TRW, Inc.
Getty Oil	United Telecommunications
Goodyear Tire	Upjohn Co.
Hewlett-Packard	Virginia Electric
Honeywell, Inc.	Warner Lambert
Houston Industries	Westinghouse Corp.

SOURCE: Standard & Poor's

STOCKS WITH INSTITUTIONAL INTEREST

COMPANY	Recent Price	AutEx Trading Interest		Institutional Holdings %Outstanding Shares
		Volume*	% Share Out.	
Kellogg Co.	20 1/4	1,362	1.8	74%
K-Mart	17 7/8	2,604	2.1	63
Searle (G.D.)	27	1,434	2.7	60
Avon Products	34 1/8	1,344	2.2	59
Deere & Co.	48	1,974	3.2	56
Texas Utilities	18 5/8	1,605	1.7	55
Citicorp	24 1/4	2,814	2.3	53
Fed. Nat. Mortgage	11 7/8	1,572	2.7	53
Phillips Petr.	58 3/4	1,527	1.0	52
PepsiCo, Inc.	27 1/4	2,733	3.0	52
American Home	28 1/8	2,163	1.4	52

* Thousands of Shares

SOURCE: Forbes Magazine

Look for Companies Earning the Biggest Profits

The single most important standard of safety is high, consistent profitability. As explained later, this can be determined by calculating the rate of return on shareholders' equity . . . a minimum annual average of 11%. By sticking to these real winners, you will always make a lot of money . . . in time.

Wright Investors' Service proved this with the stocks of the 30 companies that make up the DJIA. It made a theoretical investment of $1,000 in each company and, 15 years later, sold out. With dividends reinvested, the shares of the 10 most profitable companies gained 208%;

those of the least profitable, only 64%. Wright's conclusion: "Profitable companies listed on the NYSE will make more money with less risk than almost any other type of investment. If the investor takes time to shift to the 10 top money makers of the DJIA each year, he will be rich while he is still young enough to enjoy his money."

SOME COMPANIES WITH HIGH TOTAL RETURNS
— PRICE APPRECIATION + DIVIDENDS — 1976 - 80

COMPANY	S&P Rating	Annualized Total Return
American Medical Inter.	A—	73%
Barry Wright	A—	74
Boeing Co.	A	56
Computervision Corp.	B	139*
Dataproducts Corp.	B	53
Flight Safety Inter.	B+	70
Foster Wheeler	A+	61
General Instrument	B+	65
Heileman Brewing	A	57
Helmerich & Payne	A	60
Humana, Inc.	B+	80
Lifemark Corp.	A—	72
Narda Microwave	B	66
Nat. Medical Enterprises	A—	84
Parker Drilling	B+	65
Parsons Corp.	A—	62
Storage Technology	B+	57*
Telecommunications	C	100
Texas Oil & Gas	A	68
Waste Management	B+	70

* Paid no dividends

By comparison, the compounded annual returns of the S&P composite index, for these five years, was +14%.

SOURCE: Merrill Lynch Market Letter

Closely Held Companies

When a company has a good long-term potential, its executives and directors will be confident enough to be heavy investors in the stock. But this same advantage can be dangerous if the shares are inherited or in a very few hands because:

• Management may prefer to pay small dividends for personal tax reasons. If you want income, skip such companies.

• Death of an owner-executive may throw large blocks of stock on the market. The need for cash to pay estate taxes could force shares to be sold, possibly with a depressing effect on the stock price. Over the long term, however, such distribution can be beneficial because it will create greater public interest and if the stock has been traded OTC, may lead to listing on the AMEX or NYSE.

• Family-owned and -managed concerns may be inefficient. This fall-off in managerial ability often occurs with the third or fourth generation. These officers and directors may have neither the skill nor the interest to keep the corporation profitable and competitive.

• Closely controlled corporations are takeover targets and thus offer unexpectedly high prices for the stock. It's getting so expensive to compete in many markets that family management is unwilling, or unable, to make the

COMPANIES WITH SUBSTANTIAL OWNERSHIP BY FAMILY, FOUNDATION OR GROUP

Ahmanson (H.F.)	Lane Bryant
Alberto-Culver	Levi Strauss
Alco Standard	Levitz Furniture
Allied Maintenance	Lilly (Eli)
AM International	Loews Corp.
AMP, Inc.	Marion Laboratories
Anheuser-Busch	Marriott Corporation
Armstrong Rubber	Maryland Cup
Avery International	Mays (J.W.)
Avon Products	McDonnell-Douglas
Bard (C.R.)	McGraw-Hill
Barnes Group	Mercantile Stores
Black & Decker	Murphy Oil
Bulova Watch	New York Times
Campbell Soup	No. American Phillips
Carnation Co.	Norton Company
Carter-Wallace	Owens-Corning Fiberglas
Certainteed Corp.	Petrie Stores
Church's Fried Chicken	Reeves Bros.
Coleman Co.	Rollins, Inc.
Cone Mills	Russ Togs
Coors (Adolph)	Schlitz (Jos.) Brewing
Corning Glass Works	Seagram Co. Ltd.
Crane Company	Sears, Roebuck
Crown Cork & Seal	Simplicity Pattern
Cummins Engine	Southland Corp.
Dayton-Hudson	Sperry & Hutchinson
Denny's	Staley (A.E.)
De Soto, Inc.	Stevens (J.P.)
Digital Equipment	Stokely-Van Camp
Duke Power	Stop & Shop Cos.
Easco Corp.	Suburban Propane Gas
Ethyl Corp.	Sun Co.
Fedders Corp.	Taft Broadcasting
Fisher Scientific	Tandy Corporation
Foster Wheeler	Teledyne, Inc.
Foxboro Corp.	Thomas & Betts
General Dynamics	Time, Incorporated
General Tire	Times Mirror
Gerber Products	Trane Company
Gordon Jewelry	Upjohn Company
Great A & P Tea Co.	Warnaco, Inc.
Heinz (H.J.) Co.	Washington Post
Hershey Foods	Weis Markets
High Voltage Engineering	Weyerhaeuser Co.
IU International	Williams Companies
Jonathan Logan	Winn-Dixie Stores
Kellogg Company	Wrigley (Wm.) Jr.
Knight-Ridder News	Zayre Corporation
Kroger Co.	

SOURCE: Moody's Investors Service

heavy investments needed for research and development, modernization and expansion. The sons prefer to take cash and an employment contract, and the old folks want to enjoy the income from convertible securities. When you know of, or can spot, such possibilities, dig deeper. You may make a lot of money.

Common Stocks for Income

If you are looking for income only, common stocks may not always be the best investment. In periods of high interest rates, bonds and savings certificates will provide higher returns. But unless those fixed-income securities are bought at a discount, they will not appreciate in value so that your total returns will be limited.

The right kind of common stocks can provide income plus capital gains and, with lower taxes, can net more money. Under present laws, all income is taxed at the highest rate but only 40% of long-term profits (when the securities have been held 12 months) is subject to the federal income tax. Thus, the investor in the 50% tax bracket pays Uncle Sam 50¢ of every dollar in interest and dividends but only 20¢ of every dollar of long-term capital gains. In the 40% tax bracket, the investor keeps 60¢ of each income dollar and 84¢ of his capital-gains dollar.

The higher your total income, the greater the benefit of investments in common stocks.

Those tax advantages may not always be as real as they first appear. Lower- and middle-income investors (who pay taxes at a modest rate) may find that the higher net returns of capital gains, when compared to those of straight income, may not justify the risks.

$10,000 CAPITAL GAIN: SHORT-TERM vs. LONG-TERM

Regular Tax Rate	Short-Term Left After Tax	Long-Term		Added Income
		Tax Rate	Left After Tax	
30%	$7,000	12%	$8,800	$1,800
40	6,000	16	8,400	2,400
50	5,000	20	8,000	3,000
60	4,000	24	7,600	3,600
70	3,000	28	7,200	4,200

It is always important to project capital gains on an annual basis. If you pay federal income taxes at a rate of 37% or less, a possible 10% or even 12% annual appreciation may not be as rewarding as a sure 8% in dividends or interest. In the 50% tax bracket, however, there will be a significant difference.

High-Yield Stocks

And if you want to speculate, choose high-yielding stock with recognition of the extra risks. This is an excellent way to build capital. These equities may not be quality investments but with a 12% dividend rate, you will double your money in six years. Just be sure the company has logical prospects of adequate earnings.

Such opportunities can be found in the following groups:

Pale-blue chips. These are established companies, usually with under $200 million in revenues, that have: *(a)* paid dividends continuously for at least 20 years; *(b)* not reduced their dividend rate in the past four years; *(c)* a reasonable amount of long-term debt; *(d)* dividends that are well above those of the average stock yield (recently, about 6%).

Sleeper stocks. These are lesser-known, smaller companies that: *(a)* do not fall into other categories; *(b)* are often traded OTC; *(c)* have been ignored by most investors; *(d)* are not seasoned enough to interest institutions. If they are solid firms in sound industries, their stocks will eventually sell at a lower yield and thus at a higher price.

Unpopular industries. At different times, various industries fall out of favor with major investors, for both valid and invalid reasons. When the latter is the case,

there may be many opportunities. When it's the former, there may be worthwhile buys in a generally weak industry. Among groups that move up and down in investor favor are tobaccos, steels, coal, sugar, machine tools and automobile manufacturers.

If an industry, or a company, does not have a growth image, dividends can double with little change in the price of the stock. Eventually, however, this superior value will be recognized but, meantime, you will get an ever-higher return.

Benefit of Dividend Exclusion

For small investors, the dividend exclusion up to $200 per couple can significantly improve dividend returns.

Under federal tax laws, the first $100 of dividends is tax-free. If the stock certificate is registered in joint names, each co-owner can deduct up to $200 of the total income.

Note: Joint ownership of securities, real estate, CDs, etc. can be costly and inconvenient. In case of the death of one co-owner, total assets will be tied up and may be counted as part of the taxable estate of the deceased.

When you start serious investing, plan purchases so that each partner owns securities paying dividends of at least $100 per year. If the stocks are bought with the husband's money, they should be given to the wife and registered in her name. You are allowed to give any one person up to $10,000 a year with no lifetime maximum. If the annual amount is greater, you must file a Gift Tax report and, if the donor dies within three years of the transfer, the value of the securities will be included in his/her estate.

Watch the Percentage of Payout

When any corporation pays dividends that represent a very high percentage of earnings, there will be comparatively little money for reinvestment for future growth. With industrial and service firms, a high payout indicates that: *(a)* the company is so profitable that the retained earnings are adequate for continued growth; *(b)* management is confident of the future and anticipates that future profits will rise so that the percentage of payout, with the same dividend, will decrease; *(c)* there can be trouble ahead.

With utilities, a high payout is not so significant, as they use debt to finance expansion. But when dividends represent 80% or more of profits, it may indicate slower growth and, probably, little chance of higher dividends.

Stocks for Steadily Rising Income

Unless you are now in, and expect to remain in, a high tax bracket, the importance of dividend income increases as you grow older. In the prime of life, your earning power is usually expanding. As you near retirement, you become more concerned with regular, comfortable income from your investments and less disturbed by taxes, due to cessation of salary or business income.

This is the time to look for stocks of companies that

COMPANIES PAYING OUT HIGH PERCENTAGE OF EARNINGS

Company	1980	3 year average	Company	1980	3 year average
American Home Products	60%	60%	Marsh & McLennan	58%	55%
Avon Products	74	66	Maytag Co.	79	66
Block (H&R)	59	51	Mohasco Corp.	88	62
Castle & Cooke	71	44	Pacific Lumber	69	55
Champion Spark Plug	76	51	Pennwalt Corp.	52	46
Clorox Co.	55	43	Pittston Co.	59	103
Coca Cola	63	58	Purex Industries	56	55
Dr. Pepper	55	53	Quaker State Refining	67	54
Dun & Bradstreet	54	54	Safeway Stores	57	48
DuPont (E.I.)	57	49	Simplicity Pattern	70	49
Emery Air Freight	72	64	Tampax Co.	79	73
Household Finance	54	43	U.S. Tobacco	50	51
IBM	56	58	Universal Foods	63	45
Kellogg Co.	55	62	Warner-Lambert	55	58
Lukens Steel	76	46	Winn-Dixie	53	47
Marion Laboratories	79	59	Wrigley (Wm) Jr.	54	49
Marshall Field	83	65			

SOURCE: Moody's Investors Service

are likely to keep raising their dividends as listed in the table. These are major corporations that, over the past decade, quadrupled their payouts. Hopefully, they will keep up this pace. *Put your money where management knows how to make money and is willing to share profits with stockholders.*

HIGH YIELDING STOCKS WHERE DIVIDEND INCREASES ARE LIKELY

COMPANY	Current Yield	Current Dividend	Anticipated Div. - 1982
American Standard	6.6%	$2.20	$2.60
Carter Hawley Hale	6.4	1.16	1.25
Coca-Cola	6.4	2.16	2.32
Continental Group	7.3	2.40	2.60
Exxon Co.	8.2	6.00	6.60
General Foods	7.3	2.20	2.44
Gillette Co.	6.4	1.90	2.10
Gulf Oil	6.6	2.50	3.20
Kimberly-Clark	6.0	3.60	4.00
National Detroit	7.5	2.00	2.25
Petrie Stores	8.1	2.20	2.45
RCA Corp.	6.4	1.80	1.88
Standard Brands	6.2	1.64	1.82
Texaco, Inc.	6.5	2.60	3.20
Winn-Dixie	6.6	1.92	2.16

SOURCE: Merrill Lynch Market Letter

How to Get Monthly Income from Dividends

Investors who have to rely on dividend income often live well for a few weeks after receiving checks and then have to skimp until the next payments. Here are some ways to beat that crunch:

• Set up a portfolio of income stocks selected according to the months in which quarterly dividends are paid.

January–April–July–October: A.T.&T.

February–May–August–November: Tampa Electric
March–June–September–December: Blue Bell
Information is available in Standard & Poor's *Stock Guide* and many investment advisory letters but it's easier to ask your broker for suggestions.

• Open a special dividend account in a thrift institution, and, each month, withdraw one-twelfth of the total estimated annual income. Select a bank or S&L that pays interest from day of deposit to day of withdrawal so you'll get a few extra dollars. This set-aside requires willpower but if the dividends are raised during the year, you'll make out OK.

• Buy shares in a mutual fund and arrange for monthly checks. In some months, this may require the sale of some shares but a well-managed fund should be able to increase net-asset value of shares so your principal will remain about the same. Besides, even with a 15% annual rate of withdrawal, savings yielding 10% will last for 11 years.

Getting Average Annual Returns of Over 15%

One easy, inexpensive and almost sure way to boost your income is to buy high-dividend-paying stocks of established companies that offer automatic dividend reinvestment plans to buy new shares at a discount. You add to your holdings at a bargain price and enjoy the benefits of compounding. With A.T. & T., you can acquire new shares at a 5% discount when they are purchased with dividends. Since the recent yield was 9.8%, you start off with a 14.8% return on part of your savings . . . more with compounding. And, starting in 1982, there are tax benefits for reinvested dividends of utilities: annually, $1,500 for joint returns; $750 for singles.

Here's how to project future income/profits:

With "T" at 55 and paying a $5.40 per share annual dividend, your yield is 9.8%. At that price, the stock is selling at a modest price/earnings ratio of about 7.

Over the past decade, A.T. & T. has increased its earnings at 7% a year and its payouts at a slightly higher rate. Let's be conservative and assume that both will rise by only 5% annually in the next five years.

You buy 100 shares for $5,500 (not counting commissions) and arrange for the dividends to be reinvested at the 5% discount or a market price of 52¼. Actual purchases will be in fractional shares, part of whose extra value will be offset by the small commissions. If the price of the stock stays at 55, here are logical projections:

Year	Earnings +5%	Dividends +5%	Income	New Shares	Total Shares	Value at 55
I	$8.19	$5.40	$540	10.28	110.28	$6,065
II	8.60	5.67	583	11.15	121.43	6,679
III	9.03	5.95	722	13.07	134.50	7,397
IV	9.48	6.25	841	16.10	150.60	8,283
V	9.95	6.56	988	18.90	169.50	9,322

Thus, in five years, you'll own some 169 shares worth, at the 55 price, $9,322. That's a 70% gain on your original investment.

Logically, the shares will be more valuable. With the projected $9.95 per share earnings and that modest multiple of 7, the shares would be selling at about 70: a total value of $11,650 . . . more than double your original investment.

(Actually, these are a bit enthusiastic as they are projected on an annual basis, whereas the reinvestments will be made quarterly in smaller sums. But the concept is sound and an excellent way to invest for income and long-term gains.)

Similar opportunities are available with stocks of many high-dividend-paying companies. There are, of course, minor risks: The selected firm may not perform as well as expected; there may be unfavorable governmental or court action; the stock market may decline. But only rarely does a quality corporation reduce its dividend and, even without any boost in the payout, you will be doing well.

CHAPTER 4

The Importance of Quality

With securities, quality is like charm in a woman. If she has it, she needs little else. In the stock market, quality is primarily the record of a corporation's financial strength, its record of profitability and growth and its prospects for continuing a comparable record in the future, and the investment acceptance of its securities.

For easy reference, most investors can refer to Standard & Poor's *Stock Guide*. This rates companies on the basis of an appraisal of past performance of earnings and dividends and relative current standing: A+ (highest); A (high); A− (above average); B+ (average); B (below average); B− (lower); and C (lowest). *Never invest in any company rated below B+.*

Professional money managers have detailed standards such as these developed by Wright Investors' Service. Here's a digest, as the actual ratings are highly complex and are adjusted, by computer analysis, for historical records, stability and so forth.

Unless otherwise noted, these are the minimums for listing a company on the Approved Wright Investment List:

Investment Acceptance
   Market value of publicly held shares: $100 million
   Trading volume (annual): $25 million
   Turnover (annual): less than 50%
   Ownership by institutions: 15
   Shareholders: 5,000
Financial Strength
   Total capital and surplus: $50 million
   Equity capital as percentage of total capital (including preferred stock and long-term debt): 50%
   Long-term debt (as % of total capital): maximum 40%

Fixed charges (ratio of pre-tax income to interest and preferred dividends): 3.5:1
Working capital (ratio of current assests to current liabilities): 2:1
Convertible securities: maximum of 30% of outstanding common stock and potential dilution, maximum of 15%
Profitability and Stability
   Profit rate (return on equity capital): 11%
   Stability index: 60%
   Dividends: minimum payout of 10% of earnings; maximum of 75%
   Dividends as % of return on equity: 5%
   Operating income (as % of total capital): 15%
Growth
   Earned growth rate (unadjusted earnings growth rate per share): +4%
   Stability index: 60%
   Equity growth (annual rate per share): +4%
   Dividend growth (per share): +4%
   Sales/revenues: +4%

All of these data are calculated for at least 10 years. For the first three categories, the ratings are: A = Outstanding; B = Excellent; C = Good (acceptable). For the growth, the numbers range from 0 to 20.

Recent ratings: AMP, Inc., AAA16; GE, AAA12; IBM, AAA12; Merck & Co., AAA14; Pfizer, ABA12; Time, Inc., ABA11; Winn-Dixie, AAA14.

Now let's see how these standards can be applied to growth stocks and can be used to make rewarding selections.

In the stock market, growth has always been a magic word but in these days of high inflation, it has become essential for those who want investments whose total returns can outpace the erosion of inflation. There are several definitions of growth but, basically, with common stocks, *growth is in the eye of the beholder.*

The conservative investor wants growth, but not at the expense of safety or income; the enterprising investor seeks appreciation but also looks for some return for the use of his money; the speculator sees growth as a rise in the price of the stock and is little concerned with what happens to the company itself.

It sounds easy to pick growth stocks, but true growth equities are relatively rare because their companies must combine growth with profitability.

Regardless of what you may hear from others or read in some books, true growth is to be found in the increase of the underlying worth of the corporation as measured by stockholders' equity (often called book value), which represents the assets behind each share of common stock.

A true growth company should earn 15% a year on its equity and grow by 10% a year, year after year. What happens is this:

TRUE GROWTH

Year	Book Value per Share	Earnings per Share	Dividends per Share	Reinvested per Share
I	$10.00	$1.50	$.50	$1.00
II	11.00	1.65	.55	1.10
III	12.10	1.81	.60	1.20
IV	13.30	2.00	.70	1.30
V	14.60	2.19	.79	1.40

In the first year, on a per share basis, the book value is $10.00, earnings $1.50, dividends 50¢, leaving $1.00 for reinvestment. This boosts the book value to $11.00 per share. At the same 15% rate of return, earnings in Year II will be $1.65, dividends 55¢, and there will be $1.10 for reinvestment. And so on.

At the end of five years, on a per share basis, the book value is $14.60, earnings $2.19, dividends 79¢, with $1.40 added to book value. Thus the underlying worth of the company is up 46%, and in normal markets this will be reflected in a higher valuation for the stock. *That's true investment growth.*

Unfortunately, in Wall Street, growth is too often based on reputation or hopes, not on facts. Eventually, of course, value will out—but it can be a slow process.

Too many analysts judge growth by broad subjective standards. They assume that because a company is in a growth industry, it automatically becomes a growth company. Or they relate higher sales and earnings without digging into the reason for these increases.

Example: Pollution control is a growth industry, at least for the foreseeable future. There are a number of companies which are engaged, directly or indirectly, in one or more phases of these attempts at environmental improvement. But which are the growth stocks?

Shares of established companies may already be selling at prices that overdiscount the future potential of the industry and/or the company. *Such growth companies in a growth industry may no longer be considered growth stocks.*

There's also the danger of selecting the wrong company. If it is new and small, how do you know there can be real future progress?

If it's a more mature organization, how can you be sure that the corporation has not reached a temporary plateau?

An industry or a company that has been growing rapidly for the last 10 or 15 years may show little or no growth in the next decade. The need for its products or services may have leveled off, competition may have moved in, new techniques or equipment may be more efficient, or capital needs may be so great that profits will be limited. There's growth only if you—and other investors—think so. *Be sure the facts justify such confidence.*

On the other hand, a new company in a new growth industry may show future promise far greater than in the past. The tough, testing days may be over, and now management can turn its attention to making money. In choosing growth stocks, it is important to weigh carefully the past performance and the future *realistic* prospects. *The best choice is a company that combines a strong past record with an equally strong future. Add a little luck and you may have a real growth stock.*

Throughout *Your Investments,* you will find specific criteria to help you find growth investments. In theory, the ideal growth stock is a proven growth company, in a proven growth industry, with proven, competent management and promising prospects for continued growth in the next decade. If it's a real growth company, its executives will be alert to new developments, and if they're not creating new products and markets, they will be moving into growth areas.

In practice, you will probably have to settle for less: *conservative investors* will be willing to pay a higher price for established growth leaders; *enterprising investors* may settle for fast-growing companies in not-so-fast-growing industries—especially if they can be acquired at reasonable prices; and *speculative investors* will tend to compromise on the required past performance. They will make their decisions primarily on future *hopes,* even if they come high. *One really "hot" stock can offset a great many losers or mediocre performers!*

The most reliable index is stable and superior profit growth during both prosperous and difficult economic periods. A true winner must meet a much broader spectrum of requirements beyond the obvious growth of earnings, equity and dividends. Premium-quality companies have future prospects of a superior rate of net return on common shareholders' equity, an outstanding balance sheet and a wide institutional following.

Guidelines for Small Growth Firms

Basically, the same criteria apply to small, unseasoned companies but, for winners, you must expand your analysis:

1. Read the annual report backwards. Look at the footnotes to discover whether there are significant problems, unfavorable long-term commitments, etc.

2. Analyze the management's record in terms of growth of revenue and earnings and, especially, return on stockholders' equity. Discard any company that has not

QUALITY STOCKS LISTED ON THE NEW YORK STOCK EXCHANGE

AEROSPACE
Cessna Aircraft
Thiokol Corp.

APPAREL
Blue Bell, Inc.
INTERCO, Inc.
U.S. Shoe
V.F. Corp.

AUTOMOTIVE
Dana Corp.
Eaton Corp.
Echlin Mfg.

BEVERAGES
Coca-Cola
Dr. Pepper
Heublein, Inc.
PepsiCo, Inc.

CHEMICALS
American Cyanamid
Bandag, Inc.
Big Three Industries
Clorox Company
Colgate-Palmolive
Dexter Corp.
Ethyl Corp.
Ferro Corp.
International Flavors
Loctite Corp.
Lubrizol Corp
NCH Corp.
Nalco Chemical
Procter & Gamble
Purex Industries
Rubbermaid, Inc.
Stauffer Chemical
Witco Chemical

CONSTRUCTION
Caterpillar Tractor
Masco Corp.
Masonite Corp.
Stone & Webster
Vulcan Materials
Weyerhaeuser Co.

DIVERSIFIED
Ametek, Inc.
Eagle-Picher
Emhart Corp.
FMC Corp.
Koppers Co.
Midland-Ross
MMM
National Service Ind.
Norton Simon
Pacific Lumber
Scott & Fetzer
Textron, Inc.

**DRUGS, COSMETICS,
   HEALTH CARE**
Abbott Laboratories
American Home Products
American Hospital Supply
Avon Products
Bard (C.R.)
Baxter Travenol
Becton-Dickinson
Bristol-Myers
Chesebrough-Pond's

Johnson & Johnson
Lilly (Eli)
Medtronic, Inc.
Merck & Co.
Pfizer, Inc.
Revlon, Inc.
Richardson-Merrell
Rorer Group
Schering-Plough
SmithKline Corp.
Squibb Corp.
Sterling Drug
Upjohn Co.
Warner-Lambert

ELECTRICAL
Crouse-Hinds
Emerson Electric
General Electric
Hobart Corp.
Maytag Co.
Square D Co.
Thomas & Betts

ELECTRONICS
AMP, Inc.
Avnet, Inc.
Burroughs Corp.
Data General
Digital Equipment
E. G. & G., Inc.
General Signal
Hewlett-Packard
IBM
Motorola, Inc.
Perkin-Elmer
RCA Corp.
Raytheon Co.
Sperry Corp.
Tektronix
Texas Instrument

FINANCIAL
Bank of New York
BankAmerica
Manufacturers Hanover
Morgan (J.P.)
National Detroit
Northwest Bancorp
Texas Commerce

FOODS
Archer-Daniels-Midland
Beatrice Foods
CPC International
Campbell Soup
Campbell Taggart
Consolidated Foods
Dart & Kraft, Inc.
General Foods
General Mills
Gerber Products
Heinz (H.J.) Co.
Kellogg Co.
Nabisco, Inc.
Quaker Oats
Ralston Purina
Standard Brands

MACHINERY & EQUIPMENT
Black & Decker
Briggs & Stratton
Bucyrus-Erie
CBI Industries

Clark Equipment
Colt Industries
Combustion Engineering
Cooper Industries
Deere & Co.
Dover Corp.
Dresser Industries
Ex-Cello-O Corp.
Ingersoll-Rand
Joy Mfg.
Parker-Hannifin
Snap-On Tools
Sundstrand Corp
Xerox Corp.

METAL PRODUCERS
Carpenter Technology
Cleveland-Cliffs
St. Joe Minerals

**METAL PRODUCTS
   MANUFACTURERS**
Amsted Industries
Continental Group
Crown Cork
Harsco Corp.
Hoover Universal
Kennametal, Inc.
Norris Industries
Signode Corp.
Stanley Works
Timken Co.

**OIL, GAS, COAL &
   RELATED SERVICES**
Atlantic-Richfield
Baker International
Conoco, Inc.
Exxon Corp.
Halliburton Co.
Helmerich Payne
Kerr McGee
Louisiana Land
Mobil Corp.
Petrolane, Inc.
Phillips Petroleum
Quaker State
Schlumberger, Ltd.
Smith International
Standard Oil (Calif.)
Standard Oil (Ind)
Union Oil (Calif.)

PAPER
Dennison Manufacturing
Fort Howard Paper
Great Northern Nekoosa
Kimberly—Clark
Union Camp

PRINTING & PUBLISHING
Donnelley (R.R.)
Dun & Bradstreet
Gannett Company
Knight-Ridder
McGraw-Hill
SFN Companies
Time, Inc.
Times Mirror

RECREATION
CBS, Inc.
Disney Productions
Eastman Kodak

Milton Bradley

RETAILERS
Eckerd (Jack)
Edison Brothers
Federated Dept. Stores
K-Mart Corp.
Longs Drug Stores
Lucky Stores
Macy (R.H.) Co.
Melville Corp.
Revco (D.S.)
Rite Aid Stores
Safeway Stores
Standard Brand Paints
Winn-Dixie Stores

TEXTILES
Cone Mills

TOBACCO
American Brands
Reynolds Industries
U.S. Tobacco

TRANSPORTATION
Consolidated Freight
Delta Airlines
Emery Air Freight
Transway International

UTILITIES
American Tel. & Tel.
Arkansas Louisiana Gas
Central & Southwest
Central Louisiana Energy
Central Tel. & Utilities
Columbia Gas
Enserch Corp.
Florida Power & Light
Florida Power Corp.
Houston Industries
Houston Natural Gas
InterNorth, Inc.
NICOR, Inc.
ONEOK, Inc.
Panhandle Eastern
Peoples Energy
Pioneer Corp.
Public Service Indiana
Rochester Telephone
So. Natural Resources
Southern Union
Southwest Public Service
Tampa Electric
Texas Eastern Corp.
Texas Gas Transmission
Texas Oil & Gas
Texas Utilities
Tucson Electric
United Telecommunications

MISCELLANEOUS
ARA Services
Anchor-Hocking
Automatic Data
Engelhard Minerals
Genuine Parts
Grainger (W.W.)
Josten's, Inc.
Malone & Hyde
National Medical Care
Rollins, Inc.
Super Valu Stores

SOURCE: Wright Investors' Service

averaged a 15% profit rate over the past five and, preferably, ten years.

3. Find a current ratio of current assets to current liabilities of two to one or higher. This indicates the company can withstand difficulties and will probably be able to obtain money to expand.

4. Look for a low debt ratio with long-term debt no more than 35% of total capital. This means the company has staying power and could be a worthwhile long-term speculation.

5. Compare the price of the stock and its price/earnings ratio to that of other, larger companies in the same industry. If it's lower, this may be a sleeper. If the multiple is above 20, be wary. Such stocks tend to be volatile.

6. Look for stocks that are selling at half their growth rates, with strong management, little debt and a return on investment high enough to generate internal growth.

All of these criteria apply, to a large degree, to established corporations. You want a proven record of able management as shown by fairly consistent results over a period of time.

GROWTH GUIDELINES

Annual Per Share Earnings Growth

	Rating
Less than 4%	Below average
4% - 5%	Average
5% - 7%	Above average
7% - 10%	Good
10% - 15%	Excellent
Over 15%	Super

Annual Return on Equity

Less than 10%	Below average
10% - 12%	Average
12% - 15%	Above average
15% - 20%	Excellent
Over 20%	Terrific

Don't Confuse Growth with Price

Investing for growth is wise as long as the price you pay does not get out of line. The problems develop because of Wall Street's tendency to swing from unsupported optimism to equally false pessimism.

When growth stocks become popular, as they did in the late 1960s, institutions keep buying with little or no regard to value. This is mass mania, not investing. The higher the price of the stock, the greater the buying—for a while. Although corporate earnings of quality stocks continued to grow steadily, the prices of some of these shares soared to outlandish heights—30, 40 and 50 times profits. The rationale: "These are Famous Name companies which will continue to grow and grow, so Buy and Hold—forever."

How stupid can you get? If Xerox, with earnings of $3.80 per share, was worth 171 in 1973, how come the same stock was selling at 41 in 1978 when profits were $5.77 a share, and in the mid 50s in 1980, when profits were up to $7.73?

Such dichotomy points out the validity of the phrase, *Growth is in the eye of the beholder.* In the long run, corporate growth will determine the value of a stock; but for the short term, there may be little relationship between price and value. Even with growth, an investor must be patient!

These same self-styled professionals can cause plenty of trouble when any company, no matter how solid or profitable, fails to live up to analysts' (not the company's) predictions. When IBM reported first-quarter earnings were up *only* 13.2%, the stock was knocked down 8 points in one day. There was no logic to such selling—yet that's the way too many money managers act. They live on hope and seldom let facts get in the way of their preconceived concepts. DO NOT FOLLOW THEIR LEAD unless you are speculating. IBM is still one of the great growth stocks; in the years ahead, it will be selling at a much higher price because real investors recognize the importance of growth and profitability.

Don't Overlook Established Companies

The corporation does not have to be young to have growth potential. There are opportunities with old companies where there's new management, a turnaround situation, or R & D-based developments. Analyst James Wolpert lists these ever-important developments:

1. Strong position in an evolutionary market. Find an industry or market that is bound to move ahead and check the top half dozen corporations. The leaders are probably the best bets, but do not overlook the secondary companies. They may provide a greater percentage gain on your investment.

2. Ability to set prices at profitable levels. This is important in service industries where greater volume can bring proportionately higher profits as overhead remains relatively stable. The same approach applies to companies making or distributing branded merchandise.

3. Adequate funds for R & D. With few exceptions, future growth of any corporation is dependent on finding new and better products, more efficient methods of doing business, etc. Look for a company which is building for that sort of future.

4. Control of a market. IBM is in a dominant position, not because of price, but because of its ability to engineer new computers and office equipment and to provide good, continuing service at reasonable cost to the customer.

5. Strong technology base. This is a valuable, but not essential, asset. Growth companies usually start with expertise in specific areas and then move out into other products and markets.

6. Growing customer demand. This means a total market that is growing faster than the GNP. In the early years of new items, almost any company can prosper because the demand is greater than the supply. Later, when production has caught up, the stronger, better managed firms will survive and expand their positions.

Watch the Corporate Earnings and Dividends

American business has continued to make more money and pay out higher dividends. There have, of course, been years of downturn but they did not last long and, soon, everything started up again. Part of the gains have been due to inflation but the quality companies continue to move ahead, usually at a rate faster than that of inflation. As measured by the S&P 400, earnings have more than quadrupled in the past 20 years: from $3.37 in 1961 to $15.85 in 1980 (and that was down from $16.21 in 1979) and dividends have more than tripled: from $2.00 to $6.55 per share.

Do not buy shares of any company that has not grown at a faster *average* rate than the economy or the overall stock market. That standard should apply to sales, earnings and return on shareholders' equity. Concentrate on the *averages* because there are times when growth can be erratic. Investments are long-term commitments.

Over the short-term, psychology is the moving force but over the years, earnings determine stock values.

CORPORATE EARNINGS & DIVIDENDS
Based on S&P 400 Industrial Average

Year	Earnings	Change	Dividends	Change
1960	$3.39	− 4%	$2.00	+ 5%
1961	3.37	− 1	2.08	+ 4
1962	3.87	+15	2.20	+ 6
1963	4.24	+10	2.38	+ 8
1964	4.83	+14	2.60	+ 9
1965	5.51	+14	2.85	+10
1966	5.89	+ 7	2.98	+ 5
1967	5.66	− 4	3.01	+ 1
1968	6.15	+ 9	3.18	+ 6
1969	6.17	0	3.27	+ 3
1970	5.43	−12	3.24	− 1
1971	6.02	+11	3.18	− 2
1972	6.83	+13	3.22	+ 1
1973	8.86	+30	3.48	+ 8
1974	9.69	+ 9	3.72	+ 7
1975	8.55	−12	3.78	+ 2
1976	10.68	+25	4.25	+12
1977	11.57	+ 8	4.96	+17
1978	13.12	+13	5.35	+ 8
1979	16.82	+24	6.04	+13
1980	15.93	− 5	6.55	+ 8

SOURCE: Wright Investors' Service

Sad to say, Wall Street is slow to react to FACTS. Temporarily, pessimism or optimism is more meaningful! Remember this when you select growth stocks. Once you have spotted real growth, you may have to be patient and wait for this value to be recognized, and accepted, by investors.

Conversely, the stock market, in buoyant periods, may stick with an "established" growth stock long after its growth has slowed and all that's left is a corporation with a reputation and hopes. Polaroid remained an institutional favorite until mid 1974 even though, for the last six years, its per share profits were flat or dropping!

One, or even two, mediocre years should not be enough to remove a quality company from a watch list. In most cases, a stock should be sold when it reports two consecutive quarters with profits below those of the previous year. *Never place name and fame above proven profitability.*

But keep an eye on corporate progress. Once a company performs well enough to deserve investor attention, the odds are that its management will battle to retain that recognition, and if not successful, will be replaced.

Always find out the reason for the slowdown. It may be due to accounting changes, a shift in type of sales, or start-up costs for a new product. With quality companies, these dips can result in greater future profitability.

But do not fall in love with any stock. If the corporate future is dim, sell. You can always buy back when the outlook becomes promising.

Two Key Checkpoints for Real Growth

In selecting stocks for managed accounts, Wright Investors' Service relies heavily on two fundamental measurements of corporate growth and profitability: *earned growth rate* (EGR) and *profit rate* (PR). These reveal the ability of management to make the money entrusted to them by stockholders grow over the years.

The EGR is the annual rate at which the company's equity capital per common share is increased by net earnings after payment of the dividend—if any. *It is a reliable measure of investment growth because it shows the growth of the capital invested in the business— YOUR MONEY.* That's what successful investing is all about!

$$EGR = \frac{E\text{-}D}{BV}$$

EGR = Earned Growth Rate
E = Earnings
D = Dividend
BV = Book Value

The book value is the net value of total corporate assets, i.e., what is left over when all liabilities, including bonds and preferred stock, are subtracted from the total assets (plant, equipment, cash, inventories, accounts receivable, etc.). It is sometimes called Stockholders' Equity and can be found in every annual report. Many corporations show the book value, over a period of years, in their summary tables. A good growth company will increase its equity capital at a rate of at least 6% per year. The accompanying table shows why Johnson & Johnson (J&J) qualifies as a top growth company.

To determine the EGR for J&J for 1976, take the per share earnings of $3.53 and subtract the $1.05 dividend to get $2.48. Then divide by the book value *at the beginning of the year:* $19.83. Thus, the EGR for 1976 was 12.5%.

$$EGR = \frac{3.53\text{-}1.05}{19.83} = \frac{2.48}{19.83} = 12.5\%$$

The PR is equally important in assessing true growth. It measures the ability of corporate management to make money with your money; it shows the rate of return

JOHNSON & JOHNSON

Year	Book Value Begin Year	Per Share Earnings	Per Share Dividends	EGR	PR
1970	$ 8.30	$1.51	$ .34	14.1%	18.2%
1971	9.57	1.82	.43	14.5	19.0
1972	11.10	2.15	.45	15.3	19.4
1973	12.99	2.59	.53	15.9	19.9
1974	15.10	2.80	.73	13.7	18.5
1975	17.29	3.18	.85	13.5	18.4
1976	19.83	3.53	1.05	12.5	17.8
1977	22.35	4.23	1.40	12.7	18.9
1978	25.28	4.98	1.70	13.5	20.2
1979	28.42	5.76	2.00	13.2	20.3
1980	32.46	6.50	2.22	13.2	20.0

Before 3 - 1 stock split

SOURCE: Wright Investors' Service

produced on shareholders' equity capital at corporate book value. It is calculated by dividing the earnings per common share by the per share book value of the common stock *at the beginning of the year*.

$$PR = \frac{P}{BV}$$

PR = Profit Rate
P = Profit per common share
    for the last year reported
BV = Book Value

Again, using J&J as an example, in 1976:

$$PR = \frac{3.53}{19.83} = 17.8\%$$

J&J's EGR and PR are well above the average. In 1976, the stocks of the DJIA had an average EGR of 7.1% and a PR of 12.5%. J&J's performance was not as good as in previous years but by 1978, with a change in top management, the company moved back toward its traditional profitable growth. As usual, Wall Street was slow to recognize the improvement and waited for confirmation before buying enough shares to raise the stock price. The big gains came in late 1980 and early 1981 when it soared above 112 before a 3–1 split.

Added Checkpoints

Other factors which can be important in discovering and evaluating growth stocks are:

1. Improving profit margins. This is an excellent supplementary test for a growing company, particularly for one whose stock is just breaking into the growth category. Improving profit margins almost always mean larger earnings per share *soon*.

The profit margin (PM) shows a company's operating income, before taxes, as a percentage of revenues. It is listed in many annual reports and most statistical analyses. It can be easily calculated: divide the net operating income (total revenues less operating expenses) by the net sales.

In 1969, Boeing Company's PM was a meager 0.1 and its stock was trading below 10. By 1975, the PM was up to 2.1 with little change in the stock price but by 1977, the PM was at 5.5 and, the next year, the stock soared to over 50.

The PM is also valuable in determining when a company is getting into trouble. Carter-Wallace, a drug manufacturer, had a hefty 16.6 PM in 1971 so that its stock sold at 31¾. By 1973, when the PM was down to 1.1, the stock had plummeted to 5.

The PM has drawbacks. Internal corporate changes can result in a higher PM but not greater or faster growth. A consumer goods manufacturer, for example, could boost its PM by shifting from direct sales to wholesale distribution.

2. Plowed-back earnings. The fastest-growing companies will almost always be the stingiest dividend payers. By reinvesting a substantial part of its profits (preferably 70% or more), a company can speed expansion and improve productive efficiency. A growth company plowing back at a rate of 12% of its invested capital each year will double its real worth in about six years.

Take another look at J&J. Its maximum payout, for dividends, has been 35% of profits. That's one reason why it was able to boost its working capital from $325 million in 1970 to $1.2 billion in 1980 and, over the same period, raise its net income from about $84 million to over $400 million! That's GROWTH.

FAST GROWTH vs. SLOW GROWTH

Company	Stock Price (High)			Earnings Per Share			Price/Earnings Ratio		
	1970	1975	1980	1970	1975	1980	1970	1975	1980
FAST GROWTH									
Big Three	6	14	36	$ .26	$ .77	$2.65	23-13	18- 9	18- 9
Petrolane	4¾	8-1/8	26	.28	.73	1.60	17- 9	8- 3	16- 8
Schlumberger, Ltd.	6	27	131	.28	1.16	5.21	32-18	23-16	25-11
SmithKline	14	15	81	.75	1.07	4.65	19-12	14-10	17- 9
SLOW GROWTH									
Bethlehem Steel	30-5/8	40¼	32	2.05	5.54	2.77	12.2	5.9	5.4
Ford Motor	45	36	31	3.78	1.95	D	9.9	15.9	5.3
Goodrich (B.F.)	34	20	28	1.54	1.12	3.57	31.6	10.3	7.0
Simplicity Pattern	31	19	11-3/8	.80	1.08	.75	31.4	12.4	13

SOURCE: Standard & Poor's: Moody Investors Service

3. Strong research and development. The aim of research is knowledge; the aim of development is new or improved products and processes. A company that uses reinvested earnings largely for new plants and equipment will improve its efficiency and the quality of its products, but it will not grow as fast, in the long run, as a company that spends wisely for new and better products.

A prime test for aggressive growth management is whether the company is spending a higher than average percentage of its revenues for research, new product development and new process development. *With good management (and a little luck), dollars spent for R & D constitute the most creative, dynamic force for growth available for any corporation.* It is not unusual for the thousands of dollars used for research to make possible millions of dollars in additional sales and profits.

Another advantage of research, on a dollar-for-dollar basis, over other forms of investment is that it is fully tax deductible as a current business expense. Most plant and equipment spending must be capitalized and then written off over a period of years. Thus, up to about one-half of corporate outlays for R & D is footed by the Government via tax savings in the year the money is spent.

HOW HIGH RESEARCH PAYS OFF

COMPANY	R&D as % of Sales	Projected 5 Year Growth in Earning
Applied Materials	12.9%	26%
Advanced Micro	12.5	25
Intel	10.1	35
Instrumentation Labs.	10.0	15
Computervision	8.7	50
Hewlett Packard	8.6	23
Plantronics	8.3	20
Natl. Semiconductor	8.2	19
Tektronix	8.0	18
Prime Computer	7.9	40
Dataproducts	7.7	61
Modular Computer	7.7	20
SmithKline	7.2	20
Storage Technology	6.9	16
Millipore	6.9	19
Control Data	6.6	15
Boeing Co.	6.5	16
Watkins-Johnson	6.2	20
Motorola	6.2	17
United Technologies	6.0	14
IBM	5.9	17
Sperry Corp.	5.8	15
NCR	5.7	13

SOURCE: Merrill Lynch Market Letter

---

4. Acquisition-minded management. Back in the mid 1960s, the words *growth* and *acquisition* were almost interchangeable. Some of the hottest stocks were those of conglomerates which often appeared to be adding a new company every month. The prices of shares of Gulf & Western, Litton, City Investing, National General and other merger-minded conglomerates soared. When the inevitable collapse came, only a handful of the "new breed" firms survived and the stocks of most of these took a beating.

Acquisition is one way to grow, and some of the most successful growth companies are still looking for takeover opportunities. In the boom years, the trick was to keep the per share earnings rising, no matter by what device. Most of these "swingers" created the appearance of growth where, in many cases, none existed.

If the buyer issued $5 million in stock for assets carried on the corporate books at $2 million, the acquisition was listed on the conglomerate's books at $2 million. Later, if these assets were sold for $3 million, the big type in the annual report would show a $1 million profit even though there was a real loss of $2 million. If the acquisition had been made for $2 million cash, there would have been no question about the dollar loss!

Under new accounting rules, spurred by the SEC and Accounting Principles Board, most of these mythical profits have been eliminated but there are still situations that should be viewed with suspicion: shifts in depreciation policy, revaluation of assets, etc. These "profits" can be more paper than real.

Growth by merger and purchase can be as important as growth by reinvestment or new product development or market development. You can *buy* growth as well as make it. Internal growth is more feasible, often faster and more durable, and it avoids confrontation with government.

Caveat: Be cautious about empire-builders: corporate management that seeks growth at any price and in almost any area. It's a tough task to run one major corporation, let alone a tandem or trio, especially when they are in different areas. Look at the record. Almost daily, there are announcements of divestments of divisions/subsidiaries that once were touted as "ideal fits for future progress."

General rule: if you own the stock of a company involved in a merger/acquisition, hold it if you respect the dominant executives and their money-making skills. Do not buy the stock for at least one year and then only when you are convinced, by steadily rising profitability and growth, that the combination is working. Management styles, marketing policies and personnel practices vary widely and, in most cases, are difficult to mesh. Never buy into corporations that have problems!

CALCULATING GROWTH RATES

ANNUAL RATE OF EARNINGS INCREASE PER SHARE	JUSTIFIED P/E RATIOS			
	5 YEARS	7 YEARS	10 YEARS	15 YEARS
2%	15	15	13	12
4	17	17	16	16
5	18	18	18	18
6	19	19	20	21
8	21	22	24	28
10	23	25	28	35
12	25	28	33	48

Note that there should be only a small premium when a low growth rate remains static over the years. A 5% annual gain in EPS justifies the same P/E no matter how many years it has been attained. But when a company can maintain a high rate of earnings growth, 10% or more, the value of the stock is enhanced substantially.

SOURCE: Graham and Dodd: *Security Analysis*

What to Watch For

To spot the nonachievers among companies in a growth industry, look for these danger points:

1. Substantial stock dilution. When a company repeatedly and exclusively raises funds through the sale of additional common stock, either directly or through convertible securities, your equity is being constantly diminished. *True corporate growth must pay off to the stockholder on a per share basis.*

New SEC rules require that a corporation show per share earnings on both a regular and a fully converted basis (what the profits would be if all debentures or preferred stock were converted into common and all outstanding warrants or options were exercised).

With free-wheeling, leverage-minded outfits, dilution can be substantial and can reduce profits by 30% or more.

There's no harm in a small dilution, especially if there are prospects that the growth in earnings will continue. But beware of any company where there are heavy future obligations. It may take extraordinary growth to maintain the value of its stock.

WHAT ARE EARNINGS WORTH?

Annual Growth Rate	What $1.00 Earnings Will Become in 3 Yrs. At Given Growth Rate	The P/E Ratio You Can Pay Today to Make 10% Annual Capital Gain & Expect P/E Ratio in 3 Years To Be 15X	30X
4%	$1.12	12.6	25.3
5	1.16	13.1	26.2
6	1.19	13.4	26.8
7	1.23	13.9	27.7
8	1.26	14.2	28.4
9	1.30	14.7	29.3
10	1.33	15.0	30.0
12	1.40	15.8	31.6
15	1.52	17.1	34.3
20	1.73	19.5	39.0
25	1.95	22.0	44.0

SOURCE: Shaking The Money Tree

---

2. Overdiscounted price. In bull markets, a few stocks sell at high multiples of over 30 times earnings. This is a steep price to pay. Such optimistic evaluations are rare today but will come again as they always have. This is the time to be cautious and take your profits. When any stock sells at a P/E that is double that of the overall market, be cautious. When the multiple triples the average, sell unless it's a roaring up-market. Huge price rises are almost always followed by equally huge declines.

Look what happened to glamour-growth stocks in 1972–73 (on the soaring side) and 1974 (on the downside). Disney went up to 119, then dropped to 16⅝. But "once burned, twice shy." Despite higher earnings and a relatively strong market, Disney stock went up to just over 60, half of its previous high. *Growth is in the eye of the beholder.* But don't get starry-eyed on the upside or too teary-eyed on the downside. In Wall Street, excesses are corrected . . . in time.

Advice from the Old Master

Benjamin Graham, in his book, *Security Analysis,* looks for bargains in stocks, which he defines as the time when they trade at:

• a multiple of no more than twice that of the prevailing interest rate: i.e. a P/E ratio of 16 vs. an interest rate of 8%.

• a discount of 20% or more from book value.

Example: In 1974, Dana Corporation stock was at an adjusted price of 8. This was a multiple of about four times earnings. The interest rate was 7¼%, and the book value was $12.34 per share.

Dr. Graham's formula worked. By early 1976, DCN stock was split 2 for 1 and could (and should) have been sold at over 30: a 364% gain.

Another opportunity came in early 1980 when the stock, with a book value of $27.37, was trading at around 18. With interest rates at record highs, this criterion was no longer applicable. But the stock was a bargain and, within a year, was back over 30.

If you think such calculations are simple and thus not effective, hear this comment from Dr. Graham: "In 44 years of Wall Street experience, I have never seen dependable calculations made about common stock values or related investment policies that went beyond simple arithmetic or the most elementary algebra. *With complex calculations, you could take it that the operator was trying to substitute theory for experience and give to speculation the deceptive guide of investment.*"

How to Relate Current Prices to Future Earnings

Relating current prices of stocks to future earnings involves a combination of formulas and hope. The details vary by institution or advisory service, but the basic principles are similar.

The most conservative approach is to project earnings for a short period, three to five years. With this measurement, stocks that are selling at very high multiples of current profits often appear more reasonably priced in terms of projected future earnings.

Theoretically, the most exact formulation of a future earnings figure is the exact number of years (even fractions thereof) of estimated true earnings included in the current price of a stock. This period is called the "payout time."

The usual P/E multiple represents the number of years of current profits in the price of the stock. That is, if a stock sells at 30 times its last 12 months' earnings, it will take 30 years for these same earnings to add up to the price you now have to pay for the stock. The hope is, of course, that growth will reduce that time span.

The price/future-earnings multiple is the number of years of future earnings that add up to the stock's current price. The lower this multiple, the shorter the payout time, and other factors being equal, the better the value, or investment worth, of the growth stock being considered.

One application of this technique assumes that earnings will continue to grow at the same constant rate. This may often be true of a few large, established corporations with long histories of steady growth, but it is a rash assumption for most smaller companies. The bigger you get, the tougher it is to maintain the same rate of growth. It is a lot easier to add 10% annually to $1 million in profits than to add $10 million to $100 million in earnings!

A reasonable frame of projection reference is five years. Many firms now prepare five-year advance budgets, and with a true growth company, this is a period long enough to balance out temporary dips and yet short enough to be reasonably accurate. If you read of such a long-range forecast in an annual report, clip the notes for your research file.

A more sophisticated approach is to relate the present price of the stock to its projected future cash flow. This ratio is comparable to the P/E multiple but adds an extra assumption: that the financial structure of the company will remain much the same. Large loans or issues of fixed-income securities can make a sizable difference in the accuracy of projections.

A GROWTH STOCK PRICE EVALUATOR

HOW TO WEIGH PRICES OF GROWTH STOCKS IN TERMS OF THEIR FUTURE GAINS IN EARNINGS OR CASH FLOW

IF — a stock now sells at this many times its current earnings or cash flow:	— AND you believe its average annual growth in earnings or cash flow per share (compounded) will be:						
	10%	15%	20%	25%	30%	40%	50%
	THEN—here is how many times its projected earnings or cash flow per share five years hence the stock is currently selling at:						
12	7.5	6.0	4.8	3.9	3.2	2.2	1.6
14	8.7	7.0	5.6	4.6	3.8	2.6	1.8
16	9.9	8.0	6.5	5.2	4.3	3.0	2.1
18	11.2	9.0	7.3	5.9	4.9	3.3	2.4
20	12.4	10.0	8.1	6.6	5.4	3.7	2.6
22	13.7	10.9	8.9	7.2	5.9	4.1	2.9
24	14.9	11.9	9.7	7.9	6.5	4.5	3.2
26	16.1	12.9	10.5	8.5	7.0	4.8	3.4
28	17.4	13.9	11.3	9.2	7.5	5.2	3.7
30	18.6	14.9	12.1	9.8	8.1	5.6	3.9
32	19.9	15.9	12.9	10.5	8.6	5.9	4.2
34	21.1	16.9	13.7	11.1	9.2	6.3	4.5
36	22.4	17.9	14.5	11.8	9.7	6.7	4.7
38	23.6	18.9	15.3	12.5	10.2	7.1	5.0
40	24.8	19.9	16.1	13.1	10.8	7.4	5.3
42	26.1	20.9	16.9	13.8	11.3	7.8	5.5
44	27.3	21.9	17.7	14.4	11.9	8.2	5.8
46	28.6	22.9	18.5	15.1	12.4	8.6	6.1
48	29.8	23.9	19.4	15.7	12.9	8.9	6.3
50	31.1	24.9	20.2	16.4	13.5	9.3	6.6

This Growth Stock Price Evaluator can be used for both projections. It is most useful when studying fast-growing companies with above-average growth rates and cash flow.

Example: The stock of a small high-technology corporation is selling at 30 times net current, per share profits. That sets a time span of 30 years. You estimate that, over the next five years, earnings will grow at an average annual compound rate of 20%. The tables shows that, if this projection is correct, the stock will be selling at 12.1 times its anticipated five-years-hence profits.

This evaluation technique can be reversed. Today, the stock is selling at a multiple of 30 but you are not so sure about its future profits. From experience, you are willing to pay no more than 12 times future five-year earnings for any growth stock. Checking the table, you find that the average annual growth rate must be 20% compounded annually to meet your investment standards. This stock just meets your criteria.

The Growth Stock Price Evaluator does *not* show the *future* price-to-earnings multiple or cash flow. They might be lower than, the same as, or greater than they are today.

There is a built-in offset: when the earnings (or cash flow) growth of a company is uninterrupted, the price of its stock tends to rise faster than earnings. This is almost always the case when the stock's P/E ratio is still below the stratosphere. *Wall Street LOVES consistency and continuity.*

The greatest risk in buying and holding growth stocks lies in overestimating their probable future rate of growth in earnings. Too many investors project recent earnings growth automatically. That's OK if you have access to complete data and can make frequent revisions, but when such forecasts go awry, the price of such glamour issues can collapse. That's why it can be so costly to hold an overpriced equity.

ALWAYS be conservative in projecting future earnings and cash-flow growth rates. A sustained annual growth rate of 10% is good; 15% is excellent; only a handful of unusual corporations can maintain a 20% growth rate for many years. American business is too competitive; expansion into new products and new markets is too expensive; and unforeseen events are too frequent to permit even the best new companies to maintain supergrowth rates—30% or more—for longer than two or three years. In successful investing, be realistic. It is just as important NOT to lose money as to make profits!

How to Determine Prudent P/E Multiples

A common feature of most of the preceding measures is that they translate a current P/E ratio into another *adjusted* figure corrected for either past growth or estimated future growth. Or corrected to show cash flow per share rather than reported earnings.

But none of these figures shows the proper level for buying or selling the stock of a particular growth company.

Example: Granted that a growth company selling at 40 times its current profits per share will be selling at "only" 16 times its projected earnings per share five years from now *if* its average growth in per share earnings actually becomes 20% a year. But is this really a better buy than another growth stock that is expected to boost its profits at an average rate of 19% a year? And why do you think that 16 times a five-years-hence earnings price is reasonable?

A handy formula is **PRU PER = G R Q M T.**

PRU = Prudent.

PER = P/E Ratio.

G = Growth. This is the company's projected growth

in earnings per share over the next five years. The basic compound interest formula is $(1+G)^5$ where G is the projected growth rate, as shown in the Growth Stock Price Evaluator and Prudent P/E Multiples Table. This omits dividend yields because they are usually small in relation to the potential capital appreciation.

R = Reliability & Risk. Not all projected growth rates are equally reliable or probable. A lower projected growth rate is likely to be more reliable than a very high projected one (30% to 50% a year).

Logically, you can assign a higher reliability rating to a noncyclical company (utility, food processor, retailer) than to a corporation in a cyclical industry (steel, machinery, tools).

Another factor is the assumed length of the projected growth period. If you can realistically anticipate that the company will continue its rate of growth for the next 10 years, a 10% rate for its stock is more reliable than a 15% rate for a company whose growth visibility is only three to five years.

If you are uncertain about the corporation's consistency, you should consider the greater risk.

Q = Quality. For the investor, this is the single most important consideration. For the speculator, it is only marginally significant. A *quality* company has a long, fairly consistent record of profitable growth in both sales and earnings; a sound, strong, uncluttered financial structure; and broad public ownership including a number of institutional shareholders.

The stock of a *quality* company, growing at an average rate of 15% or more a year, could be prudently priced higher than a lower quality company expanding at a slightly higher rate.

M = Multiple of price to earnings. This is a comparative measurement. The first step is to determine the P/E for an average-quality nongrowth stock. This is done by relating the current yield on guaranteed, fixed-income investments (savings accounts, corporate bonds) to the P/E multiple that will produce the same yield on the nongrowth stock.

$$PE + \frac{D}{IR}$$

PE = Price/Earnings ratio
D = Dividend as percentage payout of earnings
IR = Interest Rate

Thus, a stock yielding 8% on a 70% payout of profits must, over a five-year period, be bought and sold at 7 times earnings to break even on capital and to make as much income as could be obtained, over the same period, via the ownership of a fixed-income investment continually yielding 10%:

$$PE = \frac{7}{10} = 7$$

Note: This is NOT a valid comparison in terms of investment alone. Since the nongrowth stock carries a certain amount of risk in comparison to the certainty of a bond or money market fund, the stock should sell at a lower multiple, probably 5 to 6 times earnings.

T = Tax position. A dollar of long-term capital gains is worth more than a dollar of interest or dividends. The higher your tax bracket, the greater the after-tax advantages of capital gains.

To the extent that *any* return from *any* common stock includes some tax-favored, long-term capital gains, it is worth proportionately more after taxes.

The taxpayer pays Uncle Sam on all income from interest and dividends but on only 40% of long-term capital gains (held over 12 months). Thus Mr. Wealthy, in the 50% tax bracket, keeps 50¢ of his income dollar and 80¢ of his realized appreciation dollar.

For the lower-income taxpayer, the spread is less. Mr. Average, in the 40% tax bracket, keeps 60% of his interest/dividend dollar and 84¢ of his capital-gains dollar.

This tax relativism is important only to investors in the 50% or higher tax bracket. *It is of some benefit to those in the next lower brackets, but it is not significant to the majority of investors.* Before you waste your time

---

PRUDENT PRICE-EARNINGS MULTIPLES FOR GROWTH STOCKS

If you project earnings per share (after taxes) to grow in next 5 years at average compounded annual rate of:	With these quality ratings*				
	B these are multiples MAXIMUM	B+ are which current	A− approximate represent price	A to pay:	A+ prudent the
5%	12.0	12.9	13.7	15.0	16.7
6%	12.5	13.4	14.3	15.8	17.4
7%	13.0	14.0	14.9	16.5	18.2
8%	13.6	14.5	15.6	17.1	18.9
9%	14.1	15.1	16.2	17.8	19.7
10%	14.6	15.7	16.8	18.5	20.4
15%	17.4	18.7	20.1	22.0	24.5
20%	20.2	21.8	23.4	25.7	28.6
25%	23.0	24.7	26.6	29.3	32.7
30%	25.2	27.3	29.4	32.5	36.2
35%	28.5	31.0	33.5	37.1	41.5
40%	31.9	34.8	37.7	41.7	46.7

*S&P designations. If not rated, use B; if new, untested firm, use a conservative rating based on comparison with similar companies, preferably in the same industry.

HOW TO FIGURE INVESTMENT GROWTH

Years of investment	Interest factors: 1 per year compounded				
	6%	7%	8%	9%	15%
1	1.00	1.00	1.00	1.00	1.00
2	2.06	2.07	2.08	2.09	2.15
3	3.18	3.21	3.25	3.28	3.47
4	4.37	4.44	4.51	4.57	4.99
5	5.64	5.75	5.87	5.98	6.74
6	6.98	7.15	7.34	7.52	8.75
7	8.39	8.65	8.92	9.20	11.1
8	9.90	10.3	10.6	11.0	13.7
9	11.5	11.9	12.5	13.0	16.8
10	13.2	13.8	14.5	15.2	20.3
15	23.2	25.1	27.2	29.4	47.6
20	36.8	41.0	45.8	51.2	102.4
25	54.9	63.2	73.1	84.7	212.8
30	79.0	94.5	113.3	136.3	434.8
35	111.4	138.2	172.3	215.7	881.2
40	154.8	199.6	259.0	337.9	1779.0

Use this to project your asset growth. With periodic investments, such as shares of funds, automatic reinvestment and personal retirement plans, multiply the annual investment by the years at the chosen % growth rate: $1,750, each year for 8 years, at 8%= $1,750 X 10.6 = $18,550.

worrying about tax savings, do your arithmetic and see for yourself how small the savings, for most people, really are. In the country club locker room it sounds impressive to flaunt your knowledge of tax benefits, but the facts seldom prove your point.

Fastest-Growing Companies

The people who have been consistently successful in locating fast-growing companies rely on formulas. They look for firms which have outstanding management, enjoy robust markets for their products or services, provide good expectations for continued profitable growth and have *proven records of past performance*.

Johnson Survey (formerly *America's Fastest Growing Companies*) specializes in young firms and so uses four-year data. Their entry criteria are less stringent than those of many professional money managers but, because they know that the growth of these firms can often be more exciting than profitable, they set strict standards and do not hesitate to downgrade or remove companies frequently.

CORPORATE SCOREBOARD: MOST PROFITABLE COMPANIES: 1980

INDUSTRY	Return on Equity	P/E Ratio	INDUSTRY	Return on Equity	P/E Ratio	INDUSTRY	Return on Equity	P/E Ratio
AEROSPACE			**FOOD & LODGING**			**PUBLISHING/RADIO/TV**		
Fairchild Industries	36.9%	6	Caesar's World	29.2	8	Commerce Clearing House	64.1	12
Boeing Co.	30.1	6	Church's Fried Chicken	29.1	10	Metromedia, Inc.	28.7	8
Composite	19.5	10	Composite	18.5	9	Composite	18.3	10
AIRLINES			**GENERAL MACHINERY**			**RAILROADS**		
Southwest Airlines	38.0	9	GCA Corp.	29.7	18	Chicago & Northwestern	46.6	6
USAir, Inc.	31.0	4	Giddings & Lewis	29.4	7	Composite	13.9	8
Composite	−0.3	NA	Composite	15.3	10	**REAL ESTATE/HOUSING**		
APPLIANCES			**INSTRUMENTS**			Lennar Corp.	32.8	7
Maytag Co.	21.2	9	Esterline Corp.	29.5	9	Composite	18.3	10
Composite	12.7	9	Western Pacific Ind.	27.5	3	**RETAILING (FOOD)**		
AUTOMOTIVE			Composite	15.4	13	National Convenience Stores	28.2	7
PACCAR, Inc.	16.1	6	**LEISURE**			Circle-K	27.3	7
Bendix Corp.	16.1	8	Technicolor, Inc.	29.4	6	Composite	14.5	8
Composite	−11.1	NM	Columbia Pictures	25.8	7	**RETAILING (NON-FOOD)**		
BANKS/HOLDING COS.			Composite	16.4	10	SCOA Industries	31.2	7
Republic New York	34.4	4	**METALS & MINING**			Wal-Mart Stores	26.6	20
Bankers Trust, NY	22.4	3	Homestake Mining	42.7	9	Composite	11.5	10
Composite	14.9	6	Newmont Mining	28.1	6	**SERVICE INDUSTRIES**		
BEVERAGES			Composite	18.1	7	Air Express International	54.6	10
Heileman (G) Brewing	31.9	7	**MISCELLANEOUS MANUFACTURING**			K-Tel International	46.8	6
Dr. Pepper	26.1	10	Trinity Industries	41.3	8	Composite	20.5	10
Composite	17.0	12	Tyco Laboratories	28.6	6	**SPECIAL MACHINERY**		
BUILDING MATERIALS			Composite	16.9	9	Caterpillar Tractor	17.6	9
Sherwin-Williams	27.7	7	**NATURAL RESOURCES**			Composite	13.4	9
Pacific Lumber	24.0	16	Petro-Lewis	50.3	16	**STEEL**		
Composite	10.9	9	Occidental Petroleum	47.0	3	Nucor Corp.	31.5	10
CHEMICALS			Composite	23.8	10	Kaiser Steel	27.9	2
Freeport Minerals	35.6	13	**NONBANK FINANCIAL**			Composite	7.8	9
Texasgulf, Inc.	33.6	6	Shearson Loeb Rhoades	62.8	4	**TEXTILES & APPAREL**		
Composite	15.3	10	Hutton (E.F.) Group	41.5	4	Guilford Mills	34.3	5
CONGLOMERATES			Composite	15.9	7	Levi Strauss	32.3	9
Southdown, Inc.	37.4	8	**OFFICE EQUIPMENT**			Composite	12.7	8
Litton Industries	26.9	9	Prime Computer	50.9	24	**TIRE & RUBBER**		
Composite	16.1	7	Computervision Corp.	34.3	35	Carlisle Corp.	29.3	17
CONTAINERS			Composite	19.2	15	Composite	3.7	10
Stone Container	21.1	6	**OIL SERVICE & SUPPLY**			**TOBACCO**		
Composite	12.9	6	Rowan Cos.	41.5	13	U.S. Tobacco	25.6	9
DRUGS			Western Co. No. America	40.4	20	Composite	21.5	7
SmithKline Corp.	37.4	16	Composite	24.2	17	**TRUCKING**		
American Home Products	32.8	10	**PAPER & FOREST PRODUCTS**			Butler International	24.8	8
Composite	20.1	12	Fort Howard Paper	23.0	11	Composite	14.6	9
ELECTRICAL/ELECTRONICS			Consolidated Papers	20.3	6	**UTILITIES**		
Tandy Corp.	37.2	16	Composite	12.6	9	Pioneer Corp.	37.2	10
Advanced Micro Devices	30.6	14	**PERSONAL CARE PRODUCTS**			United Energy Resources	31.0	7
Composite	19.3	13	Mary Kay Cosmetics	51.7	15	Composite	12.9	7
FOOD PROCESSING			Avon Products	29.1	9			
Staley (A.E.) Mfg.	29.7	6	Composite	19.1	12	**All Industry Composite**	**15.3**	**10**
Kellogg Co.	26.5	9						
Composite	15.6	8						

NA = Not Available   NM = Not Meaningful

SOURCE: Standard & Poor's Compustate Services, Inc.

The selections are based on:

- Growth in net income per share.
- Uninterrupted gain in annual profits for the last three years.
- Evidence of continued growth at the time of listing.

From a master list, they then choose those companies with the largest and most consistent year-to-year gains in earnings and those whose stocks are selling at the lowest P/E ratios.

Periodically, they eliminate companies when: (1) the average annual growth rate of profits per share, through the last fiscal year, drops below 10%; (2) annual earnings fail to rise by at least 5% over those of the prior year.

Read that over again; those are true tests of real growth and are a solid base for your investment decisions.

CHAPTER 5

Value Approach in Common-Stock Selection

The value approach is the statistician's and accountant's way of finding the right stocks for profitable investments. It is based on the *financial facts.* It relies heavily on economic forecasts and analyses of the corporation's present strength and past performance as indications of what can be anticipated in the future.

When you select stocks on the basis of *value* and the corporation's ability to make money, you are almost always sure to pick winners. It takes time for such stocks to rise to a point where you can take sizable profits. But if you have done your homework and there is no major change in the way the company operates, the products it makes and the markets it serves, you will make money over the long term.

Value is the approach used by fundamentalists. They look for situations where they are able to buy stocks of quality corporations at undervalued prices. They examine value in terms of cash, current assets and proven profits rather than the rosy, intangible promises of big future earnings.

Fundamentalists are interested in paying one dollar for two dollars, three or more, of such concrete assets. They are seldom willing to pay thirty or forty dollars for one dollar of prospective, and possibly uncertain, earnings and/or dividends. That's why the value approach is often called "the margin of safety" approach.

How to Analyze Financial Reports

Financial analysis is not easy for the uninitiated, but once you get the swing of things, you can pick the few quality stocks from the thousands of publicly owned securities, and if you are speculative-minded, you can find bargains with securities of mediocre or even poor corporations.

Basic figures and ratios show the company's current and prospective financial condition, past and prospective earning power and growth and, thus, investment desirability.

Publicly owned corporations issue their financial reports on an annual, semiannual or quarterly basis. Most of the important-to-the-investor information can be found in: *(a)* the balance sheet; *(b)* the profit and loss, or income statement; *(c)* the change in financial position or the "flow of funds" data.

In each of these you can find or derive:

1. The key quantities: net tangible assets, changes in components of working capital, sales costs, profits, taxes, dividends, etc.

2. The important rates or ratios: price/earnings, profit margins, net worth per share, growth rate, profit rate, etc.

3. The relations between significant ratios: to compare the performance of the corporation with some standard, such as its own past average performance, the industry average, or some overall business-stock-market average.

The analyses here apply primarily to industrial corporations. With proper variations, they can be used for a better understanding of utilities, railroads, finance firms and insurance companies.

The Importance of the Balance Sheet

The balance sheet shows the financial position of a company as of a given date, usually the end of either the calendar or fiscal year. Here you can find a fully detailed breakdown of the firm's capital, or assets, and liabilities (in each case, both current and long term) as well as the company's net worth, more familiarly known as stockholders' equity or book value.

Note: For convenience, the following examples are calculated only for the current year, and 000,000 are omitted. The data and explanations are digested from the valuable booklet Understanding Financial Statements *prepared by the NYSE.*

Key Balance Sheet Quantities

1. Total assets. This figure ($131.5 at the end of the current fiscal year) represents all the assets a company uses in its business, whether these assets are owned or leased. They are reported at original cost less depreciation or amortization (except for inventories which are the lower of cost or current market worth).

2. Net working capital. This is total current assets ($48.4) less total current liabilities ($21.6), for a net of $26.8 million. *Current assets* are of varying liquidity: cash and highly liquid Government securities (in the prior year), fairly liquid accounts receivable, and less liquid inventories. *Other assets* of $5.5 million include longer-term receivables (possibly holdings in subsidiaries) and the surrender value of insurance.

3. Fixed assets. This figure shows the value of buildings, machinery, equipment ($104.3) and land ($.9). Except for land, fixed assets have a limited useful life. Each year, a provision (accumulated annually) is made for depreciation ($27.6) due to wear and tear so that the value of the assets will not be overstated.

The increase in fixed assets ($104.3 in the current year versus $92.7 in the prior year) is probably due to expansion and/or improved facilities and equipment. A large boost in fixed assets should, hopefully, be followed, in the next year, by a corresponding increase in products and sales, and a reduction in costs due to more efficient operations. If there is only a small change in fixed assets for several years, the company may be heading for trouble. It may not be keeping competitive.

In well-run corporations, the accumulated reserve also includes allowances for obsolescence and loss of value due to technological and other changes.

The higher valuation for land ($.9 vs. $.7) represents the acquisition of additional property.

Natural resource companies (oil and gas producers and mining corporations) which use up some of their assets each year show depletion allowances. Despite some theories to the contrary, these are not an important factor in corporate profitability.

The best companies are those that make enough money to plow back, consistently, substantial sums in improved facilities and equipment.

Note that this balance sheet contains no items for intangible assets: good will, trademarks, patents and copyrights. *They have no direct relation to corporate profits or growth.* Under accounting rules, their value is normally amortized on an annual basis. Such items are omitted in computing the net tangible assets attributable to the common stock.

4. Current liabilities: $21.6 million. These are monies owed or debt obligations due within one year. They include:

a. Money owed to suppliers for raw materials, parts, other supplies and items needed to conduct the business. Ordinarily, when sales are expanding, there will be an increase in this category.

b. Accrued liabilities such as unpaid wages, salaries, and commissions.

c. Current maturity of long-term debt due in the next year. Many loans have provisions for repayment of a fixed amount annually.

d. Taxes due. Sometimes, the amount owed for Federal income taxes is shown separately.

e. Dividends payable—as declared by the directors but not paid by year-end.

Notice that the company, at the end of the current

BALANCE SHEET

ASSETS, LIABILITIES & STOCKHOLDERS' EQUITY	Dec. 31 Current Year Millions	Dec. 31 Prior Year Millions
ASSETS		
Current Assets		
Cash	$ 9.0	$ 6.2
U. S. Government securities	–	2.0
Accounts and notes receivable	12.4	11.4
Inventories	27.0	24.6
Total Current Assets	$ 48.4	$ 44.2
Other Assets		
Receivables due after one year	4.7	3.9
Surrender value of insurance	.2	.2
Other	.6	.5
Total Other Assets	$ 5.5	$ 4.6
Fixed Assets		
Bldgs., mach. and equipment at cost	104.3	92.7
Less accum. depreciation	27.6	25.0
	$ 76.7	$ 67.7
Land	.9	.7
Total Fixed Assets	$ 77.6	$ 68.4
Total Assets	$131.5	$117.2
LIABILITIES & STOCKHOLDERS' EQUITY		
Current Liabilities		
Accounts payable	$ 6.1	$ 5.0
Accrued liabilities	3.6	3.3
Current long-term debt	1.0	.8
Fed. income and other taxes	9.6	8.4
Dividends payable	1.3	1.1
Total Current Liabilities	$ 21.6	$ 18.6
Reserves	3.6	2.5
Long Term Debt	26.0	20.0
Stockholders' Equity		
(5% Cum. Preferred ($100 par: authorized and outst. 60,000)	6.0	6.0
Common ($10 par: authorized 2,000,000; outst. 1,830,000)	18.3	18.3
Capital surplus	9.6	9.6
Earned surplus	46.4	42.2
Total stockholders' equity	$ 80.3	$ 76.1
Total liabilities and equity	$131.5	$117.2

SOURCE: New York Stock Exchange

year, had $3 more current liabilities than in the preceding year ($21.6 vs. $18.6). That's a goodly sum when sales were up only $5.8. In this case, fortunately, much of the difference was represented by higher inventories.

Watch the liabilities in the annual report of any company in which you plan to invest. A fast-growing corporation must plan carefully for its future financial needs. When current liabilities grow faster than current assets, there can be difficulty unless the firm has adequate borrowing power. Here, current assets rose $4.2, so the extra $3 in liabilities is not out of line.

5. Long-term debt: $26.0. This shows the money due a lender (such as an insurance company) or lenders (such as individual bondholders) after one year. During the current year, the company paid off $1 in its debt but had to borrow an additional $7.

6. Stockholders' equity: $80.3. This shows the reinvested earnings ($46.4) and the amount of money invested by stockholders. This is also called book value. It is an accounting term showing what the common shareholders actually own: $80.3 in the last year—a modest $4.2 million increase from the year before.

On a per share basis (calculated by dividing the total by the number of common shares outstanding), it shows the assets behind each share of common stock. That's a low 5.5% increase, well below the 10% to 15% which is characteristic of true growth corporations.

The $6.0 figure is based on 60,000 shares of 5% cumulative preferred stock with a par value of $100 per share. In event of liquidation of the company, the holder of each share of this stock would receive $100. In many cases, such stock can be redeemed, at the company's option, at a fixed price.

$18.3 is based on 1,830,000 shares of common stock. The par value is listed at $10. Since the stock was sold at a price above par, the company received an additional $9.6 million, which is shown as *capital surplus.*

Par value, or the stated value of "no par common stock," is a legal or arbitrary amount having no relation to the market value of the common stock or to what would be received in liquidation. (Market value is the amount which investors are willing to pay to buy a share of common stock.)

7. Earned surplus: $46.4. This represents the earnings retained in the business (not paid out in dividends). It is *not* a tangible sum or an amount on deposit in a bank. That's why more companies are dropping the term *surplus* and using *earnings retained and invested in the business.*

In theory, the surplus is available for dividends, but the ability of the corporation to pay dividends depends as much on its financial position as on the amount of surplus in the balance sheet. Frequently, major creditors, such as a bank or insurance company, place restrictions on the extent to which surplus is available for dividends.

Statement of Income and Earned Surplus

Here's where you find out how much money the company took in last year, how much had to be spent for expenses and taxes, and the size of the resulting profits (if any) that were available for distribution to shareholders or for reinvestment in the business. These figures are interesting, but when expressed as amount per share of common stock, they are important for comparisons: *(a)* to corporate results of previous years, and *(b)* to those of other companies in the same or similar businesses.

1. Sales or revenues. The $5.8 increase ($115.8 vs. $110) is fair but not exceptional. If the industry boosted sales by 10%, this 5.3% gain would not be satisfactory.

When reviewing the sales figure, be sure to find out if unit sales have expanded or if the larger dollar volume is derived from price rises.

2. Cost of goods sold. This $76.4 shows the outlays for raw materials, wages, salaries, supplies, power, etc. Since sales were up $5.8, the increase in costs ($3.2)

shows that expenses were kept under control and that the profit margin remained stable. The lower the cost of goods sold, the larger the profit margin.

3. Selling, general and administrative expenses. This item varies with the type of business. In a steel company, most of the money probably would be spent for selling and administration. In a cosmetic company, the majority of such costs would be for advertising and promotion. Again, the company appears to be able to keep these expenses in line (up only $1.2).

Note: this category may include R & D costs which, in many reports, are shown as a separate item.

4. Depreciation and depletion. These expenses, as well as amortization of various types, differ from the other expenses because they are not an actual cash outlay. Every piece of machinery, equipment, etc., has a limited life. IRS rules set maximum allowances to be used and require that depreciation can be related only to cost.

Depletion is similar to depreciation and represents the reduction in the value, as used, of natural resources such as coal, timber, copper, oil, and gas.

The higher the amounts provided for depreciation and/or depletion, the lower the net reported income. Conversely, large deductions make for a high *cash flow* (the total of net income plus deductions for depreciation or depletion).

Some analysts consider cash flow a better guide to future dividend policy than net income. But consideration should also be given to other items: working capital,

STATEMENT OF INCOME AND EARNED SURPLUS

	Year Ended	
	Dec. 31 Current Year Millions	Dec. 31 Prior Year Millions
SALES	$115.8	$110.0
Less:		
Costs and Expenses:		
Cost of Goods Sold	$ 76.4	$ 73.2
Selling, General and Administrative Expenses	14.2	13.0
Depreciation	2.6	3.5
	$ 93.2	$ 89.7
Operating Profit	$ 22.6	$ 20.3
Interest Charges	1.3	1.0
Earnings before Income Taxes	$ 21.3	$ 19.3
Provision for Federal and State Taxes on Income	11.4	9.8
Net Income (per common share)	$ 9.9	$ 9.5
Earned Surplus, Begin. of Year	42.2	37.6
	$ 52.1	$ 47.1
Less Dividends Paid on: Preferred Stock ($5 per share)	(.3)	(.3)
Common Stock (per share)	(5.4)	(4.6)
Earned Surplus, End of Year	$ 46.4	$ 42.2

SOURCE: New York Stock Exchange

projected capital expenditures, new products and markets, etc.

5. Operating profit: $22.6. As a percentage of sales, this indicates the pretax profit margin, 19.5%, an improvement over the 18.5% in the prior year.

Normally, manufacturing companies have pretax profit margins (after depreciation and depletion) of about 8%.

6. Interest charges: $1.3. This is the cost of borrowed funds. It is a deductible, before-taxes expense.

Bondholders like to see at least three dollars of available earnings for each dollar's interest the company must pay. There's no trouble here because there are seventeen dollars (before provision for Federal income taxes) for each interest dollar.

7. Earnings before income taxes. This is the operating profit: $22.6 minus interest of $1.3 equals $21.3.

8. Provision for taxes. This $11.4 is just half of the operating profit. With a few exceptions at the state level, the rate of corporate income taxes has not varied much in the past several years.

9. Net income for the year. This is, perhaps, the most important-to-the-investor figure. The $9.9 was about 4.2% higher than the net of the previous year. It represents an 8.5% return on each dollar of sales: 9.9÷115.8. This was slightly down from 8.6% in the prior year.

The best companies are those which maintain or increase their profits each year: in total, in percentage of sales and in relation to stockholders' equity.

The average net income to sales depends on the type of business. Food chains are lucky to report a profit of two cents per sales dollar; manufacturing corporations average about six cents per revenue dollar; and cosmetic-drug companies do far better: twenty to thirty cents of every sales dollar.

The important figure is the return on equity, the shareholder's investment: $9.9 divided by $80.3 (the stockholder's equity) equals 12.3%. This 12.3% is a shade better than the profit rate reported by the 30 corporations which make up the DJIA.

10. Dividends on preferred stock: $300,000. This is a standard guide for the investment quality of a preferred stock. In this case, the company covered its preferred dividend 33 times!

On cumulative preferred stocks, dividends which have not been paid in the past, in addition to current dividends, must be paid before any dividends can be paid on the common stock.

11. Net income available for common stock: $9.9. This shows the amount of money which can be used to pay dividends to owners of the common stock. When divided by the weighted average of shares outstanding, it reports the per share earnings, the most widely used criterion for judging corporate progress. If a company has no senior securities (such as preferred stock), all of the net income is available for common dividends.

Fast-growing companies tend to reinvest 70% or more of their net income, thus leaving 30% or less for dividends. Steady-revenue corporations, such as utilities, usually pay out 60% or so of their profits. (In recent years, however, in order to keep attracting new capital, some have boosted the percentage of payout to 80% or more.)

This policy does not leave much for investing in the future so be wary of such companies even though the yields may be welcome. *For income:* look for stocks of companies that distribute a bit more than half their income; *for growth:* buy shares of stingy dividend payers.

12. Earned surplus. At the end of the year, the company added $9.9 (net income) to the $42.2 shown at the beginning of the year. This made a total of $52.1 before payment of $5.7 in dividends on preferred and common stock. The balance, $46.4, showed that the company was worth $4.2 more than at the end of the prior year. Reinvested earnings became part of other assets (inventories, receivables, etc.) or were used for new plants and equipment. That 10% increase in earned surplus is about double that reported by the average public corporation.

Seven Keys to Value

	Current Year	Prior Year
1. Operating profit margin	19.5%	18.5%
2. Current ratio	2.24	2.38
3. Liquidity ratio	41.7%	44.1%
4. Capitalization ratios:		
Long-term debt	24.4%	20.8%
Preferred stock	5.7	6.3
Common stock and surplus	69.9	72.9
5. Sales to fixed assets	1.1	1.2
6. Sales to inventories	4.3	4.5
7. Net income to net worth	12.3%	12.5%

1. Operating profit margin (PM). This is the ratio of profit (before interest and taxes) to sales. The operating profit ($22.6) divided by sales ($115.8) equals 19.5%. This compares with 18.5% for the previous year. (Some analysts prefer to compute this margin without including depreciation and depletion as part of the cost because these have nothing to do with the efficiency of the operation.)

When a company increases sales substantially, the PM should be widened because certain costs (rent, interest, real property taxes, etc.) are fixed and do not rise in proportion to volume.

The PM is useful for comparison but can be misunderstood when the corporation changes the types of products sold or its method of distribution. When a finance company acquires a retail chain, sales and profits may increase substantially even though the PM on combined revenues is considerably below that of the finance company's former PM.

2. Current ratio. This is the ratio of current assets to current liabilities: $48.4 divided by $21.6 equals $2.24. For most industrial corporations, this should be about two to one. It varies with the type of business. Utilities and retail stores, for example, have rapid cash inflows and high turnovers, so they can operate effectively with lower ratios.

In your analysis, check the past record and watch for any major shift in this ratio.

When the ratio is high (5:1), it may mean that a company is not making the best use of its liquid assets. It may have too much money invested in securities. They provide high yields for a while but they do not expand the business.

3. Liquidity ratio. This is the ratio of cash and its equivalent to total current liabilities ($9 divided by $21.6 equals 41.7%). It is important as a supplement to the current ratio because the immediate ability of a company to meet current obligations or pay larger dividends may be impaired despite a high current ratio. This 41.7% liquidity ratio (down from 44.1% the year before) probably indicates a period of expansion, rising prices, heavier capital expenditures and larger accounts payable. *If the decline persists, the company might have to raise additional capital.*

4. Capitalization ratios. These show the percentages of each type of investment as part of the total investment in the corporation. Though often used to describe only the outstanding securities, capitalization is the sum of the face value of bonds and other debts *plus* the par value of all preferred and common stock issues *plus* the balance sheet totals for capital surplus and retained earnings.

Bond, preferred-stock and common-stock ratios are useful indicators of the relative risk and leverage involved for the owners of the three types of securities. For most industrial corporations, the debt ratio should be no more than 66⅔% of equity or 40% of total capital.

In this instance, the long-term debt plus preferred stock is 43.1% of the equity represented by the common stock and surplus, and 30.1% of total capital.

Higher ratios are appropriate for utilities and transportation corporations.

5. Sales to fixed assets. This ratio is computed by dividing the annual sales ($115.8) by the year-end value of plant, equipment and land before depreciation and amortization ($104.3 plus $.9 equals $105.2). The ratio is therefore 1.1 to 1. This is down from 1.2 to 1 the year before.

This ratio helps to show whether funds used to enlarge productive facilities are being wisely spent. A sizable expansion in facilities should lead to larger sales volume. If it does not, there's something wrong. In this case, there were delays in getting production on stream at the new plant.

6. Sales to inventories. This ratio is computed by dividing the annual sales by year-end inventories: $115.8 divided by $27 equals a 4.3:1 ratio. The year before, the ratio was 4.5 to 1.

This shows inventory turnover: the number of times the equivalent of the year-end inventory has been bought and sold during the year.

It is more important in analyzing retail corporations than manufacturers. A high ratio denotes a good quality of merchandise and correct pricing policies. A declining ratio may be a warning signal.

Note: A more accurate comparison would result from the use of an average of inventories at the beginning and end of each year.

7. Net income to net worth. This is one of the most significant of all financial ratios. It is derived by dividing the net income ($9.9) by the total of the preferred-stock, common-stock and surplus accounts ($80.3). The result in this case is 12.3%.

This shows the percentage of return, in profits, that corporate management is earning on the stockholders' investment. In other chapters, the same basic information is shown, on a slightly different basis, as the *profit rate (PR)*.

This 12.3% is a slight decrease from the 12.5% of the prior year. It's a fair return: not as good as that achieved by a top-quality corporation but better than that of the average publicly held company. *The higher the ratio, the more profitable the operation.* Any company which can consistently improve such a ratio is a true growth company. *But be sure that this gain is due to operating skill, not to accounting legerdemain or extraordinary items.*

Ratios and Trends

Detailed financial analysis involves careful evaluation of income, costs and earnings. But it is also important to study various ratios and trends, both within the specific corporation and in comparison with those of other companies in the same industry. Usually, analysts prefer to use five- or ten-year averages. These can reveal significant changes and, on occasion, spot special values in either concealed or inconspicuous assets.

Example: When there is a wide difference between the book value of assets as carried on the balance sheet and their current market value, there may be important resources such as company holdings of valuable real estate, oil, gas or uranium.

Here are some of the interesting and often important data:

Operating ratio. This is the ratio of operating costs to sales. It is the complement of *profit margin* (100% minus the PM percentage). Thus, if a company's PM is 10%, its operating ratio is 90%. It's handy to compare similar companies but not significant otherwise.

PMs vary according to the type of business. They are low for companies with heavy plant investments (Borg-Warner) and for retailers with fast turnover (K-Mart) and high for marketing firms such as those providing information (Dun & Bradstreet), operating radio/TV stations (American Broadcasting) and for those manufacturing consumer products (Gillette).

For railroads and transportation corporations, a similar widely used test of operating efficiency is the *transportation ratio*—the percentage of revenues absorbed by the cost of handling traffic. *The lower the ratio, the greater the operating efficiency.* But because so many railroads have become holding companies that have diversified into nontransportation areas, this ratio is no longer overly useful.

Interest coverage. When a company has a large amount of senior obligations (bonds and preferred stocks), it is important to know that profits will be adequate to cover the payment of annual interest. This figure is the number of times the annual total interest ($1.3 on bonds and $.3 on preferred stock) is covered by the earnings ($22.6)—14+ times in the example. The usual acceptable minimum ratio for an industrial corporation is three to four times interest needs.

Keep in mind that when a company (except utilities or transportation firms) has a high debt, it means that investors shy away from buying its common stock. To provide the plants, equipment, etc., which the company needs, management must issue bonds or preferred shares (straight or convertible to attract investors). There are some tax advantages in such a course, but when the debt becomes too high, there can be trouble during recessive times. All, or almost all, of the gross profits will have to be used to pay interest and there will be nothing, or little, left over for the common stockholders.

On the other hand, speculators like high-debt situations when business is good. This means that when profits soar, all of the excess, after interest payments, will come down to the common stock. Typically, railroads, which have tremendous assets (almost all financed by debt obligations), are popular in boom times. An extra 10% gain in traffic can boost profits far more—percentagewise.

When corporations like utilities have small year-to-year fluctuations in earnings, a large amount of senior securities is no problem.

Payout ratio. This is the ratio of the cash dividends to per share profits after taxes. It reflects management's policy. Fast-growing corporations pay small dividends—less than 30% of each earned dollar; stable, profitable companies pay out about 50%; and utilities, which have almost assured earnings, pay 70% on the average.

It is pleasant to receive an ample dividend check, but for growth, look for companies that pay small dividends. The retained earnings will be used to improve the financial strength and operating future of the company; *and retained earnings are tax-free.*

Example: Avnet, Inc. has not paid out more than 26% of its profits since 1971. Yet its per share earnings have risen steadily: from 23¢ in 1971 to 95¢ in 1980. The reinvestments paid off as the price of Avnet stock rose from about 8 to 60 despite the generally poor market.

By contrast, National Steel Corporation, which has paid out between 32% and 96% of its profits, reported per share earnings of $2.61 in 1971, $9.44 in 1974, $6.56 in 1979 and $4.42 in 1980. No wonder the value of its stock fell from 56⅞ to 47, back to 52 and, recently, was down to 23.

Price to book value ratio. This is the market price of the stock divided by its book value per share. Since book value trends are relatively more stable than earnings trends, conservative analysts use this ratio as a price comparison. They keep in mind the historical over- or undervaluation of the stock, which in turn depends primarily on the company's profitable growth (or lack of it).

Because of inflation, understatement of assets on balance sheets—and in boom times, the enthusiasm of investors—often pushes this ratio rather high. *On the average, only the stocks of the most profitable companies sell at much more than twice book value.* Stocks of high-growth, profitable companies, such as Kodak, IBM and Xerox, do sell at higher ratios (usually) because investors believe these great corporations can continue to rack up ever-higher profits (as they have done in the past). But when there's a bear market, such stocks have further to fall than those selling at more logical price/equity ratios.

The price/equity ratio is a secondary checkpoint. Since 1971, this multiple, as measured by the S&P 400 Stock Index, has been at a high of 2.2 and a low of 1.3.

Price/earnings (P/E) ratio. This is calculated by dividing the price of the stock by the reported earnings per share for the past 12 months. Thus, the stock of Brandy-Dandy (B-D), with per share profits of $2.00 for the past year and selling at 24, has a P/E ratio of 12. This information is printed in stock tables in many financial publications.

This multiple of 12 was: *high* in comparison with that of the DJIA which, at the time, was 7; *low* when related to the company's historic range (over the past 10 years, a high of 17 and a low of 5.8).

B-D was a quality company, rated A by S & P. It was financially strong; had an outstanding record of higher revenues and profits; reported a 10 year average profit rate of 17.4% and earned growth rate of 10.2%; and earnings were up at an annual rate of over 10%—from $1.21 to $2.80 per share.

B-D had ample capital, modest debt and able management. There were no visible reasons to indicate that the future would not be as favorable, especially when the number of institutional investors was rising steadily.

By fundamental standards, the stock of B-D was undervalued. In 30 months or so, the investor can *hope* for gains of from 46% to 92% plus dividends of over 3% annually, to achieve total returns of from 53% to almost 100%. These projections are optimistic because: *(a)* the overall stock market may not move up; *(b)* the company may become unpopular with professional money managers who may not be enthusiastic about new policies or acquisitions; *(c)* there may be unfavorable governmental or legal problems affecting one or more of the industries in which B-D is involved; *(d)* the company may falter.

Two caveats: (1) Such projections can be made ONLY with stocks of quality corporations with long, fairly consistent records of profitable growth. They will not work with shares of companies that are cyclical, erratic or untested. (2) There can be no guarantee that these goals will be attained as soon as anticipated. Wall Street is often slow to recognize value and always takes time to come to intelligent decisions.

Investment tax credit. Currently corporations are allowed to take up to a 15% investment tax credit for long-life capital assets purchased. This is designed to encourage business to replace old machinery and equipment. On a $10 million new investment, there's a $1.5 million tax credit.

That's why it's important to note how much of corporate profits is due to such tax benefits rather than to profitable operations. In the past two decades, an increasing percentage of earnings of major corporations has been due to these tax advantages. To the stockholder who wants income, it makes little difference where the cash for the dividend comes from, but to the growth-minded investor, such gains are not a true measure of corporate growth.

These investment tax credits are difficult for amateurs to analyze. They are explained in the notes at the end of annual reports but not always in a way that the average investor can apply to his evaluation of the company. When you are puzzled about the failure of a stock to rise appreciably after higher earnings have been reported, ask your broker if those extra profits came from credits or operations.

Cash flow. This yardstick is increasingly popular in investment analysis. Reported net earnings, after taxes, do not reflect the actual cash income available to the company. Cash flow shows the earnings after taxes *plus* charges against income that do not directly involve cash outlays (sums allocated to depreciation, depletion, amortization and other special items).

A company might show a net profit of $250,000 plus depreciation of $1 million. Cash flow is $1,250,000. Deduct provisions for preferred dividends, then divide the balance by the number of shares of common stock to get the cash flow per share.

With changing tax laws, depreciation is becoming extremely important to many corporations. In 1950, U.S. companies set aside less than thirty cents in depreciation for each dollar in profits after taxes. Since the early 1960s, the figure has risen to about one dollar in depreciation for each dollar in net profits!

According to some analysts, cash flow isn't what it used to be. In an effort to keep earnings high in inflationary times, accountants exercise "judgments" that tend to *overvalue* some assets and *understate* depreciation expenses. As a result, some companies are paying dividends with money they do not have or must borrow and, in effect, are cannibalizing the corporate structure to keep the stock price up.

This is a complicated area that reflects management's interpretation of established accounting policies.

Examples:

• When Company A owns over 20% of Company B, Company A can book B's earnings even though there's no transfer of funds.

• A retailer reports, as revenues, millions of dollars of receivables that have not been collected (and, in some cases, may never be).

• A corporation continues to show depreciation of $10 million a year on a facility, yet, because of inflation, the real replacement cost is $15 million.

To get more accurate figures, says *Forbes* magazine, analysts have developed two new figures:

Distributable cash flow: the amount of money the company has on hand to pay dividends and/or invest in real growth. If this is negative, there are problems. If it's positive, fine, *unless* the company pays out more than this figure in dividends and, thus, is liquidating the firm.

Discretionary cash flow: distributable cash flow minus dividends: how much money is left after allocations for maintenance and dividends, to grow with. Companies do not really set aside such funds but, ultimately, they have to have the money in some form—cash savings or borrowing.

The table shows what has been happening with some major corporations. Note that companies requiring heavy capital expenditures, such as Bethlehem Steel, have negative cash flows in both categories. This is not exactly news but is another way to point out why these corporations are not good investments. Highly profitable companies,

CASH FLOW INDICATORS: 1980

Company	Net Income	Distributable Cash Flow	Discretionary Cash Flow
American Brands	$ 389.0	$ 184.3	$ 42.1
Bethlehem Steel	95.0	−399.3	−469.2
DuPont	670.0	− 35.3	−455.3
General Electric	1,490.0	852.4	152.4
IBM	3,500.0	5,390.6	3,390.6
Merck	431.0	293.8	113.8
Sears, Roebuck	475.0	−220.6	−649.6
United Technolo.	390.0	96.4	− 79.6

SOURCE: Forbes Magazine

such as IBM and Merck, have high cash flows by both measurements. They are worthwhile investments.

To a degree, these analyses of cash flow are comparable to the inflation accounting outline in the Introduction. They repeat the same conclusion: *real value* is a total concept that should be based on realistic, conservative accounting and not on judgments that may be legal and, to some extent, accepted, but artificially boost corporate profits.

Fundamentalist Checkpoints

1. Operating efficiency. This is the ultimate competitive evaluation of a corporation's management. The best test is the ratio of profits to net sales or revenues. Go back ten years to see if this ratio is improving, erratic, equal to, or better than the past.

The measure of operating efficiency is especially valuable in a turnaround situation. But be sure that the improvement is genuine and not accomplished by changes in accounting, etc. Shrewd new management may prefer to come in with a bang and then hope that business will improve enough to provide the extra income needed to offset the temporary, accounting-achieved improvement.

2. Growth trend of earnings. Look at the current earnings *before* taxes to see how they compare with the past. Companies which can report higher profits with declining or stable revenues have cost/profit-conscious (though not necessarily able) management. The earnings trend is important when a company moves into new product areas, makes an acquisition in a different field or introduces new management incentives such as stock options or a profit-sharing plan. *You want to know if such changes are benefiting corporate management or the stockholders.*

3. Dilution of earnings. When a company has outstanding convertible securities, warrants and other securities that can be exchanged for common stock, the SEC requires that the per share earnings be stated to show how much per share profits will be diluted if these options are exercised.

This information is essential in evaluating corporations which have made a number of acquisitions with securities, especially "Russian rubles" (convertibles, warrants, etc.).

A quality company will show no more than a few pennies per share dilution, but there can be a huge gap with some "empires." Before it was reorganized, L-T-V had a spread of per share earnings from $4.65 "stated" to $2.79 "fully diluted."

4. Dividend trend. If a company continues to boost its dividends in line with its growing profits, that's an excellent sign. If the company maintains or increases the dividend when profits drop or plateau, it is either a sign that management is confident of the future or is determined to keep shareholders—and the general stock market—happy. *Always check such a situation.*

If the profit dip is temporary and unusual, you can probably trust management. With an unseasoned corporation, be cautious. Management may be more interested in buttering up major stockholders (especially in a family-controlled firm) than in reinvesting for future growth.

Wall Street wisdom predicates that, to win shareholders' favor, a profitable company should keep increasing dividends. But, according to *Fortune,* this does not always work out. A study showed a drop in the prices of the stocks of 19 companies that increased dividends annually from 1971–80. Warner-Lambert shares were down 41.2% despite an average dividend rise of 8.7% and Avon Products stock fell 61.4% even though its payouts were up 10% every year. The only solace for investors was that the yields kept improving.

5. Capital expenditures. This provides a strong indication of the desire of corporate executives to remain competitive or attain industry leadership. With fast-changing technology, it is almost imperative that a major corporation continually build for the future. When capital expenditures drop significantly (especially when it is probable that this action will bolster lagging earnings), there may be serious trouble ahead.

If capital expenditures rise sharply, it may mean that former management was negligent and that, for the next couple of years, profits are not likely to rise.

On the average, it takes three years before major capital expenditures for new plants, equipment, processes or products provide reasonable profits.

6. Research and development. Almost without exception, corporations which appropriate liberally for R & D are leaders in their fields—in sales and profits and growth. The top-rated companies know that they must continue to build for the future. When a president announces that allocations for R & D are being substantially reduced—unless there is a very logical explanation—take heed. He may be sacrificing tomorrow for today.

Some enterprises, such as retail stores, cannot benefit too much from R & D, but these are the exceptions. Most business organizations need to invest continually and consistently to develop new products and processes.

7. Foreign earnings. With so many companies now doing business around the world, through fully or partially owned subsidiaries, foreign earnings can be an important factor. Under new accounting rules, all unrealized gains and losses from foreign balance-sheet translations must be reported as part of current income each quarter—not averaged out over the full year. This can make a significant difference over the short term. Black & Decker, for example, had to show a 15¢ per share loss on foreign exchange in early 1981. This was about 20% of total earnings.

Formulas for Value

Professionals use various methods to calculate value and to determine whether a stock should be bought or sold. Here are two that you can use yourself:

Corporate cash position. This was developed by Dr. Benjamin Graham, granddaddy of fundamentalists. To use:

• Subtract current liabilities, long-term debt and preferred stock (at market value) from current assets of the corporation.

• Divide the result by the number of shares of common stock outstanding.

If the asset value per share is higher than the price per share, Graham would place the stock on his Review List.

Example: Puff Publishing has $100 million current assets, $20 million bonds, $10 million preferred stock and current liabilities of $25 million: a net of $45 million. With 1 million shares, this works out to $45 per share asset value. When the stock is at 35, PP meets Graham's requirements for an undervalued situation.

Percentage buying value. This formula, developed by John B. Neff of Windsor Fund, uses the current yield plus the rate of earnings growth divided by the current price/earnings ratio. If the result is 2 or more, the stock is worth buying:

$$\frac{CY + EG}{PE} = PBV$$

CY = Current Yield
EG = Earnings Growth
PE = Price/Earnings Ratio
PBV = Percentage buying value

Here's how the formula worked, several years ago, with fast-growing, non-dividend-paying Tandy Corp. and high-yielding, stodgy A.T.&T.:

$$\text{Tandy} \frac{0 + 17\%}{4} = 4.25\% \qquad \text{BUY}$$

$$\text{A.T.\&T.} \frac{7.2\% + 6\%}{8.1} = 1.6\% \text{ SELL or DO NOT BUY}$$

But in 1980, when the price of "T" had dropped so that the P/E ratio was around 6, the formula signaled a buy:

$$\frac{10\% + 5\%}{6} = 15 = 2.5 \text{ BUY}$$

To find the rate of earnings growth, check the company's annual report for data of the last five to 10 years or ask your broker to get the information. Unless there are strong reasons to expect excellent growth in the future, do not be optimistic. Be conservative and use the historical average.

Another formula involves a weighted calculation of three values: market, earnings and assets. Assuming the market value is determined to be 10, with a weight of 25%; earnings value is set at 15, with a weight of 55%; and asset value is 25, with a weight of 20%. The ultimate value is $15.75:

Element of Value	Value	Weight	Net Value
Market	$10	25%	$2.50
Earnings (Investment)	15	55	8.25
Assets	25	20	5.00
Ultimate value		100%	$15.75

Characteristics of an Undervalued Stock Investment

1. A current dividend or 4.5% or more.
2. Cash dividends must have been paid for at least 5, and preferably 10, years without decrease in dollar payout.
3. Total debt less than 35% of total capitalization.
4. Minimum of $25 million net working capital for liquidity.
5. Current dividend protection ratio should be at least 1.4: $1.40 earnings for each $1.00 dividends.
6. Current P/E ratio of 6 or less.
7. Next year's profits should be expected to be higher.
8. Gain-to-loss ratio or minimum of 2:1: i.e. based on past market action and future prospects, the probable gain should be twice as great as the possible loss: a potential gain of 10 points vs. a 5-point decline.

Another Check for Undervalued Stocks

To judge whether a stock is undervalued, Management Asset Corp. calculates the average 10-year growth rate of earnings and then assigns a P/E ratio which is increased by .8 for each 1% of profit rise. With zero growth, the P/E is 8; with 1% average rise, 8.8; with 2%, 9.6; and so on, to 20 for a growth rate of 15% or more.

Next, multiply the average dollar earnings for the decade by the assigned P/E to find the price at which the stock should be sold. To find the buy price, subtract one-third of the final figure.

Example: XYZ has boosted its profits by 10% annually for 10 years. The assigned P/E ratio is 15.8; the average earnings per share have been $3.00. Thus, 3 × 15.8 = 47.4. Subtract 33% to get a buy price of 31.6.

Common Stocks with Total Claim on Earnings

Income investors should look for companies which have only common stock outstanding. That means that there are no interest or amortization charges to be paid on bonds, and that all profits are available to the common shareholders. This can mean more liberal dividends.

Since such corporations have no leverage, the prices of their shares are likely to be stable and less susceptible to large capital losses in either slowly declining markets or sudden price shakeouts.

Debt-Laden Companies

Conversely, be very careful with corporations that have a large amount of debt. By definition, they are not quality investments. Once in a while they can be profitable speculations, but you have to be smart and lucky.

Low P/Es Pay Off

Several studies show that stocks with low P/Es (seemingly those with the worst prospects) will outperform those with high multiples. In the 21 years from 1957 through 1977, 80% of low P/E stocks scored better than average gains, says analyst David Dreman.

He admits, "Over a sufficient period of time, earnings determine stock prices but when profits are low and there are prospects of improvement, low P/E stocks can be real winners. . . . When investors are disappointed by groups of stocks with the highest multiples, they tend to overreact and dump their shares so their prices decline. With low P/E groups, the action is reversed. If favorable developments come, they cause an optimistic reappraisal of the stock."

Dreman warns that the investor must maintain a hard-headed approach, discounting hot tips and alluring concept stocks. "He must tell himself," he says, "that he is figuratively betting black on a roulette wheel with more black numbers than red."

Here are his rules:

• *Buy large and medium-size established companies* whose stocks pay high dividends and have low P/E ratios. Such companies usually suffer less from accounting legerdemain than smaller companies do and have more staying power.

• *Select companies that are financially strong* and able to sail smoothly through the rough weather the low P/E firms can encounter.

• *Look for:* (1) current ratio (current assets divided by current liabilities) of 2:1 or higher; (2) total debt no more than 40% of capital (bonds, preferred stocks and common stock).

• *Diversify,* preferably 15 stocks in a dozen or more industries.

• *Be patient.* Success takes time, usually at least one year.

Ray Dirks, analyst-turned-author, seconds this approach but looks for stocks with very low P/E ratios. He insists that the lower the multiple, the more likely the rise in the price of the stock. His studies show that, between 1967 and 1976, the stocks with the lowest multiples gained $5 for every $1 while those with the highest P/Es returned only 84¢ on every invested $1. *His rule:* when the stock moves from 3 to 6 times earnings, sell and find another super-bargain. But you must be ready to accept some losses. In many cases, there is a sound reason why the stock is so unpopular.

Earned Yield

This is a concept that is widely used in England and can be useful in analyzing investment portfolios as well as stocks of individual corporations. The Earned Yield (EY) is the Price/Earnings ratio turned upside down: the after-tax earnings per share divided by the price of the stock. Thus, a stock trading at 20 with per share profits of $1.00 has a P/E of 20 and an EY of 1/20th or 5%. The stock's EY is $5.00 per $100 investment.

The EY is used by professionals to compare portfolios. *Example:* Willie Whizmaster manages a personal pension plan with ten stocks. Of these, nine are selling at 10 times earnings but the tenth, because of a sharp profit decline, is temporarily valued at a multiple of 100. The average P/E ratio is 19 but does not properly reflect the true market values.

But that errant stock would have an EY of 1.0%: $10 price and 10¢ earnings. So the EY for the portfolio would be a more realistic 9.1%.

DEBT-FREE COMPANIES

NEW YORK STOCK EXCHANGE

COMPANY	5 Year Earnings Growth	Return on Equity	COMPANY	5 Year Earnings Growth	Return on Equity
Amsted Industries	17%	21.3%	Longs Drug Stores	15	23.6
Campbell Red Lake	40	40.7	Maytag Co.	8	27.6
CBI Industries	8	20.4	Miller-Wohl	25	46.3
Dome Mines	47	30.9	Oakite Products	8	17.9
Dun & Bradstreet	17	32.9	Petrie Stores	12	30.9
Family Dollar Stores	18	26.6	Schering-Plough	12	25.1
John H. Harland	20	23.6	L. S. Starrett	21	17.5
Illinois Tool Works	23	16.6	Weis Markets	17	21.5
Inter. Flavors & Fragrances	20	22.5	Woods Petroleum	8	34.3

AMERICAN STOCK EXCHANGE

COMPANY	5 Year Earnings Growth	Return on Equity	COMPANY	5 Year Earnings Growth	Return on Equity
Automatic Switch	24	16.9	Gross Telecasting	21	23.2
A. T. Cross	24	34.9	Logicon, Inc.	18	18.1
Day Mines	153	26.3	O'Sullivan Corp.	20	27.7
Evans-Aristocrat	24	23.3	Park Chemical	13	20.2
Gen. Employment Enterprices	123	31.0	Penn Engineering	34	23.7
Giant Yellowknife Mines	...	26.6	SGL Industries	14	18.6
Gorman-Rupp	13	20.5	Summit Energy	15	20.3

OVER-THE-COUNTER

COMPANY	5 Year Earnings Growth	Return on Equity	COMPANY	5 Year Earnings Growth	Return on Equity
American Filtrona	13	17.3	Manitowoc Co.	6	26.8
American Welding	35	15.1	Moore Products	18	19.1
Astrosystems	19	17.5	Neutrogena Corp.	19	26.4
BBDO International	15	53.6	Page Airways	31	19.2
Bob Evans Farms	30	31.4	PBA, Inc.	24	39.2
Bolar Pharmaceutical	53	33.9	Pinkerton's	13	20.5
Brenco, Inc.	23	28.0	Research, Inc.	20	20.2
Brooks Fashion Stores	22	50.2	Roadway Express	14	24.0
Callon Petroleum	−4	17.8	SafeCard Services	95	42.4
Chemed Corp.	13	19.9	St. Jude Medical	....	17.0
Comserv Corp.	50	16.6	Servicemaster Industries	28	30.9
Drexler Technology	110	24.3	Sturm, Ruger & Co.	11	24.1
Frost & Sullivan	47	20.5	Tampax, Inc.	4	30.2
Harper Group	35	21.2	Tennant Co.	18	22.7
Hollywood Park	9	17.2	Tri-Chem	−7	27.3
Interface Mechanisms	82	36.4	Unimed, Inc.	47	17.4
Kelly Services	34	27.0	WD-40 Co.	22	68.1
Lawson Products	15	27.3	Wham-O Manufacturing	22	15.6
Liberty Homes	115	18.8	Wiser Oil	15	23.0
MacDermid Corp.	24	21.0			

SOURCE: Forbes Magazine; Standard & Poor's

Look for stocks that have low EYs. Chances are they are undervalued and ready for a rapid rise.

Companies Repurchasing Their Own Stock

When companies repurchase their own stock, it can be a bullish sign. A survey made when the market was at a low ebb found that 64% of such stocks outpaced the field in the next 12 months.

Repurchase of a substantial number of shares automatically benefits all shareholders: profits are spread over a smaller total; there's more money for dividends and reinvestments; and there's temporary market support.

During recessive periods, many corporations feel that their stocks are at bargain levels and represent a wise and fruitful use of corporate funds. With shares at 50% of book value, the purchase acquires two dollars in assets for every one dollar spent. The savings on dividends could be applied against the interest on loans made for the stock purchase.

On the other hand, a steady stock purchase is a partial liquidation of the corporation, and the critics say, why not pay out more of the surplus cash and let the shareholders decide if the stock is worth buying?

Here's what happens: A company with 1,000,000 shares earns $2 million, for profits of $2.00 per share. If 50,000 shares are acquired and the company nets the same amount the next year, the earnings will be $2.10 per share. *Note:* That's a good reason to check the number of outstanding shares to be sure that the earnings growth is genuine.

Repurchased stock can be used for stock options, employee purchase plans, exercise of warrants, acquisitions, etc. The stock must be held for two years before it can be used in a pooling-of-interest merger. When it's paid out sooner, the deal becomes a straight purchase with more costly tax liabilities.

A corporation is required to make a public announcement of its intention to repurchase. When it's a listed stock, all transactions are handled by one broker for one

COMPANIES WITH HEAVY DEBT BURDENS

COMPANY	Debt as % Total Capital Short Term	Long Term	COMPANY	Debt as % Total Capital Short Term	Long Term	COMPANY	Debt as % Total Capital Short Term	Long Term
A-T-O	10.7%	44.9%	Hospital Corp.	3.0	49.7	Rapid American	3.3%	75.3%
Albertson's	1.2	52.7	Inter. Harvester	26.6	31.2	Rohr Industries	0.8	53.7
Am. Medical Inter.	2.4	54.7	IU International	20.9	42.5	Ryder Systems	2.6	68.8
American Stores	6.9	50.2	Lamson & Sessions	0.6	54.5	Saxon Industries	12.8	55.7
Am. Water Works	9.5	59.3	Leaseway Trans.	16.2	50.1	Sea Containers	11.6	63.4
Avco Corp.	18.0	59.2	Lockheed Corp.	5.4	62.3	Southland Corp.	3.1	49.4
City Investing	7.4	57.7	LTV Corp.	1.6	64.5	Standard Oil (Ohio)	1.0	54.7
Coastal Corp.	9.8	49.3	MAPCO, Inc.	1.9	52.4	Stop & Shop	2.8	55.8
Dayco Corp.	11.2	47.3	McGraw-Edison	2.5	56.2	Sun Chemical	7.2	49.7
Fed-Mart	4.1	59.0	Memorex Corp.	10.0	41.6	Supermkts General	3.3	58.2
Fisher Foods	5.1	56.6	Metromedia, Inc.	1.1	52.5	Talley Industries	10.8	46.3
Gelco Corp.	36.6	52.4	Monogram Indust.	5.5	48.7	Texas International	2.6	50.6
Genesco, Inc.	15.1	47.8	Nat. Medical Enter.	3.3	53.9	Trans Union	20.3	56.6
Gifford-Hill	4.1	63.5	No. American Coal	1.0	54.7	United Merchants	16.1	64.3
Global Marine	6.7	62.7	NVF Industries	16.6	59.6	Wang Laboratories	9.1	48.0
Gulf & Western	12.5	47.1	Ogden Corp.	5.2	48.3	Zayre Corp.	3.3	58.0
Harte-Hanks	5.2	48.2	Outlet Co.	12.9	40.5			

Does not include airlines, food and lodging companies that rely on mortgage-type financing

SOURCE: Standard & Poor's Compustat Service

---

day with a limit of 15% of the daily average volume for the preceding four weeks. To make it convenient for large shareholders, such as estates or foundations, to act without unduly disturbing the market, block purchases of $250,000 or more can be handled without restrictions.

Another point to watch: a suddenly announced repurchase at year-end. This could be window-dressing to boost the per share profits.

CHAPTER 6

Timing for Extra Profits, Lower Losses

Read this chapter together with the next one on "How to Use Technical Analysis Profitably." You'll learn the importance of timing in successful investing.

Some analysts insist that timing is the *only* factor in stock market profits. I don't see any of them driving a Rolls-Royce. Timing is imperative with speculations; with investments, it is an aid that can help you achieve extra profits and avoid unnecessary losses. When you buy a quality stock at a reasonable price, you will always make money . . . eventually. Good timing can reduce the patience period.

The trouble with timing is the stock market itself. Many *long-term* changes in stock prices result from "rational" or "fundamental" economic, monetary, financial and corporate factors and forces. *Short-term* changes, however, are due to psychological factors—fear, hope, confidence, uncertainty—*anything but facts.* This is the area where *technical analysis* becomes important.

You can make money, temporarily, when you buy the *best* securities at the *wrong* time. If you hang on to them through their inevitable decline, you will end up a winner when they bounce back again. You can often make money by buying a *poor* security at the *right* time. But the best of all investment worlds is when you buy the *right* security at the *right* time.

Timing Errors

The gravest timing-related errors made by investors—primarily by amateurs, but frequently by professionals—are:

1. To refuse to sell after the price trend of the stock has reversed from up to down. If the stock is held at a loss and your portfolio can be strengthened by switching, the tendency is to take no action. As a result, you soon get locked in with your worst-performing stocks!

2. To refuse to sell when the stock you own soars to an unusually high level far beyond its normal range and its logical maximum value. This is the situation when stocks become popular. By definition, *this is the time to think about selling*—because the danger of a price drop is far greater than the probability of a further meaningful gain. *Best bet:* Set actual or mental stop orders at 10% to 15% below current market prices in a stable market.

3. To refuse to buy when the price of the stock is at a

low ebb and when prospects for profitable growth by the company and the industry are good. This is the point at which stocks are unpopular and bargains can be found.

It is a sad truism that when stock prices are really low, most people are unwilling to buy and that when stock prices are really high, most people forget the logical prospects and buy avidly.

The basic rules for the successful timing of investments are to buy stocks when they are undervalued and unpopular and to sell when they become fully priced and are very popular.

Types of Timing

Broadly speaking, there are two kinds of timing:

Fundamental timing: the determination as to whether or not it is a good time to invest in common stocks. This is used to improve profits, not for quick trading gains. Action is taken against a background of the fundamental factors that influence stock prices: the economic, monetary and political influences; the earnings, dividends, financial strength, ratios, yields, interest rates and, of course, future prospects for the economy, the industry and the company.

With fundamental timing, the investor acts with the confidence that the stock market, over a period of time, will adjust to price levels reflecting these rational factors. Successful fundamental timing requires a continuous business and economic forecast.

Such an approach pays little heed to the many psychological and short-run market forces that affect week-to-week, month-to-month and, often, year-to-year fluctuations in stock-market prices. With fundamental timing, the investor works in general areas: low or *buy* ranges and high or *sell* ranges.

One widely used guide is the price/earnings ratio of the stock market. The fundamentalist believes that, over a decade or so, the market tends to sell within a broad range of a multiple of profits: for the DJIA, from a high of 15 to a low of 6. This means that when the Dow stocks sell at more than 15 times earnings, the market is becoming overvalued and some stocks should be sold. Similarly, when the P/E ratio of the Dow falls below 6, it's time to consider buying. This type of timing takes patience and

can be used only for long-term investments.

Market timing: whether and when to buy and sell specific stocks. This recognizes that, most of the time, the prices of common stocks move together and that there are four kinds of market-price movements:

1. Major bull and bear market swings. These are seldom less than two years' duration. Usually, they last longer but include many short reversing fluctuations. Analysts may be able to spot the long-term trends but are more lucky than wise in predicting interim actions.

Typically, bear markets move downward much faster than bull markets move up. *Remember the psychology: Disillusion and deflation panic investors more than illusion and inflation elate them. BUT NOT ALWAYS. There is nothing more predictable in general terms and more unpredictable in specific terms than the stock market.*

2. Intermediate market movements within a major bull or bear market. These usually run several months. These are ever-present, ever-changing. They are most rewarding (or most irritating) with groups of stocks.

3. Seasonal market movements of a month or so. These can be superimposed on intermediate swings. They tend to follow established patterns and often concern only a few stock groups significantly but generally apply to all securities.

4. Immediate short-term fluctuations of weeks or days. These are of importance only to traders although, on occasion, upsetting to investors.

There are hundreds of investment timing techniques which attempt to spot and pinpoint all four of these market movements. The conservative investor wants to catch the turn of major bull or bear markets; the less conservative watches for immediate movements; the speculator relishes the seasonal swings, but only the professional plays for the short, day-to-day fluctuations. *All serious investors should understand the broad trends and movements of the stock market in order to sharpen their own timing.*

Tools and Techniques of Market Timing

Market timing is always difficult. Technicians rely on charts and indicators. Fundamentalists look for signs of

STOCK-MARKET ACTION

INVESTMENT GROUP	1980	1979	1978	1977	1976	1975	1974	1973	1972	1971
DJIA	+15	+ 4%	− 3%	− 8%	+18%	+38%	−28%	−17%	+15%	+ 6%
NYSE Composite	+26	+15	+ 2	− 7	+21	+32	−30	−20	+14	+12
S&P 500	+26	+12	+ 1	− 7	+19	+32	−30	−18	+16	+11
Value Line	+ 8	+24	+ 1	− 5	+32	+44	−34	−35	+ 1	+ 9
Groups										
Financial	+ 3	+53	+ 6	− 5	+49	+19	−36	−29	+10	+ 9
Consumer	+16	+12	+ 6	− 4	+31	+54	−23	−44	+ 4	+19
Defensive	+15	+17	+ 1	− 4	+22	+37	−17	−24	+ 7	+ 7
Cyclical	+23	+21	+ 3	− 5	+39	+53	−21	−10	+ 8	+15
Utilities	+ 9	+ 5	+ 9	− 6	+25	+39	−23	−20	+ 8	− 3
Transportation	+28	+17	+ 4	− 1	+39	+58	−13	−24	+ 6	+47

SOURCE: Wright Investors' Service

bargains or overpricing. They both recognize that there are patterns that can be used successfully. For example, they know that, on the average, the price of a stock will swing 20% to 25% every year. This spread represents the profit that most people look for.

To take advantage of such price movements, analysts develop *relativity ratios*. These measure the change in the price of a stock (or group of stocks) against a stock-market index and thus can categorize volatility.

The best known is the "beta," based on the S&P 500 Stock Index. A stock with a beta of 1.25 has 25% more volatility (and thus risk) than the overall market. This means that it is likely to fall or rise 25% more than the general level of stock prices.

In terms of investing, the conservative would choose low-beta stocks: those rated under 1.00. In a down market, their decline will be less than average; in an up market, their gain would be smaller. The aggressive investor would concentrate on high-beta stocks.

Betas are best for professionals because of the complex calculations but, with experience, the amateur learns to check them before acting.

It is important to keep abreast of developments because stock/group betas can change markedly over the years. In 1973, drug stocks had a beta of .79, so were considered defensive. But by 1979, the industry beta had risen to 1.24: 24% greater volatility than the overall market.

Stock-bond yields. This can be useful in determining when to move from bonds to stocks or back again. It has not been overly valuable in recent years because of the super-high yields of fixed-income securities but is an excellent frame of reference.

The basic premise is sound: that there is always competition for capital between stocks and bonds. The total returns of common stocks—dividends plus capital appreciation—is weighed against the interest of bonds.

Note how the relationship has changed over the years, especially since interest rates began to rise. Back in the early 1960s, the difference was small, less than 1%. Most people preferred equity to debt.

In the bull-market years of the early 1970s, when stock prices were high and thus dividend yields low, the bond advantage widened so that some investors moved into bonds, especially with the stock-market downturn in 1974.

A timing signal was flashed in 1979 when the spread widened to over 4%—a clear signal that, for income, it was wise to shift some savings to bonds. This trend was confirmed in 1980 and was still hanging in there in early 1981.

By and large, yield spreads are of more concern to professionals than to amateurs, but yield spreads can be helpful to get a better idea of what's happening in the money markets and, with experience, polish investment timing.

Value timing. This involves the use of P/E ratios for market timing: to *buy* when the multiple of a specific stock is below the long-term average range; to *sell* when it rises well above the historically high ratio. This is better in theory than in practice.

Value timing tells you when a stock is under- or

YIELDS: STOCKS vs. BONDS

Year	S&P Close	Stock Yields	Bond Yields	Difference vs. Stocks
1959	65	3.1%	4.4%	−1.3%
1960	61	3.3	4.4	−1.1
1961	76	3.0	4.3	−1.3
1962	66	3.4	4.1	−0.7
1963	79	3.3	4.2	−0.9
1964	90	3.0	4.4	−1.4
1965	98	3.1	4.6	−1.5
1966	85	3.3	5.4	−2.1
1967	105	3.2	5.8	−2.6
1968	113	3.0	6.5	−3.5
1969	101	3.1	7.5	−4.4
1970	101	3.6	7.8	−4.2
1971	113	3.0	6.9	−3.9
1972	132	2.6	6.7	−4.1
1973	109	2.9	7.5	−4.6
1974	76	4.1	9.2	−5.1
1975	101	4.1	9.0	−4.9
1976	119	3.8	8.5	−4.7
1977	105	4.5	8.2	−3.7
1978	107	5.0	8.6	−3.6
1979	121	5.2	9.4	−4.2
1980	154	4.8	12.4	−7.6
1981*	154	4.3	13.4	−9.1

* March 31, 1981

SOURCE: Wright Investors' Service

overvalued but it cannot indicate when a favorable price movement will occur. Wall Street is slow to change its prejudices. The price movements you want, and believe in, can take months, even years. They are signaled by market action which reflects psychology more than logic. Within any one year, the price of a volatile stock may fluctuate as much as 50% but there will be little or no change in its fundamental value. Thus, by buying an undervalued stock at the wrong time, you can tie up your money and miss potential profits that you might have made by buying a fairly valued stock or even an over-valued stock, at the right time.

During 1972 and 1973, the prices of glamour-growth equities zoomed up and up. They soared far beyond traditional values and the fundamentalists cried in horror and dismay. *But they still kept moving up under the pressure of institutional buying.*

According to fundamental standards, even an aggressive investor should have sold Avon Products at around 100 in 1972–73 when the P/E ratio soared above 40. But AVP roared to a high of 140 with a multiple of 65 times earnings!

As usual, the fundamentalists were right but their timing was wrong. By late 1974, AVP had fallen way, way down to 19—along with almost all glamour-growth equities.

The value approach, when combined with technical analysis, can be extremely rewarding and relatively safe. *The big losses take place when you fail to heed the signals on market action and the facts of corporate growth and profits.*

When to Buy Stocks

There are so many tips/rules/guidelines for buying stocks throughout *Your Investments* that it is not necessary to summarize the timing of purchases. They all boil down to this: *When investing,* buy only quality stocks when they are undervalued, have bright prospects and are becoming popular. You can afford to be patient. But you should buy only when total returns can be expected to be 35% to 50% in the next 24 months. That will assure you average annual total returns of at least 15% on your money.

When trading, you can be more flexible on quality, but timing must be more precise: buying *up* stocks in *up* industries in an *up* market. Or when you are selling short (where the buying comes later), the reverse. Your target goal should come faster, usually in six months or less.

There is one concept to keep in mind in timing purchases, especially in a bull market: *Buy high and sell higher.*

Normally, when you come across a stock you like, you decide that you will buy it when its price dips—e.g., when it's trading at 25, you set a buy order at 23.

It's always pleasant to get a bargain but, experience shows, the best time to buy any stock is when its price is rising (unless you are willing to wait). The key, says technician Joseph E. Granville, is "Volume. This always comes before price."

He argues that unless a substantial number of people are interested in the stock, its price will move within a narrow range. Only when there is additional activity will the stock price change significantly: *up* when corporate news/prospects are bright; *down* when they are gloomy. In other words, he says, "Do not be afraid to buy a favored stock at 26 or 27 if the rise comes with unusually high trading. *Buy high and sell higher.*"

The reasoning back of this concept is that when sales increase, people know, or think they know, more than the rest of us. When the stock move is up, they are sufficiently confident to put up their money to back their opinion. Vice versa on the downside.

Despite his showmanship and iconoclastic approach, Granville continues to rely on volume indicators. But with the huge trading of recent months, the significance of volume alone appears to be less significant than in the past. Or at least more useful for speculating than for investing. A great many people who followed Granville's famous *sell* signal in early 1981 lost a great deal of money fast. The market did tumble but it quickly recovered to new highs, and later, as Granville's forecast dropped, to new lows. Timing is a double-edged sword: it cuts profits as well as losses unless one is nimble.

When to Sell Stocks

Selling stocks is more difficult and, for successful timing, demands strict adherence to strict rules. It is never easy to sell any stock when it is high-priced, popular and profitable. Such action is contrary to human nature and fails to accomplish two important objectives: to make your spouse happy and yourself boastful.

Yet it is the most logical approach. *How can you make real profits if you do not buy low and sell high?*

Sure, you can always operate on the "greater fool theory" that, regardless of how high the price of a stock

becomes, a "greater fool" will come along and buy it from you. But what happens when the bubble bursts and there are no more devil-may-care buyers? *You can lose a lot of money FAST.*

Here are some guidelines for *selling:*

1. Take your profits when better gains are likely in another stock. In November 1980, the stock of Schlumberger (SLB), after a long and strong rise, hit 130. A check of the fundamentals showed that the company's profit rate was slipping after the acquisition of Fairchild Camera: 37.7% vs. 41.4% earlier in the year.

This peak price assured a handsome profit and, since the risks were now greater than the potential rewards, this was the time to sell and put the proceeds in a more rewarding situation. Soon, SLB fell below 100!

2. Sell when the original reasons for purchase no longer hold. There are three basic reasons to buy any stock:

a. Your study shows that this is a sound company with good prospects for profitable growth.

b. You believe that something good is going to happen: the stock may be split, the company is getting a big new contract, a new, profitable product, acquisition, etc.

c. Reports and/or charts show that smart money is moving into the stock.

Items *b* and *c* are usually reasons for a quick rise in the price of the equity. There should be quick action. If there is not, *sell.* You were wrong.

3. Use stop orders. These can protect your profits or minimize your losses. There are two handy ways to do this:

a. *Enter a good-until-canceled stop order.* This will vary with the price range and the volatility of the stock, but as a rule, 10% to 15% below the purchase price or, if higher, the current value. With a stock at 50, set the stop at 45¼ or 42½. Use fractions because in a fast-falling market your round-number stop may not be executed. If the stock goes up to 55, move the stop up.

b. *Use a mental stop order.* This requires determination and constant surveillance of the stock market. It is valuable only for the disciplined investor. He should set a price below which he does not want to own the stock. Each night he checks the closing price and then decides his next day's action. If the price trend is down and the volume is up for several days, he should act promptly.

The difficulty with this approach is that it is too easy to delay, to get busy or to change your mind. Most people wait for a rally. By the time they do act, they have lost a couple of points more than anticipated.

4. Sell when an industry becomes unpopular. In early 1981, it became clear that there would be a surplus of oil and, with a free market in the U.S., this indicated lower prices and lower profits for major energy companies. The market values of oil stocks began to decline: Exxon, from 90 to below 70; Phillips Petroleum, from 65 to the low 40s. For weeks, oil stocks, with ever lower prices, were among the Most Actives, indicating that major investors were unloading at any price. The oil stocks were out of favor, and once that happens, it can take months and even years for them to come back.

The wise investor sells and watches for bargains. But he is patient and slow to buy back. After you are *sure* the stock has hit bottom, wait another couple of weeks. It will probably go lower!

This advice is also important when your stock holds within a narrow range for a long time. You make money *only* when the stock is going up (unless you sell short). If you are not enthused with the dividend yield, sell and look for more rewarding opportunities.

5. When the charts show a confirmed downtrend. This applies to both the market and specific stocks. In his excellent book *Follow the Leaders,* Richard Blackman sells when:

The trendline on the DJIA (or any other standard stock-market indicator) clearly reverses. On the long-term chart, at Points A:

- In early 1969 when the average fell below 900.
- In the winter of 1973 when it fell after edging over 1000.
- In early 1977 when the chart showed the start of a year-long drop.

The chart signaled buying opportunities (B) in mid-1975 and again in early 1980.

By heeding the overall trends and then using them as a framework for the action of individual stocks, the investor would have cut losses (or eased profits) and would have achieved far greater returns than if he held on in hope—or listened to the recommendations of most market letters. Most of the A and B signals indicated a shift of 20%, more than most people make on their savings each year.

6. When the stock's volume reaches a six-month high. On bar charts, the number of shares traded is shown at the bottom. When a stock is in a downtrend, strong volume will accelerate the decline. Vice versa on the upside. *Volume precedes price.*

7. After a big hit. If you have just sold at a substantial profit, take your time before reinvesting. Do not let your broker persuade you to sell and buy another stock. He's trained to "get the other side of every trade." Stop. Clear your head. Let the market go for a week. Then make sure that the next stock you buy has a potential gain of at least 25%. Otherwise sit on the sidelines.

8. After three straight losses. Blackman says, "When this sad situation occurs, sell everything. If you struck out three times in a row, it's not you if you have been playing by the rules. You're in a bad market and should recognize it."

9. After 12 months if you are fully invested. At this point, the market and up-moving stocks are likely to pause under the pressure of sales by profit-taking investors. They take control and, for a while, virtually stop the market from going up.

"When you judge this time span, do so from the week the uptrend started, not the date you bought the stock. Check the chart and make believe you bought at the bottom. Then mark your investment calendar one year ahead.

"This is a tough rule for most investors to accept. It should be used flexibly but it's backed by common sense and proven-profitable results."

HOW FAMOUS NAME STOCKS HAVE CHANGED

1981 LIST

STOCK	Earnings Growth Annual Rate	
	5 years	10 years
Abbott Laboratories	+22%	+17%
AMP, Inc.	+37	+18
Automatic Data	+21	+22
Baker International	+22	+27
Baxter Travenol	+21	+22
Big Three Industries	+21	+23
Digital Equipment	+30	+29
Dun & Bradstreet	+18	+13
Engelhard Minerals	+34	+29
Fluor Corp.	+23	+24
Gearhart Industries	+28	+36
Halliburton Co.	+17	+25
Helmerich & Payne	+25	+27
Hewlett-Packard	+24	+26
Hospital Corp.	+23	+24
IBM	+13	+13
Johnson & Johnson	+15	+16
Lubrizol Corp.	+20	+18
Merck & Co.	+13	+14
Nat'l Semiconductor	+26	+42
Perkin-Elmer	+25	+18
Pioneer Corp.	+26	+28
Raytheon Co.	+24	+19
Schlumberger, Ltd.	+35	+34
SmithKline Corp.	+34	+20
Tandy Corp.	+30	+32
Texas Instruments	+28	+21
Texas Oil & Gas	+31	+33
Warner Communications	+23	+17
Waste Management	+37	+35

1972 LIST

STOCK	Earnings Growth Annual Rate	
	5 years	10 years
American Home	+12%	+13%
AMP, Inc.	+37	+18
Avon Products	+11	† 9
Black & Decker	+22	+15
Burroughs Corp.	+ 4	+10
Chesebrough-Pond's	+15	+13
Coca-Cola	+11	+11
Colgate-Palmolive	+ 5	+ 9
Delta Airlines	+27	+12
Eastman Kodak	+12	+11
Emerson Electric	+16	+12
Halliburton Co.	+17	+25
Holiday Inns	+15	+ 8
Honeywell, Inc.	+26	+14
IBM	+13	+13
K-Mart	+ 1	+11
McDonald's Corp	+20	+27
Merck & Co.	+17	+14
MMM	+20	+13
PepsiCo, Inc.	+17	+14
Polaroid Corp.	+12	+ 3
Procter & Gamble	+13	+11
Schering-Plough	+12	+17
Schlumberger, Ltd.	+35	+34
Sears Roebuck	+ 1	+ 1
Sperry Corporation	+13	+13
Texas Instruments	+28	+21
Warner-Lambert	+ 2	+ 6
Xerox Corp.	+11	+12

SOURCE: Wright Investors' Service

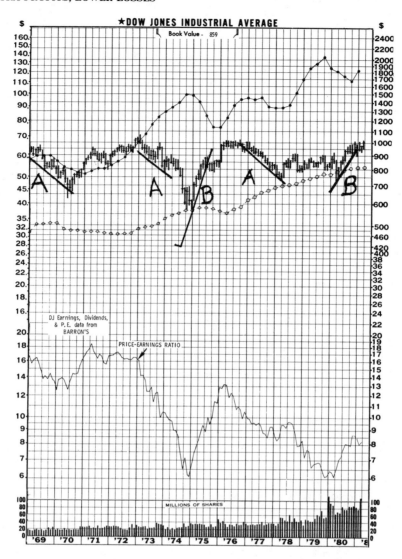

10. When stocks break out of a consolidation pattern. This is a variation of Blackman's break in the uptrendline. Stocks seldom rise to a peak and then fall off. They usually form a consolidation area where the price moves up and down within a relatively narrow range. Charts show this quickly.

As long as the stock stays within this channel pattern, *hold*. But the minute there's a breakthrough on the downside, get ready. If the penetration is confirmed in the next day or so, *sell*.

Advice: Never try to outguess the market. A stock does not care who owns it. You will never get the absolute top price. When there's a down break with heavy volume, don't wait for an explanation. Make your move. The stock could turn around after you've sold, but better half a loaf than none.

11. When you have a short-term profit (if there's a good chance that you might lose 20% before the 12 months' period is over). You will have to pay full taxes on your gains, but you may cut your losses.

The mathematics work out this way. For every $100 short-term profit, you will net $80 after taxes (assuming a modest tax bracket). If you can hang on for a year, the net will be increased to $84. But if your $100 profit is cut 22% to $78, your after-tax net will be only $50 even with the lower capital-gains tax.

This is a handy rule for volatile stocks. Suppose you bought 100 shares of Blowhard, Inc. at 36 in November. It jumps to 46 in March, so you have a $1,000 profit. Under this rule, you can afford to lose only $200 of the $1,000 profit. That's a two-point drop. Any stock that rises ten points in five months can fall two points in seven months more. *It is better to sell and be happy.* (Blowhard did go to 50⅞, but at the end of six months, it was down to 30.)

12. When the dividend income falls short of your needs. People who need maximum income on their money should not hesitate to sell and take their capital gains if the return on their current investment is considerably lower than could be obtained elsewhere.

Example: You own 1,000 shares of Earache, Ltd., bought at 10 and paying 50¢ a share for a $500 annual income. Within the year, the stock becomes popular and jumps to 26. The profits are not up enough to justify much of a dividend increase, so your yield is now 2% with a possibility of a slight raise.

You sell the shares, pay taxes and commissions and have some $20,000 to invest in 1,000 shares of a utility yielding 10%. That's income of $2,000 a year with the possibility of future raises: at least $1,500 more than before.

13. When the company plans to issue convertibles (debentures or preferred stock). Potentially, this puts more shares on the market and thus will dilute the corporate earnings. More important, CVs are usually issued when the market is most favorable and the securities can command the highest prices.

Of 141 NYSE companies which issued CVs in the buoyant market of the late 1960s, the common stock of 70% of these companies fell 25% or more within the next nine months.

14. When your stock runs up on news that the company is to be taken over by another. There are several good reasons to sell *promptly.*

First, proposals do not always end in marriage (on Wall Street anyway); second, there is no guarantee that the merger will be successful. Most important, the stock market sours quickly on acquisitions. Of 56 stocks that moved up on news of a proposed merger, seventy-one percent of the stocks fell 25% or more within the next nine months!

Sell quickly because most of the declines occur in the first three months. Of course, if you have reason to believe the takeover will be completed and then result in a much stronger organization, you will make your judgment on a different, sounder basis. *But get all the facts first. That's more than most of the people who boosted the price of your stock will have done.*

15. When your stock moves up too fast. If you are lucky enough to pick a stock which moves up 40% or 50% in a couple of months, sell or set a stop order. Here again the track records show that a sale is best: of 55 NYSE-listed stocks that achieved a 50% gain in a short period, 39 fell 25% or more within the next six months.

Always sell too soon. When a stock becomes overpriced, the risks of a severe decline are far greater than the rewards of further gains. Take your profits and run to another stock that will provide similar profits in the future.

Remember: Very few securities reach prices reflecting P/E ratios beyond their average parameters. When they do, it's usually wiser to let others test the unfamiliar ground. Or set stop prices to protect your profits.

16. When insiders are selling. When there are twice as many (or more) sellers than buyers, something unfavorable must be coming up. Get out before the bad news hits the wires.

One final, handy check: Ask yourself, "If I were making a new investment, would I buy this stock at this price at this time?" If the answer is an unqualified YES, hold. If there are minor doubts, get ready to sell at a target price on both up- and downside. If the answer is NO, sell at once.

Short Selling as an Aid to Timing

Short sales are made when speculators sell stocks (usually borrowed) in hopes of buying back at lower prices. Obviously, short sellers anticipate a decline in the value of the shorted stocks and, usually, of the overall market.

Information on short sales can be useful in timing buying and selling but is not easy to interpret correctly. These are the most widely used checkpoints:

Total short sales. The short interest of all stocks traded on the NYSE and AMEX is published about the fifteenth of the month in financial publications. It shows stocks in which: *(a)* there has been a month-to-month change of at least 2,000 shares sold short; *(b)* 5,000 or more shares have been sold short.

The data also report the total number of the company's outstanding common shares, the short interest of the previous month and those stocks that are involved in arbitrage because of a merger/acquisition.

According to technical theory, a large short interest is bullish because this provides a cushion for the market. Eventually, short sellers will have to cover their positions. This demand will boost volume and prices. Stocks with large short positions often show the greatest gains.

Similarly, a low and shrinking short interest warns that speculators are becoming bullish and that a market top may be approaching.

Maybe so. But traders have different objectives, and institutional investors, who dominate trading, seldom sell short. So, in effect, short selling represents the action of a small group and is not always accurate. Yet, when enough people believe something, it becomes self-fulfilling.

Short-interest ratio (SIR). This shows the short interest as a percentage of average trading volume for the preceding month. The potency of any short-interest total depends on how it compares with the total volume of trading. If the average volume is 30 million shares daily and the short interest is 30 million shares, the ratio is 1.00. Generally, it takes a ratio of 1.70 or higher to act as a bull-market prop.

When the ratio falls below 1.00, it's usually a bear-market signal. In most cases, a falling ratio is unfavorable and bull markets often start when the ratio is 2.00 or higher. Many technicians start buying when the SIR hits 1.7. In fact, since 1932, no *sustained* market rise has taken place without the short-interest ratio moving above 1.7.

Specialist short sales. These are made by professionals who have intimate knowledge of the market and specific stocks. When they risk their own funds to go short, they believe that the prices of certain stocks are going to decline. When their short sales are high (over 67%), it's a bearish indicator. When they reduce their short positions (under 40%), an improved market can be expected. These data are reported by several financial services and major financial publications. These are reliable for timing both sales and purchases but they must be followed carefully and interpreted correctly. They should never be used alone.

These are all better theories than practice. Studies show that *(a)* the short position must be of some magnitude to have any effect on the price action of the stock; *(b)* certain stocks seldom attract much short selling even after massive moves; *(c)* some short sales are artificial in that they represent arbitrage because of a proposed merger when the shorted shares will never be repurchased.

There is some evidence that the short-interest theory affects the overall market, but there are doubts as to its validity with individual stocks. An analysis by Randall Smith found that a high and rising short interest does not have an upward impact on a specific stock. But these same stocks do show greater volatility both up and down than the overall market.

Conclusions: (1) If you have a strong opinion that stocks are going to rise in price, buying short-interest stocks will give you more bang for the buck; conversely, if you are bearish, the fact that a stock has a high short interest is no reason to short it. (2) Stocks that make big moves in bull markets or that do not go down much in bear markets and which show a short interest beginning to decline from a high level often have a final, climactic upward spurt.

Watching these factors could improve the timing in a profitable sale of long stock. But analyst Barton Biggs says, "Read the short-interest tables to find out what the volatile stocks are. They do not prove anything else."

CHAPTER 7

How to Use Technical Analysis Profitably

Technical analysis (T.A.) concentrates on supply and demand to determine which stocks to buy or sell and when to do, or not to do, so. The key factors are not the underlying values of the companies but the behavior of the market and stocks: price movements, volume, trends, patterns and, most important, supply and demand.

Basically, T.A. is concerned with what *is*, not with what *should* be. The dyed-in-the-wool technician cares little for what a *company* does but much about what its *stock* does. He operates on the basis that (*a*) the action of the market is the best indicator of its future course; (*b*) 80% of a stock's price movement is due to factors outside the company and 20% to factors unique to that stock; (*c*) the stock market, over the short term, is rooted 85% in psychology and 15% in economics.

Broadly speaking, T.A. is more useful for trading than for investing, but even die-hard fundamentalists pay attention to T.A. in timing of their purchases and sales. When properly used, T.A. can be a valuable tool to improve stock-market profits. *Everyone who wants to be a successful investor should understand technical analysis.*

Technical analysis is such a broad area that only its major areas/tenets can be summarized here. For details, read the books listed in the Bibliography.

The Dow Theory

This is the most popular and widely used of "follow the market" concepts. All such techniques are based on the belief that stock prices cannot be accurately forecast but that stock-price trends persist long enough to be utilized successfully. The key factors are well proven: that the market itself prolongs movements—investors buy more when the market is rising and sell more when it's dropping.

This "follow the crowd" approach is useful for investors and essential for traders. It enables them to buy when the market is going up and to sell, or to sell short, when it turns down. But, for amateurs with small holdings, such activity can be expensive because of the commissions. For those with limited resources and time, this type of T.A. can be better in theory than in practice.

The Dow Theory is named after Charles H. Dow, one of the founders of Dow Jones & Company, Inc., the financial reporting-publishing organization. The original hypotheses have been changed somewhat by followers, but, broadly interpreted, the Dow Theory signals both the beginning and the end of bull and bear markets.

Dow believed that the stock market is a barometer of business. The purpose of the theory is not to predict movements of security prices for traders but, rather, to call the turns on the market and to forecast the business cycle or longer movements of depression or prosperity. It is not concerned with ripples, the day-to-day fluctuations.

Basically, the Dow Theory states that once a trend of the Dow Jones Industrial Average has been established, it tends to follow the same direction until definitely canceled by *both* the Industrial and Railroad (now Transportation) averages. The market cannot be expected to produce new indications of the trend every day, and unless there is positive evidence to the contrary, the existing trend will continue.

Dow and his disciples saw the stock market as being made up of two types of "waves": *the primary wave,* which is a bull or bear market cycle of several years' duration, and the *secondary* (or *intermediary*) *wave,* which lasts from a few weeks to a few months. Any single primary move may contain within it a score or more of secondary waves, both up and down.

The theory relies on similar action by the two averages, which may vary in strength but not in direction. Robert Rhea, who expanded the original concept, explained it this way: "Successive rallies penetrating preceding high points with ensuing declines terminating above preceding low points, offer a bullish indication . . . (and vice versa for bearish indication). . . . A rally or decline is defined as one or more daily movements resulting in a net reversal of direction exceeding 3% of either average. Such movements have little authority unless confirmed by both Industrial and Transportation Averages . . . but confirmation need not occur in the same day."

Dow did not consider his theory applied to individual stock selections or analysis. He expected that specific issues would rise or fall with the averages most of the time, but he also expected that any particular security might be affected by special conditions not applicable to the averages.

Dow made the point that "the business community has a tendency to go from one extreme to the other. It is either contracting business under a belief that prices will be lower or expanding under a belief that prices will be higher. It appears to take five or six years for public confidence to go from the point of too little hope to the point of too much confidence and then five or six years to get back to the conditions of hopelessness."

The key indicators of the Dow Theory are:

1. A bull market is signaled as a possibility when an intermediate decline in the DJIA stops above the bottom of the previous intermediate decline. A bull market is *confirmed* after this has happened, when the next intermediate rise in the DJIA goes above the peak of the last previous intermediate rise.

2. A bull market is in progress as long as each new intermediate rise goes *higher* than the peak of the previous intermediate advance, and each new intermediate decline stops *above* the bottom of the previous one.

3. A bear market is signaled as a possibility when an intermediate rally in the DJIA fails to break through the top of the previous intermediate rise. A bear market is *confirmed* after this has happened, when the next intermediate decline breaks through the low of the previous one.

4. A bear market is in progress as long as each new intermediate decline goes *lower* than the bottom of the previous decline and each new intermediate rally fails to rise as high as the previous rally.

A pure Dow theorist considers the averages to be quite sufficient in themselves to do a forecasting job. It is not necessary to supplement them with statistics of commodity prices, volume of production, carloadings, bank debts, exports and imports, etc. If one of the averages shifts from a bull market pattern—or vice versa—and if the shift is confirmed by the other average, the course of future economic activity is clear.

Interpreting the Dow Theory

The Dow Theory leaves no room for sentiment. A primary bear market does not terminate until stock prices have thoroughly discounted the worst that is apt to occur. This decline requires three steps: (1) "the abandonment of hopes upon which stocks were purchased at inflated prices"; (2) selling due to decreases in business and earnings; (3) distress selling of sound securities despite value.

Primary bull markets follow an opposite pattern: (1) a broad movement, interrupted by secondary reactions averaging longer than two years, where successive rallies

penetrate high points with ensuing declines terminating above preceding low points; (2) stock prices advance because of demand created by both investors and speculators who start buying when business conditions improve; (3) rampant speculation as stocks advance on hopes and expectations.

These broad swings may take years. Markets do not normally go straight up or straight down but, according to Dow, "are subject to periodic interruptions by countermoves that are likely to retrace one third to two thirds of the original move before starting again in the primary direction. Thus, a bull market that rises 30 points will probably lose 10 to 20 points of its gain before resuming its ascent."

There's no question that the stock market today is vastly different than in the early years of the century when Dow formulated his theory. The number and value of shares of publicly owned corporations have increased tremendously: in 1900, the average number of shares traded annually on the NYSE was 59.5 million. Now, it's not unusual for total daily volume to exceed 50 million shares and soon, predict the optimists, 100 million!

The sharpest criticism is leveled against the breadth, scope and significance of the averages. The original Industrial Index had only 12 stocks and, say the critics, the 30 large companies whose stocks make up the present average do not provide a true picture of today's broad, more technologically oriented market. The Transportation Average, they insist, is hopelessly outmoded even with the substitution of airlines and trucking corporations for railroads. When first selected, the rails accurately mirrored business activity. Today, with the geographic disbursement of industry, transportation is no longer a reliable guide to the economy.

Finally, they wonder if Government regulations and institutional dominance of trading have so altered the original concept of individual investors that the Dow Theory can no longer be considered all powerful and always correct.

To most investors, the value of the Dow Theory is that it represents a sort of "think for yourself" method which will pay worthwhile dividends for those who devote time and effort to gain a sound understanding of the principles involved. Whether or not you agree with its conclusions, it is a strong force on Wall Street. When enough people believe a particular theory, their own actions will make the theory come true—partially, anyway.

Under the Dow Theory, a new primary bull market got underway in early March 1978. Here's what happened, according to Robert W. Ross, vice president, Boston office, Shearson/American Express:

The Dow Jones Industrial Average and the Dow Jones Transportation Average made bear market lows on February 28 and March 9, 1978, at 742.12 and 199.31 respectively. Then came a strong rally. Under the Dow Theory, the validity of the surge called for a pause and decline. The retracement would have to exceed 3% of the price of each average.

By May 17 the DJIA soared to 858.37, and the DJTA rose to 231.30 on May 22. By May 26, the Industrials had fallen to 836.9 and the Transportations to 223.70, fallbacks of 3.1% and 3.3% respectively.

The rally came in early June when the DJIA jumped to 863.83 and the DJTA moved up, narrowly, to a new high of 231.35. The bull market was off and running. There were secondary reactions in the fall of 1978 and in late 1979, but in January 1980, the DJIA hit a new recovery high of 1005. But the DJTA, at 403, was short of its November 28 close of 426: a clear warning of an impending secondary reaction (which occurred).

On March 25, 1981, when the DJIA closed at 1015.21, the DJTA was at 433.55—confirmation of the primary bullish trend.

DOW THEORY PRACTICE IN RECENT YEARS

Type Market	Date Confirmation	% Move Between Dignals
Bull	1/27/75	+25%
Bear	10/24/77	−23
Bull	3/9/78	

Bull market confirmation:

Date	DJIA	DJTA
1/7/80	1005	403
3/3/81	990	417
3/25/81	1015	434

Interim signals:

1/7/80	1005	403
3/13/81	990	417
3/25/81	1015	434

SOURCE: Robert W. Ross

Bellwether Techniques

Many Wall Streeters watch the stock leaders to determine future trading strategy and, on occasion, to anticipate longer-term trends. Usually, it is a single important market heavyweight; sometimes, it's the average of an industry group (autos, drugs, chemicals, etc.); more frequently, it's a market-oriented group (institutional favorites, most-active stocks, low-priced stocks).

The bellwether theory relies on the market action (or inaction) of a leading stock, average or index. It postulates that in a rising market, when the chosen leader hits a new yearly or cyclical high, it's a bullish signal. When it fails to reach a new high for three or four months, a market top is near. In a bear market, the leadership is the opposite, though not as firm nor as reliable.

Historically, the stock of General Motors has been a key bellwether but, because of problems peculiar to the auto industry, its forecasting value has not been as useful recently as in the past.

Here's how Robert H. Stovall, vice president of Dean Witter Reynolds, Inc., explains the use of this bellwether:

"In a rising market, if GM goes for four calendar months without setting a new high, it's giving a sell signal. Conversely, in a down market, each time GM makes another low, add four months of waiting time before a trend-reversing buy signal is possible.

"The GM bellwether has been 80% accurate since the 1920s but its accuracy rating has dropped to about 60% in recent years."

In September 1979, GM peaked at 65⅞ to flash a bullish signal. Four months later, on January 24, it stood at 55, thus indicating a bearish trend, then dropped to a lower low of 52⅞ on February 11 and to 48 in March.

With mounting problems in the economy and in the automobile industry, GM fell further by the end of 1980. Then the stock started up again and, by mid-spring, hit 58⅞, a 12-month high. Technically, the bellwether's *buy* signal did not become "official" until the stock price held above 43⅞ on May 20, the end of the four-month span.

Thus, unless the stock falls further (as it has not done at this writing), the next checkpoints were September 20 and January 20, 1982.

London Stock Market Index

This is a fairly reliable indicator of what is likely to happen in the U.S. market in the following two weeks to two months. It is the London *Financial Times* Index, sort of a Dow Jones Industrial Average for the London Stock Exchange. Its closing price, as of the previous day, is published in the financial pages Tuesday through Saturday.

Its value is that it reflects stock markets worldwide and, often, forecasts trends of U.S. securities. Its greatest use is to improve timing: to buy when the London Index moves up, to sell when it declines.

Most traders rely on a chart with channels and trendlines. When these are broken, they act immediately. In the majority of situations, such an early decision will boost gains or cut losses. As London is five hours ahead of New York, check this index before the opening of the NYSE before making a major commitment.

Volume and Velocity

Joseph E. Granville, one of the most skillful technicians, is convinced that volume is always a key indicator. He has developed a special system, cumulative net volume, which he calls *On-Balance Volume.*

In his calculations, every time the stock under study closes at a higher price, he adds the daily trading volume to the cumulative total. When the stock closes lower, he subtracts the daily trading volume from the running total. When there's no price change, no volume is recorded.

His reasoning: When volume rises with price, smart money is buying; soon others will follow and there will be a strong upmove.

Granville also relies on *Velocity:* the cumulative volume as a percentage of corporate capitalization. This measures turnover and thus demand. If a stock has 10 million shares, and records cumulative volume of 10 million shares, the velocity is 100%.

Says Granville, "Every time the stock turns over its entire capitalization in a relatively short period of time, it's like a giant spring getting tighter and tighter. When the velocity approaches 100%, the spring will snap and the price will break out. If the stock is in an uptrend, there will be a sharp advance."

Granville is a master showman and, with complete

self-confidence, does not hesitate to make strong recommendations, usually to *sell* (or sell short) or to *buy* with equal enthusiasm. In recent years, he's been a powerful force in the stock market and never ceases to gloat over his ability to influence "investors" as evidenced by his famous *sell* signal in February 1981 that sent the market reeling for a few weeks. But, because fundamentals were strong, the market quickly worked its way up again, to new highs. T.A. is always better for traders than for fundamentalists.

Buying-Power Indicators

Since T.A. is designed principally to measure the flow of money into and out of the market, especially by those with special knowledge (or hopes), the quantity and quality of trading can be an important indicator.

Market strength is shown by:

• Rising volume in rallies. Investors are eager to buy, so the demand is greater than the supply, and prices go up.

• Shrinking volume on market declines. Investors are reluctant to sell.

Market weakness is indicated by:

• Rising volume on a market decline. Investors are getting nervous and fear still lower prices.

• Declining volume on market rallies. Investors have little faith in the higher prices.

With this technical approach, volume is the key indicator: it rises on rallies when the trend is up, and rises on reactions when the trend is down.

Full information on daily upside and downside volume on both the NYSE and AMEX is provided by Quotron, Financial Information Service and *Barron's*.

Note: Volume trends are apt to reverse before price trends. Shrinking volume almost always shows up before the top of a bull market and before the bottom of a bear market.

For pinpointing short-term price/volume trends, consider the "enthusiasm" index devised by Arthur A. Merrill. This relates the NYSE volume for the five most recent trading days on which prices rose to the volume for the five most recent days on which prices fell. A high ratio (1.05 or above) is bullish; a low ratio (0.85 or below) is bearish.

If you become intrigued with the value of volume as a trading guide, set up two separate charts: one for the volume of advancing stocks, the other for the activity of declining issues (the data are available in the *Wall Street Journal* and *Barron's*). Plot the moving average for each and when the lines cross, this will indicate a reversal of the recent trend and forecast the probable short or intermediate movement.

Most-Active Stocks

These tables, usually found at the top of the stock data of major stock exchanges and OTC, show the volume leaders. When you see the shares of the same company or industry group listed two or three times in a fortnight, you can be sure that something is happening. But do not act on this guide alone. It takes two to make

MOST ACTIVE STOCKS
For full week

Yearly High	Low	Stock	Sales	Last	Change
54 3/8	29 1/8	Texaco	3,748,800	35 7/8	−2 3/8
18 1/4	6 1/4	Sony Corp.	3,122,400	17 7/8	+ 1/8
55 1/4	23	Kennecott	3,095,000	54 1/8	+ 3/8
28	11 7/8	Stor. Tech.	2,998,470	63 1/8	+4 3/4
72 3/4	50 3/8	IBM	2,829,100	63 1/8	− 1/8
13 1/4	9 1/4	Rals. Purina	2,745,000	12	+ 3/4
19 5/8	14 1/2	Sears Roeb.	2,675,400	17	− 1/8
58 7/8	39 1/2	Gen. Motors	2,502,400	54	+3
24 7/8	17	Citicorp.	2,398,900	24 5/8	+1 7/8
21	10 3/4	Fst. Charter	2,021,400	17 3/4	+1 3/4
24 1/8	8	LTV	2,014,300	23 7/8	+1 3/4
33 7/8	22 7/8	I T & T	1,980,800	32 7/8	+2 5/8
26 1/2	15 1/2	K-Mart	1,950,400	18 1/2	− 1/2
91 1/2	42 1/4	St. Oil (Ohio)	1,865,000	49 7/8	−2 1/8
12 3/4	5	Schlitz	1,846,100	11 7/8	+2 1/2

SOURCE: Barron's; New York Stock Exchange

headlines: one major investor who wants to buy and another who feels it's time to sell.

Forget about Exxon, GM, and IBM. These giants have so many shares outstanding that they are almost always among the NYSE leaders.

Keep an eye out for:

Newcomers, especially small and medium-size corporations. When the same name pops up two or three times in a short period, such heavy volume probably indicates that something is happening: a pending acquisition, new product, unexpected problems and so on. When such a price trend is confirmed by other indicators, it's usually smart to follow the leaders and profit: *buying* when there's a rising trend (in price and volume) and *selling* when the opposite occurs. Let the institutions carry the ball for you.

Companies in the same industry. Stocks tend to move as a group. Activities in retailers such as Sears and K-Mart *could* signal interest in this field. But wait for confirmation.

Advances/Declines

This is an excellent guide to the trend of the overall market. The data are usually translated into a chart. This shows the cumulative total of the difference between advances and declines on the NYSE, as published in the financial press. The chart should show action over a period of time, at least one week and preferably longer.

This was an erratic week: on Monday, the declines were slightly more than the advances. On Tuesday, the market moved up, eased a bit on Wednesday, stayed

ADVANCES/DECLINES

Issues Traded	Mon.	Tues.	Wed.	Thur.	Fri.	Weekly
Traded	1,894	1,926	1,925	1,919	1,894	2,135
Advances	677	1,156	932	769	638	1,178
Declines	816	416	614	753	888	738
Unchanged	401	354	379	397	368	219

almost even on Thursday and dipped on Friday. Note, too, that the unchanged remains within a narrow range.

Let's use a weekly chart. There were 2,135 issues traded: 1,178 advances, 738 declines, with the rest unchanged. That's a net advance of 440 for the week. Add this to an arbitrary base, say, 20,000, to get a cumulative A/D of 20,440.

The following week, 710 stocks were up and 832 down. That's a net decline of 122. Subtract this from 20,440 to get 20,318. If you are working on a 20-week basis, divide by 20 to get a current week *moving average* for that A/D line.

All presentations show a broad, *nonprice* picture of the current trend of the whole market. A/D data are most useful when its action is compared with that of narrower market-price averages or indices such as the DJIA. With charts, it is often possible to spot the difference in behavior that may indicate a turning point ahead.

Near market peaks, the A/D line will almost invariably top out and start declining several weeks—to months—before the popular blue chip averages. This is a signal that all is not well with the stock market.

At market bottoms, its action is also helpful, even if less predictive. It usually turns up with, or shortly after, the DJIA.

Until a few years ago, most technicians preferred to calculate their A/D action in terms of daily advances or declines. Now, a weekly A/D line is more popular. It provides more "dimension" and "direction" since it smoothes out minor daily fluctuations which, if only ½ or ⅛ of a point, may not be significant.

Highs and Lows

This is an excellent confirmation guide. It shows how many issues moved to record highs or lows. In this week, the overall market was ebullient. Investors were enthusiastic and willing to pay peak prices to many issues. Only a handful of stocks fell to new lows. For the week, this was a positive market: 321 new highs and only 16 new lows.

WEEKLY HIGHS AND LOWS

	Mon.	Tues.	Wed.	Thurs.	Fri.	Weekly
New Highs	57	130	153	135	93	321
New Lows	5	8	6	6	4	16

Again, this can be charted and revised periodically. Then it should be compared to the Dow or S&P Index. Keep in mind that these figures report on the full NYSE while the standard averages reflect the actions of a relatively few stocks of major corporations.

In a rising market there are usually more highs than lows; vice versa for a declining period. *As long as the high-low indicators stay closely in step with the averages, there's little value, but when the high-low line starts dipping while the averages move up, WATCH OUT: internal market conditions are deteriorating.*

Conversely, an upturn in the high-low line while the DJIA is still declining probably indicates impending market strength.

This index exposes the underlying strength or weakness of the market, which is too often too easily masked by the action of the DJIA. In an aging bull market, the DJIA may continue to rise, deceptively showing strength in a mere handful of stocks while most stocks are too far below their highs for the year to make new ones. Thus, a small total of new highs at such times is one of the most significant manifestations of internal market deterioration. The reverse is the telltale manner in which the total of new lows appears in bear markets.

Broad-Based Indicators

As defined at the end of this book, the major indices—the Dow Jones Averages, Standard & Poor's Indexes and New York Stock Exchange Composite Index—are either limited or weighted, so do not reflect what's really happening. The two most accurate indicators are those of *Value Line* and *Indicator Digest*, which report the price movements of all stocks traded on the Big Board.

The *Indicator Digest Composite Index* is constructed so that each stock has the same weight. Thus, the percentage changes are equal without distortion due to market price or number of shares outstanding.

All indices follow similar patterns but the watchful analyst can catch differences that can be utilized for profit. Note that in mid-1978 the IDA was moving up while the DJIA was still down. This meant that the overall market was more favorable than of the 30 big companies. And in 1980, the IDA moved almost straight up while the DJIA hesitated at the outset. Well, every extra couple of points through early buying counts!

And to make it easy for amateurs, IDA shows the Index against a set base: above is favorable; below is negative.

Moving-Average Lines

A moving average (MA) is just what the name suggests: an average that moves with the unit of time covered. A 30-week MA of the DJIA shows the average closing price of the 30 stocks for the 30 most recent Fridays. Each week, the total changes because of the addition of the latest Friday's closing figure and the subtraction of the Friday closing figure for 30 weeks ago. Then the new total is divided by 30 to get the MA.

Some technicians prefer to use a 200-day MA. In both cases, the MA is compared to a regular average, such as the DJIA. Here's how it serves as a trend indicator:

1. As long as the DJIA is *above* its MA line, the outlook is bullish.

2. As long as the DJIA is *below* its MA, the outlook is bearish.

3. A confirmed downward penetration of the MA is a *sell* signal.

4. A confirmed upward penetration of the MA is a *buy* signal.

But always beware of false penetrations and delay purchases or sales until a substantial penetration (2% to

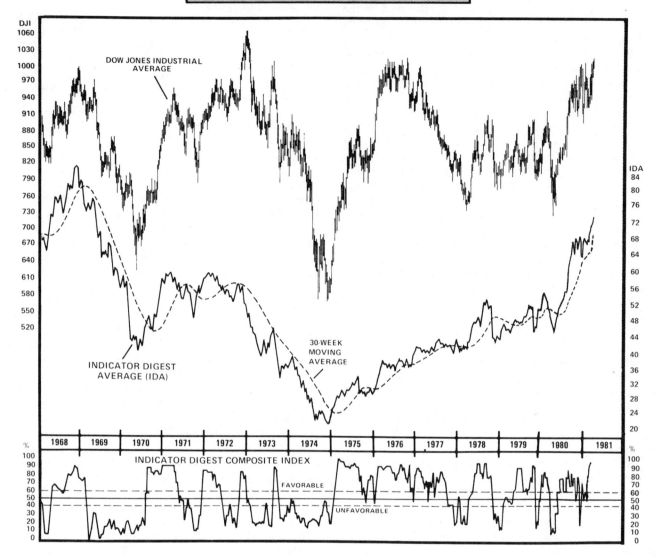

INDICATOR DIGEST COMPOSITE INDEX

3%), *upward or downward, has been confirmed within a couple of weeks.*

More cautious technicians look for comparable action with a second MA line, which is frequently plotted for a ten-week period.

Professional money managers, more concerned with long-term performance for pension-fund investments, believe that the most reliable and effective way to measure their results is by a three-year moving average. This period is long enough to compensate for stock-market fluctuations and to enable clients to judge the true capability of the investment adviser.

MAs are vulnerable to swift market declines, especially from market tops. By the time you get the signal, you may have lost a bundle because prices tend to fall twice as fast as they rise.

If you enjoy charting, develop a ratio of the stocks selling above their 30-week MA. When the ratio is over 50% and trending upward, the outlook is bullish. When it drops below 50% and/or trending down, there's trouble ahead. Like many technical indicators, this is a hybrid: part price index and part a breadth indicator.

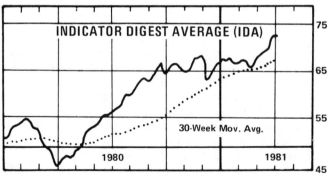

IDA MONTH-END CLOSING PRICES												
Mar 80	Apr 80	May 80	Jun 80	Jul 80	Aug 80	Sept 80	Oct 80	Nov 80	Dec 80	Jan 81	Feb 81	Mar 81
44.79	48.56	52.97	55.60	60.37	62.43	63.84	64.69	67.87	66.63	66.76	67.87	73.47

The Importance of Psychological Attitudes

Keeping in mind that "the stock market is 15% in economics and 85% in psychology," here are two ways to get a reading on that psychology:

Barron's **Confidence Index** (BCI). This is published weekly in the financial news magazine. It shows the ratio of the yield on ten highest-grade bonds to the yield on the broad Dow Jones 40-bond average. The ratio varies from the middle 80s (bearish) to the middle 90s (bullish).

The theory is that the trend of "smart money" is usually revealed in the bond market before it shows up in the stock market. Thus, *Barron's* Confidence Index will be *high* when shrewd investors are confident and buy more lower-grade bonds, thus reducing low-grade bond yields: *low* when they are worried and stick to high-grade bonds, thus cutting high-grade yields.

Many market technicians use the BCI as a *primary* indicator. If you see that it just keeps going back and forth aimlessly for many weeks, you can probably expect the same type of action from the overall stock market.

Speculators' Confidence Index (SCI). This is based on the same principle as *Barron's* index but uses the ratio between two sets of stock prices. You can make your own by dividing S & P's index of 20 low-price stocks by either S & P's index of 25 high-grade stocks or the broader, more representative S & P 500 stock index. You may be able to spot turning points when:

1. *The SCI stops declining and starts to reverse.* This is usually one of the first clues to the end of a bear market. It shows that investors' hopes are reviving. At the bottom of the decline, confidence is negligible and the SCI is low.

2. *The SCI rises to a high point as the advance roars on and speculation rises.*

3. *The SCI falls just before the top of a major rise— when investors lose confidence and start to sell speculative issues.*

SCI is a valuable tool of T.A. Unfortunately, its signals come at a time when people are so pessimistic that they are reluctant to believe anything positive or are so overoptimistic that reason and logic are forgotten. *Next time the stock market moves to an extreme—either way—take time and construct your own SCI and watch the signals for a few weeks.*

Block Transactions

If you assume that "big money" investors are usually right, you should analyze the price trends of large transactions on the NYSE (1,000 shares or $100,000 minimum). These can provide useful clues to market trends. If the upticks (transactions at a higher price than the immediately preceding transaction) persistently outnumber the downticks, the outlook is bullish. If it's the opposite, the prospect is bearish.

Barron's carries reports of trades of over 25,000 shares each week or you can subscribe to The Worden Tape Reading Service, where similar data are based on computer readouts, and which also includes activity on both AMEX and NASDAQ.

Rely on Consensus

Never (well, hardly ever) rely on one technical indicator. Only rarely can a single chart, ratio, average or index be 100% accurate. There can be false signals or no

LARGE BLOCK TRANSACTIONS ON NYSE

Company	Price	Volume	Previous Sale
Texaco	37 5/8	80,000	37 5/8
Geico Corp.	19 1/2	65,000	19
Norton Simon	16 3/4	150,000	16 3/4
Engelhard Minerals	51 1/2	50,000	O.T.
Sterling Drug	25 7/8	100,900	26 1/8
Union Oil Calif.	39 7/8	146,800	40
Fluor Corp.	45 1/2	277,400	O.T.

O.T. = Opening Trade

SOURCE: Barron's

signals at all. When an indicator breaks its pattern, look for confirmation from at least two other guidelines. And then wait a bit longer to see if the original indicator continues to move as anticipated.

There will be times, especially for traders, when such delays will reduce or eliminate profits. But such cases are few except in erratic markets. The stock market represents a focal point for a vast number of forces and a vast number of people; significant changes seldom come rapidly, and they are almost always clearly forecast.

The same consensus counsel applies to technical investment advisory services. If you can afford to do so, subscribe to more than one service. If you don't want to spend the extra money, pick one which provides a series of indicators, such as *Indicator Digest*. Here are some of its guidelines:

Composite indicator. This blends indicators which have proven to be the most reliable in forecasting major trend changes in the stock market. Its big advantage is the infrequency of its signals, thus lessening the chances of a whipsaw.

Overbought-oversold index. This is a handy measure of the short-term trend's likely duration. Minor upswings or downturns have limited lives. As they peter out, experienced traders say the market is "overbought" or "oversold" and, presumably, ready for a near-term reversal.

This indicator (also known as the *ten-day advance/ decline*) provides an objective measurement instead of the traditional seat-of-the-pants approach. It is a ten-day accumulation of the NYSE's net advancing or declining stocks.

A reading of around 1500 means that the market is starting to be overbought. At 2000 or above, it indicates that the advance is ripe for a correction. Under 2000 usually means that the selling has been overdone for a while.

Short-term trading guide (SGA). The initials SGA stand for Speculative Group Activity. If the speculative trading favorites start to display real activity in a new direction, the rest of the market is not far behind.

This chart is maintained on a weekly basis by rating the action of hundreds of stocks, divided into 26 separate industry groups. Each week, each group is rated from +2 to −2 points on the basis of the relationship of the group's average price for the week to a moving average of its weekly prices. The direction of the M.A. is important. The aggregate points will range from +52 to −52. Signals are given when the week's Guide value crosses the five-week M.A. but only if (1) the weekly Guide and the M.A. are traveling in the same direction or (2) the M.A. has leveled out.

Note that at this time (late April), the SGA was continuing to move straight up but, in the last week, had turned down a trifle. To technicians, this indicated that a consolidation might be developing and, if maintained, could provide a broad base for a rally. But if the SGA dropped a few more points, there could be another roller-coaster. Clearly, this was a time to delay action.

Speculation Index. This is the ratio of the ASE/NYSE volume. When trading in AMEX (generally more speculative) stock moves up faster than does that of NYSE (quality) issues, speculation is growing. It's time for traders to move in and investors to be cautious.

A companion indicator is the **CD/QT (Cats and Dogs vs. Quality).** This is the ratio of S&P's Low Priced Common Stock Index and S&P's High Grade Common Stock Index. This tells whether low-priced speculatives are being buoyed by speculative enthusiasm or whether interest is shifting to higher-quality issues. At the start of a bull market, the CD/QT is usually about 1.00.

233 Key Stocks. This indicator is one of the most useful tools because it measures the market movers from the solid, old-time blue chips to the proven growth favorites. Since these generate a large proportion of the market's capitalization and volume, no major market move would be worth its salt without their support. The batting average of this index has been high.

When the five-week moving average of this stock group rises to over 60%, the outlook is promising; over 70%, look for a durable advance.

Mutual fund cash-balance ratio. As mutual funds buy more stocks, their cash (or available buying power) reserves diminish. The opposite occurs when their cash reserves mount in fear of a bear market.

Whenever the amount of money available for investment has risen above 9.5% of total fund assets, the market has almost always been at an important buying area. A bear market is signaled when the level of cash falls into the 5 or 5.5% range.

Most-active indicator. This shows the trend in terms of *up* stocks and *down* stocks. It's a variation of the item outlined earlier and can be easily plotted if you do not care to buy the printed charts. Here's how:

On a daily basis, set down the net difference between the number of stocks *up* and the number *down*. If 9 are up, 5 down and 1 unchanged, the net is +4. Total the results for the last 30 market days, then divide by 30. On the 31st day, remove the oldest data, add the newest. Record the results on your chart.

Buy when the indicator is +3; *sell* when the indicator falls below −3. Readings in between are neutral.

How to Use Charts to Maximize Profits and Minimize Losses

Most chart readers believe that "one picture is worth a thousand words." They are convinced that charts of various types, properly prepared and interpreted, can reveal the technical factors and clues, previously discussed, more clearly than any other means. *In a word, charts promptly convey the "net current verdict of the market place."*

Charts may not be as speedy as computers, but many investors find them clearer and easier to understand. Combined with electronic data, they have become an important factor in the analysis of stock-market action. *Most investors and ALL speculators should understand and be able to use charts.*

Charts are a graphic ticker tape. They clearly show the highs and lows, how volume rises or falls on an advance or decline and, in summary form, the long-term patterns of the stock market and individual stocks. *Charts are the best way to follow "smart money," which usually has inside information.* If better earnings are imminent, these investors buy aggressively and cause a solid uptrend in the chart formation. If higher profits are far off, buying is slow and, probably, occurs on weakness. All

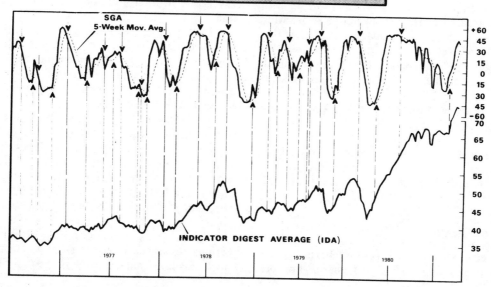

SHORT-TERM TRADING GUIDE (SGA)

SGA
5-Week Mov. Avg.

INDICATOR DIGEST AVERAGE (IDA)

1977   1978   1979   1980

these actions will be shown on the stock's chart.

Charts measure the flow of money into and out of the stock market, industry or specific stock. Once looked upon as an arcane, esoteric practice—one step above reading tea leaves for portents of the future—charts are now an accepted part of technical analysis and have become an essential part of the stock market and security analysis. Two premises: (1) What happened before will be repeated again; (2) a trend should be assumed to continue in effect until such time as the reversal has been definitely signaled.

There are some people who depend solely on technical indicators to make investment decisions, but most analysts agree with the philosophy of *Babson's Reports:* "Perusal of charts . . . can serve as a useful adjunct to fundamental analysis . . . [Investors] should pay attention if only because a substantial amount of buying and selling on the stock market is done by investors who do depend at least partly on technical indicators."

Charting is simple; interpretation is complex. Even the strongest advocates of T.A. disagree among themselves on the meaning of various formations. Broadly speaking, charts are most valuable to provide corroboration. Once you have made up your mind to buy, sell or hold a stock, check the charts. But as James Dines, a leading chartist, warns: "*Be careful.* Charts are like fire or electricity. They are brilliant tools if intelligently controlled or handled. But they are also dangerous."

Dines, who has built a successful business on chart-based recommendations, points out that "most stocks have distinct personalities." They almost always follow established patterns as they reflect the type of person who buys them. There are few false or erratic moves with AT&T; this is a favorite of cautious, older people. New issues bounce like a yo-yo; they are of major interest to traders. And some stocks tend to have recurring patterns, even after many years.

Says Dines, "By watching for the same configuration for the stocks you own or plan to buy, you can boost your profits and cut your losses."

Charts are not infallible, but they can:

1. Help determine when to buy and when to sell by indicating probable levels of support and supply, and by signaling trend reversals.

2. Call attention, by unusual volume or price behavior, to something happening in an individual company that can be profitable to investors.

3. Help determine the current trend: up, down, or sideways, and whether the trend is accelerating or slowing.

4. Provide a quick history of a stock and show whether buying should be considered on a rally or a decline.

5. Offer a sound means for confirming or rejecting a buy or sell decision that is based on other information.

Charts do reveal the past but, at best, can only suggest the future.

Major Types of Charts

The most commonly used types of charts are bar charts and point and figure (P & F) charts. For best results, both should be constructed on a daily or weekly basis and, when you become more practiced, by months or years.

Excellent charts on almost every major publicly owned stock can be purchased at nominal cost. But if you are a do-it-yourselfer, all you need is the daily stock-market listing and a pad of graph paper: plain squares for P & F charts; logarithmic paper or standard paper for bar charts.

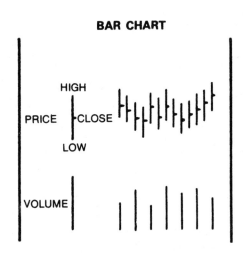

BAR CHART

Bar charts record price changes in relation to time. The horizontal axis represents time—day, week or month; the vertical coordinates refer to price. To follow volume on the same chart, add a series of vertical lines along the bottom. The higher the line, the greater the volume.

Using a daily stock-market report, the chart-maker enters a dot to make the highest price at which the stock was traded that day, then another dot to record the low. A vertical line, drawn between these dots, shows the price range and a short horizontal nub on the line marks the level at which the stock closed. After a number of entries have been made, the lines begin to form a meaningful pattern.

P & F charts are one-dimensional graphics. They show only price changes in relation to previous price changes. There are no indications of time or volume. The key factor in interpretation is the change in price direction.

In making a P & F chart, the stock price is posted in a square: one above or below another, depending on the upward or downward movement of the price. As long as the price continues in the same direction, the same column is used. When the price shifts direction, the chartist moves to the next column.

In the accompanying point and figure chart, GM fell in a downward sequence from 68 to 67 to 66. Then it rose back to 67, so the chartist moved to column 2. After GM went down to 62 and then up to 63, he shifted to column 3 and so on. A new column is started only when the price change is a full unit—usually one point, though, occasionally, half a point or, for longer projections, two or three points.

Again, the plotting forms a pattern and shows the various resistance levels, that is, where the price of the stock stayed within a narrow range (57–56, and later 48–

POINT AND FIGURE CHART

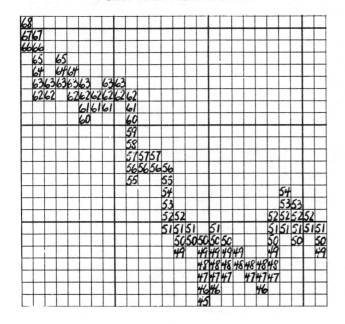

47). The chart signals when there's a shift from such a base: down from 56 to 51; up from 47–48 to 52.

The best way for an amateur to learn about P & F charts is to copy them. Take a stock which has been plotted for many years and slowly recopy its action on a piece of graph paper. Then draw in the trendlines: the uptrendline on the high points, the downtrendline along the low points. Then draw your channels.

Caveat: DO NOT FOLLOW YOUR OWN AD-VICE AT THE OUTSET. It takes years to develop confidence in charts and to understand how wrong they can be.

Some professionals think that P & F charts are oversimplified and prefer to use them for short-term guides. One veteran technician finds them valuable in "helping to choose between two or three selected stocks. These charts quickly identify stocks on the way up and on the way down."

P & F charts do have disadvantages: they do not portray intraday action or consider volume. The information on the financial pages reports only the high (62), low (59¼) and close (61½). This does not show that the stock might have moved up and down from 60 to 62 several times during the day.

Despite the omission of volume on P & F charts, many technical analysts feel that volume should always be checked once there is a confirmed trend on the chart. Usually, rising volume on upside movements and dwindling sales on the downside indicate that the stock has ample investor support. It's always wise to be on the same side as volume.

Unusual Charts

Almost every chartist has his favorite configurations. They include such descriptive titles as: the rounding bottom, the flag, the pennant, the tombstone top, the Prussian helmet formation, the megaphone top, the lat-

tice formation, etc. One of the most popular formations is *Head and Shoulders.*

Oversimplified, the Head and Shoulders Chart portrays three successive rallies and reactions, with the second reaching a higher point than either of the others. The failure of the third rally to equal the second peak is a warning that a major uptrend may have come to an end. Conversely, a bottom H & S, formed upside down, after a declining trend, suggests that an upturn lies ahead.

Left shoulder. This forms when an upturn of some duration, after hitting a climax, starts to fall. The volume of trading should increase with the rally and contract with the reaction. *Reason:* people who bought the stock on the uptrend start to take profits. When the technical reaction takes place, people who were slow to buy on the first rally start buying on the technical reaction.

HEAD AND SHOULDERS CHART

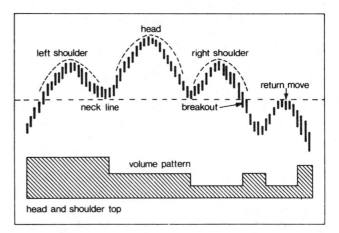

Head. This is a second rally which carries the stock to new highs and is followed by a reaction that erases just about all the gain. Volume is high on the rally, yet lower than when forming the left shoulder. *Reason:* investors who missed both the earlier actions start buying and force new highs.

This is followed by another drop as those who hesitated earlier see the second reaction and start acquiring the stock as it is sold by early buyers.

Right shoulder. The third rally fails to reach the height of the head before the reaction. This is a sign of weakness. Watch the volume. If it contracts on a rally, it's likely that the price structure has weakened. If it increases, beware of a false signal.

Breakout. This occurs when the stock price falls below the previous lows. At this point, most of the recent buyers have sold out—many of them at a loss.

No H & S should be regarded as complete until the price breaks out below a line drawn tangent with the lows on the left and right shoulders. This is called the neckline.

Chart Reading Is an Art

Technical analysis, especially chart reading, is an art and a skill rather than a solid body of objective, scientific information. Both can be aids to intelligent speculation and investing, but they are not sure-fire systems for beating the market. It is not surprising, therefore, that there are sometimes wide disagreements among different technical and chartist services, not only about the state and direction of the market but also about the desirability of specific stocks.

Charting is an aid to stock analysis, not an end. It is valuable to catch short-term movements and to provide the investor with an overview of the market action of a particular stock or, when dealing with industry groups or types of stock transactions, to make comparisons.

There is nothing certain about any chart signal. Interpretation varies with individuals and specific situations.

The biggest disadvantage of charts is that, invariably, they do not work at precisely the times they are needed most—when the market is putting the finishing touches to a major top or bottom. Charts reflect what has happened, so that at market bottoms almost every chart pattern will seem bearish and point to a much lower level of prices. At market tops, it's the reverse.

The best combination, for maximum profits and minimum losses, is fundamental analysis supplemented by graphic technical analysis. Charts report what volume and price changes occur. Proper interpretation can predict the direction and intensity of change because every purchase of every listed stock shows up on the chart.

Watch the bottom of the chart as well as the progress lines. This shows volume, and *volume precedes price*. A strong inflow of capital eventually pushes up the price of the stock; an outflow of dollars must result in a decline. To the charted results, it makes no difference who is doing the buying or selling.

Charts are a history of an individual stock. By studying past action, it is possible to make a reasonably valid prediction of the future.

Interpreting Charts

The Legend Chart is typical of those available from technical services. It provides the basic tools needed to improve the timing of purchases and sales.

Left side: Per share earnings and dividends scaled from 0 to $5.50.

Bottom: Months, from February 1977 through November 1978. Similar charts have information for periods of one day or one week to 12 years.

The vertical bars above the months show volume in thousands of shares. Trading was light in May and July, then rose considerably in September and again in February, April, July and August of the current year.

Right side: The price range, equal to 15 times the earnings-and-dividends scale at the left. When the price bars and earnings line coincide (as in the summer of 1978), the stock is selling at 15 times its last 12 months earnings. When the price pattern is above the line, the P/E ratio is higher; when below, lower.

The price range, earnings and dividend data of all stocks are plotted on uniform-ratio semilogarithmic grids. Here the linear distance for a 100% move is the same any place on the chart whether the rise is from $5 to $10 or from $20 to $40.

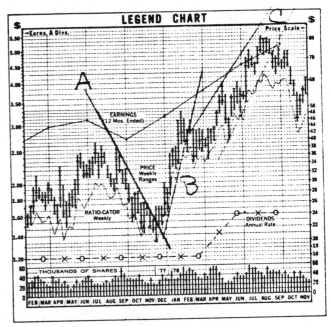

SOURCES: Securities Research Company

This uniform system also makes it possible to compare charts of different stocks as to their advances, declines, P/E ratios and percentage yields.

Earnings line: The straight line above the plotted bars. This is for a "12 months ended" period and is read from the left side of the chart. Deficits (not shown here) are typed in.

Dividend line: The interrupted line below the bars. This is plotted on an annual-rate basis and is also read from the left side. An X indicates the week of the ex-dividend date; an O shows the week the dividend payment was made. Extra, year-end and special dividend payments are typed in.

Ratio-Cator line: The wavy line, which in this case is below the price entries; in erratic markets it could be above. This line shows whether the stock has kept pace, outperformed, or lagged behind the DJIA. It is plotted from data obtained by dividing the closing price of the stock by the closing price of the DJIA on the same day. The resulting percentage is multiplied by a factor of 7.0 to bring the line closer to the price bars. It is read from the right-hand scale.

The Importance of Trendlines

Trendlines are important in chart analysis. They are easy to draw and use and are reliable about 80% of the time, more often when you have patience enough to wait for confirmation from other technical indicators.

Trendlines are formed by connecting the lower points of the stock movement when the price of the stock is rising; the higher points when it's dropping. In the Legend Chart, the downtrendline (A) is the straight line drawn at the *tops* of the last two or three high quotations of the stock. The uptrendline (B) connects the last few *low* prices. By drawing more or less parallel lines (C) on the opposite side of the trendline over the same time span, you form channels.

Once a trendline is formed, the stock tends to move along that line. There may be interim swings but most stocks return to their established patterns. Remember your high-school physics: "A trend in motion is assumed to be intact until there is a clear change."

By spotting the trend, you can get an edge in determining your tactics. By projecting the trendline, you can get an idea of where the stock price *should* go and by updating charts, you can watch where and when the market/industry group/stock *does* go.

The trendlines establish a base. The uptrendline is a support level—a reference point to time the purchase of an upmoving stock and the sale of a downmoving one.

A downtrendline is the opposite. As long as the direction is down, the stock should not be bought and, if held, should be sold or sold short.

The way to make money in normal and bull markets is to look for uptrendlines (B and C). They indicate a favorable momentum which is likely to continue until there's a clear reversal in the price of the stock. *Buy stocks which are moving up and sell them when they turn down.* The earlier you can buy in the formation of an uptrendline and the closer to the line, the greater your profit. This is almost always true in up markets and usually true in flat markets.

In bear markets, the downtrendline (A) is used: selling in the fall of 1977 and, again, in late 1978.

Example: In September 1977, the market turned and the stock price started down from 38. A trader might have sold, or sold short, at 36. An investor, with a quality stock, would probably hold a bit longer and get out at 32 in October. Both will be glad because, within weeks, the stock dropped to 20.

In December, the situation brightened and, slowly and steadily, the chart pattern showed an uptrendline (B). The speculator would come back at 24; the investor would probably wait for confirmation and pay a little more. Both would more than double their money if they held until January/February 1978 when there was a break, down, of the trendline.

Note how clearly the chart portrays the fluctuating, but generally rising, market of the first six months of 1978, the August break and the fall debacle. Granted these are hindsights but, with experience, you can make fairly accurate projections.

Charts are important for short-term decisions but, as we'll see, they are valuable in spotting patterns. To technicians, the tendency of repetition is very important. They believe that what has happened before is likely to happen again.

One of the most reliable of these "repeats" is the 50% rule.

When a stock moves up or down significantly, there is likely to be a technical reaction which will lose or recover a good share of the move. What happens is that traders move in: taking profits with the rise, picking up bargains on a dip. Usually they time their action within the channel drawn on the stock's chart: *selling* when the stock price hits the bottom of the channel, *buying* when it bounces off the bottom.

The 50% rule is valuable in predicting reactions from strong gains. *Example:* When a stock jumps from 30 to 50 without serious interruption, the chances are good that it will back off to 40 (50% of the original advance from 30 to 50).

At all times they watch for a meaningful penetration. If it's on the upside, with an uptrending stock, they may sell if they have an adequate gain, but more likely, they will hold to see if the breakout continues. Once a stock hits a new or interim high, the momentum will probably continue, so let the profits ride.

If the move is on the downside and breaks through the trendline, there is generally a drop of between 7% and 15%, but this is dependent on the type of stock, type of market, volume and past chart pattern. Traders know that a quick, small loss is almost always smart strategy. Once a stock reverses direction, there's no way to tell how far it will fall.

Channels

These are a more sophisticated form of trendlines. The bottom line connects the recent lows, and the top line joins the recent highs. Or once you have established a trendline, you can draw a more or less parallel indicator preferably against the uptrendline.

Channels are most useful for traders who move into and out of positions rather quickly. They want their profits in a hurry. Speculators who can watch charts almost daily will buy and sell on the basis of movements within the channel: with the Legend Chart, buying at about 46 in April 1978 and selling at around 56 two weeks later; buying again at 52, in June, and selling, at 68, in July, and so forth. Or selling short at 56 in May and covering their position in the low 40s in May. Channels are guidelines. They are most significant when there is a clear breakthrough, as occurred in September. As this was on the downside, the trader would sell or sell short.

Before you risk any money in trading by charts or channels, make a dry run with your target stock for several months. This exercise can be tedious (and frustrating if your predictions prove out) but the lessons learned can save you from unnecessary losses.

Using Charts

After you have selected a quality stock, ask your broker for copies of a current chart of the industry group

TRENDLINE CHART

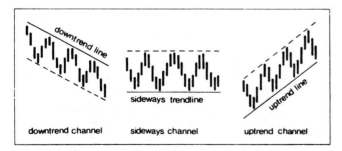

SOURCE: William L. Jiler, *How Charts Can Help You in the Stock Market*

Short-Term

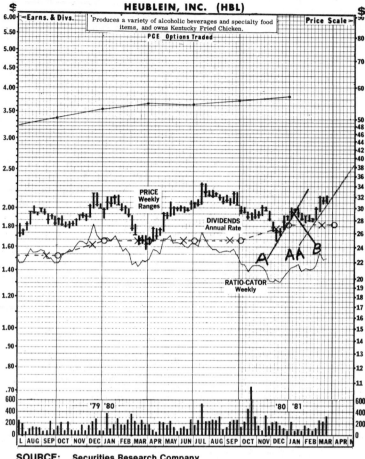

SOURCE: Securities Research Company

and two charts of the stock: short-term, covering the last 20 months, and long-term, recording 12 years of market action.

When both the industry and stock charts point up, you have a *buy* candidate *if* the fundamentals are favorable. Next, draw your own trendline by joining the last two or three low points and project this to the edge of the chart. The potential gain should be at least 25%. The time span for reaching this goal will vary with the type of stock and market. A volatile mover, like Disney, can jump 10 points in 60 days; a slower Exxon may take a year to achieve the same percentage rise.

To show the timing value of charts, here's an example with Heublein, Inc. (HBL). This is a quality company with a long-term history of profitable growth. But, due to problems with the acquisition of Kentucky Fried Chicken, earnings dropped and investment acceptance plummeted. By mid-1980, the situation appeared to be under control and prospects favorable. The stock was a worthwhile investment as well as a good trading vehicle.

The charts can be valuable for both objectives. First, check the short-term record—from August 1979 through March 1981. Note: (1) the trend is generally up; (2) the price swings are fairly wide, about 5 points over 2–3 months.

Keeping in mind that patterns tend to repeat, go back

to the previous upmove that started in November 1980 and draw Trendline A through the low points: from about 25 to just over 30 when a modest decline set in. To get the full picture, draw line B to check the pattern of the decline. This was short and within a narrow range so could be considered as a consolidation period.

In late February 1981, HBL moves up from about 28 to 30, then to 32. Draw trendline AA by connecting the recent low points. This projects to a potential price of 38: a 19% jump from the 32 base.

To get a broader frame of reference, turn to the long-term chart that shows the 12-year market action. Note that the most recent high was in mid-1980 when the stock bounced above 34. If HBL breaks through this level, it will probably take off. But there may be a temporary dip because this is also the point where investors who bought at that high start selling to break even. This extra supply will dampen enthusiasm. But the trendline is still favorable.

Obviously, these projections assume a steady or rising market. If there's a sharp decline in the DJIA, wait until things brighten.

OK, you buy HBL at 32 (or possibly a fraction lower on a temporary price dip). You set a target price of 38 (as indicated by the trendline AA). As an investor, sit tight and wait.

Long-Term

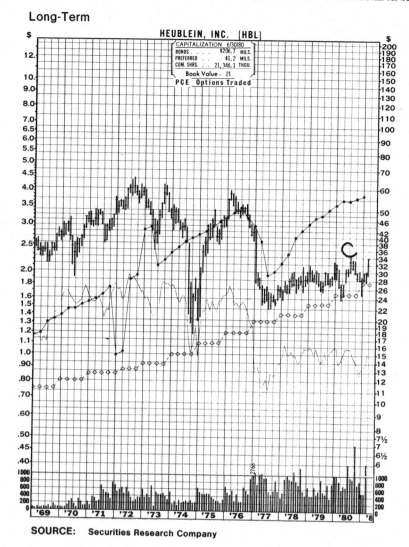

HEUBLEIN, INC. (HBL)

CAPITALIZATION 6/30/80	
BONDS	$206.7 MILS.
PREFERRED . .	$1.2 MILS.
COM. SHRS. . .	21,346.1 THOU.

Book Value - 21

PCE Options Traded

SOURCE: Securities Research Company

But if you want to trade, protect your position by setting a stop-loss order at 29¼, about 10% below your cost. If the stock moves up, keep raising that floor: at 35, to 31¾, etc.

If and when the stock hits 38, review the situation to decide whether it is wise to sell or to set a new target, probably around 45, the point (on the long-term chart) from which the big drop started.

If you have time and money enough to be a trader, get a daily or weekly chart and draw channels. Then, move in and out according to the price swings within those lines: selling at 35, buying back at 33, selling at 36, etc. But, with commissions, you must deal in fairly large blocks to make any real money.

Heed the advice of technician Richard Blackman, author of the best-selling *Follow the Leaders:* "Buy an

UP stock in an UP group in an UP market. If you cannot logically hope for a 25% gain in a few months, stay out of the market." That's sound counsel even though an investor should be willing to wait a little longer.

Technical analysis, especially charts, can be a valuable aid to stock-market timing. Unless you are extremely optimistic and can afford to tie up your money for a while, *never* buy any stock until its chart is pointing up. And *always* check the chart action before you sell. If it's still favorable, even though the fundamentals may be shaky, hold until there's a downturn.

From personal experience, I can testify that charts and trendlines provide substantial benefits in the management of portfolios. They save money by preventing too-early buying and avoiding too-late selling. Besides, charts can be fun!

CHAPTER 8

Canadian Investments: Best for the Future

With Canadian investments, be selective. There are profitable opportunities but, generally speaking, major publicly owned corporations do not meet the quality standards of financial strength, investment acceptance, profitability and growth. And there are economic and political problems. The economy is shaky and the government is torn by dissension. In most cases, the risks are greater and the rewards less than can be obtained in the U.S.A.

Basically, the problem is the Canadian economy, not the industries or individual companies. What happens in the United States is repeated north of the border. Canada does not have the population, the financial resources or the management/labor skills to support many major enterprises and, in most cases, these companies must rely on the United States, which accounts for 70% of all exports and imports.

The best investments are in these areas:

Natural resource corporations: paper and pulp, mining and metals, oil and gas. Most of these are doing well and all of them have great potential. But the prices of their stocks are influenced by political pressures, primarily for limited ownership by non-Canadian investors.

Real estate trusts. These are aggressively buying and building in the U.S.A. They are worthwhile for those who understand real estate but not for most investors. And with the high cost of money, their growth has been slowing and their profits dwindling.

Regulated firms such as banks, telephone companies and utilities. These are safe but their dividends are not as high, nor increasing as fast, as those of American companies.

Future Potential

Long-term prospects for Canadian industry are excellent but you must be patient.

1. Canada is the only industrial nation in the Free World that has within its borders all known energy sources: an ample supply of hydroelectric power, oil, natural gas, coal and uranium. But, too often, the cost of release and transportation is enormous and will require government participation—an unwelcome partnership for many investors.

2. Canada is rich in essential minerals, metals and timber, all needed around the world.

3. Agriculture is booming and will continue to be a major export. Here again, government will be involved, and this limits the potential profits for private investors.

4. Cheap power is of increasing importance, giving aluminum producers a price advantage and improving the foreign trade balance by sales of electricity to American utilities.

5. Retail outlets are concentrated in a few strong, publicly owned companies. In many cases, there can be quick gains from takeovers, as when Hudson's Bay Company acquired Zellers, Ltd.

6. Government favors investments in Canadian corporations by such policies as mandating that 90% of personal pension plan holdings must be made in Canadian securities/assets.

7. Stocks are relatively cheap, with price/earnings ratios seldom over 10.

8. Corporate growth can be rapid because most firms are small. A "big" Canadian corporation is one with revenues over $100 million.

9. Profit margins are somewhat higher than those of similar American corporations.

Tax Situation

For Americans, taxes can be a problem but are easing. There's a withholding tax on dividends and interest but this can be used as a credit on U.S. tax returns. Major changes will come if a new U.S.-Canadian tax treaty is approved by the U.S. Senate. This will reduce the tax on dividends, lower taxes on royalties and rents, exempt interest on municipal bonds and eliminate the departure tax which applies to U.S. citizens who live and work in Canada for more than five years.

DO's and DON'Ts for Investing in Canada

DO invest, don't gamble. Look for securities which will benefit from the long-term growth of the country. Forget about "penny" oil and gold mining stocks. There is almost no way you can be sure of the integrity of the promoter or the authenticity of the salesman's claims.

DO deal with a broker with good research facilities. Information on many Canadian issues is limited in the United States. Look for a large, established American brokerage firm with offices north of the border.

DO subscribe to a worthwhile investment advisory service such as Canadian Business Service, 55 York Street, Toronto 1, Canada.

DON'T deal in shares of Canadian companies listed only on Canadian stock exchanges until you are familiar with the corporation. There are plenty of Canadian firms listed on American exchanges.

DO consider investing in mutual funds specializing in

Canadian securities. This will enable you to take advantage of professional research and judgment.

DON'T ever buy any security over the telephone. Despite attempts of authorities to control bucket shop operations, they still exist and, unfortunately, lure naive speculators.

DO arrange for all investments to be made in U.S. currency. At times, the Canadian dollar is worth less than the U.S. dollar. By specifying U.S. currency, you will minimize the losses from temporary fluctuations.

Where You Can Buy Canadian Securities

Many leading Canadian securities are listed on the NYSE and on other American stock exchanges or traded over the counter in the United States. Most Canadian stocks, however, are traded on one or more of the four Canadian stock exchanges: the Montreal Stock Exchange, the Canadian Stock Exchange (in Montreal), the Toronto Stock Exchange and the Vancouver Stock Exchange.

Commission rates are close to those in the United States, but there are stock transfer taxes in several provinces.

For information on the market activity of Canadian stocks, one of the best sources is the Toronto Stock Exchange *Monthly Review,* which is obtainable directly from the exchange, from a bank or from your broker. This shows the latest price ranges and value, capitalization and dividend record plus indices from major stock groups.

Current data on stock trading are carried in many daily newspapers and, on an expanded scale, in the weekly *Financial Post* and *Financial Times.* Reports on individual companies are available from *Financial Counsel, Canadian Analyst* and, in considerable detail, from *The Canadian Business Service Investment Reporter* (see Bibliography).

CANADIAN STOCKS FOR INVESTORS

Company	Recent Price	Yield	Earnings Per Share	P/E Ratio	Company	Recent Price	Yield	Earnings Per Share	P/E Ratio
Very Conservative					MacMillan Bloedel	37	4.7	5.03	7.4
Bank Montreal	31	5.4%	$5.85	5.3	Molson "A"**	27	5.3	3.25	8.3
Bank Nova Scotia	31	5.4	5.50	5.6	Newfoundland L&P**	21	6.7	2.48	8.5
Bell Canada**	19	9.5	2.40	7.9	Norcen	30	3.3	3.55	8.5
Calgary Power**	19	5.5	1.80	10.5					
Canadian Pacific**	42	4.5	7.80	6.2	**Average**				
Canada Trustco**	29	5.2	2.20	13.2	Abiti Price	29	5.5	4.25	6.8
Dofasco "A"**	41	6.1	6.10	6.7	CHUM "B"	15	1.9	1.08	13.9
Hudson's Bay Co.	25	4.8	2.60	9.6	Consol. Bathurst	25	8.3	5.00	5.0
Imperial Oil "A"	32	4.4	4.15	7.7	Hudson Bay M&S	30	4.0	4.80	6.3
Inco "A"**	24	3.4	3.00	8.0	Imasco "A"	32	3.8	4.15	7.7
Moore Corp.	40	4.5	4.30	9.3	Standard Broad	14	3.6	1.45	9.7
Noranda "A"**	27	5.2	4.06	6.7	Steinberg's "A"	30	3.3	3.55	8.5
Nova	39	2.9	3.70	10.5	Torstar "B"**	19	4.0	2.20	8.6
Royal Trustco	20	5.6	2.10	9.5	Woodward "A"	31	3.4	3.20	9.9
Seagram Corp.	68	2.1	6.90	9.9	Zellers	18	1.9	1.75	10.3
Shell "A"	25	3.6	3.15	7.9					
Stelco "A"	36	5.6	4.05	8.9	**Higher Risk**				
Walker-Consumers	28	4.7	3.70	7.6	DRG "Z"	7	5.7	1.47	4.8
					Electrohome "A"	16	. . .	3.07	5.2
Conservative					Great Lakes Forest	74	3.8	15.50	4.8
Alcan Aluminium	40	4.5	6.00	6.7	Ivaco "A"	24	2.7	3.70	6.5
Brascan "A"	33	4.2	2.75	12.0	McIntyre Mines	56	. . .	8.10	6.9
Canadian Tire "A"	32	2.3	3.07	10.4	Placer Develop.	23	2.6	2.29	10.0
Cominco	65	6.8	9.44	6.9	Reichold Chemicals	14	3.4	1.90	7.4
Hudson's Bay O&G	23	2.5	2.15	10.7	Weldwood	27	3.7	3.10	8.7
Interprov. P.L.	15	10.0	1.90	7.9	Westburne Indus.	25	2.8	3.70	6.8
Labatt "A"	27	4.9	3.05	8.9					
MacLean-Hunter	11	2.3	.76	14.5					

* Either actual or estimated   ** Automatic dividend reinvestment

SOURCE: Canadian Business Service

CHAPTER 9

Picking the Right Industries Groups

Nothing is more certain in Wall Street than change, especially in investor attitudes toward industry groups, and, to some extent, toward specific companies. Today's favorites are likely to be tomorrow's disasters; stocks scorned yesterday may become popular almost overnight; and there are always special groups that should be judged by popularity rather than by fundamentals. That does not mean you should ignore quality but it does mean that you should recognize that, over the short term, Wall Street is seldom rational. That's why worthwhile investment profits usually take time.

For maximum profits (and minimum losses), it is important to stay flexible: to be ready to shift a portion of your portfolio to shares of companies in industry groups that are popular. When Wall Street falls in love with an industry, even the poorest stocks in that category can rise and the leaders will soar to heights unjustified by fundamental considerations. Look at the record: for three years, 1977–78–79, military and commercial aircraft stocks rose sharply but they were not listed in the Stron-

gest category in 1980. Wall Street always boosts popular stocks to unwarranted heights and then shifts to another field—if only to show how "smart" they are as professional money managers.

In 1978, stocks of personal loan companies were up 42%, but soon they were in the doghouse: down 11% in 1979 and another 8% in 1980.

In the early months of 1980 gold stocks were hot, and for the past three years oils have been winners: refiners in 1978 and international companies in 1980. In most cases, the initial enthusiasm is justified but, with few exceptions, that euphoria continues months after the industry/corporate situation has weakened. The time to buy is when groups are becoming popular—as shown by listing on the Most-Active List and by news reports and analyses.

It's nice to know the reasons why there's such heavy buying but it's really not *that* important. If Wall Street likes a group, the prices of stocks of companies in that industry will go up. *Buy, hold and be wary.* In a short

FASTEST-MOVING INDUSTRY GROUPS

1980 STRONGEST	% Change	1979 STRONGEST	% Change	1978 STRONGEST	% Change	1977 STRONGEST	% Change
Gold	+89.61	Oil Refiners	+40	Food Chains-Local	+72	Motion Picture	+87
Construction/Engin.	+84.69	Steamship Lines	+33	Sulfur Producers	+68	Hotel-Motel Chains	+50
Oils/International	+66.87	Copper Producers	+31	Printers	+59	Apparel Stores	+47
Railroads	+61.64	Military & Comm.Aircft.	+30	Gauges & Meters	+52	Magazine Publishers	+36
Electronics/Meters	+59.74	Automotive-Diver.	+25	Militry & Comm. Aircrft	+49	Miltry&Comm.Aircrft	+28
Electronics/Defense	+57.13	Aerospace	+23	Personal Loan Cos.	+42	Shoe Stores	+27
Conglomerates	+53.79	Machine Tools	+22	Machine Tools	+41	Gold	+25
Electronics/Divers.	+52.93	Aluminum Producers	+22	Motion Pictures	+40	Book Publishers	+25
Crude Oil	+47.67	Conglomerates	+19	Photo Equipment	+38	Government Defense	+23
Gas Pipelines	+44.60	Electronics-Defense	+17	Crude Oil & Natural Gas	+36	Scientific Equipment	+23

1980 WEAKEST		1979 WEAKEST		1978 WEAKEST		1977 WEAKEST	
Discount Stores	−24.45	Plumbing/Heating	−14	Paints & Resins	−28	Sulfur Producers	−48
Auto/Trucks	−23.82	Savings & Loan	−13	Bakers	−27	Oil Refiners	−38
Auto/Diversified	−21.80	Personal Loan	−11	Liquefied Propane Gas	−25	Radio, TV, Phono	−33
Confectionary	−20.09	Local Food Chains	− 5	Commercial Finance	−22	Brewers	−31
Plumbing/Heating	−17.17	Gas Operating Cos.	− 4	Brewers	−21	Integrated Oil Cos.	−27
Steel/Non-Integrated	−13.97	Electric Power & Gas	− 4	Department Stores	−18	Steel Cos. Integrated	−26
Electronics Systems	−13.73	National Food Stores	− 4	Steel - Integrated	−17	International Oils	−23
Distillers	−10.90	Electric Power Cos.	− 3	Trucking	−16	Commercial Finance	−23
Electric Power	− 8.75	Dairy Products	− 3	Electric Power	−16	Household Chemicals	−23
Personal Loan	− 8.22	Variety Stores	− 6	Variety Stores	−16	Auto Parts	−22

GROUP AVERAGES		GROUP AVERAGES		GROUP AVERAGES		GROUP AVERAGES	
Number Advances	77	Number Advances	75	Number Advances	55	Number Advances	50
Number Declines	23	Number Declines	25	Number Declines	43	Number Declines	49
Number Unchanged	0	Number Unchanged	0	Number Unchanged	2	Number Unchanged	1

SOURCE: Wright Investors' Service

time, many of these original "investments" will have become so high that these stocks are speculations selling above their true values. That's the time to set stop-loss orders and be ready to sell in a hurry if the price slides past your limit. When major investors sour on an industry, shares of even the most profitable firms in that industry will decline. That's what happened to oil stocks in the spring of 1981.

By and large, stocks move with the overall market. But, as the table shows, there are exceptions which can be turned to gains by buying at the beginning of the upswing and selling, or selling short, when there's a confirmed downtrend.

What these data show is that, at any specific time, certain industry groups are in the news, attracting institutional attention and, someone feels, have something extra going for them: high dividends in a period when investors choose yield over growth (metalworking, cyclicals, utilities); low debt, strong cash positions in times of tight money (drugs, foods); basic assets in years of economic and political uncertainty (natural resources such as oil and gas, gold, silver, etc.).

For the short term, the best gains will come from swinging holdings such as warrants and options. In bull markets, buy popular groups on margin; in bear markets, sell unpopular issues short.

For the long term, buy quality stocks when they are undervalued and shunned, and sell them when they become fully priced when, by definition, they are popular.

In both situations, technical analysis can be valuable in catching shifts in trends: Upmoves with high volume are bullish; downswings, with heavier than usual trading, are bearish.

The tough decision comes in determining whether unpopularity is irrational or deserved. Professionals are often able to spot signs of trouble that are not readily visible in financial reports. Corporate management may utilize accounting to report higher earnings or stronger finances than would be shown by more conservative methods. This may not reflect on the integrity of management. These executives are trying to present the best possible case—as we all do in our business, professional or personal life.

Soon you may find a full explanation of those small-type footnotes that refer to "methods of inventory valuation," "other assets," and especially, off-balance-sheet financing such as leasing. Time was when most of these accounting concepts were used only by aggressive companies with limited capital, temporary problems, and corporate ambitions exceeding their financial capabilities. But in these days of tight credit and competition for capital, even large, conservative corporations are turning to "unusual" accounting.

There is nothing wrong in such tactics except that omission tends to create an incomplete, if not inaccurate, summary of corporate finances.

Under pressure from the SEC, stock exchanges and the accounting profession, more data are being made available to stockholders. Usually, the information can be found in 10K reports that are filed with the SEC. (You can get a copy from the corporate secretary or by writing to the SEC.)

The fact is that accounting is not an exact science. Financial statements always contain figures which are the result of estimates or approximations, for example, estimating the useful life expectancy of fixed assets for the purposes of depreciation; approximating the collectibility of receivables; etc. *Accounting information is incompatible with absolute precision and truth in reporting.*

Always watch for changes in the traditional method of accounting when they boost profits. That's a danger signal for all but financially strong corporations; they usually indicate that management is trying to present a brighter picture than really exists.

Example: A steel company might change its depreciation schedule on a $100 million furnace from an accelerated rate (say, $5 million a year for 20 years) to a straight-line rate (say, 30 years or $3.3 million annually). By allowing a smaller amount for depreciation, the company can show $1.7 million more in gross earnings.

This shift may be fully justified by experience, but the result is that earnings appear to be higher than in previous years when, actually, there is no real change. In prosperous times, companies may reverse the process and "hide" some of their extra profits.

To achieve spectacular profits, you do not have to change management procedures, just accounting—or accountants.

Gulf & Western used another tactic. They gave an equal face amount of 7%, 30-year debentures for 5½%, 20-year convertible debentures. G & W determined that the new debentures were worth about $650 and so recorded a profit of $350 per debenture tendered—a $15 million gain listed in the annual report.

But if G & W gained that much, who lost? A little arithmetic would have shown that the present value of the 7% CVs had a true cost of $652.79. Hence, the company reported a bookkeeping profit of about $350 on each bond tendered. But this was really an out-of-pocket cost of $90.21. *Result: a true loss of $3.8 million instead of the reported $15 million profit.*

If you concentrate on quality companies, you will have no such problems. But you still have to decide your overall strategy: to buy growth and hold, to look for ever-higher earnings and dividends or to take advantage of special situations that can provide extra benefits under certain conditions.

Buy Growth and Hold?

This approach is based on the logical premise that, over the years, you can make money by picking sound growth industries and companies and holding their stocks for decades. This enables you to participate in the steady, natural growth of the U.S.A., to earn ever-higher dividends almost continuously, to protect your savings against inflation, to feel secure in deflationary periods, to avoid costly commissions from in-and-out trading and to keep your taxes at a reasonable level. Unfortunately, with the slow growth of the U.S. economy, such a strategy is becoming more difficult. To win, the investor must be highly selective; buy stocks of profitable, growing companies; time purchases wisely and be patient.

If you begin such a program at the peak of a boom and happen to die near the bottom of a depression, your heirs will not fare well. But if the reverse occurs and you make your major commitments near bear-market lows, the results can be sensational. In 1974, when per share profits were $5.14 (adjusted for a split), the stock of Mobil Corp. sold at 15. In 1980, profits were $9.46 and the stock was at 90. Profits were up 84% but the stock price was six times as high!

In Wall Street, popularity is always more important, over the short-term, than profits. Between 1974 and 1980, the stock of Avon Products fell from 65 to 31 but per share earnings rose 107%!

If you subscribe to the Buy Growth and Hold theory, you'd better put those stocks in your pension-plan portfolio or anticipate a long life. You will always do better by managing your holdings: buying when undervalued, selling when fully priced and repeating this process over the years.

Selection Is Not Easy

One problem with growth industries is that they keep changing. Automobiles were a true growth group in the '20s; mediocre performers in the '30s and '40s and boomers in the '60s. In 1980–81, they were disasters.

Since 1974, electronics has been a "hot" industry but it's becoming more mature and, with few exceptions, corporate growth has slowed with size. Now you have to be very selective.

One checkpoint that is becoming of increasing importance: the ability of the industry to generate capital internally. With the high costs of money, every extra dollar of profits does double duty: It makes possible expansion and it reduces the drain of expensive interest payments on debt. This is the reason why steel companies are poor long-term investments. There's no way that most of these corporations can earn enough to provide even a fair percentage of the $30 billion needed for capital improvements in the next decade.

On the other hand, retailers relying on cash customers and fast turnover can build capital from within. In the years ahead, cash and cash flow will become of greater importance in the selection of equity securities.

Another consideration, especially for conservatives, is stability and security of income. These characteristics apply to noncyclical industries supplying or selling necessities: electricity, food, money, drugs, cosmetics and so forth. None of these industries—or the companies in them—are depression-proof. But, overall, they offer a high degree of earnings stability through good times and bad.

Special Groups

Usually, stocks move with the market and those within a group move with the industry. But this is not always true. In 1979, stocks of automobile replacement parts makers went up 21% while all other groups fell. These aberrations make it difficult for the amateur to take advantage of shifts. So the best course is to pick an uptrending industry and then select the best-moving stocks. Or to avoid downtrending industries even though there may be a few winners. DO NOT TRY TO OUT-GUESS WALL STREET. Those professionals have more money than you have and thus pack a lot more weight.

How to Find What Companies Are in an Industry

The best place to get a breakdown of industry groups is from your broker. The tables here show general categories but, for more detailed data, check your local library for a copy of Moody's *Industrial Manual,* Standard & Poor's *Corporate Records* or Standard & Poor's *Stock Guide.*

You can also find periodic listings in publications of the New York Stock Exchange and, if you own shares of investment companies or bank common-trust funds, check the categories shown for their portfolios.

To Check "Normal" Prices

This criterion is discussed in detail elsewhere but to find out when an industry is out of line with its historical pattern, use this table. It shows the median returns on stockholders' equity: how much money the average company in that group has made, on invested dollars, in the past—in this case, the year 1980.

RETURN ON STOCKHOLDERS' EQUITY

Mining/crude oil production	21.0%
Tobacco	19.8
Petroleum refining	19.4
Broadcasting/movies	18.0
Pharmaceuticals	17.9
Scientific/photo equipment	17.1
Soaps/cosmetics	16.9
Aerospace	16.2
Electronics/appliances	16.2
Publishing/printing	15.9
Beverages	15.6
Metal Products	15.3
Office equipment	15.1
Food	14.5
Chemicals	13.9
Metal Manufacturing	12.9
Apparel	12.8
Paper/fiber/wool products	12.8
Textiles	8.1
Motor vehicles	8.1
Rubber/plastic products	5.0
ALL INDUSTRIES	14.4

SOURCE: Fortune

Buy the Leaders for Best Profits

If you are the type of investor or money manager who insists on diversifying by industries, do so only with companies that are leaders in their fields. Their stocks will perform better than the group average and with less volatility and greater appreciation than low-quality, marginal firms. BUT: (1) if you cannot find quality companies in a specific area, don't strain to fill the category; (2) remember that even the best stocks will not be able to buck the unpopularity of an industry group.

Here are comparisons between "good" and "poor"

companies in several major industries. Note how the prices of the shares of the well-managed firms moved up more or less steadily over the 1971–80 decade while those of the problem companies seesawed, up for a short term and then down because of lower, inconsistent profits.

Generally, the price/earnings ratios for an industry swing within similar ranges, so earnings become of major importance in profits—or losses.

The point is that, even if you correctly appraise the outlook for an industry, it makes a vast difference which stock you buy. Stick with *quality* companies that are leaders for the surest, most rewarding investment returns.

Company	High Stock Price			Price/Earnings Range
	1971	Interim	1980	
Retailing				
Melville Corp.	21	40	42	22–7
Sears Roebuck	52	62	15	27–7
Utilities				
Houston Nat. Gas	8½	42	63	23–9
Northeast Util.	15½	17	7½	11–7
Steel				
Carpenter Tech.	7½	36	53	24–4
U.S. Steel	24	60	35	23–D

CHAPTER 10

Special Situations and Techniques

This chapter discusses unusual speculative/investment opportunities. The one common factor is that the stocks involved all have distinct characteristics and do not fully conform to standard analyses and actions. Most of them are speculations but some, such as banks and utilities, can be investments.

Special situations offer the prospects of substantial capital gains in a relatively short time, often with comparatively small risk. Special industries are groups that require somewhat different analysis than is used with most securities. Special techniques are concerned with short-term trading that is usually best for professionals but should be understood and, occasionally, used by amateurs.

Special Situations

These include a variety of opportunities: pending recapitalization or reorganization; mergers, acquisitions or liquidations; stock splits and spin-offs; well-known stocks that, for one reason or another, are "sleepers" selling well below their historic multiples or their present book values; companies involved in new developments or in areas of fast growth; firms with a small number of shares; corporations loaded with cash; companies whose stocks are traded OTC that are ready and eligible for listing on a major stock exchange; new issues and so on.

There are two bases for special situations: internal and external changes.

Internal action is the result of management or stockholder-induced shifts: new executives, mergers, new products, expanded marketing, refinancing, etc. When these involve an outside group, start your research on the new management or investment team. Do they have a record of successful takeovers or are they predators who are likely to sell off corporate assets and leave a worthless shell?

Once you are convinced that the new owners are serious about rebuilding a business, check the old company reports to try to discover the reasons for their interest. Your broker may be helpful, but the best source will probably be special advisory services such as those published by Value Line and *Forbes*. Be cautious of comments by friends unless they have been close to the situation.

Basically, your decision should reflect confidence in the new owners/managers. Swingers may want to move in early; speculators should wait until at least some of the promises have been fulfilled; investors should not act until there is strong, steady progress.

Example: General Dynamics was a troubled aerospace, natural resources company in 1970 when financier Henry Crown took control. Crown had a long record of successful takeovers and reorganizations.

At the outset, the stock dropped from the low 20s to 16. The new management worked slowly, and for several years the stock yo-yoed between 28 and 14. There were no real gains until 1975, when Wall Street became convinced that Crown had not lost his magic touch. Earnings were strong and consistent and, with a huge new fighter plane contract, the future looked bright. The stock shot up to 60 and, after a few fluctuations, soared over 90 before the first of two stock splits: 2½–1 in 1979 and 2–1 in 1980. The profits were tremendous but took about eight years. Keep that time frame in mind. With all special situations, you may be lucky and win early but, in most cases, worthwhile gains take time.

External changes that make a company's stock "special" include: (1) population, economic, regional and governmental shifts or developments which provide new markets, lower production costs, higher prices, etc.—all items which can be translated into greater profits; (2) scientific and technological developments that create additional opportunities for alert management—microwaves, lasers, etc.; (3) national monetary strengths or weaknesses that expand or restrict major corporations; and (4) availability and cost of raw materials—oil, bauxite, copper, iron ore, timber, and so on.

Generally, these are most beneficial to established corporations with substantial holdings in the essential resources.

Checkpoints for Special Situations

Worthwhile special situations are hard to come by. One approach is to watch the market behavior of active stocks, notably those on the AMEX or OTC. When there is a sudden burst of popularity, chances are something favorable is in the wind. But unless you are willing to settle for a quick five-point profit, take your time, get the facts and wait until there is a confirmed uptrend. You may lose the first 10% of profits, but when you hope for a 100% gain, that's not important.

In most cases, the discovery of a special situation will be sparked by public information: a news announcement, a feature article in a business publication or a special report from a research department or organization.

Here are some guidelines for special situations. Each should be judged on the basis of your financial resources, willingness to speculate, recognition of the reward/risk ratio and time frame. Once in a while a special situation will develop quickly, but significant gains will usually take twice as long as anticipated!

New products. In most cases, these produce better publicity than profits. There is a long gap between the announcement and the ultimate earnings: on the average, two years.

Despite what your broker may tell you when touting a new small company, new developments are most significant to established corporations which have the capital and manpower to exploit the breakthrough.

Example: In 1970, Bausch & Lomb stock was selling around 13 (adjusted). As the result of its control of a new soft lens, the stock soared to over 90 within a year. But when there were delays due to governmental requirements and production difficulties, the stock fell to 17. With all special situations, always set a stop-loss order to lock in your profits.

Favorable court decision. Wall Street dislikes uncertainty. Litigation can depress a stock's price, and legal approval can bring a fast, sharp rise.

Example: When Connecticut's State Insurance Commission approved ITT's acquisition of Hartford Fire Insurance Company, ITT's stock rose 60% in eight months. Then the Big Boys started to take their profits and the stock fell sharply—another example of the importance of a stop-loss order with special situations.

Investor disfavor. This often occurs before the market recognizes the significance of corporate changes.

Example: Burroughs was a stodgy manufacturer of adding and calculating machines. Quietly, its management transformed it into a highly successful producer of electronic data processing equipment. By 1966, Wall Street discovered BGH's rapid earnings growth; in three years, the stock price nearly tripled and, with interim fluctuations, it has continued to go up. But you gotta be patient.

Spin-off assets. This occurs when subsidiaries are worth more when they are distributed than when they are held. These spin-offs may result from governmental edict or management's decision to concentrate in other fields.

Generally, spin-offs are accomplished through a tax-free distribution of a division of a subsidiary so that the shareholders own an interest in one or more new companies. Spin-offs can involve slow-growing, low-profit units or, better, fast-growing companies. The result is that the sum of the parts is greater than the value of the whole.

Obviously, the stockholder benefits most when the divested company is a winner. One of the most successful spin-off firms is Tandy Corp. Shares of Tandy Brands, worth $1,000 at the outset, grew to $8,800; with Tandy Crafts, each $1,000 rose to $4,623 plus shares of another spin-off, Color Tile, originally $1,000, recently trading for $2,121.

With almost all special situations, you are speculating, so try to diversify. You may not always pick a winner, but the rewards can be so substantial that one or two big hits can more than make up for small winners or a few losers.

Historically (and according to the mythology of Wall Street), many of the best special situations have been with unlisted stocks. But these days, with the shortage of credit and venture capital, worthwhile opportunities may develop with established companies—sometimes those in trouble but, more often, small-to-medium size corporations with unique capabilities. There are few better ways to speculate than with special situations—when you do your homework, time your transactions and are patient.

Stocks Selling Below Book Value

In discovering certain types of special-situation stocks, the analyst reverses the normal approach of watching for companies which show ever-increasing sales and profits. Rather than *buy dear and sell dearer,* the idea is to *buy cheap and sell dear—fast.* Instead of looking at the daily list of new yearly highs, the analyst checks the lows for possible bargains that have prospects.

Many stocks fall behind the market for purely temporary reasons, then are forgotten by the majority of investors. They continue to be unpopular even after the original reason for their fall from grace has been corrected.

The trick is to spot undervalued situations ripe for a turn. Do not buy any stock just because it is historically cheap and therefore "bound to rise eventually." The ideal time to buy an undervalued stock is when selling pressure has been exhausted and there appears to be some sustained investor/speculator interest and good prospects for the corporation. Always avoid hopeless laggards: stocks of companies that have been, and still are, going nowhere fast.

One starting point is *book value* (what the shareholders actually own after paying all debts). Time was when book value, especially of manufacturing companies, was a convenient way to judge per share worth. But no more. Some companies, such as drug manufacturers, have few facilities and thus report a relatively small book value. Steel firms, on the other hand, have huge investments in plants and equipment and thus have a high book value.

The real key to the value of the corporate stock is

the ability of management to use these assets profitably.

When a stock sells below book value, and the company reports average to good profitability and growth, its stock may be a bargain. You are buying, at a discount, assets which can provide a strong base for progress.

Note: This criterion does not apply to railroads, which have vast properties and, generally, low earnings. Their stocks are seldom priced above book value.

Speculative Opportunities in Volatile Stocks

Both cyclical and leveraged common stocks in *all* price ranges can be highly volatile. Speculators take advantage of such situations by buying the most volatile stocks in rising markets or selling such stocks short in falling markets. Both approaches can be risky and profitable. *They are definitely special situations.*

Here's how the arithmetic of volatility works: suppose the DJIA moves from 800 to 1000 in a given period of time, say 16 months. This is a gain of 25%. In the same period, the stock in which you are interested moves from 10 to 14: up 40%. Divide .40 by .25 to get 1.6, which (because you are dealing in percentages) becomes 160%. That means your stock is far more volatile than the stock market average during this period of time.

Before you speculate in any stock, you should be aware of its relative volatility. A chart is also valuable. You can make your own or check *The Financial Weekly* (if it is a listed stock) or buy one from a professional service. Then compare the movements of your stock with that of the stock market as a whole. In combination with your own research, this information can give you a valid estimate of the volatility of any stock. Here's a scale for reference:

Use broad ranges. The volatility of a particular stock varies. On one market move, it may be 140%, on the next 110%.

Relative Degree of Volatility	Percent Range vs. DJIA as 100%
Very high	140 and over
High	115–140
Average	85–115
Low	60–85
Very low	less than 60

Also check the action in different markets. Some stocks move up faster than they move down; others move down faster than they move up. If a stock tends to lose more rapidly than it gains, it is a candidate for short selling, but it probably is not suitable to the average investor. Conversely, true growth stocks will normally retain some of their previous market gains even in market dips—and so they are usually not considered special situations.

If you want to make this distinction, add a + to the stock that is more volatile on the upside; a – to indicate the reverse; and an = to show comparable volatility on both rises and declines.

Candidates for Stock Splits

Another fertile field for special situations is the corporation which may split its stock, i.e., issue one, two, three or more shares for each share outstanding. It is psychologically easier to buy 100 shares of a stock priced at 40 than 50 shares at a price of 80. And, of course, commissions on round lots are less than those on odd lots.

Splits usually occur when the price of the stock moves to a historically high level and management becomes fearful that the high price will discourage individual investors.

Stock splits can be welcome and profitable. The speculator who owned 300 shares of Houston Oil & Minerals in 1972 ended 1977 with 6,000 shares.

The NYSE encourages stock splits as part of its efforts to broaden public ownership of listed stocks. When more shares are available at lower prices, more investors become interested. This helps to assure both an adequate supply for daily trading and a more orderly market.

On the Big Board, the most popular price range has been 15 to 29. About 60% of all NYSE orders (in number, not in volume orders) to buy and sell stocks involve $4,000 or less, that is, an average per share price of $40 or less.

The possibility of a stock split is of primary interest to traders because it provides an opportunity for extra short-term profits. Serious investors buying for long-term capital gains should focus their attention on basic financial considerations. If a stock is not a good value at 100, it is no better at 50 after a two-for-one split.

The greatest immediate profits from stock splits often occur in the last six to three months before the directors take positive action. During this period especially when there are earnings and dividend increases, anticipation can push up the price of the stock.

With stock splits, the Wall Street adage *buy on the rumor, sell on the news* is applicable most of the time. The typical pattern is as follows:

1. The price of the stock rises fairly rapidly before the public announcement: on the average, about 20%. This is due to the pressure of insiders, information leaks or shrewd guesses.

2. The price reaches a peak from two to 24 weeks before the announcement of the split. On the rare occasions when the secret has been kept, the peak comes just after the announcement.

3. For two days after the news, the price remains high. Five days later, a study shows, half the split stocks have declined in price.

4. Just before the actual split takes place, there is likely to be another rally, especially if the overall market is bullish.

How to Determine Whether a Stock Is Likely to Split

1. Is it to the corporation's benefit to attract more stockholders? This is a primary consideration in companies which deal with goods and services which stockholders can buy. The best candidates are companies involved with consumers: retail stores, manufacturers of

SOME COMPANIES THAT HAVE SPLIT THEIR STOCK OR
PAID STOCK DIVIDENDS FREQUENTLY IN RECENT YEARS

Aetna Life & Casualty Co.
Air Products & Chemicals
Allright Auto Parks, Inc.
Amerada Hess Corp.
American Family Corp.
American International Group
American Medical International
American Shipbuilding Co.
Amsted Industries
Analog Devices, Inc.
Apache Corp.
Archer-Daniels-Midland
Arkansas Louisiana Gas
Atlantic-Richfield Co.
Baker International Corp.
Bally Manufacturing
Barry (R.G.) Corp.
Barry Wright Corp.
Beckman Instruments, Inc.
Best Products Co.
Big Three Industries
Boeing Co.
Brush Wellman Inc.
Cabot Corp.
Caesar's World, Inc.
Castle & Cooke, Inc.
Cessna Aircraft Co.
Cincinnati Milacron, Inc.
Cleveland-Cliffs Iron Co.
Combustion Engineering Co.
Computervision Corp.
Conagra, Inc.
Cooper Industries, Inc.
Crane Company
Crouse-Hinds Co.
Dayco Corp.
Dennison Manufacturing Co.
Dome Mines Ltd.
Dover Corp.
E-Systems, Inc.
Elgin National Industries
Engelhard Minerals
Fairchild Industries, Inc.
Federal Co.
Federal Signal Corp.
Filmways, Inc.

Flight Safety International
Fluor Corp.
Fort Howard Paper Co.
Foster Wheeler Corp.
Freeport Minerals Co.
Frontier Airlines
GCA Corp.
Gearhart Industries, Inc.
General American Oil
General Cinema Corp.
General Dynamics Corp.
Gibraltar Financial Corp.
Guardian Industries
Handy & Harman
Harland (John)
Helmerich & Payne, Inc.
Hewlett-Packard Co.
Honda Motor Co., Ltd.
Hospital Corp. of America
Houston Oil & Minerals
Huffy Corp.
Hughes Tool Co.
Humana, Inc.
Hutton (E.F.) Group, Inc.
Insilco Corp.
Intel Corp.
Internorth, Inc.
Interpublic Group, Inc.
Iowa Beef Processors, Inc.
Josten's, Inc.
Kemper Corp.
Keystone International, Inc.
Knight-Ridder Newspapers
Kollmorgan Corp.
Lamson & Sessions Co.
Lance, Inc.
Lee Enterprises
Levi Strauss & Co.
Lifemark Corp.
Litton Industries, Inc.
Louisiana-Pacific Corp.
Lucky Stores, Inc.
M/A Com Inc.
Mary Kay Cosmetics, Inc.
Matsushita Electric Industrial
MCA Inc.

MGM Grand Hotels, Inc.
Miller-Wohl Co., Inc.
Mitchell Energy & Development
Morrison-Knudsen Co., Inc.
Morse Shoe, Inc.
Murphy Oil Corp.
National Medical Care, Inc.
National Medical Enterprises, Inc.
National Semiconductor Corp.
Natomas Energy Co.
Nevada Power Co.
New England Nuclear Corp.
Noble Affiliates, Inc.
Norton Simon, Inc.
Nucor Corp.
NVF Company
Overseas Shipbuilding Group
Papercraft Corp.
Parker Drilling Co.
Parker Pen Co.
Payless Cashways, Inc.
Pay Less Drug Northwest, Inc.
Peabody International
Petrolane, Inc.
Philip Morris, Inc.
Pioneer Corp.
Prime Computer, Inc.
Quaker State Oil
Quanex Corp.
Raybestos-Manhattan, Inc.
RLC Corp.
Rochester Gas & Electric
Rowan Companies
Ryder System, Inc.
SCA Services, Inc.
Schlumberger, Ltd.
Sedco, Inc.
Shearson Loeb Rhoades, Inc.
Shell Oil Co.
Signal Companies, Inc.
Smith International
SmithKline Corp.
Snap-On Tools Corp.
Southdown, Inc.
Southland Corp.
Southland Royalty Corp.

Staley (A.E.) Manufacturing
Standard Oil (Indiana)
Standard Oil (Ohio)
Stanley Works
Stauffer Chemical Co.
Stevens (J.P.) & Co.
Storage Technology Corp.
Sun Chemical Corp.
Sun Co. Inc.
Sun Electric Corp.
Sunshine Mining Co.
Super Valu Stores
Tandy Corp.
Teledyne, Inc.
Texas Industries, Inc.
Texas Oil & Gas Co.
Tidewater, Inc.
Tokheim Corp.
Trane Co.
TRE Corp.
Trinity Industries, Inc.
Tyler Corp.
UNC Resources, Inc.
Union Oil Co. (Calif.)
United Cable Television
United Guaranty Corp.
United Refining Co.
U.S. Fidelity & Guaranty
Universal Foods Corp.
Universal Leaf Tobacco Co.
Wackenhut Corp.
Wallace Business Forms
Wallace-Murray Corp.
Wal-Mart Stores
Wang Laboratories, Inc.
Warner Communications, Inc.
Washington Post Co.
Western Co. of North America
Wetterau Incorporated
Williamette Industries, Inc.
Wometco Enterprises, Inc.
Wrigley (Wm.) Jr. Co.
Wynn's International, Inc.
Xtra Corp.
Zapata Corp.

SOURCE: Securities Research Company

food and drugs, oil companies and franchise firms. But there are also opportunities in fast-growing fields such as electronics.

Stock splits help a company to expand markets, make acquisitions and attract additional financing. When the stock is more widely held and more favorably known, the company can move ahead more rapidly.

2. Does management hold a small percentage of the outstanding stock? When there is a threat of an outside raid, companies often split their stock, thus making more shares available. Management, which retains its shares, hopes the lower price will attract more shareholders.

Conversely, if a few people own a substantial block of the shares, there will be little benefit for them in a split, unless there are future problems because of taxes, acquisitions or estate diversification.

3. Is the stock price above $75? The most attractive range for investors is $35 to $50 a share, so a stock almost has to be selling at a fairly high price to justify a split.

4. Has the corporation split its stock before? This is not always a reliable indicator, but it does provide a clue to management's thinking. Some companies seem to have a policy of frequent splits. Since 1977, Lifemark Corp. has announced four splits; Hospital Corporation of America, three; and Schlumberger, Ltd., three with prospects of another soon.

5. Are the earnings likely to continue to grow substantially? There will be little benefit from a stock split when the prospects for future earnings are dim. When the stock of a strong, continually growing company gets into a relatively high range, there are good reasons to look for a stock split. Higher profits enable a company to increase dividends at the time of the split.

6. Is an OTC company progressing so well that management may be considering listing the stock on a major stock exchange? The NYSE requires 2,000 stockholders, at least one million shares of common stock publicly held, and annual corporate earnings, in the latest year, of $2.5 million before Federal income taxes and $2 million pretax in each of the preceding two years. When a corporation reports such profits but has too few shares and stockholders, a stock split may be coming.

Welcome Stock Dividends

Stock dividends are extra shares issued to current shareholders, usually on a percentage basis. A 2% stock dividend means that two new shares will be given for every 100 old shares. Most companies continue such a policy over the years, especially when the prices of their stocks keep rising. For example, since 1968, Air Products & Chemicals, Inc., has declared 9 stock dividends and two stock splits. On an adjusted basis, the price of each share has moved from about 6 to a high of 55.

For the corporation such distributions have two goals:

• To expand the number of available shares at minimal cost. They are offered by small companies which want to have sufficient shares to qualify for listing on an exchange (this may be a long, slow process). Larger corporations feel that the extra shares encourage shareholder loyalty.

• To conserve cash. This is a temporary benefit because, when cash dividends are declared, they will have to be paid on many more shares of stock.

For shareholders stock dividends are tax shelters. Instead of paying the maximum tax on cash dividends, the stockholder pays the lower capital gains tax when he sells the appreciated stock.

Do not let the extra shares cloud your investment judgment. Corporations which declare stock dividends should be examined carefully to see if they are really growing. The actual dollar profits (before and after taxes) should increase every year. If earnings stay about the same or decline, stock dividends may not be so welcome.

How to Find Profits in Merger Candidates

Despite more stringent Federal regulations and threatened enforcement of antitrust laws, mergers are still increasing, and they can provide special situation profits to investors who are willing to do their homework.

The best opportunities are in acquisition candidates: medium-size firms which are limited in products, capital or management; and smaller companies with positions in, or access to, growth markets. Look around for local firms in your own hometown! Or those with whom you do business!

Fear of the future, by executives and/or owners, is the underlying reason for a willingness to sell or merge, but *whatever the reason for a sellout or merger, the investor can often profit if he buys judiciously at the right time.* That's not easy. By the time the merger is announced, the stocks of both companies may have already risen substantially due to buying by insiders.

Still, there are always insiders who, through shrewd guesses or, more likely, informational leaks, start buying early. Watch for unusual action in the stock of a target company. Two weeks before LTV Corp. offered to buy

Pneumo for cash and a new preference stock, Pneumo shares rose from 37 to 47. In the month before Diamond Shamrock announced it was acquiring stock of Tesoro Petroleum, TSO shares jumped from 20⅞ to 26¼. If you bought then, you would have made another four points in two weeks.

You can buy on the rumor, but this is speculative because a high percentage of acquisitions fall through. But once a company has started down the "for sale" path, the odds are good that it will be acquired—eventually.

Note: An excellent source for merger candidates and for stocks which are attracting unusual interest is *The Financial Weekly*'s Stocks in the Spotlight. This shows the past week's price and volume action in relation to the overall stock market, the same stock 200, 30 and 5 days ago. The figures are in percentages to show how much the stock has gained or lost relatively.

With the 30-day data, a figure of 1.0 indicates that the stock is gaining on the market at a rate of 1% for the period or a total of about 30% during the time frame. During a down market, a stock could be declining but will have a plus percentage because it was dropping at a slower rate than that of the market.

When the name of any company starts appearing on several of these lists, watch out. Some group must know something or have some plans which involve a substantial number of shares.

Tender Offers for Quick Profits

Tenders are offers made by a corporation or group to buy a stated amount of stock at a stated price for a stated period. With this approach, the acquisitors hope to buy a substantial block of stock without the risks that open market operations will run the share price up excessively. The tender price is always above the recent market value.

Under NYSE and federal regulations, all tenders must be made pro rata rather than on a first-come, first-served basis. Shareholders can also withdraw before the deadline if they change their minds.

With tenders, you have to be lucky as well as smart. Most offers are originally viewed as unfavorable by the target company's management. As a result, there's an irate outcry that the price is too low and a scurry to find another potential partner who will boost the proposed purchase price. This can prove profitable for shareholders.

Example: ESB stock, at $19.50, was courted by International Nickel with a tender offer of 28 per share. Then United Aircraft, anxious to diversify, bid 34. Finally, Inco settled at 41, and the stock traded at 41¼—more than double the price the week before.

Most offers are in cash, but Crane Co. acquired a substantial position in Anaconda Company with a convertible. Later, Crane sold its holdings to Atlantic Richfield.

Advice: Wait until all offers are in before you make any decision. Chances are very good that you will get more than the original tender price.

If the deal involves exchanging securities, consider whether you want to own shares in the acquiring company, and project income, not just current yield. Almost certainly this will be greater than what you are now getting.

Sell on the open market rather than waiting for the tender closing date. This eliminates risks that: (*a*) the tender will be withdrawn (which can be done without legal penalties); (*b*) only part of your shares will be acquired and you will end up with an odd lot; (*c*) poor timing will be costly.

Example: Macmillan stock was selling at 10 when a tender for 1.2 million shares, at 13, was announced. It rallied to 12, then dropped back to 10 the morning after the tender expired, when the company announced that it would accept only 32 of each 100 shares offered.

To find companies that may be acquired, use this checklist:

- Stock selling at a low price/earnings ratio
- Declining earnings
- Excess liquid funds that can be used to finance acquisition
- Concentrated share ownership
- Substantial cash flow
- Undervalued tangible or intangible assets
- Low debt
- Flat or lower dividends
- Poor market performance of stock
- Absence of strong management

Do your homework but do not commit your money until there is a logical reason to anticipate action: a statement by an officer or director; a major change in personnel; or an upsurge in the price and volume of the stock.

New Issues: Profitable but Risky

New issues are back. In 1980, Wall Street sponsored some 150 issues with a total value of over $700 million. This compared with 51 issues, valued at $360 million, in 1979. Add the hundreds of penny stock issues and it's a wild and wooly area of speculation. From early reports, it seems probable that 1981 will see more new issues than ever before.

All new issues are speculations. Most of those sponsored by established brokerage firms have a reasonably sound basis if the company has a fairly consistent record of profitable growth. Their shares can be worthwhile for those who have spare savings, are willing to take quick, after-issue profits or can afford to wait for the long pull. All penny stocks are 100% gambles!

Before getting into details of new issues, let's look at the record. Of 500 new issues floated in the hot market of 1961–62, 12% vanished, 41% went bankrupt, 25% are operating at a loss; 20% are still profitable but only 2.4% can be considered worthwhile holdings.

Penny stocks. Most of these are centered in Denver but, with their success, similar offerings are popping up around the country. If you are lucky, you can make a lot of money. But the odds for long-term success are always unfavorable.

As you'll soon learn, most companies with penny stocks are better for their promoters (and their friends)

than for "investors." Their markets are more or less controlled; their initial price is "negotiated" by the company, the selling shareholders and the underwriter; and, once the initial enthusiasm is past, there may be almost no real market interest.

Most penny stocks involve companies in the oil and gas business; a few are technology oriented or involve new inventions/concepts. The one surety is that, under SEC rules, there must be full disclosure in the prospectus. Read it for laughs more than for information.

In the offering for Beef & Bison Breeders, who set out to bring the "beefalo" to the American dinner table, the prospectus states: "The offering price . . . bears no relationship to assets, earnings, book value or other criteria of value . . . there is no trading market for the securities . . . no assurance that the market will develop . . . Purchasers should be financially able to sustain the loss of their entire investment."

Well, you can't say they didn't warn you!

SOME PENNY STOCK WINNERS

Company	Offering Date	Offering Price	1980-81 High
Calvin Exploration	8/80	$2.50	$ 7.62
Centennial Petroleum	11/80	.10	1.41
Dakota Resources	10/80	1.00	4.50
Deca Energy	12/80	7.00	12.00
Denver Western	10/80	.10	1.75
Eagle Exploration	9/80	5.00	8.75
Nova Petroleum	1/80	.25	3.12

SOURCE: Going Public; OTC

The big attraction is the low price and the huge number of shares. For $1,000, gamblers can own thousands of shares and profit from a slight price rise. The profits are awesome: Centennial Petroleum came out at 10¢ per share and, within a couple of months, was selling at $1.41; Denver Western started at 10¢ and soared to $1.75.

Usually, these gains are temporary. With each new offering (and that's where the promoters make their money so there's a steady stream), interest in outstanding shares dwindles and, with lessened demand, the stock prices fall. No one pays attention to whether the company has a genuine role, is actually operating or makes money. You are shooting dice and the house sets the odds.

Legitimate (well, usually) New Issues

With the current high cost of debt, more companies are seeking equity capital, so there may be excellent opportunities in the year ahead.

Generally, the purpose of the new issue is to provide capital for expansion. The more of the proceeds that go back to the company, the better the deal. The best situation occurs when the new money is used to boost operating capital, broaden markets or improve profit margins. It's probably OK if some of the new money is used to pay off high-interest debt. But be cautious when a high percentage of the proceeds goes to bail out existing shareholders.

New issues, sponsored by established brokerage firms, often a local or regional underwriter in cooperation with a Wall Street organization, fall into two types: (1) family-controlled corporations whose managements want to establish a market value for shares for estate planning; (2) small, unseasoned companies that need money to continue their strong progress.

With both of these:

Check the type of business. New ventures have the best chances for success in established growth areas such as electronics, retailing and energy exploration. The risks are greatest with unproven fields such as solar energy, thermal power and fish culture. These are exciting concepts but, in most cases, profits will require many years and additional capital.

Look for a reputable sponsor: a well-known, established brokerage firm that will maintain interest in the stock by making a market (standing ready to buy and sell shares in the future).

Avoid issues underwritten by small, local organizations who work on a "best efforts" basis. They do not have to pledge one cent of their own funds to guarantee the sellout of a new issue. They merely promise to do their best.

Check the auditor. Skip any offering where the statements are certified by an unknown local firm. There's too much chance for favorable interpretations or even collusion.

HOW SOME NEW ISSUES FARED

Company	Offering Price	High	Low	Recent Price
Agripost, Inc.	1	7 1/8	1	4 1/4
Apple Computer	22	37 1/4	21 1/2	26
Digital Switch	5	7 3/4	2 1/4	6 7/8
Enzio Biochem	6¼	27 1/4	10	27 1/4
Genetech	35	88	35 1/4	39 1/2
Up-Right, Inc.	11	15 1/2	8	9 1/4

SOURCE: Barron's

Read the prospectus. This must spell out the history of the corporation and the background of its officers and directors, detail its financial record and, believe it or not, list the risks of ownership of its stock.

Look for *executives* who have held key positions with successful corporations, are willing to work for small salaries and who hold large equity positions that will be valuable only if the company succeeds; *directors* associated with major organizations or, better yet, with successful venture-capital firms. At least you will know that someone has made a thorough investigation.

Avoid companies run by lawyers. By training, they are conservative and that's not what builds profitable growth.

With all new companies, the skill and competency of management are more important than the products or services offered.

Study fiscal data such as:

Financial strength. Ideally, current assets should be twice current liabilities: debt (bonds, preferred stock and bank loans) no more than 50% of total capitalization; cash enough to handle unexpected problems such as delays in start-up of new facilities, introduction of new products and so forth.

Financial performance. There should be sales of at least $10,000,000 with profitable growth for five years as shown by:

1. Operating income, before taxes, over 10% annually.
2. Return of equity averaging 15% a year. Calculate this by the profit rate: the per share profit divided by the book value (e.g., a company with 1 million shares and stockholders' equity of $5 million has a book value of $5.00 per share; to meet the 15% standard, the annual net profit should be $750,000 or 75¢ per share).

Conservative accounting. There should be no inflated property values nor trick allocations of costs or unusually rapid depreciation to boost reported earnings.

Determine the realistic value of the new shares. As a rule of thumb, the offering price should be less than 10 times earnings for the last 12 months. Investors are seldom willing to pay over $10 for each $1 of corporate earnings.

For a stock issued at 15, the per share profits should be at least $1.50. This multiple is higher than that of most stocks of established companies.

Recognize the risks. Little companies have to be watched and nursed along. Their profits can yo-yo and clobber the price of the stock.

Example: The stock of Tesdata Systems, a $15 million-a-year computer company, dropped 15% in one day when an interim financial report showed a small earnings decline. Yet the company's average sale was $150,000, and one order, booked a week earlier, would have reversed the profit picture.

In taking profits with new issues, set your goals before you buy. *If you are investing,* plan to hold the stock for three years but be ready to sell if the price: (a) rises sharply as the result of a takeover offer; (b) falls because of declining profits or managerial changes.

If you are speculating, sell by formula of time or profit:

• On the nineteenth day after issue (when the underwriters have eased or withdrawn their support so that the stock will start to trade on its merits).

• When you have a 50% gain. This is a high return but if you are still enthusiastic, sell half your stock to get back your capital for new ventures.

With both investments and speculations, set a stop-loss order about 10% below cost or recent high price. If the stock continues to move up, raise that figure proportionately. But do not lower that protection price. The first loss is almost always the smallest. If you hang on in hope, you will be bucking the odds. *Remember:* Two of every three new issues sell below their offering price within the next 12 months!

Companies with a Small Number of Shares

Corporations with a relatively small capitalization—say, with around 500,000 shares, or fewer—can offer interesting opportunities for both speculators and investors.

In most cases, such corporations are closely held and their shares are not actively traded. As a result, they sell at relatively low multiples and have relatively high dividend yields. They are excellent prospects for mergers, stock splits and new management—all aimed at broadening the market for the stock and at raising the market value. *But some of these companies prefer to remain single.*

COMPANIES WITH SMALL SHARE CAPITALIZATION
(Under 600,000 shares of common stock)

AFA Protective Systems	Kiddie Products
AGM Industries	Kleer-Vu Industries
Alamon Savings	Lynden Transport
Alaska NW Properties	Mangood Corp.
Allen Organ	MAPI, Inc.
American Underwriters	Michaels (J)
Andrea Radio	Miller Bros. Industries
ANRET, Inc.	Mooney Broadcasting
Archie Enterprises	MPO Videotronics
Autodynamics, Inc.	National Mobile Concrete
Base Ten Systems	National Valve & Mfg.
Berkshire Gas	Newport Electric
Bozzuto's Inc.	Norwesco, Inc.
Braun Engineering	Park Chemical
Chesepeake Utilities	Paxall, Inc.
Clarostat Mfg.	QONAAR Corp.
Computer Data Systems	Raycom Industries
Comtel Corp.	Realist, Inc.
Consolidated Accessories	Ripley Co.
Consumat Systems	St. Louis Steel Casting
Crowley, Milner & Co.	Scope Industries
Danners, Inc.	S-G Metal Industries
Dellwood Foods	Shorewood Corp.
Drewry Photocolor	Southwestern Electric
Driver-Harris	Standard Alliance
Edwards Industries	Stocker & Yale
Electro-Catheter	Summer & Co.
Empire Airlines	Sunset Industries
Espey Mfg. & Elec.	Synergistic Commun. Group
Esquire Radio & Electronics	Tensor Corp.
Evans, Inc.	Trailer Equipment
Excepticon, Inc.	Transmation, Inc.
Exolon, Inc.	Trion, Inc.
Firchburg Gas & Electric	Uniflite, Inc.
Florida Public Utilities	UniShelter, Inc.
GBC Closed Circuit TV	United Consol. Industries
General Real Estate	United McGill
Gray Communications	Valley Resources
Groff Industries	Viatech, Inc.
Heights Finance	Village Supermarkets
Hiller Aviation	Walker Color
Holly's, Inc.	Walter Scott
HS Group	Watsco, Inc.
Jefferson Corp.	Wellco Enterprises
Kahler Corp.	Wells-Gardner Electronics
Kenwin Shops	Wisconsin Southern Gas
Keystone Portland Cement	

SOURCE: Standard & Poor's

Special Groups

Usually, as shown in the Price Trends table, stocks in an industry move together. In 1980, all types of drug stocks moved up briskly. But there can be significant variations: with beverages, stocks of brewers and soft drink companies did well but those of distillers faltered. With utilities, shares of communication firms edged ahead, those of electric power companies declined, but those of gas-related corporations soared.

The point is this: most research organizations use broad categories in making their pontifications. Glance at them if you are interested but, before you invest, get more detailed information.

The best course is still to pick an uptrending industry and then uptrending stocks with the best prospects. Conversely, avoid downtrending groups even though there may be a few winners. Unless you are rich, smart and lucky, do not try to outguess Wall Street. The professionals may be wrong over the short term, but over the long pull of investing they will be right if only because they have more money than you do.

Bank and Utility Stocks

According to traditional Wall Street wisdom, two stock groups, banks and utilities, move together and, within those groups, also in unison: *up* when interest rates drop; *down* when they rise.

Broadly speaking, those aphorisms are still true but becoming less so. More than ever before, it is essential for investors to look at individual banks and utilities as to their financial strength, profitability, growth, political environment and, most important, management. Gone are the good old days when all banks could be considered safe, steady-dividend-paying investments or all utilities could be counted on for ever-rising income. No matter what your father told you, be skeptical about the stability of regulated corporations, get all the facts and make your judgment on the basis of *quality* and *value*. In the near future, hundreds of financial institutions and scores of electric and gas companies will be merged or reorganized.

Bank Stocks

There's not space here to discuss the significant changes that are taking place in the financial world. The major money-center banks are redirecting their assets and redefining their markets: *internationally,* some are slimming their overseas operations and others turning to joint ventures with foreign banks; *nationally,* some, like Bankers Trust (New York), are selling off their retail branches and concentrating on wholesale business including innovative services such as packaging commercial paper, setting up repurchase agreements and developing stand-by commitments to speed new debt issues.

Others are moving into broader areas to lessen taxes and escape interest rate ceilings: Citicorp is shifting its credit card services to South Dakota and J. P. Morgan is opening a subsidiary in Delaware with its liberal laws.

With regional and state banks and bank holding companies, the big changes are ahead. As the result of the NOW accounts where interest is paid on checking accounts and thrift institutions can make consumer loans, the difference between commercial and savings banks/savings and loan associations is narrowing. Soon, it may be hard to tell them apart.

Since there are a limited number of publicly owned savings and loans, let's concentrate on bank stocks, especially those whose shares are traded on the New York Stock Exchange.

All banks face increased competition: from brokerage

PRICE TRENDS – 100 INDUSTRY GROUPS

INDUSTRY GROUP	1981 INDEX PRICE HIGH	LOW	LAST	WEEK % CHANGE	YEAR TO DATE 1981 (5/1)	1980 (5/2)	1980 YEAR
AEROSPACE							
ENGINES & PARTS	309.44	267.59	300.85	-2.78%	+4.83%	-11.8%	+16%
MILITARY & COM	241.66	205.03	205.03	-4.12%	-11.64%	-13.4%	+38%
APPAREL							
CLOTHING	198.76	161.03	192.61	-3.10%	+21.81%	-8.4%	+10%
SHOE	418.77	336.47	402.65	-3.85%	+24.15%	-2.5%	+39%
AUTOMOTIVE							
DIVERSIFIED	42.37	32.96	39.12	▼-7.41%	+22.58%	-9.6%	-22%
ORIGINAL PARTS	326.10	278.64	313.85	-3.75%	+10.58%	-19.3%	+10%
REPLACE PARTS	407.21	357.82	391.94	-3.33%	+11.34%	-21.5%	+11%
TRUCKS-TRAILERS	84.26	75.71	79.43	-.59%	+.15%	-19.5%	-24%
BEVERAGES							
BREWERS	64.32	47.83	60.68	-5.65%	+22.32%	+.3%	+36%
DISTILLERS	290.87	263.08	263.98	-6.76%	-6.64%	-12.7%	-11%
SOFT DRINKS	338.20	293.03	319.25	-1.74%	+11.92%	-8.7%	+13%
CHEMICALS							
DIVERSIFIED	117.75	104.00	114.55	-1.56%	+9.49%	-11.2%	+10%
HOUSEHOLD	251.52	214.38	242.29	-3.67%	+7.88%	-5.4%	+5%
INDUSTRIAL	265.59	215.06	254.50	-1.97%	+18.33%	-10.8%	-1%
PAINTS & RESINS	151.23	120.65	124.16	-3.69%	+21.85%	+1.8%	+15%
RUBBER & TIRES	156.37	119.18	146.16	-4.43%	+27.31%	-9.9%	+41%
SULFUR PROD	649.82	558.65	609.66	-3.63%	+11.59%	-17.0%	+39%
CONSTRUCTION							
CEMENT PRODUCER	289.80	253.63	284.58	+.43%	+13.30%	-10.5%	+15%
CONST MACHINERY	276.73	216.41	255.69	-4.47%	+13.23%	-16.5%	+33%
DIVERSIFIED	221.24	195.56	213.08	-3.69%	+2.91%	-8.6%	+5%
ENGINEERING SVC	1165.45	879.90	881.58	+.18%	▼-26.05%	+9.4%	+85%
LUMBER	232.11	197.83	225.22	-2.97%	+11.56%	-13.7%	-6%
PLUMBING,HEAT	316.00	248.74	308.39	-2.41%	▲+51.44%	-21.5%	-17%
DIVERSIFIED							
CONGLOMERATES	257.84	219.14	257.84	+.10%	+19.73%	+3.0%	+54%
GENERAL	273.20	234.76	271.13	-.76%	+11.17%	-13.4%	+8%
DRUGS							
COSMETICS	313.75	270.89	298.34	-4.51%	+12.43%	-.3%	+25%
DIVERSIFIED	296.35	258.68	285.98	-3.35%	+14.18%	-6.9%	+25%
ETHICAL	329.93	299.10	329.93	+.66%	+8.53%	+2.4%	+36%
MEDICAL SUPPLY	556.69	513.08	541.19	-.79%	+5.66%	+1.3%	+24%
ELECTRICAL							
APPLIANCE MFG	275.77	221.51	265.12	-1.50%	+18.03%	-10.6%	-4%
DIVERSIFIED	170.55	134.70	164.98	-3.26%	+18.29%	-.4%	+38%
INDUS,COMMERC'L	669.71	560.99	669.17	-.08%	+12.68%	-5.7%	+38%
ELECTRONICS							
DIVERSIFIED	239.73	203.13	218.02	-6.24%	-6.89%	+1.1%	+53%
PARTS & COMPON	666.01	543.85	630.72	-5.83%	+2.76%	-10.1%	+24%
SYSTEMS	197.31	164.82	193.43	-1.97%	+11.79%	-24.9%	-14%
GOVT DEFENSE	596.02	489.19	568.72	-4.87%	-1.84%	+3.2%	+57%
GAUGES & METERS	914.35	542.13	659.56	-5.86%	-8.20%	-5.2%	+60%
RADIO,TV,PHONO	70.55	58.45	70.55	+1.71%	+10.23%	+5.3%	+109%
FINANCIAL							
COMMERCIAL	247.32	211.25	218.98	-4.49%	+6.05%	-18.3%	-6%
MULTI-BANK HOLD	220.71	196.29	217.87	-1.29%	+8.54%	-12.2%	+7%
ONE-BANK HOLD	163.96	146.46	162.87	-1.79%	+9.89%	+1.3%	+19%
PERSONAL LOAN	160.51	132.99	151.35	-5.71%	+16.21%	-16.5%	-8%
SAVINGS & LOAN	329.68	266.56	293.55	▼-6.58%	-9.60%	-17.8%	-3%
FOOD							
BAKERS	284.45	206.44	266.86	-3.73%	+29.93%	-7.6%	+5%
CANNERS,PROCESS	264.36	230.27	255.36	-3.41%	+11.28%	-11.4%	+18%
CONFECTIONERY	146.51	119.40	146.51	-1.47%	+32.22%	-27.9%	-20%
DAIRY PRODUCTS	153.50	128.94	148.26	-3.41%	+15.55%	-7.1%	+6%
DIVERSIFIED	198.69	172.56	193.41	-2.66%	+13.30%	-5.5%	+2%
GRAIN,FLOUR,CER	369.41	329.18	353.80	-2.69%	+7.84%	+3.8%	+7%
SUGAR PRODUCERS	418.18	359.46	364.69	-.53%	▼-16.84%	-3.6%	+41%
GLASS							
GLASS PRODUCTS	231.21	192.77	223.32	-3.41%	+7.73%	-1.9%	+18%

INDUSTRY GROUP	1981 INDEX PRICE HIGH	LOW	LAST	WEEK % CHANGE	YEAR TO DATE 1981 (5/1)	1980 (5/2)	1980 YEAR
MACHINERY & EQUIPMENT							
DIVERSIFIED	181.14	159.30	172.44	-1.88%	+1.26%	-21.2%	+5%
INDUSTRIAL	664.88	564.68	636.96	-1.12%	+3.14%	-4.1%	+21%
MACHINE TOOLS	498.76	425.64	498.76	+1.85%	+7.66%	-6.9%	+37%
OFFICE EQUIP	138.23	116.90	116.90	-5.31%	-16.10%	-8.8%	-7%
SCIENTIFIC	353.01	316.88	353.01	+2.36%	+1.55%	-12.1%	+28%
TRANSPORTATION	276.46	222.74	276.46	+1.73%	▲+40.56%	-17.3%	+14%
METAL PRODUCERS							
ALUMINUM	155.16	132.23	141.56	-5.47%	+5.00%	+.7%	+21%
COPPER	339.45	191.90	339.45	▲+4.71%	▲+52.81%	-11.7%	+3%
DIVERSIFIED	162.25	122.06	145.96	+.71%	+9.62%	-19.3%	+11%
GOLD	1272.48	1022.90	1192.22	+1.35%	-9.52%	+5.2%	+90%
STEEL-INTEG	110.85	85.80	108.20	-2.40%	+18.96%	+1.2%	+12%
STEEL-NON-INTEG	150.21	115.56	146.51	-2.47%	+30.76%	-10.3%	-14%
METAL PRODUCTS MFRS							
DIVERSIFIED	204.18	177.42	195.74	-4.14%	+19.53%	-12.6%	+6%
METAL CONTAINER	264.20	216.46	246.62	-4.38%	+13.93%	-19.9%	-5%
WIRE,CHAIN,SPRI	230.24	193.75	220.20	-2.47%	+13.70%	-7.5%	+10%
OIL, GAS & COAL							
CRUDE OIL	759.34	522.64	560.41	▲+7.23%	-9.92%	-1.5%	+48%
DOMESTIC	354.72	288.02	300.25	▲+4.25%	-16.28%	+2.6%	+54%
INTERNATIONAL	236.16	163.28	171.52	▲+5.04%	▼-26.38%	+13.2%	+67%
LIQUEFIED P.G.	651.47	565.79	569.79	-1.82%	-8.22%	-9.1%	+11%
REFINERS,DISTRB	205.66	160.07	160.44	+.23%	▼-42.48%	+2.5%	+28%
PAPER							
DIVERSIFIED	300.04	254.37	274.86	-2.15%	+5.08%	-7.3%	+19%
PACKAGING PROD	670.56	473.33	656.66	-2.07%	▲+44.19%	-13.6%	+10%
PRINTING & PUBLISHING							
BOOK PUBLISHERS	246.26	214.65	236.93	-3.79%	+9.85%	-12.9%	+22%
MAGAZINE PUBLI	446.45	341.95	434.86	-2.59%	+23.04%	-10.4%	+40%
PRINTERS	351.22	278.46	341.69	-2.72%	+11.99%	-10.3%	+27%
RECREATION							
HOTEL,MOTEL	1304.61	923.57	1243.06	-4.73%	+19.48%	-10.5%	+24%
MOTION PICTURE	839.51	639.23	807.70	-3.79%	+22.47%	-1.7%	-4%
PHOTO EQUIP	149.52	123.76	144.96	-3.77%	+1.87%	-5.6%	+21%
BROADCASTING	483.55	378.94	455.58	-5.04%	+21.83%	-17.2%	0%
RETAILERS							
APPAREL STORES	557.80	441.48	550.74	-1.27%	+21.14%	-17.7%	+23%
DEPT STORES	142.76	104.98	129.20	▼-9.50%	+21.61%	-10.3%	0%
DISCOUNT STORES	117.58	98.37	105.49	-4.40%	+.17%	-11.1%	-24%
DRUG STORES	263.19	204.52	260.63	-.97%	+24.99%	-12.0%	+21%
FOOD-LOCAL	118.69	88.54	118.69	+1.24%	+20.63%	-20.5%	-11%
FOOD-NATIONAL	152.94	121.68	146.93	-3.93%	+17.27%	-13.1%	-2%
SHOE STORES	834.87	674.63	834.37	+.80%	+24.37%	-9.1%	+24%
VARIETY STORES	99.45	84.67	93.11	-6.37%	+3.01%	-8.8%	+7%
TEXTILES							
APPAREL FABRICS	189.53	142.03	188.53	▲+7.95%	▲+43.72%	-6.6%	+9%
TOBACCO							
CIGARETTES	423.45	354.58	407.74	-3.72%	+7.01%	+10.1%	+41%
TRANSPORTATION							
AIRLINES	109.22	72.67	97.56	▼-9.65%	+38.78%	-17.4%	-6%
RAILROADS	308.20	250.65	293.21	-4.87%	+14.21%	+2.7%	+62%
STEAMSHIP	494.10	301.43	301.43	-1.40%	▼-36.95%	+32.2%	+21%
TRUCKING	415.66	290.00	398.91	-3.28%	+37.53%	-17.0%	+2%
UTILITIES							
COMMUNICATIONS	88.31	81.34	86.87	-.40%	+.46%	-2.1%	+4%
ELECTRIC POWER	59.70	55.38	58.65	-1.75%	+.70%	+6.1%	-1%
ELEC PWR HOLD	53.36	49.28	51.49	-1.16%	-2.89%	-4.0%	-9%
ELEC PWR & GAS	68.61	64.65	66.93	-1.99%	+1.21%	+1.5%	-8%
GAS OPERATING	199.49	169.15	185.58	-1.50%	+7.52%	-3.6%	+23%
GAS PIPELINES	456.59	384.14	397.79	+3.55%	-15.44%	-4.9%	+45%
GROUP AVERAGES							
GROUP COMPOSITE	306.43	249.63	285.51	-2.23%	+9.34%	-7.2%	+17%
NO. OF ADVANCES				20	82	22	75
NO. OF DECLINES				80	18	78	23
NO. OF UNCHANGED				0	0	0	2

NOTES: INDEX PRICE for each group is based on 100 on 12/31/65. WEEK % CHANGE is the average % change of the stocks in each industry group. 100 GROUP COMPOSITE is index price based on the arithmetic average of 100 Industry Group Index prices at 12/31/67 and has been adjusted for subsequent weekly % price changes. *These industry groups are averages of 3 to 6 companies as distinguished from the Industry Group Averages of all companies in each group published in Wright Comparative Investment Analyses.* ▲Fastest rising groups. . .▼Steepest price declines. <u>Underline</u> indicates new high or low this week.

SOURCE: Wright Investors' Service

firms with expanding financial services; mutual funds that make loans on shares; retailers and steel companies that own savings and loans, etc. If you own shares in any local financial institution, stay alert. If management is able and aggressive, you may do well. But if it's small or shaky, you may be lucky to get your money out.

The basic problems with banks involve the source of funds. Ideally, they borrow cheap—through demand deposits—and lend dear. In the past few years, this process has been reversed. Many banks have been locked in with 10% mortgages and 14% consumer loans and forced to pay 20% for new money or to sell off, at whopping losses, long-term bonds. In most cases, the crises have passed. If the bank has survived, it will probably do better in the years ahead. But the wise investor should keep an eye on the criteria summarized in the table.

There are, of course, other considerations but these provide a good starting point for analysis.

MAJOR BANKS: MOST AND LEAST PROFITABLE (1980)

Company	Total Assets $ mil.	% Domestic Demand Deposits	Loan Loss % Loans	Long-Term Debt/Capital	4 Yr. Growth Equity	Per Share Earnings	Return on Equity
Allied Banc. (Tex)	$ 2,855	41.0%	1.8%	22.6%	18.5%	24.2	23.6%
Republic (N.Y.)	6,447	9.3	2.1	36.4	16.9	30.6	21.1
Mercantile Texas	5,460	41.2	1.3	29.5	13.8	17.5	19.9
Texas Commerce	11,287	39.5	1.2	8.9	14.4	20.2	18.7
BankAmerica	111,617	14.7	0.9	24.5	12.4	16.1	18.3
First Inter. (Tex)	13,781	31.0	1.1	36.3	12.9	17.3	18.3
Valley National	5,733	32.7	1.3	0.2	13.1	26.1	18.1
U.S. Bancorp (Ore.)	4,879	30.2	0.9	38.0	13.6	15.3	18.1
Banc One (Ohio)	2,824	30.3	1.2	15.0	11.7	14.3	17.6
First City (Tex)	11,275	35.4	1.4	11.1	12.6	19.4	16.9
Michigan National	5,757	24.3	0.6	27.5	13.0	8.0	16.6
Security Pacific	27,794	28.6	1.0	35.6	11.1	21.8	16.6
Western Bancorp	32,110	34.9	1.3	32.9	11.6	23.8	16.5
Cont. Illinois	42,089	19.2	1.0	30.7	10.8	12.2	16.0
Seafirst	9,588	29.8	1.1	20.3	11.9	13.6	16.0
Citizens & Southern	4,341	47.9	2.0	7.7	5.8	25.2	7.4
Marine Midland	17,480	25.4	1.2	31.6	4.2	38.6	7.1
Nat. North America	5,693	27.1	1.0	6.2	5.7	10.9	6.1
Fidelcor (Penna.)	3,316	38.6	1.7	31.7	0.4	−0.5	2.8
First Penna	5,497	27.5	1.4	75.3	−11.7	Deficit	−6.2
Medians		32.1	1.2	24.9	8.9	15.2	13.8

SOURCE: Forbes Magazine

Demand deposits as percentage of total deposits. Historically, no interest was paid on demand deposits so the higher this percentage, the less costly the loan base. With NOW accounts, this is no longer fully true but it's still a good indication of financial strength.

Loan losses as percentage of total loans. The lower this figure, the less the bank has to deduct from earnings.

Long-term debt in relation to total debt/capital. Note that Citicorp, the nation's largest bank, is not included in this list. *Reason:* its debt is over 50% of total capital. This is double that of BankAmerica.

Citicorp argues that its bond debt earns its own redemption and, therefore, is really a source of retained earnings equity. But debt is debt and always less profitable than equity capital. With banks, low/modest debt ratios are a favorable, but not always a key, factor.

As with all investments, the two best tests are the ability of management to make money as shown by the growth in equity and earnings per share. Consistency is important so start with these data and get more detailed information from your broker. You don't want 30% growth one year and 5% the next.

This table gives you an idea of what to look for when investing in bank stocks. The most profitable companies are candidates for purchase; the least profitable may be coming back but don't spend your money until their progress is confirmed. It's a tough, increasingly competitive business. The banks most likely to hold up in the coming years are those that are well capitalized, have the broadest deposit base, the smallest amount of debt and have been able to keep their loan losses low and their growth high.

Utility Stocks

Traditionally, these have been favorites of conservative investors. The dividends have been ample and steadily rising. But now it's essential to look behind the profits and payouts. Be cautious when the earnings are the result of accounting or special credits such as Allowances for Funds During Construction (AFDC).

Not long ago, Consolidated Edison told shareholders that it earned $207.7 million while it told the IRS that it lost $41.4 million. The company did pay an ample dividend but only by the use of tax credits and deferred and capitalized costs. In effect, the payout represented borrowed money.

The situation is just as dangerous with AFDC. Here, new construction and interest expenses, on the new plant, are shifted off the income statement (where they reduce earnings) onto the balance sheet (where they become part of the base used to ask for higher rates). This is legal, logical and generally approved by regulatory commissions but it's a danger signal for investments.

What happens is this: The new $100 million Hotflash P & L plant won't be operating for three years. To offset the cost of the cash tied up in construction, the utility debits its balance sheet and credits to earnings the Allowance for Funds used During Construction (AFDC).

This amounts to 8% ($8 million a year). When the plant is capitalized, HF has inflated its net by $24 million and shows its value as $124 million. The money is not there but is expected to materialize as income and depreciation from the new plant.

Rationale: It's unfair to soak today's customers for tomorrow's cost. If the construction item was included in the present rate base, current bills would be much higher.

When construction programs were small and interest costs low, AFDC amounted to 7.2% of the industry's reported net income for common stock. More recently it has been averaging about 35%, and for some much more: Duke Power 84%, Florida Power 70%. Their management, and state public utility commissions, want to keep down consumer rates. So many utilities pay dividends greater than their AFDC.

In selecting utility stocks you must be choosy and get full information about:

1. The attitude of the public utility commissions which set their rates. In some areas government officials have recognized the need for adequate returns on investment to permit the companies to raise new capital for ever-rising needs. But this has not been the case in many states where the utilities are called on to fulfill social services such as discounts for the poor and elderly, financing of insulation, and other nonprofit operations.

2. The heavy costs of conversion from oil to coal. These can be spread out over several years, but they will dent profits and probably result in some delays in higher rates.

3. The problems of environmental controls caused by governmental agencies and public pressure. In most cases present laws require that coal-burning plants be equipped with scrubbers. These are costly and may not be able to reduce the pollution levels anyway, especially when plants turn to readily available high-sulphur coal.

4. Accounting changes are being forced by the SEC and the Financial Accounting Standards Board. Their target: the deferring of major costs. Under generally accepted accounting principles (GAAP), utilities are allowed to report income to shareholders on the basis of costs permitted by their regulators in the setting of rates. But in an attempt to smooth out rates, some commissions require utilities to defer to future years some costs that other companies, also using GAAP, must write off immediately.

Storm damage to a manufacturing plant would have to be taken out of that company's current-year profits. But losses from the same damage to a utility plant would probably be deferred and written off over several years—at a current benefit to profits.

And under new FASB rules, companies must capitalize leases used to finance long-term, single-purpose assets, such as new plants. But in setting rates, most utility commissions require that such leases be treated as operating costs or rent.

As a result, utilities turn to off-balance-sheet financing to improve earnings because when a lease is capitalized, a greater portion of its costs is written off in the early years. To financial analysts, this procedure makes it almost impossible to compare the operating results with those of other enterprises.

What it comes down to is that the traditional yardsticks are no longer valid and no one knows, for sure, just what is happening to the financial stability of many electric, gas and telephone companies. Since Wall Street dislikes uncertainty, the prices of utility stocks are likely to reflect income far more than growth.

(See Chapter 24 for tax benefits of owning shares of utilities with dividend reinvestment plans.)

Checkpoints for Utility Stocks

1. Favor utilities that use *normalized* **tax accounting** (setting up deferred tax reserves that increase operating expenses on which rates are based). This means higher rates to consumers while giving management extra cash to invest. (It is used by such firms as Louisville Gas & Electric, Public Service of Indiana and Kansas Power & Light.)

2. Avoid those which use *flow through* **tax accounting** (skipping deferred tax reserves and flowing tax savings through to consumers by reducing operating expenses). Customers pay for higher debt and equity requirements and the costs of inflation. (It is used in the East and West Coast urban areas: Southern California Edison; Potomac Electric; etc.)

3. Beware of depreciation under 3%. Any lower figure is in effect watering the stock.

4. Check the base on which rate of return is calculated. A 7% return on a plant figured at *fair value* or *reproduction cost* can be higher than 8% on the plant's original cost.

5. Be skeptical about fixed-charges coverage (the amount of earnings available to pay bond interest or preferred dividends).

6. Beware of a low effective tax rate. It may mean too liberal accounting.

7. Watch rate structure revisions such as "lifeline" rates to smaller users through discounts keyed to the time of day, season or age of the customer. These are substitutes for the traditional sliding scales which have been so important in maintaining the stability of utility earnings. While some of these special charges may benefit shareholders, most of them amount to public subsidies at the expense of private profits.

8. For the short term concentrate on utilities using coal and/or natural gas. After the Three-Mile Island accident, major money managers became reluctant to become involved with companies relying on nuclear power because of possible protests from shareholders.

So they have turned to utilities using gas on the basis that since 90% of gas is produced within the United States, supply and price problems will be minimal. As price controls eased, the values of many of these companies have jumped: Enserch from 17 to over 60; Southern Natural Resources from 28 to 75.

9. Diversification. More utilities are moving into the exploration for, and ownership of, wells. They use the gas for their own operations and sell the surplus. Houston Lighting is now Houston Industries (HOU) and has extensive holdings in gas wells. Arkansas Louisiana (ALG) derives 75% of its revenues from natural gas and oil exploration. Such diversification provides additional, and profitable, revenues and makes their stocks more attractive, as can be quickly seen by the fact that their stocks sell at higher-than-industry price/earnings ratios.

Best checkpoint: NEVER buy any utility, for investment, rated below A by Standard & Poor's.

Profit Opportunities from Foreign Business

More American corporations are finding that overseas business can be an important source of revenues and profits. In some cases, the expansion has been through fully or partly owned subsidiaries based abroad. In Europe, the Common Market has made expansion and centralization easier. In Japan and the Far East, joint ventures are becoming common.

Foreign operations have many advantages: antitrust

restrictions are limited; growth opportunities are developing because of the higher standards of living; and there's an increasing push toward greater sophistication in industrial and scientific areas.

In recent years, the low value of the American dollar has boosted U.S. exports. Many specialized products, such as automatic machinery, precision instruments, electronic items and aircraft, can be produced here and shipped abroad at competitive prices. To a significant degree, the future of many American corporations is tied to world markets . . . as shown by the table.

This foreign business is usually quite profitable but there are often accounting problems that affect the market price of the company's stock. Time was when a multinational corporation could set up reserves for unrealized gains and losses from foreign-exchange transactions. Over the full year, these would more or less balance out.

Now, however, the company must report these results in their quarterly statement. Often, this distorted earnings, and ever-nervous Wall Streeters panicked a bit, usually selling when there was a loss even though the overall prospects for the company remained excellent.

This rule does bring uniformity in accounting, but as a practical matter, the changes are fictitious. Unless the money is actually converted into dollars, there is no effective cash flow. This situation has led to pressure for modifications which are being seriously considered.

It is possible for a company to hedge against wide swings, but no system can cover every contingency. Often, the cost of goods is reported in the old, high currency, while sales are shown in the new, lower rates.

Advice: Concentrate your search on stocks of major multinationals that are selling at low multiples and of those companies, of any size, which are able to report fairly consistent profits despite foreign-exchange losses.

Avoid small, thinly capitalized companies and any larger firms that have a big stake in one foreign country where the currency swings widely.

For most international firms, the overseas markets are still growing at a faster rate than domestic markets. Able management built strong positions abroad and will be able to develop techniques and procedures to continue that growth. There will be few booms but more steady, long-term progress. And foreign profits will no longer be able to bail out inadequate management.

Foreign Investments

With the turbulent American market and decline in the value of the American dollar, more sophisticated investors are buying shares in foreign corporations. Most of these are dominant in their domestic markets and expanding their interests throughout the Free World.

Fortunately, you do not have to worry about buying and selling abroad, as shares of many of these major firms are available in the United States as American Depositary Receipts (ADRs).

These are issued by an American bank acting as depositary for shares of the foreign corporation held abroad. Each ADR is a contract between the holder and the bank. It certifies that a stated number of shares of the

SOME COMPANIES WITH LARGE FOREIGN INTERESTS

Company	% of Foreign Sales	Company	% of Foreign Sales
Abbott Laboratories	34.5%	Ingersoll-Rand	33.6
American Brands	31.1	IBM	52.4
American Cyanamid	34.8	International Flavors	66.9
American Home Products	35.0	International Harvester	33.1
American Standard, Inc.	46.3	International Minerals	35.1
AM International Inc.	33.0	International Multifoods	34.3
Avon Products	42.9	Johnson & Johnson	43.1
Baker International	35.2	Lilly (Eli) & Company	39.2
Bally Manufacturing	33.6	Memorex Corporation	45.1
Baxter Tranvenol	35.4	Merck & Co., Inc.	46.9
Beker Industries	51.8	Mobil Corporation	62.6
Bendix Corporation	39.4	Morrison-Knudsen	36.6
Black & Decker	56.8	Natomas Corporation	68.3
Boeing Company	40.8	NCH Corporation	48.5
Borg-Warner	36.4	NRC Corp.	56.7
Bristol-Myers	34.1	Northrop Corporation	62.2
Bucyrus-Erie	50.0	Occidental Petroleum	49.0
Burroughs Corporation	42.3	Parker Drilling Company	50.4
Carnation Co.	31.8	Pfizer, Inc.	55.9
Caterpillar Tractor	48.5	Polaroid Corporation	40.6
Champion Spark Plug	36.7	Quaker Oats	30.8
Chicago Pneumatic Tool	36.1	Raymond International	42.2
Cincinnati Milacron	47.2	Raytheon Company	33.6
Clark Equipment	38.4	Resorts International	31.5
Columbia Pictures	33.4	Reynolds Industries	36.4
Continental Group	33.8	Robertson (H.H.)	52.9
Continental Oil	36.6	Robins (A.H.) Company	32.8
Control Data	33.6	Rohm & Haas	34.9
Cooper Industries	33.2	Rore Group	31.0
CPC International	63.1	Sante Fe International	76.3
Crown Cork & Seal	39.4	Schering-Plough	43.9
Cummins Engine	30.1	Schlumberger, Ltd.	81.0
Curtiss-Wright	41.7	Searle (G.D.) & Co.	35.2
Deere & Company	34.9	SmithKline Corporation	42.5
Dentsply International	56.5	Sperry Corporation	42.7
Digital Equipment	37.6	Squibb Corporation	34.1
Dow Chemical	47.1	Standard Oil (Calif.)	61.4
Dresser Industries	35.5	Sterling Drug	47.3
DuPont (E.I.)	36.3	Superior Oil	34.0
Eastman Kodak	38.3	Sybron Corporation	38.5
Emhart Corporation	44.3	Syntex Corporation	43.1
Exxon Corporation	77.6	Texaco, Inc.	49.3
Firestone Tire & Rubber	35.0	Trans-Union Corporation	36.4
Ford Motor Co.	35.0	TRW Inc	34.5
Foster-Wheeler Corp.	48.4	Union Carbide	41.6
Gillette Company	57.7	Uniroyal, Inc.	36.9
Goodyear Tire & Rubber	36.2	United Technologies	37.2
Grace (W.R.) & Co.	33.0	Upjohn Company	34.0
Gulf Oil	56.7	Warner Communications	30.0
Hercules, Inc.	32.6	Xerox Corporation	47.2
Hughes Tool	41.9	Zapata Corporation	32.7

SOURCE: Standard & Poor's

overseas-based company has been deposited with the bank's foreign office or custodian and will be kept there as long as the ADR remains outstanding. The U.S. purchaser pays for his stock in dollars and receives dividends in dollars. The bank, acting for the seller, notifies its foreign office, which provides the equivalent number of shares in London or Paris or Tokyo. When the foreign corporation has a large capitalization so that its shares sell for the equivalent of a few dollars, each ADR may represent more than one share: 10, 50 or even 100 shares in the case of some Japanese companies where there are tens of millions of shares of common stock.

Financially speaking, ADRs bridge the gap between foreign and American concepts of publicly owned securities. Outside of the U.S., Canada and, to some extent,

**SOME FOREIGN CORPORATIONS WHOSE SHARES ARE TRADED ON U.S. EXCHANGES
DIRECTLY OR THROUGH AMERICAN DEPOSITARY RECEIPTS**

Australia Broken Hill Proprietary G. J. Coles & Co. MIM Holdings Santos Union Carbide of Australia Woodside Petroleum **France** Aquitaine Machines Bull Perrier Peugeot St. Gobain Schneider et Cie. **Germany** AEG-Telefunken BASF, AG Commerzbank Deutsche Bank Deutsche Texaco Dresdner Bank Hoechst Siemens Volkswagenwerk **Holland** Akzo, N.V. Heineken, N.V.	Philipps Gloeilampen Royal Dutch Unilever, N.V. **Israel** American Israeli Paper Bank Leumi IDB Banking **Italy** Fiat Olivetti Pirelli **Japan** Canon Fuji Bank Fuji Photo Hitachi, Ltd. Honda Motor Japan Air Lines Kirin Brewery Kubota, Ltd. Matsushita Electric Mitsui & Co. Nippon Electric Nippon Optical Sharp Corp. Tokio Marine & Fire Toyota Motors Wacoal	**South Africe** Anglo-American Corp. Anglo-American Gold Blyvooruitzicht Gold Bracken Mines Buffelsfontein Gold Burma Mines Charter Consolidated Durban Roodepoort East Driefontein Gold East Rand Proprietary Elsburg Gold Harmony Gold Hartebeesfontein Gold Kinross Mines Kloof Gold Leslie Gold Libanon Gold Loraine Gold President Brand Gold President Steyn Gold Randfontein Estates St. Helena Gold Southvaal Holdings Stilfontein Gold Vaal Rees Mining Welkom Gold West Driefontein Gold Western Areas	Western Deep Levels Western Holdings Winkelhaak Mines Zandpan Gold **United Kingdom** Associated British Foods Beecham Group Bowater Corp. B. A.T. Industries British Petroleum Burmah Oil Gestetner Glaxo Holdings ICL Ltd. Imperial Chemicals Marks & Spencer Plessey Rank Organisation Rothman's International Shell T & T Tate & Lyle Tube Investments Vickers, Ltd. **Other** I.E.M., S.A. Telef. de Mexico Tubos de Mexico Ericcson Telephone

SOURCE: **Bache Model Roland International**

Japan, stock ownership usually has been confined to a small group of insiders, often a family. Managements have tended to view investors, especially Americans, with suspicion. They prefer to deal with familiar institutions, such as their bank, which may be a correspondent for, or a branch of, a U.S. bank.

ADRs enable foreign companies to tap American capital and Americans to seek profits abroad. ADRs are easily transferable and are traded the same as other securities: a few on the NYSE, many on the AMEX, and an increasing number OTC.

American international banks, such as Morgan Guaranty and Citicorp, handle all mechanical transactions at nominal cost. Almost all major brokers have specialists in ADRs, and many firms make markets in the U.S. and gain extra profits for themselves by arbitrage, that is, by the small, temporary differences between the prices of stocks on foreign exchanges and of ADRs in the U.S.

ADRs present no security problems because they are registered like regular stock. Most foreign securities are in bearer form. If they are lost or stolen, they can be sold by anyone who presents them to a broker.

ADRs eliminate many headaches: Britain imposes a stamp tax on 1% of a security's value; when investors want to sell overseas, they have to send in their shares and wait for their money; and some foreign corporations are not accustomed to keeping stockholders informed on dividends, subscription rights, merger proposals, etc.

Negatives for ADRs include:

Scant information. You will get little or no financial data unless you ask the ADR bank, in writing, to add your name to the corporate financial mailing list.

Taxes. Most foreign governments withhold a tax on dividends and interest from securities held by nonresidents. You can get an offset on your U.S. tax return by filing IRS Form 116. Capital gains made from foreign stock transactions are taxed at the same rate as domestic deals.

Problems with rights. ADR owners may not exercise rights issued by foreign corporations unless the new stock issue is registered with the SEC. Such rights are automatically sold by the depositary bank, and the proceeds are sent to the beneficial owner.

Foreign investments do have additional political and economic risks not possessed by U.S. stocks. But most of the corporations which have ADRs are large, international organizations which are not likely to be severely affected by shifts in their home country. For the average investor who does not have access to extensive research facilities, ADRs are a handy way to buy a position in the expanding world economy.

Between the surge in the U.S. market and the economic difficulties abroad, ADRs are not growing in popularity. But as more foreign corporations move into the American market, they will probably turn to ADRs to raise funds.

Currently, only a few foreign companies pay the extra costs of transfers and bank fees of ADRs, but with the competition for attention, this may change. Check your broker to find which ADRs offer this benefit.

Foreign Securities and Funds

Other ways to invest abroad include both debt and equity holdings. In addition to the regular attraction of high interest on debt or appreciation of the stock, there's the possibility of capital gains as the result of favorable currency fluctuations. With a weak dollar, prices advance. (But with a stronger dollar, they can decline.)

Yankee bonds. These are debt issues of foreign governments and corporations funded in U.S. dollars and registered with the SEC. Their yields have been as much as 1% higher than equivalent domestic debt; their maturities are relatively short (6 to 15 years); and many have mandatory redemption requirement retirement of the whole issue in equal annual amounts, usually after a grace period of five years. Thus, a 15-year issue would be retired in ten equal payments between the sixth and the fifteenth year.

Mutual funds that

1. *Invest in foreign denominated debt.* Their sales pitch: "Steady income from interest plus appreciation: if the dollar continues to fall, the value of foreign securities will rise; if the dollar rises, profits by buying dollar-denominated securities issued by non-U.S. borrowers such as foreign governmental agencies and international banks." In other words, the best of two worlds.

But there will be double taxation: U.S. shareholders must pay their usual taxes on income and gains, and there will also be foreign levies on a portion of the interest. If the sponsors can figure out how to calculate the foreign taxes, they can be used as a tax credit or deduction from the U.S. return.

And such glowing projections can work IF the fund managers are able to catch changing trends in foreign exchange. That's a tough task—as the financial officers of many multinational corporations have learned.

2. *Specialize in foreign stocks.* (See chapter on investment companies.) Templeton Growth Fund has been a top performer for the past ten years (but is now switching to U.S. securities); International Investors has done well with South African gold mining shares; and the Japan Fund has been a big winner for many years.

According to professionals who specialize in foreign securities, these investments should not be made in hopes of a quick killing. They should be considered more like insurance policies to cope with inflation as indicated by weakness in the U.S. dollar and corporate performance. Usually, foreign stocks move in the opposite direction of American equities. Their greatest value is the reduction of volatility of a portfolio.

Arbitrage for Quick Profits

One of the most exciting, rewarding and risky special situations involves arbitrage: "the simultaneous purchase and sale of the same or equivalent security in order to profit from price discrepancies." It is used primarily by professionals who do not have to pay commissions and so can shoot for small gains.

Yet, according to *Fortune,* a shrewd investor who became involved in arbitrage on 35 deals made money on 27, broke even on 2 and lost on only 6. It took from 6 to 251 days for completion. The quicker the win, the more profitable since less capital was tied up.

The recent wave of mergers and tender offers has opened arbitrage to sophisticated amateurs. The risks are high, but it's one of the fastest ways to accumulate capital in Wall Street. If you pick a winner, gains can be big and quick. *But it's no game for the neophyte.* One brokerage firm limits arbitrage accounts to those who will put up $100,000 ($50,000 on each side of the deal); another won't touch an account unless the customer has had "considerable experience and looks as if he won't flee after his first loss."

The mechanics of playing merger-arbitrage are complicated and depend on the ability to calculate percentages, act quickly, and obtain accurate information promptly.

Basically, you buy the stock of one prospective merger partner and, at the same time, sell short the stock of the other. If the merger is completed, you trade in the stock of the acquired company and receive shares of the surviving firm which are sold to pay back the loan on the short shares. *There is always the risk that if the deal falls through, you could lose on both positions.*

Closely allied to arbitrage is the speculation with stocks of companies which are to be acquired. Their values can soar, but this is one time when it may not pay to let your profits run. When Applied Digital Data announced that merger discussions were starting, the stock was at 12. Almost overnight, it jumped to 17, then to 20. But hindsight showed this was the time to sell. The talks broke down and the stock fizzled to about 14.

Or the late-arrival amateur can pay too much. The stock of Lehigh Portland zoomed from 18 to 25 after the announcement of merger plans. By the time Phil Philm got the word from his broker, the stock was at 23. Reluctant to sell with less than a 20% gain, Phil did not take his broker's advice to sell when the stock hit 27. *Sad ending:* the merger was consummated at 25 so Phil spent a lot of time, money, and commissions for a puny profit.

To spot candidates for arbitrage:

• Work with a trading-minded broker who is tuned in to Wall Street's rumor network.

• Watch the *most active* stocks on both the NYSE and AMEX. If the name of a small or medium size company appears twice within a week or so, something is happening.

• Study *The Financial Weekly* for lists of unusually active stocks. Tables show listed and unlisted stocks as to:

a. The number of shares traded in the past week as a percentage of total shares outstanding. When the figure is over 5%, check further.

b. The trend versus the market: for 200 days, the last 30 days, and the last 5 days. These stocks are the big movers on both the up and downside.

c. Volume as a percentage of a 20-day moving average. This is a good indication of the stocks which are attracting investor interest. Not all these leaders will be candidates for arbitrage, but it's a good starting place.

• Watch for cash-rich companies and those where control is closely held. The cash assets make a tempting target and the acquisitor can deal with a few people to establish a base for a tender offer.

Guidelines for Arbitrage

• Have at least $50,000 in cash and nearly as much in reserve.

• Always use margin: Greater leverage is what arbitrage is all about. With the current high cost of borrowing, your potential returns will have to be higher and come faster than in the past.

• Welcome friendly takeovers; stay away from proxy battles. The rewards may be lower but so will be the risks.

• Never speculate on the basis of rumors or tips. Stick with publicly announced agreements to merge, liquidate or go private. One bomb can wipe you out.

• Look for a good spread between the current market price and the cash or cash-and-securities package to be received when the transaction is completed.

Example: When Hartz Mountain announced that it planned to go private by buying back shares at 14, one arbitrageur bought at 12. Two points doesn't sound like much, but in 101 days the total percentage gain was 16.7%, a profit rate of 4.96% a month.

• Buy stock of the company that is being acquired; sell short the shares of the company whose name will survive.

Example: Brandy-Dandy (BD) offers to acquire Snookie-Cookie (SC) on the basis of 0.8 shares of BD for one share of SC. BD is selling at 28 so each SC share could be swapped for stock valued at $23.24. But SC stock is at 22¾, so there's a 49¢ per share spread. The arbitrageur would buy SC and sell BD short. *Get out your handy calculator and figure how many shares you would have to handle to make a worthwhile profit.*

• Calculate the "expected value" of the deal. This involves the odds of completion and the ultimate rate of return, usually annualized for easier comparisons. Professionals look for 20% to 30% on their investment.

Example: Company A offers $30 cash for each share of Company B, then selling at $20. After the announcement, Company B stock jumps to $27. At this point, the speculator hopes for $3 per share if the offer is accepted but, if the deal is nixed, he would lose $7 per share because the stock would probably fall back to its old level.

To determine the "expected value," the arbitrageur sets the odds—say, 80% for completion and 20% for failure. He multiplies the percent amount he might win or lose; to win: 80% times $3.00 or $2.40; to lose: 20% times $7 or $1.40. The difference between the two figures is $1.00 per share. If he buys Company B stock, he divides $1 by 27 to get a return of 3% in four months or 11.2% a year. That's below the target so he would probably pass this one up.

Example: On March 18, Atlantic Richfield made a tender offer for Anaconda stock at $27 each for six million shares. Anaconda stock was at 23.

The arbitrageurs stepped in with an offer of $26 per share. The holders sold despite the probability of a better price a few weeks later. The speculators then resold at 27 on March 31 for a 5.8% profit—or a whopping 163% annual return.

But if the transaction had fallen through after the purchase, the arbitrageurs would have been stuck with the stock, which probably would have dropped in price.

What to Do About Defunct Securities

The typical defunct security is as worthless as a buggy whip, but every now and then one provides a windfall for its owner.

An estimated 2,000 defunct companies still hold money for holders of stocks and bonds. The most fertile field is railroads and recently, with the soaring prices of gold and silver, shares of old mining concerns.

Example: Chinese railway bonds issued in 1908 and 1910 for the Tientsin-Pukou line are curious securities which were printed in German, denominated in 20 British pounds each and "guaranteed" by the old Chinese government. The bonds stopped paying interest in 1937, but they still trade on the London Stock Exchange.

Take another look at those forgotten securities in grandma's trunk in the attic. You might be lucky if China decides to honor debts of the previous regime.

If you find an old yellowed certificate in your files, it may pay you to contact firms that specialize in ferreting out obsolete securities. These organizations maintain extensive files of out-of-business corporations and, for a fee, will trace your stock. For $15 per issue, they'll give you a prompt appraisal:

R. M. Smythe Co., 170 Broadway, New York, New York 10038.

Stock Market Information Service, 235 Dorchester Boulevard East, Montreal, Quebec, Canada.

To check any old security, ask your local library for a copy of *Manual of Valuable and Worthless Securities,* by Robert D. Fisher. There are 2.5 million securities listed.

CHAPTER 11

How to Read and Profit from the Annual Report

The single best source of investment information is the corporate annual report. In a 15-minute check, you can learn whether to hold or sell a stock; in 30 minutes of study, you can decide whether to buy more shares now or wait until later to do so.

The latest reports are more rewarding than before. As the result of new standards set by the SEC and the Financial Accounting Standards Board, the report must contain more detailed information: source of volume and profits; data on off-balance sheet financing such as store/plant/equipment leases; allocations of hard-to-check sources of expenditures for interest and research and development.

In all areas, look for:

Trends: in sales, earnings, dividends, accounts receivable and debts.

Information: *from the tables:* corporate financial strength and operating success or failure; *from the text:* explanations of what happened during the year and what management expects in the future.

Positives: new plants, products, personnel and programs.

Negatives: plant closings, sales of subsidiaries, discontinuance of products and future needs for financing.

Always read the report Chinese style: from back to front. Start with the auditor's report. If there are hedging phrases such as "except for" or "subject to," be cautious.

They can signal future problems and/or write-offs.

Next, review the financial summary (usually toward the end). This is a digest of financial data for the past five or 10 years and provides an overall view of corporate performance.

In the stock market, past is often prologue. The corporation with a long, fairly consistent record of profitable growth can be expected to do as well, or better, in the years ahead and thus prove to be a worthwhile holding. The erratic performer is likely to continue to move from high to low profits (or losses) and should be considered a speculation.

For comparison, here are two major corporations with statistics digested from their annual reports starting with the most recent data (Year 5) and going back four years.

• **Company I (for Investment)** is a financially strong, diversified corporation that has increased its sales, earnings and dividends regularly. Its stock is the kind that should be in every investment portfolio.

• **Company S (for Speculation)** is a debt-heavy corporation with a cyclical pattern of earnings and deficits. Its stock is not a suitable investment but, under some conditions, may be an attractive speculation.

The categories were selected to indicate areas for review:

Statement of Income. This explains how much money

FINANCIAL SUMMARIES
Statement of Income

	COMPANY I (Invesment)					COMPANY S (Speculation)				
	Year 5	Year 4	Year 3	Year 2	Year 1	Year 5	Year 4	Year 3	Year 2	Year 1
Revenues	$6,314	$5,288	$4,690	$4,192	$3,541	$5,370	$4.248	$4,977	$5,381	$4,138
Operating Income	536	444	373	333	280	222	491	529	803	554
Depreciation	78	64	57	52	47	300	276	234	211	196
Net Income/Share	2.41	2.13	1.86	1.71	1.55	(10.27D)	3.85	5.54	7.85	4.72
Dividends per Share	.96	.82	.74	.68½	.62¾	1.50	2.00	2.75	2.30	1.65

Balance Sheet

	Year 5	Year 4	Year 3	Year 2	Year 1	Year 5	Year 4	Year 3	Year 2	Year 1
Gross Property	1,243	1,067	928	822	730	6,402	6,450	6,168	5,687	5,309
Inventories	729	596	516	502	412	626	834	620	510	443
Acc'ts Receivable	625	491	434	383	339	631	421	402	497	454
Current Assets	1,574	1,291	1,107	997	826	1,496	1,657	1,388	1,682	1,376
Cur. Liabilities	718	571	456	402	346	978	784	719	1,032	713
Long-Term Debt	297	258	268	275	208	1,155	1,023	857	648	663
Shareholders'Equity (Book Value/Share)	13.39	12.15	10.62	9.55	8.56	49.93	61.66	59.82	57.02	51.59

All figures are in millions so add 000

came in and, in broad terms, how the results affected shareholders.

Revenues, primarily from sales of products. With inflation, these totals should rise annually but, now and then, lower revenues may be a sign that the company is concentrating on profits rather than volume.

Operating income. This is what the company has left over after paying production, sales and administrative expenses. Use this to determine:

1. The source of earnings: whether entirely from operations, the result of accounting changes or the inclusion of the proceeds of the sale of buildings/division, etc. Neither of these last two reflect management's money-making skill.

Watch for trick data—e.g., a utility reported a 27¢ per share rise in net income but, as explained in a footnote, 14¢ of that extra income was the result of a new billing policy whereby the income included estimated profits from services rendered but not yet billed!

2. The profit margin: the ratio of income to sales. To calculate this, divide income by revenues. In Year 5: for Company I, 8.5%; for Company S, 4.1%. Note, too, that I's PM remained fairly steady over the years but that of S bounced up and down.

Depreciation. This represents the accounting allocations for wear and tear of equipment and property. It is tax-free money that will be used for replacement and expansion so should be an ever-rising figure. Watch for a sharp shift in any one year, as this could boost reported (but not real) profits.

Net income. This is the well-known "bottom line," expressed on a per share basis. If earnings are flat or down, read the president's message to find out why and what steps were taken to improve the situation. This is a key factor in the trend of corporate profitability.

Even if earnings are up, remember that they should be discounted because of the effects of inflation: i.e. a stated 15% gain should be reduced to a real increase of about half as much. You'll be surprised at how many corporations fail this test.

Dividends. Here again, watch the trend more than the dollars. Company I has raised its payout by about 10% a year while Company S paid out less last year than five years ago.

Check the percentage of dividends to earnings. Except with utilities, a dividend of more than 50% means too little money is left for future growth. And when a company reports a deficit and still pays a dividend (as Company S did), watch out.

Balance sheet. This shows the financial condition of the corporation and, here, spotlights the substantial difference in assets required by industries.

Gross property. Usually, ever-higher values reflect expansion, replacements and acquisitions. But a lower figure could be beneficial if it is the result of the sale of unprofitable operations or unused plants. Company S, a heavy-industry manufacturer, needed six times as expensive properties as did Company I. But the important factor is not the size of assets but the earnings they produce.

Inventories. With inflation, these should increase at the same rate as sales. If there is a sudden rise, check the text of the report to find out why. Management may be smart in stocking up in anticipation of higher costs of raw materials. Or it may have miscalculated customer demand. As a rule of thumb, a 10% jump in inventories equals a 30% decline in net earnings.

With Company I, that sharp increase in inventories in Year 5 reflected the acquisition of a company which needed more goods in order to move into new marketing areas.

Accounts receivable. When these rise at a rate faster than that of sales, it's a yellow signal. With the current high interest rates, financing customers can be mighty costly and can lead to a future cash squeeze or write-offs. Refer to the president's letter to learn if the increase represents higher sales in the future.

Current assets and liabilities. These show cash and liquid assets and currently payable bills. Generally, the ratio should be 2:1. That means that, after all accounts are paid, 50% of the current assets are available to stockholders. Company I's ratio is well over double, but that of Company S is a marginal 1.5:1.

The current ratio varies with the type of industry. Utilities and retail stores have rapid cash inflows and high turnovers so can operate effectively with low ratios. Again, watch the trend.

Long-term debt. This is an important check of financial strength. The lower the debt, the less the fixed payments will cut into profits. It's true that current debt will be repaid in ever-cheaper dollars but when long-term loans keep rising, profits should be up even more. The money has to be repaid sometime.

Stockholders' equity or book value. This is the net worth behind each share of common stock: what's left after deducting all liabilities from all assets.

This is a key figure. It can be used to calculate two very important indices: profit rate (PR), the return on invested capital, and Earned Growth Rate (EGR), the annual rate at which retained earnings are plowed back into the corporation.

As explained in the chapter on growth stocks:

• To find the PR, divide the per share income by the per share book value. In Year 4, Company I reported per share profits of $2.13 and book value of $12.15 per share. Divide 2.13 by 12.15 to get a PR of 17.5%. This is well above the 12.12.1% PR of the 30 DJIA companies for the past decade and shows why Company I is solid, worthwhile investment.

• To find the EGR, subtract the dividend from the earnings, then divide by book value: 2.13 − .82 = 1.31 divided by 12.15 = 10.8%. This is nearly double the 6.6% EGR of the Dow companies in the 1970s.

With Company S, the PR was a measly 6.2% and the EGR a weak 3.2%. That's why its stock is a speculation.

Reading the Report

When you review the text, you can get an idea of the kind of people who are managing your money, learn what and why they did, or did not, do, and some idea of future prospects. If you save previous annual reports, compare what was predicted and what happened.

Always read the president's message and look for possible danger signals such as:

Unfulfilled promises. If there were failures, there should be logical explanations. Management is not always right in its decisions but, in financial matters, frankness is the base for confidence. If you cannot believe the chief executive officer, do not hold the company's stock.

Double-talk. Clichés are integral parts of business writing but they should not be substitutes for proper explanations. If you find such meaningless phrases as "a year of transition" or "we have identified the problem and are taking corrective steps," be skeptical.

Inadequate information. For competitive reasons, no president can reveal everything but he should not neglect to mention important problems such as a major lawsuit, governmental litigation, delays in operation of a new plant, etc. These subjects are too important for footnotes alone.

Projections. Be wary when any chief executive promises "a 25% increase in sales" or "earning of $3.00 per share." Modern business is too competitive and too subject to unexpected pressures for such assurance. Make your own calculations on the basis of past performance and never be as optimistic as your broker.

In much the same way, denigrate overenthusiasm about new products, processes or personnel. Usually it takes at least three years to translate new items into sizeable sales and profits, to get new plants running smoothly and to find out whether the reputation of the new marketing vice president is deserved.

Follow-Up

Once you've read several annual reports and made notes, take advantage of what you've learned.

First, sell any of your present holdings if you cannot say a loud "OK" to the three original criteria: profitability, growth, and character. There are plenty of other opportunities that will prove more rewarding and make you and your spouse feel more comfortable.

Second, ask your broker for recommendations on new investments. When you have narrowed this list to five companies, get their annual reports and start your homework over again. This should be easier since you will know what to look for, and, presumably, the broker's research department has screened its selections.

Third, review your final choices against the stocks you continue to hold. You may prefer to add to your present portfolio. But do not become too enthusiastic about new choices. As far as you are concerned, their management has yet to prove itself. And always concentrate on quality and value as shown by a strong financial position and high, consistent, growing profits.

CHAPTER 12

Preferred Stocks: Better for Corporations Than for Individuals

A preferred stock is just what the name states. It has preference on all income available after the payment of bond interest and amortization and before dividend payments on the common stock. It is a "middle" security: halfway between a bond and a common stock.

Most preferred dividends are fixed, but when the corporation does not earn enough money, they may be skipped. Usually they are cumulative and can be paid when profits become ample.

Compared to common stocks, preferreds are safer, but unless they are convertible to common stocks, they cannot provide the ever higher income of common stocks in growing, profitable companies. In addition, that fixed income is vulnerable to changes in the interest rate. When the cost of money goes up, the value of preferred stocks goes down.

To individuals, the attractions of preferred stocks are: their low cost, typically $100 per share (but occasionally $25 or $50) compared to the $1,000 or $5,000 face value of bonds, and their more frequent payments, quarterly dividends rather than semi-annual interest. *To corporations,* preferred stocks offer the tax shelter of dividends in that 85% of the income received is deductible. Thus a corporation in the 46% tax bracket can enjoy an after-tax return of 93.1%. That's why preferreds are favored investments for life insurance companies, mutual savings banks and all types of corporations from industrial giants to professional organizations of physicians, dentists and so on.

Possible long-term advantage: If Congress should reduce the double taxation of corporate dividends, by permitting companies to deduct dividends from taxable income, preferred stocks could become a cheaper financing vehicle for corporations and more rewarding for investors.

Checkpoints for Preferred Stocks

In selecting preferred stocks, look at these factors:
Quality: those rated BBB or better. The difference in

yield between well and poorly rated preferreds is seldom significant. The slightly lower dividend rate is more than offset by the added safety.

Low debt: capitalization that is not overloaded with bonds. Since bond interest must be paid first, the lower the debt ratio, the safer the preferred stocks.

Call provision. Be sure that there are no special items, in small type, that permit early redemption. Usually, there will be few restrictions with preferred stocks of large, listed corporations but you cannot be so sure with those of new, small companies that have had difficulty in obtaining capital.

Take nothing for granted: call protection can be illusory. In recent years, some utilities have taken advantage of obscure provisions in their preferred charters to refund prior to the expiration of the five-year, nonrefundable call date.

Sinking fund. This permits the corporation to buy up a portion of the outstanding preferreds each year so that the entire issue is retired before the stated maturity date: i.e. starting five years after the original sale, the company buys back 5% of the stock annually for 20 years. Usually, these yields will be less than those of straight preferreds.

Corporate surplus. When this becomes substantial, there will be pressure to retire some of the preferred. For the common stockholder, this means less interest to be paid and thus a chance for higher dividends. For the preferred shareholder, prospects of redemption tend to raise the market price if the stock is selling below par.

Junior preference issues. Many of these permit refunding prior to the stated date through the issue of common stock. These carry a lower rating and tend to be more volatile than their senior companions.

STRAIGHT PREFERRED STOCKS

COMPANY	Dividend	S&P Rating	Recent Price	Recent Yield
American Brands	$2.75	BBB	23	11.9%
A. T. & T.	3.64	AA	33	11.0
Beneficial Finance	2.50	A—	18	13.9
Commonwealth Edison	12.75	BBB	90	14.2
General Telephone	2.48	BBB	18	13.8
Iowa-Illinois G&E	2.31	A—	15	15.4
Johns-Manville	5.40	BBB+	44	12.3
Niagara-Mohawk	3.60	BBB	24	15.0
Penna. P&L	4.50	BBB+	33	13.6
Public Service E&G	1.40	A+	10	14.0
Utah P&L	2.80	AA—	20	14.0

SOURCE: Standard & Poor's; New York Stock Exchange

Marketability. Preferred stocks of quality corporations listed on major exchanges are actively traded. Those of small companies, especially when sold OTC, may have thin markets and be subject to sharp price differentials. You can see this by the daily reports, where price changes can be as much as two points—far more than the swings of common stocks.

Full voting rights. Preferred stockholders should not be shut out from having a say in the management of the company. The NYSE lists only preferreds with the right to vote if the company gets into trouble.

Restrictions on common dividends. Adequate working capital and a satisfactory surplus should be required before dividends on the common stock can be paid. This helps protect you against a dip in earnings.

Restrictions on new preferreds or bonds. There should be some workable provision to limit management from issuing new preferred stock or bonds—preferably approval by at least two-thirds of the preferred shareholders.

Premiums. Always consider the value of the preferred in relation to straight debt issues. As a rule of thumb, buy preferreds only when the yield is 25% greater than that of bonds of similar quality (or the same company).

Heed the counsel of fundamentalist Benjamin Graham: "The preferred holder lacks both the legal claim of the bondholder and the profit possibilities of a common stockholder. All investment-grade preferreds should be bought by corporations, not by individuals."

Experienced broker. If you plan substantial investments in preferred stocks, deal with a brokerage firm which has a research department that follows preferreds and can provide you with fully detailed information on available shares. Many registered representatives neither understand nor like preferreds.

Higher fees for brokers. Indiana and Michigan Electric paid Wall Street firms $890,000 in commissions to sell its $100 million bond issue but $1.34 million to market its $40 million preferred stock issue.

Furthermore, brokers are allowed to net twice as much for low-par preferreds as they do for the standard $100-par preferreds of equivalent quality.

How to Make Up to 36% a Year

Sharp traders can get as many as 12 dividends a year by rolling over preferred stocks. This extra income is possible because, unlike accrued interest on bonds, dividends on preferred stocks are not included in the sale price. By buying the shares just before the dividend date, you get the full payout. Then, you sell and buy another preferred with an upcoming payment date. Because of commission costs, it's best to deal in large units of 500 shares or more.

In theory, those 12 annual dividends could yield 36%. Realistically, however, you'll probably have to settle for about 8 checks a year. With a 12% yield, that will total a 24% annual rate of return.

Timing is important because, after the payout date, the price of the preferred will drop, typically from 25% to 50% of the dividend. Thus, a 12% preferred might trade at 103 before the dividend and drop back to 101½ in the next couple of days. If you sell, you will take a small loss. If you wait a week or so, you may not lose anything but you will not be able to roll over as often.

This tactic is best for corporate investments because, as noted, the corporation pays taxes on only 15% of the dividends. For a corporation in the 46% tax bracket, that 24% yield would be equivalent to 41.38% taxable income.

Unique Mutual Fund for Tax Benefits

The 85% tax deduction allowed corporations on dividend income has triggered new types of investment companies: *Qualified Dividend Portfolio I* (common stocks) and *Qualified Dividend Portfolio II* (preferred stocks). Their objective is to provide income that qualifies as dividends and is therefore eligible for the tax deduction.

The unusual aspect of QDPs is that funds are invested for maximum income through dividends and short-term capital gains. QDPs can do this because Federal tax laws treat both short-term gains and interest income as dividends as long as they pass through a regulated investment company. The QDPs can sell all holdings in which there are capital gains within 12 months of purchase, take the profits and their tax benefits and, if the securities still look good, buy them back.

The tax savings are dramatic. A corporation that invests $4 million for a 9% total return ($360,000) in a mix of capital gains and dividends would be liable for income taxes of $80,355. With the same sum in QDPs, the tax would be only $24,840. Similar savings are possible for individual investors with smaller accounts. There's one danger: the value of the portfolio could decrease—but that could happen anyhow!

Comparison of Results of Account Managed Internally (AMI) and Same Investment in QDP Fund

Type Income	Funds	Gross	Tax Rate	Net
Dividends	AMI	$195,000	6.9%	$181,545
	QDP	195,000	6.9	181,545
Interest	AMI	65,000	46.0	35,100
	QDP	65,000	6.9	60,515
Short-term gains	AMI	50,000	46.0	27,000
	QDP	50,000	6.9	46,550
Long-term gains	AMI	50,000	28.0	36,000
	QDP	50,000	6.9	46,550

SOURCE: The Vanguard Group, Valley Forge, Pa.

CHAPTER 13

Convertibles: Income Plus Potential Appreciation

Convertible securities (CVs) combine the features of senior securities, with their fixed income, and the growth potential of common stocks. As the name implies, CVs can be converted into shares of the related common stock at specified ratios, usually until a specified date, but occasionally indefinitely. Convertible bonds (usually called debentures) represent a debt of the issuing company. They can be viewed as a debt with a warrant attached or as an issue of stock with a put option. In most cases, both types of CVs are callable prior to maturity but not during the first few years after issue. This encourages the initial sale.

Convertible preferred stocks are similar but not as secure, for they are not as likely to be paid off in case of corporate liquidation. Their big plus is their lower price: $25 to $100 each, compared to a usual par value of $1,000 for CV bonds.

CVs are a conservative way to play the equity market and an aggressive way to play the fixed-income market. Investors like the comparatively high yields; speculators become excited about the possible gains from a rise in the price of the related common stock. CVs are best in bull markets, can be profitable, with careful management, in bear markets, but in flat markets are seldom worthwhile. The key is the ability of the corporation to make more money. Otherwise, the losses can be substantial.

Usually, CVs are protected against major dilutions (over 5%) of the related common stock (because of stock splits or stock dividends) by appropriate adjustments of the conversion terms.

Note: When the term *convertible* is used alone in this chapter, it refers to both preferred stocks and bonds.

Value Determinants

CVs have been extolled as permitting the investor to "have his cake and eat it, too." This optimism is based on the theory that there are two value determinants:

Investment value: the estimated price, usually set by an investment service, at which the CV would be selling if it had no conversion feature. It is supposed to be a floor price under which the CV will not decline regardless of the price action of the underlying common stock. This investment value is always related to the prevailing interest rate, so it will fluctuate. Thus, when the stock is selling well below the conversion price, an 8% CV, issued at par, will trade at about 66 when the yield on straight bonds is about 12%.

Conversion value: the amount a CV would be worth if it were exchanged for shares of the common stock. It is almost always higher than the investment value. A bond convertible into 50 shares of common stock has a conversion value of $1,000 when the stock is at 20 per share. If the price of the stock rises to 30, the conversion value will be $1,500—probably more because of the ever-present element of hope.

The point of conversion depends on the yield, not the market prices of the securities. *Example:* Whistle Stop 6s, '98 entitle the holder to 30 shares of common, now selling at 36 and paying a dividend of $2 a year. The CV would probably be trading at around $1,100.

The yields of both the bond and common are the same: $60. If the stock's payout is raised to $2.25, the income will be $67.50 for the stock versus $60 for the bond. It's time to think about a swap.

Always keep in mind that: *(a)* there will be a constant yield on the CV as long as the corporation is solvent; *(b)* there may be a boost in the dividend of the common stock.

A CV will usually sell at the higher of its two current values and, in a strong market, at a premium. But don't let anyone kid you; by their nature, all CVs are better speculations than investments. Despite what some brokers may tell you, CVs are no sure road to financial success.

As one corporate treasurer told me, "With marginal corporations, convertibles can be the worst of all possible worlds. They are debt obligations with the potential of diluting the common stock if the proceeds of the issue fail to produce profitable growth. They complicate the capital structure by adding another layer of securities. By and large, CVs are issued by companies that cannot get the lowest rate on straight bonds or can wangle extra tax benefits. And when you pay a premium of 25%, you are, in effect, betting that the Dow Average will move up from 800 to 1000 in a relatively short time."

Definitions Used with Convertibles

Issue. This names the issuing company, the interest rate of the bonds and the date of maturity when the bond will be redeemed. Some securities have a deadline for conversion. After that date, you may get fewer shares of stock.

Rating. This is based on a company's financial well-being, as considered by a financial service (for details, see the chapter on corporate and government bonds). The top rating is Aaa, then Aa, A, Baa, etc. The B ratings flash a warning signal. All C ratings apply to bonds of poor standing.

Amount outstanding. The dollar value of the bonds now outstanding. As a general rule, be wary of small issues—less than $20 million. Their market will be limited.

Call price. This is the price you receive if all or part of the bonds are redeemed in advance of the maturity date: 102.63 means you get $1,026.30 per bond.

Conversion price. To determine how many shares of common stock your bond will convert to, divide the conversion price into the par value ($1,000). Thus, a conversion price of 50 equals 20 shares of common. Your broker has printed material to save you the arithmetic.

Conversion premium. The percentage of difference between the conversion value and the market price of the CV. With Dayco, each CV can be swapped for 47.8 shares of common stock. When the common is trading at 12¼ ($12.25), the conversion value is $585.55 ($12.25 × 47.8).

Since the CV is selling at 61½ ($615), the difference is about $30. Divide $30 by $615 to get a premium of 4.88% (rounded out, in the table, to 5%).

Yield of CV. The interest rate divided by the current price. With Dayco, 6% at $615, this is 9.76% (rounded out to 9.8%).

Yield of common. This is the dividend on the stock divided by the price of the stock. With Dayco, 56¢ per share at 12¼, it's 4.57%, rounded out to 4.6%.

Note: These data, plus other information such as the value of the CV based on the price of the common stock and the value of the common based on the price of the CV, are available in printed reports from Moody's and Standard & Poor's. Ask your broker for a copy or check your local library.

Formula for Premium on new CVs

To calculate the premium on a new issue, use this formula:

PC = the price of the common stock
SC = the number of shares by conversion
PV = the par value of the convertible
$P = the dollar premium you pay
CV = the present value of the convertible
 P = the percentage of premium

$$CV = PC \times SC;$$
$$PV - CV = \$P;$$
$$\frac{\$P}{CV} = P$$

Example: Tall Timbers convertible debentures 8% due in 1996, rated A, are selling at 100. Each bond is convertible into 32.39 shares of common stock, which is trading at 29. To find the percentage of premium:

$$CV = 29 \times 32.39 = 939.31$$
$$1000 - 939 = 61$$
$$\frac{61}{939} = 6.5\%$$

This is a low premium for a CV of a well-rated corporation. If the corporate prospects are good and the

---

KEY DATA ON CONVERTIBLE DEBENTURES

Company / Issue	Rating*	Price		Call Price	Conversion		Yield	
		CV	Common		Ratio	Premium	CV	Common
Am. Airlines 5¼, '98	Ba	62	13	100	40.0	19%	8.5%	None
Citicorp. 5¼, '00	NR**	64 1/8	22 5/8	103.75	16	16	9.0	6.3
Dayco 6, '94	B	61 1/2	12 1/4	102.33	47.8	5	9.8	4.6
Eastern Air 11¾, '05	B	83 1/3	8 1/2	111.75	76.9	28	14.1	None
U.S. Steel 5¾, '01	Baa	61 1/2	30 3/4	104.60	15.9	26	9.4	6.5
Wickes 9, '99	Ba	78	14	106.30	44.2	26	11.5	7.4

* Moody's Investors Service   ** Not Rated

SOURCE: Merrill Lynch Market Letter

stock is attracting investor interest, Tall Timber CVs could be worthwhile.

CVs Benefit the Issuer

In judging the merits of any investment, it is wise to consider the benefits to the issuer. With common stock, shareholders are partners; with bonds, they are creditors. With CVs, they are potential shareholders with hopes sustained by promise of a steady income. CVs are a call on the stock, so they are alternatives to common stocks, not bonds.

Generally, CVs enable the corporation to:

1. Sell stock at a higher price than could be obtained with a straight issue. To raise $10 million through an equity offering, a company would have to sell 100,000 shares of common at $100 (disregarding financing costs). Since CVs usually command a premium of about 15%, the $10 million could be raised by selling CVs at 115. When converted, they would require only 85,000 shares of common! In effect, the corporation is selling common stock at higher than current prices, and without presently diluting equity.

2. Obtain a lower interest rate. There's usually a substantial savings in the interest rate of CVs as compared to straight bonds. Depending on the caliber of the issuing company and market conditions, CVs bear interest rates as much as 2% below those of regular bonds. On a $10 million issue, that means a savings of $100,000 to $200,000 a year.

3. Achieve gradual dilution of the common stock. The company hopes the funds obtained from the CVs will enable greater and more profitable growth. When the price of the common stock rises above the conversion point, some CV holders will convert and the dilution will be largely offset by higher earnings. At the end of the option period, all CVs become stock, so the debt, if debentures, will be wiped out. Almost all CV debentures are unsecured and usually subordinate to other debts of the issuing corporation (this assumes that the CVs are not redeemed earlier).

4. Secure tax benefits. Financing by CV bonds rather than by preferred or common stock has tax benefits: bond interest is tax deductible, while dividends on both preferred and common stock must be paid *after* all costs and corporate taxes.

There may also be situations where a corporation can use convertibles to borrow millions of dollars with no, or little, interest. Here are two recent examples:

In May 1980, when yields of new corporate bonds were 14%, Wang Laboratories floated $50 million of 8% debentures with a conversion price of 38⅜ when the common stock was at 33. For such a fast-expanding computer company, this 17% premium was in line so the issue sold out quickly. Investors were happy with the modest yield and prospects of long-term appreciation.

But in October, before the first interest date, Wang called the entire offer. Since the stock was selling between 51 and 64, investors averaged gains of 47%. But this was far below the 72% profit that they would have made if they bought the stock directly. The big winner was Wang because the company had the use of the $50

million for 4½ months without paying one cent of interest. This saved the company about $2.6 million!

Similar "opportunities" have not been so rewarding. When Digital Equipment tried to force an exchange, a few months after the new issue of 8⅞% CVs, investors balked. They pointed out that this would dilute the number of shares of common stock by 12% and dumped their shares. When the stock price fell 10 points, the swap was canceled.

Advice: With all CVs, check the call provisions to be sure that there are at least four years of protection.

The corporate benefits can be even greater when the new CVs can be exchanged for stock in another company. Textron, Inc. issued $85 million in 7¾% debentures, due in 2005, and convertible to shares of Allied Chemical which were held by Textron. On the surface, this appeared reasonable but, under IRS rules, such an exchange qualifies as a capital gain so, when the swap is made, there will be taxes to be paid. The real winner was Textron.

The original cost of the Allied stock was $61 million: $42.50 per share. If Textron had sold the stock at the current price of $50, the company would have made an $11 million gain. After $3 million in taxes, the net return would be $69 million.

By using CVs, with an 18% premium, Textron boosted the per share stock value to 59 and thus netted $84.6 million, almost $16 million more. This maneuver did require first-year interest payments of $6.5 million but, since the issue proceeds were used to pay high-cost, short-term debt, the after-tax cost was about $3.5 million. This was reduced further by the $3.2 million dividends from the Allied stock: 85% tax-free. *Result:* shrewd Textron got the use of an extra $16 million for about $500,000, a net cost of 3%!

Checkpoints for CVs

The common stock. The plus value of any CV lies in the worth of its related common stock. If a stock is speculative, the CV will be risky, too. If it's a stock of a stodgy company, the conversion privileges of the CV won't make the corporation grow faster or more profitably.

Buy CVs only of companies whose common stocks you want to own on the basis of quality, value and prospects.

Trade-off. With all CVs, the investor faces a trade-off between the premium and the yield: i.e. the difference between the income of the convertible and the dividend on the related stock. Professionals look for issues where the spread can be made up in about three years.

Example: A $1,000 par value, 9% debenture can be exchanged for 20 shares of common stock. The stock is at 42 so the difference is $160 ($1,000 − $840). That's a 19% premium.

The stock pays a $2 dividend or a total of $40 if a swap were made. The difference between the $90 interest and the $40 dividends is $50 a year.

To calculate how long it will take for the extra income from the interest to make up the conversion premium, divide $160 by $50 to get 3.2 years. Thus, with a prosperous company, that 19% premium is acceptable.

Duration of the conversion privilege. If the conversion period is short, the company may not be able to show growth and profits fast enough for the common stock to appreciate to the point at which the option will be valuable. If you are looking for long-term gains, you may be better off with the common stock than with the CV, especially if there is a chance of an early call at a price which is well below the market value.

Don't assume that the conversion period runs for the life of the bond. Sometimes, the convertibility of a debenture, preferred or related warrant lapses before the senior security matures. Often, too, the conversion price rises so that today's attractive option may be purely theoretical several years hence.

Buying time. In weak stock markets and in the first phases of a business downturn, it's best to concentrate on CVs of companies in defensive industries: utilities, food processors, food chains, dairy product makers, finance companies, etc.

In strong markets and in the early stages of business recovery, maximum capital gains are generally found in CVs of companies in cyclical industries: steel, machinery, aerospace, construction, etc.

Be wary in ALL bull markets. When stock prices are high, new issues of CVs are floated to take advantage of investor optimism. If you buy new CVs, you may pick up a few points quickly but the long-term prospects are likely to be based on rather enthusiastic projections. *Be sure the related stock is not selling at or near its all-time high.*

In bear markets, relax and be patient. You will get a reasonable yield and if the company moves ahead, the price of its common stock will rise with an upmove of the overall market. Remember: In most cases, CVs are issued by corporations that have difficulty floating straight debt.

Interest rates. The toughest time to own CVs is when the cost of money is rising. A small upmove of ½% will cause a drop of 5 to 7 points in the investment value of the CV.

Comparable yields. As a rule of thumb, the yield of the CV should be no more than 25% below that of a nonconvertible issue of comparable quality or the price of a nonconvertible bond.

When you find a bargain, be cautious. Once in a while, you can find a winner but usually there's a reason (logical or not) for the low price of any security. There is no free lunch in Wall Street . . . well, hardly ever, and then, not usually planned.

Timing. The investor should make the swap when the income from the dividends on the common stock is greater than the interest of the debentures or the dividends of the preferred.

Example: PDQ $4.00 preferred is convertible to 1.05 shares of common stock. The owner of 100 shares of preferred is sure of $400 annual income. By converting, he can own 105 shares of common that, with a $5.00 per share dividend, brings in $525.

The speculator must stay alert. When the price of the CV moves above its conversion value or call price, he should act immediately: sell or set a stop-loss order. The

company may start redemption to improve its balance sheet or the price of the stock may drop.

Example: In 1978, when airline stocks were popular, Pan American 9⅞, '96s, convertible into 166.67 shares of stock, were trading at $1,791.70 when the stock was at 10¾. The bond redemption price was $1,086.20. This was the time to take a profit.

A few months later, when PN stock fell to 6, the debentures were down to $1,000, so some folks missed the boat.

Pros: As Stated by Some Enthusiasts

Floor but no ceiling. High-grade CVs do have some sort of price floor but almost no price ceiling. But this applies to their common stocks, too. In bear markets, the values of CVs can fall just as fast, and far, as the common stock and, when interest rates rise, their declines are almost certain.

More favorable margin requirements. Usually, brokers require less collateral for CVs than for common stocks and most banks will loan more: normally, 80% of their value compared to 50% for stocks. Thus, there's greater leverage than with stocks. And, when the yields are high, the income will reduce the net payment to the lender.

Lower commissions. As bonds, CVs carry commissions that are below those for an equal dollar amount used to buy stock. To purchase five CVs selling at 80 might cost $25. The same $4,000 used to acquire 200 shares of stock at 20 would cost about twice as much.

N.B.: Do not be lured by the no-commissions of new CV issues. That handling cost is built into the offering price. The best CVs to buy are those in the after market, when they are selling at deep discounts.

Worthwhile investments for your children and grandchildren. While you live, the income is ample and after you're gone, your heirs can hope for appreciation.

Cons: Based on Experience

Large investment. Most brokers charge a minimum $25 commission for buying or selling CVs, so it's expensive to buy fewer than five bonds at a time ($5,000 at par). Above that figure, commissions drop to $2.50 each.

Specialized analysis. The profitable selection of CVs requires careful comparison and analysis. You have to study the CVs as well as the issuing corporation. If your broker does not have specialists in CVs, his firm probably relies on outside services which use computers to make their selections. Or you can watch for weekly or periodic reports issued by investment advisory services such as Moody's, Standard & Poor's, United Business Service, Babson's Reports and Canadian Business Service.

Limited marketability. Both CV debentures and preferreds have limited investor acceptance. As a result, their trading volume is modest and prices can swing substantially. That's an important consideration if you have to sell in a hurry. Take a look at the daily quotations and you'll see that, with many CVs, prices can fall (and, occasionally, rise) rapidly: 2 or 3 points a day.

If you plan to speculate with CVs, check the trading

volume and price movements over a couple of months. With investments, of course, temporary fluctuations are not important.

High premiums. The prices of both CV preferreds and bonds are often overpriced because of their well-publicized advantages. This is especially true with new issues in prosperous times. Naturally, CVs are issued when the underwriter feels they can command the maximum price.

Follow these criteria:

• *Premium of 15% or less:* risk is small with quality or well-rated (B or better) companies.

• *Premium of 15% to 25%:* getting risky. The CV yield should be high enough to justify the risk or the prospects for the company should be very good.

• *Premium over 25%:* the yield should be relatively high and corporate prospects outstanding. Otherwise, you're speculating.

How to Project Returns with CVs

Here's an example of how to guesstimate what your profits will be with a $1,000 debenture convertible to 25 shares of common stock, now trading at 32.

If the stock goes up:

By the second year after the issue of the CV, the company reports a hefty rise in profits and continuing good prospects. As a result, the price of the common stock jumps 25% to $40 per share. The CV goes up too, but at a slower rate, say 20%, from 100 to 120. There is good reason for this. As the bond price increases, the CV acts more like a stock and less like a bond. The investment value is of diminishing importance, the risk increases and the yield declines—all factors which tend to hold back the price of the senior security. *Conversion is unrealistic but some holders might want to sell the CV and take their profits.*

XYZ continues to do well, and with a buoyant stock market, the price of the common stock hits $60 per share:

an 87½% gain. But the CV price goes up only 50% to 150. At this point, virtually all the bondlike characteristics are lost and the CV is interchangeable with the stock—as indicated by the disappearance of the conversion premium.

Before you decide to convert, check the comparative yields of the CV and stock. Interest is $50 per year. The dividend on the stock must be $2.00 per share to equal that income!

When a CV's conversion value and market price become the same, the stock and the CV should move up and down together.

When a CV sells with a negative conversion premium (that is, below its conversion value), professional traders move in for arbitrage. They buy the CV and simultaneously sell the stock short. Converting the CVs enables them to replace stock borrowed for the short sale.

Example: If the XYZ CV is priced at 145 while the conversion value is $1,500 the trader will buy 10 bonds for $14,500. He will then sell short 250 shares of XYZ common for $15,000 for a quick profit of $500!

If the stock goes down:

The other possibility is that XYZ runs into trouble and its profits dwindle so that the price of the common stock is cut in half to 16. The price of the CV will fall but will be cushioned by its investment value of 75: a 25% dip.

The price of the CV might go lower as the investment value would have to be readjusted. If the interest rate rose sharply, the price of the CV would fall even further.

If the CV had started out with a high coupon, say 9%, and the prime interest rate declined substantially, the price of the CV would rise as a reflection of its investment value. The reverse would be true if the CV originally carried a low rate and the interest rate rose sharply.

The Advantages of CV Preferreds

CV preferreds have many of the above advantages (except tax savings) for corporations PLUS:

WHAT A CV IS WORTH

		At Issue		Stock Goes Up		Stock Goes Way Up		Stock Goes Down	
Market price of CV	100	($1,000)		120	($1,200)	150	($1,500)	75	($750)
Yield	8%			6.66%	$\dfrac{80}{1200}$	5.33%	$\dfrac{80}{1500}$	10.66%	$\dfrac{80}{750}$
Conversion ratio	25								
Conversion price	$40	$\dfrac{1,000}{25}$							
Market price stock	$32			$40		$60		$16	
Conversion value	$800	(25 × 32)		$1,000	(25 × 40)	$1,500	(25 × 60)	$400	(25 × 16)
Conversion premium	25%	$\dfrac{1000-800}{800}$		20%	$\dfrac{1200-1000}{1000}$	0	$\dfrac{1500-1500}{1500}$	87½%	$\dfrac{750-400}{400}$
Investment value		75 ($750)							
Premium over Investment value	33%	$\dfrac{1000-750}{750}$		60%	$\dfrac{1200-750}{750}$	100%	$\dfrac{1500-750}{750}$	0	

SOURCE: Based on data from New York Stock Exchange

No fixed obligation. Preferred stock is not a debt which may have to be repaid at a specific time or which may have to be retired by a fixed date—directly or through sinking fund provisions.

Continuity. Preferred stock will remain outstanding until it becomes advantageous for holders to exercise their conversion privileges.

Income. A CV preferred is usually issued in connection with an acquisition. The dividend rate is attractive to selling stockholders who want income. The convertibility provides other shareholders with the potential of capital appreciation.

For investors, high-grade CV preferreds are attractive. They are virtually as safe as bonds, have as much or all the capital gains potential of the related common, and are usually easily bought and sold. *For corporations* (and for regular or professional retirement funds), they provide a strong tax benefit: 85% of dividends received are exempt from Federal income tax.

SOME CONVERTIBLE PREFERREDS

COMPANY	Income	No. Shares Conversion	Price Stock	CV
AMAX, Inc.	$3.00	1.310	58	73
Arcata Corp.	2.16	1.036	28	30
Armco, Inc.	2.10	1.275	38	48
Arvin Industries	2.00	1.600	15	24
Brunswick Corp.	2.40	1.720	14	26
Carter Hawley Hale	2.00	1.688	18	31
Champion Inter.	4.60	1.667	25	52
Consolidated Foods	4.50	2.357	28	64
GAF Corp.	1.20	1.250	13	16
General Dynamics	4.25	2.273	34	76
Household Finance	2.50	1.500	16	24
I. T. & T.	5.00	1.437	29	46
Kidde (Walter)	1.64	0.787	44	34
RCA	2.12	0.714	30	24
Tesoro Petroleum	2.16	1.724	16	28
United Technologies	7.32	2.667	54	142

SOURCE: New York Stock Exchange

Hedging with CVs

For sophisticates, CVs offer excellent vehicles for hedging: buying one security and simultaneously selling short its related security. The hedge is set up so that, if the market goes up, you make more money on the purchase than you lose on the short sale or, if the market goes down, vice versa. Such trading works best in volatile markets.

Example: With the aid of an investment service or your broker's research department, you discover that the stock of Rootie-Tootie goes up more than that of its related convertible preferred: +50% compared to +41%, and that the CV falls less than the common: −25% vs. −50%.

The common stock is at 15 and the CV $1.10 preferred, convertible to 1.25 shares, is at 19 . . . almost no premium. You buy 1,000 shares of preferred and sell short 700 shares of common. The cost, without commissions, is $19,000 in cash or $9,500 with margin. Here's what can happen:

If the common goes up 50%, the CV will be worth

HEDGING WITH CONVERTIBLES

IF COMMON PRICE	Goes Up 50%	Stays Unchanged	Goes Down 50%
1. Common Stock	22½	15	7½
2. Convertible preferred	26¾	19	14¼
3. Common gain (loss)	($5,250)	0	$5,250
4. CV gain (loss)	7,750	0	(4,750)
5. Subtotal (line 3 plus 4)	2,500	0	500
6. Dividend on CV	1,100	1,100	1,100
7. Commissions*	(500)	(500)	(500)
8. Net gain (loss) lines 5, 6, 7, 8	3,100	600	1,100
9. Percentage return Line 8 divided by $19,000	16.3%	3.2%	5.8%
10. Margin interest @ 16%	(1,520)	(1,520)	(1,520)
11. Net gain (loss) using margin line 8 minus line 10	1,580	(920)	(420)
12. Percentage return with margin Line 11 divided by $9,500	16.6%	negative	negative

* Brokerage commissions vary

$26,750 for a $7,750 profit. The loss on the short sale will be $5,250 for a net profit of $2,500. Since this takes place over a year, there are $1,100 dividends from the CV and no payout for the dividendless stock.

If the market goes down, the stock will lose half its value (down to $4,750) so when covered, the short sale will bring in a profit of $5,250. There will be a $4,750 loss on the CV so the net profit will be $500 plus $1,100 dividends for $1,600—less commissions.

Best bet: Try hedges out on paper until you are sure you understand what's happening. There's no guarantee the gains or losses will repeat past performance but that's one of the risks of speculating.

Writing Options vs. CVs

For investors, CVs can be used to boost income by selling calls or buying puts.

Example: In March, K-Mart 6s, '99, each convertible to 28.17 shares of common stocks, are selling at 68¾. The common is at 19, and September 25 calls command a premium of 1¾.

You buy 11 CVs for about $7,600. This gives you control of almost 310 shares of common stock so you write 3 September calls (100 shares each) at the exercise price of 25 for $175 each. These are six-month calls so make your calculations on that time basis. You are sure of $855 income: $330 from the interest of the CVs plus $525 premiums from the calls. Not counting commissions, this is an 11.25% return in six months or a net, after commissions, at an annual profit rate of about 20%.

The risk is that the price of the stock will rise to 25 so that the calls will be exercised. That's not likely because such a gain is a whopping 31.5%. If this does happen, you can either buy back the calls and reduce your profits or you can convert the CVs, turn over the 300 shares of stock to the buyer of the call and still own 10 shares.

With puts, do the opposite. (See the chapter on options.)

Warning: This is not for amateurs and should be

undertaken only with the counsel of a knowledgeable broker.

Converting Convertibles

In the ebullient 1960s, new CV issues flooded the market and, with hopes of ever-rising values for the common stocks, were selling like hotcakes. But as with most promotions, success was fleeting. When the price of the related stocks dropped far below the conversion price, CV buyers were stuck with low-yielding bonds and the corporations ended up with debt instead of equity on their balance sheets.

With UAL, Inc., for example, there was little prospect of conversion of its CVs 4¼s, '92, at $77.79 when the common stock was selling at 20. And the debt made new borrowings difficult.

To solve these problems, UAL came up with a swap package. To exchange new CVs for old, it offered an 8% debenture, maturing in 2003, and convertible into common at $22.50 per share. Each $1,000 of the old CVs could be turned in for $644 of the new issue. There was a similar offer of other CVs.

In a sense, everyone won. The investor got $51.52 in annual interest, versus $42.50 before, and the new CV converts to 28.6 shares compared to 12.9 shares before.

The company brought conversion closer and thus looked forward to saving on interest payment, cut its debt by $55.8 million, and as the result of accounting procedures, reported a profit equal to the debt reduction from the paper transaction.

If you're offered a similar deal, better take it!

SOME CV DEBENTURES WITH LISTED OPTIONS
(By writing calls, you can boost income)

COMPANY & CV	Convertible to shares of common	Price Stock	CV
Alcoa 5 1/4, '91	12.50	34	123
Ashland Oil 4 3/4, '93	30.00	31	95
Becton Dickinson 4 1/8, '93	20.48	48	100
Citicorp 5 3/4, '00	24.39	23	63
Eastern Air 11 1/2, '99	62.50	8	78
Ford Credit 4 7/8, '98*	18.04	21	50
Grace (W.R.) 4 1/4, '90	17.45	49	86
Greyhound 6 1/2, '90	54.42	17	92
Heublein 4 1/2, '97	14.39	32	55
Inter. Paper 4 1/4, '96	26.32	46	72
K-Mart 6, '99	28.17	18	64
Lockheed 4 1/4, '92	13.79	27	68
Pfizer, Inc. 4, '97	21.05	50	106
RCA 4 1/2, '92	16.95	30	67
Ralston Purina 5 3/4, '00	65.23	11	76
Trans-World 4, '92	14.86	20	41
Whittaker Corp. 4 1/2, '88	21.28	26	84
Xerox Corp. 6, '95	10.87	55	76

* Convertible to Ford Motor stock

SOURCE: The Wall Street Journal

CHAPTER 14

Fixed-Asset Investments for Safety

Fixed-asset investments are those where you are certain (or reasonably sure) of getting back your money. In most cases they are loans for which you receive interest, so there is no chance for capital appreciation. But with the growing demands for money, financial institutions are coming up with a number of attractive new types of accounts/investments.

The portion of your savings to be allocated to these static holdings depends on your sleep-well level. If safety is paramount, buy and hold nothing else. If you want the highest total returns, use fixed assets only for reserve funds. When interest rates are high they can be rewarding, but they are seldom worthwhile as long-term holdings because their set value is eroded by inflation.

The safest, but not always the most rewarding, investments are those that are guaranteed or insured, as to dollar principal, by the U.S. Government or its agencies. Such coverage differs from the usual bond guarantee of repayment of principal at maturity because it also assures *nonfluctuating prices at all times*. You *always* get back the same number of dollars you invested.

These include savings accounts and certificates of deposit issued by savings banks, commercial banks and federally insured savings and loan associations; and U.S. savings and retirement bonds.

Fixed and Variable Prices and Yields

Most fixed-asset investments pay fixed incomes, so their prices/values move with interest rates: *down* when the cost of money rises; *up* when it falls. There are a number of variations:

Fixed price, fixed yield. Here, both the price and the return on investment are fixed in advance for the life of the instrument.

Example: Certificates of deposit for which both the principal sum and the interest rate are specified to a set date of maturity. With a 30-month, $1,000 certificate at a thrift institution, you are sure of getting back your $1,000 plus the interest at the stated rate, currently about 14%. At that rate, your money doubles in six years when the income is compounded.

Fixed price, variable yield. There are two types:

• Government savings bonds where the price remains

the same but the yields rise. Thus, a $100 bond paid 3.25% interest in 1959; 4.25% in 1969; 6% in 1979; and currently, 8.5%.

• Bank and S&L accounts. These have risen from 3% in 1950 to 5.25% today and, before too long, may be higher when federal limits are removed.

Variable price, fixed yield. In this group are marketable bonds and mortgages. The interest rate is fixed but the market price fluctuates with business and money-market conditions.

Example: A 4% bond issued at 100 ($1,000) would sell at about 80 when the interest rate on new bonds is 5%; to 40 when new issues pay 10% and to the low 30s when they yield 12%. (The actual price will depend on the years to maturity, as the investor will profit by the appreciation from market price to face value at maturity.) The old issue price will provide income competitive to that of new offerings.

In considering all forms of fixed-income holdings, it is essential to remember the erosion of inflation. The dollar invested 20 years ago will buy only 20% of the same goods and services today! And the same decimation applies to the interest income. When you choose fixed-asset investments, you place security over total returns and you will ALWAYS lose purchasing power.

Savings Institutions

Historically, there have been three major types of banking institutions for individuals but, under new legislation, the differences are narrowing and within the next few years the services and investment opportunities will be similar. Soon there will be a wave of mergers and acquisitions, first within the county or state and, later, regionally or even nationally. These should benefit the investor.

• *Commercial banks* offer checking accounts, business and personal loans and, increasingly, savings opportunities.

• *Savings and loan associations.* Originally, these were organized as membership groups where neighbors pooled their resources to lend money to each other for housing. These have grown to be major factors in the financial world, have extended their lending activities to apartments, commercial buildings, land development, mobile homes, home repairs and personal and commercial needs. Most S&Ls are federally chartered but in some states, notably California, Texas and Ohio, they are for-profit organizations that operate under state laws but, generally, are subject to federal regulations. In recent year, to increase their capital (and to provide profits for directors), more of these associations have been going public. Their shares can be worthwhile investments.

• *Mutual savings banks.* Most of these are located in the northeastern and north-central states. They offer services/accounts similar to those of S&Ls and already are taking over other types of thrift institutions.

Regardless of the type of bank/savings account, there is $100,000 insurance: for commercial banks through the Federal Deposit Insurance Corporation (FDIC); for S&Ls, by the Federal Savings and Loan Insurance Corporation (FSLIC).

There's no direct charge for this protection because the institutions are assessed on the basis of their deposits. In any one institution (including branches), the maximum coverage for one individual is $100,000 but you can exceed this when the accounts are held in different rights and/or capacities.

For example, you and your wife can have three fully insured accounts: in your name, in her name and in joint name. You can set up joint accounts with your children or where you are a trustee or guardian; these are treated separately.

Savings Accounts/Certificates

The most widely used fixed-asset investments are savings accounts and certificates. The basic interest rates are set by federal authorities but there can be differences in total yields because of different methods of compounding.

This means paying interest on accumulated interest. Over the long term, this is the single most important factor in successful investing. See the table "The Power of Compound Interest" in the Introduction.

The more frequent the compounding and the longer it continues, the greater the benefit. Always look for an institution where interest on all savings accounts/certificates is compounded daily. Just because the advertisements stress "daily compounding," do not assume that this policy extends to all certificates.

Points to check:

Terms of payment. Some institutions pay interest only on deposits held on a specific date: January 1, April 1, etc. Thus, if you add to your savings on January 15, you will not draw interest on that extra money until April 1. If you withdraw the money before the end of the interest period, you get nothing.

The best deal is when interest is paid from the exact date of deposit through the exact date of withdrawal or maturity. Always make sure that your money continues to earn interest after the certificate comes due, preferably as a rollover into a similar investment, not back to the passbook rate.

Grace period. Interest is paid retroactively to the start of an interest period or calendar month when the deposit is made soon after the starting date, usually up to ten days.

Example: You get full interest for May if you make your deposit on May 9.

Some institutions also offer "rear end" grace periods by permitting withdrawals during the last three business days of an interest period without loss of interest.

More than ever before, it will pay you to shop around to find the most rewarding rates and terms for your savings. There may be special offers/techniques that can boost returns slightly (but not as much as the advertisements indicate). An extra ½ of 1% yield, even when compounded, won't make you rich but can be welcome.

Choose Carefully; Stay flexible

Savings accounts of all types are safe but, with the exception of Treasury-bill-related certificates, are not very rewarding. Their greatest appeal is safety: that you will never get back less than you deposited (unless there are penalties for early withdrawal).

Unlike bonds, their values do not fluctuate with the cost of money. But neither does their rate of return. This can be costly when interest rates rise. Back in 1976, the 8% interest on an eight-year certificate was attractive but by 1981, when interest rates were over 15%, the return was far below that of money market funds, bonds and special Treasury-bill-related, short-term certificates.

INTEREST RATES

Year	Treasury Bills	Prime Rate	Corporate Bonds	Municipal Bonds
1929	4.4%	6.0%	4.2%	4.3%
1934	0.3	1.5	3.4	4.2
1939	0	1.5	2.3	2.8
1944	0.4	1.5	2.1	1.6
1949	1.1	2.0	2.0	2.2
1954	1.0	3.1	2.6	2.4
1959	3.4	4.5	4.4	3.6
1964	3.6	4.5	4.4	3.2
1969	6.7	8.0	7.5	5.7
1971	4.3	5.7	6.9	5.5
1973	7.0	8.0	6.7	5.2
1975	5.8	7.8	9.0	7.0
1976	5.0	6.8	8.5	6.6
1977	5.3	6.8	8.2	6.1
1978	7.2	9.1	9.2	6.8
1979	11.9	15.0	10.9	7.6
1980	13.2	20.5	15.0	8.15
1981*	12.9	17.2	13.4	9.80

* Spring

SOURCE: Wright Investor's Service

Currently, there are these major types of savings investments (but watch for changes). None of them involve commissions or fees so all of your money goes to work.

Passbook account: 5½% interest, usually with compounding depending on the amount and time span of the deposit. *These are primarily for convenience.*

6-Month Money Market Certificate: yield is tied to that of six-month Treasury bills. There is no compounding. New certificates are offered every Tuesday at a yield based on that set at the Monday Federal Reserve Board auction.

The minimum purchase is $10,000: in cash or by a combination of cash and a loan, usually with interest at 1% above that of the yield of the certificate.

30-Month Certificate of Deposit. Minimum deposit from $100. The yield is set at a figure slightly lower than that of the six-month CDs. Interest is compounded daily so a 12% yield works out to an annual rate of return of 12.74%.

There are still traditional accounts/certificates with one- to eight-year maturities and different methods of compounding. These are most useful when you want to be sure of money at a set future date.

With all special CDs, there are penalties for early withdrawal: for those held less than one year, the loss of three months' interest. If the penalty is greater than the interest, you get back less than you deposited. For those held more than one year, the loss of six months' interest.

The penalty is waived when:
- The owner dies or is found mentally incompetent;
- The time deposit is in a Keogh or IRA retirement plan and the depositor is over 59½ years old.

When interest rates are very high, it may pay you to take the penalty on an old, long-term, relatively low-yielding CD and put your money in a high-return, short-term CD. Ask your thrift institution to make the calculations.

If you do this at year-end, watch out for problems with the IRS. When the deposit is in one year and the penalty is assessed in the next, the IRS requires that all of the interest be added to your income in the year of receipt, but it will not grant a credit for the loss until the year of the penalty.

Special Variations and Benefits

In their drive to hold savings accounts, some thrift institutions have come up with unusual opportunities. They may not all be available in your area but if you want a high, short-term return, ask around. They all involve loans at, of course, high interest. Here are typical offers:

Freedom certificates. These are six-month certificates issued in combination with a preauthorized collateral loan agreement. They enable the investor to borrow up to 95% of the value of the certificate with interest on the loan at 1% above the savings-certificate rate.

Example: You invest $10,000 in a six-month Treasury bill certificate paying an annualized yield of 12.65%. After 90 days, you find you need $5,000, so you borrow that amount against the certificate.

$10,000 @ 12.65% for six months	$10,630.81
Less: interest @ 13.65% for 90 days:	168.30
loan principal	5,000.00
At end of six months	$5,462.51

At maturity, you can take your money or roll over both the certificate and loan for another six months.

Purchase loan. You have $5,000 to invest, so you borrow $5,000 more to buy a $10,000 certificate. You pay interest at 1% higher than the certificate yield. At maturity, the $336.60 interest is deducted from the $10,630.80, so your net is now $10,294.20—hardly a worthwhile return but you have something to talk about!

84-Day CDs. This is a very short-term investment that requires a minimum purchase of $10,000. It's a repurchase agreement that pays a little less than that of T-bill CDs, currently 12%. You receive a certificate from the bank stating that you own a U.S. government security, held by the bank, and that the bank will buy it back, unconditionally, for the principal plus the interest. At the end of 84 days, you can renew the CD.

Because the maturity is less than 90 days, this CD is not subject to federal regulations and limitation of interest. *Hard to beat for short-term holdings.*

18-Month option. This gets around the penalty for early withdrawal by involving a loan. You deposit $1,000 on a 2½-year CD and state that you want the "18-month option." After a year and a half, you can either exercise the option by taking out the total, say $1,188.53, or you can let the money stay and, at the end of 30 months, get back $1,355.72.

What happens is that the institution lends you $1,188.52 for the 12 months remaining on the certificate's 30-month term. The interest charge is 1%.

Buying bank stock. This is offered by some small banks seeking to boost their capital. Union Bank & Trust Co. of Erie, Penna. offers depositors part of their interest payable in bank shares. The minimum investment is $10,000. The interest is the maximum allowed for a 30-month CD. The interest is split: 1.12 percentage points is prepaid in the form of bank shares. The balance accumulates.

Thus, on one day, a depositor could get 8.13% cash interest plus 16 shares of stock valued at $28 per share. The bank increases deposits and capital, saves money in cash interest outlays; the depositor gets ownership in a local institution and can count on ample dividends and possible appreciation.

Pooling resources. With $50,000 from your own savings and that of friends/relatives, you borrow $50,000 to buy a $100,000 certificate of deposit. By law, the bank can pay whatever interest they choose, usually higher than that paid on $10,000 units. If the big CD pays 17.75% and the cost of the loan is 1% above the yield, the net return is 16.75%, probably more than could be obtained with a $50,000 investment.

Tax Deferral. If you are retiring soon and expect to be in a lower tax bracket in another year or so, ask your thrift institution to post the interest at maturity instead of crediting it quarterly. Every little bit helps.

Beware of Gifts

It's always nice to get something "free" but before you take advantage of any special offer for new or added savings, do your homework. The true return may be lower than that of a comparable regular investment and, because of taxes, not as rewarding.

Example: A local thrift institution offers a 19-inch color TV set and $150 cash for a $10,000 six-months savings certificate. A rival advertises cash interest of 12% on the same deposit: $600 after six months. If the TV is worth $450, it's a good deal. Otherwise, take the cash and look for a retail store.

The choice becomes more significant with big-ticket items. Not so long ago, a New York bank offered a $77,600 Rolls-Royce for a $160,000 deposit for eight years. That works out to less than 8% annual interest.

The real problem, however, is the tax due. The merchandise qualifies as interest and, probably, taxable in the year of receipt, not over the period the investment is held. If you can afford to put up $160,000, you are in a very high tax bracket. You will have to pay a 70% tax on the full market price: $54,320. And if you are not in that top tax bracket, that expensive car will put you there.

A variation of this is the "bring a friend" offer. Here there's a gift, in cash or merchandise, to anyone (other than a member of the household, and over age 18) who brings a "friend" to the bank who deposits $10,000 or more in a six-month term account with the deposit to remain one year. The sponsor gets $100—more with large deposits. Again, watch the tax angle.

Savings Certificates vs. Treasury Bills

When you can afford to invest $10,000 or more, compare six-month money market certificates with straight Treasury bills. In most cases, the T-bills are a better deal. Here's why:

1. The CD minimum is $10,000. The T-bill is sold at a discount so the cost is less. To calculate the price you pay, use this formula:

$$D = \frac{L \times SY}{360}$$

D = discount per $100 face value
L = life span of security
360 = number of days in financial year
SY = stated yield

With a 180-day instrument and a 12% yield:

$$D = \frac{180}{360} = 5 \qquad 5 \times 12 = 6.00$$

Multiply 6.00 by 100 to get $600. Subtract $600 from $10,000 to get the cost of $9,400.

2. The true yield of the T-bill is more because T-bill trading uses a 360-day year but your money works 365 days and the stated yield is based on the cost.

$$TY = \frac{D}{C} \times \frac{365}{L}$$

TY = true yield
D = discount
C = cost
L = life span of security

Again, with a 180-day T-bill, the yield of 12% and a cost of $9,400, the true yield is 12.76% for a year or 6.38%—12 divided by 94 divided by 2.

$$TY = \frac{6.00}{94.00} + 6.38 \times \frac{365}{180} = 2.03 \quad 6.38 \times 2.03 = 12.95\%$$

Thus, the T-bill annual yield is 12.95%.

3. Interest in T-bills is exempt from state and local income taxes. That of the certificate is fully taxable. This can be important in states with an income tax and very important where there are also local levies.

4. If the certificate is cashed in before maturity, there's a penalty of 90 days' interest. With T-bills, there's an active after-market, so you will always get more than you invested since the sales price includes accumulated interest. There might be a small loss in the first few weeks if there was a sharp rise in interest rates.

EE and HH Savings Bonds

The old Series E and H savings bonds have been replaced by new issues, Series EE and HH. They pay a trifle more for a longer period but they are still poor investments and, with higher yields available elsewhere, getting worse.

Traditionally, the major attraction of the Es and Hs was the fact that no taxes on accrued interest had to be paid until redemption. Some folks kept pushing back their tax date by swapping Es for Hs. But even that small benefit is being curtailed. E bonds issued before April 1952 will pay no interest after they've been held for 40 years. E bonds issued after that date get one ten-year extension and then stop paying interest.

H bonds bought before May 1959 stop paying interest after 40 years, too. Those acquired after that date will have 10 more years of life and will come due 20 to 30 years after their original purchase. *If you have any E or H bonds stashed away, get them out, cash them in and put your money to work for more rewarding returns.*

Buying the new EE and HH bonds may be patriotic but it's not very profitable. EE bonds are available at 50% of face value: e.g. a $50 one costs $25, a $100 one, $50, etc. They pay 9% interest. They cannot be cashed in until after the first six months and the maximum annual purchase, by an individual, is $15,000 face value.

DEADLINES FOR INTEREST ON E BONDS

Date of Issue	Date of Maturity
May 1941-April 1952	May 1981-April 1992
May 1952-January 1957	January 1992-September 1996
February 1957-May 1959	January 1996-April 1998
June 1959-November 1965	March 1997-August 2003
December 1965-May 1969	December 1992-May 1996
June 1969-November 1973	April 1995-September 1999
December 1973-June 1980	December 1998-June 2005

No interest will be paid after maturity. The bonds may be exchanged for Series HH bonds within one year after maturity.

The HH bonds, in denominations of $500 to $10,000, mature in 10 years and pay 8.5% interest semi-annually. There's a penalty for early redemption when bought for cash but not when exchanged for E bonds. Maximum annual investment: $20,000.

With both of these new issues, there are modest tax savings:

• Interest is free of state and local income taxes.

• Federal taxes can be deferred until the bonds are redeemed in most cases. When E bonds are swapped for HH bonds, the taxes on the accumulated interest of the E bonds does not have to be paid until the HH bonds are cashed in or mature. But the interest on the HH bonds is taxable in the year received.

Government Retirement Bonds

These are issued in denominations of $50, $100 and $500 through Federal Reserve Banks and the U.S. Treasury. They are designed for investments of funds in Individual Retirement Accounts. They pay 9.0% interest compounded semi-annually. They are suitable only for those who place safety above income and growth. (See chapter on retirement.)

How to Locate Unclaimed/Lost Savings Bonds

If your savings bonds have been lost or stolen, get form PD 1048, an Application for Relief, from the U.S. Treasury. Fill it out, giving such information as serial number; issuance date; name, address and Social Security number of owner, where possible. These are helpful but not essential. Mail the form to Bureau of Public Debt, 200 Third Street, Parkersburg, W.Va. 26101.

Corporate Notes for Good Yields and Convenience

Investors who want competitive yields and flexibility should find out about corporate notes. These are issued by major companies and, in many cases, their maturities can be tailored to meet your time schedule: 135 days; 2 years, 3 months; etc.

General Motors Acceptance Corporation (GMAC) offers both short- and medium-term notes. The short-term debt is bought at a discount (interest is deducted on issue, and the investor receives face value at redemption). Longer-term debt is on an interest-bearing basis. Yields are competitive.

For minimum investments of $50,000: 30–59 days, 13.5%; 60–89 days, 13%. For minimum investments of $25,000: 90–119 days, 12.75%; 120–179 days, 11.75%; 180–279 days, 11.50%.

Medium-term notes: minimum investment of $25,000: 9 months to 3 years, 13%; minimum of $10,000: 3 to 5 years, 13.75%.

At maturity, the notes can be rolled over or collected through your local commercial bank.

The notes, in bearer form, can be obtained through GMAC offices in Atlanta, Boston, Chicago, Dallas, Detroit, Kansas City, New York, Philadelphia, Pittsburgh and San Francisco. For information, call the toll-free 800 number available from your local GM car dealer.

Floating-Rate Notes

These are notes issued by major bank holding companies and some money-hungry corporations. They were heralded as a hedge against inflation but have not worked out too well for investors.

The interest rate shifts with that of six-month T-bills. Usually there are minimum and maximum yields: from a guaranteed low of 6% to a high of 19%. Typically, the notes are sold for $5,000 but can be resold in units of $1,000.

The first offering was made by Citicorp in 1979. The yield was the higher of 11.05% or 1.05% above the rate paid on 180-day T-bills. Changes were made every six months. There was no federal insurance but there was a substantial sinking fund. The notes could be bought and sold in an active market but were not redeemable for 10 years.

Popularity waned when interest rates jumped from 12% to 15.75% in less than two months. To correct against such sharp shifts, recent issues set the coupon according to a formula that includes the yield of bank CDs as well as that of T-bills.

Continental Illinois Corp. tried six-year notes with a yield of 0.5% above that of six-month T-bills and convertible, through May 1986, into 8.5% debentures due in 2004. Investors have not been excited about the low yield of the bonds but things may change in the future.

European CDs

For the wealthy and wise, there are European CDs— bank IOUs denominated in U.S. dollars held abroad.

Most mature in six months. Their yields are a bit higher than those of similar U.S. debt.

For those who are not familiar with international finance or have limited funds, an alternative is shares of investment trusts. Typically, their holdings are: 50% in CDs issued by foreign branches of U.S. banks; 25% each in debts of foreign banks. The minimum investment can be $1,000 and there's no penalty for early redemption. BUT there can be losses due to currency fluctuations.

Tax Certificates

For shrewd, locally savvy investors, delinquent tax certificates provide high returns in a short period. These represent unpaid property taxes. They are sold at public auction with yields of up to 20%. If the property owner pays up quickly, the buyer gets a minimum of 5% interest. If the payment is made within three months (as 80% are), the investor makes out well. And if the property owner fails to redeem the certificates, the buyer can apply for a tax deed and, ultimately, take possession of the property by paying one year's taxes. These certificates can be highly profitable if you know what you're doing, work with a knowledgeable attorney and invest sizable sums.

Monthly Checks with High Yields

Among the most convenient, highest-yielding and safest fixed-income investments are Government National Mortgage Association (GNMA) securities. They are shares in a pool of Federal Housing Administration (FHA) and Veterans Administration (VA) mortgages, primarily on single-family homes. They pay monthly interest of over 14% plus amortization and, after a few years, periodic extras as loans are prepaid or refinanced. They are called "pass-throughs" because the mortgage banker who packages the original loans "passes through" income to investors.

There are two types: *Ginnie Maes,* pools of regular, level-payment mortgages, and *Jeeps,* packages of graduated-payment mortgages (GPMs), a new type of loan that permits smaller monthly payments in the early years and then gradually rising payments as the homeowner presumably earns more money.

Both have double protection: the insurance of FHA and the guarantee of VA plus the overall guarantee of GNMA. The original package is made up primarily of 30-year mortgages but, because of prepayments and refinancing, the average life of the pool is 12 to 15 years.

Here's how they work: A large brokerage firm buys a multimillion-dollar package at wholesale and sells portions at retail, usually $25,000 each. (But you can buy shares in funds for $1,000 each with a sales commission of about 3%.)

For easy arithmetic, let's assume that you invest $50,000 in certificates of a $1 million, 11.5% package of Ginnie Maes. You own 5% of the offering. The first monthly checks will be around $500—almost all representing interest. Gradually, more of the payment will be for amortization and, soon, a $50,000 mortgage will be paid off so you will receive 5% of this cash-in, roughly

$2,500 extra. Thereafter, your monthly check will be smaller as there will be less interest and amortization. But the annual rate of return will be more than 11.5% because payments are made monthly.

The *Jeeps,* first offered in 1979, provide a better rate of return than Ginnie Maes because, in the first five years, the amount of the underpayment is added to the principal of the loan at the original interest rate. Thus the buyer reinvests part of his income at the high, original interest rate even though the cost of money may have dropped over those early years. Of course, this has not happened recently because interest costs have risen.

T-BOND CALCULATOR

This is a printed form that quickly translates T-bond prices into approximate yields, and vice versa. The yields are based on 8%, 20 year bonds. This is available from the Chicago Board of Trade for $1.00 each.

Here's an example with a Ginnie Mae contract:

GNMA Interest Rate	Amount Equivalent to $100,000 Principal Balance of 8% Contract	GNMA Interest Rate	Amount Equivalent to $100,000 Principal Balance of 8% Contract
9 1/4%	$91,603.10	10 1/4%	$85,714.30
9 3/8	90,840.30	10 3/8	85,046.10
9 1/2	90,032.20	10 1/2	84,328.90
9 3/4	88,560.90	11	81,743.90
10	87,146.00	12	76,972.40
10 1/8	86,393.10	13	72,674.40
		14	68,823.10

Digested from Chicago Board of Trade

With older Ginnie Maes, the yield can be excellent because of a combination of:

1. Discount prices due to rising interest costs. A pool of mortgages with an 8% interest rate will sell in the 60s when new-issue package loans carry a 12% yield.

2. Faster-than-expected prepayments and refinancing. With a smaller principal, the same monthly payment works out to a higher yield. Here's a real-life example that occurred two years ago when interest rates were lower:

The original Ginnie Mae unit was $25,000. After three years, $7,115.77 of the principal had been repaid, thus reducing the balance to $17,884.23. At that time, each unit was selling, at a 19% discount, at $14,486.23. By buying at this time and price, the investor had a yield of 11.92% and if the paybacks continued at the same pace, he would have had a hefty 15.45% rate. But when interest rates dropped, the value of the units rose and the yield became more competitive.

With Ginnie Maes, all of the first income is taxable interest. But as amortization rises and mortgages are repaid, a large, but not regular, portion is a nontaxable return of capital. With Jeeps, the individual investor pays no tax on the interest until it is actually received—five years or more in the future. The fund provides detailed data for tax returns.

Both Ginnie Maes and Jeeps are excellent investments for: *(a)* those who need sure, regular income and can benefit from the extras of repayments; *(b)* retirees whose actuarial life span is less than 12 years. The check arrives every month, even if some debtors default.

In real life, Ginnie Maes may, or may not, be as rewarding. It depends on the rate of repayments. When interest rates are high, this will slow because home owners will not refinance so quickly. That's when selection needs the counsel of an experienced broker.

The key is what's called "FHA speed." This is the rate by which the FHA calculates the speed of repayments: 100% FHA speed is equal to the national average life of FHA mortgages—in recent years, 11.2 years. When the speed is higher, there's a faster payout, so the Ginnie Mae yield is higher. Here's the calculation base:

FHA Speed	New Pool Years	4-Year-Old Pool Years
100	11.2	9.2
150	8.5	6.7
200	7.0	5.2
300	5.3	3.5
400	4.4	2.6

Keep in mind that the older pools, issued when interest rates were lower, will sell at a discount. Buying them gives the investor a competitive yield plus a built-in increase in the eventual yield if the mortgages in the pool are prepaid. It's like owning a long-term bond whose maturity is shortened. With a FHA speed of 200%—a pay-down rate twice as fast as the national average—the investor boosts his return.

Here's an example digested from a column by Jill Bettner in the *Wall Street Journal:* Dealer Dan buys a $50,000 piece of a four-year-old Ginnie Mae 8% pool with a speed of 300% at a price of 75½% of the remaining principal balance of the mortgages. At this pay-down rate, 39.79% of the original principal would have been paid off, leaving 64.21% in the remaining principal, or $32,105: $50,000 × 64.21%.

At the price of 75½, Dan would pay $24,239.28 ($32,105 × 75½) for this block. Now he offers this same interest to an investor at an anticipated yield of 13.75%, based on the assumption that the 300% speed will continue. The price would be 83¾% or $26,887.94 ($32,105 × 83¾%).

The risk is that the pay-down rate may slow. At 200%, the yield would be 12.60%; at 150, 12%. Still, it's a welcome return.

For smaller investments, see Ginnie Mae funds as outlined in the chapter on Investment Companies.

Private Mortgage Funds

Similar opportunities are offered by bank holding companies, thrift institutions, and major brokerage firms. In some cases, all mortgages are insured by private firms; with others, the sponsor guarantees to pay the first 5% to 10% of defaults. All funds make full monthly payments, yields are about 1% greater than those of Ginnie Maes and units are available for as little as $1,000 each. Here are typical examples of what to look for:

• BankAmerica certificates representing units of a pool of 3,000 real estate loans on single-family homes.

• Milwaukee's Republic Savings & Loan Association offered a $10 million issue to depositors with shares priced at $10,000 each. The mortgages are all five-year notes with a final balloon payment so that most of the early payments represent interest and you get your investment back at the end of five years.

• New York's Dime Savings Bank floated a $10 million pool of low-interest-rate mortgages. Since they were at a discount, purchasers could count on income and appreciation.

• Merrill MBS, Inc. pass-through certificates with each pool consisting of no less than 250 conventional mortgage loans with fixed interested rates and original maturities of from 26 to 30 years. There's insurance to cover not less than 5% of the principal balance.

NOW Accounts

Starting in 1981, all banking/savings institutions were permitted to offer interest-bearing checking accounts called Negotiable Orders of Withdrawal (NOW). The initial maximum interest rate is 5¼% but ceilings will be phased out over six years.

In selecting a NOW account, shop around and compare the costs and benefits with your present arrangements. The yields are the same but the conditions vary widely as to minimum balance, monthly service charge, method of payment of interest and whether you get back your checks or a computerized printout of transactions.

NOW ACCOUNTS

Institution	Minimum (no charge)	Service Charges	
Chase Manhattan	$3,000	$2,999-$2,000:	$2.50 month
		below $2,000:	$5.00 month
Chemical Bank	2,000	below $2,000:	$4.00 month
Citibank	3,000	below $3,000:	$4.00 month
County Federal S&L	2,000	$1,999-$500:	10¢ per check
		below $500:	$3.00 month
First Federal S&L	1,000	below $1,000:	$4.00 month
West Side Federal	500*	below $500:	$2.00 month
Dry Dock Savings	1,000	$999-$500:	$2.00 month
		below $500:	$2.00 month +15¢ per check
East New York Savings	1,000	below $1,000:	no interest
NY Bank for Savings	2,000	$1,999-$1,000:	$1.00 month
		$999-$400:	$2.00 month
		below $400:	$3.00 month

*No minimum balance for senior citizens.

The table shows the variety offered by a few New York City institutions. They are typical of what you will find in your area. If you like to get the most for your money, watch local ads and call several convenient institutions. Generally, the least expensive will be the S&Ls who are battling to boost the number of depositors. But their service for check cashing and personal loans may be less efficient than that of a commercial bank.

And, as you will soon learn, unless you keep a substantial account, the end-of-the-year benefits may not be worth the bother.

N.B.: When you discuss the minimum balance, find out if this includes savings accounts/certificates. If so, one $10,000 money market certificate will assure that your checking account always draws interest.

CHECK LIST FOR INTEREST RATES

Check your answer to each of the following four questions. Add up your answers. A total of six or less means you think interest rates will drop. Seven or eight calls for stable rates. A score of nine or more means you look for higher interest rates.

A. A recession in business activity
   1. Has already begun
   2. Will begin within a few months
   3. Won't come for another year

B. Over the next few months, the overall rate of inflation will:
   1. Decline
   2. Stay about the same
   3. Increase

C. Over the next few months, the value of the U.S. dollar in foreign markets will:
   1. Appreciate
   2. Remain stable or decline slightly
   3. Depreciate rapidly

D. Money growth in the next quarter will be:
   1. Slow—below the Fed's long-term goals
   2. Moderate—in line with Fed goals
   3. Rapid—similar to 1979's summer

SOURCE: Argus Research Corp.

Mexican Savings Accounts

Interest rates on Mexican savings accounts have changed drastically in the past year. Short-term deposits, with a minimum of $8,999 U.S. dollars, pay only 12% while those of $100,000 start at 14.12%—both less than can be obtained in CDs and money market funds in the U.S.

If you save in pesos, the returns can be exceptionally high: from 26.50% for 90-day accounts to an interest at maturity of 36.15% for two-year, $100,000 deposits. By law, all deposits are subject to a 21% withholding tax.

According to Eugene C. Latham, editor of *Mexletter,*

MEXICAN SAVINGS ACCOUNTS
DOLLAR DEPOSITS: $8,000 Minimum

Time	Gross Interest	Tax	Annual Net Rate Monthly	At Maturity
3 mo.	15.19%	21%	12.00%	12.01%
6 mo.	15.51	21	12.25	12.19
12 mo.	15.82	21	12.50	12.60

$100,000 Minimum

Time	Gross Interest	Tax	Annual Net Rate Monthly	At Maturity
3 mo.	17.88	21	14.12	14.13
6 mo.	17.88	21	14.12	14.17
12 mo.	17.88	21	14.12	14.22

PESO DEPOSITS: $100,000 Pesos

Time	Gross Interest	Tax	Tax-free Interest	Annual Net Rate Monthly	At Maturity
3 mo.	12.00%	21%	17.02%	26.50%	26.80%
6 mo.	12.00	21	19.02	28.50	29.45
12 mo.	12.00	21	20.27	29.75	31.95
18 mo.	12.00	21	20.77	30.25	34.05
24 mo.	12.00	21	21.27	30.75	36.15

SOURCE: Mexletter, Apartado Postal 1335, Mexico 1, D.F. Mexico

---

once a deposit has been made, the gross and tax-free interest rate is frozen for the life of the account. Depositors may elect to: (1) receive a monthly check; (2) compound monthly interest (only with accounts under 30 days); (3) have interest paid in a lump sum at maturity (with accounts for 3–24 months); (4) transfer interest from a time deposit to a short-term account. Interest rates fluctuate under rules of the Central Bank. With longer-term deposits in pesos, specific maturity dates can be selected: i.e. 7 months, 22 days.

Warns Latham: "The best deal with Mexican savings accounts is when the retiree, living in Mexico, saves in pesos. The returns are high but living costs are rising. And there's always the possibility of another devaluation of the peso. But any loss could be used against U.S. taxes."

U.S. tax law allows Americans to take a foreign tax credit against U.S. taxes for the amount of income taxes paid to Mexico. To do this, attach IRS Form 1116 to your federal tax return. If your U.S. tax rate is below 21%, you cannot take full credit but may carry the balance forward.

CHAPTER 15

Taxable Corporate and Government Bonds

Bonds are no longer the safe, secure securities they used to be. They do provide steady income and you're almost always sure to get your money back but, in recent years, their values have fluctuated as much, or more than, those of common stocks. In less than nine months, the price of top-quality A.T.&T. 8¾% bonds fell from 98 ($980) down to below 68 ($680).

What this means is that investors who buy bonds must: (1) do so with an eye on total returns—interest income plus appreciation; (2) be willing to trade, not to hold. To be profitable in the future, bonds must be managed.

Bonds are debt. When you buy a bond, you are loaning money to a corporation or government. In return, you receive a certificate that states the issuer will pay interest at a specified rate, usually twice a year, until the debt is repaid, at a specified date, 5, 10, up to 40 years hence.

For corporations, bonds are a relatively inexpensive way to obtain funds for capital improvements and expansion. The interest is a tax-deductible business expense, so the cost of a 12% bond for a firm in the 46% tax bracket is 6.48% (.12 × 54%).

This recent debacle is in addition to the basic disadvantages of all debt securities:

• *Inflation.* As fixed holdings, the dollars invested and the income received are worth less every year. With 10% inflation, each $1,000, after 20 years, will buy only about $150 worth of the same goods and services.

• *High taxes.* All interest (except that of tax-exempts) is taxable at the highest personal income-tax rate. With capital gains, only 40% of the realized appreciation is taxed.

• *Difficulty of compounding* (earning interest on interest). Unless you buy shares in a bond fund, there can be no automatic reinvestment as with stock-dividend in-vestment plans. The interest payments will have to be held in a low-yield savings account until there is money enough to buy a new bond. Over a couple of years, the 7% difference between a 5½% thrift account and a 12½% bond yield will add up to over $70 per year.

• *Lack of appreciation* unless the bonds are bought at a discount and held to maturity (or, when traded, sold at a higher price). If you buy a new bond for $1,000, you will get back exactly $1,000 at maturity. The only chance for a profit is if interest rates decline sharply so that the bond value rises.

What to Look for in Bonds

Quality. This is essential in choosing bonds for investment. Since you buy bonds for safety, stick to quality and forget the small extra interest ($5 to $10 per year per bond) which can be obtained with the debt of a secondary corporation.

Most corporate and municipal (but not Federal Government) bonds are rated by statistical services in nine categories from gilt-edged to extremely speculative. These ratings represent carefully calculated estimates of the degree of protection for both principal and interest. They are based on past performance, current financial strength and future prospects. By and large, the two top services, Moody's and Standard & Poor's, come up with about the same opinion.

Prices for high-grade bonds, rated A or better, reflect money-market conditions and interest rates almost exclusively. Farther down the scale, bond prices are more closely attuned to business conditions generally and to the quality of the specific corporation. Medium-grade Baa or B bonds are the lowest category which qualifies for commercial bank investment. *Anything below this rating is speculative and should NOT be purchased as an investment without close analysis of updated financial statements and considerations of industry prospects. Of course, if you want to speculate, Baa-rated bonds pay over 15% and junk bonds as high as 17%.*

Watch for changes in ratings. Upgrading is beneficial; downgrading may signal future trouble. Among recent revisions by Moody's:

HOW BONDS ARE RATED

General description	Moody's	S&P
Best quality	Aaa	AAA
High quality	Aa	AA
Upper medium	A	A
Medium	Baa	BBB
Speculative	Ba	BB
Low grade	B	B
Poor to default	Caa	CCC
Highly speculative default	Ca	CC
Lowest grade	C	C

Ratings may also have + or − sign to show relative standings in class.

TAXABLE BONDS

Up: Central Illinois Light, from A to Aa
Down: Dana Corp., from Aa to A
      Inter. Harvester, from Baa to Ba
      Union Electric, from A to Ba

Terms: *Serial bonds* are redeemed at various dates over a period of years. This enables the buyer to select the exact maturity he desires: in seven years when daughter Delphinium starts college, for example. Usually, all of the debt comes due at once, but there's extra safety when there's a sinking fund (explained later).

Corporate collateral. This is the property behind each bond. *Secured bonds* are: (1) first-mortgage bonds backed by the company's real estate, plants, trucks and so on *or* equipment trust certificates secured by railroad equipment—locomotives, freight cars, etc.; (2) bonds guaranteed, as to principal and interest, by another corporation or by the Government or a Government corporation or agency. Examples of the former are foreign bonds offered for sale abroad by foreign subsidiaries or affiliates of U.S. corporations and guaranteed by the parent company.

Unsecured bonds or debentures are backed only by the general credit standing of the issuing company. The investor should translate this credit into the company's ability to pay annual interest and amortization plus the principal sum when due. The projection should consider recent historic ratios and trends and should apply to the *total* debt.

In practice, for most bonds, the ability of the corporation to pay is much more important than theoretical security because legal obstacles to investors collecting a bond's security in the event of insolvency are often formidable and time-consuming, quite possibly requiring litigation.

A handy formula for determining investment-grade bonds (interest charges should be covered over a period of five years):

	Before Federal Income Taxes	After Federal Income Taxes
Industrial Bonds	5×	3×
Public Utility	3×	2×
Railroad	4×	3×

Type. *Bearer or Registered Bonds.* Historically, most bonds were issued in *bearer* form with interest coupons attached. Interest was paid, usually twice a year, by presentation of the detachable coupons to the paying agent. This is the origin of the phrase *clipping coupons.*

There are still some of these bonds extant. Since the mid 1950s, the majority of all bonds that have been issued are in registered form. Their owners receive interest checks by mail just as with dividends. Since the names of the owners are recorded, holders are protected against loss, theft and fire, and automatically receive notice of redemption calls.

Larger corporations may float both bearer and registered bonds for the same issue, giving buyers a choice.

For institutions specializing in handling large amounts of bonds, registered issues may be somewhat less convenient than those in bearer form. Transferring a registered certificate is more complicated and usually takes at least four business days. Institutions are, therefore, sometimes willing to pay slightly more for bearer issues than for registered issues of identical quality. *For most individuals, registered bonds are more convenient and slightly more rewarding.*

How Bond Interest Is Paid and Calculated

Interest on bonds is added to the sales price but does not include the day of delivery. It is calculated on a daily basis. For U.S. government issues other than Treasury bills, the base is the exact number of days in a 365-day year. With other bonds, it's a 360-day year or twelve 30-day months.

From the:	
1st to 30th of the same month	29 days
1st to 1st of next month	30 days
1st to 28th of February	27 days

If interest is payable on the 30th or 31st, from the:	
30th or 31st to 1st of next month	1 day
30th or 31st to 30th of next month	30 days
30th or 31st to 1st or 2nd of next month	1 month, 1 day

To figure the yield superiority of 360-day bonds versus 365s, divide the interest rate by 360 to get the daily return, then multiply the result by 365. With a 12% interest rate, the daily rate works out to 0.333%, so the annualized rate for 365 days would be 12.16%

How to Read Bond Quotations

The first line shows that, during the week, 142 A.T.&T. bonds, due in 1986, with a coupon of 2⅝%, were sold at prices between 67½ and 68½. The last sale, at 67⅞, was ⅛ above the closing price of the previous week.

Each bond paid $26.25 annual interest, so the yield was 3.9%. Investors will accept this low return because they know that in five years, the bond will be redeemed at $1,000 for a per bond, long-term capital gain of $321.25. Over the previous 52 weeks, the price of this debt issue moved from a low of 63⅝ to a high of 73.

HOW CORPORATE BONDS ARE QUOTED ON THE NYSE

52 Weeks		Issue	Cur. Yld.	Sales $1,000	Weekly		Last	Net Chg.
High	Low				High	Low		
73	63 5/8	ATT 2 5/8, '86	3.9	142	68 1/2	67 1/2	67 7/8	+ 7/8
78	57	Cleve. El. 8 3/8, '11	13	5	63	60 3/4	63	+2 1/4
122 3/8	96 7/8	Pac T T 15 1/2, '20	15	51	102 7/8	100	102 1/4	+3 1/8

SOURCE: New York Stock Exchange

The Cleveland Electric bond is selling at a few points lower than that of Ma Bell but its current yield is a high 13%, more than three times greater. *The reason:* this bond will not mature for 25 years later. People want to be paid for waiting for their money. Its price has been volatile (typical of long-term debt issues) with a high of 78 and a low of 57. That's a swing of 27%, just about the same as that of the common stock. Clearly, bonds are not more stable than quality stocks.

The Pacific Telephone bond shows that when debt issues have high coupons, their prices can move up well above par. Usually, the investor thinks of capital gains with bonds, in terms of appreciation from a discount, but when the cost of money is dropping, newly issued high-yielding debt can be profitable, too. By selling at or near the 122 high, the investor could have made a lot of money to add to the ample $155 annual interest.

Government bonds, which are traded OTC, are quoted in thirty-seconds and show the yield to maturity: the coupon rate plus the appreciation to par.

GOVERNMENT NOTES/BONDS

Rate	Maturity	High	Low	Last	Chg.	Yield
11 3/8	April 1982 n	98.24	98.9	98.24	+ .26	12.62
7 1/4	Feb. 1984 n	87.5	86.8	87.4	+1.2	12.69
7 1/2	Aug. 1988-93	71.30	70.30	71.16	+ .27	11.96

SOURCE: Barron's

These are summaries of weekly quotations for $1,000 face-value bonds with high and low rates of interest. The first line, for the short-term debt due in April 1982, shows that the high trade was at 98 24/32 ($987.50) and the low at 98 ($980). Both prices are before the accrued interest that has accumulated since the most recent semi-annual payment. The last transaction was 26/32 higher than that of the closing price of the previous week. The yield to maturity was 12.62%: the 11⅜% coupon plus the few dollars to the $1,000 redemption price.

The 7½s, 1984 traded at almost the same yield to maturity but, because of the lower coupon and somewhat longer maturity, were worth about 11 points ($110 each) less.

The prices of the 7½s due in 1988–93 were even lower because of the 7-to-12-year wait for redemption. The yield to maturity was a bit less than the others, probably a temporary situation that might prove profitable for sharp professional traders. Generally, yields to maturity tend to be competitive and are the basis for selection.

Prices and Yields of Bonds

The interest rate is the important factor in the price of bonds, not supply and demand as with common stocks.

Bond values rise when interest rates decline; conversely, bond values fall when interest rates go up.

Yields on short-term issues tend to fluctuate more than those on equal-quality longer-term bonds. Short-term *yields* react more quickly to business cycles and monetary changes, and move to greater extremes in both directions. In tight money markets, short-term interest rates are usually appreciably higher than long-term ones. In easy money markets, when interest rates are relatively stable, short-term issues typically yield less than long-term ones. Shrewd traders take advantage of this differential.

By contrast, *prices* of long-term bonds fluctuate more than those of short-term issues. *The reason:* time is money. A change in interest rates calculated for a few weeks or months involves a lesser change in price than the same change projected for years ahead.

A rise of 1% in the interest rates will mean a drop of about $10.00 for a $1,000 short-term T-bill but it can force a decline of $100 or more for a bond with 20 years to maturity.

How to Figure Bond Yields

Yield is a matter of definition and objective.

The nominal or coupon yield. This is the interest rate stated on the bond: 10%, 11.25%, etc. It depends on the quality of the issuing corporation and the prevailing cost of money at the time the bond is issued.

The actual yield on the purchase price. This is the rate of return per year that the coupon interest rate provides on the *net* price (without accumulated interest) at which the bond is purchased. It is *higher* than the coupon yield if you buy the bond below par, *lower* if you buy the bond above par.

The current yield. This is the rate of return on the current market price of the bond. This is *higher* than the yield on the purchase price if there has been a decline in the price, *lower* if there has been a rise in the market value of the security.

The yield to maturity (YTM). This is the rate of return on a bond held to redemption. It includes the appreciation to par from the current market price when bought at a discount from par, or the depreciation to par when bought at a premium.

To approximate the YTM for a discount bond:

1. Subtract the current bond price from the face amount.
2. Divide the difference by the number of years to maturity.
3. Add the annual interest.
4. Add the current price to the face amount and divide by two.
5. Divide (3) by (4) to get the YTM.

Example: A $1,000, 5% coupon bond, due in 10 years, is selling at 57 ($570). The coupon yield is 5%; the current yield is 8.8% (5 ÷ 57); the YTM is 11.8%.

1. $1,000 − 570 = 430
2. 430 ÷ 10 = 43
3. 43 + 50 = 93
4. 570 + $1,000 ÷ 2 = 785
5. 93 ÷ 785 = 11.8%

This is approximate, as an exact figure would have to include the accrued interest and number of days to maturity.

YIELDS OF CORPORATE BONDS

Year	Corporate				Averages	
	Aaa	Aa	A	Baa	Utilities	Industrials
1975	8.79%	9.25%	9.67%	10.56%	9.78%	9.26%
1976	7.98	8.24	8.53	9.12	8.61	8.33
1977	8.19	8.40	8.57	8.99	8.65	8.42
1978	9.16	9.33	9.53	9.94	9.67	9.31
1979	10.74	11.15	11.46	12.06	11.68	11.02
1980	13.21	13.78	14.03	15.14	14.48	13.60

SOURCE: Moody's Investors Service

The discount yield. This is the percentage from par or face value, adjusted to an annual basis, at which a discount bond sells. It is used for short-term obligations maturing in less than one year, primarily Treasury bills.

Roughly, this is the opposite of YTM. If a one-year T-bill sells at a 12% yield, its cost is 88 ($8,800). The discount yield is 12 divided by 88 or 13.64%.

Types of U.S. Government Bonds

There are five principal kinds of U.S. Treasury securities of interest to individual investors. In order of declining maturity, they are:

1. U.S. Treasury bonds. These have both medium-term (5 to 10 years) and long-term (over 10 years) maturities. All Treasury bonds come in either registered or bearer form and are interchangeable. Interest is paid semi-annually.

2. U.S. Treasury notes. These mature in from one to five years, are issued in bearer form only and pay interest semi-annually.

3. U.S. Treasury bills. These mature in 91 days, six months, nine months and one year. The first two maturities are issued weekly, the latter two once a month. They come in bearer form only, so they should be kept in a safe deposit box or given to a bank for custody. The minimum amount of new bills that can be purchased is $10,000 (face value), but you can buy smaller amounts on the after market.

T-bills are sold on a discount basis that reflects the YTM. Thus, a one-year 12%-yield bill would be bought at 88 ($8,800) and, 12 months later, be redeemed for $10,000. This is a true return of 13.64% because the 12% yield is on an investment of $8,800. This gain is interest and thus taxable at regular federal income-tax rates but it is not subject to state and local income-tax levies.

Individuals can buy T-bills via a form available from the nearest Federal Reserve Bank. This is done by a noncompetitive bid (to arrive by mail on Friday or, in person, before 1:30 P.M. on the day of the auction).

The price you pay will be the average of all competitive offers from large institutions that buy millions of dollars' worth each week. With the form, enclose a personal certified check or an official bank check drawn on a bank in the Federal Reserve district. The check should be made payable to the "Federal Reserve Bank of (District)." A third-party check endorsed by you to the Fed will not be accepted.

A few days after the auction, the Fed Bank will mail you a "discount" check, representing the difference between the purchase price and the face value of the bills. With this will be a receipt as proof of your purchase.

The details of the acquisition are entered in a government ledger, with no extra charge. This book entry reduces the risk of loss or theft, saves printing costs and eliminates delivery and clearance problems.

If you prefer to buy through a broker or a bank, charges will be $15 to $25 per transaction.

To roll over a T-bill at maturity, you can indicate your wishes at purchase or send in Form PD 4633–1 at least 20 business days before the maturity date.

For more information, request "Basic Information on Treasury Bills" from your nearest Federal Reserve Bank or Federal Reserve Bank of New York, 33 Liberty Street, New York, N.Y. 10045.

4. U.S. Treasury tax anticipation bills and certificates. These are issued to mature a few days after Federal income tax payment dates (April 15, June 15, etc.). They can be used to pay income taxes at par (or with full interest to maturity), thereby giving the taxpayer a bonus of several days' interest. They are used primarily by corporations with large tax bills.

Federal Agency Bonds and Participation Certificates

There are well over 100 series of notes, certificates and bonds issued by Federal agencies as instrumentalities of the U.S. Government: Federal Intermediate Credit Banks, Federal Land Banks, Banks for Cooperatives, Federal Home Loan Banks, etc.

They are backed by the full faith and credit of Uncle Sam and carry maturities from a few months to many years. They are among the highest quality securities available. Their yields are as high, and often higher, than those of most Aaa- or Aa-rated industrial bonds.

Problems: in odd lots, Government agency bonds may be less liquid than corporates, so you could take a small loss if you have to sell quickly. The point spread between bid and asked prices has been as high as ½ of 1% versus a normal spread of ¼ of 1%. *But most people buy bonds for long-term holdings.*

Some of these difficulties have been overcome by a new market on the AMEX. This deals in odd lots of T-bills and Federal notes and bonds. This reduces commission costs and makes it possible to buy in comparatively small units. You do not get possession of the certificates, which are held in trust in a bank. Credits for interest and transactions are made to the account, with copies to you and your broker.

How to Make Profits with Bonds

To most people, a bond is a secure, static investment that provides a fixed annual income and, at maturity, can be redeemed for the same amount of dollars used to purchase it when issued. *Just buying bonds and storing them in a safe deposit box is a foolish way to invest.*

With all kinds of bonds, there are plenty of *conservative* opportunities to attain capital gains and to increase total returns: income plus appreciation. Nowadays, bonds

FIXED-INCOME SECURITIES

Type	Minimum Purchase	Maturity Range	Liquidity	Interest	Where Available
Short Term					
U.S. Treasury Bills	$ 10,000	3-12 mos.	Best	Discount	Brokers, Banks Federal Reserve Banks, AMEX
Local Authorities	1,000	3-12 mos.	Average	Straight	Brokers, Banks
FNMA notes (Federal National Mortgage Association)	50,000	30-270 days	Good	Discount	Large Dealers
COOP Bank Bonds	5,000	180 days	Good	Straight	Brokers, Banks
Federal Inter-mediate Credit Bank Bonds	5,000	270 days	Good	Straight	Brokers, Banks
State-Local Government Notes	5,000	1-12 mos.	Average	Straight	Brokers, Banks
Bankers' Accep-tances	5,000	1-270 days	Average	Discount	Brokers, Banks
Negotiable CDs	100,000	1-12 mos.	Average	Straight	Brokers, Banks
Commercial Paper	100,000	1-270 days	Poor	Discount	Dealers
Medium Term					
U.S. EE Bonds	25	9 years	None	Discount	Banks, U.S. Treasury
U.S. HH Bonds	500	10 years	None	Straight	Fed. Reserve
U.S. E Bonds	25	5 years	None	Discount	Banks, U.S. Treasury
U.S. H Bonds	500	10 years	None	Straight	Fed. Res. Banks, U.S. Treasury
U.S. Treasury Notes-Bonds	1,000	1-20 years	Good	Straight	Brokers, Banks
Federal Financing Bank Notes-Bonds	1,000	1-20 years	Good	Straight	Brokers, Banks
Farmers Home Ad-ministration Notes-Certificates	25,000	1-25 years	Average	Straight	Brokers, Banks
GNMA Securities/ Certificates (Government National Mortgage Association)	5,000	1-25 years	Average	Straight	Brokers, Banks
GNMA Pass-Through Certificates	25,000	Avg. -12 years	Good	Straight	Brokers, Banks
Federal Land Bank Bonds	1,000	1-10 years	Good	Straight	Brokers, Banks
Corporate Notes and Bonds	5,000	1-50 years	Good	Straight	Brokers
Eurobonds and Notes	1,000	3-25 years	Poor	Straight	Brokers, Foreign Banks
Long Term					
Local Housing Authority Bonds	5,000	1-40 years	Good	Straight	Brokers, Banks
Federal Home Loan Mortgage Certificates	100,000	15-30 years	Average	Straight	Brokers, Banks
FNMA Bonds (Federal National Mortgage Association)	25,000	2-25 years	Average	Straight	Brokers, Banks
State and Local Government Notes-Bonds	5,000	1-50 years	Average	Straight	Brokers
TVA Notes-Bonds (Tennessee Valley Authority)	1,000	3-25 years	Average	Straight	Brokers, Banks
International Bank for Re-construction and Develop-ment, Asian Development Bank and Inter-American Development Bank notes and Bonds	1,000	3-25 years	Average— down	Straight	Brokers, Banks
Foreign notes and bonds denominated in dollars and foreign currencies, issued by US and for-eign corporations and governmental bodies	1,000	1-30 years	Below average	Straight	Brokers and Overseas Banks
Corporate Preferred Stock	25 up	no maturity	Average	Quarterly Dividends	Brokers

SOURCE: **The Complete Bond Book** by David M. Darst

should be bought for trading, not holding, unless you are willing to swap the ultimate security for interim paper losses or actual profits.

Capital gains result from changes in interest rates. *Straight bonds almost always reflect the cost of money.* Buy short-term, high-coupon bonds when there is a prob-

---

SELECTED SHORT TERM BONDS
With Standard & Poor's Ratings

Maturing in 1983
Allied Chemical 8 3/8 (A)
Duquesne Lighting 3 5/8 (AA)
GMAC 8.7 (AA)
N.Y. Telephone 8 (AAA)
Standard Oil (Ind) 4 1/2 (AAA)

Maturing in 1984
American Can 9 1/4 (A)
Florida P&L 9 1/8 (A)

No. Illinois Gas 8 1/4 (AA)
Pacific G&E 3 1/8 (AA)
Texas Gas Trans. 8 3/4 (A)

Maturing in 1985
GE Credit 8 1/4 (AA)
Ingersoll Rand 8 3/4 (A)
Masco Corp. 12 1/4 (A)
Sears Roebuck 7 3/4 (AA)
Southwest Bell 2 3/4 (AAA)

LONG TERM BONDS
With Standard & Poor's Ratings

Maturing in 2000
Beneficial Corp. 7.45 (A)
Dow Chemical 8 7/8 (A)
Monsanto Co. 9 1/8 (A)
Standard Oil (Ohio) 8 1/2 (AA)
Weyerhaeuser 8 5/8 (A)

Maturing in 2005
Bank America Corp. 8 7/8 (AAA)
Dow Corning 9 3/8 (A)
General Motors 8.05 (AAA)
Procter & Gamble 8 1/4 (AAA)
Union Carbide 8 1/2 (A)

Maturing in 2010
Comm. Edison 11 1/4 (A)
Duke Power 14 7/8 (A)
N.E. Telephone 9 1/2 (AA)
Pacific NW Bell 8 5/8 (AAA)
So. Central Bell 9.2 (AAA)

Long Maturities
Amer. Fgn. Power 5, 2030 (A)
Bell Penna. 11 7/8, 2020 (AAA)
Mich. Bell 9 1/8, 2018 (AAA)
N.Y. Tel. 8 7/8, 2017 (AAA)
So. Bell 12 7/8, 2020 (AAA)

SELECTED INTERMEDIATE TERM BONDS
With Standard & Poor's Ratings

Maturing in 1986
A. T. & T. 2 5/8 (AAA)
Caterpillar Tractor 5 1/8 (AA)
Honeywell Finance 8.7 (A)
Shell Oil 4 5/8 (AA)
U.S. Steel 4 1/2 (A)

Maturing in 1987
Avco Financial 9 7/8 (A)
Beneficial Corp 8.85 (AA)
Marathon Oil 10 1/4 (AA)
Niagara Mohawk 4 7/8 (A)
Southern Bell 2 7/8 (AAA)

Maturing in 1988
Consolidated Edison 4 (A)
Dow Chemical 4.35 (A)
Ford Motor Credit 7.85 (A)
McDonald's Corp 8 5/8 (A)
Mont. Ward Credit 7 3/8 (A)

Maturing in 1989
Chesa. & Ohio Rail. 4 (AA)
Columbia Gas 9 5/8 (A)
Heller (W.E.) 9 1/2 (A)
May Dept. Stores 9 (A)
Reynolds Tobacco 7 (AA)

Maturing in 1990
Baltimore G & E 3 1/4 (AA)
General Foods 8 7/8 (AAA)
No. Natural Gas 9 1/2 (A)
Shears.Loeb Rhds 15 1/4 (A)
Sun Oil 4 5/8 (AA)

Maturing in 1991
Cleveland Electric 8 3/8 (AA)
Macy Credit 13 7/8 (A)
N.Y. Telephone 4 1/2 (AAA)
Pacific G & E 5 (AA)
Tenneco 8 1/4 (A)

Maturing in 1992
Bendix Corp. 6 5/8 (A)
Corn Products 5 3/4 (AA)
Liggett Group 6 (A)
Standard Oil (Cal.) 5 3/4 (AAA)
United Technologies 4 1/2 (AA)

---

ability of higher interest rates; buy long-term, low-coupon bonds when there is good reason to anticipate a decline in interest rates in the next six to twelve months.

Example: A 4⅜ U.S. Steel bond, issued at $1,000, and maturing in 1996, sold at 55 when the interest rate was 8%. When the cost of money went below 7%, its value moved up to about 59. This was the time to consider selling unless you felt that interest rates would go lower.

But, later, when interest rates soared to over 18%, its price fell to 39. When they started to fall again, the price jumped to about 66.

N.B.: Since you are giving up some current income when you buy discount bonds, always look for a higher-than-current yield.

Discount bonds are excellent investments for a Subchapter S corporation (basically a family holding company where profits are funneled through the corporation to the individual shareholder). These investments can earn "tax-free" income for shareholders because appreciation is long-term: since only 40% of long-term capital gains are taxable to an individual, the result is to convert part of the investment income into tax-exempt income.

Sidney Homer, the dean of "Bond Street," points out how to increase your income with straight bonds. He feels that investors should recognize the value of reinvesting bond interest. Over a 20-year period, he points out, more than half the total return of a bond comes from interest on interest. *This is the magic of compounding interest.* To build capital and boost your income over the years, always reinvest the semiannual interest in more bonds. If the check is small, hold the money in a savings account until you can add savings and buy more bonds.

In *The Yield Book,* Homer explains that all bonds do not act the same when there is a change in interest rates. Other things being equal, the volatility of bonds is greater: *(a)* the longer the maturity; *(b)* the lower the coupon; *(c)* the higher the starting yield.

Thus, 20-year 8s are more volatile than 30-year 12s; 15-year 10s are almost as volatile as 30-year 12s; etc. *If you have substantial holdings in bonds, it will pay you to ask your registered representative to discuss your portfolio with an experienced bond analyst and/or trader.* Since 1980, bonds are a brand new ball game.

Generally:

• *If you look for higher interest rates,* buy short-term bonds. If you're right, reinvest the redemption proceeds in high-yielding long-terms.

• *Be cautious about locking in high yields* unless you are happy with income alone. Over a period of years, their prices can swing widely and their total returns will always run behind inflation.

• *If you look for lower interest rates,* buy low-coupon, long-term bonds and sell when you have an adequate capital gain. When interest rates fell 1%, the value of Ohio Bell 7.5, 2011 bonds rose from $594 to $645. The percentage gains would be higher if you used margin.

• *With bonds, don't worry about "wash" sales—* selling and buying back similar securities within 30 days (see chapter on Taxes). With stocks, these losses are not tax deductible. With bonds, there are no such limitations.

• *Watch out for maintenance fees* if you leave the bonds with your bank as custodian. Typically, the charge will be about $5.00 per month. This will lower your rate of return because $60 a year is quite a dent in the $1,200-a-year interest on 10 12% coupon bonds.

Buying on Margin

Stock exchanges and brokerage firms limit margin accounts with bonds: usually about 33% for long positions, 50% for short selling. But banks are more liberal and will lend up to 80% on quality corporate bonds and over 90% on U.S. Government securities. A few years ago when the cost of money was lower and the interest rate on bonds reasonably close to that of the loan, it was often profitable to buy on margin. The income from the bonds paid a good share of the loan cost. If interest rates declined and the price of bonds rose, you could sell for a low-taxed, long-term capital gain. Or if you were a swinger and felt that interest rates were going to go up, you could sell short and cover your position at a profit. Such speculations do not work well in periods of high interest.

For High Taxpayers: 45% Annual Rate of Return

If you pay taxes at a 70% rate and are willing to borrow heavily, government bonds bought at the right time can provide after-tax returns of over 45%. This is possible because of a combination of deductions for interest and low—3% to 8%—margins on the loan. The benefits may be worthwhile at a somewhat low tax bracket. Here's how this was done in 1980, before the tax bill:

Dr. Ogilvie, in the 70% tax bracket, bought $1 million 7% coupon U.S. Government bonds, due in 13 months, at 94.4375 ($944,375). He put up $29,540 in cash and arranged a fixed-interest loan for the balance. (For tax purposes, everything had to be over one year).

His interest payments were $44,710. In the 70% tax bracket, this meant an after-tax expense of $13,414. His total investment was $42,954.

When the bonds are paid off at par, the capital gain will be $45,625. Since this will be taxed at a 28% rate

(40% at 70%), the after-tax net will be $19,437. On the investment base of $42,954, that's a net return of 45.25%.

The danger: that the price of the bonds will drop, so that Dr. O. will have to come up with more cash. But with such a short maturity, this is not likely. If this should happen, it would be expensive: every rise of 1% in the cost of money means an extra $10,000 a year.

Before you try such a deal, be sure to check with your tax adviser. In some cases, the net interest expense that can be written off in one year is limited to $10,000 although the excess can be carried forward.

The Yield Curve

A yield curve traces on a graph the yield to maturity of a group of securities, compared with the time remaining in each security's life. To draw a yield curve, the professional sets out the maturities on graph paper on a horizontal line, from left to right, starting with the shortest maturities (30 days) and continuing to the most distant (30 years). Then he plots the yields on the vertical axis and connects the dots with a line which becomes the yield curve.

The value of this chart is that it shows what investors THINK future interest rates will be. It is helpful in choosing maturities of debt instruments to meet specific investment needs.

This illustration shows the yield curve as of early April 1981:

In January 1978, the curve was flat but tending upward.

In January 1979, the curve started down to forecast a decline in the cost of money. So, too, in January 1980, when interest rates were quite high. By June 1980, the rate was down but the forecast was for higher yields. By December 1980, money costs were at a peak.

Note that, at that time, short-term rates were over 18% but the forecast was for a sharp drop. This occurred by the end of March 1981. Now the yield curve was steady, indicating that investors did not expect much change.

Here's how the yield curve can be used. Let's suppose

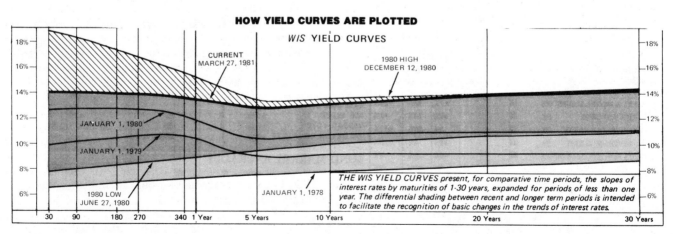

HOW YIELD CURVES ARE PLOTTED

WIS YIELD CURVES

CURRENT MARCH 27, 1981

1980 HIGH DECEMBER 12, 1980

JANUARY 1, 1980

JANUARY 1, 1979

1980 LOW JUNE 27, 1980

JANUARY 1, 1978

THE WIS YIELD CURVES present, for comparative time periods, the slopes of interest rates by maturities of 1-30 years, expanded for periods of less than one year. The differential shading between recent and longer term periods is intended to facilitate the recognition of basic changes in the trends of interest rates.

30   90   180   270   340   1 Year   5 Years   10 Years   20 Years   30 Years

SOURCE: Wright Investors' Service

you inherited $10,000 and want to have it available in ten years. You have these debt choices:

• A ten-year bond to be held to maturity. This would be OK if you expected interest rates to stay high.

• A six-month Treasury bill which will be rolled over at maturity repeatedly over the ten years. This would be wise if you might need the money and if interest rates are high and expected to rise.

• A two-year Treasury note which, at maturity, would be turned into an eight-year note. This would be fine if short-term rates are high and expected to drop and long-term rates are low and expected to rise.

• A 15-year bond to be sold after ten years. This would be worth considering if you expect interest rates to fall. But it carries the greatest risk.

The yield curve can aid investors to visualize the profit potential of various investments with different maturities. As with all technical indicators, it is not always correct (or, more likely, not correctly interpreted), but it's a useful tool in predicting future interest rates. Ask your broker for regular charts of yield curves from his research department.

Special Types of Debt Issues

With tight money and continuing needs for major capital investments, corporations (with the shrewd aid of their friendly underwriters) have come up with unusual debt offers, some involving special inducements, others government guarantees. In most cases, the interest rates are higher and the terms of the loans shorter than standard issues. Usually, they are best for wealthy investors.

Equipment Certificates. These are floated by airlines and railroads to finance the purchase of new planes or rolling stock. Their yields are excellent and there's little chance of a default because the company would then be out of business. Certificates are issued in serial form so they mature at different dates.

Optional maturity. These are bonds that can be redeemed anytime after the first five years or so. This provision protects the investor against unfavorable shifts in the cost of money by setting a floor on the value of the debt.

Example: In 1979, Beneficial Corporation, the big finance firm, offered an 8% bond redeemable in any year from 1983 through 2001. In 1984, if interest rates are above 8% (and thus the market value of the bond will be below 100), the investor can get back his $1,000 and reinvest the proceeds in higher-paying securities. If, at that time, interest rates are below 8%, he is locked in with what is a better-than-average rate of return.

FHA-backed bonds. These are private debt issues 90% guaranteed by the Farmers Home Administration. The proceeds are used to finance business acquisition, plant expansion or equipment purchases when the project is in a rural area and shows promise of providing permanent jobs.

For investors, these bonds provide longer maturities and the assurance that Uncle Sam will make good on any loan in default. To the borrower, they offer a lower interest rate than could be obtained on its own credit.

Typical issue: $15.25 million, 20-year, 8.9% bonds for Perdue, Inc., a poultry processing firm.

Eurobonds. These are issued by foreign subsidiaries of U.S. companies. They pay 50 to 100 basis points (0.5% to 1%) more than similarly rated domestic bonds.

Since these have heavier sinking funds than most U.S. issues, there's less risk of loss of capital when interest rates rise. Buy only in units of 10 or more because these bonds are sold in a dealer's market oriented to major investors.

Foreign bonds. These are issued in native currencies and are therefore subject to a decline in the value of the currency in which the bonds are denominated. As the dollar bounces back and the Swiss franc, German mark or Japanese yen declines, American holders will see the value of their holdings drop. With rising interest rates, that slide could worsen.

James Sinclair, a Wall Street bond expert, warns, "Avoid Swiss franc issues of private companies, regardless of the currency involved. Their managements follow local accounting practices so can just as easily hide assets as losses. . . . To buy a Swiss security, you must first buy Swiss francs, often selling at a premium."

If you want to gamble, put some money in Danish five-year installment bonds, traded on the Copenhagen Stock Exchange. Each year a drawing is held and a certain percentage of the bonds is picked to be redeemed at par (1,000 kroner, about $177). If your bonds are chosen, you get a yield of over 26%. When held to maturity, you get a yield of over 14%. There's no Danish tax on the interest, and the brokerage fees are 1.75% to buy, 1.5% to sell. You must report the income on your U.S. tax return. For information: Den Danske Bank, 75 Rockefeller Plaza, New York, NY 10020; Privatbanken A/S, 450 Park Avenue, New York, NY 10022.

Yankee bonds. These are foreign issues floated in dollars. They include debt of governments, governmental agencies and publicly owned corporations. Their yields are good, and there are possibilities of extra profits due to shifts in exchange rates, but their marketability is limited. You had better know something about the issuer or have a money-savvy adviser.

New Types of Bonds

Wall Street, ever alert to changing trends, has come up with innovative packaging of debt issues. Usually these involve lower-rated (BB and B) companies, so there are risks. But there are also extra rewards because corporations are willing to make concessions to borrow the money they need.

New ideas are coming up every month, but these will give you an idea of the unusual opportunities that are currently available. Be selective. In a credit crunch, some of the companies may not be able to meet all their commitments.

Indexed to inflation. Sunshine Mining Company, a major silver producer, offers investors a chance to profit from future increases in the price of silver. Their 15-year, 8.5% debt can be redeemed for the greater of $1,000 cash or the going value of 50 troy ounces of silver (equivalent to $20 an ounce).

Super-discounts. These are bonds that are issued far below par. The corporation saves taxes and gets a low cost; some investors lock in a high yield and can count on certain appreciation (unless the company fails).

Example: Martin Marietta floated 7% bonds due in 2011 at a 46% discount. The YTM was 13.25%,

To the corporation, the after-tax cost per bond, for interest, was $30.72 vs $37.80 otherwise. In effect, MM deferred part of the interest payment to maturity. In 30 years, it will have to come up with $165 million to pay for an initial loan of $94.2 million.

By tax regulations, the company must charge a portion of the discount against income each year as though it were an interest expense even though this does not involve cash outlays. For tax purposes, the non-cash charge amounts to 1/30th of the discount each year. When deducted from corporate taxes, there's a bigger tax flow.

The appreciation may look like capital gains but not to the IRS. The taxpaying investor must count a portion of the bond discount as gross income and pay taxes on it in that year. These discount bonds are worthwhile investments ONLY for tax-exempt portfolios such as those of foundations and pension plans. They can lock in good yields for 30 years with little chance of call.

Indexed to oil prices. These are bonds where the interest rate fluctuates with the price of oil. Petro-Lewis sold 20-year bonds with an initial coupon of 13%. This yield goes up annually if the price of "sweet crude" from West Texas rises 10%, The rate cannot drop below 13% or go above 15.5%. Apparently, investors were not overly impressed: the original bonds, offered at $1,000 each, were selling recently at $860.

Tied to earnings. Allegheny Beverage, a Pittsburgh-based bottler, sold 10-year bonds with a face coupon of 14%. If pre-tax income goes above $12 million, the rate will rise ½ point to a 15% limit. The only flaw is that the company has never earned more than $10 million.

Equity kicker. Pettibone Corp. offered a package of debt and equity. For $838, the investor got one $1,000, 12⅜% bond plus six shares of common stock.

Variable rate. General Felt Industries offered 20-year bonds at a discount to yield, to maturity, 17.42%. The rate is pegged to the YTM of 20-year Treasury bonds and is reset every three months. If interest rates decline, the return goes down, too.

Now do you see why the bond market is fast approaching the speculations of common stocks?

Automatic Bond Reinvestment

Just as with common stocks whose dividends are used to buy new shares, corporations now offer interest-reinvestment programs. Illinois Power Company permits the interest to be used to buy shares of common stock at a 5% discount from the average price of the stock on the first trading day of the month in which the interest is paid. Over a three-year period, this formula plan boosted the total return of the 8⅞, '08 bonds to 10.57%.

N.B.: To the IRS, this interest is still taxable as ordinary income whether received or converted to stock.

Always Check the Call Protection

When a major investor buys a large block of bonds, he wants to be sure that this can be a long-term holding and will not be redeemed when interest rates decline. Usually, bonds have call protection that rules out redemption for the first five or 10 years and then only at an above-par price—e.g., at 105 ($1,050 for a $1,000 bond).

The corporation can save money because there will be less interest to pay over the years IF the cost of money drops—roughly more than 1% below the original coupon (e.g., a 12% bond would probably be refinanced when the interest rate goes below 11%).

Watch for corporate policy changes that may save the company money at your expense. In late 1979, A.T.&T. reduced the extra interest paid on called bonds from 12 to 6 months' premium.

It's nice to get the extra money but you will have to reinvest the proceeds at a lower rate of return. *Do not buy long-term bonds without adequate call protection.*

Double-check the call provisions for high-coupon utility bonds. With Niagara Mohawk Power 10%, '85s, the *big type* set the call price at 103.54 after 1981 but the *small type* referred to a replacement fund, a reserve for the repair and maintenance of mortgaged property, to be used to redeem the bonds at any time. So, four years before the anticipated protection date, investors had to turn in their bonds.

Sinking-Fund Provision

This requires the corporation to make periodic, predetermined cash payments to the trustee of the bonds. With this money, the trustee buys back a portion of the outstanding debt: in the open market when the bond price is below par; by lot when it is trading above face value.

With a sinking fund, the corporation pays less total interest. With a 25-year issue set up to buy back 3.75% of the debt annually, 75% of the bonds will be retired before maturity. This means that the average life of the bonds will be about 17 years, not the 25 years anticipated by the investor. And, again, the proceeds may have to be reinvested at a lower yield.

A similar situation to the early-call provision is the use of the "funnel." This allows the company to satisfy sinking-fund requirements for its entire mortgage debt by zeroing in on and retiring bonds of a single issue. Obviously, the called bonds will be those with the highest coupons. The same threat of early retirement applies to some preferred stocks.

Another special situation with sinking funds is "doubling the option." This allows the corporation, at the time interest payments are due, to call up twice the normal number of shares at a special call price. Thus, with a 6% sinking fund, started in the fifth year, this will amount to an annual call of 12% of the entire issue. To the investor, this would be worthwhile only if the call price were well above par.

About the best thing that can be said for sinking funds is that they reduce the risks by lowering the total debt and, to some extent, providing price support for the bonds. In most cases, the investor loses and only the corporation wins.

To Swap or Not to Swap

Swapping bonds is important in serious bond investing. On the surface it appears profitable to sell a bond yielding 6.5% to purchase a similar quality bond selling to yield 8%. In theory, this is a gain of 150 points a year to maturity.

This is wrong. The conventional yield to maturity assumes a reinvestment rate of 6.5% for one and 8% for the other. Actually, the reinvestment rate will be identical for both issues. Thus the yield gain from the switch is narrowed and, depending on the time to maturity, may be almost eliminated.

In the same way, there's a problem in relating present and future yields. Is it more profitable to accept $1 income today or $1.20 three and a half years hence?

Homer uses this formula to find the answer:

$$\frac{1}{(1 + R)T}$$

T = number of semiannual interest periods
R = interest rate per period, expressed as a decimal

$$\$1.20 \times \frac{1}{(1 + .035)7} = \$1.20 \times \frac{1}{(1.035)7}$$

$$= \$1.20 \times \frac{1}{1.272} = \$1.20 \times .786 = \$.943$$

Answer: Take the $1 yield today!

If you add a number of bonds to your portfolio, review them every six months, use the interest productively and consider swaps whenever there is a change of 1% in the prevailing interest rate.

Homer says, "A $1,000 8% bond compounded semiannually will grow to $2,000 in 9 years, $7,106 in 25 years and $50,504 in 50 years."

Flower Bonds Are Blooming Again

Once again, "flower" bonds are worthwhile investments for older people. These are U.S. Government obligations that carry low coupons and therefore sell at a discount. They are accepted at face value in paying estate taxes when they are owned by a person at death.

Example: February 3½, '90 bonds are selling at

about 84. A senior citizen who buys ten of these for $8,400 will get a $10,000 credit against estate taxes when he or she dies.

"Flower" bonds do not pay top interest but the tax savings can be welcome. See your tax adviser if you are elderly or are responsible for estate planning for an older relative.

Plan Bond Portfolios by Age

Bond investments should be as carefully planned and diversified as a stock portfolio. Consider present and future needs, tax bracket, lifestyle, and age. Here's a conservative recommendation:

Age Bracket	Corporates	CVs	Tax-Exempts	Gov'ts
30-39	50%	50%	—	—
40-49	33	33	33	—
50-59	25	25	25	25
Over 60	20	20	20	40

High-Yielding Bonds for Speculation

These bonds are of two types: (1) Those of well-established corporations which have run into temporary trouble, usually not entirely of their own making. Under normal conditions, such securities would be safe investments. (2) Those of highly leveraged companies whose issues are of questionable quality (usually unrated) and not suitable for institutional portfolios.

Currently, both types are selling at low prices (and thus high yields) because investors can get somewhat comparable returns with much less risk.

The second group are classified as "junk" bonds. Generally, these bonds are used to massage the corporate balance sheet. A bond exchanged for common stock, for example, provides leverage for the company to produce an instant earnings increase. This is because the after-tax interest cost is always less than the earnings attributed to the acquired common stock. To cover stock that is selling at five times earnings, the company must earn 40% before taxes. By swapping for a 10% bond, it can save three-quarters of that cost. Shrewd speculators take advantage of this situation and obtain high yields and, with a little luck, appreciation as well.

FLOWER BONDS TO REDUCE ESTATE TAXES

Issue	Recent Price	Yield
3 1/2, Feb. 1990	84.22	5.72%
4 1/4, Aug. 1987-92	84.16	6.16
4, Feb. 1988-93	84.14	5.83
4 1/8, May 1989-94	85.	5.77
3, Feb. 1995	84.14	4.52
3 1/2, Nov. 1998	84.16	4.81

SOURCE: Barron's

SOME HIGH YIELDING BONDS

Company / Security	Moody's Rating	Recent Price	Recent Yield
Alabama Power 13½, '00	Baa	83 1/4	16.20%
El Paso Electric 15, '00	A	96 1/8	15.10
Ford Credit 9.7, '00	Aaa	61 1/4	15.83
Georgia Power 14½, '10	Baa	92 1/2	15.67
Pacific Tel. 15½, '20	A	97 5/8	15.88
Phila. Electric 9 5/8, '02	A	61 1/4	15.70
Portland GE 9½, '06	Baa	61	15.57
Pub. Service, N.H. 14½, '00	Baa	92 1/8	15.74
Standard Oil (Ind) 16, '89	Aaa	100	16.00
UNC Resources 12, '98	Ba	73 7/8	16.23
World Airways 11¼, '94	Ba	71	15.84

SOURCE: New York Stock Exchange; Moody's Investors Service

Be very cautious with these securities. Marginal companies often offer to swap for lower-coupon CVs or preferred stock. But the replacements may be just as risky and pay less.

N.B.: Once in a while, because of unusual circumstances, junk bonds can be debt of well-rated companies. Teledyne 10% subordinated debentures, 2004, were selling recently to yield 12.1% at 825. They were rated BB because they were subordinated to other corporate debt. But Teledyne's cash flow could pay them off in a minute if management so decided.

Defaulted Railroad Bonds Still Highly Profitable

If you have followed previous editions of *Your Investments* and bought defaulted railroad bonds, you made a lot of money. Typically, in the Penn Central reorganization, 4% bonds, bought at around 40, were paid off with securities that have risen twenty-fold, and now that the company is a profitable real estate/pipeline firm, have excellent growth/income potential.

The boom is over but there are still opportunities for sure gains and, according to Hans Jacobsen, railroad specialist with Herzog, Heine and Geduld (170 Broadway, New York, N.Y. 10038), "You won't have to wait much beyond 1982."

Still-traded railroad bonds will be swapped for a combination of cash, short-term mortgage bonds, and common stock of a new corporation—when approved by a Federal Court. The cash comes from the sale of assets and continues to compound at 8% annually.

Here are the remaining opportunities:

Boston & Maine. If a pending offer is approved, the bondholder will get par plus accumulated interest. With the 6s: about $1,750 for those now trading at $1,350. With the 4s, with 24 years of interest, more than $1,000 for debt that can be acquired for less than $750.

Erie Lackawanna. Again, the potential profit is the gain to par plus interest: for the 3⅛s (which rose from 33 last year to a recent 85), a 50% total return.

Morris & Essex. Scheduled payout for a 50% gain: for the 3⅛s, selling in the low 80s, an estimated $830 in A-1 and A-2 bonds; $145 in B-bonds and the balance in cash.

Lehigh Valley: 3¾s, '95 at 48 will get 12 years' interest plus bonds for a total value of over $1,000.

Jacobsen is not enthusiastic about the defaulted debt of other railroads but repeats that "The risks are minimal and largely a matter of time: how fast the courts act. You will tie up your money for a year or two but you are sure to profit . . . if you deal with a knowledgeable broker."

How a Small Investor Can Buy Bonds

If you do not have ready resources to buy a block of bonds, take a look at bond funds. They provide competitive yields, can be purchased for a minimum investment of $1,000 or so (usually with a sales commission), and permit reinvestment of income for compounding. The shares of many funds sell at discounts so there can be extra profits. These are the most popular types:

1. Closed-end funds whose proceeds are invested in fixed-income debt securities and whose shares are publicly traded on the NYSE or OTC. They operate like regular mutual funds. Their yields are slightly less than those of new issues; recently about 13%. The actual returns, of course, depend on the composition of the portfolio and the skill of the money managers. Pricewise, they have been losing investments with annual losses of over 30% because of rising interest rates.

Costs of doing business are comparatively high. Some loads are 8.5%; management fees are around 0.5% of assets plus 0.5% for operational expenses plus 2.5% of the fund's cash income. Thus, the yield to shareholders will be about 1.5% less than the return of a bond average.

To beat competition, some fund managers look for income from trading or other noninvestment tactics. They buy high-yielding commercial paper, lend part of their portfolio to major underwriters short of certain bonds. The underwriter pays a small fee and thus avoids bank borrowings or having to cover a short position in an erratic market.

Always check the portfolio and the policies of the fund before you invest. Special techniques may be profitable but they can be risky and the concept of a bond fund should always be SAFETY FIRST.

2. Open-end funds which invest either wholly or largely in Government notes and bonds. They are geared to the small and medium investor. They diversify their portfolios by maturities rather than by types of bonds. Sales charges are low, and often there are no redemption fees.

Usually the prices of fund shares drop further than their net asset value (the worth of the underlying securities). In one year, the assets back of one share of a major fund fell from $15.99 to $15.51, but the market value of each share declined 72¢ more: from $15.37 to $14.65.

Since there are no maturity dates for the fund shares, an investor always takes an extra risk: that the spread will become greater rather than smaller. The discounts vary according to the type of bonds held and the management fee charged. Don't worry if you buy for income, but be cautious if you want capital gains.

Advice: Consider buying shares of any bond fund which sells at more than 15% below net asset value, especially if the underlying securities are sound and relatively risk-free.

3. Small bond funds. These are the latest pitch, by brokerage firms, to cash in on investor interest in fixed-income securities. Usually, the redemption of bonds is at the will of the issuer. But with these new bond funds, which can be purchased for $1,000 with additions in $100 units, the bondholder may redeem part of the total each year at par plus accrued interest.

4. High-yield bond funds. These specialize in low-grade issues with extra high rates of return: up to 15% a year. They are better speculations than investments but, at 15% compounded, you will double your money in about five years.

They do have special features:

• *Greater upside leverage* as compared to typical bonds. When interest rates fall and bonds rally, the funds get double pressure from: (*a*) the rise of the overall bond market and (*b*) the enthusiasm of investors who bid up prices until they are almost equal to net-asset values.

• *Downside cushion in a down market.* Shares of bond funds selling at deep discounts will decline less than the prices of individual bonds.

Extra checkpoints in choosing bond funds:

Evaluate the portfolio. *For safety,* choose those with the most AA- and A-rated holdings. *For income,* look for those that buy lower-quality issues. Stay away from any fund that has large holdings of NR (Not-Rated) issues.

Be skeptical about claims of diversification. With well-rated bonds, there's little chance of failure to pay interest or redemption.

Check the repurchase price. If the fund buys only at the lower side of the price spread, you will lose a few dollars when you cash in. At redemption, Nuveen pays the bid side price. Merrill Lynch pays the offering price as long as the fund is one in which it makes a market.

Look for frequent distributions. A fund that pays monthly assures a steady cash flow and, if the income is reinvested, compounds at a higher rate. Buy just before the distribution-declaration date.

Calculate the average discount. When a fund is selling below its average annual discount from net-asset value, it's probably a good buy. If it's priced well above that average, be cautious. Usually, the discount will reflect the composition of the portfolio.

Bond Immunization for Pension Funds

To fight GIC (Guaranteed Investment Contracts) offered by insurance companies, Manufacturers Hanover Trust has developed a *bond immunization* plan. It may be copied for smaller investors.

The rate of return is not guaranteed but simulations by actuaries have shown a 95% chance of hitting a target rate of return. The method is based on the actuarial fact that a change in a bond's price equals what is known as the "duration" of that bond multiplied by the shift in interest rates.

Duration is the mean cash flow: the mean time it takes to receive all the coupons and the principal over the life of the debt. After about 25 years, the weight of the coupon flow is primarily principal, so the duration level stays around 10.

To meet the duration rate, the fund managers mix the bonds by rate and maturity date. The duration of the bond must always equal the period of time for which they want protection. Thus, if they want a set yield for ten years, the bond must have a duration of ten years. After one year, the protection number drops to nine, so part of the bond must be sold and replaced with a bond with lower duration. This rebalancing of the portfolio is done annually. Well, it's a good theory and only time will tell whether it works in practice.

CHAPTER 16

Tax-Exempt Bonds: for Income, Not for Total Returns

When interest rates were low, tax-exempt bonds were rewarding investments primarily for the wealthy: those who paid income taxes at a rate of 39% or more. But today, with tax-free yields of over 10% and inflation-fattened income boosting tax brackets, almost every serious investor should consider placing a portion of his savings in tax-exempt securities. For those in the 32% tax bracket, a 10% tax-free yield is equal to a taxable return of 14.71%—just about what's available with short-term Treasury bills and money-market funds and long-term quality bonds.

Unless you are wealthy or a shrewd trader, tax-exempts should be bought for income and should be held to maturity. There's not much chance for appreciation and costs are relatively high: for commissions and price differentials for purchases or sales in small lots of less than $10,000. If and when interest rates decline, tax-exempt bonds will become less attractive

Tax-exempt bonds (also called municipals) are just what the name states. They are debt issues of states, local governments and certain public authorities whose interest is exempt from federal income taxes and from state and local income taxes when the bonds are issued in that state. The tax benefit does not extend to capital gains.

The higher your tax bracket, the greater the attraction. And if you substitute sufficient tax-exempt interest for currently taxable income, you may move down to a lower tax bracket. The specific percentage advantages are shown in the table. When you get out your home calculator, use your *effective* tax rate, not the one that is shown for your gross-income bracket. In most cases, this will be the tax rate finally used after all deductions and adjustments. This can be much lower than the percentage figure in the table (before the 1981 tax law).

The table should never be the sole or final answer. The situation is different with every investor today and will be more so in the future. Get all the facts before you assume that a tax-free income is best for you.

In the 37% tax bracket, the investor who buys a 9.50% municipal bond receives the equivalent of a taxable 15.08%—about the same yield of some well-rated corporate bonds. And in the 49% tax bracket, that 9.50% yield provides the same net income as an 18.62% taxable corporate debt issue—available only with a few low-quality securities.

When you have to pay state income taxes, the benefits are greater: in the 41% tax bracket, that 9.50% tax-exempt is the same as a taxable 16.10%. In the 50% tax

TAX-EXEMPT VS. TAXABLE INCOME

IF YOUR NET JOINT TAXABLE INCOME IS * (Married) (000s Omitted)	Your Federal Income Tax Bracket Is	TO EQUAL THESE TAX FREE RATES						
		7.00%	7.50%	8.00%	8.50%	9.00%	9.50%	10.00%
		YOU WOULD HAVE TO EARN THIS MUCH FROM A TAXABLE INVESTMENT						
$24.6 - 29.9	32%	10.29	11.02	11.76	12.50	13.24	13.97	14.71
29.9 - 35.2	37	11.11	11.90	12.69	13.49	14.29	15.08	15.87
35.2 - 45.8	43	12.28	13.15	14.03	14.91	15.79	16.67	17.54
45.8 - 60.0	49	13.72	14.70	15.68	16.66	17.64	18.62	19.60
60.0 - 85.6	54	15.21	16.30	17.39	18.47	19.56	20.65	21.73

DOUBLE EXEMPTION FROM FEDERAL AND NEW YORK STATE INCOME TAXES

25.0 - 29.9	41	11.86	12.71	13.55	14.40	15.25	16.10	16.94
35.2 - 45.8	50	14.00	15.00	16.00	17.00	18.00	19.00	20.00
60.0 - 85.6	60	17.50	18.75	20.00	21.25	22.50	23.75	25.00

TRIPLE EXEMPTION FROM FEDERAL, NEW YORK STATE AND NEW YORK CITY INCOME TAXES

20.2 - 21.0	39	11.47	12.29	13.11	13.93	14.75	15.57	16.39
30.0 - 35.2	49	13.72	14.70	15.68	16.66	17.64	18.62	19.60
35.2 - 45.8	53	14.89	15.95	17.02	18.08	19.14	20.21	21.27
60.0 - 85.6	62	18.42	19.73	21.05	22.37	23.68	25.00	27.02

* Net taxable income, after exemptions and deductions

SOURCE: Lebenthal & Co., Inc.

bracket, the equivalent is a hefty 19%. (Broadly speaking, these figures, which apply to residents of New York State, would be similar for those who live in states where there's an income levy.)

The greatest benefits accrue to investors who pay the highest total income taxes: in New York City, for example, with a modest 39% total tax rate, that 9.50% tax-free return would require a taxable yield of 15.57%; in the 49% tax bracket, 18.62%. And in the 62% group—income of $60,000 for a married couple—that 9.50% nets the same as a 25% taxable return!

It's also wise to compare yields with those available from quality common stocks held for more than one year. With a 15% return—5% dividends and 10% appreciation—the taxes will be lower: for residents of non-income states in the 32% tax bracket, the net yield will be 12.12%: 32% of the 5% income (1.60%) plus 32% of 40% of the 10% capital gain (1.28%), for a tax bite of 2.88% or a net return of 12.12%. That's equivalent to a tax-free return of about 8.25%.

In the 49% tax bracket, the figures are 2.45% on the income and 1.96% on the capital gains for a tax of 4.41% or a net of 10.59%. That's the equivalent of a tax-free return of about 5.25%.

But remember that: (1) unless you buy municipals at a discount, there's not likely to be the 35% to 50% appreciation that characterizes common stocks of growing, profitable companies; (2) after retirement, most people will be in a much lower tax bracket.

If your goal is income and your tax bracket is high, the bond is a better investment. But the stock, with its ever-higher dividend and, hopefully, rising price, will provide greater net returns over the years

How to Calculate Equivalent Yields

To figure the exact equivalency between any tax-exempt and taxable yield, use these formulas:

1. To determine the percent yield that a bond or other fully taxed security must provide to give an after-tax return that matches a given tax-exempt yield:

$$\frac{TEY}{(100) - TB} = TY$$

TEY = Tax-Exempt Yield
TB = Tax Bracket
TY = Taxable Yield

If a tax-exempt bond yields 9% and the investor is in the 43% tax bracket, the equivalent taxable yield is 15.78%.

$$\frac{9}{(100) - 43} = \frac{9}{57} = 15.78$$

2. To determine the percent yield which a tax-exempt bond must pay to match the after-tax return of a bond or other security with a given, fully taxable yield or a taxable capital gain, reverse the formula:

$$TEY = TY \times (100) - TB$$
$$15.8 \times (100 - 43) = 15.8 \times 57 = 9.00\%$$

Safe but . . .

Most tax-exempt bonds are safe and will be repaid at maturity. When issued by a municipality, for example, they have a prior lien on all taxes but if there is not enough income to meet operating expenses, interest will have to be delayed or the repayment date extended. This is possible because of tax revolts and decreased Federal funding.

Before investing solely because of tax advantages, consider that:

1. Prices are not guaranteed. Bond prices are influenced by: *(a)* The cost of money. When interest rates rise, their values drop, regardless of the quality of the issue. If you have to sell, you will lose a lot of money. *(b)* The supply and demand for tax-exempt securities and various types of such issues. The difference may appear small but can total $30 to $40 per $1,000 face value.

2. Poor marketability. This applies primarily to lots of 5 or less and to uneven lots of 8, 14, 19, etc. These are the units most individuals buy when they invest a fixed sum. Prices of tax-exempts, except for large issues of turnpikes, toll bridges, etc., are not available in the daily press. Odd-lot prices, in selling, may be as much as five points ($50 per $1,000) below those of units of 100 bonds.

Tax-exempt bonds are NOT for investors who need or want quick and full liquidity. They are best suited for those who plan to hold them for redemption at maturity.

3. Decline in real value. As with all fixed-income holdings, tax-exempt bonds are subject to value erosion through inflation. Over its 30-year life, the typical "municipal" will lose almost all its purchasing power. At maturity, you will get the same number of dollars as you paid at issue, but unfortunately, those dollars will be worth far less in the real world!

Your best bet is to buy tax-exempts when they are selling at a discount. You can be sure of an eventual profit when the bonds are redeemed at par—even though this may be years away.

Types of Tax-Exempt Bonds

There are some 15,000 municipalities listed in Moody's *Bond Record* and nearly as many more communities/states/agencies with outstanding debt issues. They range from multi-million-dollar AAA-rated state/highway bonds to unrated $50,000 obligations of a local parking authority. Their total face value is over $200 billion. Trading is dominated by professionals who view $100,000 as a small lot.

In recent years, individuals, with ever-higher incomes and taxes, have become major investors in this field and, in the future, their role is likely to expand.

Broadly, these are the most widely used, and traded, forms of tax-exempt securities:

1. General-obligation bonds. These are the most common. They are backed by the full taxing power of the issuer. The payment of their interest and redemption is a primary obligation, so they usually have the highest ratings and the lowest yields.

A new variation of the customary $5,000 municipal bonds is the "minibond," issued directly to the public in denominations of $100, $500 and $1,000. In 1978, the State of Massachusetts sold $1 million worth of five-year, 5.7% bonds with a maximum individual purchase of $5,000. The bonds, rated AA by Standard & Poor's, sold at a discount with redemption at face value. Several municipalities in other states have made similar offers.

2. Limited-tax bonds are backed by the full faith and credit of the issuing body but not by its full taxing power. The issues might be secured by the receipts of a particular tax or even a portion of a particular tax.

3. Revenue bonds are based on revenues from projects built or maintained by local governments: waterworks, sewers, dormitories, etc. Their quality varies with the financial success of the underlying enterprise.

Time was when the most popular revenue bonds were those secured by income from motorists: toll roads, bridges and tunnels. But as states and communities seek added income aside from regular taxes, the revenues come from a variety of sources. In each case, analyze the issue as you would a corporate bond: Evaluate the soundness of the project and the income coverage of debt service. For a good electric or water system, net revenues need be only 120% of annual debt-service requirements; with new toll roads, look for 200% coverage. And keep checking the credit. A lot can happen in a few years, as shown by the fall and rise of the price of Big Mac bonds in New York City. Watch out for special provisions such as these:

• Turnpike Authority of Kentucky 7½s, '09 are paid by toll revenues but also have a call on the proceeds of a "severance" tax assessed on all coal produced in the state. Thus, the true coverage of interest and principal is 3.32 compared to 1.5 for most revenue issues.

• New York State Dormitory Authority bonds are paid from rentals to students. Their acceptance had been tainted by slow payments so that several major universities pledged their endowment-fund securities as collateral. New York University series D, 6s, '09, discounted to yield over 9%, are covered 2.1 times.

Revenue bonds have higher yields (generally about 20% more) than do general obligations of the same quality because revenue bonds are not regarded quite as safe in that the latter are backed by the full faith, credit and taxing power of the issuer.

4. Special-assessment bonds are usually small, almost neighborhood issues. They are secured by special levies on taxpayers benefiting from improvements such as new sewers or streets. Their investment values are limited.

5. Authority bonds can be either general obligations, revenue, or a combination of both. For example, when local housing authorities issue bonds under contracts with agencies of the Federal Government, these securities are fully backed by Uncle Sam and thus become high-quality investments. All these types of bonds carry modest interest rates.

You can get high yields with excellent security from the debt of publicly owned utilities: Colorado's Platte River Power Authority, Nebraska's Omaha Public Power District, and Arizona's Salt River Project.

Many of these bonds are rated A or better and carry tax-exempt yields of over 9%. Lower-quality issues, such as those of the New York City's Municipal Assistance Corporation, pay as much as 10⅝%—equivalent to a taxable yield of 21.24% for those in the 50% federal tax bracket, more when there are state and/or local levies.

6. Industrial-development bonds result from efforts to attract industry. Many states and some local governments issue tax-exempt bonds to finance the construction of plants, buildings, and facilities which are then leased to private companies. The bonds are backed by the rents or revenues of the project. The tax exemption applies only to small issues (under $5 million), so there's little after-market liquidity.

These bonds, originally used by small Southern communities to attract industry, are now available in almost every state. Ask your broker about small lots of local issues at discounts. They may yield 10% tax-free. Be sure that the guaranteeing corporation is solvent!

7. Pollution-control bonds are a new version of double-guaranteed debt, that is, they are secured by the state or local agency and the credit of a major corporation.

You may never have heard of Coconino County, but with the Arizona Pollution Corporation, it issued tax-free bonds paying 8.5% for A-rated Tucson Gas & Electric Co. Look around home for similar issues backed by such quality corporations as Exxon, General Motors, and major utilities.

8. Hospital bonds are available for single institutions, but more frequently, they are issued through state or regional hospital authorities. They are not as liquid as other debt issues but carry high coupons, long call protection, and because of federal restrictions on competition, they are safe long-term investments.

Variations of these include bonds that are guaranteed as to payment of principal and interest:

• *Industrial revenue bonds* issued by municipal agencies to finance construction of hospitals such as those operated by Hospital Corporation of America (HCA). This guarantee sounds better than it is because, if HCA should go broke, the bondholders will have to stand in line with other creditors. Realistically, however, that's not likely. HCA is rated A by Standard & Poor's and is the largest company in its field with anual revenues of over $1 billion and net income of some $55 million.

• *Health service bonds* guaranteed by the U.S. government such as Massachusetts Health and Educational Facilities Authority debt. These are collateralized by the Government National Mortgage Association. They are backed by an FHA mortgage (insured by Uncle Sam) that bears interest and principal equal to the debt service payments by the benefiting hospital.

9. Life-care Bonds, more aptly described as retirement-community bonds. These are debt issues, made under state auspices, whose proceeds are used to build housing units for well-to-do tenants who do not qualify for government aid. Usually, the operators are nonprofit religious groups.

10. Federal tax-exempts. These are bonds and notes of local public-housing authorities guaranteed by the U.S. government. There have been no long-term issues in recent years, but outstanding bonds are available at discounts.

There are also short-term (three- to six-month) notes that can be excellent for temporary funds. They pay around 8.50% and have an excellent secondary market.

Another variation is Section 8 Bonds. These are issued by state and local housing authorities to build low- and middle-income rental housing. There is no guarantee by Uncle Sam but the payments are secured by a federal rent subsidy with bondholders having first claim in case of financial trouble.

11. Puerto Rican bonds. These are fully exempt from federal, state and local income taxes regardless of where you live in the United States. They are rated A, are readily marketable and yield over 9%, reflecting investors' fears that the Commonwealth may not be as stable as mainland issuers.

12. Subsidized-housing bonds. In an effort to reduce the cost of home ownership, some municipalities have floated bonds at interest rates some 3% below those of taxable debt and then loaned the proceeds to qualified home buyers. These are good deals for investors but the concept has been criticized as, in some cities, the money has gone to affluent rather than poor families.

Congress may outlaw such cheap money but don't worry. There will probably be a grandfather clause to protect your holdings.

13. Pre-refunded issues. These are bonds, secured with U.S. Treasury obligations, that mature well in advance of their stated maturity date. They usually sell at a premium above par.

PRE-REFUNDED BONDS
TAX EXEMPTS

Issue/coupon	Original Maturity	Call Date	Recent Price	Recent Yield	Yield to Call
N.J. Sports 7.50%	2009	1984	108.98	6.88%	5.70%
Salt River 8.125	2013	1985	111.16	7.31	5.70
Suffolk Cty. 8.875	2006	1986	116.04	7.65	6.00
Mass (State) 9.00	2001	1987	116.00	7.76	6.57

Example: Suffolk County, N.Y., refunded an old issue with a pre-refunded loan. After the first call date, the U.S. Treasuries matured and were used to pay the old bonds at their call price. The new bonds were scheduled to mature in 2002 but will be called in 1986 at 103.

Their early call feature does not keep their price up but the tax loss, when held to the call date, is not tax-deductible. Still, if you sell the bonds at a loss before the call date, that amount can be used to reduce your total tax payment to Uncle Sam.

14. Put option bonds. These permit the investor to turn in the bonds, at face value, for cash, after a five-year waiting period. You must give six months written notice. With such protection, these bonds always sell at close to par, regardless of interest rate trends. The repurchase is guaranteed by a letter of credit issued by a bank for a fee of 0.45% of the value of the outstanding bonds.

Example: $50 million, 11¾% Washington Public Power Supply Systems nuclear-power projects #4 and #5 bonds due in 2010.

How Tax-Exempts Are Issued and Sold

Most of these "municipal" bonds are offered in serial form, with specific amounts maturing annually for the life of the issue, 20 years or more. There is usually a series of coupons attached. These denote the date when interest becomes due, normally semi-annually. The bondholder detaches the coupons and presents them for payment either to the paying agent or a commercial bank. The bonds can be registered for specific ownership either as to the principal only or as to both principal and interest.

Few "municipals" come out at par. Those with short maturities usually are priced at a premium. Those with long maturities may come out at discounts. The key factor is always the *yield to maturity* (YTM). There is only a tiny difference in the investment value between a 9.40% bond selling at a premium to yield 9%, and a 9% bond selling at par to yield 9%. Both bonds are paying 9% on the dollar.

Bonds are traded by dealers on a bid and asked basis. They make their profits by buying in quantities at lower "wholesale" prices and selling at higher "retail" prices. Most dealers maintain a substantial inventory but if you want specific bonds, they will get them from another dealer . . . probably at a slightly higher cost. Choose a dealer whom you trust and rely on his judgment. With small lots, it does not pay to shop.

Bargain opportunity. Most bonds are issued in bearer form, but some are available in registered form, that is, recorded in the owner's name. These registered bonds sell at bargain yields because large buyers do not want to bother with the expense and time of registration. If you don't mind getting a check directly from the municipality, you can get extra income for your invested dollars by watching for these opportunities.

How the Market Operates

Municipal bonds are one of the few investment situations where the small investor gets a better break than the big buyer. An individual with $25,000, or less, buys small blocks of bonds traded in the secondary market. As these are odd lots, they can often be acquired at a lower cost (and thus higher yield) than that paid by a big institution for a large block of identical securities. The bank is willing to trade off some yield for the convenience of handling $100,000 or more. The individual who buys 10 bonds may wind up with earnings of 1% or more tax-free ($10 per $1,000 bond).

The public's entry into the bond market has changed the bond business. Where once bond dealers looked askance at any order under $100,000, many firms are now aggressively pushing $5,000 units for the individual investor. Some may even settle for orders of $1,000 if this is the start of a savings/investment program.

Typically, Lebenthal & Co., Inc., in New York City, provides full information on bid and asked prices and uses a computer to locate the best bond buys at specific maturity dates, etc. Now you know what you are buying.

Not only is this a valuable service but it also shows competitive opportunities. Unlike listed stocks, which are sold at auction on exchanges, municipal bonds have no frame of public price reference. Each dealer sets his prices on the basis of cost and demand, or in the case of larger houses, at prices for which similar lots of the same bonds can be sold or acquired.

How to Choose Tax-Exempts

The factors (aside from tax considerations) to review in selecting tax-free bonds are:

1. Ratings. All major bond issues are rated on their quality by Moody's, Standard & Poor's or Fitch's: from Aaa (highest), Aa (high quality), down to C (lowest). *For details see chapter on corporate bonds.*

These criteria are set by professionals who have developed statistical yardsticks to judge the ability of a state or local government or agency to pay its obligations, especially under adverse economic conditions.

For investments, buy only bonds whose ratings start with "A" or "a." They are safe and, in most cases, their yields will be only slightly less than those of lower-quality issues.

For speculations, a "Baa" rating involves as much risk as anyone seeking income should take. If you want to gamble, do not buy tax-exempt bonds!

On the other hand, there are many good local bonds that are not rated because the municipality does not have enough outstanding debt and can sell issues easily. These do not have an active market and, usually, are bought in toto by a local financial institution.

N.B.: Generally, ratings by the services are similar but there are times when they do not agree. This can provide an opportunity for extra income.

Example: In 1980, Moody's rated Chicago School Finance Authority bonds a low "Baa-1" while Standard & Poor's considered them "AA." This difference of opinion reflected the uncertainties of municipal finance. Moody's felt that the school board might run into difficulty refunding older debt issues; S&P argued that the city could, and would, raise taxes.

The investor who was willing to accept the Moody's rating was about to get a 9% yield compared to the 7.85% return on comparably rated debt issues.

2. State and local tax exemption. Usually, in cities and states that have income taxes, the income from bonds issued in that state (and from Puerto Rico) are exempt from such levies. Whenever you can do so, choose bonds that will give you this extra advantage—e.g., if you live in New Jersey, buy bonds issued in that state.

3. Maturity date. For bonds with the same rating, the shorter the maturity, the lower the yield and the greater the price stability. Unless you plan to buy tax-exempts continuously and indefinitely, it is usually prudent to stick to bonds with maturities of not more than ten years.

You should select maturities according to your financial needs and time schedule. If you plan to retire in 10 years, pick a discount bond which will mature a decade from now. You will get a capital gain which will be taxed at your lower after-65 tax rate.

4. Economic base. Look for communities where: *(a)* the assessed valuation of property is considerably less than the full valuation; *(b)* there's a strong, diversified economic base not dependent on any one industry; *(c)* there is stable, fairly competent local government and *(d)* a low debt that is not likely to rise sharply in the near future.

Guidelines: Look for net debt that is less than 10% of actual property value, and debt service that is under 12% of total expenditures.

There are distinct regional differences with municipal bonds. Generally, debt of states in the Sunbelt sell at higher prices (and thus provide lower yields) than those of other regions of the country. This is due to the strength of their economies, more conservative governments, lower welfare/social costs and expanding rather than deteriorating tax bases.

5. Hidden debt. This represents unfunded pension

liabilities—that is, the shortfall between the benefits due retired and active employees, and the assets in the pension fund. The gap must be bridged sometime or the fund will be declared bankrupt.

This caveat applies to *(a)* older states such as Pennsylvania where, a survey showed, 25% of all municipal pension funds paid out more each year than was contributed; *(b)* major cities with financial problems. In Los Angeles, the police and fireman's fund has unfunded liabilities four times available assets. That's a sure sign of future trouble and, possibly, difficult situations such as have been faced by New York City. Such municipal bonds are not safe investments.

6. Marketability. The most readily salable tax-exempts are general obligation bonds of state governments and revenue bonds of large, well-known authorities. Smaller issues have few price quotations, and the cost of selling, especially in odd lots, can be more than the half-year interest payment!

The most dangerous holdings are those of small municipalities or authorities. How can you expect to get a quick sale of 22 bonds of the Dogpatch Septic Tank Authority?

7. Call provisions. Many issues permit the bonds to be redeemed, at a price above par, after the first five or ten years. With older low-coupon issues, there's no problem because these bonds can be bought, at below par prices, in the open market.

But with high-coupon issues, early redemption can save money. The borrower can float a new loan at lower interest: i.e. if the outstanding issue carries a 10% coupon and interest rates drop to 8%, the bond would sell at around 122. If it could be called at 105, it would pay the borrower to float a new 8% issue and force early redemption. But the investor would take a beating.

With some new bonds, however, an early call can be welcome. These are debt instruments of communities that have had difficulty in borrowing. These early call provisions are similar to a kicker and can be very profitable.

Example: In January 1981, the New York City Municipal Assistance Corporation 9¾% bonds, due in 1992, were selling at 92 ($920). This meant a tax-free return of 10.60% currently and a 10.99% yield to maturity.

Under the special provisions of the loan, these bonds were callable each January 1 and July 1, at premiums, so the yields to call were much higher. If interest rates fell, M.A.C. might refund and issue new debt at lower rates. Here's what could happen:

Call Date	Call Price	Yield to Call
7/1/81	102	32.073%
1/1/82	102	20.862
7/1/82	101.5	16.903
1/1/83	101.5	15.192
7/1/83	101	13.901

With such potential profits, these bonds are hard to find, especially in small lots.

How to Interpret Information on Municipal Bonds

Issuer: the name of the state, governmental unit or agency that borrows the money: Allegheny County, Penna. (where Pittsburgh is located).

Coupon: 4.25%. By clipping the coupon, you will receive $42.50 interest a year: $21.25 semi-annually.

Maturity: 1992 (actually, there is a specific day and month but the year is used for convenience). At this time, each bond will be redeemed at $1,000.

Recent price: the closing price at which the last transaction took place: 57 17/32nds or $575.12 each. This price is expressed as a percentage of the $1,000 face value. Price alone does not indicate whether a bond is an attractive value. The dollar quotation is an arithmetic function of the coupon rate, maturity and yield. It is not important unless the coupon rate and maturity of different bonds are the same. The important factor with bonds is always the yield to maturity. In the settlement of the purchase, the final price includes the interest accrued since the last payment.

Current yield: the rate of return at the present time. It is calculated by dividing the coupon rate (4.25%) by the current price ($575.12). This comes out to 7.389% so is rounded off to 7.4%.

Yield to maturity: the rate of return received if the bond is held to maturity in 1992. This is the sum of the coupon yield (4.25%) plus the appreciation to par

SOME TAX-EXEMPT BONDS

Issuer	Coupon	Maturity	Recent Price	Current Yield	Yield to Maturity	Rating*
Allegheny Cty., Pa.	4.25%	1992	57.17	7.4%	10.9%	AA
Baltimore, Md.	3.00	1987	66.63	4.6	10.7	A
California (State)	4.50	1988	75.88	5.9	9.4	AA+
Hartford Cty., Conn.	2.24	1993	40.54	5.6	11.1	AA
Commonwealth Puerto Rico	5.00	1992	60.86	8.2	11.3	A
Massachusetts (State)	4.80	1992	62.24	7.7	10.7	AA−
New Jersey (State)	5.00	1995	63.48	7.9	10.0	AAA
New York (State)	5.00	1991	68.38	7.3	10.1	AA−
Ohio (State)	3.75	1991	59.41	6.3	10.1	AA+
Wisconsin (State)	5.65	1998	65.86	8.6	9.9	AAA

* Rated by Standard & Poor's

SOURCE: Money Reporter

($424.88) at redemption. This is the key factor in judging debt issues.

Rating: the quality of the bond as determined by Standard & Poor's. With Allegheny County, it's a high AA.

For Higher Returns, Buy Discounted Municipals

Just as with corporate and government bonds, investors who can afford to defer current income for a higher return at maturity should consider buying tax-exempts that are selling at discounts. The capital gains on the appreciation will be taxed but the net income will be greater than that from bonds bought at or near par.

Example: Jim Rogers, who expects to retire in ten years, has $50,000 to invest. He pays federal taxes at the 50% rate. If he buys $50,000 of A-rated municipals at par, he'll get a tax-free 9% return: $4,500 a year or $45,000 over the next decade plus the return of the $50,000: a total of $95,000.

With the same $50,000, he can buy a package of discounted tax-exempts with par value of $70,000, a coupon rate averaging 7% and a yield to maturity of about 11%. He will receive less income—$3,500 a year for a ten-year total of $35,000—but at maturity the bonds will be worth $70,000. After paying the tax on the capital gains ($4,000), he'll have $16,000, so his total worth will be $121,000—$26,000 more than from the bonds purchased at par. Unless you want to lock in a very high yield for many years, look for discount bonds if you pay taxes at a fairly high rate.

When to Swap Tax-Exempts

Generally, tax-exempts should be held to maturity but there are times when it pays to swap: when you need more money at retirement or when you want to set up a tax loss.

Example: At the end of 1979, Bob Allen owned 10 New York State Power Authority 3.20,'95s. They provided $320 income and were trading at 89. The bonds were subject to call, at par, under a sinking fund so the average life was five, not the apparent 15 years.

As Bob was due to retire in 1980, he sold out, added $1,100 and bought 10 New York State Power Authority 8s, '09 at par. Now he could count on $800 annual income (an increase of $480). He knew he would get his extra money back in less than three years and that the maturity would be extended to about 15 years ... about as long as he could expect to live. Furthermore, he set up a tax loss of $1,100 that he used against earned income.

Do's and Don'ts on Tax-Exempts

DO keep tax-exempt securities in a safe place. They are fully negotiable. Title passes with possession. This makes it imperative that the bonds be kept in a safe-deposit box or with your broker.

DON'T report either ownership or income on your income tax return. The only information that is required is the capital gain or loss on a sale.

DO check whether you need a tax shelter. This applies especially to professional men and women such as physicians, lawyers, etc. They can create their own retirement funds, where the income earned by the plan is free of all current income taxes. Not until they draw down benefits after retirement is there any tax on the basic contributions.

Municipal bonds are tax-exempt so should not be held in pension plan portfolios unless your vested assets are so large that the withdrawals will be taxed at the highest rate. Even then, it's much smarter to buy tax-exempts with personal savings.

DO deal only with a reputable brokerage firm. Bond selling, by an unscrupulous operator, can be very profitable—for the promoter. The growing popularity of tax-exempts with individual investors has spawned a modern version of the bucket-shop technique. Glib salesmen telephone prospects to offer bargains in "tax-free municipals." They lie about the bond's quality, issuer, return, yield, maturity date and true market price. Even if they tell the truth, the buyer has almost no way to check the quotations because they concentrate on secondary securities. These "fast-buck" operators prey on ignorance by selling bonds from their inventory (which was probably acquired at bargain prices). You can take a terrible beating if you end up with a mess of different bonds of little-known governments or agencies.

If you get a hard sell on tax-exempts, by telephone or in person, be cautious. You will always be safer to deal with your regular broker.

DO take advantage of serial maturities. Unlike most corporate bonds, which usually have the same redemption date, municipals mature serially: a portion of the total debt comes due each year until the final redemption. For example, the $400 million North Carolina Municipal Power Agency Number 1, series 1978, had such breakdowns as: $3.4 million, maturing in 1986, carrying an interest rate of $5\frac{1}{5}$%; $4.47 million, due in 1991, $5\frac{7}{10}$%; and $240 million, due in 2020, $6\frac{7}{8}$%.

Such a feature can help financial planning. The investor can buy bonds to come due when extra money will be needed—for college tuition, for retirement, etc.

DON'T buy tax-exempts on margin. Banks will lend up to 80% of the current market value of municipal bonds. But the interest paid to buy or carry previously purchased tax-exempt securities is *not deductible* on your income tax return. Furthermore, all capital gains, no matter how they are obtained, are subject to full taxes.

DO buy in December. This is bargain month for the municipal bond market. Many investors swap bonds at this time to set up tax losses. This selling pressure tends to lower prices so, temporarily, yields are higher.

Special Tax-Exempts

Two of the newest types of tax-exempts are designed for specific investment needs:

• **For short-term:** commercial paper with maturities of less than 270 days. They are ideal parking places for temporary funds as, when you buy a sizeable unit, you can tailor the redemption date to your schedule. *Examples:* $75 million Government Development Bank for

Puerto Rico; $53 million issue for the Illinois Educational Facilities Authority.

• **For offsetting inflation:** floating-rate notes issued by local authorities and backed by major corporations. *Example:* U.S. Steel 30 year pollution-control bonds whose returns are adjusted weekly to the higher of 67% of 90-day T-bills or 75% of the 30-year government bond rate with a 6% floor and a 14% ceiling. Good deal if you can get 'em.

Warrants with Tax-Exempts

The latest wrinkle by Wall Street is a warrant tied to municipal bonds. To attract buyers, the New York City Municipal Assistance Corporation (M.A.C.), with the eager help of underwriters, marketed bonds with a warrant attached. The $100 million debt was due in July 2008. Each $5,000 bond carried a 10⅜% coupon and was offered at par. The kicker was a warrant that entitled the purchaser to buy a new bond, within the next two years, with an identical return maturing one year earlier than the main issue. The warrants soon were trading on their own.

According to the underwriter, this sweetener cut the interest rate by ⅝ to ¾ of a percentage point over a conventional M.A.C. issue for total savings of $14 to $17 million. In addition, this gimmick is expected to eliminate some $2 million that would be required for a new offering in the future.

Well, if you gotta get money, you have to pay for it! If you are in a fairly high tax bracket, these bonds-with-warrants can be very profitable.

Insured Municipals

If you would like to lend your money locally, find out about insured tax-exempts. These are general-obligation and revenue bonds of small communities with the payment of principal and interest guaranteed by private insurers: American Municipal Bond Assurance Corp. (AMBAC), sponsored by MGIC, the mortgage guarantee company; or by Municipal Bond Insurance Association (MBIA), a consortium of Aetna Casualty, Connecticut General, Firemen's Fund and U.S. Fire Insurance. The premium, $10 to $20 per bond, is paid either by the issuer or the underwriter. This cost is more than offset by the lower interest paid. Standard & Poor's, for example, rates all insured issues AAA.

These bonds are ideal for safety and high tax-free income, but deal only with a firm that makes a market so that you can sell quickly and at a fair price.

Tax-Exempt Bond Funds

Investors who want: *(a)* to be relieved of the job of choosing individual bond issues; *(b)* diversification; *(c)* to have interest reinvested for the benefits of compounding, should consider tax-exempt bond funds. These are the current choices:

Unit trusts. These are closed-end funds. All receipts from the sale are invested in a fixed portfolio. No new bonds are added. The funds themselves do not have a final maturity date but as a fund's holdings mature (or as the bonds held are paid off by the state or local government through sinking funds or other redemption operations), the proceeds are distributed on a pro-rata basis to fundholders. These funds are self-liquidating so that when assets drop to about 20% of the original investment, the fund goes out of business.

Unit trusts are safe and assure regular income based on the yields at the time of the issue: about 7% for funds started in 1976; 8% for those floated in 1979; and up to 9% for those offered in 1980.

But because their base yields are fixed, the market value of their shares declines when interest rates rise, as they did in 1980. If you cashed in early, you had to take a bath. A $10,000 unit of one fund, issued in 1972, was worth less than $7,000 eight years later!

State bond unit trusts. These invest in tax-exempt issues only in one state where income taxes are high. Recently, they were available in California, Massachusetts, Michigan, Minnesota, New Jersey, New York, North Carolina, Ohio, Pennsylvania, Virginia and Puerto Rico.

The latest variation is the New York Insured State Municipal Bond Fund. It buys only tax-exempts issued in that state and insured, as to payment of interest and principal, by MGIC Indemnity Corp. or AMBAC. As a result, all bonds are rated AAA by Standard & Poor's.

Each unit has a par value of $1,014 but is sold for $1,000. After a management fee of 4.7%, $953 is invested. There are annual costs for the trustee, annual evaluation and annual insurance premium. You can have all income reinvested for daily compounding or can get interest checks monthly, quarterly, semi-annually or annually. And, after eight months, for a fee of $25, units can be exchanged for shares of other bond funds under the same management.

Managed tax-exempt funds. These are similar to stock mutual funds. The professionals invest in and manage a portfolio of municipal bonds. The shares are bought and sold on the open market and their values fluctuate with the changing worth of the underlying securities.

In theory, the trading will produce capital gains as the professionals shift holdings in anticipation of changes in interest rates. But it doesn't always work out that way. Only a handful of managers have been smart enough to sell, or sell short, as interest rates have soared. But some managers do seem to be learning the hard way—on investors' money.

Short-term tax-exempt bond funds. These are sort of short-term, tax-exempt money-market funds. The money received from the sale of shares is invested in short-term municipals, with an average maturity of 170 days.

The yields are a bit lower than available from regular funds but the chances of capital loss are small because of the frequent maturities. Advantages of tax-exempt bond funds:

• *Small investment.* $1,000 to start, $25 additions.

• *Diversification.* Bonds are balanced by types, geography, maturities and ratings (usually a minimum of Baa).

• *Automatic reinvestment.* All interest and capital

gains are used to buy additional shares, thus taking advantage of the magic of compounding.

• *Swapping.* For shares of other funds under the same management company. Thus, with an older unit trust yielding 6%, you can cash in (at a loss these days) and get shares of a new fund paying 9% or more.

• *Convenience.* Monthly, quarterly, semi-annual or annual checks for interest.

• *Detailed reports for tax returns.* These are valuable when you sell shares after retirement and there are realized capital gains which, of course, are taxable.

Check the Costs

Unit trusts are sold with a load of 3.5% to 4.7% so you have less money working for you. But over 20 years or so, this is not an important consideration. There are modest management/administration fees but with funds managed by Vance Sanders & Co., there's a 40% savings because their funds are limited partnerships and thus subject to lower reporting costs.

Open-end funds are no-load but charge management fees, usually 0.5% plus some fees.

Comment: Generally, the managed fund is a better investment if you expect to sell in less than ten years. The shares react to the fluctuating interest rates.

Unit trusts are better for long-term holdings as shifts in value tend to balance out over the years.

Always check the track record of the fund manager and look for funds that have achieved their stated goals for at least three consecutive years.

CHAPTER 17

The Profits and Perils of Leverage

Leverage involves the use of borrowed funds to enhance profits. With securities, it means buying on margin: using stocks, convertibles or bonds as collateral for a loan from your broker or banker. This tactic is most valuable in periods of moderate interest rates as the income from dividends/interest may offset the cost of the loan. But even when money is expensive, buying on margin can be effective for aggressive investors who have the temperament and financial resources to assume the added risk.

With securities, the margin regulations are set by the Federal Reserve Board but your broker may set higher limits. Under current Fed rules, you can borrow only when you have at least $2,000 in cash or securities. The margin requirements are 50% initially and 25% for maintenance: i.e. with $5,000, you can borrow $2,500 and must maintain $1,250 in equity—the difference between the market value of your portfolio and the amount owed the lender.

With $5,000 cash, you can buy 100 shares of a stock at $50 each. By using margin, you will have $7,500 so you can buy 150 shares.

Like most stock market ploys, leverage is most effective when stock prices rise. If the stock moves to 55, you will have a $500 (10%) profit in your cash account or $750 (15%) gain in your margin account. At this point, your cash-account assets will be $5,500 or the margin-account assets will be $8,250. The equity will be $5,750 ($8,250 value minus $2,500 loan). This will be above the maintenance minimum of $1,375. Now you can increase your loan.

But leverage can work both ways. If your stock starts to slide, you will lose money that much faster. With a 5-point drop in the price of the stock, the cash-account loss will be $500; that in the margin account, $750. If the decline is substantial so that your equity falls below 25%, your broker will issue a margin call and you will have to come up with more cash or other collateral.

Typically, brokers charge interest on the margin loan that is 1% above that of the current call money rate at which brokers borrow from banks. In years past, when interest rates were nominal, there was a small spread between the income from dividends/interest and the interest paid on the debt. This made margin attractive, especially to those in high tax brackets because the interest on the loan was tax deductible.

But these days when the cost of money is so high, borrowing can be expensive. If you pay 20% interest on that $2,500 loan, the out-of-pocket cost is $500 a year. If you receive only $250 in dividends on the extra shares of stock, that means a pre-tax loss of $250. The price of those extra 50 shares will have to go up over 5 points to break even.

Margin borrowing might make better sense for an investor in the 50% tax bracket. He could deduct $250 (half of the interest) but for those paying taxes at a lower rate, the benefits must be calculated in advance and, usually, will not be worthwhile.

Undermargined Accounts

If the value of your margin account falls below minimum maintenance requirements, it becomes undermargined and, even if the deficit is only $4.00, there will be a margin call. To check when you're approaching this 25% level, divide the amount of your debit balance by three and add the result to your net loan. Thus, one-third of $5,000 is $1,666, plus $5,000 equals $6,666. If the portfolio value is less, your account becomes restricted.

This limits the withdrawals. Here, the base is what is

called the Special Miscellaneous Account, representing the funds in excess of margin requirements which come from price appreciation, dividends, proceeds of sale and cash deposits made to meet a margin call. At this point, you can withdraw funds above the maintenance minimum but you must deposit assets equal to the lesser of 70% of the market value of the securities taken out or the amount needed to bring the remaining equity back to 50%.

There is one way to get around these rules: *Buy and sell, on the same day, stocks of equal value.* But the 70% retention rule applies if the transactions are made on different days.

The Fed's rules are specific. On same-day deals, if the cost of the stock you buy is greater than the value of the one sold, you deposit 50% of the difference between the two prices. If the new stock is worth less than the old, only 30% of the difference is credited to the SMA.

If the equity drops below 30%, your account becomes *super-restricted.* All purchase and sales, even on the same day, are treated separately with each purchase requiring 50% margin and each sale releasing only 30% of the proceeds.

Advice: If you use margin, don't let your equity fall below 50%. In a volatile market, you can get in trouble mighty fast.

Margin Rules

FRB rules apply to stocks listed on registered U.S. exchanges, to stocks listed with NASDAQ and to unlisted securities whenever they are purchased "for the purpose of carrying listed stocks." Brokers cannot margin other stocks.

You can, however, use unlisted stocks, including Canadian issues, to borrow from your bank. On some high-quality, actively traded OTC stocks, banks often lend substantially more than permitted for listed stocks when purchases are *not* "for the purpose of carrying listed stocks."

While shares of most mutual funds are unlisted, their portfolios contain stocks and bonds listed on major exchanges. Therefore, mutual fund shares are subject to FRB margin requirements at banks.

The NYSE sets special margin requirements on individual issues which show a combination of volume, price variation or turnover of unusual dimensions. These requirements are intended to discourage the use of credit in certain issues because of undue speculation.

In addition, customers whose accounts show a pattern of "day-trading" (purchasing and selling the same marginable issue on the same day) are required to have the appropriate margin in their accounts before transactions in securities subject to the special margin requirements can be effected.

How to Figure Your Yield when Buying on Margin

To determine exactly what yield you get by buying on margin, you have to ascertain the return on your actual investment: the *margin equivalent yield.* You can calculate this from the accompanying formula or from the accompanying table.

The *cash yield* % is the return on securities bought outright. The same formulas can be used for both pre-tax and after-tax yields.

$$MEY = \left(\frac{100}{\%M} \times CY\% \right) - \left(\frac{100}{\%M} - 1 \right) \times DI\%$$

MEY = Margin Equivalent Yield   CY% = Cash Yield %
%M = % Margin   DI% = Debit Interest %

Example: You are on a 50% margin base, receive 12% cash yield from dividends and pay 20% in your debit balance.

$$MEY = \frac{100}{50} \times 12 - \frac{100}{50} - 1 \times 20$$

$$MEY = 2 \times 12 = 24\% \ - \ 2{-}1 \times 20 = 20\%$$

$$MEY = 24\% - 20\% = 4\%$$

Thus, the 12% return, with margin, dwindles to 4%.

What You Can Buy on Margin

With stocks, the margin formula is: *Add two zeros and divide by the margin requirement* (currently 50%). This gives you the dollar amount you can buy with the cash you have available (except in restricted and super-restricted accounts).

With $10,000 cash, you can buy any one of the following:
$20,000 worth of marginable stocks.
$20,000 worth of listed convertible bonds.
$40,000 worth of nonlisted convertible bonds.
$100,000 face value of municipal bonds.
$200,000 face value of government bonds.

There can be problems in down markets. In margin evaluation, when the price of a stock falls below a full dollar figure, the next lower round-dollar value is used. Thus, when a stock drops from 100 to 99⅞, its new margin value is 99: a loss of less than 1% of its worth.

But a stock selling at 10 that falls to 9⅞ is valued at 9, a 10% loss.

How to Get Extra Leverage

Many professionals purchase a company's convertible securities on margin rather than the common stock. With convertibles (assuming a purchase price reasonably close to investment and conversion value), risk is substantially reduced on the downside due to the price resistance encountered as the CV nears the floor provided by its investment value. On the upside, there's no such resistance and the full benefits of leverage are enjoyed. With a margined position in CVs, the risk may be no greater (and can be less) than would be incurred by nonleveraged ownership of the common stock of the same company, while the appreciation potential may be substantially greater.

Here's an example, based on an actual situation, that

took place a few years ago when interest rates were lower. It compares a leveraged investment in Toonerville Trolley 6½% convertible bonds with a $10,000 investment in the common stock of the same company. The CV was at par; the common stock at 8.

To buy 20 CVs, the investor put up $10,000 and margined the balance. At the same time he bought 1,250 common shares for $10,000 cash. The stock declined to 6 (down 25%). The CV, reflecting the downside support due to its inherent investment value and adequate interest, dipped 7% to $930 per bond (a 14% loss on the $10,000 investment).

In a few months, both securities were back to their original level. In the next 18 months, the bonds rose 80%, so their value was $36,000—a net profit of $16,000. The stock went up 50% to 12, or $15,000—a gain of $5,000. The leveraged position in the CVs produced both superior protection on the downside and superior capital appreciation on the upside.

Furthermore, over a year, the bond interest of $1,300 would have covered the $1,200 cost of carrying the margin account at 12%.

Note: If you had margined the stock, your risk would have been greater and your offsetting income less, but you would have done well. But if the prime interest rate had risen sharply during that period, the price of the CVs would have dropped farther.

Financing Stocks via Insurance Funding or Vice Versa

Until the scandal of Equity Funding (which reinsured nonexistent life insurance policies), there was wide interest in combining the sale of insurance with mutual fund shares. The idea was to persuade people to use existing collateral to borrow money in the expectation that the earnings generated by the borrowed money would be greater than the interest cost. The steps:

1. *Invest:* buy shares of a mutual fund.
2. *Insure:* select a life insurance program.
3. *Borrow:* using your mutual fund shares as collateral, get a loan (from the friendly insurance-mutual fund company) to pay each annual insurance premium.
4. *Repay loan:* at the end of 10 years you pay the principal and interest on the loan: either in cash, from insurance cash values or by redeeming shares.

Result: Any appreciation from your investment in excess of the amount owed is your profit. If you die, your heirs get full value because the loan will be paid by the insurance.

In effect you bought securities on margin to acquire life insurance rather than extra shares of stock. *Objective:* double mileage from invested dollars.

This concept has considerable validity in periods of rising stock prices and low interest rates. Presumably, the value of the mutual fund shares will reflect the long-term rise in the stock prices! And the dividends will help pay the interest on the loan.

Before you become entranced with the "logic" of this dual approach, consult a competent, impartial insurance adviser and make your calculations on the basis of a decline in the value of the stocks you buy.

A HYPOTHETICAL EXAMPLE OF THE REWARDS AND RISKS OF LEVERAGE

Capitalization	ULC (Millions)	HDC (Millions)
5%	—	$15.0
Common & Surplus	$20.0	$ 5.0
Total Capital	$20.0	$20.0
No. Shares $20	1.0	.250

	Operations Net Before Taxes and Interest	Interest	Balance (In millions)	Taxes	Net	Earnings Per Share
ULC	$2.0	—	$2.0	$1.0	$1.0	$1.00
	2.6	—	2.6	1.3	1.3	1.30
	1.4	—	1.4	.7	.7	.70
HDC	2.0	.75	.625	.625	2.50	
	2.6	.75	1.85	.925	.925	3.90
	1.4	.75	.65	.325	.325	1.30

Profit Opportunities from Corporate Leverage

Corporate leverage offers the possibility of reaping big rewards from a modest investment. There are two general types of such opportunities:

1. Capitalization leverage, which involves the use of either *(a)* senior securities (bonds or preferred stocks) or *(b)* borrowed funds to increase profits as a percentage of the corporation's investment or equity.

2. Operating leverage, where a firm uses its fixed or overhead costs as a lever which enables it to convert a relatively small change in sales or revenues into a relatively large change in earnings. This type of leverage becomes most interesting as revenues approach the firm's break-even point. The best companies for leverage are those with high fixed expenses for plant, equipment and machinery and low variable costs for labor, materials and marketing. They require substantial volume, but once the fixed outlays are paid, profits soar. In poor times, however, watch out: most of the earnings will be needed to keep the company operating. The higher the profits, the greater the price swing in the stock; the lower the net income, the lower the market evaluation of the stock.

Example: Two hypothetical companies, each capitalized at $20 million—UnLeveraged Company (ULC) with no senior debt and one million shares of common stock, and Heavy Debt Company (HDC) with $15 million in senior debt, $5 million in equity capital and 250,000 shares of common stock.

Note that total capital is the same in each case, but stockholders own *all* of ULC while bondholders, in effect, own three-quarters of HDC. The effect of the different structures shows up in the interest column: ULC pays nothing; HDC shells out $750,000 each year. The interest costs are, however, a deductible tax expense, so HDC pays less of its income to Uncle Sam.

In good, normal and poor years, ULC shows a better net profit, but because of the greater number of common shares, its earnings per share are lower. HDC shows a lower net profit, but with one-quarter as many shares, it reports higher per share profits.

The leverage takes effect in the best and worst years. ULC, with no debt, holds its profits within a reasonable range from the median: up to $1.30 per share in the best year, down only 30% in the poor year.

But HDC's profits swing from a normal $2.50 per share, up to $3.90 with prosperity and down to $1.30 per share in the poor year, when interest payments take over half the gross profits.

If the stocks of both companies sell at ten times earnings, ULC would range between 13 and 7, HDC between 39 and 13!

Note: The same principle applies to real estate, which involves leverage more than almost any other type of investment—usually, a little cash and a lot of debt. This takes advantage of the tax benefits of depreciation and interest payments.

Here's a real example of leverage: back in 1966, the prospects of corporate leverage sent the stock of Williams Bros. soaring from 10 to 89. Williams, a designer and builder of pipelines, had a net worth of $23 million. It planned to take over Great Lakes Pipe Lines Co. for $287.6 million: $9.6 million in cash and the rest in debentures and debt. The idea of Williams ending up with earnings of $10 million, almost 10 times previous profits, sent its stock to new highs!

Soundly leveraged common stocks are attractive instruments for investors seeking long-term growth and inflation protection. Here's why:

Tax benefits. Under our tax system, interest paid is a fully deductible corporate expense *before* taxes. Dividends are an expense *after* taxes. Bonds with a 12% coupon cost corporations about 5.5% after taxes. On new common stock, to pay about the same percentage of dividends, the company would have to earn close to 20%—no easy task.

Inflation benefits. With inflation a permanent part of our economic system, borrowed funds will be repaid with ever cheaper and more easily earned dollars. And if convertible bonds are used, a rapidly growing company may be able to escape repayment of all or most of its debt by completing the conversion into common stock.

Low multiples. Stocks of corporations with heavy debt often sell at a relatively low price/earnings ratio and with a comparatively high dividend yield. *The reason:* As a company's debt or other prior obligations increase or hold, the risk attached to owning its common stock rises, and ownership in that company is not as attractive as ownership in an equivalent low-debt or debt-free company.

The stocks to watch for are those of companies with substantial debt, whose earnings records indicate that, even in recessionary times, the company will be able to meet its basic money obligations.

Warning: The search for leverage should not trap you into the serious danger of investing in companies that are overburdened with debt. Debt is worthwhile only when it leads to high earnings.

Significantly, companies with a high percentage of debt show smaller earnings per dollar of invested capital than do low-debt or debt-free corporations (with the possible exception of regulated corporations such as utilities). Maybe it's natural to be careless with someone else's money!

True growth companies seldom have heavy debt; they are able to generate the capital needed for expansion from retained earnings. Heavy debt firms provide greater leverage for speculators, but they are not suited for long-term investments.

Leverage with Bonds

The margin regulations for bonds are stricter with brokers: with corporate bonds, the initial and maintenance requirements are both 30%; with governments, 8% to 10% at the outset and 5% thereafter.

If you borrow against debt securities, get the loan from your bank. With A-rated bonds, you can get 90% (and sometimes 95%) of the market (not face) value. With careful selection and timing, you can profit from such leverage with short-term issues. The cost of the loan will be partly offset by the interest which, in turn, is tax deductible (except with municipal bonds) and you'll profit from the sure appreciation when the bonds are bought at a discount.

Example: Dr. Pershing thinks that interest rates are near a peak and will fall in a year or two. He buys $1 million worth of 7.625% Treasury bonds due in 16 months, at 91.37 with $50,000 cash and a loan of $913,750 at 18.4% interest.

At maturity, the bonds will appreciate to $1 million for a long-term capital gain of $86,250 ($62,100 after taxes). Interest expense will be $54,024 (total interest of $158,868 minus income of $104,844) or $16,207 after taxes (assuming a 70% tax bracket). Thus, there's $45,893 return on an investment of $50,000 over 16 months: 66.75% a year on his money!

Do not borrow against bonds that will not mature for many years. Their prices can fall sharply if interest rates rise so that the bank will insist on more collateral. These may be good speculations but, when used as collateral, they are not good investments.

Margin Insurance

If you use margin frequently, consider buying credit life insurance that will repay your broker in case you should die. This is available in two forms:

• *Blanket policies,* from the brokerage firm, to cover all margined customers under 65 years of age. This is sold by Aetna Life and Casualty. So far, not many firms have been willing to pay the premiums.

• *Individual policies,* paid for by the investor: i.e. Margin Life, underwritten by Federal Home Life under the sponsorship of the New York Stock Exchange. Rates vary according to the age of the customer: per $1,000 per month, from 27¢ for those under 35 years of age to $3.08 for those aged 60–64. The rate is figured in terms of the customer's average daily debit balance during the prior month and is billed, by the broker, as part of the regular monthly statement. Currently, the coverage is limited to $15,000.

CHAPTER 18

The Wonderful, Speculative World of Warrants

According to the dictionary, "To speculate is to buy or sell in expectation of profiting from market fluctuations." Speculation involves risk-taking so cannot be considered part of a true investment program. But wise speculating can be profitable and an important means of building capital. *But it should be undertaken only with funds you can afford to lose.* It is not for amateurs but as you become knowledgeable and experienced, the risks of speculation diminish. When you have time to do research and to watch the market, you will find it worthwhile to allocate a part of your savings to volatile situations where the rewards justify greater risks.

Warrants are one of the most valuable and profitable vehicles for speculation when properly selected and carefully managed. They offer high leverage because of their relatively low cost and fast market movements. But they can be tricky and, as a rule, warrants should be bought only in bull markets and sold short in bear markets.

In the late 1960s, warrants became popular when conglomerates were making acquisitions. To assure a tax-free exchange, the merger makers needed 80% control. They sweetened the deal by adding warrants to convertible debentures. Most of these are no longer available.

More recently, the role of warrants has diminished as the result of changes in corporate financing and the growth of listed options. Still, for speculators, warrants are important, potentially profitable securities.

A warrant is an option to buy a stated number of shares of a related security (usually, common stock) at a stipulated price during a specified period (5, 10, 20 years or, occasionally, perpetually). The price at which the warrant can be exercised is fixed above the current market price of the stock at the time the warrant is issued. Thus, when common stock is at 10, the warrant might entitle the holder to buy one share at 15.

Generally, warrants are used by corporations in connection with new senior securities such as bonds or preferred stocks.

To the buyer, they are a "kicker," an inducement to purchase. They are often part of a loan package made by big lenders such as insurance companies. They give them a piece of the action by providing an opportunity to have an equity position and to make extra money if the price of the stock rises (e.g., if the common stock of the company mentioned above goes from 10 to 25, the warrant holder will have an instant profit of $10 per share when he buys the stock at 15). And when the stock is sold, the capital gains will be taxed at a lower rate.

To the seller, warrants provide:

1. *Lower interest costs* than would be needed to issue regular bonds. Typically, bonds packaged with warrants will have coupons as much as 2% points below the prevailing cost of money: 9% vs. 11% for straight debt.

2. *Tax benefits* in that net costs are lower. With a $1,000, 7%, 25-year convertible bond with a warrant attached, the value, for tax purposes, would be $680 for the bond and $320 for the warrant. The corporation can write off the $70 annual interest as an expense and amortize the $320 as a bond discount over the 25 years, thus creating an additional $13-per-year tax deduction. The after-tax cost of the bond/warrant would be $28.50 compared to $35 for straight debt or convertible.

Leverage

The big attraction of warrants is leverage. Compared to the related stock, the warrant is always low-priced and thus more volatile. Since the two securities tend to move somewhat parallel to each other, an advance in price creates a higher percentage gain for the warrant than for the stock.

Example: A warrant to buy a stock at 20 has an intrinsic value of 5 when the stock is selling at 25. When the stock moves up to 35, the gain will be 40%. A similar 10-point rise to 15 for the warrant is a 200% jump.

But the downside risks with warrants can be greater than those of the stock. A 5-point drop for the stock, from 25 to 20, is a 20% decline, but a similar loss for the warrant, from 15 to 10, is a 33% swing.

As a general rule, leverage is not advantageous when the warrant has little or no intrinsic value: when the stock is trading well below the exercise price. But, as with all speculations, there's seldom logic in the evaluation in an erratic market.

Profits with Warrants

Warrants are pure speculations. They have no voting rights, pay no dividends and have no claim on the assets of the corporation. They are not registered with the company and are generally issued in bearer form. If they are lost or stolen, there's almost no way for brokers or an exchange to "flag" them.

Warrants represent *hope.* When the price of the common stock with a related warrant is *below* the exercise price, the warrant has only speculative value. Thus, a warrant to buy a stock at 20 is theoretically worthless when the stock is at 19.

In practice, however, the warrant has a value reflecting the prospects for the company, the life of the warrant, stock-market conditions, etc. Not so long ago, the common stock of a major utility was trading at 44 and the warrants to buy the stock at 52 were selling at over 7. *That's hope!*

When the price of the stock rises above the specified exercise price, the warrants acquire a tangible value that is usually inflated by speculation. Thus, when that utility stock rose to 52, the price of the warrant soared to 11½. *Now do you see why warrants are 100% speculations?*

The closer a warrant gets to its expiration date, the smaller the premium it commands. After expiration, the warrant is worthless. Conversely, the longer the life of the warrant, the higher the premium if there is real hope that the price of the stock will rise.

With perpetual warrants, faith can pay off. *Forbes* magazine describes a classic example of the potential. In 1942, Tri-Continental Corp. (TY), a closed-end investment company, with holdings in conservative stocks, was not doing too well. Its warrants were trading at 3¢ each and were used primarily for tax losses. The warrant could buy 1.27 shares of TY at 22¼, far above the current value.

By 1969, the stock market was rising. The value of TY common was up and that of the warrants exploded. An investment of $312 in the common stock, at the 1942 low, was worth $29,000 but the same amount "invested" in the warrants zoomed to $703,000!

The gyrations can be amazing: fantastic profits when hopes are high; disastrous losses when ardor cools. In 1969, Atlantic Richfield offered 500,000 warrants to buy stock at $110 per share for three years. As ARC stock rose from the 50s toward 100, the warrants sold at an emotional and overexcited top of 47¼. *Their total market value was $23.6 million.*

By late 1971, the common had dropped 40%, back to about 55. The warrants, with only nine months of life, fell to 1½, a total market value of $500,000!

How to Figure the Value of a Warrant

The speculative value of a warrant is greatest when the warrant price is below the exercise price. If the stock moves up, the price of the warrant can jump fast.

Under guidelines set by warrant expert S. L. Pendergast, the maximum premiums to pay are as follows:

Stock Price as % of Exercise Price	Warrant Price as % of Exercise Price
80%	28%
90	34
100	41
110	48
120	55

Note that the maximum premium to pay for warrants with a few years of life is 41% when the stock is at 100% of its exercise price.

Keeping in mind that that market price of warrants is hard to predict, here are two guidelines:

• *Rule of thumb:* A warrant is worth 40% of the exercise price plus or minus 50% of the difference between the market price and exercise price of the common stock. If the market price is higher than the exercise price, add half the difference. If it's lower, subtract.

Example: The common stock is at 25. The warrant is exercisable at 30. Thus, 40% of 30 equals 12. Now add

SOME WARRANTS FOR LISTED STOCKS

COMPANY	Exercise Terms	Expiration	Recent Price Common	Warrants
Alleghany Corp.	$ 3.75	Perpetual	27 3/4	31 1/2
American Airlines	14.00	1984	13 3/8	4 3/8
Atlas Corp.	31.25	Perpetual	15 1/4	5 1/2
City Investing*	1.02 @ 27.70	1983	26 1/4	1 1/2
Comm. Edison A	1/3 share	none	18 1/8	5 7/8
Comm. Edison B	1/3 share	none	18 1/8	5 7/8
Eastern Air Lines	10.00	1987	8 1/2	3 1/2
Frontier Airlines	10.29	1987	19	11 3/8
Greyhound Corp.	23.50	1983	17 1/4	2 1/2
Mattel, Inc.	4.00	1986	9 3/4	6 7/8
Resorts Intrntl.	53.00	1984	28 3/4	5
Sterling Bancorp	15	1983	33 3/8	1 1/8
Textron, Inc.	11.25	1984	29	19 7/8
Towner Petroleum	22.12	1986	23	11 1/2
Transcontntl Oil	16	1985	17	10 1/8
Trans-World Corp.	31	1986	20 1/8	8 1/8
Tri-Contntl Corp.	4.12 @ 5.64	Perpetual	20 3/8	55
USAIR, Inc.	1.04 @ 18.00	1987	20 7/8	11 1/8

* For shares General Development

SOURCE: Barron's

half of 5 (2½) to get 14½, the value of the warrant.

With the common stock at 35, the formula would be 12 minus 2½ for a value of 9½.

• A more precise calculation is used by investment adviser T. J. Holt. Here, the current intrinsic value (CIV) of the warrant equals the sum of the stock price (SP) plus the number of shares per warrant (N) minus the exercise price (EP): CIV = (SP + N) − EP.

To determine the percentage of premium: Here WP = warrant price; PP = percentage premium.

$$\frac{WP - CIV}{SP \times N} \times 100 = PP$$

With the stock at 35:

$$\frac{14.5 - 6}{35 \times 1} = \frac{8.5}{35} \times 100 = 24.3\%$$

How to Pick Warrants for Capital Gains

In a bull market:

• **Buy only warrants of a common stock that you would buy anyway.** If the common stock does not go up, there is little chance that the warrant's price will advance.

• **Buy warrants of active, growing companies.** The best profits come from warrants associated with stocks that have potential for strong, upward swings due to sharp earnings improvement, a prospective takeover, newsmaking products or services, etc. Look for volatile stocks or ones that are temporarily popular.

In most cases, the warrants for fast-riding stocks, even at a high premium, will outperform seemingly cheap warrants for issues that are falling.

At the outset, stick with warrants of fair-to-good corporations whose stocks are listed on major exchanges. They have broad markets.

When you feel more confident, seek out special situations, especially warrants of small, growing firms. Many of these "new" companies rely on warrants in their financing. Their actual or anticipated growth can boost the price of their warrants rapidly.

But be wary of warrants where the related stock is limited or closely controlled. If someone decides to dump a block of stock, the values can fall fast.

• **Buy warrants when they are selling at low prices.** The percentages are with you when there's an upmove, and, with minimal costs, the downside risks are small. But watch out for "superbargains" because commissions will eat up most of the gains.

• **Buy warrants that are priced within 20% of their exercise value.**

• **Watch the expiration/change date.** After expiration, the warrant has no value. Generally, stay away from warrants with a life-span of less than four years. When you know what you are doing, short-life warrants can bring quick profits if you are smart and lucky. But be careful. You could end up with worthless paper.

Some warrants have changing conversion values: e.g. Textron, Inc., warrants could be exercised at $10 until May 1979, then rose to $11.25 until 1984. Lazy warrant holders who did not keep informed lost money.

• **Avoid dilution.** If there's a stock split or stock dividend, the market price of the stock will drop but the conversion price of the warrant may not be changed. The same caveat goes for warrants subject to call. Generally, warrants of listed companies will be protected against such changes, but take nothing for granted.

Once in a while, warrants will be reorganized out of their option value. This occurs with troubled corporations taken over by tough-minded operators who are unwilling to pay for past excesses or to provide profits for speculators.

• **Spread your risks.** If you have sufficient capital, buy warrants in five different companies. The odds are that you may hit big on one, break even on two and lose on the others. Your total gains may be less than if you had gambled on one warrant that proved a winner, but your losses will probably be less if you're wrong.

• **Look for special opportunities such as "usable" bonds.** When warrants are part of a package, both the warrants and the bonds may be used to acquire stock. If the bonds trade at a big discount, use them to buy the stock.

Example: Brandy Snifter, Inc., sold a package of bonds/warrants that permitted the bondholder to exercise the warrants on the basis of the par value of the bond. The warrant was to buy the stock at 20. With the stock at 15, there was only hope. But since the bonds were down to 60 ($600), they could be used to buy 50 shares of stock, with a market value of $750.

Always buy warrants to sell, not to exercise.

Selling Warrants Short

In bear markets, the leverage of warrants can be profitable with short sales. Basically, it's the opposite of buying long. You assume that the same relationship between the stock and warrants continues when their prices fall.

But short selling is always tricky and, with warrants, there can be other problems: *(a)* limited markets because of lack of speculator interest; *(b)* exchange regulations— e.g., the American Stock Exchange prohibits short selling of its listed warrants several months before expiration date; *(c)* the possibility of a "short squeeze": the inability to buy warrants to cover your short sales as the expiration date approaches; *(d)* the life of the warrants may be extended beyond the stated expiration date. This advances the date when the warrants become worthless, so a short seller may not be able to cover his position at as low a price as anticipated.

Hedging with Warrants

Warrants provide an excellent vehicle for hedging by both speculative and conservative investors.

For speculators. For short-term trading, hedge by buying warrants and selling short the related common stock. If the stock goes up, you will profit because the value of the warrants will rise proportionately more than the price of the stock. If the stock goes down, you can make a profit in most cases: The total loss on the warrants will be less than the gain on the short sale.

Example: General Earache stock is at 100. The warrant, exercisable at 55, is at 50. You believe a bear market is coming so set your hedge on the basis that both securities will fall back close to their original prices. This would mean a 50% drop for the stock (from 100 to 50) and a 70% decline for the warrant (50 to 15). The downside leverage is a welcome 1.4 to 1.

You sell GE stock short and buy the warrants. If everything goes according to plan, you make 15 points. You cover your short position at 50 for a 50-point profit; you sell the warrant at 15 for a 35-point loss. These figures do not include commissions and, if GE stock pays dividends, any payments you have to make to the owner of the borrowed stock.

A variation of this speculative tactic is the *reverse warrant hedge.* Here's how this worked with A.T.&T. stock and warrants:

In July 1970, Jim Marine bought 100 shares of T at 44 and sold an equal number of warrants short at 7. His total investment was $4,400 because the stock was used as collateral for the short position.

There were three possible movements before the warrant expired on May 15, 1975:

1. If the 1975 price was the same (44), there would be no profit on the stock, but there would be almost $700 from the short sale of the warrants because they could be acquired for next to nothing. Add some $1,300 in dividends (assuming the present $2.60 per share payout continued) for a total return of about $2,000 in less than five years. That's not bad for a stock whose price remained unchanged.

2. If the price of the stock soared to 60, there would be a $1,600 profit on the stock plus $1,300 in dividends for a total income of $2,900. Offsetting this: a net loss of $800 from the cost of covering the short sale (assuming the price of the warrants jumped to 15). Total gain: $2,100, about the same as in Example 1.

3. If the price of T fell to 40, there would be a stock loss of $400 and a $700 profit on the warrants. To this $300 gain, add the $1,300 in dividends for a small but

welcome return even when the price of the investment fell 10%.

What actually happened? The price of T rose to just under 52 in early May 1975. Mr. Marine got out for a $775 profit on the stock *plus* $700 on the short sale *plus* $1,409 in dividends: a total of $2,884. This was a return of over 65% in less than five years with no risk.

Granted, both the investor and the speculator could have fared better if they had correctly predicted the trend of the stock. There would have been no losses to reduce profits but the hedge provided protection against almost any movements.

For conservatives. Suppose that you feel the stock market is moving too high. You become nervous but do not want to sell out completely. Many of your holdings are fine-quality equities which you would not hesitate to retain for the long term.

You can hedge by shifting 50% or so of your funds into bonds, T-bills or savings accounts and using the balance to buy fast-moving warrants. If your forecast proves wrong and the market rises, the money in warrants can show as much capital gains as if you had not sold your stocks and you will still have the income from your fixed assets investments.

If the market drops, you can limit your losses by using stop orders on the warrants.

The reverse warrant hedge can also provide profits in erratic markets. Here's an example of a *conservative* hedge as cited by Leroy Gross, vice president, Dean Witter Reynolds, Inc.

In May 1974, the stock of Carrier Corporation (CRR), listed on the NYSE, was at 11¾; its warrants were trading on the AMEX at 2⅜ and were exercisable at $27.33 until July 1976.

Buy 100 shares of CRR at 50% margin by putting up $587.50; sell short 200 CRR warrants for $475. The dividends of $52 a year from the stock will more than offset the cost of interest on the margin account.

About a year later, the warrants were covered at ⅞ ($175 for 200), for a gross profit of $300. In early 1976, the stock was sold at 17¾ ($1,775) for a gross profit of $600. After adding dividends and subtracting interest and commissions, the return was over 40% on the invested capital.

The risks were minimal. Losses could have resulted only if: *(a)* the price of the stock fell below 7 (11¾ less 4¾ from the sale of the warrants); or *(b)* the company extended the life of the warrants (a moot point since the repurchase was made before the expiration date).

Risks of Warrant Hedges

Despite the fact that, theoretically, hedges provide full protection, the results may not always be rewarding because:

• Commissions cut into, even eliminate, profits.

• Speculators miscalculate the future warrant price in relation to that of the stock. They may not always move together—e.g., a warrant is trading at 16 and you

calculate that it is worth 12. But there can be trouble if speculators grow cautious and are willing to pay only 6 for the warrant.

• Common-stock dividends. Since the short seller must pay the dividends on the borrowed shares, this outlay can be expensive.

• Lack of action. If the price of the stock holds steady, so will that of the warrant. This is not what you hoped. You tie up your money with no income, and since the value of the warrant depreciates with time, you may be spinning your wheels.

• All profits and losses on short sales, regardless of the time the securities are held, are short-term. Loss can provide tax benefits but profits are taxed at the highest rate.

Using Warrants with Options

Swingers use warrants to speculate in options. The costs are low, the risks modest and the profit potential high, especially in erratic but uptrending markets.

Example: In October, TP Industries stock was at $14.50, and the warrants, exercisable until August the next year, were at $4.50. Trader Tom bought 1,000 warrants for $4,500 and sold ten January options with a striking price of 15 for 1⅜, to net about $1,250 after commissions. If TPI stock stayed the same or went down by January, Tom would let the options expire and sell another ten calls with an April expiration. If these also expire, he will sell ten more options with an August closeout date.

If the stock went up, he would buy back the January options and sell ten April calls at a higher premium, etc. He hoped to sell three sets of options, at an average return of $1,250 each, to net $3,750.

In August, if the stock was at $16.50, the warrants would be worth $2.75. He would sell them for $2,750 and deduct the $1,750 loss from the $3,750 profit on the options for a pleasant $2,000 profit on a net investment of $3,250.

If the warrants expired worthless, he would still be ahead of the game. That's what hedging is all about.

Tax-Exempt Bonds with Warrants

As explained in the chapter on tax-exempt bonds, the newest Wall Street gimmick is a municipal bond with an attached warrant. This was helpful in floating a $100 million debt issue for New York City's Municipal Assistance Corporation. The warrant entitled the holder of each $5,000 bond to buy a new bond, within the next two years, with an identical rate of return but maturing one year earlier than the original issue.

The warrants soon developed a market of their own and, as interest rates dropped, rose in value. Be sure that your broker understands how these are traded. Each unit controls five bonds so that a market price of 7 ($7) means that you have to come up with $350!

CHAPTER 19

Profits in Stock Rights

Rights are a special form of option. They give shareholders the opportunity to buy corporate securities, usually common stock, ahead of the public and at a more favorable price: at, say, 22 when the stock is trading at 25.

Rights are issued by corporations seeking additional equity capital, especially utilities anxious to issue more common shares to balance their heavy debt obligations. Their discount reflects the fact that the new shares will dilute the value of the outstanding stock (total assets and earnings of the company are now divided among a larger number of shares). There are no commissions and if the shareholder does not want to exercise any or all of his rights, he can sell them in the open market.

To the issuing corporation, rights:

• *Lower costs of raising capital.* Existing stockholders are already favorably disposed toward the company so are likely to be anxious to subscribe, especially if they feel that the added capital will create greater profits.

• *Build shareholder good will* as the result of being able to acquire new stock at discount prices.

• *Broaden stock ownership at small cost.* With more shares, there are likely to be more shareholders. And because some people will not exercise their rights, from lack of interest or lack of money, the options can be sold, hopefully to new investors who are looking for bargains.

Values of Rights

To be eligible for rights, you must own the stock before it goes "ex-rights." Thus, the worth of the stock will decline after the ex-date.

Rights have an intrinsic value but they are also speculative because of the high leverage: A 10% rise in the price of the stock can mean as much as a 30% jump in the value of the right. Or vice versa on the loss side.

Let's assume that the stock is trading at $31 per share; that shareholders get one right for every five shares; and that each right entitles the holder to buy one new share at $25 each.

VR = value of right   MP = stock's market price
EP = exercise price   NR = number of rights needed to buy one share

$$VR = \frac{MP - EP}{NR + 1}$$

To calculate the value of one right *before* the ex-date, add 1 to the number of rights:

$$VR = \frac{31 - 25}{5 + 1} = \frac{6}{6} = \$1.00$$

Thus, each right is worth $1.00 and the stock, at this time, is worth that much more.

After the stock has gone ex-rights, there'll be no built-in bonus for the stock, and the right will sell at its own value or, possibly, higher if the price of the stock advances, or lower if it declines.

NEVER LET RIGHTS LAPSE. You lose not only on the actual value of the right but you may also lose a tax benefit if there's a loss.

Special Benefits

The most important investment advantage of rights is that their exercise enables the investor to purchase the common stock on very low margin in a special subscription account (SSA).

This is a margin account set up to use the rights to buy extra stock within 90 days after the rights issue.

To open an SSA, deposit rights—your own or purchased—with your broker. In addition to no commissions for purchase, the *advantages* are: (1) a 25% margin compared to 50% for stocks; (2) no interest charges so you can use the full credit balance; (3) a year to pay if you come up with 25% of the balance each quarter.

Example: You have rights to buy Kwick Kick common, selling at 63, for 56 on the basis of one new share for 10 old shares. You acquire 100 rights so you need $5,600 to complete the purchase. You can borrow up to 75% ($4,200) so can make the deal with only $1,400 in cash or collateral. Every three months you must reduce the outstanding balance by 25%. Once 80% of the purchase price has been paid, you can sell or transfer the stock to your regular margin account.

The *disadvantages* of SSA are: (1) The price of the stock may decline so you will have to come up with more margin; (2) you cannot draw cash dividends or use the securities for collateral as long as they are in this special account.

• Tax savings. Neither the receipt nor the exercise of the right results in taxable income to the stockholder. But you will have to pay taxes on ultimate profits when the stock is sold.

Benefits to Stockholders

• **Maintenance of ownership position.** If you like a company well enough to continue as a shareholder, pick up the rights. According to *Barron's,* 80% of stocks bought with rights outperformed the market in the year following the issue.

• **Bargain price.** When American Electric Power offered rights on 9 million shares at 22, the stock had been trading at 23¾. If you owned 100 shares, you could pay $2,200 for new stock with a market value of about $2,350 (with the extra shares, the value of the stock on the open market will drop a bit).

But you will have to act fast because most offers have limits—often 16 days, seldom over one month.

• **No commissions.** By using rights—those you own or those you purchase—you can buy more stock without brokerage fees. You can save as much as $75 per round lot.

• **Profits from rights themselves.** If you do not want to acquire more stock, you can sell the rights in the open market. You can do this through your broker or through a bank designated by the company.

Or you can buy rights, either to exercise or for speculation. Trading in rights starts as soon as the offer is announced. For a while, the prices of both the basic stock and the rights are quoted—the latter on a "when issued" (wi) basis. Here's an example with Florida Steel.

52 Weeks High	Low	Stock	Sales 100s	Week's High	Low	Last	Net Change
51⅞	18⅛	FlaSt	31	52	51	52	+1⅛
25⅝	25⅝	FlaSt wi	5	26¼	25⅝	26¼	+ ⅝

As a rule, it's best to BUY rights soon after they are listed in the financial press; to SELL a day or two before the lapse date. Always look at the total costs: commissions and taxes on the rights and the future sale of the stock. You are dealing in odd lots so the costs can be significant.

N.B.: *Foreign rights (including those of Canadian corporations) may not be exercised by U.S. residents except in the rare cases in which the issuer has registered the related securities with the SEC. Best bet: Sell and avoid possible problems.*

• **Extra rights through additional subscription privilege.** Some shareholders will not exercise their rights so, after the expiration date, there will be an opportunity to buy these rights, usually on the basis of your original allotment. You must indicate your wish to participate in the oversubscription early, preferably when you send in your check for the new shares. Better do this yourself as small orders, handled through a major brokerage firm, can be lost in the back office.

There is a slight tax break. If the value of the rights received is *less* than 15% of the cost of the stock at the time of the offer, the rights are assumed to be without cost for determining the taxable gain on the sale of the rights and for setting the cost of the new stock.

If the value of the rights is *more* than 15% of the cost of the stock, you must allocate the cost of the rights proportionately: reducing the cost basis of the old stock and raising that of the new securities. *High-income-tax-bracket investors will do better by selling their rights.*

If stock rights are allowed to lapse, you can take a capital loss if their fair market value, at date of issue, is 15% or more of the market value of the old stock. The loss is proportional to the allocation of rights. If the value of the rights is less than 15%, you can take a tax loss only by notifying the IRS in writing, usually more bother than it's worth.

Profits or losses on the sale of the rights themselves are subject to regular tax rules.

CHAPTER 20

How to Select Investment Companies

Investment companies (commonly called mutual funds) are back in style. The public is buying shares at a greater pace than ever as the result of new types of funds, no or low sales charges, good-to-excellent performance and aggressive marketing techniques. Apparently, most people feel that that can buy better returns than they can obtain by themselves. There's some merit in this view but it's a better sales pitch than fact.

All investment companies operate pretty much the same way. They pool the money received from the sale of shares to buy and sell different types of securities for different investment goals: income, growth or various combinations. For this service, there's a fee, sometimes clearly stated but, more likely, included in the operational costs.

The two most significant features of all investment companies are diversification and liquidity. The invest-

ments are made in at least 50, and usually closer to 100, corporations/governments and you can always get your money quickly: by redemption on demand or by sale through regular stock-trading channels.

Investment companies can be divided into two types in two ways: by structure and by sales acquisition costs.

Open-end funds, officially termed mutual funds, stand ready to sell new shares or redeem old ones at net asset value: the current worth of the underlying securities.

Closed-end funds are similar to corporations. Closed-end funds have a fixed number of shares, often listed on major stock exchanges, that are bought and sold like regular stocks with standard commissions.

All funds can also be categorized as:

Load funds. These are *sold,* primarily by registered representatives of brokerage firms but also by qualified-by-law individuals who work full- or part-time.

A sales charge, typically about 8.5%, is deducted from the amount of the investment. Then come fees for service, custody, management, reports and administrative expenses. Even after two years, only 85% of the investor's money may be working for him. But his sales representative handles all details.

Note: For estate- and gift-tax purposes, shares of load mutual funds are valued at the *bid* price (without commissions), not the *asked* price (which includes the sales cost).

When you buy shares of a load mutual fund, the sales charge may be shown in two ways: the stated commission, say 7.5%, or the percentage of your investment, 8.11%.

When you invest $10,000, the salesman/broker keeps $750, so your money is only $9,250. But the true charge is 8.11%: $750 divided by $9,250.

No-load funds. These are *bought* directly from the sponsoring company with no sales charge.

With both load and no-load funds, there is no cost for redeeming the shares, and management fees run from ½% to 1% of the value of the invested money. This seems small but can eat up a good chunk of your investment income. With $100,000 invested, a $8,000 annual return could be reduced by $750 every year.

Example: You have $10,000 to invest, and shares of both types of funds, with comparable records, are quoted at $10 each. Your money will buy 1,000 shares of a no-load fund but only 920 shares of a load fund with an 8% sales commission. At the end of 20 years, the load fund must earn an average of ¾ of 1% more than the no-load fund to provide the same return.

On larger purchases, load-fund commissions are lower, usually on a sliding scale that drops to 3% on a single $100,000 purchase or commitment.

HOW INVESTMENT COMPANY SHARES ARE QUOTED

	NAV	Offer	Income	Capital Gains
Acorn Fund	27.29	N.L.	.84	2.44
Amer. Gen. Group				
Am Gen Grth	37.61	N.L.	.25	8.95
Am Gen Harbor	12.12	13.25	.66	.66
Am Gen Hi Yld.	9.41	10.09	1.265	....
Am Gen Mun	16.36	17.18	1.48	....

NAV = Net Asset Value per share.

Offer: Price at which shares may be purchased. This includes NAV plus maximum sales charge.

N.L. = No Load. All shares are traded at NAV.

Income: when dividends, payments for last 12 months.

SOURCE: **Barron's**

How Funds Distribute Their Income

To qualify for exemption from corporate income tax, a fund must meet these tests:

• At least 90% of its gross income in any taxable year must consist of dividends, interest and capital gains from securities.

• Not more than 30% of gross income in any taxable

year may be from sales of securities held under three months.

• The fund must distribute to its shareholders as taxable dividends at least 90% of its *net* income for any taxable year, excluding long-term capital gains (which may be distributed or retained, in whole or in part). When distributed, they are taxable to the shareholder.

Closed-End Funds: Buying Assets at a Discount

Shares of closed-end funds are usually available at discounts up to 30%. Investors feel that their fixed capitalization limits opportunities to take advantage of unusual situations. They would have to sell current holdings to make new commitments.

When the discount narrows (this is a slow process that does not usually occur in the early stages of a bull market), the patient investor can do well. At all times, the same amount of money invested in one or two stocks can buy ownership in a number of companies and probably receive a higher income.

Example: You are ready to start planning for retirement and want to shift from your $100,000 low-income ($2,200 in dividends), growth stocks to a more diversified, better-yielding portfolio.

After selling your shares and paying the capital gains tax, you have $80,000. You locate a closed-end fund which is selling at a 20% discount. You buy 4,000 shares at 19, pay the commission costs of about $2,530 and have enough left over for a vacation.

SOME CLOSED-END STOCK FUNDS

Fund	Net Asset Value	Price	Difference
Adams Express	17.75	14 1/2	−18.3%
Baker Fentress	102.69	75 1/2	−26.5
Gen. American	20.44	19 3/4	− 3.4
Lehman	16.53	14 1/2	−12.3
Madison	26.82	22 3/4	−15.2
Niagara Share	22.03	21 3/4	− 1.3
Overseas Securities	6.28	8 1/4	+31.4
Source	27.21	22 7/8	−15.9
Tri-Continental	29.19	23 1/4	−20.3
U.S. & Foreign	29.80	21 7/8	−26.6

SOURCE: **Barron's**

Your share of the underlying stocks of the fund has a market value of $100,000. Annual income has averaged almost 8%, so you can count on about $6,000 more than before. And, if the market moves up, you have an excellent chance of capital appreciation because this is the time when closed-end funds usually rise faster than the overall average.

Over the years, closed-end funds have sold at an average discount of about 15%. Only rarely (usually when they hold large blocks of popular stocks), do their shares command a premium price. These special funds can be good investments but don't be lured by the discount alone. It may be greater when you sell!

Buy closed-end funds only for the long term and be ready to sell when you have a substantial capital gain.

According to Thomas J. Herzfeld, who specializes in closed-end fund investments, the best time to buy is when the discount is over 25% and the market is turning up. If and when the discount drops to 10%, you'll be happy.

Dual Funds: $2 or More for Each Invested $1

An interesting variation of closed-end funds is the dual fund, which offers two separate investment vehicles: capital shares and income shares. You can buy one or both.

All money paid in, for both types of shares, is placed in a single pool. All capital growth from investments is retained by holders of capital shares. All income (dividends and interest) received by the entire fund is paid to holders of income shares. Thus, every shareholder has $2 serving his investment goal for every $1 he invests—more when the shares sell at a discount. Dual funds use leverage for investment rather than speculative goals.

Shares of most dual funds are listed on the NYSE. The prices of both types of shares are quoted in the daily financial tables when there are sales. More detailed data on net asset value, percentage of discount or premium and closing market prices as of the previous Friday are shown in tables published in the Monday editions of major financial publications.

The *income shares* resemble preferred stock in that they have a stated minimum dividend which is cumulative. Dividends are paid at rates of 8% to 10% on the original offering price. This means that, with the usual discounts of 25%, the real returns are higher.

Dual funds were started in the late 1960s and since their life span was 12 to 18 years, several have already terminated and many more will do so in the next few years. At dissolution, all income shares are paid off at a price guaranteed in the prospectus or swapped, on a dollar-for-dollar basis, for capital shares. Then, the entire fund becomes a standard, open-end investment company.

Example: When American DualVest closed out, the income shares were redeemed for $15 each; the capital shares which were switched to a regular fund were valued at $11 each. This was less than the original $15 cost but the net asset value per share of the new fund was $13.80.

Income shares sell on a yield basis so have been depressed recently. They are of interest to tax-exempt organizations for their assured redemption price and to corporations because 85% of the income is deductible.

Right now, there's a chance for some gains with capital shares when they are at attractive discounts. Dual funds are another example of Wall Street's ability to offer "investment opportunities" whose package is more attractive than the contents.

Investment Objectives

Investment companies come in all sizes, shapes, and combinations. Fund managers have become merchandisers, just like food and drug manufacturers.They find an area of public interest (or create one) and develop a fund to meet this "need." They are, in effect, selling the sizzle, not the steak.

The broad objectives can be summarized as follows:

SOME DUAL FUNDS

Fund	Income Shares Price	Income Shares Yield	Liquidation Date	Liquidation Value	Capital Shares Price	Capital Shares N.A.V.*
Gemini	14½	16.5%	1982	$11.00	33	$39.68
Hemisphere	4¼	17.6	1985	11.44	4 1/8	3.04
Income & Capital	9½	14.5	1985	11.81	11 1/2	13.03
Leverage	13	5.8	1982	10.10	27 7/8	31.58
Scudder Duo-Vest	9	11.2	1982	9.15	15	16.68

* Net Asset Value

SOURCE: Wall Street Journal

Income—concentrating on preferred stocks, common stocks that pay high dividends, and bonds with high yields. These funds are not adverse to capital gains, but it's a secondary consideration.

Conservative balance—primary goal: preservation of capital; secondary objective: moderate growth and income. Typically, portfolios contain a large percentage of bonds and preferred stocks plus quality common stocks.

Aggressive balance—aiming for capital gains from a diversified list of leading stocks plus, in some cases, a varying proportion of bonds. Companies which are fully invested in common stocks, except for a small cash balance, are known as *all-common-stock funds.*

Growth—investing for long-term capital appreciation and future income. In early years, dividends are small because the focus is largely on "stocks with a future."

Performance—these companies seek maximum capital gains by any and every means: fast turnover, use of "letter" stock and warrants, and concentration on limited-stock new issues which can be whipsawed, with the help of cooperating brokers and funds, to unreasonably high levels.

Special situations—these funds are, usually, venture capital sources which provide money to new companies. They combine their equity investments with senior securities such as convertible debentures and/or rights and warrants. Hopefully, these "kickers" *may* become valuable.

Tax shelters—operated primarily to give shareholders tax-favored income or capital gains or to defer capital gains. They are not true investment companies.

Specific types of special funds include:

Letter stock funds. These are strictly for the venturesome. They aim at capital growth and operate on the theory that gain comes first and risk second. They put most of their assets in "letter stock" (that is, in securities which have not yet been registered with the SEC for public sale and which must be held in the fund portfolio for a specific period of time or until registration).

Funds purchase these unissued shares at discounts of 25% to 30% below the price of the same, or comparable, securities which are traded on the open market. With few exceptions, the issuing companies are new firms, long on hope and prospects but short on cash and experience.

Corporate directors are willing to sell the shares because they like the ideas of quick cash and avoiding the bother and expense of SEC registration.

By every standard, letter stock is a gamble. The fund

manager is hoping that the company will do so well that his shares can be sold, in a year or two or three, at a handsome profit. So far, there have been few successful letter stock funds, but hope—and the lure of a big killing—springs eternal.

Private debt bond funds. These are funds which are usually sponsored by financially oriented firms such as insurance companies. At the outset, the idea was to combine privately placed debt and preferred stocks with equity. MassMutual Corporate Investors, for example, invested in loans and mortgages for income and took allied warrants and stock options for capital appreciation. The investments were made in partnership with the fund sponsor, Massachusetts Mutual Life Insurance Co.

Private placements historically have commanded a premium yield of 0.5% to 1% above publicly traded bonds of comparable quality. On the other hand, they are less liquid with no secondary market. Still, over 30 years, Connecticut General says that its losses on private placements have been 1/20th of 1%.

The big plus is the potential of capital gains from the conversion of debentures of the exercise of warrants added to sweeten the loan. MassMutual realized a $1.3 million profit when an 8% note was converted to common stock. But there can be lemons, too. The same fund took a $1 million loss on its "investment" in a book distributing firm.

High-yielding funds. These are another sales gimmick. They are designed for speculators who are willing to have their money invested in unrated, or low-rated, bonds that pay high interest and have prospects of capital appreciation.

Nicknamed "Super Income," they are popular with swingers and with registered representatives because they carry a hefty sales commission. Never buy them with money you will need in a hurry. Their prices can swing 30% a year, not exactly the mark of investment quality.

Index funds. These are composed of securities that make up a stock-market average such as Standard & Poor's Composite 500 Stock Index and are selected on a proportional basis. The idea is that by owning the average you will do as well as the overall market.

Since Wall Street seldom settles for mediocrity (at least not in the sales pitch), some funds try to beat the market by indexing only 200 of the most profitable S&P corporations.

There's no research, commissions are few because of the small turnover and the management fee is a low 2/10 of 1% of share value. Usually, however, there's a sales load of 8.5% and a quarterly maintenance fee of $6 no matter how many shares you own.

Other sponsors have special attractions such as exchanging fund shares, dollar for dollar, for stocks of well-known corporations. With the Vanguard Group, 100 shares of A.T.&T., at 52, will get you about 371 shares of The First Index Fund with a net-asset value of 14 per share.

Equity and bond funds. This type of investment company invests 75% in discount bonds and 25% in equities that are indexed to the S&P 500 stock average. The Merrill Lynch offering will self-destruct on December 31, 1990. By that time, the investor will get back his money

from the matured bonds (barring defaults) and will still own common stock that, hopefully, will be worth much more.

These are long-term holdings because: *(a)* the sales load is 4%; *(b)* the redemption fee is ½ of 1%; *(c)* there's no assurance that the bond discount will close much before the liquidation date; *(d)* the early returns of 4.5%, adjusted for operating expenses, won't move over 8% for some time; *(e)* the possibility of capital gains is better over the years.

SOME FUNDS FOR HIGH INCOME

Fund	Recent Price	Recent Yield
Am. General Bond	16 ½	12.4%
Federated Hi-Income	12.32	12.4
Fort Dearborn Income	9 7/8	12.6
John Hancock Bond	14.46	11.0
Lincoln Nat. Dir. Place.	15.00	13.3
Mass Mutual Income	13 ¼	12.4
St. Paul Securities	9	12.0
USLIFE Income	7 3/8	12.2
Vestaur Securities	9 7/8	13.0

SOURCE: Barron's

Socially conscious funds. With these, investments are not made in stocks of industries involved in area that some people consider immoral, unethical or questionable. Provident Fund for Income won't buy shares of companies in liquor or tobacco. Dreyfus Third Century buys only shares of corporations producing products for safety, purity, health, education, housing, environment, minority hiring, civil rights or consumer protection. With such investments, you have to sacrifice performance for ideals. That's not exactly a profitable financial criterion.

Fund funds. These are mutual funds that invest in other mutual funds. The idea is to keep moving out of poor-performing funds into those with the best current record. As usual, this is a better sales concept than investment vehicle. And you have to pay two management fees and hope that the "professional" managers are shrewd enough to time their investments profitably.

Commodities funds. These offer shares in professionally managed portfolios of commodities futures contracts. The commissions/charges are high, but similarly managed private portfolios, with broad diversification and computerized controls for signaling buy and sell points, have produced good results. (See the chapter on Swinging Investments.)

Split-income/commodities funds. The goal is income plus capital gains. A portion of the money is invested in high-yielding debt and the balance in commodity-futures contracts. The theory: If inflation increases, the value of fixed-income holdings will decline but that of the commodities will rise. Or vice versa.

Example: The Income & Price Index Fund (The Boston Company, Inc., One Boston Place, Boston, MA 02106) invests $85 of every $100 in bonds and $15 in liquid assets. Between $7.50 and $10 of that $15 is used as margin to acquire commodity-futures contracts having an aggregate face value of $50 at the time of purchase.

The commodities portion of the fund is managed passively—like an index fund. Futures are bought and sold to maintain the weights assigned to each commodity—e.g., 9% for gold, etc.

The fund has a "nonrecourse" margin agreement whereby the commodity brokers release the fund and its investors from any liability to the broker for any losses sustained on the liquidation of contracts if margin previously deposited is insufficient to cover losses. In exchange, the fund initially makes a higher than typical margin deposit and pays the highest brokerage commissions.

Well, if you want to be a swinger, this is one way to start.

Tax-free distribution funds. These provide an interesting, and profitable, way to save taxes on income, because: (1) they reinvest all income/appreciation for compounding; (2) they avoid paying taxes by taking the 85% dividend exclusion available to corporations by investing in preferred stocks and by taking short-term losses to offset operating expenses; (3) they pay out capital, not income, to shareholders who need money. This is not taxable. With modest withdrawals and high tax-free yields, savings compound rapidly.

One of the most successful of these special funds is American Birthright Trust, 247 Royal Palm Way, Palm Beach, FL 33480. Over the past 11 years, the yields of one of its funds (concentrating in utility stocks) have averaged 22%.

Bond funds (taxable and tax-exempt). As explained earlier, there are two broad types: *unit trusts,* which buy bonds and seldom make changes; *managed funds,* where the money managers try to gain extra profits by guessing the shifts in interest rates.

Option funds. These specialize in selling calls and puts for extra income. When conservatively managed, this approach can add 10% or more to the fund's normal return and can also limit losses. But, in an effort to beat competition, some fund managers speculate: buying and selling options without owning the related stocks. If they guess right, they can make a lot of money for shareholders. And even when they are wrong, the losses are relatively small. For details, see the chapter on options.

Money Market funds. These are a special breed so are covered in a separate chapter.

Advantages of Mutual Funds

1. Diversification. Unless you have $50,000, it is almost impossible to have a properly diversified portfolio. It's costly to buy in odd lots, and if you buy round-lot shares of quality corporations, your average per share cost will be about $40, so you can own only about 12 different stocks at maximum. That's about a minimum for diversification in industries and types of investment objectives.

To buy just 10 shares of each of the 30 stocks which make up the DJIA would cost about $15,000. With a small investment (preferably supplemented by regular savings), you can buy wide diversification in professionally selected securities with mutual funds.

2. Systematic supervision. Investment companies have the personnel, research, facilities and experience to handle efficiently all details of stock transactions, dividends, warrants, rights, proxy statements and other details of stock ownership. Well-run funds mail dividend checks promptly, provide accurate year-end summaries for income tax purposes and are ever ready to answer questions.

3. Professional management. While the records of a few funds look as if their money had been managed by astrology or advice from an African witch doctor, the great majority of investment companies reflect the time, experience and knowledge of skilled money managers. Most of the top executives are professionals. Even when they make mistakes, they do so after what they considered thorough research, study and analysis.

As a business, investment companies are relatively new. A few are still controlled by the individuals who pioneered the pooled money concept. Today most funds are operated by professionals who have been trained in the art of money management. Many of them have lived through a number of bull and bear markets and recognize the necessity to maintain high standards, do intensive research and make use of mechanical, statistical and technical tools to improve their investment performance.

HOW SOME LEADING FUNDS PERFORMED OVER THE YEARS

FUND	1980	1979	1978	1977	1976	1975	1974	1973	1972
Market	+14.9	+ 4.28	+ 2%	−12%	+18%	+18%	−30%	−17%	+17%
Price New Horizon	+53.7	+33.4	+20.5	+12.6	+11.0	+38.9	−38.3	−40.0	+21.4
Istel Fund	+35.5	+27.0	+15.1	− 1.8	+ 3.6	+21.4	−10.4	− 5.6	+ 7.6
Investors Research	+70.9	+15.7	+14.2	+ 5.8	+11.7	+22.7	−12.8	−14.4	+20.3
Security Equity	+44.1	+29.9	+11.3	− 0.2	+33.1	+29.8	−23.8	−23.5	+14.5
OTC Fund	+18.9	+51.2	+30.1	+21.5	+33.0	+23.0	− 7.9	−15.0	+14.1
Axe-Houghton Stock	+34.1	+20.2	+10.0	−11.2	+21.1	+17.5	−10.8	−12.7	+10.6
Financial Income	+13.0	+21.7	+ 1.6	+ 3.9	+40.6	+34.3	−12.5	− 4.2	+10.5
Am. Gen. Harbor*	+26.0	+16.5	+ 8.8	+ 2.7	+26.5	+24.6	−11.3	− 6.8	+ 4.8
Am. Gen. Enterprise**	+72.1	+47.9	+21.0	− 6.8	+14.8	+33.6	−30.5	−20.5	+ 6.4
Pioneer Fund	+25.8	+23.1	+11.5	+ 3.4	+36.3	+38.1	−17.2	− 3.4	+14.9
Provident Fund	+ 3.0	+ 1.7	+ 7.3	+ 3.6	+26.8	+22.7	− 9.9	−15.3	+ 1.4
Chemical Fund	+26.8	+21.0	+ 1.3	− 8.1	+ 8.6	+21.0	−24.0	−14.0	+29.3

* Formerly Harbor Fund   ** Formerly Enterprise Fund

SOURCE: Wiesenberger Service; United Business Service

With better understanding of the informational-recording/reporting capabilities of computers, more fund managers are doing a better job. Unfortunately, there are still some individuals who set rigid formulas which trigger unwise and unwarranted selling of good stocks which experience temporary setbacks. Overall, however, the professional competence of many managers is improving, as has been shown by their better than average performance recently.

Unless you have ready access to current statistical information and can devote many hours to studying the economy, the stock market, industries and specific stocks, investment companies will get you results that are as good as, and usually better than, you can achieve on your own.

The true professional money manager establishes strict standards for the stocks he wants to buy and hold, acts primarily on the basis of facts and makes decisions which are keyed to the investment goals of the fund for which he is responsible.

4. Awareness. This includes direct and comparative knowledge of the conditions which affect the stock market: *(a)* money supply, interest rate, gross national product, industrial capacity, productivity, tax laws, etc.; *(b)* new developments in industrial technology and techniques which will influence the future of many corporations; *(c)* technical data on price and volume movements as best displayed on charts; *(d)* stock market activity such as insider purchases or sales, unusual transactions, etc.; *(e)* news reports of the Dow Jones News Wire. By the time the amateur gets the word or understands the significance, a stock may have moved a couple of points.

5. Lower costs. When you buy stock directly, you pay the full costs of commissions and taxes. When you buy shares of a mutual fund, these expenses are lower (because of the volume involved) and are spread over a broader base.

It is unfair to compare the cost of buying 100 shares of stock at, say, $40 with the cost of buying $4,000 of mutual fund shares. Your broker will charge up to $116 for a round-trip transaction. The load fund sale will cost about $34.

The proper comparison should be with the cost of investing $4,000 in the shares of a large number of securities. The total expense would be far more than that of acquiring the fund shares.

You can reduce the cost of buying load shares by larger commitments, either directly or through a letter of intention. This is a written statement that you plan to invest a stipulated amount over a given period of time.

6. Better performance. Don't believe the downgrading of the performance of investment companies. Of course, they did not do well in the bear market of the early 1970s, but over the years, very few individuals have done as well as the consistently high-ranking funds.

See for yourself. Pit your average annual returns (dividends and interest and capital gains) for the past ten years against those of the funds you are now considering. All funds provide detailed information, and while you may have to dig below the fancy charts and chest-beating, the facts are there. Look for consistency rather than erratically brilliant performance—unless you are

willing to spend the time and money to make frequent switches.

7. Switching privileges. When a management company sponsors more than one type of fund, all shareholders have the privilege of swapping on a dollar-for-dollar basis as the market or personal needs change. Usually, this involves a small fee of $5 per transaction.

Example: in 1976, Dr. Kneecap buys 1,000 shares of Super-Duper Growth Fund and arranges for reinvestment of all income and realized capital gains. The fund performance is fair with total returns averaging over 6%.

By 1978, Dr. K., taking a look at the 9% yield of a bond fund under the same sponsorship, arranges to switch from growth to income.

In late 1979, when interest rates soar, Dr. K. switches to a money market fund to get a 13% yield. In the summer of 1980, as interest rates decline, he moves part of his savings back to the growth fund.

In early 1981 when interest rates move up, he shifts part of his portfolio back into the money market fund and when yields drop below 14%, he goes back to equities.

Most brokers offer similar alternatives. Once you have set up an account in a money market fund (usually with $5,000), you can use it as a bank: drawing out to pay for new purchases; putting in proceeds of sales, dividends and interest. You won't have the leverage of a margin account but you'll be getting, instead of paying, the interest.

Caution: Watch the tax angle with every switch. To the IRS, this is both a sale and a purchase. All realized capital gains on sales are taxable, short or long-term depending on the holding period. Similarly, all capital losses are tax deductible.

FUNDS WITH BEST PERFORMANCES

Year	Fund	Type	Gain
1970	Founders Special	G	+ 21.0
1971	Nicholas Strong	G	+ 85.5
1972	Templeton	I	+ 65.6
1973	Inter. Investors	I	+ 92.8
1974	Sherman Dean	G	+ 24.8
1975	Amer. Gen. Venture	G	+ 86.8
1976	Sequoia Fund	G	+ 67.4
1977	Value Line Leverage	G	+ 51.3
1978	20th Century	G	+ 41.7
1979	United Services	G	+190.2
1980	Hartwell Leverage	G	+ 93.9

G = Growth   I = International

SOURCE: Wiesenberger Services

Disadvantages of Investment Companies

Shares of investment companies are like all investments. The most important factor is the caliber and competency of management. Just as with corporations, there are able, mediocre and poor money managers. *The mutual fund concept is sound and wise for most investors. The disadvantages crop up within the funds themselves.*

If you are an investor, be wary of highly publicized, aggressively promoted funds. If you are a speculator, you should realize that the risks do not vanish just because there's professional management. *Investment companies provide no magic formula for investment success.*

There are some operational disadvantages which can be avoided by wise planning. For example, you can postpone, but you cannot avoid, all taxes on gains. When periodic capital gains distributions are made, you must pay a tax on that gain even if you immediately reinvest the proceeds. If you do not reinvest this money, you not only have the tax to pay but also must face the problem and cost of reinvestment elsewhere.

When you decide to buy fund shares, do so AFTER the capital gains distribution. Otherwise, you will be getting back part of your own money on which you will have to pay a tax.

This distribution policy works against older persons and long-term investors who plan to hold fund shares indefinitely. If they had bought good quality growth stocks and held on to them, these holdings (under present tax laws) would become part of their estate so there would be no capital gains taxes during their lifetime. With investment company shares, the capital gains tax will have to be paid when distributions are made.

Watch out for penalties. Some mutual funds have heavy penalties for failure to maintain contractual accumulation plans under which half or more of the first year's payment is used for sales commissions and expenses. The fund promoters argue that this so-called *front-end load* acts as a prepaid penalty and helps to prevent lapses in the early years of the plan.

But it also serves to cut down long-term investment results because there's much less money available for investment. If you should be unable to continue payments, a contractual plan can be very expensive. *It is better to have a voluntary accumulation plan or, if possible, a nonpenalty program.*

Judging Mutual Funds

Here are some guidelines for selecting mutual funds and, to a lesser extent, closed-end investment companies.

Performance record. This is the key. New management may make improvements, but the only way any investor can judge the future is on the basis of past performance.

When you look at the record, keep in mind the objective of the fund: income, growth, balance, speculation, or whatever it may be. What you want to know is how and if the goal has been attained, preferably over 10 years.

Unless you are willing to settle for safety and income alone, the fund should have attained average annual total returns (realized gains, reinvested income, and unrealized appreciation) 2% greater than the yield of a quality corporate bond: recently, 15%.

Pay attention to that *average.* Several major funds have never been first in performance in any one year, but they do better than the market in good years and not as poorly in bear markets. Look for the fund's *total record*—in both *up* and *down* markets. In *up* years, the fund should beat the market. In *down* years, the losses, if any, should not be greater than that of a stock-market average such as the DJIA.

One of the best guides is the annual *Forbes* magazine mutual fund report (August 31 issue). This rates funds on the basis of performance, since 1968, in each of three rising and three declining markets. To get a high score, the fund must have had an average annual total return of 8% over the 13 years and must perform consistently with not less than a B in either *up* or *down* periods.

Data includes reinvestment of realized capital gains and income. There are no deductions for sales charges.

Investment portfolio. Most funds provide information on the securities bought and sold, the percentage of assets in cash or equivalents, in bonds, in preferred stocks, etc. These data can be revealing. A fund that holds a lot of cash after the start of a confirmed bull market is not making the best use of its funds.

A fund whose holdings are dominated by big-name favorites (Exxon, GE, GM, and IBM) is neither aggressive nor research-minded. The managers are buying reputation and security. You can do as well yourself.

If the names of some of the stocks are unfamiliar, management is speculative-minded. That's OK if you're willing to accept the risks, but be cautious when more

---

STRONG GAINERS IN 1980

Fund	Type	Yield	% Increase Net Asset Value
Hartwell Leverage	M	0.0%	93.9%
Stein Roe Cap. Oppor.	G	0.9	76.0
Constell. Growth	M	0.0	74.5
20th Century Growth	M	0.0	73.3
Am. Gen. Enterprise	M	0.2	72.1
Security Ultra	M	0.4	71.7
Investors Research	G	1.4	70.9
Weingarten Equity	M	0.4	64.7
United Services	S	7.1	64.4
Am. Gen. Growth	G	0.5	63.0
St. Paul Special	G	0.6	62.2
St. Paul Growth	G	0.6	61.7

M = Maximum Capital Gains; G = Long-Term Growth; S = Specialized Portfolios

SOURCE: Warren, Gorham & Lamont, Inc.

BOND AND PREFERRED STOCK FUNDS PERFORMANCE

Fund	Average Annual Total Returns 1968-80	1980 Capital Growth	Income
Axe-Houghton Income	1.3%	−2.8%	8.2%
Babson Income	1.9	−4.2	8.9
Investors Selective	6.4	−9.1	10.6
Keystone B-1	5.8	−4.7	10.2
B-2	6.2	−5.9	11.1
B-4	6.3	−7.0	10.6
Liberty Fund	−0.5	−4.0	8.0
National Securities	3.7	−9.2	11.1
Northeast Investors	5.5	−6.1	10.6
Steadman Associated	3.2	2.9	6.8
United Bond	5.0	−13.0	10.7

SOURCE: Forbes Magazine

GOOD PERFORMERS IN UP AND DOWN MARKETS

Fund	Type	Up	Ratings Markets	Down	Average Annual Total Return 1968-80
ASA Limited	CE	B		A+	+22.8%
Inter. Investors	L	B		A+	21.0
Templeton Growth	L	A		A+	18.9
Petrol. & Resources	CE	A+		B	13.1
Charter	L	A+		A	12.2
Mutual Shares	NL	B		A	12.1
20th Cent. Select	NL	A		A	11.0
Founders Special	NL	A		A	10.7
Madison	CE	B		B	9.3
Guardian Mutual	NL	B		B	8.6
AMCAP	L	A+		B	8.4

Adapted from Forbes Magazine.

than 30% of assets are in stocks traded on the AMEX or OTC. Only rarely do these qualify as quality investments.

For a check on the growth potential, average the price/earnings ratios of the 20 major holdings. If the resulting multiple is far above that of the DJIA, the chances of substantial capital gains in the near future are small.

If you have time to do so, get copies of annual reports for the past several years and check the portfolios to discover the stocks bought, held, and sold and when the changes were made. This will give you a good idea of management's skill in selection, objectivity, timing, and patience—the marks of true professionalism.

Watch the timing in different stocks and types of markets. Did the fund sell Avon at 140 or at 19? buy Williams Cos. at 38 or 14? Engelhard Industries at 25 before the split or at 50 after the split?

Just as with individuals, most funds make their biggest gains in a few stocks. They concentrate about 40% of their holdings in some 25 stocks. Check this emphasis. In the long run, proper selections can pay off. For the short-term, this strategy can be devastating if a few of the stocks decline.

Finally, relate the results to the goals. A fund which opts for income may have most of its money in high-dividend-paying utility stocks or bonds. In periods of rising interest rates, changes are hard to make and will reduce real returns. The income will be offset by paper losses.

Size. The larger the assets of a mutual fund, the smaller the amount each investor pays for administration. If you choose funds with assets over $50 million, this should not be important. The management fee of $250,000 to $275,000 operational charges should be adequate to pay for able management and staff.

Stay away from funds whose assets have been under $50 million for over 10 years. If the fund hasn't grown, its performance must have been so poor that new shares could not be widely sold. If it's a new fund, there's no track record.

Conversely, when a fund becomes huge (over $500 million), there's a tendency for the managers to confine their investments to the relatively few major corporations that have millions of shares outstanding. In order not to

offset the market, large holdings must be purchased and sold over a period of time and so may not always be traded at the most advantageous price.

This lack of agility makes it difficult for major funds to beat the averages. In a sense, they are the market. By contrast, smaller funds can score welcome gains if they pick three or four winners. But large funds are likely to be more consistent in their returns.

Turnover. This shows the dollar amount of stocks sold in relation to total assets. Thus, if a fund had assets of $100 million and sold $75 million in stocks in one year, the turnover would be 75%. This is high and may indicate that the fund managers are either speculating for short-term profits or are anxious to generate big commissions to reward a related brokerage firm or registered representative who pushes the sale of fund shares.

According to *Forbes,* the best performing funds are slow on the draw: They buy slower, sell slower, and hold longer than the funds as a group. Frequent buying and selling means that the managers made wrong decisions at the start and repeated their errors over and over again.

Fund Extras

Not all funds offer all services, but here are some of the most frequently available extras:

1. Automatic reinvestment. This means that all dividend and capital gains disbursements will be automatically and systematically reinvested to compound your earnings. This can be beneficial because there's magic in compound interest. As outlined early in *Your Investments,* consistent savings (which this is) is one of the most important factors in making money make money. With a total average annual return of 12%, your money will double every six years.

Note: This automatic reinvestment is a form of dollar cost averaging, but it may not always be in your best interests. Mutual funds pay their largest dividends in capital gains when the stock market is relatively high. Instead of reinvesting at the high level, you may do better to take the cash and wait for the market to decline. Your cash will buy more shares.

2. Beneficiary designation. With both single-payment and contractual plans, you can name your beneficiary by means of a trust agreement. This will assure that the investment will go directly to your designated heir when you die. There will be none of the delays and expenses of probate. Consult your lawyer because some states prohibit this transfer.

3. Term life insurance. This is available with long-term, contractual plans. The insurance guarantees that your survivors will receive the full amount of your investment commitment. The cost is reasonable and is deducted from your regular monthly payment. Most mutual funds provide the life insurance without examination to investors under the age of 55 and with a total investment of under $18,000.

4. Open account. This enables you to invest whenever you have extra funds. The money buys shares immediately and avoids the bother of needless separate certificates for small lots or fractional shares.

5. Regular income checks. These are available (by

the month, quarter or other specified period) in several ways: *(a)* by buying shares in several funds, each with different dividend months; *(b)* by arranging for regular quarterly dividends to be paid in monthly installments; *(c)* by opting for a fixed income each month by permitting the sale of some shares to supplement the dividends. In addition, most funds will ease your tax reporting—and taxes—by providing printouts to show that the redeemed shares were those with a loss or with the least capital gains.

This is an ideal setup for retirement. Suppose you have $100,000—from savings and the sale of your home. You want a steady income of $12,000 a year or about $1,000 per month. That's a total return of 12%. A *good* fund should reach this target. If it does, your capital remains intact. If management improves this performance, the reinvested balance will keep growing and make possible money enough for a special vacation or a new car.

6. Master retirement plan. All pension plans must meet the regulations of the IRS to allow you to claim full deduction for your retirement contributions. Most mutual funds have special forms to save you paper work, provide the information needed for tax returns and, of course, invest your retirement funds.

7. Loan program. Fidelity Group permits shareholders to use their investment as collateral for loans at interest rates tied to the broker's call money rate. The minimum loan is $5,000 on a 50% margin. There are no set repayment terms, and you can defer interest by raising your balance.

Measuring Risks in Mutual Funds

Wiesenberger Services, Inc., which monitors mutual funds, rates performance in a risk context by three criteria:

1. Reward Factor: the percentage of change, over a period of time, in the net asset value of the fund when all realized capital gains and income distributions are reinvested.

2. Risk Factor: the *beta* coefficient. This is the measure of the fund's sensitivity to—or volatility relative to—that of the market as a whole (usually the S & P 500-stock index with dividends added back). This base is always 1.00.

3. Reward-Adjusted-for-Risk Factor: the *alpha* coefficient (AC). This represents the difference between actual net-asset-value performance and the performance that might be expected on the basis of the calculated *beta* factor.

Example: The S & P index gains 8.44%. Fund X, with a *beta* factor of 1.50, gains 15.55%.

Multiply 1.50 by 8.44 to get a +12.66 Anticipated Fund Return (AFR) on the basis of measured *beta*.

Subtract the AFR of 12.66 from 15.55 to get a +2.89 (AC).

On the other hand, Fund Y has a *beta* factor of 2 and also gains 15.55%.

2 times 8.44 equals +16.88 (AFR).

15.55 less 16.88 equals −1.33 (AC).

Thus, says Wiesenberger, Fund X is better. Fund Y

has twice the risk of the general market yet fails to provide comparable rewards as promised in the fund's stated investment policy and objectives.

Tax Treatment of Retained Capital Gains

A special provision of the tax law offers some tax advantages to shareholders of investment companies that retain gains and pay taxes on all or part of their realized capital gains. The only limitation is that it must be a *regulated* investment company.

Under IRS rules, the capital gains tax paid by an investment company on retained gains is, in effect, credited to the tax account of each shareholder in proportion to the number of shares held on the last day of the taxable year. *The extra benefit:* buying the fund shares a few days before the end of the tax year.

Fill out Schedule D of Form 1040 of your federal income tax to include, as a long-term gain, the amount of retained gain designated by the fund in its year-end report. Then calculate the tax due at *your* capital gains rate.

On Form 1040 take credit for the company payment and attach Copy B of the notice sent from the fund.

The credit comes because the mutual fund pays the maximum tax on capital gains. Chances are that your effective tax rate on capital gains is less, so the excess payment by the fund can be used to offset your tax on other income. You get a refund if the credit exceeds your tax liability.

Furthermore, you increase the per share tax-cost base of your shares by the undistributed gain per share remaining after the tax paid by the mutual fund.

Tax Treatment of Distributed Gains

Most long-term capital gains are distributed to shareholders by all types of mutual funds. When you receive your check, you can treat it as a long-term gain on your Federal return *even though* you may have held the fund shares for less than 12 months (after January 1, 1978).

Such distribution is treated as ordinary income on tax reports to Alabama, Arkansas, California, Delaware, Illinois, Mississippi, North Carolina, Pennsylvania, and Wisconsin.

The rest of the states follow the Federal practice of taxing all capital gains distributions of mutual funds as capital gains except Florida, Nevada, New Hampshire, South Dakota, Texas, Washington, and Wyoming, where there is no appreciable tax.

Converting Gains from Short to Long Term

To well-to-do investors, it makes a big difference whether profits on sales of fund shares are taxed as short- or long-term gains. In the 50% tax bracket, a $10,000 gain achieved in five months would be cut in half by the federal income tax (more when there are state and local levies). But if that gain is long term, the tax will be 20%, so there will be $3,000 extra in your investment account.

With sharp timing, it's possible to make this switch by buying shares of a closed-end fund before the declaration of the annual capital gains distribution, typically in January or February, and holding for 31 days. This tactic works best when the investor has substantial short-term capital gains that can be offset by short-term capital losses.

According to Section 852(b) (4) of the IRS code, a long-term gain on capital gains dividends from mutual funds can be established *if the shares are held for more than 31 days*. Since the price of the fund shares will decline in line with the distribution, a sale will probably be at a loss.

Example: Cosmic Closed End Fund (CCE), with a net asset value of $20 per share, is selling at $17, a 15% discount. In early January, Pat Flanagan, a bachelor in the 50% tax bracket, buys 5,000 shares at 17.

In mid February CCE declares a $2 per share long-term capital gains distribution. This forces the net asset value down to $18 and the stock price to $14.75.

Pat receives $10,000 that qualifies as a long-term capital gain, sets aside $2,000 for taxes, and adds $8,000 to his portfolio. He sells the shares for a short-term capital loss of $11,250 (5,000 shares at a $2.25 loss). This can be applied, dollar-for-dollar, against short-term capital gains he scored on other investments.

CHAPTER 21

Money Market Funds: Profitable Parking Places

Money market funds are the latest Wall Street fad. And, for once, they offer a good deal to individual investors: excellent liquidity (telephone redemptions); high yields (often over 15%) and convenience (check-writing privileges and, once an account is established, additions of modest sums). These are investment companies that invest only in liquid assets: Treasury bills and notes, CDs, commercial paper, repurchase agreements, etc. They pay daily interest and thus compound income. Their yields reflect the current cost of money . . . with a slight lag when rates shift.

The growth of these funds has been astounding: from zero a few years ago to over $300 billion today. William E. Donoghue, publisher of Donoghue's *MONEYLET-TER* and author of *The Complete Money Market Guide* calls them "a sure way for American investors to fight inflation. Now, everyone can have a form of a savings account with a variable rate of return floating with general interest rates."

Donoghue, who obviously is enthusiastic, points out that:

• **Your money is always at work** because interest is compounded daily. With Treasury bills, you buy at a discount and get full value at maturity . . . no compounding.

• **There are no costs** and all of your money goes to work immediately. With T-bills, bought through a bank, the cost is about $15 and you lose 3 days interest and 4 days discount on the discount. If you deal direct and mail in your check on Thursday to the Federal Reserve Bank, you lose a week's interest and, at maturity, get no interest for 5 more days.

• **Safety.** Your money is used to buy prime debt of well-rated corporations or the U.S. Government or its agencies. If you choose a fund that invests only in U.S. securities, your yield will be ½ of 1% lower but you can count on Uncle Sam's guarantee.

• **Easy redemption:** by telephone when proper procedures are set up at the outset.

• **Check-writing privileges plus extra income.** Since it takes a week or so for the check to clear, you get more interest.

Example: A California shareholder, using checks supplied by a New York–based fund, pays his $1,000 monthly rent. It takes 7 days for clearance so he picks up 84 days of "free" interest a year.

• **Quick benefits when interest rates rise.** You get the extra return immediately rather than having to wait until you make new investments in bills or notes. And, when interest rates fall, you continue to get the high yields for another month or so.

• **The privilege of shifting to other mutual funds** under the management of the same advisory firm. Thus, you can use money market funds as a parking place while you decide which and when investments are to be made. This can be done directly or with your broker whose firm will keep your cash working by buying shares of a fund as soon as the proceeds of a sale are available.

Currently, there is pressure from banking and thrift institutions to require these new funds to set up reserves and thus reduce yields to be more competitive with CDs. Their arguments: fair play and to provide more money for mortgages. To Donoghue, this would deprive the small investor of the opportunity to get these high yields.

Both sides are writing to Congress but, apparently, there is little chance of a change. If you want high yields, put some of your savings into these special funds as long as their returns are greater than those of other fixed-income holdings.

But remember:

(1) Based on historic conditions, these present yields are unusually high. When and if interest rates decline, you can do better with investments in intermediate and long-term bonds bought at par or at discount.

(2) All income is taxed at the highest rate. In the 50% tax bracket, that 15% return drops to a net of 7.5%. When you buy common stocks that provide total returns of 15%—5% dividend and 10% appreciation—your net will be greater. When the stocks are held for more than 12 months, the realized gains will be taxed at the low capital gains rate. For that 50% taxpayer, the tax will be 20%, so the net will be 10.5%: 2.5% on the income plus 8% on the gains. But, of course, with money market funds, you will probably get your money back while the values of stocks will fluctuate.

(3) Money market funds are not insured. CDs in banks and thrift institutions are covered, up to $100,000, by an agency of the U.S. government.

(4) In an effort to beat competition, some fund managers are buying European securities and paper of lower-grade corporations, both comparatively risky.

(5) There can be temporary losses if the money market fund managers guess wrong on interest rates. This occurs as the result of the method used in evaluating the share values.

How Fund Assets Are Valued

All money market funds price their shares at $1.00 each. The stated yield, as reported weekly in the financial press, reflects the interest earned on investments. But the methods of calculating the value of the underlying assets and the earned income varies. The base is the net asset value (NAV) per share. This is determined by subtracting all liabilities from the market value of the fund's shares and dividing the result by the number of shares outstanding. Here are the most widely used systems of calculation:

Amortized Cost. This technique values each security at cost at the time of purchase and assumes a constant rate of amortization, to maturity, of any discount or premium. It does not take into account the impact of fluctuating interest rates on the market value of the holdings. The concept is that, since the securities will be held to maturity, price is not important.

Example: DD Fund invests $10 million in 15.75%, 6-month commercial paper. It expects to get the money back plus interest.

But if the cost of money rises to 17.75% in the next month, the market value of the $10 million holdings will decline. A new investor might pay $1.00 for a share worth, say, 99¢.

To keep the share value at a constant $1.00, the fund must lower the daily dividend by the amount of the change in the underlying values. With a large fund, the effect is minuscule. A one-day drop in the NAV might decrease the dividend rate by only 1/200th of 1%.

But other funds, investing at a higher rate, will report a better yield so some DD shareholders will redeem their shares and, with new investors, buy shares of the higher-yielding funds. If this continues, the DD fund will be in trouble.

That's what happened in 1980 with Institutional Liquid Assets (ILA), set up by a group of Chicago banks. In anticipation that the cost of money would decline, ILA managers lengthened the maturities of new purchases in order to lock in what they thought would be higher yields than might be available a few months hence.

They were wrong: rates turned around and headed up. At this point, ILA's yields were no longer competitive. Investors sold their shares. To meet these redemptions, ILA had to sell securities. In a few weeks, the shares were backed by assets worth 99.5¢ per dollar. To avoid losses, the sponsors had to put in more money at lower yields than could be obtained elsewhere. Other funds, with less affluent sponsors, might have folded.

Mark to market. This is like an equity mutual fund. At the end of each day, the managers value the shares. The "pure interest" yield is computed to reflect the interest income earned on the portfolio. Then they (1) mark their holdings to the day's closing market prices; (2) figure the per-share capital appreciation or depreciation; (3) add or subtract the gain or loss from the pure interest yield to arrive at an "actual yield."

A variation of this is to mark to market on a variable NAV basis. This does not factor capital gains or losses into the interest figure but adjusts the NAV (the price of the fund shares paid by investors).

Straight line accrual. This recognizes pure interest income only and does not reflect market value fluctuations, so provides stability of principal and yield.

Advice: These are complicated calculations and are really not important to investors. Forget about the seven-day figures and look at the 30-day average yields. In practice, most funds will return about the same rate over a period of time. It is foolish to switch for a few extra percentage points for a few weeks.

Yet, too many people look only at the current yield. Not long ago when the returns of one fund were listed at 19% and most other funds were reporting returns below 18%, there was a tremendous surge of investors into the higher-paying fund. But since all funds have a limited number of authorized shares, the winning fund had to stop selling shares and, later, expand the number of available shares.

How to Select Money Market Funds

Know the manager. Look for a well-known, established management firm. Strong sponsorship is essential. No major brokerage firm, insurance company or mutual fund group will endanger its reputation by risky investments or trick accounting.

Don't chase after high yields. Look for reasonable rates of return and remember that you are investing, which, by definition, means fairly long commitments. As a frame of reference, compare the yields to those of 90-day Treasury Bills.

Buy late in the day: after 3 p.m. This means you will pay the closing price and will start getting interest immediately.

Look for low average maturities: 60 days at the most. This assures flexibility and the opportunity to move with interest rates. With long maturities, there can be problems when the cost of money changes suddenly. These maturities are published weekly in the financial press or you can get the information from your fund by calling the toll-free number.

MONEY MARKET FUNDS
(Digested from Donoghue's MONEYLETTER)

Fund	For Period Ended 4/22/81 7 Day	30 Day	30 Day Month Ago	12 Mo. Yield 3/31	Ave. Mat.	U.S.	Repos	CDs	BA	CP	Foreign
Alliance Capital	13.5%	13.7%	15.2%	12.7%	22	1	1	13	11	74	
American General	14.4	14.5	16.8	13.1	25		2			98	
Cash Reserve	14.0	13.9	16.2	13.6	22	8	1	8	6	69	
Daily Cash Accum.	14.4	14.6	16.0	13.0	26			10	2	77	11
Delaware Cash	14.7	14.7	15.5	13.1	13			8	5	49	38
Dreyfus Liquid	14.4	14.4	15.3	12.9	30	3		31	12	22	32
Federated Master	14.3	14.6	16.0	12.7	25		2			97	1
Fidelity Daily	14.3	14.0	15.4	12.8	28	4	3	48	22	23	
Intercapital	14.8	15.9	16.1	12.8	37	11		53		36	
Kemper Money Mkt.	14.9	15.1	16.9	13.4	37					56	44
Mer. Lynch Ready	14.4	13.5	16.3	13.2	36	38	1	37	10	14	
Rowe Price Prime	14.5	14.4	15.7	13.3	29		2	10	1	48	39
Reserve Fund	14.6	14.6	15.3	13.2	20		19	8			64
Shearson Temp.	14.7	14.8	16.0	12.3	31	10	3	31	15	41	
Average Maturity	29	32	29								
Previous report	30	32	29								

U.S.= U.S. Government Securities;   Repos = Repurchase Agreements;   CDs = Certificates of Deposit;
BA = Bankers' Acceptances;   CP = Commercial Paper;   Foreign = European CDs and Yankee $ CDs

In the table, the average maturity dropped from 32 to 29 days in the last month and one day from that of the previous report (two weeks before). Commented Donoghue: "If the average maturity shortens again next week, this is a signal of rising short-term interest rates." He was right. Within 10 days, the prime rate was up again.

After you follow these tables for a couple of months, you'll see that there are other signals:

• When the average rate of maturity moves within a narrow range, interest rates are likely to remain stable.

• When the maturity jumps, say, from 36 to 40 days, there will probably be a sharp decline in returns.

Check the 7-day data but focus on the 30-day figures. These funds are so huge that it takes time to make shifts.

This table also shows how to check the composition of the portfolios. The most conservative funds are those that buy primarily U.S. Government obligations; the most aggressive are those which hold European instruments and Yankee dollar CDs. If you invest a large sum, always ask for the minimum standards for Commercial Paper and watch out for any fund that OKs ratings under A.

SLY System

This is an indicator, developed by Donoghue, to predict the trend of interest rates. It is an acronym for Safety, Liquidity and Yield which, he believes, are the key characteristics of all money market funds. The probable future trend of yields is forecast by the average maturity of the underlying securities which, in turn, reflects the opinions of the professional money managers. When the average maturity of a fund, or groups of funds, shortens, it's a good bet that interest rates will rise. The pros are getting ready to take advantage of hgher yields.

Conversely, when the average maturity lengthens, it's a sign that the fund managers believe interest rates will decline, so they strive to lock in the current high yields.

Right now, money market funds are rewarding short-term investments for those who look for income, but when the yields drop below 14%, get ready to move some of your savings into quality stocks or, if you want to lock in high yields, to bonds. At 12% (and that's the future projected by many analysts), use these funds only for temporary parking places for cash. You can do better with other types of securities.

HOW TO MAKE THE MOST MONEY WITH SHORT-TERM FIXED-INCOME INVESTMENTS
(conservative investor)

When interest rates are rising
• Invest in money market funds
• Never invest in anything else—you'll lose higher yields tomorrow.
• Borrow at fixed rates to invest at higher rates. Make sure that there are no prepayment penalties in the loans.

When you think rates are about to peak
• Put 25% into CDs or unit investment trusts; 75% in T-bills if rates are under 9%.
• Put 50% in normal money market funds.
• Put 25% into superyielding money market funds.
• Wait for the peak.

When interest rates peak
• Move another 25% from money market funds into CDs or unit investment trusts.

When interest rates are falling.
• Keep investments in superyielders.
• Add to CDs and unit investment trust holdings.
• Sell CDs and unit investment trust holdings for three months after buying them if they can be sold at profit.
• Reinvest in CDs and unit investment trusts, if available, or in superyielders.
• Move back into a 75% money fund, 25% CD/UIT profile.

When interest rates begin to climb.
• Move back into money market funds.
• Shift out of superyielders quickly.

Adapted from Complete Money Market Guide, William E. Donoghue with Thomas Tilling.

CHAPTER 22

Tax Savings and Tax Shelters

These days, inflation boosts income, earned and unearned, so that more people are moving into higher tax brackets. As a result, there are benefits from tax savings and, at the highest rates, from tax shelters. The more you make, the more fully Uncle Sam becomes a "silent partner." You will have to pay taxes on: income and capital gains while you live; on assets after you die *unless* you take advantage of the tax-saving, tax-deferring opportunities available in many types of investments.

Some people feel there's something shady about tax shelters: "They may be legal but not entirely ethical." *This is not true.* The benefits of tax shelters were legislated by Congress to encourage investment in areas that, otherwise, might not attract sufficient capital. With real estate, the deductions for interest and depreciation make it possible to build and own apartments and office buildings at a lower cost than would otherwise be possible. With oil and gas deals, the write-offs of intangible costs for exploration and drilling and the depletion allowance help to offset the high risks. Properly structured tax shelters are a vital force in our economy. They are not only legal but also can be rewarding for investors.

It's always wise to take advantage of tax savings but, with tax shelters, heed this comment by Dean LeBaron, a successful professional money manager/adviser: *"Tax shelters are worthwhile only for the very wealthy who have specialists structuring deals for them. By the time offers are put out on a merchant basis to a sales force, the individual investor has cause to be very wary of the prospective investment result."*

Three of the most useful tax shelters—tax-exempt bonds, personal pension plans, and real estate—are discussed elsewhere. This chapter concentrates on tax-saving investments in securities, and tax shelters such as oil and gas deals, cattle and equipment leasing, and adds a few suggestions useful in estate planning.

The primary objective of investing is to make money, not to avoid taxes. Yet, tax savings are important in that they are net *after* taxes. They do not have to be shared with the tax collector, as do cost savings and higher earnings. In the 50% tax bracket, each tax dollar saved is worth twice as much as an increase in income of the same amount.

Tax Savings Through Investments

Tax savings are available through safe securities by: *(a)* holding for more than 12 months to benefit from the lower tax rate on capital gains: *(b)* investing for growth rather than for income; *(c)* buying shares of companies whose dividends are fully or partially tax-free.

Hold for over 12 months. The easiest, most logical and most effective way to reduce taxes is to choose long-term capital gains over dividends or interest. The federal income tax applies to only 40% of the profit on property held over one year: For most people, this means a tax rate below 20%—e.g., in the 40% tax bracket, the levy is 16% (40% × 40%).

The holding period is actually 12 months and one day; for securities, the starting date is the settlement day, and the eligibility date is the settlement day for gains, the trading day for losses. This information appears on your broker's confirmation slip.

If the purchase was made on the last day of any month, the long-term gain does not take effect until the last day of the twelfth following month regardless of the number of days in each month.

When you buy a stock that is moving up, check the calendar: (1) on the anniversary of the day you made the purchase; (2) for the date when the chart first showed a confirmed uptrend with rising volume. One year later, if there are gains, major investors will often start to take their profits so that the price may decline temporarily. By careful monitoring, you may be able to sell at or near this interim peak.

Profitable companies that pay no dividends. Their management believes in reinvesting all earnings. Such stocks can be excellent for those in high tax brackets.

SOME PROFITABLE COMPANIES THAT PAY NO CASH DIVIDENDS

COMPANY	Standard & Poor's Rating
Aydin Corp.	B
Cray Research	NR
Computervision	B
Crown Cork & Seal	B+
Data General Corp	B−
Datapoint Corp.	B
Digital Equipment Corp.	A−
Dome Petroleum	B+
Modular Computer	B−
National Semiconductor	B
Prime Computer	NR
Recognition Equipment	B−
Tandy Corp.	B+
Teledyne, Inc.	B+
Wyly Corp.	B−

SOURCE: Standard & Poor's

Stingy dividend payers. Most true growth companies build their capital value (and, eventually, the market price of their stocks) by reinvesting a large percentage of their earnings rather than paying them out as dividends. As long as the corporation prospers, the investor wins. If a company earns 20% on shareholders' equity, pays out 5% in dividends and reinvests 15%, everything will double in about five years.

Example: Revlon, Inc. earned 20.3% on each invested dollar during the 1970–79 decade. Its per share dividends rose from 50¢ to $1.63; its book value, per share, jumped from $6.34 to $24.08 and 67¢ of earned dollar profit was reinvested for growth. Despite the poor market, the price, adjusted for a split, rose from 24 to over 53.

Aggressive corporations that continue to reinvest a large share of profits in research, development, new plants, new facilities and new markets: Automatic Data Processing, Digital Equipment, Hewlett-Packard and Schlumberger, for example.

As long as the growth is real (based on substantial gains in stockholders' equity) and consistent (lasting for at least five years), the company will prove to be a profitable investment. Sometimes that superior performance will not be immediately recognized in the market price of the stock but, eventually, quality and value will pay off.

The careless stockholder who fails to do his homework will take a beating when the company promises more than it can produce. Litton Industries, Boise Cascade, LTV, Whittaker and other one-time wonder stocks soared but failed to stand the test of consistent performance. Eventually, some of these come back and become worthwhile investments but it usually takes many years.

Companies where control is closely held by: *(a)* a foundation—e.g., Kellogg Co. and Campbell Soup; *(b)* family-dominated firms such as Anheuser-Busch, Avery Products and Gordon Jewelry. Often, these wealthy people prefer long-term appreciation to current income. But because of the limited number of public shares, gains can be slow.

Research-minded corporations that plow back large sums into long-term investigations and development. If and when these studies pay off, they create new markets—e.g., AMP, Inc., Johnson & Johnson, Intel Corp., Merck and Xerox.

As an investor, you sacrifice current income for future hopes. Pick an established company with a long record of solid, profitable growth through new products and you will get a sizable payout if you buy the stock at a reasonable price and are patient—usually three years.

New, small companies that need every nickel to hold and improve their competitive position. Some of these are marginal investments but good speculations. There is almost no way to be sure that any new company, no matter how exciting its prospects or how glowing its promise, will become successful.

The odds are 10–1 against skipped dividends ever coming back but the gamble lessens with time. After five years, the odds may be down to 5–1, so your risks are still high. But if the company does make it, the rewards can be substantial. You must decide how long you are willing to wait.

In looking for tax savings in common stocks, concentrate on companies where there are solid profits that are being reinvested in the business. With good management,

these funds will enhance the value of the corporation and you'll sell with a welcome capital gain.

If you are an investor, review the past record for five to ten years to see if there are sound reasons to anticipate real growth. If you are a speculator, pick a company in a group that is currently popular and hope. A rabbit's foot also helps.

Check historical stock dividend pattern. Buy stocks of companies that have a history of declaring stock dividends. Such a policy keeps increasing the number of shares and, until you sell, there's no tax to pay. When you do take a profit, you will have a lower tax base because the cost declines each time there's a bonus.

To find your tax base, divide your original cash investment by the total number of shares. With Southland Corp., which has paid stock dividends annually since 1968, the 100 shares bought for $11 each ($1,100) now total 139 shares so the cost base is about 8.

NON-TAXABLE DIVIDENDS: 1980

Company	Percentage Tax-Exempt
Arizona Publice Service	60%
Cleveland Illuminating	100
Commonwealth Edison	92
Dayton P&L	85
Eastern Utilities	86
Long Island Lighting	100
Middle South Utilities	98
Niagara Mohawk	65
Ohio Edison	100
Pacific P&L	45
Pennsylvania P&L	100
Philadelphia Electric	47
Portland G&E	63
P.S. New Hampshire	100
Public Service E&G	79
Rochester G&E	100
San Diego G&E	95
Toledo Edison	100
United Illuminating	84
Virginia Electric	100

SOURCE: Standard & Poor's

Tax Savings from Utility Stocks

Partially tax-free dividends are available from shares of a dwindling list of corporations, primarily public utilities. With these, there are in effect two sets of books: one for shareholders, one for the IRS. There are different charges for depreciation and amortization, so these companies can pay dividends on current and accumulated earnings that do not exist on their tax returns. Recent legislation has limited this practice, but the following table shows recent examples of tax-free income.

Tax Shelters

Tax shelters are one of the few ways an individual can offset inflation. They make it possible for the investor to retain more of his earnings as he moves into a higher tax bracket. But before you shell out your savings in any tax shelter, make sure that it is a sound investment.

With too many tax-sheltered investments, most people are so intent on avoiding taxes that they do not check the assumptions or the facts. An accountant can verify figures, but he seldom looks behind them. That's the big advantage of using securities as tax shelters. The benefits may not be as spectacular or conversational, but they will be understandable and easily verified. *Tax shelters are fine—when you understand all their ramifications.*

Almost all tax shelter deals are complex and, to be really worthwhile, expensive. For the well-to-do, they can be rewarding not only in tax savings but also in long-term capital gains and, eventually, income. The risks are substantial, so you should always start with money you can afford to lose; be willing to invest more if necessary and, most important, be patient—usually for at least three years.

D. Bruce Trainor, head of Omni-Exploration, Radnor, Pa., warns, "If anybody is thinking about tax shelters to make money, somebody must do a lot of hard work. You need an independent expert—mining engineer, geologist or cattleman—to check the procedure used in packaging the deal. Then, you must study the structure to make sure it benefits you."

The term *tax shelter* refers to an "expense"—a payout of cash or a charge representing the using up of capital that can be deducted from gross income in arriving at the amount of an investor's income subject to tax.

Among typical tax deductible expenses are: depreciation, interest, the cost of feed in fattening livestock, the intangible drilling costs connected with oil and gas exploration, etc.

Most of the "expense" items are non-cash charges. You subtract depletion and depreciation from taxable income, but you do not actually pay the cash to anyone. Thus, it is possible to have *losses* for tax purposes while having *income* in a cash sense.

Example: You are in the 50% tax bracket and make a $10,000 investment in a tax shelter that will, hopefully, generate $10,000 in deductions. As income, that $10,000 would be cut to $5,000 after taxes. If the investment can generate a $10,000 deduction, you have "saved" $5,000 in taxes.

The most common tax shelter is built around a limited partnership. This involves a *general partner* who has expertise in the operations of oil, cattle, crops, etc.,

and *limited partners* who are the investors seeking specific profit opportunities and tax benefits.

The general partner assumes management responsibilities and makes all decisions. Under recent IRS rules he must have a minimum 1% interest in partnership losses as well as gains. Generally, he is a knowledgeable individual who puts up a little money, receives a sizable share of the profits, is assured of income while the project operates, and accepts liabilities for losses in excess of partnership capital.

Private offerings, involving about 35 partners, start with an investment of $25,000. Public offerings, with more than 100 participants, must file a prospectus with the SEC and meet certain financial standards. In an oil-gas deal, the manager must have substantial net worth, not less than 15% of the money raised or $250,000.

Several states set minimal requirements for investors: in California, you must be in the 50% tax bracket and have $200,000 in assets; in Illinois and Texas, the minimums are $5,000 for investments and $200,000 for net worth.

Increasingly, investors are getting greater protection: members of the NASD must exercise "due diligence": discovering whether the general partner is competent and honest; comparing the proposal with similar deals; evaluating the likelihood of the proposed tax benefits; and determining the fairness of the proposed method of sharing profits and expenses.

With almost all tax shelters, off-the-top costs are substantial; usually 6% to 8% sales commission; a 1% management fee; reimbursement of all expenses including, with oil-gas deals, salaries up to a preset maximum. Typically, the general partner gets 25% of the payout up to the investment total, then 50% of the balance. The limited partners supply most of the money but never get most of the profits: usually, 75% of after-costs income until they get their money back, then 50% of the balance. They can include the tax benefits on (or off) their personal income tax returns. In case of failure, they can claim total tax losses not greater than their equity investment in the last two years.

Remember, too, that if you are well-heeled, tax shelters can push you into a higher tax bracket: (1) the top tax rate on personal service income is 50% but on invest-

TAX SHELTER vs. INCOME-EARNING ASSET

	With Tax Shelter			With Profitable Investment		
	Business Income	Tax Shelter + Income	Total = Income	Business Income	Investment + Income	Total = Income
Gross Income	$100,000	$4,023	$104,023	$100,000	$4,023	$104,023
Cash expenses	−50,000	−8,309	−58,309	−50,000	0	−50,000
Depreciation	0	−3,668	− 3,669	0	0	0
Taxable Income	50,000	−7,954	42,046	50,000	4,023	54,023
Tax @ 50%	−25,000	3,977	−21,023	−25,000	−2,816	−27,816
Net Income	25,000	−3,977	21,023	25,000	1,207	26,207
Plus depreciation	0	3,669	24,692	0	0	0
Net cash flow	$25,000	−308	$24,692	$25,000	1,207	$26,207

SOURCE: Managing Your Money. Paul A. Randle & Philip R. Swensen.

ment income (as from tax shelters) is 70%; (2) the 15% add-on minimum tax applies to tax-preference items when such income exceeds the greater of $10,000 or half the taxpayer's regular tax; (3) the alternative minimum tax, broadly speaking, applies to total capital gains, not just the 40% that is taxable under regular tax rules. (N.B.: Check changes under new law.)

In all tax shelters, be wary and use common sense. Most troubles result from ill-founded tax opinions prepared by lawyers as part of the offering proposal. The SEC requires only full disclosure. There can be no legal action unless there is proof of violation of Rule 10(b): "misstatements or omission of material facts that may be considered fraudulent even if not made for the specific purpose of cheating."

As Edwin Hall, vice president of Merrill Lynch Tax Investment Marketing Group, warns: "Tax shelters are like fire. They can be valuable tools if intelligently selected and managed. But they can be dangerous unless you are in a high tax bracket, deal with reputable sponsors and realize that, in most cases, if they won't work as investments, they won't work at all. They are seldom worthwhile for investors who need ordinary income, not tax deductions."

To summarize: the ultimate tax shelter is an investment so profitable that it increases your income tax bracket dramatically and, despite the higher tax liability, you have more after-tax dollars. Here's an example that can be used to make your calculations on the next offer by your friendly "tax-adviser" salesman:

Oil and Gas Tax Shelters

With the energy crisis, the most popular tax shelters are oil and gas deals. The sponsors are specialists or, increasingly, divisions of major brokerage firms.

Broadly speaking, there are two types of programs:
• **Private funds,** which involve fewer than 35 participants and require a minimum investment of $150,000;
• **Public funds,** with hundreds of investors and units available for $5,000 to $10,000 each.

The drilling operations are either: **developmental,** where wells are drilled in previously discovered oilfields to exploit already producing formations; or **exploratory,** where drilling is speculative but, usually, close to known production areas.

Generally, the developmental deals have lower risks, provide income earlier and are not as rewarding as exploratory projects. In both cases, the tax benefits are similar.

Investors can deduct from earned income all intangible drilling costs and, if the well comes in, depletion allowances as well. These are calculated by a complex formula to a maximum of 22% of revenues (under current laws).

Each deal is different but, typically, a $10,000 investment, for an individual in the 50% tax bracket, would mean a $4,500 tax benefit in out-of-pocket expenses. Thus there would be only $5,500 at risk.

The table shows what may happen in a hypothetical, but realistic, situation. With $10,000, the investor takes a first-year deduction of $7,500, a net tax savings of $3,750. In Year II, the deduction is $1,500: a $750 net tax saving. If all goes well, the cash flow starts in Year III with $1,000, rises to $4,000 by Year V and then drops, gradually, to $800 in Year XII. The total taxes saved will be $4,500 so the true cost, to the investor, is $5,500. And over the 12 years in which a typical deal lasts, the investor should receive income of $20,000, partially sheltered by the percentage depletion allowance.

Warns Hall: "There's no way of knowing the future value of the program. Some wells start off with a good flow while others require additional money for full development. Don't let anyone kid you. All oil and gas deals are speculations."

In the last year or so, there's been an added benefit: the opportunity to swap drilling-fund partnerships for shares of a public corporation. The new companies are smaller independent producers that want to expand and/or cash in on the current popularity of energy investments. The high prices commanded by oil and gas stocks make such conversions attractive to both managers and investors.

For the professionals: Such deals permit them to expand their operations, improve their balance sheet, cut operating costs, add new reserves and, often, list their shares on major stock exchanges.

For the limited partners: a tax-free conversion (after two years to assure time for fair appraisal of reserves), continued tax write-offs for the intangible drilling costs, receipt of a share in any oil and gas that is recovered and exchange of illiquid holdings for stock that, often, trades at multiples of 30 times earnings.

These swaps are profitable for investors but of course, they benefit the oil companies by improving cash flow, strengthening the balance sheet and cutting the heavy costs of collection and distribution of income and explanations of tax benefits.

Checkpoints for Oil and Gas Drilling Deals

1. At least 85% of the investment should be devoted to drilling-related activities. The more money spent to

CASE HISTORY: OIL & GAS DEAL
(Projected for 12 years; investor in 50% tax bracket)

Year	Investment	Tax Deductions	Taxes Saved	Cash Flow
I	$10,000	$7,500	$3,750	0
II		1,500	750	0
III				$1,000
IV				3,000
V				4,000
VI				3,500
VII				2,500
VIII				1,600
IX				1,400
X				1,200
XI				1,000
XII				800
	$10,000	$9,000	$4,500	$20,000

SOURCE: Merrill Lynch

seek oil and gas, the better the chances for success. If it's only 50%, forget it!

2. The general partner should not benefit at the expense of the limited partner. One of the main reasons for the poor repute of oil and gas deals has been the ability of the general partner to profit no matter what happens. He's in Texas and you're in Philadelphia, so there's almost no way to check operations. Be sure to get, in writing, a statement that there is not, and will not be, any conflict of interest.

3. About 60% of the revenues should go to the limited partners. The investors' money should be used solely for intangible (deductible) costs. The general partner should pay all tangible (completion) costs.

Typically, sharing should be *(a)* before program payout: 75% to limited partners and 25% to sponsor; *(b)* after program payout: 50% each.

4. Assessments should be spelled out in detail. Preferably, these extra funds should be limited, but if the well is successful, few people will object to adding to their investment.

5. All investors should be able to get out without undue penalties. Terms should be described in the prospectus. With oil-gas deals, you'll get only the discounted redemption price of the shares and be lucky to break even.

Exit ability is important if you plan to donate all or part of your shares to charity or to another member of the family. They may not want to stay in the oil business!

6. Diversify and be cautious. Plan to invest in three programs; use only money you do not need; and be patient.

7. Avoid year-end deals. These are sold, frantically, in November and December because too many wealthy people leave tax planning to the last minute. This does not allow time for proper analysis. Promoters unload their slow sellers and drillers offer a prepayment feature so that investors can take a fast deduction. But the IRS is tightening rules and, in the rush, some details may be overlooked so that, five years from now, the latecomer may be smacked with an unexpected tax bill.

8. Check the promoter's long-term performance. With the risks of oil/gas drilling, buy shares *only* in partnerships/companies where the value of previous investments has doubled in three years.

Other Popular Tax Shelters

In recent years, Congress has limited tax deductions and set rules for the time of write-offs but there are still viable tax shelters for the wealthy and wise. Basically, they defer taxes but they can also be profitable deals. Always discuss the terms with a taxwise attorney and, until you become experienced, use only money that you can afford to lose.

Equipment leasing. These take advantage of depreciation and investment-tax credits. They are best with heavy items that maintain high residual value and, often, provide appreciation when sold. They are not wise, for individuals, with equipment such as computers, whose worth is likely to fall rapidly because of technical obsolescence.

Here's how a typical lease of a railroad car works:

The investor buys a hopper car (used for shipping grain) for $30,000. He can pay all cash or cash plus a loan from his local bank. The deal is managed, under contract, by a railroad leasing company that assumes responsibility for purchase, maintenance, accounting, leasing and selling (at a hefty fee of at least 12%).

The car is leased to a railroad or shipper. With a fixed-rate lease, there will be regular income for a stated period (assuming the lessor is credit-worthy). With a per-diem lease, the returns will be greater when utilization is high but lower during recessionary months. The tax benefits are: (1) a first-year tax credit of 10% of the cost of the equipment plus accelerated depreciation and, in many states, a bonus depreciation that tends to boost deductions; (2) tax credit for interest on the loan; (3) deduction of all operating expenses; (4) sheltered cash flow; (5) in the early years, ordinary losses to offset income from other sources.

Plus the fact that rail-car technology rarely changes much. With inflation, a well-maintained car becomes more valuable each year. The car that cost $30,000 new in 1977 has a current replacement value of over $40,000.

But there are dangers:

Hidden costs. When management firms supply cars, they often mark them up and, of course, charges for maintenance, insurance and property taxes are hard to check.

Delivery. Cars are in short supply. Your tax shelter can vanish if the promoter cannot get cars to sell, and some entrepreneurs have been known to walk away with your down payment.

Residual values. They are high now but could plummet in a depression.

Leases. With the embargo on grain shipments to the Soviet Union and the slowdown in housing and automobiles, demand for certain types of cars is lagging. You could go months without income.

Liquidity. If you need your money in a hurry, you may have to take a whopping loss and lose some of your tax credits.

River barges. These deals are similar to those of freight cars. They involve river hopper barges used to transport liquids, chemicals and dry cargo on major waterways. They require less capital: $5,000 for five units. According to one salesman, the investor will get a 10% return for 10 years, be able to deduct substantial depreciation and interest and sell at a "big" profit after about seven years. *One possible drawback:* if the taxes proposed by the Reagan administration are adopted, barges will not have such a cost advantage over trucks and railroads.

Coal mining. Time was when coal mines were a prime tax shelter. Advance royalties, paid with a little cash and a large long-term note, were tax deductible. But no more. The IRS limits tax deductions to the advance royalties paid in one year.

Still, with the expanding demand for coal, there are opportunities to save taxes and make money, too. But be cautious and look for:

Experienced operators. Coal-mining companies currently involved with a producing, operating, economic mine and seeking capital for a new property that is an extension of a going business.

Engineering evaluation. A realistic estimate of coal deposits made by an objective, unrelated authority.

Firm orders. Contracts or orders for the delivery of coal to nearby docks.

Transportation. Convenient railroad sidings and trucks in place with easy access to nearby markets.

Financial strength. Mining equipment at work with the new investment for added facilities; estimates of the quality of the coal; expected selling price; anticipated costs, tonnage and profits.

Yield. Assurance of regular profits of $1.50 per ton to provide a monthly return on investment of 15%.

The tax deductions can be substantial:

Depletion allowance. 10% of gross income (but not to exceed 50% of taxable income before deducting depletion). If coal sells for $28 per ton and the investor receives $1.50 per ton, then 10% of $28 would allow 50% of the investor's revenue to be tax-free.

The depletion can go to the owner of the property, holder of the lease, owner of net profits or royalty interest. Or the benefits can be split.

Exploration costs. These can be deducted as expenses. Predevelopment items are usually capitalized but those previously deducted must be recaptured after the mine goes into production.

Mining development expenditures. For road construction, excavation, drilling of shafts, control of water seepage, etc. In some cases, these can be deferred to a later year.

Prepayment of royalties. Generally, the IRS allows a deduction of up to two years.

Movies. For $5,000, you buy one unit in a $2.5 million partnership to produce a low-budget film. To break even, the gross must be $10 million, possible with TV and foreign rights.

After expenses, the first $2.5 million of disbursable cash goes 99% to the limited partners. Then, each further $1 million is split: $600,000 to investors; $250,000 to general partners; $150,000 to the producer.

Exotics such as books, plants and gems. These are the typical partnerships and, according to the glib promoters, offer quick tax write-offs and a chance to reap a bountiful return in later years. Most of these are outright frauds and unacceptable to the IRS (despite what the promoter may claim).

The "special representative" sells you 500 Bibles at a "wholesale price" of $10,000. You hold them for one year and then, with his help, donate them to various tax-exempt institutions at a $30,000 "retail value." This "assures" you of an immediate $30,000 charitable deduction on your income-tax return. But, almost before you know it, the IRS creams the deal and you have to come up with $5,000 more if you are in the 50% tax bracket.

Another book sham involves engraved plates of a hardcover book, bought with small cash and a large note to be paid out of profits of the paperback edition. You take several deductions: a 10% investment tax credit,

HOW TO COMPARE TAX SHELTER INVESTMENTS

Investment A: annual depreciation of $15,000;
Investment B: Tax-deductible interest $15,000

	Normal Income	Normal Income + Investment A	Normal Income + Investment B
Taxable income	$50,000	$60,000	$60,000
Depreciation (A)	0	−15,000	0
Interest (B)	0	0	−15,000
Taxable Income	50,000	45,000	45,000
less tax @ 45%	−22,500	−20,250	−20,250
After-tax income	27,500	24,750	24,750
Plus depreciation	0	15,000	0
Net cash flow	$27,500	$39,750	$24,750

SOURCE: Managing Your Money.
Paul A. Randle & Philip R. Swensen

accelerated depreciation and interest. One deal never even got to the IRS: $2 million, in handy units of $5,000 each, for the acquisition of plates for 36 books and films. The promoters admitted taking $1.7 million for expenses!

Energy-related projects such as manufacturing wind turbines; installing small hydroelectric generating plants on fast-moving streams and at abandoned dam sites; processing waste and plants for fuel for small boils; and even a "new" type of windmill. All of these involve double risks: unproven techniques/products and non-approved tax deductions.

Royalty trusts. These are shares in the income from oil/gas wells. The trust controls oil rights for large areas. If oil or gas is discovered, the drillers (usually major oil firms) pay a percentage of the revenue to the trust. These royalties are "off the top": i.e., if the oil company drills a dry hole, there will be no royalties but neither will there be any costs to the trust.

All earnings are paid out so the trust pays no taxes and the shareholder gets the full revenue from the royalty. IRS recognizes that shareholders have a personal stake in the assets that provide income to the trust so part of the cash payout is regarded as a return of capital and not taxable. For example, you buy a trust share at $40. Its assets are depleted at 8% in Year 1, so $3.20 of the total yield is tax sheltered. If the payout is less, there's no tax. If it's more, the tax applies to the excess: at $4.00 per share, 80¢ is income. You must pay a capital gains tax on this money. Each year, your cost figure is reduced, for tax purposes, by the amount of the depletion. When you sell for more than the adjusted cost, you pay a capital gains tax on the excess.

Mostly royalty trusts are traded OTC but there are three on the NYSE: Mesabi, Mesa Royalty and Houston Oil Royalty.

Cattle Breeding and Feeding

These programs are best for the wealthy and patient but can be worthwhile for those who have special knowledge or enjoy investing in interesting situations. They require expertise and capital.

There are two major types of cattle investment partnerships as outlined in this interview with Garrett P. Cole, vice president of Oppenheimer Industries of Kansas City, Mo., a professional management firm with over 30 years experience.

Q: Why are tax shelters in cattle worth considering now?

A: Because farmers need capital and, to encourage greater production of cattle, Congress has approved special tax benefits for investors: cash basis accounting, accelerated depreciation, investment tax credits—all deductible from regular income plus, in most cases, low taxes on long-term capital gains when the cattle are sold.

Q: What is the most popular tax shelter with cattle?

A: Breeding cattle. This refers to a herd of cows, their calves and in-between female cattle known as yearlings. Commercial herds are sound business propositions. Markets exist in hundreds of rural centers; prices are quoted in daily newspapers; the ranchers who raise cattle are experienced businessmen; and costs are well known through governmental studies.

Q: Where and how does one start?

A: Locally if you live in a rural area; with a professional manager when you live in a city. The minimum investment should be $20,000 plus about half that amount each year thereafter.

TABLE A

CATTLE BREEDING TAX SHELTER

Current year

Buy 100 cows @ $600 each		$60,000
90% loan @ 12%	$54,000	
10% cash down payment		6,000
Expenses paid to December 31		17,500
Total cash outlay		23,500
Depreciation/net expenses for year		23,500
Percentage deductible from income		100%
Investment tax credit		6,000

Five years later

Proceeds from sale of herd	$110,000	
Ordinary & capital gains tax	(32,000)	
Investment tax credt recapture	(2,000)	
Net sales proceeds		76,000
Total cash investment	106,000	
Tax savings: 50% tax bracket	57,500	
After-tax cost		48,500
After-tax profit		$27,500

SOURCE: Physician's Management 1/81

Table A shows a typical situation. You buy 100 cows at $600 each: $60,000, 10% cash and the balance by a non-recourse loan. You prepay some interest and advance money for breeding fees and a portion of the feeding expenses. The total cash outlay is $23,500: $6,000 down, $2,500 for prepaid interest; $1,800 for breeding; and $13,200 for feed and management.

Since you are trying to make money, you can deduct most of the investment in the year of payment.

Q: What are the tax advantages?

A: There are three:

1. Depreciation: a 20% bonus on the first $20,000—$4,000 when you file a joint income-tax return.

2. Added annual depreciation calculated up to a 200% declining balance over 7 years or less: $2,000 in the first year; $10,000 in the second year and so forth.

3. Each cow is a qualified asset so you can deduct 10% of gross value to a maximum of $10,000 a year. The total tax savings, for an individual in the 50% tax bracket, is $17,750. And you own property that can be expected to increase in value.

Q: How long does this tax shelter last?

A: Cattle breeding investments are continuing tax shelters. Each year, your new outlay, about $10,000, is fully tax deductible under the same terms.

There will be a death loss of 2% to 3% but many ranchers provide an annual indemnity for those above 3%. You also get credits for the proceeds of the sale of steer calves and unfit animals. And the size of your herd keeps increasing when the heifer calves become cows.

With cash basis accounting, all cattle born to the herd start on a zero cost basis. When sold after 24 months, the proceeds become low-taxed, long-term capital gains. In about five years, a sale of the herd should net about $110,000, depending on the market at the time.

At this point, calculations get tricky. In that 50% tax bracket, the taxes will be $32,000. But the law requires a recapture of the original $6,000 investment tax credit deducted in the year of purchase. So the $110,000 drops to $76,000. In five years, your $106,000 investment has created $57,500 in tax deductions so the after-tax cost is $48,500 and your net profit is $27,500.

Q: What about cattle feeding?

A: This provides greater leverage but the risks are higher in that market prices are subject to wider fluctuations and the investment is higher, usually over $250,000.

Q: For example?

A: Let's say Bill Bush buys 500 steers at $160 each: $180,000 with $9,000 down and a 95% loan of $171,000 at 12% interest.

He must also advance $125,000 for the purchase of feed and the payment of fees and operating expenses. This can be deducted immediately so, in the 50% tax bracket, he saves $62,500.

Bill makes his money by selling the cattle at the end of the feeding period, hopefully when prices are high. Usually, he rolls over his profits into a new deal and so defers taxes until a year when he has other major deductions or is retired and in a lower tax bracket.

Under IRS rules, feeder cattle are business inventory so do not qualify for capital gains. The profit is always taxable as ordinary income.

Table B shows that Bill gets a tax deduction of $125,000 in the first year. This is 93% of his cash input of $134,000: $9,000 down payment plus $125,000 operating expenses. If he sells the cattle in the second year for $308,000, he must repay the $171,000 loan. This leaves him $137,000: a $3,000 cash-on-cash profit for his short-term investment. Taxwise, he must report, as ordinary

TABLE B

CATTLE FEEDING TAX SHELTER

First Year
Buy 500 steers @ $360 each		$180,000
95% loan at 12%	$171,000	
5% down payment		9,000
Purchase of feed, fees, etc.		125,000
Total cash outlay		134,000
Deductions for operating costs		125,000
Percentage deductible from income		93%
Tax savings in 50% tax bracket		62,500

Second Year
Cash flow
Gross proceeds from sale of steers		308,000
Less repayment of loan		171,000
Cash received		137,000
Taxable income		
Sales price cattle	$308,000	
Cost basis cattle	180,000	
Ordinary gain		128,000
Tax due in 50% bracket		64,000

SOURCE: Physician's Management 1/81.

income, $128,000: the difference between the $180,000 cost and the $308,000 sales price. All that he has done is to defer taxes.

Cattle breeding is an excellent tax shelter; cattle feeding is more risky and not as rewarding. But both have their place in the portfolio of wealthy individuals.

What to Do Before Investing in Any Tax Shelter

Read the prospectus. Too many people are so anxious to avoid taxes that they hear the story they want, not the truth. Remember the well-publicized Home-Stake Production Company scandal that involved so many prominent business and professional people? The prospectus clearly stated that the company was being investigated by the SEC, there was a conflict of interest in ownership of land adjacent to the oil drilling area and the promoters had a history of legal controversy. But the "investors" were greedy and failed to do their homework.

Make sure it's a good business proposition, not just a tax dodge. Look for a without-tax-benefits return of at least 2% above that of quality corporate bonds; tangible results within 18 months; and, in four or five years, the probability of getting back two or three times your original stake. With tax benefits, boost those targets to 4 to 1, or even 6 to 1.

Have the ability to get out quickly and profitably. With private deals, you may be able to find a friend to buy you out. With public programs, look for those where the prospectus spells out a liquidity provision that allows any partner to ask for an independent evaluation after the first two years.

Note: The problem of getting out of a tax shelter carries over to your estate. If you should die, your heirs have only nine months to pay estate taxes.

Check the sponsor's record and reputation. The majority of tax shelters are put together by small, regional brokerage firms, but increasingly, major financial organizations are getting into the field. ALWAYS check the sponsor and, if possible, talk to someone who has been involved with the same people before. If it's a large deal, spend a few extra dollars to have it reviewed by a specialist.

Have your own resources. *With a tax shelter, never invest any money you will need—ever.* Think ahead five to ten years. There's the risk that you will lose all or most of your money if there are unexpected hazards: an oil well blow-out, a fire in an apartment, a blight of crops, etc. The only thing limited about a partnership is that when it's properly structured, you can't lose more money than you put in.

Ask why the promoter is working your area. If the deal is so good, why isn't it picked up by people living where the property is located? In North Carolina, a Kansas-based company offered to sell physicians a package deal: to buy cattle at a set price, to feed and fatten them for a set fee and to sell them at a predetermined profit plus life insurance for the herd. When nothing happened for a year, investigation found that some of the feedlots were nonexistent and that there were no contracts for the sale of the cattle at any price. None of the "investors" have gotten back their money but some of the salesmen are guests of Uncle Sam.

Warning Signals After You Invest in a Tax Shelter

Tax shelters need to be watched, reviewed and often revised. Here are danger signals to watch for:

Cash calls from the general partner. Don't panic. There may be logical reasons for extra money, especially these days when costs are rising so rapidly. The realtor may have to pay more than the anticipated points to get the mortgage; the rancher may have underestimated feed costs; or the oil driller, desperate to get pipe, may pay overtime delivery charges.

When there's a cash call, get direct confirmation from the tax shelter's accountant. If this is unavailable, *beware.*

Late accounting reports and tax returns. If these important papers are a month late, the general partner is inefficient, if not corrupt. *Get out fast.*

Skips promised cash distribution. If you don't get that check on time, find out why and start making plans to ask for your money. If it's a large deal, the general partner probably will pay you off to avoid trouble with big investors. If he refuses, call your lawyer.

Investigations by a regulatory unit or notice of default. These are difficult to determine. The promoter is not likely to volunteer such information, and defaults are filed by creditors preliminary to foreclosure—too late to do much good.

Protections: (1) Watch the financial pages for news that the syndicate is in trouble. There may be a chance to get some of your money out or to join with others to take control. (2) Ask the general partner to inform you of *any* legal action against the corporation or partnership or individuals involved. Keep a copy of the query for the IRS and possible court action.

Tax Shelter Roll-Overs

A sound tax shelter will eventually start turning out considerable taxable income. Eventually, you will have to pay up, but there are ways to defer the income tax liability:

1. Roll your investment over by investing the taxable income in another tax shelter. This *may* be OK if you move into a similar type of investment (from one oil-gas deal to another), but be wary if you shift to another area.

The idea of a roll-over is to turn short-term gains into long-term ones. You sell at a loss, buy, and hold for 12 months before taking your gain. Under a new IRS ruling, you lose the tax advantage if the roll-over is to a different type of holding.

A taxpayer with a short-term gain in real estate set up a roll-over late one year by buying silver futures and simultaneously selling them short. The loss taken on one side of the hedge was matched against the real estate gain. This eliminated most of the short-term gain. In the following year he closed out the other side of the hedge for a long-term gain roughly equal to the eliminated short-term gain.

Said the IRS: "The loss was not part of a closed and completed transaction because the taxpayer kept a balanced position while creating his loss. The investor lacked an expectation of profit so could not take a deduction on the loss side of the hedge." The ruling is being appealed.

2. Give the investment to a member of your family who's in a lower tax bracket. Unless this is carefully structured, you may trigger a tax liability.

The problem stems from the nature of the tax shelter. When you went into the deal, there was plenty of leverage. Your share of the partnership's debt was considered a "contribution" of money. That increased your tax basis, so you deducted losses greater than your original investment.

But when you get out, that "contribution," says the IRS, is a cash distribution. You may have to pay income taxes on the excess liabilities even if you don't make a cent on the transaction—such as on a gift to a son or daughter.

3. Place the deal in a trust with yourself as owner. As long as you control the trust, you probably won't be taxed. But when you try to get rid of the ownership or revoke the trust, the IRS may consider this a taxable event.

4. Transfer ownership to a corporation set up for that purpose. You will have to pay a capital gains tax but can escape the higher income levy. To avoid any recapture of ordinary income, say from depreciation, you and your family must own less than 80% of the corporation.

5. Effect a tax-free exchange for a similar asset— e.g., with real estate, for another building; with oil and gas deals, for units of a deal managed by the same group. There are no taxes to pay IF you can find a taker, but consult a tax expert, as the IRS watches for unusual swaps.

Tax Shelters in Your Family

Corporations. Since these often pay taxes at a lower rate than does a wealthy individual, it can pay for you to transfer some personally owned securities to a company that you or your family control. This can be especially valuable when the corporation invests in preferred stocks whose dividends enjoy an 85% deduction.

Transfers to children/grandchildren. This takes advantage of the tax exemption and tax exclusion of dividends (currently, a maximum of $100). Over a ten-year period, this tax-free income can grow to a sizable sum.

N.B.: If you are a doting grandparent making a gift of securities, be sure they carry the Social Security number of the child, *not your own.* If you make the common mistake of failing to make the change, the IRS computer may force you to pay taxes on the interest/dividends.

Check with your lawyer before you set up any type of custodianship. If a grandparent transfers securities to his grandchild, naming the child's uncle as custodian, the child's father will still be taxed on any income used to discharge the father's legal obligation to support the child.

Be careful in giving stock to minors and naming yourself as custodian. Such shares must be registered in the name of the custodian. If you die while the children are minors, the stock will be taxed in your estate. *Solution:* name someone else as custodian.

Family partnership. This can be most useful with property where management is needed. This format lets you transfer income to a family member in a lower tax bracket. Except for your partnership interest, the property transferred will not be included in your estate.

Be sure to spell out everything in detail and maintain a business structure: regular meetings with minutes, distributions based on each partner's interest, salaries/fees related to actual work performed and operational involvement by everyone.

Limited partnership. This is similar to the family partnership with one individual as general or managing partner. You can keep control because limited partners, legally, cannot vote. But you cannot restrict the rights of the other participants and, as general partner, can be sued for omissions and failures.

Sub-chapter S. This enables the investor/shareholder to pass corporate income/gains/losses directly to his personal income-tax statement. Because it involves a corporation, individual liability is limited.

This is usually best for a family group owning real estate. It is complicated, hard to form, requires someone to spend time in management and must be conducted under restrictive rules. Financing can be difficult because all shareholders must agree to assume individual liability. The loss pass-through cannot exceed the amount of the shareholder's basis plus any loans made to the corporation. This means that the investor cannot claim a share of any mortgage to leverage the total investment. But, properly structured, this special corporation can be an excellent tax shelter for the wealthy and wise.

Tax Shelter Through Deferred Annuities

Deferred annuities permit the accumulation of tax-free income, assure a steady lifetime income, and are one of the few investments that provide greater benefits than ten years ago.

These are lump-sum payment contracts that can be bought from most insurance companies by almost any adult. At age 65, the purchaser is assured a fixed income as long as he and, if he so designates, his spouse live.

Over the years, all income accumulates tax-free until withdrawal. At that time, part of the monthly income is tax-exempt as a return of capital. The rate of accumulation depends on the return from investments made with the money. Currently it is about 11%, although the guaranteed rate is much lower. If the investments yield more than projected, the annuitant will have a larger retirement income. If it's less, he is still sure of the predetermined amount.

Example: Mr. Vieser, age 45, purchases a $100,000 deferred annuity. To be conservative, let's assume an average interest rate of 7% over the next 35 years. For the first 10 years, he lets the $100,000 accumulate at interest. At age 55, he starts withdrawing $100,000 over the next decade. This is tax-free as a return of capital. At 65, he has $246,534 and takes half of this to buy an annuity for himself and his spouse.

If Mr. Vieser lives to age 80 (and he comes from long-lived ancestors), he will have $316,290 left to be paid to himself or his widow over the next 20 years. This is taxable.

The table shows how this works. Over 55 years, the annuity, purchased for $100,000, will provide $803,033. If both die before the first withdrawal, the policy proceeds go directly to a beneficiary: tax-free with proper planning.

Warning: Sales charges are high: 5.5% to 8.5% of the payment. This means less money at work.

Deferred annuities are excellent tax savers for those who want security, have sufficient funds to tie up for a long time, are in a high income bracket and can expect to live beyond actuarial expectancy.

$100,000 DEFERRED ANNUITY

Age	Cash Value	Cash Out	Taxes
45	$100,000	0	None
55	196,715		
55 to 65	(withdraw $100,000)	$100,000	None
65	246,534		
	Uses $123,267 to buy annuity; leaves balance at interest		
65 to 80	With a 15 year life certain annuity for $123,267, $11,241 per year to total $168,629.	168,629	Yes
80	316,290	534,404	Yes
	20 year fixed period annuity will give beneficiary $26,720 per year for total of $534,404.		
		$803,033	

Installment Sale Within Your Family

For individuals with substantial holdings, preferably in one stock, an installment sale can be a real money saver. It can increase income, reduce the tax bite on large capital gains and enable the seller to escape the 15% minimum income tax of "tax preference items" that otherwise escape the regular tax (such as the untaxed half of a net long-term capital gain). This minimum tax is due when the preference items are in excess of $10,000 or half the regular income tax for the year, whichever is greater. The installment sale spreads the gain over several years and thus reduces, or eliminates, the minimum tax.

Here's an actual case history that took place in 1978. The interest rate on the sale was 5%. Today it may be higher, so check with your tax advisor first. But the concept is still sound.

Many years ago, Mr. Beane invested $25,000 in a good growth stock. Over the years, the original 200 shares had grown to 5,000 shares with a market value of $250,000. The annual dividends were a skimpy $2,500 and since Mr. Beane was ready to retire, he wanted more income.

A direct sale would have meant a hefty tax bite, at least $50,000. So he sold the shares to his son for a note requiring payments of $1,666.50 per month for 234 months (19½ years). The total payments would be $389,961: $250,000 for the stock plus $139,961 interest computed at the 5% rate. In his tax return, Papa Beane listed the transaction as follows:

Stated sales price	$389,961
Less interest	139,961
Adjusted sales price	$250,000
Less cost	25,000
Capital gains reported on installment basis	$225,000

Since there was a 10–1 relationship between the sales price and the cost basis, the monthly installment would be 10% tax-free as a return of capital, and the 90% would be taxed as a long-term capital gain:

Interest	$589.12
Long-term capital gain	961.54
Tax-free return of capital	106.84
Total monthly payment	$1,666.50

Mr. Beane, Sr.'s, taxes would depend on his tax bracket each year, presumably at a modest rate after retirement.

Mr. Beane, Jr., deducts from his income-tax return the $7,069.44 annual interest (12 × $589.12).

To provide more income for his father, Beane, Jr., sells the stock and reinvests the $250,000 (less commissions) in mutual-fund shares. He arranges for a systematic withdrawal plan to cover the monthly payment, a total of $19,998 a year, almost eight times the previous income.

Since the fund yield is over 10% annually, Beane, Jr., comes out well ahead and, hopefully, by the end of the 20 years, will have a welcome nest egg of his own.

Note: T. Rowe Price Associates, Inc., Investment Research and Counsel, suggests an alternative method of payment: at level interest. This can be advantageous to the seller since it enables a greater amount of tax-free return of capital and long-term capital gain to be transferred to the buyer in the early years of the contract. Since the interest portion of the payment remains the same in each year, the seller is not forced into a higher tax bracket in the earlier years because of high interest payments. (The Price firm does not market this financial technique, as do many mutual funds.)

No-nos: Prearranged deals where you sell appreciated property on the installment plan to, say, your spouse, who then sells it to someone else. At a minimum, the sale should be delayed for one year and then only with the approval of a knowledgeable tax adviser.

Repeat: for most investors, tax shelters are better for conversation than real profits. Always do your homework first; use only money you can afford to forget; and consult a wise and wary lawyer. And then take another look at real estate and tax-exempt bonds.

CHAPTER 23

The New Options Market

No area of the securities markets has changed more dramatically than options since formal trading, on exchanges, started in 1974. At the outset, the number of options was limited, the volume small and the price changes closely related to those of the related stocks. Generally speaking, the options market was predictable.

But no more. Today, annual volume is over 100 million contracts representing 10 billion shares of stock. With many options, prices move on their own with little relation to the shifts in their stocks. Increasingly, the options market is dominated by professionals who do nothing but trade in calls and puts. Always remember this when you deal in popular options. You are competing with men and women whose livelihood depends on their ability to guess (and, occasionally, manipulate) option prices.

Still, everyone who owns securities should understand and, at times, use options as part of investment strategy. With careful selection and constant monitoring, *selling* options can boost income; *buying* options can bring quick, short-term gains; and both techniques can be structured for tax benefits.

Options are a cross between trading in stocks and trading in commodities. They permit holders to control, for a specified period of time, a relatively large amount of stock with a relatively small amount of capital. They are rights to buy or sell a specified number of shares (usually 100) of a specified stock at a specified price (the striking price) before a specified date (the expiration date).

In effect, options are limited-life warrants. They pay no dividends and, by definition, are diminishing assets. The closer the expiration date, the less time there is for the value of the option to rise or fall as the buyer anticipates.

Buying options is speculation. Selling options can be investing.

The most popular and widely used option is a *call*— the right to buy the underlying stock. A *put* is the opposite—the right to sell the stock. For sophisticated traders, there are complex combinations: spreads, strips, straps and straddles.

Options have been available, on a limited basis, for many years but major interest started in 1974 when they were listed on major exchanges. Today, calls and puts on over 300 stocks (primarily those of NYSE companies) are traded on one or more of four markets: Chicago Board of Options (CBOE), American Stock Exchange (AMEX), Philadelphia Exchange and Pacific Exchange.

These listed options have expiration dates (the Saturday after the third Friday) every three months: January, April, July and October; February, May, August and November; March, June, September and December. Trading is limited to three of the four maturities: January, April and July, and then April, July and October.

The cost of the option is called a premium. It varies with the duration of the contract, the type of stock, corporate prospects, and the general activity of the stock market. Premiums run as high as 15% of the value of the underlying stock: for example, for a volatile stock selling at 50 ($5,000 for 100 shares), the premium for a far-out call to be exercised in nine months from now might be 7½ ($750). Shorter-term calls carry smaller premiums: from 2% for those expiring in a month to 7% for those callable in about six months.

For the trader, the lures of options are low cost and high leverage. For about $900, he can control 100 shares of Eastman Kodak selling at 80 ($8,000). Once the price of the stock moves close to the exercise price of the option, both stock and option will usually move together, often in fractions of a point. Thus, the $900 can be just as profitable as the $8,000 investment—not counting the dividends.

Buying calls is risky. When the price of the stock declines, the value of the call can drop faster and farther, percentagewise, than that of the stock and, probably, will expire worthless. There are times when options can be used to protect positions, but most trades in calls and puts are speculations.

Selling (writing) calls on stocks you own can be conservative. With experience, a knowledgeable broker and a good market, an investor can obtain total returns, at an annualized rate, of 18% to 20%: 13% to 15% from premiums and 3% to 5% from dividends received as long as the stock is owned. Usually, such profits are before commissions but, with practice and a little luck, they can be net.

Definitions in Options Trading

Striking price: the price per 100 shares at which the holder of the option may buy the related stock.

For stocks selling under $60 per share, these are quoted at intervals of five points: 25, 30, 35, etc.

For stocks over $60 per share, the difference is 10 points: 70, 80, 90.

Options are added when the stock price reaches the high or low strike price: i.e. a 40 strike price will be listed when a stock hits 35 and a 25 option when the stock sinks to 30.

Expiration date: Saturday following the third Friday of the month in which the option can be exercised.

Premium: the cost of the option, quoted in multiples of $\frac{1}{16}$ for options priced below $3, $\frac{1}{8}$ for those priced higher. To determine the percentage of premium, divide the current value of the stock into the quoted price of the option. When there's a difference between the exercise price of the option and the quoted price of the stock, add or subtract the spread.

Here's how calls are quoted in the financial pages:

HOW OPTIONS ARE QUOTED

Option/ Price	April Vol.	April Last	July Vol.	July Last	Oct. Vol.	Oct. Last	Stock Price
Eas Kd 50	1	31 1/2	b	b	b	b	80
Eas Kd 60	7	20 1/2	a	a	13	22 3/4	80
Eas Kd p 60	a	a	71	5-16	12	11-16	80
Eas Kd 70	1180	10 3/4	175	13	31	14 1/2	80
Eas Kd p 70	687	3-16	195	1 5/8	22	3	80
Eas Kd 80	1484	2 5/16	292	6 5/8	60	8 3/4	80
Eas Kd p 80	2143	2 7/16	211	5 1/8	15	6 5/8	80
Eas Kd 90	b	b	239	2 3/4	52	4 3/4	80

Volume in 100s. "p" = put; a = not traded; b = no option offered.

SOURCE: Wall Street Journal

Explanation: On this day, in early April, when Eastman Kodak stock was at 80, the last trades on April calls were: 31½ ($3,150) at the striking price of 50 with one contract (controlling 100 shares) traded; 20½ ($2,050) at the striking price of 60 with 7 contracts traded; 10¾ ($1,075) at the striking price of 70 with 1,180 contracts; 2⁵⁄₁₆ ($231.25) at the striking price of 80 (its current quotation); and no option offered at the strike price of 90. *Obviously, those who bought EK calls with a low striking price made a lot of money.*

On the puts, there were no trades at 60; 687 contracts at ³⁄₁₆ ($18.75) at the striking price of 70; and 2,143 contracts changed hands for options at the striking price of 80 at 2⁷⁄₁₆ ($243.75) each.

As with all publicly traded securities, the prices of premiums reflect temporary hope and gloom, but over a week or two, call quotations tend to follow standard patterns that move in close concert with the underlying stock.

Usually, the most stable relationship is between the prices of options with the same striking price and different expiration dates. Analyst Richard A. Brealey states that "the dispersion of stock price changes increases

RELATIVE PREMIUMS

As % of price of underlying common stock when common at exercise price

Months to Expiration	Low	Average	High
1	1.8– 2.6	3.5– 4.4	5.2– 6.1
2	2.6– 3.9	5.2– 6.6	7.8– 9.2
3	3.3– 5.0	6.7– 8.3	10.0–11.7
4	3.9– 5.9	7.9– 9.8	11.8–13.8
5	4.5– 6.8	9.0–11.2	13.5–15.8
6	5.0– 7.5	10.0–12.5	15.0–17.5
7	5.5– 8.2	10.9–13.7	16.4–19.2
8	5.9– 8.9	11.8–14.8	17.7–20.6
9	6.4– 9.5	12.7–15.9	19.0–22.2
10	6.8–10.1	13.5–16.9	20.2–23.6
11	7.2–10.7	14.3–17.9	21.4–25.0
12	7.5–11.2	15.0–18.8	22.5–26.2

roughly in proportion to the square root of the period of the option. A stock will fluctuate $\sqrt{2}$ or 1.41 times as widely over a six-month period as over three months."

Thus, a fair value for a six-month option should be 1.41 times as much as the short-term one. And a one-year call should cost 1.41 times as much as a half-year option.

These ratios apply at the outset of the transaction. The time value of every option will fall rapidly as the expiration date nears.

Dividends and rights: As long as you own the stock, you continue to receive the dividends. That's why calls for stocks with high yields sell at lower premiums than those of companies with small payouts.

A stock dividend or stock split automatically increases the number of shares covered by the option in an exact proportion. If a right is involved, its value will be set by the first sale of rights on the day the stock sells ex-rights.

Commissions: These vary with the number of contracts traded: for a single call, a maximum of $25; for 10 calls, about $4.00 each. For calculations in multiple units, use $14 per contract.

When you are writing options and income is paramount, it's a good idea to try to work with a base unit of 300 shares of owned stock. For each side of the transaction the commission per call is about half that of a single option (about $15 versus $25).

Money-saver: Write long-term calls for ¹⁵⁄₁₆ ($93.75) instead of 1 ($100). The commission is $8.39 versus $25, so your net is greater: $85.36 compared to $75 for the one premium.

Restricted options. An option is "restricted" when its previous day's price closed at less than 50¢ per share and its underlying stock price closed at more than 5 points *below* its strike price for calls or more than 5 points *above* its strike price for puts. Opening transactions (buying or writing) of restricted options are prohibited, but closing transactions (liquidations) are permitted. Check your broker, as there are exceptions.

Writing Calls

In writing calls, you start off with an immediate, sure profit rather than an uncertain, potentially greater gain. You have these choices:

On-the-money calls. These are written at an exercise price which is at or close to the current price of the stock.

Example: In December, Mr. Horwitz buys 100 shares of Almost Always (AA) at 40 and sells a July call at a striking price of 40, for 4 ($400). The buyer acquires the right to buy this stock at 40 anytime before the expiration date at the end of July.

Mr. Horwitz will not sustain a dollar loss until the price of AA goes below 36. He will probably keep the stock until its price moves above 44.

At this price, the profit meter starts ticking for the buyer, so let's see how the speculator fares. By July, AA is at 50. The buyer can exercise his option, pay $4,000, and acquire the shares which are now worth $5,000. After deducting about $500 costs (premium plus commissions), he will have a net profit of $500, thus doubling his risk capital.

But if the price of the stock moves up to only 42, the buyer will let the call expire and take the loss. Mr. Horwitz will keep about $475: the $400 premium plus two quarterly dividends of, say, $50 each, minus the $25 commission paid for the call sale.

If the price of the stock soars, Mr. Horwitz can still work out if he is willing to come up with cash to keep the stock with its paper profit.

When AA stock hits 50, the July call will be quoted at about 11⅝. New corporate developments make Mr. Horwitz enthusiastic about further gains, so he buys back the call for $1,162.50. He takes a cash loss of about $787 (the $762.50 deficit from the $1,162.50 purchase price minus the $400 premium plus the commissions). But he has a $1,000 paper profit on AA stock.

Now, Mr. Horwitz can write a new call, at 50 with an October expiration date, for 3 ($300). This will cut his out-of-pocket loss. If the stock is called, in October, at 50, he is still ahead of the game.

With all calls, there's flexibility and, often, several alternative strategies.

In-the-money calls. This is a more aggressive technique that requires close attention but can result in fine profits and tax benefits for those in high income-tax brackets. The calls are written below the current stock price.

Example: You buy Glamour Electronics Co. (GEC) at 209 and sell two in-the-money calls, at a striking price of 200, for 25 ($2,500 each). If GEC goes to 250, you buy back the calls at 50 ($5,000 each), chalk up an ordinary loss of $5,000, then sell the shares for a $4,100 gain. In a 50% tax bracket, the loss saves $2,500 in taxes, and the after-tax gain is $3,280.

If GEC declines, there are no ordinary losses for tax purposes. But you can still make money if the stock ends its option period between 209 and 185. Between 209 and 201, everything is a capital gain. At 201, if the call is exercised, there's an initial $5,000 capital gain. You must deliver the shares for an $800 loss and can buy another 100 shares at market for another $100 loss. But the net is a welcome $4,100—all taxable at the low long-term rate.

At 200 or lower, the calls are worthless, so you pocket $2,500, after taxes, as ordinary income. From this, deduct the $900 loss on the stock for a net gain of $1,600.

Deep-in-the-money calls. These are calls that are sold at striking prices *below* the current quotation of the stock. Writing them is best when the investor is dealing in large blocks of stock because of the almost certain commissions which have to be paid when the underlying stock is called. The ideal selection is a dividend-paying, low-volatility stock of a well-known company. The seller always accepts a certain, limited profit rather than a potentially bigger gain.

There are two approaches:

• *Using the leverage of options:* when the exercise price of the call is below that of the current value of the stock, both securities tend to move in unison. Since the options involve a smaller investment, there's a higher percentage of return and, in a down market, more protection against loss.

Example: Pistol Whip, Inc. (PWI) is selling at 97⅝. The call price at 70 two months hence is 28, so the equivalent price is 98. If PWI goes to 105, the call should keep pace and be worth 35.

If you bought 100 shares of the stock, the total cost would be about $9,800. Your ultimate profit would be about $550, close to a 5.5% return. If you bought 10 options, the dollar profit would be a 22.4% return on the smaller $2,900 investment. If the stock does not move, you can let it go or buy back the calls at a small loss. If PWI declines, your maximum loss is $2,900, probably much less than that of the stock.

N.B.: All too often, this is more theory than practice. When an option is popular, it may trade on its own and not move up or down with the price of the stock. This separate value will shift only when the expiration date is near.

When Williams Cos. stock was in the low 40s in March, the Nov. 45 call traded at 2¹⁄₁₆. Yet, a few weeks later, when the stock fell to 35½ (−16%), the call edged down only to 2 (a 3% decline).

• *Creating cost:* basing your return on the total income received from the premium and dividends.

Example: In January, you buy 1000 shares of Well-known Chemical at 39½. You sell April 35 options for 6⅞ each, thereby reducing the price per share to 32⅝. There's a 45¢ per share dividend due before the exercise date.

If the call is exercised, the total return will be $7.21 on a $32.62 investment: a 22% gross profit in four months. Even after commissions, the annual rate of return will be excellent, and the stock will have to drop below 33 before there's a paper loss.

Out-of-the-money calls. These are written at exercise prices well above the current quotation for the stock. They are best suited for investors who want to combine modest income and capital gains and still retain ownership of the stock.

Example: In March, Reggie Rich buys 300 shares of Big Blue Chip (BBC) at 50½, then writes three October calls, at the striking price of 60 at 1 ($100) to get $300 immediate income.

If the stock stays below 60 for the next seven months, he keeps the premiums, dividends, and stock and writes new calls. If BBC goes above 60 before the end of

October, Reggie can protect his position by buying back the calls just before the exercise deadline. He will probably have to come up with cash to do this but, like Mr. Horwitz, will keep the stock with its 9½ points of paper profits. By repeating this process, he will strengthen his portfolio and add to his income.

This approach has hazards: *(a)* in a rising market, such good deals are hard to find because the price of the stock must have declined sharply and quickly in order to have the 60 option still listed; *(b)* the stock may move up just as rapidly and be called before the expiration date; *(c)* the price of the stock may continue to drop. Reggie takes in cash but has paper losses. Still, with quality stocks, the risks of substantial declines are small if calls can be written again and again, as explained herewith.

Buying Back

Time and a fluctuating market are the option writer's best assets. The premium decreases as the time value vanishes. If the price of the option drops, the writer can cover his position at a price that is 50% or so below that of the original premium. Then, he sells a new out-of-the-money call and starts over again. With this tactic, it is possible to wrack up substantial profits even though the price of the stock stays about the same and even more when it drops temporarily. Here's what happened with Xerox (XRX)—after deducting commissions and fees.

1979	March: Bought 300 XRX at 57¼ for net cost of $5,800.	
	September: Sold 3 calls, 70 April, @ 3¼	+928.78
	October: Bought back 3 calls @ 1 1/16	−355.88
	Net profit	+572.90
1980	March: Sold 3 calls, 70 October @ 2¼	+632.92
	March: Bought back 3 calls @ 1	−226.87
	Net profit	+406.05
	April: Sold 3 calls, 60 July @ 1 1/16	+288.44
	May: Bought back 3 calls @ 3/16	−123.82
	Net profit	+164.62
	October: Sold 3 calls, 70 April @ 4¾	+1,372.58
1981	January: Bought back 3 calls @ 2⅛	−697.03
	Net profit	+603.55
	February: Sold 3 calls, 70 July @ 1½	+406.71
	March: Bought back 3 calls @ ⅝	−206.52
	Net profit	+200.19

Over this period, the dividends on XRX stock totaled $1,215 so the total returns were $3,162.31: an average annual rate of return of 15.7%. And the stock price stayed almost unchanged at about 58.

Writing Naked Calls

If you maintain a substantial margin account and have experience in trading options, you can write "naked" calls (that is, without owning the stock). This can be risky if the price of the stock moves up substantially. But with listed options, you can always cover your position by buying another call even though it's at a higher price than that at which you made the sale of the option. You will lose part, or all, of your premium but will keep the stock and its paper profit.

Rules for Writing Options

When you write an option, you are betting that the stock will not fluctuate greatly: *(a)* that it will not go up by more than the amount of the premium (if the exercise price is below the present market price), or *(b)* that it will not go up beyond the exercise price plus the amount of the premium (if the exercise price is above the present market price).

Here's a digest of rules for a successful approach to writing options as outlined by LeRoy Gross, vice president of Dean Witter Reynolds Securities, Inc., and other options authorities:

1. Work on a programmed basis. Have a minimum of $25,000 in securities and be ready to write options every month or more often if the situation looks unusually promising. Do not have all your money in the same types of securities and try to space the dates on which the options can be exercised, preferably a month apart. With the addition of more options on the exchanges, it is possible to select any month you want.

2. Set a target rate of return. If you want a 15% annual return, you will have to wait for premiums of over 10% for six-month contracts or 6% for three-month expiration dates. The dividends and turnover will bring such income.

A good rule: get out when you double your money or can buy back the option at a net cost half of that of your investment. If you bought a call at 1, get ready to sell at 2½ (the extra pay for commissions). If you sold a call at 4, buy it back when its value drops below 2. You can make more if you hang on but, with the short-term volatility, that's risky.

3. Concentrate on stocks you would like to own on their own merits. *A convenient guide:* stocks on the *quality* list and those recommended by brokers and investment advisory services.

4. Try to write long-term calls (six to nine months) until you are experienced. The longer the option period, the greater the percentage of premium. With most stocks, profitable changes require at least four or, in erratic markets, six months.

5. Keep your capital fully employed. Well before the expiration date of your option, be ready to buy another stock and start over again. You are dealing in percentages, so keep those premiums rolling in. Except in a roaring bull market, the odds are that you will retain the stock.

Have a list of ten stocks: five in your portfolio, five others for replacements. Generally, the premiums move with the price of the stock. But watch for unusual opportunities which your broker should catch as the result of his firm's computer printouts.

6. Own the stock on which you sell a call. When you become an expert, you can buy the stock immediately after you write the option. Before then, don't try to outsmart the professionals.

It's best to buy the stock and then wait for a profitable option. Once you have decided that the stock is fairly priced or, better yet, undervalued, wait for a temporary dip to buy. Then be patient and do not write a call until you are sure of the total percentage return you want.

7. Calculate your net return. Add the premium, dividends and appreciation (if any), then subtract the commissions and fees. With 100 shares of stock bought at 30, and a call sold and exercised at 30, the total commissions are about $145. That's a cost of nearly 5%, so the premium should be a minimum of 10% and, preferably, 15%.

8. Don't average down. Gamblers on a losing streak double up. If they bought an option at 4 and it drops to 2, they double up to get an average cost of 3. Now the option price need only move up one point to get out even. If it zooms, they make more money.

Like most theories, this sounds better than it is. A trend in motion is more likely to continue (in this case, down) than to reverse over the short life of an option.

9. Keep a separate bookkeeping system. Options are a special breed. Separate accounts make it easier for your accountant to prepare your annual tax return and to provide corroboration if the IRS makes an audit.

10. Be persistent. Once you have decided that you will write options as part of your investment plan, keep on doing so regularly regardless of what the stock market does. With the premium check in the bank (or your margin account), you are off to a good start. If you pick the right stocks, you will be able to maintain, and enhance, your capital.

11. Watch your timing. It's best to write a call when the stock has risen to a price which you think is too high. If you bought the stock at 45 and it has moved to 57, look for a setback. Then write an out-of-the-money call at an exercise price of 60. If you can get a 4-point ($400) premium, you gain downside protection to 53. If the stock is called at 60, you still do well: a 15-point profit in the stock plus 4 points on the call for a total $1,900 return plus dividends.

Timing is also a major factor in the value of the option premium. The closer the expiration date, the lower the premium. In July, premiums on January calls will be one half a point or more less than premiums on comparable February options. *The reason:* the demand dwindles because investors looking for gains are beginning to move out of the market. This leaves fewer buyers, primarily short-term speculators, to make the market.

12. Protect your capital. When the price of your stock has dipped below your net-after-premium price: *(a)* sell the stock and simultaneously buy a call with the same striking price and expiration date as the one originally sold (this maintains most of your capital for reinvestment); *(b)* buy a call to close out your position and write a new call for a more distant expiration date. (See the example of Mr. Horwitz earlier.)

This is the kind of information that can be discovered by an alert broker or through special options advisory services.

13. Use margin. Leverage boosts profits. Under present regulations, stocks can be purchased on 50% margin. Since long-term call premiums run up to 12%, buying the stocks on margin makes sense. If the stock price is unchanged or declines by expiration time, the option buyer loses his entire investment. If the price rises 12%, the cash buyer comes out about even. But if he uses

margin, he has a 24% gain (ignoring commissions and interest costs).

But these days, when interest costs are so high, margin is not as attractive, or as profitable, as it was when you borrow at 8% or less.

14. Watch the record dates of high-dividend stocks. An option which appears comfortably above parity may be exercised by a wily trader to capture the large dividend.

15. Define your investment goals. If you want maximum safety, write calls on stable stocks which pay sizable dividends. The lower premiums will be offset by the higher yields.

If you want greater total returns write out-of-the-money calls on stocks which pay modest dividends and are moving up in value.

If you are aggressive, concentrate on volatile stocks where the dividends are low and the market action volatile. The premiums will be high, but the odds are that in an up market the calls will be exercised and you'll lose your stock. Or, in a down market, the price of the stock will decline for a paper loss.

Buying Options

Buying options is speculating. In some months 90% of all calls purchased expire worthless. This sounds devastating, but in real life most options are traded before the striking date.

It's best to buy options in a rising market, and on stocks in a rising industry group.

There are two broad approaches:

1. Buying long-term, out-of-the-money options at a low premium (usually 1 or less). By diversifying with three or four promising situations, you may be lucky to hit it big with one and make enough to offset losses on the others.

2. Buying short- or intermediate-term in-the-money or close-to-the-money options of popular, volatile stocks (e.g., a call with two months to expiration date, a stock within 5% of striking price and a low time premium). If the stock moves up sharply and pushes the premium to double your cost, sell. If you have three or more options, sell when you have a 50% gross profit. Advice from one expert: "Never pay a premium of more than 3 for a call on a stock selling under 50 nor more than 5 for one trading over 60. Both prices should include commission costs."

Rule of thumb: The striking price of the option and the market price of the stock should change by about one half as many points as the change in the stock price: for example, if a 30 option is worth 5 when the stock is at 30, it should be worth 2½ when the stock falls to 25, and worth 8 when the stock moves up to 36.

Here are guidelines for determining how much to pay for newly-listed calls where the time premium is at its peak:

Watch the spread prices. When trading a July option, look at the premiums on the October and January options to see if they are in line.

Watch for unusual situations. Normally, the prices of options move with the prices of the underlying stocks. But there are periods when premiums move up and down

PRICE RANGES FOR NEWLY-LISTED OPTIONS

Stock Price	3 Months	6 Months	9 Months
10	1 5/8 - 1 1/2	1 3/4 - 2 3/8	3 - 3 3/8
20	2 1/8 - 2 1/4	3 1/8 - 3 1/2	4 - 4 1/2
30	3 - 3 1/4	4 - 4 1/2	5 - 5 1/2
40	4 - 4 1/4	5 1/4 - 6	7 - 7 1/2
50	4 3/4 - 5 1/4	6 1/4 - 7	8 - 8 3/4
75	7 - 7 3/4	0 1/4 - 11	12 - 13

on their own. Often, premiums drop more than the related stocks. *Example:* In November, when Hello Dolly stock was at 23⅜, the May 25 calls were quoted at 2⅜. By the end of December, the stock was up a fraction to 24, but the option, which, theoretically, should have dropped about 5% with the time factor, fell 30% to 2. If this unusual spread continues, it might be worthwhile to buy back the call and wait for more rewarding premiums for the August calls.

Conservative strategy. Put 90% of your investible cash in money market funds and use the balance to buy calls. The interest, of 12% or more, will offset some of the losses in options. Over the short life of an option, the most you can lose will be about 5% of your money, and you might pick some winners.

Example: Elmer Emrich owns 10,000 shares of CBA stock currently selling at 28. He sells 100 six-month calls at 30 for $2 each ($20,000) and buys shares in a money market fund yielding 12%. At the end of six months, CBA is trading at 27 so he keeps the stock, has $1,200 extra income from the fund and can start writing calls again.

If the stock price soars to 35, he buys back the 100 calls at 5 ($50,000). He loses $30,000 but his stock is now worth $70,000 so he's still ahead. Now he can sell new options at 40, etc.

Options with Takeovers

Options are a great way to play the takeover market. In one day, after the announcement of an acquisition offer by Standard Oil (Calif), one call on AMAX stock soared from a cost of $175 (1½ premium plus $25 commission) to $9,000! A handful of insiders made a fortune but currently are being investigated by the SEC. For the amateur, the only way to make so much money so far is to be very lucky.

How to Trade Options

The new options market has opened new vistas for speculators. Trading is for cash, so there are no margin calls. The investments are relatively small, the potentials large, and there are always opportunities to hedge. Instead of risking their money in junky, low-priced stocks, speculators can get action with the same outlay for options on top-quality equities.

There are scores of speculative situations, so the examples have to be limited. Once you get the swing of trading options, find a skillful broker, do your homework and play the odds. Success in options is a matter of

percentages. Because calls are traded daily, there's instant information, and gains or losses can be taken any time during the life of the contract.

You can dabble with one or two calls but to really play the options market, you should work with $8,000 a month, spend time enough to make frequent checks and have a fast, reliable source of information: daily from your broker or weekly from specialists in options' information.

If you have time to watch developments closely, you can let your profits run, but for most amateurs, the best rule is to set target prices for gains of 10% to 25%—after deducting commissions and depending on the size of your investment, the prospect of the stock market, and the volatility of the stock.

The sale of multiple options against a single stock position can assure extra protection in a decline, added income if the stock stands still and bigger returns when there's a modest advance. This works best following a strong market advance, when there's likely to be a temporary lull or fallback.

Example: You own 300 shares of So Long, Inc. (SLI), trading at 25. You believe the market is topping out, so you sell six calls at premiums of 2½ each: $1,500. Here's what could happen:

Price SLI	Gain/Loss	Price Call	Gain/Loss	Net
20	-1,500	0	+1,500	0
25	0	0	+1,500	+1,500
30	+1,500	5	-1,500	0
35	+3,000	10	-4,500	-1,500

You will profit as long as the stock stays between 20 and 30, but you'd better be ready to cover your position if the stock zooms over 30. Some shrewd buyers may exercise the calls before the expiration date.

Caveat: Don't try this multiple writing with volatile stocks. Their rapid price swings can narrow that profit zone in a short time.

Checkpoints for Trading Options

In trading, it's important to have a frame of reference for the value of the option, follow the market trend, concentrate on volatile, low-dividend-paying stocks, and watch the time factor.

The action of the stock will be the determining factor in profits and losses, but gains are easier to come by when you:

1. Check these points.

Time before expiration. The longer the period before the exercise date, the greater the chance for appreciation. Unless you are sharp, observant, and lucky, it seldom pays to trade in calls with less than two months to run. Profits can be made only with volatile stocks in an erratic market and that's no spot for the amateur.

Volatility. The best bets are options on stocks which swing over 25% a year. This criterion rules out slow movers such as utilities, steels, and financial institutions. It highlights swingers such as Pennzoil, Tandy, and Williams Cos.

Price of the stock. The greatest percentage gains can be made with low-priced stocks; the lowest percentage gains, with costly equities such as Superior Oil. But each has its day of glory.

Striking price of the option. This selection depends on your experience and trading goals. Buying deep-in-the-money calls offers the best leverage because their premiums are relatively small.

Yield of the stock. The higher the dividend rate of the stock, the lower the premium of the option—usually. For quick-profit trading, stick with low or no-dividend payers.

2. Follow these rules suggested by Peter deHaas of Lehman Brothers:

Buy the option when the market is going down but when you **anticipate a turnaround soon.** This will give you the benefit of both the temporary and long-term price rises.

Buy options where the underlying stock is trading below, but close to, its striking price. The premium will be smaller and will rise when the stock moves above the exercise price.

Pick options with small premiums and the stocks appear to have prospects of fast, upward action.

Stick with high-quality stocks until you are experienced. With options, the risks are enough without adding the danger of poor investments.

Don't enter market orders. Give your broker a specific price or, if you are anxious, a price range at which to buy. In fluctuating markets, an active option can move more than ½ point and can cut deeply into your potential profits.

Spreads for Profit and Protection

Hedges can be profitable with calls when the spread is right, usually no more than ½ point between the cost of the calls exercisable at different dates and/or different prices.

A hedge involves buying one option and selling another short, both in the same stock. *Your goal:* to capture at least the difference in premiums. Dollarwise, these are inexpensive because, under present margin rules, your long option is adequate to cover the short option. Thus, your cash outlay is small: $50 for that ½-point spread.

LeRoy Gross used this example in the spring when A.T. & T. was just under 50. Calls, at a striking price of 50, were trading at 3½ for July and 4 for October.

Sell July 50 for 3½	+$350
Buy October 50 for 4	− 400
Cash outlay	50

Add a $25 commission for the full transaction to make a net investment of $75, so it's not expensive to deal in units of 10 or more.

If T is below 50 in July, you keep $350 and still own an option worth $250 to $300.

If T goes up by October, the option will be worth, say, $500 or more. Profit: $850+.

If T is at 60 by the end of July, that month's option will be worth 10, so you have to buy it back at a loss of about $650 plus in-and-out costs. But the October call

might be 14, so you could sell that for a gross profit of $1,000 or more to offset the July loss.

If the stock falls below 46½, you will lose money unless there's a recovery by October. But with such a stable stock in a rising market, this is not likely. The key factor is the small spread which keeps the maximum loss low.

Perpendicular spread. This is based on buying and selling options with the same exercise date but different striking prices.

Example: Easy Rider (ER) is at 101¾. The market is moving up and you are bullish. Sell 10 ER October 100s at 12¼ and buy October 90s at 16⅞. This requires an outlay of $4,625. Your maximum loss will occur if ER plunges below 90.

If it goes to 95, you will still make $375. At 100 or higher, your profit will be a welcome $5,375, a 120% return on your investment.

If the market is declining, set up a bearish spread. Psychologically, the risk is greater, so it is best to deal with lower-priced stocks, selling at, say, 24⅝.

Buy 10 October 25s at 2⅛ and sell 10 October 20s at 5⅜. This brings in $3,250 cash. Since the October 20 calls are naked, you'll need $5,000 margin (but the premiums cut this to $1,750) to control nearly $50,000 worth of stock.

If the stock goes to 22, you will make $1,250. At 20 or below, your profit is $3,250 for a 180% return. With perpendicular spreads, you know results at any one time. With horizontal spreads, there's the added risk of time.

Butterfly, or sandwich, spread. In this case you are multihedging. Here's what to do: In the spring, when your stock, hypothetical Busty Bertha, is at 96¼, with July 80 calls at 17⅛, July 90s at 12⅛ and July 100s at 7⅛, *buy* one July 100 and one July 80 and *sell* two July 90s. This provides $2,425 in cash, but it requires at least $1,000 margin.

If you can set up such a combination, *you cannot lose money.* If the stock ends July at 80 or below, or at 100 or above, the buy and sell sides offset each other.

You make money if BB stock is between 81 and 99 (that profit zone again). At 94, you will lose $800 on the sell side but make $1,400 on the buy side for a $600 gross profit.

At 90, you get the best profit. The July 80 call is worth 10 (a loss of $712.50), and the July 100 expires worthless for a loss of another $712.50. But the two July 90s also expire at zero, so the investor pockets $2,245 on the sell side for a net gain of $1,000, or 100% on the money he put up.

There are dangers in such complex combinations:

1. With one call each, the commissions will eat you up.

2. Such spreads are difficult to execute at the same time.

3. Early exercise by the buyer can destroy the hedge and create a new ball game.

4. Lifting a leg of the spread can: *(a)* increase the risk from temporary market fluctuations, *(b)* create an unprofitable tax situation. The potential profit on the short side could be larger than the loss on the long side. If

both are closed out or expire, the taxes could take all the gains.

Advice: Set up butterfly spreads *only* if you have a shrewd, knowledgeable broker, time enough to watch changes, and money enough to make such speculations worthwhile. Otherwise, your broker will be the winner.

Mistakes with Options

These comments are based on counsel from veteran Max G. Ansbacher, vice president of Bear, Stearns & Co., New York City.

Failing to include all costs in calculating profits. Since the profit from writing calls is always limited, be sure to deduct—mentally and actually—the costs of commissions.

Example: Mr. Flack buys 100 shares of stock at 22 and writes a call, at 20, for $3. That's a gross spread of $1.00 per share. This appears to provide reasonable returns:

• when bought for cash, of 5.2% ($1 divided by the net cost of $19).

• when 50% margined, of 12.5% ($11 cash minus $3 premium equals $8, which is divided into $1).

With four months to run before expiration, the annualized rates of return would appear to be 15.6% and 37.5% respectively.

But with 200 shares and two options, the per share commissions total $1.01: to buy the stock, 43.7¢ ($87.40); to sell the options, $15.90 per option; and, if the call is exercised, 41.6¢ ($83.20). So Mr. Flack really lost money!

Being too bullish. No matter what your long-term forecast for the stock market, it will have little effect during the short life of most options.

Over the short term, it is just as likely that the market will go down as well as up. This applies especially to buying options. *Advice:* If you trade, never put all your money in options on one side of the market.

Forgetting loss potential. When selling calls, your profit is limited but your potential loss is almost unlimited if the stock goes down. Use a stop-loss order to sell the stock when it has declined to a predetermined price. At that point, the call can be continued naked or bought back.

Puts for Protection and Profit

In the past few years, puts have become more popular and more widely used as the result of being listed on major options exchanges. Properly handled, they can extend the range of investment and tax strategies, open new profit opportunities, provide bear market protection and, in fast-moving periods, yield excellent rewards.

A put is the opposite of a call. It gives the option owner the right to *sell* a specified number of shares (usually 100) of a specified stock at a specified price before a specified date. Puts have the same expiration months, dates, and prices as do listed calls.

But a put is a distinct entity. Its intrinsic value increases with a decrease in the value of the related stock. You buy a put when you are bearish and anticipate the

market/stock will decline. But a put is a wasting asset as its value will diminish with the approach of the expiration date.

As with calls, the attraction of puts is leverage. For a few hundred dollars you can control stock worth thousands. Generally the premiums will be smaller than those of calls because of lesser demand. In the stock market few people are pessimistic.

The best candidates for stocks involving puts are:

• *Stocks paying small or no dividends.* You are hoping for the value to decrease. Dividends tend to set a floor for stocks as, even in bear markets, yields are important.

• *Stocks with high price/earnings ratios.* These are more susceptible to downswings than stocks with lower multiples. A stock with a P/E of 20 has a lot more leeway for a drop than one with a P/E of 10.

• *Volatile stocks.* These are issues with a history of sharp, wide swings. Stable stocks move slowly, even in active markets.

With all combinations of puts, check your tax adviser. Puts can be used to postpone taxes, but they must be properly timed and executed.

Selling Puts

In selling (writing) puts, you receive an instant profit but must be ready, with cash or collateral, to buy the stock if it is selling at or below the exercise price.

Example: The stock is at 53. You think it will go higher, but you would welcome extra income. You write an in-the-money put at 50 and receive 2 ($200).

As long as the stock stays above 50, the put will not be exercised. But once it falls below 50, you must be ready to buy the stock or buy a comparable put.

Many traders write puts against cash. This provides income and also the opportunity to buy stocks at below current prices.

These are naked options, so you must meet substantial margin requirements and probably have readily available assets of $25,000 or more. Brokers are wary of all naked options.

If you guess right and the value of the stock drops, you can do well. You have the premium and can acquire the stock at a bargain price.

Using Naked Puts

Naked options, by definition, have risks, but they are risks which are inherent in any investment founded upon stock prices. This is especially true when selling naked puts because they are equivalent to writing covered calls. Actually, the puts have several extra advantages: lower commissions because, unless you are writing out-of-the-money calls, you must include the cost of selling the stock when called; less margin money than needed to write the same amount of covered calls; and, when T-bills are used as margin, you get a higher yield on your money than you can receive from dividends on the stock. Here's how a conservative can use puts:

Mr. W. believes shares of H-D are a sound, long-term investment. In July, its shares are at 56 in a weak market. Mr. W. thinks the stock would be a buy at 50. The option quotes are:

Stock	Strike Price	Put	Oct.	Jan.	April	Close Price
H-D	50	P	¾	1¼	1¾	56

Mr. W. writes a naked January 50 put and collects $125.

If the stock stays above 50, he pockets $125 (less commission). In January he can write a new put at a later expiration date and keep earning short-term capital gains.

If the stock falls below 50, he buys at an equivalent price of 48¾ (50−1¼).

Advice: Write naked puts only: (a) on fundamentally strong stocks; (b) when you have funds enough to complete the purchase. Diversify with at least three puts. And do not be afraid to buy back the put if you change your mind or the market does it for you.

Using Puts with T-Bills

If you become involved with puts, set up a liquid base of six-month T-bills as collateral. These will earn income greater than the dividends paid on owned stock against which calls are written. When you sell a naked put, you get instant cash; if the put is exercised, you will have funds to buy back the option, possibly with tax benefits, or to acquire the stock at a bargain price.

Example: Dr. Wheeze has $11,000 to invest. In late January he buys 200 shares of Pointy Head stock at 54½, for $10,900 and sells two July 50 calls at a premium of 6¾ ($675) each for $1,350. That's a net difference of $450. Before the expiration date, he receives two 65¢ per share dividends ($260), so he takes in $710 (without commissions).

He will do better if he buys a six-month T-bill with a 12% yield for $9,400 and leaves the $1,600 in his margin account. With the T-bill as collateral, he sells two July 50 puts at 1¹⁵⁄₁₆ ($193.75 each) for $387.50. In July, he has a $600 profit on the T-bill for a total of $987.50.

High-Risk Hybrid Options

For sophisticated traders, there are combination options that provide high rewards with high risks.

Straddle—a double option, combining a call and a put on the same stock, both at the same price and for the same length of time. Either or both sides of a straddle may be exercised at any time during the life of the option—for a high premium. These are profitable when you are convinced that a stock will make a dramatic move but are uncertain whether the trend will be up or down.

Traditionally, most speculators use straddles in a bull market against a long position. If the stock moves up, the call side will be exercised and the put will expire unexercised. This is more profitable than writing calls because the straddle premiums are substantially higher than those of straight calls.

But this can be costly in a down market. If the underlying stock goes down, there's a double loss: in the call and in the put. Therefore, when a straddle is sold against a long position, the straddle premium received must, in effect, protect 200 shares.

OPTION STRATEGIES
(in order of benefits)

Very Optimistic
  Buy call with strike price above market
  Buy call with strike price at market
  Buy call with strike price below market
  Buy stock on margin
For speculations, combine one of these:
  Sell put with strike price above market
  Sell put with strike price at market
  Sell put with strike price below market
Moderately Optimistic
  Buy stock, sell put
  Buy stock, sell call with strike price above market
  Buy stock, sell call with strike price at market
  Buy stock, sell call and put, both at market
  Buy stock, sell call and put, both with strike prices away from market
Neutral
  Buy stock, sell one call with strike price above market, one at market
  Buy stock, sell two or more calls with strike price above market
  Sell put and call both with strike prices at market (straddle)
  Sell call with strike price at market, put with strike price below (combination)
  Buy stock and one put with strike price at market (call)
Moderately Pessimistic
  Buy stock and two puts
  Sell call with strike price at market or lower, buy call at higher strike price (bear spread)
  Sell naked call with strike price above market
  Sell stock short, buy two calls
  Sell stock short, buy one call at market (synthetic put)
  Sell naked call with strike price at market
  Buy one call and two puts, all with strike price at market
Very Pessimistic
  Buy put with strike price at market
  Sell naked call with strike price below market
  Sell stock short, buy call with strike price above market price (partial put)
  Buy put with strike price below market
  Sell stock short

SOURCE: Max G. Ansbacher, *The New Options Market.*

In a bear market, it might be advantageous to sell straddles against a short position. The odds are better.

Here's an example that was given to me by a broker who prides himself on his trading ability:

"In January, Honeywell (HON) stock is at 100. In the past year, its price has bounced between 65 and 100. Since the best straddle usually is short-term, I settle on the February expiration date and, simultaneously, buy a call and a put, both at 100; 5($500) for the call and 4($400) for the put. Add $100 commissions ($25 each for buying and future selling) and my exposure is $1,000.

"To make money, HON must rise above 110 or fall below 90. At 112, the call will be worth 13 ($1,300) while the value of the put will fall to about ½ ($50). I make $350 in one month!

"If HON falls to 88, the call will be worth about 1 ($100) and the put will be at least 12 ($1,200) so I take away $300.

"If the stock stays between 90 and 110, I will lose a portion of my investment. If it ends up at 100, I'm wiped out. I always play for one big hit because I know that 25% of straddles do not work out. But with a profit of 200% or more, I can afford that percentage of losers."

Well, I told you he was a trader.

Spread—a variation of a straddle in which the call will be at a price above the current market and the put at a price below the current market. Essentially, this is a cheaper form of straddle, carrying a lower premium because of the lower risk to the seller.

Strip—a triple option: two puts and one call on the same stock with a single option period and striking price. A strip writer expects the stock to fall in the short term and rise over long term. He offers to sell 100 shares he owns above the market price or take 200 shares below the market. The premium is higher than for a straddle.

Strap—also a triple option: two calls and one put on the same stock. The writer gets top premium. He's bullish over the long term, but more negative than the strip seller on short-term prospects.

Insurance. (1) To protect against severe loss on a stock you own. (2) To lengthen the holding period to qualify for the lower long-term tax rate. The date of the purchase of the put can be the starting point, so shares held short term can be shifted by the acquisition of a put.

Let's assume you own 100 shares of Long Shot Electronics (LSE). It is now 60 and has risen from your cost of 30. You are convinced of the long-term potential and do not want to sell. But you are edgy and anticipate a price drop. You can either buy a put or sell short.

June:

Buy one October put for 4, exercisable at 60	−$ 400
or	
Sell 100 LSE short 60	$3,000 margin
By October if LSE is at 50:	
Sell October 60 put 10	+$600 ($1,000 profit on the put minus $400 cost)
or	
Buy 100 LSE 50:	+$1,000 minus interest costs

The cost of the put reduces the profit but also the risk and the amount of collateral.

If LSE is at 70:

October put expires worthless	−$ 400
But the stock profit is	+$1,000
So your gross profit is	+$ 600
or	

If you buy the stock to cover the short position:

You will have to pay	$7,000
So you will be	−$1,000
If LSE stays at 60:	
The October put expires	−$ 400
or	
Buy the stock at 60 to meet the commitment	Even

The leverage is high: The return on the $3,000 margin is $1,000, or 33%. For the $400 cost of the put, the gain is $600, or 150%.

Lock in capital gains. The same general techniques can be used to lock in those capital gains. By buying the put at 60 for $400, you reduce the stock value to 56. If the stock falls to 50, you sell the stock at the exercise price of 60 for $6,000. Deduct the $400 put premium from the $3,000 profit and you still have $2,600. That's $600 more than if you had held the stock until its price fell to 50.

Money-saver: Buy restricted puts: those selling at less than ½ point with a strike price more than 5 points out-of-the-money. You must own equivalent shares of the underlying stock or convertible. This is less expensive than selling out and buying a call and more flexible than a stop-loss order.

Example: You own a stock bought at 20, now selling at 42. To protect your profit, you buy a future put at 35 for ⅜. If, by exercise date, the stock does not decline to or below 35, let the put expire, lose the $37.50, and sell the stock at a gain.

Option Mutual Funds

If you prefer to let someone else deal in options, ask your broker about new types of special funds which deal in calls and, occasionally, puts:

Money/market/options funds. These utilize a variation of the minimal risk strategy by putting 90% of fund assets in high-grade money-market instruments (T-bills, CDs, etc.) with average maturities of nine months. This provides income and flexibility. If interest rates rise, the fund manager converts to higher-yielding holdings.

The remaining 10% of the assets is used to buy options as speculations. To qualify for tax exemptions, these funds must not derive more than 30% of their profits from securities held less than 90 days. Thus, some calls must be written for long periods, at higher premiums. In most cases, the real profits from such funds have come from the liquid assets, not from the premiums on the calls.

But there have been exceptions, notably with calls on stocks involved with takeovers. In 1977, Money/Market Options Investments paid $3.73 for calls, exercisable at 50, on J. Ray McDermott stock, then selling at 49. When the battle for control started, the option value jumped to 9! Well, even professionals have to be lucky now and then.

Writing-options funds. These invest your money in high-yield stocks and then sell calls for additional income. They keep cash so that the calls can be bought back if the values of the calls shift sharply.

Example: In early April, the fund buys PDQ at 55 and writes August calls, at the striking price of 55, for 2½. This means a maximum profit per 100 shares of $250 (not counting commissions).

In June, PDQ is up to 58 and the option is at 4⅛. Management, believing that the rise will continue, buys back the call for a 1⅝ loss, which is "justified" because of the three-point paper profit. If the stock continues to rise, they might write a new call at 60, etc.

This policy eliminates the possibility of substantial capital gains, so income is limited to the combination of dividends and premiums.

On the other hand, if PDQ falls to 53 by August, the $250 premium is added to income, but there will be a paper loss in the stock.

There are other problems: there are relatively few high-paying stocks on which calls can be written, the sales load is as much as 9% and the management fee takes another ½% to ¾%. *The only certainty is that the money managers and brokers always win.*

Variable annuity/options fund. This enables the investor to postpone taxes on income and profits. The fund invests in common stocks and writes calls. Normally, all income would be distributed annually to shareholders who must pay taxes at their regular income-tax rate.

Under a plan offered by Oppenheimer Management Co., investors can exchange their fund shares for participation units in variable annuities backed primarily by shares in the options fund. All income is paid into the variable annuity where there will be no taxes until the payout, presumably years hence at retirement time. The minimum investment is $2,500 with a sales charge of 8.5%, but you pay nothing for the swap. Withdrawals can be made at any time, but, to meet IRS regulations, these takeouts should be limited to three in the first seven years.

Tax Treatment of Options

The tax treatment of options is important to those in high tax brackets. It is not overly significant for small sums used for investment or speculation by people subject to modest-to-low income levies. Under new laws, all option premiums, profits and losses are short-term. With their short life, always a practical maximum of nine months with listed options, there can be no low-taxed capital gains.

But when you write calls, there can be tax benefits in that when the option on owned stock is exercised, the tax holding period is determined by how long you have held the stock. The premium becomes a part of the purchase or sales price of the stock:

• *With calls,* the premium increases the amount realized by the writer on the sale of the stock: i.e. when a stock is bought in June at 30 and, in January, a July 30 call is sold for 3 and exercised in July, the tax-effective sales price is 33.

• *With puts,* when the option is exercised, the writer subtracts the premium from the price paid for the stock: i.e. when the stock is acquired at 30 and the put was sold at 3, the tax base is 27.

"Before you start dealing in options on a major scale," LeRoy Gross of Dean Witter Reynolds, Inc., advises, "check with your tax adviser. If you are in the 50% tax bracket, double-check.

"Under present tax laws, start out on the basis that profits will be taxable at your full tax rate and can be used to offset short-term or long-term losses. There are exceptions, but most traders and all investors who deal in options should forget about taxes and look for returns high enough to withstand a sizable tax bite."

There are still opportunities for choices in tax strategies, as shown by these examples prepared by the American Stock Exchange in its publication, "Tax Planning for Listed Options":

In September, you buy 100 shares of XYZ at 97¾ and write a January 90 call for 13¾. In mid-January, the stock is at 94¼ and the call at 4¾. You must decide whether to close out the call or wait for exercise.

If the stock went below 90, the call would expire and you would have a short-term gain of $1,375 plus an unrealized loss in the stock.

Closing Purchase

Premium income	$1,375.00
Cost of buy-back	−475.00
Short-term gain	$900.00
Unrealized loss on stock	($287.50)

Exercise

Exercise price	$ 9,000.00
Premium received	1,375.00
Total proceeds	$10,375.00

...or Gain

Proceeds of exercise	$10,375.00
Tax basis of stock	−9,737.50
Short-term gain	$637.50

*No commissions, costs included.

Your decision should be made in consideration of your total tax picture, especially when you have short-term losses to offset.

A similar situation develops with profits from writing puts. If the price of the related stock rises, you have a short-term capital gain from the lapse of the put. If the trend is down, you have a short-term loss but may be able to acquire the stock at a more favorable price. Again, the tax decision should *never* be the key determinant.

Some Tax Details

When an option you own expires unexercised, its tax value is zero, and you have a short-term capital loss which can be applied against short-term capital gains or against ordinary income up to a maximum of $2,000 (see Chapter 32).

If the option is exercised, the entire transaction is treated as a purchase or sale of the underlying stock. The holding period of the option cannot be added to the holding period of the stock.

Here are some tax-saving ideas:

Writing out-of-the-money calls. Near the end of any taxable year when calls you have written are up in value, you can set up a roll-over by buying back the calls, taking a loss on this year's tax return, and selling a similar call with an exercise date in the following year. This profit (hopefully) will be taxable in the next year.

Writing in-the-money calls. If you wrote the call naked, you can extend the holding period by buying the underlying stock and thus become a covered writer.

If the price of the stock keeps moving up, you face the possibility that the option will be exercised and you will have to sell the stock before holding it more than 12 months. In such a case you could buy another 100 shares and deliver the "new" stock for a short-term loss and hold the "old" stock for a long-term capital gain.

There are several other tax-postponing techniques, but with small investments, they are seldom worthwhile. The savings are small and the calculations bothersome.

Watch Taxes on Special Combinations

Since it is no longer possible for a writer to have ordinary income or loss with any type of option, there are no chances for tax tricks with spreads, straddles, strips, or straps.

You can still close out the legs of a spread in different taxable years and thus split tax liabilities or benefits. And you can still set up a spread which involves writing a call that is likely to be exercised on a long-term, profitable stock which can be delivered against that exercise. You may be able to realize a long-term capital gain on one side and a short-term loss on the other. The same benefits apply to a shrewd put spread. But these depend on luck more than on skill.

Before you become heavily committed to such complex situations, consult your tax adviser. If you purchase and sell options with identical maturity dates and striking prices, the IRS could consider these as a single transaction and thus eliminate the tax advantages.

With straddles, however, the taxes still apply to the components. All premium income or loss to writers from a closing purchase or lapse of an option is considered a short-term capital gain or loss, as with all straight options.

Whether you write or buy options, do so with the belief that taxes will be short-term: Losses will have limited use, and gains will be taxed at your regular rate. If you are able to shift burdens on some transactions, count yourself lucky—and smart.

CHAPTER 24

How to Make the Most of Formula Plans

Formula plans are *always* better than the "lock-'em in the safe-deposit box" approach; *usually* superior to random, impulsive choices; and *never* as effective as thoughtful, well-planned, well-timed investing. They average out, missing maximum profits and skipping big losses. Carried out consistently (which rarely happens), most formula plans buy relatively cheap and sell relatively dear. They are safe and, if you are patient and persistent, can provide better-than-average profits. But they remove the fun, thrill and pride of judgment-based investing.

These days when the stock market is so volatile— with the Dow moving up and down as much as 100 points in a few months—formula plans have extra appeal for long-term investors. There's no system that can guarantee that a fool cannot lost money but, when carried out, formula plans can avoid the two most common investment mistakes: buying too high and selling too low.

Some mechanical systems are worthless; others may seem to have certain limited usefulness; and others show flashes of brilliant success at times, giving the illusion that they are the answers to the vagaries of the stock market. The difficulty comes when, flushed with success, the investor begins to believe he has found the magic formula and neglects to do his homework and use common sense.

Types of Formula Plans

With investment by rote, there are two broad categories: (1) ratio plans where action is based on predetermined criteria to buy, sell or revise holdings; (2) automatic plans where investments are made with fixed dollars and/or fixed time periods.

Ratio Plans

Ratio plans compel caution in bull markets and bravery in bear markets. The force purchases as prices rise and switches or sales as prices decline. They are best for cyclical stocks in cyclical markets and require frequent attention. Here are the methods most widely acclaimed by professionals:

Percentage of stocks. With this plan, you decide what percentage of your investment funds should be in stocks: 25%, 50%, 75%, etc. At convenient time intervals, you sell or buy stocks to restore or maintain the set ratio regardless of the level of stock prices.

Example: You start with $20,000 and plan to have 80% in good-quality common stocks and the remaining 20% in bonds or a savings account. You buy $16,000 worth of stocks.

After six months, you find that the stock market has risen so that the total value of your holdings is now $23,000. The stocks are now worth $19,000, or approximately 83% of the total $23,000. Therefore, you must sell $600 worth of stocks to reduce these holdings to $18,400 (that is, to the predetermined 80% of the total $23,000). You then add the $600 (less commissions and taxes) to your savings account.

If the stock market declines in the next half year so that your total holdings are worth only $18,000, with your stocks valued at $14,000, you buy more stocks. Because the stocks are now only 77% of the total, you shift $400 from your savings to buy more stocks to reach that 80% mark.

You obey the formula no matter how scared you are that the market is going to drop more. *With all formula plans, you must learn to regard falling prices as a chance to buy more stocks at lower prices to help make up for paper losses.* That's not easy!

Percentage changes. With this type of formula plan, actions are taken when the value of the portfolio increases or decreases by a set percentage. The change can be the same each way or varied—e.g., sell when the value of the portfolio goes up 25%; buy when it drops 20%. You start with $2,000, equally divided between stocks and bonds.

When you have a 25% gain, sell some stocks and buy bonds. Or when the value dips 20%, sell some bonds and buy stocks to get back to the original balance.

Compared to a buy-and-hold strategy, this plan provides a 5% gain. With wider swings, the profits can be greater. For most folks, this is more interesting than practical. Most of us are not willing to accept such strictures because we believe that a rising stock (and market) will continue to go up and that a falling stock (or market) will somehow reverse its trend. But, statistically, over several market cycles, this will work out well.

A variation is the 10% approach. There are no value judgments or complicated calculations. Each week, you add up the worth of your portfolio based on the closing prices. Then, you set up a 30-day moving average (MA) (see chapter on Technical Analysis). As long as the MA continues to rise or hold steady, you maintain a fully invested position.

When there's a dip of 10% or more below the previous high, sell out or, if you're cautious, sell the losers. Do not start buying again until the MA rises 10% above the monthly low point. Then, go back to a fully invested position.

This sounds better for trading than for investing but, surprisingly, this doesn't work out that way. Most trends continue longer than anticipated and, with a diversified portfolio of quality stocks, that 10% decline will not come as quickly nor as often as you may think. Vice versa for that 10% upswing. But not with volatile holdings where you can be whipsawed and hurt by too many commissions.

Variable ratios. These apply primarily to mixed portfolios. The key is the percentage of stocks held: up as stock prices decline, down as they rise. It's a defensive plan that works best when the market moves within a fairly limited range. In a bull market, the percentage of stocks might drop from 75% to 50% or less. Toward the end of a bear market, the buying starts again. In each case, the shift is from stocks to fixed-income holdings.

The focal point is a central average that calls for investments half in stocks, half in bonds—e.g., when the DJIA is at 850. You buy more stocks at low prices and sell more at high prices.

The problem is to determine that central price average. If stock prices zoom up past your selected median, you'll be almost out of stocks and miss maximum appreciation. On the downside, however, you will always build protection but you will not get back into stocks at the right time—unless you're lucky.

A compromise is to tie the central zone to some outside-the-market criterion such as (1) growth of Gross National Product (this is hard to follow, and you will miss sharp, temporary rallies; still, that's the idea of formula plans—you act on rote, not judgment) or (2) determinants of stock prices rather than the stock prices themselves. Thus, if the P/E ratio of the DJIA is between 13 and 15, the ratio might be 50% stocks, 50% bonds. When the multiple falls below 10, the percentage of stocks might rise to 60%—and so on. The difficulty is that there is no way of knowing how long the new base will continue. In the late 1960s, a P/E of 12 was low; by 1979, it was high.

How to Improve Formula Plan Results

The essence of all formula plans is to sell most stocks before bull market peaks and to buy most stocks before bear market bottoms. Since you are operating under a formula, you cannot use judgment in deciding whether a bull or bear market will continue. But there are some supplementary techniques which can help improve your profits:

1. **Wait 30 to 60 days before buying or selling.** Once the formula has given a signal, wait for confirmation of this trend. You will have to develop your own timing schedule, but a month is minimal and two months may be too long.

2. **Act only at the midpoint of the zone.** This is another delaying tactic. It shifts the action point up or down.

3. **Use stop orders.** When your formula stock-selling point is reached in a rising market, place stop orders to sell a few points below the current market level. If the uptrend continues, you will not sell your stocks too soon.

In the opposite direction, when your formula buying point is reached in a declining market, put in an order to buy at a few points above the current market. If the downtrend continues, you will not buy too soon.

4. **Change ratios or zone.** When you find that the formula plan is out of step with realities, you probably have been too conservative. Any change at or near the top of a bull market will not be effective. You will be almost out of stocks anyway. This is the wrong time to invest more heavily in stocks.

It is probably more effective to make a zoning change at the time when the market drops into the middle or lower ranges. You will hold more stocks, so your profits should increase as the prices rise.

Automatic Investing

With these formula plans, investments are made in fixed dollars and/or at fixed times. They rely on consistency and, in most cases, prompt reinvestment of all income from dividends or interest. Since the same dollars buy more shares at low prices than at high, these plans must be maintained for years to be truly worthwhile.

Dollar-cost averaging (DCA). This is the most widely used direct-investment formula plan. It eliminates the difficult problem of timing. You invest a fixed amount of dollars at specific time intervals: one month, three months or whatever time span meets your savings schedule. Your average cost will always be lower than the average market price during the accumulation period.

The table illustrates how DCA works: what happens when you invest $100 regularly, regardless of the price of the stock. The lower the market value, the more shares you buy. Thus, the per share average *cost* is $4.255 but the average *price* per share is $5.80. The profits come over the long term as the price of the stock rises.

With DCA, the type of stocks acquired is more important than with strict formula plans. You want quality stocks that have these general characteristics:

• *Volatility* . . . but not too much. Preferably, the 10-year high price should be 2½ times the low. These swings

DOLLAR-COST AVERAGING

Price per share	$100 will buy
$10	10 shares
8	12.5
5	20
4	25
2	50
Total shares	117.5
Total investment	$ 500
Average cost per share	$4.255
Average price per share	$5.80

are more common with cyclical stocks such as motors, machinery and natural resources but they can also be found with industries whose popularity shifts: drugs, electronics and food processors.

In bear markets, your dollars buy more shares but your paper losses on already held stock will be high so you will have to have a stout heart and confidence enough to maintain your commitment. That's where quality counts.

• *Long-term growth.* These are stocks of companies that can be expected to continue to boost revenues and earnings and outperform the overall stock market. If your stock fails to keep pace with the market comeback, you will lose the main advantage of DCA. Look for stocks that are more volatile on the upside than on the downside.

• *Steady, ample dividends.* It is true that dividends, as such, have little to do with formula plans but they can help to provide regular sums needed for periodic investments, especially when you find it difficult to scrape up spare cash.

STOCKS FOR DOLLAR-COST AVERAGING

Aluminum Co.	Heublein, Inc.
Archer-Daniels-Midland	Honeywell, Inc.
Baxter Travenol	Houston Natural Gas
Black & Decker	Lilly, Eli
Blue Bell	Long's Drug Stores
CBS, Inc.	Melville Corp.
Coca-Cola	Pillsbury Co.
Deere & Co.	Pitney-Bowes
Delta Airlines	Procter & Gamble
Dow Chemical	Revlon, Inc.
Emhart Corp.	Rollins, Inc.
Fort Howard Paper	Rubbermaid, Inc.
General Electric	Texas Instruments
General Foods	Times-Mirror
Goodyear Tire	Upjohn Co.
Heinz (H.J.)	Winn-Dixie

With the right stocks and modest commitments, you may find that, in a few years, the dividends will be enough to meet those periodic payments. *Timing hint:* Start your program a week or two before the date you expect to receive a dividend check from the company whose stock you plan to buy.

If you use margin, your dividends should more than cover the cost of the interest.

• *Better-than-average profitability.* The average profit rate of the company, over a decade, should be at least 10%. It's fine to be able to buy more stock when the price is low, but there's little benefit if its value does not

move up steadily over the years. Corporations able to show consistent profitable growth will always be worth more in the future. With DCA, you are striving to accumulate greater wealth. This can always be done best by buying stocks of companies that make better-than-average profits.

• *Good quality.* This means stocks of companies rated not less than B by Standard & Poor's. More conservative investors should stick with A-rated companies.

Avoid companies with high debt ratios. In recessionary times, they may find it difficult to meet their debt obligations, let alone show a profit.

Shares of mutual funds are excellent vehicles for DCA. They provide diversification, generally stay in step with the stock market as a whole and usually continue to pay dividends.

Note: A study by *Forbes* magazine raised doubts as to the true value of DCA. A survey of 12 NYSE stocks over a five-year period found that: *(a)* the average cost under DCA exceeded the median for all purchase prices; *(b)* with eight of the stocks, the investor would have beaten DCA by buying a single block on any randomly chosen date; *(c)* the gains of the four "successes" averaged only 7.9% a year; *(d)* the commissions of DCA cut the gains in half.

With experience, it is possible to improve DCA results. This involves timing and judgment, so, to a large degree, counters the chief advantage of DCA.

1. Instead of buying at a specific date, wait until after a technical reaction when the stock price falls back 5% to 10%. This can be risky but with charts and volume checks, if the purchase is not too long delayed, it can save money.

2. Use a system such as Synchrovest. Its inventor, Robert Lichello, explains this in his book *Superpower Investing.* This calls for monthly investments of a fixed amount in both stocks and a savings account. The proportion that goes into each is determined by the previous month's performance of the stock or investment-company shares.

Example: You set aside $300 per month. Invest $225 in American Widget common and $75 in savings.

At the beginning of each month, compute the cost per share of the stock you own and compare it with the market price per share.

Then divide the market price per share into the cost price: If your AW cost was $33 and it's now at $34, $34 into $33 gives a multiplier of .97.

Next, multiply your basic monthly investment of $225 by .97 to get $218, the amount you invest in AW this month. The balance, $82, goes into your savings account.

If the market price of AW sinks below your cost per share, say, to $32, you repeat the process. $232 goes to buy AW shares and $68 for savings.

Now you add cash from your savings. Multiply the entire balance in your savings by .03 (the excess over 1 in your multiplier) and use that amount to buy additional AW shares.

For success, you must choose a stock or fund that will go up and, of course, make allowance for commissions.

Dividend reinvestment. This is a variation of DCA

that involves prompt reinvestment of dividends, often with a discount on new stock purchases. This service is offered by a number of corporations to strengthen stockholder relations and raise additional capital at low cost; for investors, it is a handy, inexpensive means for regular savings. It avoids the nuisance of small dividend checks and forces regular investments. It's good for growth but not for current income as you never see the dividend check. Many companies offer these new shares at a discount and some permit extra cash deposits, typically to a maximum of $3,000 each dividend time.

SOME COMPANIES WITH DIVIDEND-REINVESTMENT PLANS

ACF	No. Indiana P.S.
Allied Chemical	Northwest Energy *
AMAX	Ohio Edison *
American Electric Power *	Oklahoma G&E
A. T. & T. *	Panhandle Eastern Pipe Lines
Baltimore G&E	Potomac Electric Power
Bell Canada	Public Service E&G
Carter Hawley Hale	Pullman
Commonwealth Edison	So. California Edison
Continental Telephone *	Southern Co.
Detroit Edison	Southern Railway
Fleming Companies	Sperry Corp.
Florida P&L	Standard Brands
Illinois Power	Suburban Propane Gas *
Interpace *	Texas Utilities
Kansas Power & Light	Texasgulf
Kemper Corp. *	Union Carbide
Louisville G & E	United Telecommunications
Macy (R.H.)	Wells Fargo *
Middle South Utilities	Western Bancorp.
Nevada National Bancorp. *	Wisconsin Electric Power
N.E. Electric	Wisconsin P&L
Nicor	Wisconsin P.S.

* Offers 5% discount

SOURCE: Forbes

Under such a plan, all dividends are automatically reinvested in the company's stock. With the shareholder's OK, a bank or broker buys the required number of shares in the open market. The company then credits the full or fractional shares and pays dividends on the new total holdings. The commissions are pro-rated among participating shareholders and average about 1% of the value of the investment; there is also a service charge of about 5%, with a maximum of $2.50 per transaction. The savings are welcome: with $100 in dividends from a stock selling at $20 per share, the five new shares would carry a commission cost of $7.25 plus tax if they were bought directly. The bank charges only about $3.81. You get credit for fractional shares, and your dividend rate is adjusted accordingly. On closeouts, you receive the shares or cash. And under current IRS regulations, the service charge can be taken as a deduction in computing your Federal income tax.

With A.T.&.T., there are small commissions and the stock is available at a 5% discount. When the stock is sold, the base price, for tax purposes, is the actual cost, not the then current market price. In an up market, this can mean a few dollars less in taxes.

Starting in January 1982, there are extra tax benefits for shares of qualified utility companies with dividend reinvestment plans. Investors get tax deductions annually: up to $1,500 for joint returns; $750 for singles.

Stock investment. This program is being promoted by a number of major banks. Purchases, limited to shares of large, NYSE-listed companies, are made in bulk.

You approve a regular monthly deduction from your bank account ($20 minimum, $500 maximum). You pay a service charge ($1–$2) plus a proportionate share of the brokerage fees, which are reduced by the more favorable brokerage commissions from large-volume buying. Shares purchased are credited on a fractional basis.

When you withdraw from the plan, the bank sends you a stock certificate for the shares you own outright, and cash equal to the market value of the fractional shares.

Note: Remember that unlike stock dividends, the cash value of the dividend is income, and the tax thereon must be paid from out-of-pocket funds.

CHAPTER 25

Techniques of Buying and Selling

The more active you become in trading securities, the more important it is to understand techniques of buying and selling. As auction centers, stock exchanges have developed numerous types of orders that assure flexibility and/or protection against unexpected price fluctuations. Some of them can also be money savers. All are governed by strict regulations.

Here are definitions of the most widely used market and limit orders:

Market order. This specifies that the broker must buy or sell at the best price obtainable. If the order is to buy, he must keep bidding at advancing prices until he finds a willing seller. If it's to sell, vice versa. The customer is always certain that a market order will be completed.

When you buy at market, you may make or lose a fraction of a point over a day's trading but when you are shooting for a 25%, or more, profit, that's not important. In selling, however, you may have to accept a loss greater than anticipated but you'll be sure of making the sale.

Contingent order. This specifies the purchase of new securities at a given price after the prior sale of other securities at some other stated price. Various time limits can be set for the prior sale. Usually, this means that you want to be sure to dispose of old holdings before you make new commitments.

Good Till Canceled order. This is good until the last trading day of each month. At that time, if it has not been executed, it is automatically canceled.

Open order. This is also known as Good Till Canceled (GTC): to buy or sell at a set price until the order is either executed or canceled.

Time order. This is usually associated with a limit order. It can be for a day, week, month or, occasionally, GTC—e.g. a Good This Week (GTW) order holds for one week and expires at the end of the last trading day.

Fill or kill (FOK). This is for immediate action. If it cannot be filled at once, in its entirety, at the stipulated price, it is canceled and a fresh quote is given from the floor.

Stop order to sell. The sell price is placed below the current price. It becomes a market order when the price of the stock is at or below the stop sell price.

Stop order to buy. This is placed above the current market price. It becomes a market order when the stock trades at or above the stop buy price.

Stop limit order. To *buy,* placed above the current market price. It becomes a market limit order when the price of the stock trades at or above the stop limit price. *To sell,* it is placed below the current price. It specifies a price below which the order must not be executed.

Examples: If the price of Pill Pusher is 70 and you enter a limit order to sell a round lot at 72, the limit order becomes effective only when the stock price rises to 72. Vice versa for selling at a limit of, say, 68. Limit orders may not be completed.

Limit orders are best when dealing with a volatile stock or a large number of shares (500 or more). But there's always the danger that your order may miss being executed by a fraction of a point and you will have to start over again.

How to Use Stop Orders

Stop orders are valuable tools in trading, especially in selling. They can cut losses short and can also be used to acquire a security at the lowest price if and when the stock price rises to or above a set price.

When setting a stop price for selling, it's wise to enter the order at a fraction above a round figure: at 50⅜, for example. Hopefully, your order will be executed before the stock drops to a round figure (50) that most investors will designate. According to one professional, the best fractions, for all types of stop orders, are ⅜ and ⅞.

Remember: There is no guarantee that your stock will be sold at the exact stop price. In a fast-moving market, the stock may drop rapidly, skip the stop price and thus the sale will be at a lower-than-anticipated figure.

Stop orders are useful to:

1. Limit losses on stocks you own. You buy 100 shares of Allied Wingding at 50 in hopes of a quick gain. You are a bit queasy about the market so, at the same time, you enter an order to sell the stock at 47⅜ stop. If AW drops to 47 2/8, your stop order becomes a market order and you've limited your loss to 2⅝ points per share.

With investments, the problem is where to set the stop. Unless you plan to hold a quality stock for years—for your children or in your retirement-plan portfolio—always set stop prices that will keep your losses low. The trigger point depends on the type of stock, the market conditions and the percentage of loss you are willing to accept. Always be ready to take quick, small losses if the stock, or market, does not do what you expected.

Generally, traders set their loss target at 10% below cost or recent high. Investors, who are concerned with long-term gains, are more cautious and prefer a loss figure of about 15%: for a stock bought at 50, 42⅜. *For best results, set stop prices on the downside and have courage enough to back up your decisions.* Once any stock starts to fall, there's no telling how far down it will go. And if you are like most people, you will hang on in hope (and embarrassment). Only rarely will such a loser bounce back within the next 6 to 12 months. *Cut your losses short and let your profits run.*

2. Limit losses when you sell short. In anticipation of a bear market, you sell short 100 shares of AW at 50. To reduce your risk if you are wrong and the market rises, you enter an order to buy 100 shares of AW at 52⅞ stop. If the stock price advances that high, you'll limit your loss to $287.50 (plus commissions).

With a stop-limit price, you specify a price below which the order must *not* be executed. This is useful with a volatile stock in an erratic market. If the price of the stock slips past the stop price, you won't be sold out.

You enter an order to sell 100 AW at 50 stop-50 limit. The price declines from 50½ to 50. At that point, your order becomes a *limit* order at 50, *not a market order.* Your stock will *not* be sold at 49⅞, as can happen with a stop order at 50.

Traders also use a variation of this technique by specifying two different prices, one for the stop and one for the limit. You tell your broker to sell 100 shares of AW at 50 stop, limit 48. Thus, if AW falls to 50 or below, your order to sell at 48 takes over. The broker will sell, hopefully at a price above 48, but if the decline continues, the stock will not be sold.

3. Assure a profit. A year ago you bought 100 shares of General Cocktail at 50 and it is now 55. You are planning a vacation trip and do not want to lose too much of your paper profit so you give your broker an order to sell at 50 stop, good until canceled. If the market declines and the sale is made, you are sure of a 10-point-per-share gain.

Similarly, the stop order can protect a profit on a short sale. This time, you sell GC short at 55. The price falls to 40 so you have a $15-per-share profit. You look for a further price decline but want protection while you're away. You enter a buy order at 45 stop. If the stock price does jump to 45, you will buy 100 shares, cover your short position and have a $1,000 profit (assuming the specialist is able to make the purchase on the nose).

You can apply the same technique in a series of steps, going up on purchases, down on short sales. This provides a continuous guarantee of sliding-scale profits. But be cautious. These machinations can be very tricky.

4. Touch off predetermined buy, sell and sell-short orders. If you rely on technical analysis and buy only when a stock breaks through a trendline on the upside and sell or sell short when it breaks out on the downside, you can place advance orders to "buy on stop," "sell on stop" or "sell short on stop." These become market orders when the price of the securities hits the designated figure.

Example: AW stock is at 48¾ and appears likely to shoot up. But you want to be sure that the rise is genuine because, over the years, there's been resistance at just about 50. You set a *buy stop order* at 51⅜. This becomes a *market order* if the stock hits that peak.

Special Situations

In most cases, the decline in the price of a stock will be the result of investor pessimism but, once in a while, snowballing can occur when there is a temporary imbalance between supply and demand. Here again, you must be a trader and maintain close contact with your broker.

Example: GC trades at 50¼, after dropping rather sharply. The specialist has, in his book, orders to sell 1,000 shares at 50 stop, 300 shares at 49¾ stop, 1,000 shares at 49½ stop and 1,200 shares at 49¼ stop.

The sale at 50 is made to the specialist (in his role of making an orderly market). The next sale, of 300 shares, is at 49¾. Now the snowballing begins, and, if warranted, the floor governors of the NYSE will step in and suspend stop orders. This cancels orders already received and prohibits acceptance of additional stop orders until further notice. This ban goes into effect only after the close of the market.

Toward the same end, the AMEX outlaws the use of stop orders on round lots (but not on odd lots). Stop-limit orders are permitted on round as well as odd lots provided the stop price and the limit price are the same.

This is a good example of how exchange rules protect the customer and help the specialist to maintain an orderly market.

Stop orders can be an important tool for traders and a useful aid to investors. They provide protection against the unexpected. Many veterans, both professional and amateur, rely on stop orders. They review them periodically, raise or lower them according to their view of the future but they *never* cancel them. They recognize a basic truth: *Most investors will not close out a position that has gone against them unless it is done automatically by means of a stop order to buy or sell.*

Stopping Stock

This is a market procedure which sounds as though it should be a close relation of the stop order. It's really a distant cousin.

Stopping stock calls for no instructions by the investor. It is a procedure whereby your broker is, in effect, guaranteed a specific price for a stock at no extra charge to the investor. Brokers use this technique to get the best possible price for their customers. Usually, the privilege is granted by the specialist in the stock although any broker may stop stock for another broker.

Example: Broker Beane has an order to sell 100 shares of AW at market. He finds the last transaction was at 50⅜ and the only bid is for 200 shares at 50. He could sell your 100 shares at 50 but feels that he can get a bit better price. He asks the specialist to stop 100 AW at 50. When this is OK'd, there are two possibilities: (1) the next transaction takes place at 50, so the specialist buys your 100 shares at that price; or (2) broker Winslow has a buy offer for 100 shares of AW. The specialist, acting on broker Beane's order, offers 100 shares at 50¼. Broker Winslow buys, so your friendly broker has been able to get 50¼ for the stock without the risk of getting less than 50. With a sizable order, stopping stock may be applied to only part of the transaction or, because of market conditions, none at all.

Breaking Even

Before you hang on to a stock in hope that its price will rise so that you can break even, check this table. A stock needs to rise 100% to correct a 50% decline! If your stock declines from 100 to 50, it has dropped 50%. But it will take a doubling in price (a 100% move) to rise from 50 back to 100. *Moral:* Take losses early; set stop orders to protect profits; stop dreaming!

If a stock drops the following percentage	It needs to rise this percentage for you to break even
5% (100 to 95)	5% (95 up to 100)
10% (100 to 90)	11% (90 up to 100)
15% (100 to 85)	17% (85 up to 100)
20% (100 to 80)	25% (80 up to 100)
25% (100 to 75)	33% (75 up to 100)
30% (100 to 70)	42% (70 up to 100)
40% (100 to 60)	66% (60 up to 100)
50% (100 to 50)	100% (50 up to 100)
60% (100 to 40)	150% (40 up to 100)
75% (100 to 25)	300% (25 up to 100)

Space Your Transactions

If you are making a large investment (500 shares or more) in any one stock, consider spacing out your purchases over a period of several days or even weeks. The commissions will be higher (roughly, 15% more to buy five 100-share lots than one 500-share block) but, in many cases, you'll save money because, with modest fluctuations, your average cost will be lower. And if you decide your choice was wrong, you can cancel the rest of the order.

Timetable for Ex-Dates

Always check the ex-dates before you sell. This will assure extra income benefits.

Ex-dividend means without dividend. On the stock tables, this is shown by the symbol "x" after the name of the comany under the "sales" column.

The buyer of a stock selling ex-dividend does not receive the recently declared dividend. The payment goes to the shareholder whose name is recorded on corporate books on a date fixed by the company's directors. With A.T.&T., here's how the data are shown in Standard & Poor's *Stock Guide:*

Name of Issue	Date	Ex. Div.
American Tel & Tel	4/1/81	2/23

But since five business days are allowed for delivery

of the stock in "regular way" transactions, the NYSE would declare its stocks "ex dividend" earlier—e.g., if the official date was Friday, the NYSE would list the stock with an "x" on Monday.

Once you have decided to sell a stable stock, delay the sale until a few days after the ex-dividend date because, on that day, the price of the stock will usually dip to reflect the loss of the income.

(N.B.: With securities traded on Canadian exchanges, the time span is three business days.)

Ex-rights means without rights. As outlined earlier, rights offer stockholders the opportunity to buy new or additional stock at a discount. The buyer of a stock selling ex-rights is not entitled to this bargain after the announced date.

Ex-interest means without interest. It applies to the interest paid on certain types of income bonds. Here again, the payment is made only to bondholders of a set date.

To check the ex-dates, use this table:

If the record date falls on:	Mon.	Tues.	Wed.	Thurs.	Fri.
Then the security sells ex-(dividend, interest, rights) on the preceding:					
U.S. exchanges	Tues.	Wed.	Thurs.	Fri.	Mon.
Canadian exchange	Thurs.	Fri.	Mon.	Tues.	Wed.

Odd-Lot Transactions

Normally, when you buy or sell fewer than 100 shares of a listed stock, you have to pay a premium charged by the specialist handling the transaction. Typically, this is 1/8th of a point; it may be more.

Recently, several major brokerage firms have eliminated this odd-lot differential by executing these small orders themselves. Dean Witter Reynolds, Inc., explains: "When the bid price is $20 and the offered price is $20¼, a buy order in our odd-lot program would cost $20¼."

On the NYSE, there's still no differential if you enter the order 10 minutes before the 10 a.m. opening of the exchange.

If you are dealing with a volatile stock in a volatile market, an odd-lot short sale may get an edge over the round-lot short. The "prevailing" round-lot price for a stock is determined by odd-lot brokers every minute, but in a busy market, many round-lot sales can be made in that minute.

Since the round-lot seller has to wait his turn in the specialist's book, the price of his short sale may be lower than the "minute" price, especially when short sales can be made only on the "uptick." When prices are dropping fast, a short sale of up to 99 shares at a stated price can be executed by the odd-lot broker on the next registered uptick, which may occur before the specialist reaches the round-lot order.

The point is: when such situations occur, you cannot know your exact cost until after the transaction.

Discount Brokers: Best for the Sophisticated

Discount brokers handle orders to buy and sell securities for less commission than do regular stock brokerage firms. They do have a role in stock transactions, but they should be used only by active traders who are knowledgeable and experienced. They are seldom a satisfactory alternative to an effective Registered Representative.

For most investors, the savings are small and not significant when related to the profits gained from a well-researched recommendation or the losses avoided by questions about the quality of the investment or by quick selling when the trend of the stock, or market, turns downward.

Discount brokers can be compared to discount retailers. At a super-store, you can buy branded merchandise at a savings, but, usually, you will have to pay cash, cart the product home, arrange for installation, and, if there are defects, argue with the manufacturer.

With a department store, you may pay more, but you can charge the purchase, get free delivery and inexpensive installation, and count on replacement or repair if you are not satisfied.

Despite the similarity of their low commissions, all discount brokers are not the same. Many are simply telephone order takers: you call and place your order with whoever picks up the phone. Others assign a particular staffer to a customer. Some provide services gratis or for a small fee: i.e. alerting a customer when a stock's price has reached a predetermined point at which the investor had said he wanted to sell or buy.

Some discounters are members of leading stock exchanges and handle their own transactions. Others clear their orders, for a small fee, through Wall Street firms. And there are also significant differences in how accounts are handled: with an "omnibus" account, all orders are executed in the firm's name after which it debits or credits the customer; with a "fully disclosed" account, the brokerage firm gives the name of the actual trader.

As guidelines, use a discount broker if you:

• Have a portfolio of $100,000
• Trade at least twice a month in units of 300 shares or more
• Have a clear understanding of what you're doing as the result of experience and research
• Do not need in-depth studies of a stock and an industry group, technical analysis, or tax information
• Feel so confident of your stock market skill that you do not want someone else to monitor or question your decisions
• Are sure that the savings in commissions are worthwhile: at least 20% below rates negotiated with regular stock brokerage firms
• Can keep close tabs on corporate activities: stock splits, stock dividends, ex-dividend dates, etc.
• Are not involved with special securities such as convertibles, options, or warrants where accurate information is difficult to obtain.
• Are retired and have ample experience and time to follow the market.

One final comment: discount brokers have not all proven to be good businessmen. One major firm reported that bad debts and execution errors cost 11% of total commission income. By comparison, the same figure for all NYSE firms was 1.4%!

SAVINGS WITH DISCOUNT BROKERS

Share Price	100 Shares NYSE	100 Shares Discount	200 Shares NYSE	200 Shares Discount	500 Shares NYSE	500 Shares Discount	1000 Shares NYSE	1000 Shares Discount
10	$30.00	$30.00	$55.00	$37.50	$106.70	$65.24	$213.62	$119.89
15	34.65	30.00	67.10	43.55	148.42	79.21	269.51	125.00
20	41.80	30.90	77.00	48.50	176.30	93.18	325.40	125.00
25	48.95	34.18	86.90	54.06	204.31	107.15	362.66	125.00
50	71.50	45.37	154.01	82.00	325.40	125.00	499.28	125.00
100	80.73	45.37	161.46	85.73	403.65	125.00	747.68	125.00

SOURCE: Olde & Co., Incorporated

For Extra Profits

Check the advice in the chapter on timing and keep these comments in mind. They are not always applicable but, often, they can add a few dollars to your profits and save you from unnecessary losses.

Follow the leaders. About two weeks before the end of a calendar quarter (March 31, June 30, etc.), buy high-grade stocks that have had a big move in the past 70 days. These are the stocks that institutional investors will use to enhance their performance. This extra demand will boost their prices and you can probably pick up a quick 2 or 3 points. (In their reports, the institutions list ownership as of the end of the quarter, so there's no way for outsiders to know whether the shares were bought before or after their price rise.)

Similarly, keep an eye on block transactions of institutionally favored blue chips. These are available in *Barron's*. When there are more sales on upticks (at prices higher than that of previous trades), it's a bullish signal . . . sometimes. Major investors tend to act like a herd of wild buffalo. They follow blindly.

Don't get wrapped up in temporary surface changes. Obviously, an in-and-out trader should not bother with long-term trends, but it is important to relate the short-term fluctuations to the market's medium-term trend. With a strong market, individual stock prices tend to have wide short-term advances. Vice versa when the market is weak.

Is the stock currently overbought or oversold? When an advancing stock rises far ahead of its rising trendline, it is temporarily overbought and some profit-taking is imminent. Avoid buying at this point. Conversely, a weak stock may become temporarily oversold and a technical rally is likely to follow.

Study the chart pattern. As explained in the chapter on technical analysis, stocks develop a character of their own. Utilities, for example, tend to move within a relatively narrow range and as a group; speculative stocks, such as Bally Manufacturing and Twentieth Century-Fox, yo-yo; and even quality top stocks fluctuate in a repetitive manner (though usually within a rather limited range and before a strong rise). In 1978 and 1979, Upjohn Co. stock went from 38 to 55, down to 40, up to 50, down to 42 and then rose steadily to 69 before settling down at a slightly lower level. Such high-grade swingers can be excellent for trading both stocks and options.

Guidelines for Trading Profits

Set sights on whole numbers. A trader is more likely to give his broker an order to buy at a whole number (40, 45, 50) than at a fraction (40¼, 45⅛). When the price of the stock hits that round number, usually there will be a flood of orders which will create a support or resistance level.

Concentrate on industries in the news, not stocks alone. Stocks tend to move together. First action is with the leaders (because of institutional interest), then the public moves in, often with secondary stocks.

Check the technical pattern. The closer the chart action resembles the theoretical textbook figure, the more likely your chances of success. Make certain that the movement is substantial. This is one area where size is always critically important.

Watch the volume. All things being equal, bullish price movements exhibit expanding volume on rallies while trading declines in sell-offs and consolidation areas.

Trade with the trend. In a rising market, take a position on the upside. Vice versa on the downside breakout.

When news is negative, specialists sell, or sell short, from the opening bell. They do not come back into the market and, by day's end, have made money. Too often, amateur investors start selling but, during the day, have second thoughts and start to buy again. They lose money.

Have a system and stick to it. Presumably you selected the system after study and expert recommendations. Follow it closely until there are strong, logical reasons to change. Jumping around is a matter of luck, not skill. Be patient. Even in trading, profits usually take time to develop.

Double up on low-priced stocks. If the price of a stock selling under 10 rises quickly, double your commitment and watch its action twice as carefully. At the beginning, a trend is more likely to continue than to reverse itself but *be sure that the direction of the stock's price is clearly established.*

Act promptly. Successful trading can be a matter of hours or days. If you cannot keep close watch, don't trade.

Anticipate, don't follow. The value of T.A. in trading is its ability to anticipate trend reversals. This technique is more successful with industries than with individual stocks.

CHAPTER 26

How to Profit by Selling Short

Selling short means selling a stock you don't own. It is the most misunderstood of all securities transactions. It is surrounded by an aura of fear and suspicion, considered a rank speculation and is seldom recommended by brokers (most of whom have never sold short in their lives). Yet when properly executed, selling stocks short can preserve capital, turn losses into gains and, under some conditions, defer or minimize taxes. With few exceptions, the *only* people who made a lot of money in the bear markets of the 1970s were those who sold short at one time or another.

Most investors buy stocks long: they purchase at what they believe to be a low price—say, 40—and hope to sell at a higher price—say, 50. Short selling is the opposite. The investor sells high, at 50, and hopes to buy low, at 40 or less. *Since the stock market is down one-third of the time, short selling can be a profitable investment strategy.*

When you sell short, think of these examples and scoff at such false fears as that selling short is un-American or will result in unlimited losses. With stock you own, the maximum loss will be 100% if the stock becomes worthless. But with a short sale, if your projections are wrong and the price of the stock, instead of going down, moves up, say from 50 to 500, you could lose 1000% of your investment. But you would have to be mighty foolish to let this happen.

Short selling is not for the faint of heart or for those who rely on tips instead of research. You may have some nervous moments if your timing is poor and the price of the stock jumps right after you sold short. But if your projections are correct, the price of that stock will fall— eventually. You must have the courage of your convictions and be willing to hang in there for months, even years.

The idea of profiting when a stock goes down may be hard to take, so when you decide to sell short, find a brokerage firm with an experienced trader.

How Short Selling Works

Short sales are made with borrowed stock, but for tax purposes, some people sell short with stock they own (that is, they sell against the box).

Professionals prefer to make their short sales with warrants, which never pay dividends, or with stocks that pay little or no dividends. (As long as you control the stock, you are responsible for paying the dividends you receive to the real owner.) Since these professionals do not have to pay commissions, they can afford to take greater risks and sell short in buoyant markets to take advantage of the almost inevitable temporary declines.

Amateurs will make more money—and sleep easier—if they sell short only in primary bear markets—*with the trend.*

Example: After watching the Dow drop week after week, you become convinced that there's a real bear market. Your research shows that some of the fund favorites are still trading at high P/Es of 20 or more. You conclude that one of the most overpriced glamour stocks is General Headache at 80, about 20 times its last 12-month profits of $4.00 per share.

1. You arrange with your broker to borrow 100 shares of GH.

2. You sell short at 80 and, to boost your profits, do so on a 50% margin so you're risking only $4,000.

3. In a few months, GH is down to 50. You cover your short position by buying back the stock for $5,000. After deducting commissions and fees, your pretax profit is about $2,900.

The speed of the stock's fall depends on the type of bear market, the extent of the overvaluation of the stock and whether institutions have been unloading large blocks of stock to accelerate its price decline.

Selling short, for the first time, takes courage. The investor who started shorting Disney at 100 (adjusted for stock dividends) had to have a lot of confidence in his judgment to stand by while DIS went up to 115. But by hanging on, he was able to reap high profits when he covered his position at 50. (Of course, if he had more courage, he might have waited until the stock fell below 20!)

To set target prices, use long-term charts to find the points of resistance in the past. See the chapter on technical analysis.

Rules/Conditions for Short Sales

Because it's a special technique, short selling of all securities is subject to strict operational rules:

Margin. All short sales must be made in a margin account, usually with stock borrowed from another customer of the brokerage firm under an agreement signed when the margin account was established. If you own stock, you can sell "against the box," as will be explained.

The minimum collateral must be the greater of $2,000 or 50% of the market value of the shorted stock but not less than $5 per share on issues selling at $5 or more nor less than either $2.50 per share or 100% of market for stocks trading under $5 per share. These provisions take care of any dividends or rights due the lender of the stock.

For amateurs who may have to wait out a temporary price rise, it's best to maintain a margin balance equal to 90% of the short-sale commitment. This will eliminate the necessity for coming up with more collateral.

Commissions. You pay regular commission, taxes and fees on the initial short sale and subsequent purchase of the stock. If you deliver your own stock, you save the buying costs.

Interest. There are no interest charges on the margin account.

Premiums. Once in a while, if the shorted stock is in great demand, your broker may have to pay a premium for borrowing, usually $1 per 100 shares per business day.

Dividends. All dividends on shorted stock must be paid to the owner. That's why it's best to concentrate on warrants and stocks that pay low or no dividends.

Rights/stock dividends. Because you are borrowing the stock, you are not entitled to the use of rights or the receipt of stock dividends.

If you know or suspect that a company is going to pass or decrease its payout, you can get an extra bonus by selling short. The price of the stock is almost sure to drop. *But be careful.* The decline may be too small to offset the commissions.

Sales price. All short sales must be made on the uptick or zero uptick—i.e., the last price of the stock must be higher than that of the previous sale. If the stock is quoted at 80, you cannot sell short when it drops to 79⅞ but must wait for a higher price: 80 or better. Or, with a zero uptick, the last two sales must be at the same price.

Taxes. All gains or losses on all short sales are short-term and thus taxable at the highest personal income-tax rate. But the profit on owned stock against which the short sale is written can become long-term when the shares are held over 12 months.

Selling Against the Box

This is a technique for freezing your paper profits or postponing taxes. Here's how it works:

On March 1, Dr. Mary buys 100 shares of Geewhiz Electronics at 40. By July, the stock is at 60 but the market is weakening and Dr. Mary gets nervous. She sells short 100 shares of GW with her own shares as collateral.

• If the price of GW stays around 60, she will lock in her gains minus commissions. She will sell the stock at 60 for a $20 per share profit: the 60 sale price minus the 40 cost.

• If the price of GW rises to 70, she'll still do OK. She delivers her own stock. She won't make that extra 10-point profit (from 60 to 70), but she will still have a $2,000 gain: the difference between her 40 cost and the 60 selling price.

• If the price of GW drops to 50, Dr. Mary has two choices:

1. To cover her short position by purchasing new shares. She will break even because her 10-point profit on the short sale will be offset by a 10-point loss on the value of the stock. Her net will be cut by the commissions.

2. To cover her short position with the shares she owns. She makes $1,000 profit on the short sale but has a smaller profit on the stocks she owns: $1,000 versus the $2,000 gain she had before.

Selling against the box is a favorite year-end tactic. The short sale brings in immediate cash, and the profit (or loss) is deferred until the short position is covered the following year or even two or three years hence.

But be careful:

• Commissions can eat up profits rapidly.

• Once the trend of the stock turns up, it is more likely to continue to rise than to fall. You may postpone some taxes, but you may also find that your year-end profit, from a lower-than-sold price, will be narrowed or eliminated.

• Under the wash sale rule (see chapter on tax rules), there will be no tax loss if the short sale is covered by buying the same or identical securities within 31 days after the date of the original short sale.

• With gains, the taxes can be long-term when the shares are held for more than 12 months. This can be tricky so check with your registered representative. The holding period for the owned stock stops when the short sale is made and begins again when the short sale is covered by a stock purchase. Thus, to qualify for long-term capital gains, a stock must be held for one year—i.e., nine months before the short sale is made plus 91 days after the short position is covered.

Selecting Stocks for Short Sales

In choosing stocks for short selling, professionals use computers to analyze economic, industry and corporate factors. Amateur investors can rely on three checks: insider transactions, volatility and relative strength as measured by stock market performance. This information is available in financial publications.

Insider transactions disclose the number of corporate officers, directors and major shareholders who bought or sold stock in the previous few months. The assumption is that when the number of insiders selling exceeds the number buying, the stock is at a high level and these knowledgeable people believe a decline is due.

It's best to wait for reports of at least two quarters to confirm the trend.

Stock	Quarter 1		Quarter 2		Last Month	
	Sold	Bought	Sold	Bought	Sold	Bought
Digital Equip	18	0	11	0	3	0
Owens-Corning	14	0	14	0	5	0
Texas Instruments	18	0	13	0	10	0

Volatility. The Zweig Security Screen, an investment advisory letter, measures volatility by Beta, the historical relationship between the price movement of the stock and the overall market and interest rates.

Each stock has a Beta number: 1.0 moves with the market; 1.5 is highly volatile (Holiday Inns, which swings 50% more than the market); 0.7 is relatively stable (General Motors, which is 30% less swinging than the stock-market averages).

Relative strength with emphasis on poor performers is a calculation that takes into account the consistency and growth of earnings and whether the last quarterly earnings were lower or higher than anticipated by Wall Street. These data are available from statistical services such as Value Line and Standard & Poor's Earnings Forecast, which reports estimates of earnings made by analysts of major brokerage firms and advisory services.

When corporate earnings are lower than the estimates, the stock is a candidate for short selling. When they are higher than projected, the stock should not be sold short.

Case History

Here's an example cited by Andrew Kern, vice president of Avatar Associates, in 1979.

In early September, the portfolio of a local physician totaled $425,000. The first $50,000 was invested in short-term Treasury bills and became collateral for short selling.

The DJIA, which had been over 900, was falling and a number of stocks appeared to Kern to be temporarily overpriced. He started to sell short, first Teledyne and then five other stocks. He was right; the overall market dropped to 806, and by late October all positions were covered for a gross profit of $5,837 on a net investment of $37,475.

Stock	Sold Short at	Covered at	Profit
100 Teledyne	100	89	$1,100
100 Caterpillar	58½	53½	500
200 Res. Cottrell	22¼	18	900
200 Mapco	34⅜	28⅝	1,150
300 Sambo's Rest.	16¾	11⅞	1,462
200 Overseas Ship.	26⅜	22¾	725

Do's and Don'ts for Short Selling

1. DON'T buck the trend. Avoid short sales unless both the major and intermediate trends are down. If it's a bull market, why try to buck optimism?

You may be convinced that a stock is vastly overpriced, but unless you have great patience, don't sell short until there is clear evidence of a decline in the market generally and your stock specifically.

2. DO short well-known stocks which are becoming unpopular. When institutions sour on a company, they get out at almost any price. This constant pressure sparks more selling and you'll be sure of your profit. Choose industries and companies whose charts show a downtrend, especially those with past histories of sharp, long swings up and down: Charter Co., Compugraphic Corp., Data Products, Gulf & Western, Kaufman & Broad, Merrill Lynch, National Semiconductor, Tesoro Petroleum, and Trans World Corp.

3. DON'T short issues with thin capitalization. When there is a limited number of shares, trading volume will be small. If large blocks of stock are closely held, you could be caught in a squeeze and have to pay a stiff premium to get your stock.

4. DO look for warrants. They are good for short selling because they are volatile, low-priced and never pay dividends.

5. DON'T short big dividend payers. You have to turn the dividends over to the owner of the stock. This is bothersome and expensive, and to some extent, it provides a floor for the price of the stock.

6. DO consider hedges. Once you have decided to short a stock, find out if there are related warrants and/or convertible bonds or preferreds. These can be used in hedges to reduce risk exposure without sacrificing too much of the potential gain.

7. DON'T be impatient. Stay in there for three to six months or, sometimes, even a year if you are still convinced that your down-drop analysis is correct. Forget about intermediate market rallies. Use charts and trendlines. As long as the major trend is down, hold your short position. Cover when there's a reversal into a *confirmed* uptrend.

8. DO check the volatility. The best stocks to short are those which move widely and, at the time of the sale, are trending down—fast.

9. DON'T short stocks with a large short interest (equal to three days of normal trading). Every short seller is a potential buyer. If there are too many shorts, the stock can rally sharply when short sellers start to cover their positions.

A high and rising short interest usually indicates that investor bearishness is being overdone and that the market is ready for a rise. When short sellers fear higher prices, they run for cover and buy heavily, thus boosting the market.

A low and shrinking short interest warns that investor bullishness is excessive, that there's little short selling and that a market top is approaching. Here again, there are many indications that the short sellers are almost always wrong. *Explanation:* Many traders have different objectives than investors.

Short-interest figures of the NYSE and AMEX stocks are published midmonthly in *The Wall Street Journal* and *Barron's*.

10. DO set protective prices. *On the upside,* 10% or more above the sale price—with flexibility for volatile stocks; with a stock bought at 50, at 55 or 57½. *On the downside,* below your sale price: 15% if you are conservative, 20% if you are aggressive (42½ and 40, respectively).

Be careful with stop orders. You may be picked off if the stock rises to the precise point of the stop order and then declines. To maximize your profits, move that stop price with the decline: to 40½ or 38 when the stock falls to 45.

11. DO rely on the odd-lot selling indicator. This is calculated by dividing the total odd-lot sales into the odd-lot short sales and charting a 10-day moving average (or getting information from your broker or an advisory service).

When the indicator has been under 1.0 for several months, sell short. When it's down to .50, the odds are even more favorable for a short sale. But do not sell short when the indicator rises above 1.0, and cover all shorts when the one-day reading bounces above 3.0.

12. DO cover short sales on weakness. And always cover when, as well as you can determine, all bearish news is out and your stocks are down to a reasonable price level.

13. DON'T put up more money when you get a margin call. You guessed wrong so get out fast.

14. DO your homework first and make certain you understand the risks and rewards.

Hedging with a Short Sale

Hedging is a strategy that makes it possible to profit if your stock goes up, down or stands still. It involves buying one security and simultaneously selling a related security short. If the market goes up, you make more money on the security you bought than you lose on the one sold short; and if the market goes down, you make more on the one you sold short than you lose on the one you bought. For another example, see chapter on convertibles.

Example: Easy-Does-It (EDI) common stock is trading at 15; its preferred, convertible to 1.25 shares of common, is at 19. From your broker's research department you learn that, based on past performance, if EDI common goes up 50% to $22.50, the preferred will rise

41% to $26.75. And if the common drops 50%, to $7.50, the preferred will fall only 25% to $14.25.

Set up a hedge by buying 1000 preferred and selling short 700 shares of common: $19,000 with cash, $9,500 at 50% margin plus commissions and fees.

See the table to find what can happen. When the common is at $22.50, the preferred will be worth $26,750, a profit of $7,750. Buying back the common will cost $15,750, a loss of $5,250. Overall, you'll be $2,500 ahead, less costs. If this action takes several months, you'll have an extra $1,100 in dividends from the preferred.

If the value of EDI common drops 50%, you'll have a $5,250 profit but will lose $4,750 on the CVs, so will net $500 plus the $1,100 in dividends.

CALCULATING POTENTIAL PROFITS OF SHORT SALE

If common's price (now 15):	Goes Up 50%	Stays Same	Goes Down 50%
1. Common stock	22½	15	7½
2. Convertible preferred	26¾	19	14¼
3. Common gain (loss)	($5,250)	0	$5,250
4. CV preferred gain (loss)	7,750	0	(4,750)
5. Subtotal (Lines 3 + 4)	2,500	0	500
6. Dividend on CV preferred	1,100	1,100	1,100
7. Commissions	(500)	(500)	(500)
8. Net gain (loss) lines 5, 6, 7, 8	3,100	600	1,100
9. % return (line 9 divided by investment of $19,000	16.3%	3.2%	5.8%
10. Margin interest on $9,500 at 16%	(1,520)	(1,520)	(1,520)
11. Net gain (loss) using margin (line 8 minus 11)	1,580	(920)	(420)
12. % return when using margin (line 11 divided by $9,500	16.6%	(negative)	(negative)

Combining a Short Sale with an Option Purchase

When you sell short, there is always the danger that your calculations are wrong and the price of the stock will skyrocket. To limit your liability, buy a call.

Example: You sell 100 shares of WOW short when the stock is quoted at 50. You calculate that the stock will fall to 40 or below. After a couple of weeks, there's little movement, so you become worried that the stock price will rise sharply. At this point, buy a long-term call at the exercise price of 50 for, say, 3 ($300).

If you are wrong about the decline and the stock jumps to 60, your loss will be only $300 because you can buy the stock at 50 at any time before the expiration date.

You will still be OK if the stock does go down to, say, 40. You will lose your $300 paid for the call, but you will make $1,000 when you cover the short sale.

CHAPTER 27

Investing for a More Rewarding Retirement

IF YOU ARE NOT ENROLLED IN A PENSION PLAN, ACT IMMEDIATELY. For most people, a qualified-by-IRS retirement plan is the single most rewarding vehicle for successful investments. And, under the 1981 tax law, many people can have *two* pension plans to assure a comfortable, money-carefree retirement.

• *Immediate tax credit for annual contribution.* Each set-aside can be deducted from income reported for federal taxes. For every $1,000 placed in a qualified pension plan, the real cost is $500 for those in the 50% tax bracket; $667 for those paying federal taxes at a 33% rate.

• *Tax-free accumulation of income and realized appreciation* of all savings while in the pension fund. When untaxed income is left to compound, the average annual return will mount at an astonishing pace. Over 25 years,

a 12% annual return will average out to 64% per year.

• *After retirement, special tax advantages on withdrawals and, at death, tax savings for heirs.*

Broadly speaking, these benefits apply to all pension plans but, in this chapter, the explanations are centered on personal retirement programs where the individual has something to say about how much he can contribute and how savings are invested. With regular savings, wise investment and prompt reinvestment, almost every successful professional or employer can become a millionaire. Over 40 years, monthly savings of less than $100, when invested at 12%, will grow to that magic million!

If you are a professional or own a small business, your pension plan should be your investment program. Few people can regularly set aside more than the amount permitted with a Keogh Plan: 15% of earned income to a maximum of $7,500 through 1981 and up to $15,000 thereafter. Over 30 years, this minimum means total savings of $225,000. When invested at 12%, this will compound to over $2 million at retirement . . . and assure annual income double to quadruple that earned while working! Even after inflation, that will buy a lot of luxury.

WHAT IT TAKES TO BE A PENSION MILLIONAIRE

Rate of Return	Annual Contribution for		
	20 years	30 years	40 years
8%	$20,235	$8,174	$3,547
10	15,870	5,527	2,054
12	12,390	3,700	1,164
15	8,488	2,002	489

As the table shows, almost anyone who starts early, saves consistently and invests wisely can be a pension millionaire. With a readily available 12% yield, a 25-year-old needs to set aside only $1,164 each year. With a 15% return (which can be achieved by following the counsel explained in this guide), that $1 million goal can be reached in 30 years with as little as $167 per month.

Granted, the million dollars will not buy as much in 2022 as today but it's a nice target!

Personal Pension Plans

Personal pension plans are of three types, all with common characteristics: (a) they must be qualified by the IRS; (b) annual contributions are tax-free, thereby reducing your income tax base; (c) all earnings from interest, dividends and realized appreciation accumulate tax-free until they are withdrawn, presumably when you will be in a lower tax bracket.

Starting in 1982, there's an extra bonus: anyone who is already enrolled in a government or corporate pension plan can also have an Individual Retirement Account (see next section).

Even in as short a time as 10 years, an annual contribution of $2,000, at a 12% yield, will compound to almost $40,000 and provide extra lifetime income of some $6,000 a year.

1. Limit of contributions.

• Individual Retirement Account (IRA)—a maximum contribution of $2,000 a year ($2,250 for yourself and a nonworking spouse). If the employer makes the full allocation, the annual set-aside can be 15% of compensation to $7,500.

• Keogh Plan—15% of earned income to a maximum of $15,000 a year, with limited voluntary contributions and sizeable additions under special arrangements. With the latter, called a Maxi-Keogh, the annual savings can be determined by setting an after-work benefit and basing the contribution as a percentage of income based on age at the start of the plan and at retirement and IRS tables. If the fund investments earn more than actuarially projected, the annual contribution must be decreased.

• Professional Corporation—up to 25% of salary to a maximum of $41,500 and, under a Defined Benefits Plan, money enough to assure a maximum payout of $124,500

a year. Both figures will be increased to offset inflation.

2. Withdrawal date.

• IRA and Keogh Plans—optional at age 59½, mandatory at age 70½. Early withdrawals are subject to nondeductible penalties and may cause cancellation of the pension plan.

• Professional Corporation—anytime.

3. Eligibility.

• IRA—(a) part-time workers who do not earn enough to justify a Keogh or Professional Corporation plan; (b) anyone who can afford to make the contribution, (from regular salary and/or outside earnings) even when enrolled in a corporate/government pension plan; (c) individuals who withdraw lump-sum retirement benefits early.

• Keogh Plan—self-employed individuals and proprietors of small companies with few employees. Immediate vesting (contributions belong to the individual) and the percentage of salary contributed must be the same for all full-time employees who have worked three years or longer unless a special program is adopted.

• Professional Corporation—all employees, but vesting is gradual:

After five years of service: (1) 25% of accrued benefits with an additional 5% annually for the next five years, then an additional 10% annually for the next five years; (2) 50% if age plus years of work equals or exceeds 45, plus an additional 10% annually for the next five years; (3) 100% if age plus years of service equals or exceeds 55.

After ten years of service: 100%, available at age 65.

When employees leave before retirement, nonvested funds are forfeited and added to the remaining account or used to reduce corporate contributions for the year of departure.

4. Trustees. All personal pension plans require trustees and custodians.

• IRA—most investments are handled through model plans where management is assumed by an institution or mutual fund. But you can direct your own investments through your broker who works with a custodian.

• Keogh Plan and Professional Corporation—with these plans, which involve much more money, the same procedures can be followed, but the role of the trustees is much more important. Larger funds almost always designate individual trustees who can be either participants or outsiders.

5. Borrowing. Any individual participant in a personal retirement plan can borrow from the plan if: (a) there's a provision written into the plan to permit such loans; (b) interest charges are comparable to those for similar loans from banks in the area; (c) repayment is to be made within a specified period. If you borrow more than your share of the fiduciary funds, you will have to put up more collateral.

6. Inclusion in estate. With IRA, if the individual dies when there is a balance in the savings-account plan, the money can be entirely tax-free if the named beneficiary is someone other than your estate. Then the beneficiary must agree to withdraw the balance in substantially equal periodic payments over the lesser of life or 36 months.

With Keogh and Professional Corporation plans, if a

beneficiary receives a lump sum as the result of the death of a participant (other than a self-employed person) before the participant starts to receive a retirement pension, the beneficiary pays no taxes on the first $5,000.

Special Pension Programs

With almost all types of qualified personal pension plans, there can be special arrangements to permit larger contributions by principals or employers. In some cases, this may result in smaller set-asides for employees. This is a complex subject, so check with your accountant or tax adviser before you make a decision. Here are summaries of the most widely used special pension programs:

IRA Simplified Employees Pension (SEP). This permits the employer to make direct contributions, fully tax-deductible, to individual IRAs of eligible employees. The maximum allocation is 15% of compensation or $7,500. The employee does the investing.

The annual amount can be increased or decreased but if the employer's contribution drops below $1,500 or 15% of the employee's income, the worker can contribute the difference and take the tax deduction.

Maxi-Keogh. This is a Defined Benefits plan that sets an after-work income based on IRS tables. The base is a maximum working income of $50,000. Here's how it worked before the 1981 changes.

DEFINED BENEFIT PLAN FORMULA

Age	Statutory Percentage
30 or less	6.5%
35	5.4
40	4.4
45	3.6
50	3.0
55	2.5
60 and over	2.0

SOURCE: R & R Newkirk: The Keogh Manual.

To calculate the permitted retirement income, there's a formula that multiplies the annual compensation by the statutory percentage (set by IRS) by the years to retirement:

$$AC \times SP \times YP = ARB$$

AC=Annual Compensation; SP=Statutory Percentage; YP=Years of Participation; ARB=Annual Retirement Benefit

Thus, for a 50-year-old male, earning $50,000, and retiring in 15 years, the maximum after-work income would be $22,500 a year.

$$\$50,000 \times 0.03 \times 15 = \$22,500$$

This benefit is a straight annuity with no pre-retirement death payments. If life insurance is included in the plan, the annual after-work payment will be 91% or $20,745. And if the widow gets a 75% pension, the figure drops to $19,969.

Actuarially, this $22,500 is based on the accumulation of $213,400. To build that in 15 years, the worker

must contribute $8,649 at the outset. The projections assume a 6% yield. With a Maxi-Keogh, he can shelter $1,149 more than with a defined contributions plan. But if the rate of investment return is higher, future contributions must be lower. With a 10% yield, the annual allocation would be cut to $6,105. Make your projections before you make a choice.

The contributions for employees under a Maxi-Keogh use the same formula with a lower multiplier. For a 40-year-old female aide earning $15,000, the after-work income would be $16,500: $15,000 × 0.44 × 24. This would require $160,000. With a 10% yield, the annual set-aside would be $1,479, less than the $2,500 possible with a straight Keogh plan.

There's another regulation when the participant earns more than $50,000 a year. Here, the percentage of contribution for employees is reduced according to the over-base $50,000 income. If this man earns $100,000, the plan must use a 3% rate because the benefits for the employees will be calculated at 1.5%. Again, check your accountant first.

Now let's see if this $19,969 will be enough to live on. Since there was an original tax deduction, the withdrawal is taxable. At an after-work tax rate of 24%, the annuity would drop to $15,175. But, in another 15 years, Social Security, if the current indexing continues, will be about $32,000 for both man and wife. This is tax-free, so total income will be a hefty almost $48,000.

Professional Corporation. Here there are a number of alternatives other than set-for-working-life contributions.

Profit-sharing. When this format is used, the annual contribution can be up to 15% of compensation, variable each year. The current maximum is $41,500, adjustable for inflation at the beginning of each new year.

Money Purchase. With this, the allocation maximum is 25% of compensation, fixed in advance, to $41,500 now but also adjusted annually.

Combined Plan. Here the allocation is partially fixed, partially variable. The maximum is 25% of compensation to $41,500, adjusted annually.

Defined Benefit Plan. There is no maximum. The amount needed to fund the predetermined benefit is set at the outset and annual contributions are made to reach this goal. At retirement, there's a limit: 100% compensation to a maximum of $124,500, also adjustable annually.

Target Benefit Plan. This permits contribution of the amount needed to fund a predetermined benefit to a maximum of 25% of compensation or $41,500 annually, also adjustable. At retirement: no more than 100% of compensation or $124,500 plus or minus investment gains or losses. Again, this is adjusted annually for inflation.

Double Plan. Money purchase: up to 10% of compensation fixed in advance. Fixed benefit: the amount needed to fund the predetermined benefit, no maximum. At retirement, the predetermined annual income is limited to 100% of compensation to a maximum of $124,500, adjusted annually for inflation.

Other Uses for an IRA

An IRA can be a temporary parking place for pension funds when switching jobs, waiting for eligibility in a new pension plan, or as a rollover of funds withdrawn from a plan in which the participant has been enrolled five years. The transfer into the IRA must be made within 60 days of the receipt of the pension money and can be done only once every three years.

Example: Mrs. Colson, after 21 years of faithful service, leaves to take another job. She receives a lump-sum distribution of $15,000 from the corporate pension plan. She reinvests the money in an IRA where all income/appreciation will accumulate tax-free until she retires, even if she joins a new pension plan.

An IRA rollover is valuable for an executive who retires early. If he or she receives lump-sum settlement, the recipient can put the money in an IRA trust and pay no taxes until withdrawal—no later than age 70½.

Example: Mr. Gehle, a 62-year-old corporate officer taking early retirement, had three options:

1. Take a $19,000 annual pension, with half payments to his widow should he predecease her. Because this was a noncontributory plan, annual payouts are taxable at regular rates, and when both husband and wife die, there will be nothing for their heirs.

2. Take a lump-sum payment of $255,000 and invest it in securities of his choice. He would have to pay stiff taxes immediately despite special tax treatment. Taxes would also have to be paid annually, at regular rates, on the income from the investments made with the balance of the money.

3. Take a lump-sum payment of $255,000 and roll it over into an IRA trust where new investments can be planned to provide an annual income of $24,000 for 24 years (under the IRS tables for joint life expectancy). This includes payout of the principal. At Gehle's death, his widow's income would be reduced, but it would still be greater than under Item 1. Unlike Item 2, there is no tax on the rollover although all annual income will be taxed at regular rates.

Mr. Gehle chose the IRA trust, then structured his portfolio to yield 12% from diversified holdings of corporate bonds, preferred stocks and quality common stocks.

All money must be paid out at the end of 24 years. If either lives longer, he or she will have to depend on other savings and Social Security. If the annual rate of return is greater than 12%, the invasion of capital will be less. If fortunate investments boost the portfolio value, the payout will be increased. These are under IRS regulations.

If Mr. Gehle goes to work for another company, the $255,000, with that 12% return, will grow to about $668,000 by age 70½. The risk: If he dies before withdrawing any money, all IRA assets will be included in his estate and taxable as if they were a lump-sum payment. When you're dealing with such large sums, consult your attorney for advice on trusts.

Pension Plan Investments

With all pension-plan investments, the key criterion is the prudent-man rule, first stated in 1830 by Judge Samuel Putnam: "All that can be required of a trustee to invest is that he shall conduct himself faithfully and exercise a sound discretion. He is to observe how men of prudence, discretion and intelligence manage their own affairs, not in regard to speculation, but in regard to the permanent disposition of their funds, considering the probable income as well as the probable safety of the capital to be invested."

It may be that, with comparatively large portfolios, a portion of retirement funds can be placed in offbeat investments, but the balance had better be in safe, income-yielding holdings. Under the law, the employer is responsible for the proper management of all retirement contributions. Unless you are an expert in a field and are willing to defend your decisions before a governmental agency, you'd better concentrate pension fund money in assets which meet the prudent-man rule.

Here are some of the most widely used:

Thrift accounts. These are the traditional investments but in recent years they have not been the most rewarding. Basically, they fund the pension plan with eight-year savings certificates where the original 8% grows to 8.33% or 8.45% depending on the type of compounding.

There's a penalty of six months' interest so it may not pay you to switch to higher-yielding holdings. Ask your thrift institution to figure out what you'll get at maturity, then deduct the penalty and add the higher yields. Generally, if you have less than two years to go, it won't pay to switch. But if you can boost the return from 8% to 12.5%, you'll make up the loss in one year and then count on an extra 4.5% return.

A better alternative, as your thrift institution officer will explain, may be a short-term investment such as the 6-month Treasury-bill-related certificates or 30-month CDs. With the 6-month holdings, you will have to keep rolling them over, probably at ever-lower yields. With the 30-month accounts, you lock in a lower return for a longer period. With all of these thrift accounts, there are no commissions or administration fees but the returns are not always competitive. At this time, these are safe investments, little more.

U.S. Government retirement bonds. These are sold by Federal Reserve Banks and the U.S. Treasury in denominations of $50, $100 and $500. They are eligible only for retirement plans. They yield 9% compounded annually. They can be redeemed at any time. They are poor *investments* but may have some use as a continuing tax shelter after retirement. When you own these special bonds, you can make partial withdrawals at a rate based on your life expectancy. A man, age 70, with an actuarial life expectancy of 10 years, can take out 10% annually and leave the remainder to draw tax-free interest.

Mutual funds. Your savings are pooled for investment according to your plan goal. You have a wide choice and, in most cases, can switch funds under the same management for a modest fee. You can choose money market funds for high income; bond funds for steady returns; growth funds for capital gains and low dividends; or diversified funds for those who cannot make up their minds.

As explained in the chapter on investment companies, there are numerous extras: the opportunity to borrow with the shares as collateral; computer read-outs to keep track of purchase dates so that taxes, at withdrawal, can be kept low; low-cost life insurance (when you're not too old); and, of course, convenience in that all you have to do is send in checks.

In most cases, the total returns will be less than you can achieve yourself. Even with no-loads, your net will be cut by about 1% because of administration fees and other costs. And once in a while, the returns will be unusually high if the manager was smart and lucky. *Put your pension money in mutual funds for convenience, not the best returns.*

Real estate. Once your pension plan contains more than $50,000, investments in real estate can provide diversification, ample income and capital appreciation. But success requires patience, expertise and a continuing flow of funds.

In some areas, banks offer participation in real estate pools of conservative, long-term mortgages. North Carolina's Wachovia Bank & Trust Co. has had a generally favorable record with average annual rates of return of over 12% (at times). This is not outstanding these days when interest rates are high but when there are properly selected properties, there will eventually be substantial appreciation. . . . if you live long enough.

There are disadvantages: (1) *Lack of liquidity*—once an investment is made, most banks require a year's notice for withdrawal. That should be no problem for a pension fund. (2) *Large investment*—generally a minimum of $10,000, with promises of continuing contributions.

If your plan has a substantial flow of money and you've had experience in real estate, set up your own real estate pool—either directly or with other pension plans or with a local bank or S&L. Residential properties should yield about 15% and commercial buildings more.

Some brokerage firms are also offering real estate limited partnerships, that run for 7 to 10 years, in unleveraged commercial real estate. There's current income and, hopefully, future appreciation.

When you make any investment with pension funds in real estate, take the income and let the promoter/developer have the tax deductions for depreciation, interest on loans, investment tax credit, etc. Since the pension fund does not want tax-related benefits, use the pension money to buy land underlying an income-producing building. Do this with an escalator clause so that your investment will benefit from higher rentals Or buy into a new or refinanced building by taking all or part of the mortgage with a provision for capital gains if the property is resold or refinanced profitably. Builders always need cash, so you can make a good deal with high income and first call on assets.

Guaranteed-income contracts (GICs). These are sold by insurance companies and, recently, guaranteed yields of over 11% for 3 to 20 years. The minimum investment is usually $200,000 with an agreement for regular future contributions.

GICs can be tailored to meet pension plan needs: (1) a lump-sum investment with the provision that additional deposits will earn the same guaranteed interest rate for the life of the contract; (2) a single-sum *participating* contract that provides a minimum guaranteed return plus a share of anything earned above that amount; (3) a *nonparticipating* contract that pays a specified yield. Interest is compounded annually and accumulated until

maturity. Variations on these basic contracts can be worked out—such as higher interest rates on new contributions if interest rates rise, etc.

Annual interest can be used to meet payments to retirees, be automatically reinvested by the insurance company or be returned to the pension fund trustees for other outside investments. The fees are modest—typically an entry charge of $250 plus annual reporting costs.

The disadvantages are that you lock yourself into what may become a low rate of return when interest payments are rising and find you have to accept a lower yield, after a few years, when the cost of money declines.

Offbeat investments: art, antiques, stamps, coins, and so forth. Under the 1981 tax law, Congress banned these collectibles from self-directed personal pension plans. By self-directed, Congress means IRAs, Keoghs, and company plans that give employees control over plan investments.

The solons made one exception: portfolios directed by an outside trustee. With these plans, collectibles are still OK. Presumably, Congress feels that these professionals will act with prudence either because of their skill or the necessity to adhere to legal and ethical standards.

This prohibition may be a blow to people who understand these unusual investments, but for most investors it will be beneficial. After soaring for several years, the prices of these offbeat holdings started to fall in 1981. Shares of one diamond fund fell to $764 from $994; fine prints sold at 50% below their year-before bids; Persian rugs were not even offered at auctions; and the price of gold was cut in half.

Self-Directed Investments

You can still manage your own money through your own broker by placing your IRA or Keogh Plan with fiduciaries such as Farmers State Bank of Delaware, Delaware Charter Guarantee & Trust Co. (both of Wilmington, Delaware) and ADP Pension Services of Newport Beach, California.

You make the investment decisions, your registered representatives handle the purchases and sales of securities and the specialists serve as trustees and record-keepers.

Typical charges: for banks, a one-time opening fee of $25, annual minimum administration of $40, and a per transaction levy of $3; for ADP, a set-up charge of $50 for IRA or $100 for Keogh, an administration fee of $55 for IRA or $75 for Keogh, plus a trustee cost of .75% to .10% of portfolio value.

Some swingers use their pension fund savings for trading. They speculate for quick gains in new issues, options, warrants and even futures. They take advantage of the fact that there are no taxes to be paid until withdrawal.

This may be OK if you are the only participant and your spouse is the only beneficiary. If you're smart, and lucky, you can pile up a lot of money. But, according to one knowledgeable broker whose customers include a number of these swingers, only 50% made worthwhile profits over a three-year period and all of them "have so much money that they will be paying taxes of more than 50% when they start withdrawals after retirement." And these "successes" took place in a period when the stock market was rising.

Don't Save Too Much

Too many high-income people, such as physicians, dentists, and lawyers, save too much money in their personal or corporate pension plans. Entranced by the idea of tax deductions for their contributions, they set retirement income goals above their present earnings and make the largest possible annual allocations. As a result, they accumulate $1 million or more. When they start withdrawals, they will have to pay taxes at a rate of 50% or higher. To a large degree, this is self-defeating. They take a tax deduction on a relatively smaller amount while working and pay as high, or even higher, a levy on a larger after-retirement income.

It's true that inflation will require greater assets in the future but many people who save too much will retire with a higher gross income than they ever attained while working.

As a rule of thumb, it's wise to check with your tax adviser when your share of retirement savings is more than $500,000.

Buy Retirement Benefits, Not Life Insurance

Life insurance is not a wise investment for pension and profit-sharing programs. It is not permitted in Individual Retirement Accounts, is of minimal value with Individual Retirement Accounts, and can be used effectively through professional corporations only under special circumstances.

The primary purpose of *life insurance* is protection against death: to build an instant estate and assure assets for your heirs in case you die early.

The primary purpose of a *pension fund* is to provide income after retirement.

Life-insurance policies are structured, generally, so that premiums are paid over a long period of time. The annual income is used to build reserves on the basis of actuarial assumptions of mortality rates and the life expectancy of the insured. A sizable portion of all premiums goes for sales and administration costs, with the balance invested at modest rates of return.

The insurance company must price its policies so that there will always be sufficient money to meet the death obligation or the annuitant's monthly benefit. With pension plans, the total accumulation is used for after-work income.

Life insurance policies are, relatively, expensive. The salesmen are compensated by commissions that run as high as 40% of the first year's contribution with additional deductions of about 10% from the premiums of the next several years. That means that less money can be invested.

Most important, the premiums for life insurance are not tax deductible so there's less money for retirement benefits. The most effective use of life insurance is with a Defined Benefits Plan because it can guarantee the ultimate benefit to the beneficiary if the participant dies early.

For those with high compensation paid by a professional corporation, life insurance in the pension/profit sharing plan can be worthwhile when combined with an annuity. The IRS rules permit tax deductions by the corporation on the corporate contributions, but the participant must pay taxes under U.S. Government Table P.S. 58 or the Section 162 Alternative.

To give you an idea of what's involved, here is an example: Dr. Clark, a 45-year-old male, sets up a retirement plan under which the corporation buys a $100,000 straight life policy in combination with other investments. The annual premium is $2,566. Under P.S. 58, the "cost" of pure life insurance is $6.30 per $1,000 of protection. So Dr. Clark must add $630 to his taxable income.

TABLE A

$100,000 WHOLE LIFE INSURANCE BOUGHT THROUGH PENSION PLAN

Male, age 45. Annual Premium: $2,566

Year	Death Proceeds	Additional Income Taxable under P.S. 58
1	$100,355	$ 630
2	100,991	678
5	104,807	732
10	114,061	1,374
15	129,407	2,073
20	149,232	3,151

SOURCE: Steven C. Glenn, CLU, 2055 Reyko Road, Jacksonville, Fla. 32207

Over the years, the premium remains the same but the includable income rises: at age 50 the base is $9.22, so the taxable income is $922. In the 50% bracket, Dr. Clark must earn $1,844 to meet this commitment.

After retirement at age 65, Dr. Clark can recapture, tax-free as he has already paid taxes on this income, about $18,000. This is payable in a lump sum or by periodic installments.

Dr. Clark does get back his tax payments but he loses the use of these savings and has fewer dollars to invest for after-work income.

TABLE B

BUYING YEARLY RENEWABLE TERM INSURANCE THROUGH PENSION PLAN

IRS Section 162 Alternative

Male, age 35. Fixed death benefit: $667,950

Year	Premium	Dividends	Net Payment (Taxable Income)
1	$1,226	000	$1,226
2	1,279	000	1,279
5	2,288	788	1,500
10	3,403	1,115	2,288
15	5,240	1,757	3,483
20	8,186	3,093	5,093*

* No payment needed after 20th year because the annuity values exceed the initial, static death benefits.

SOURCE: Steven C. Glenn, CLU, 2055 Reyko Road, Jacksonville, Fla. 32207·

The Section 162 Alternative combines an annuity with renewable term life under IRS regulations. Since this involves term life, the death benefits remain the same: $667,950. But the premiums, even after using dividends to reduce payments, keep rising: from $1,226 in the first year to $2,288 in the 10th year and to $5,093 in the 20th year. At this point, there are no more premiums to be paid because the cash value of the annuity, compounded at an assumed rate of 9.75%, will exceed death benefits, which will always be $667,950 plus the value of the annuity.

Again, the premiums are tax-deductible by the corporation but must be included as income by the participant. Under Section 162, the imputed income (the official description of the amount of money taxed) will be about the same as under P.S. 58 but there is no recovery of taxes during retirement. The insured accepts the fixed death benefit in return for no premium payments after age 55.

Annuities in Pension Plans

One of the most aggressively promoted investments for retirement is the deferred annuity. The savings can be made by a lump sum or in installments to provide monthly income after retirement, presumably when you are in a lower tax bracket. The sales pitch: Buy now when you have money; enjoy tax-free accumulation while you work; and, at 65 or so, start withdrawals, generally about 7% of accumulated principal plus interest, without penalties or taxes, until you get back the original investment.

This is another example of a deal that sounds better than it really is. None of these savings are tax-deductible and the ultimate receipts are less than can be obtained with other types of investments.

With an annuity, the method of payout must be chosen two years before retirement. Once the decision is made there can be no change. But most plans permit you to take cash at 65 and buy the best-paying annuity, even from another company. This can be important, as the monthly payments vary widely: as much as $100 per month with a $10,000 annuity!

Annuities come in two forms:

Fixed-income. Your money is invested in bonds, mortgages, etc., to provide a specific sum per month.

Variable. Your investment is split between bonds and common stocks. Their income and value fluctuate, so if you retire when the stock market is high, you will have more assets than could be obtained with a fixed-income annuity. But in a down market, you would lose.

You also have several choices on the method of payment: for life; for life with 10 years guaranteed (the balance goes to your heirs); for the life of both husband and wife; for period certain (5, 10, 20 years, etc.); in a lump sum on which you will have to pay a tax on accumulated income.

For most people, the attraction of an annuity is that it eliminates the worry of living too long. If you and your spouse live well beyond your actuarial age expectancy, you win. But otherwise, it's not a profitable investment. But, as an insurance contract, the proceeds will not be subject to probate.

The actual payments vary according to age, sex and type of option but, as a rule of thumb, a male at age 65 will receive $100 per month for each $10,000 annuity investment. The check is a combination of interest and principal so that, in most cases, there will be nothing left at death.

Furthermore, the return is fixed and will be constantly depreciated by inflation, plus the fact that there is no opportunity to take advantage of higher rates of return available from other investments where the principal remains intact. Four years ago, when Uncle Al retired, the 8% guaranteed yield looked good. But today he can get 14% with money-market funds or government bonds. And he, or his heirs, can get back his money: immediately with liquid assets; 15 or 20 years with bonds.

In many cases, the purchase of tax-exempt bonds will work out better. Here's an example cited by Executive Wealth Advisory with a one-time investment of $100,000:

With an 8% tax deferred annuity, the total accumulation will be $216,000 in 10 years; $466,000 in 20 years . . . BEFORE TAXES.

In the same time periods, $100,000 invested in a tax-exempt bond fund that yields 6% and automatically reinvests all interest will grow to $179,000 and $321,000 respectively . . . TAX-FREE.

The annuity wins only when the recipient is in a low or modest tax bracket: in 10 years, less than 17% ($216,000 minus 17% tax equal $179,000); in 20 years, under 31% ($466,000 minus 31% tax equal $321,000).

As with all investments, do your homework, make your projections and understand exactly what will happen to your savings. In this example, $100,000 is an awful lot to pay for a secure income that will leave little or nothing to your heirs.

Calculating the Value of Your Pension Plan

To guesstimate the value of your retirement savings, use these tables. Table C lists the factors to use, at varying time spans and yields, to project growth of assets and, later, inflation. (Remember: the real rate of inflation, especially for retirees, is much less than the official rate.)

Table D shows the compounding factor to be used for annual contributions. Table E is a work sheet.

This example applies to an individual who plans to

TABLE C

COMPOUNDING FACTOR

For Annual Yield or Inflation

Years To Go	8%	9%	10%	12%	15%	18%
5	1.5	1.5	1.6	1.8	2	2.3
10	2.2	2.4	2.6	3.1	4	5.2
15	3.2	3.6	4.2	5.5	8.1	12
20	4.7	5.6	6.7	9.6	16.4	27.4
25	6.8	8.6	10.8	17	32.9	62.7
30	10.1	13.3	17.4	30	66.2	143.4

SOURCE: ABCs of Investing Your Retirement Funds.
C. Colburn Hardy

retire in 20 years, contributes $5,000 annually to a Keogh plan and makes investments yielding 12%. He saves $120,000 and, after work, will have $552,000—enough to assure more than $60,000 a year as long as both husband and wife live. That's a *real* investment.

TABLE D

COMPOUNDING FACTOR ON ANNUAL CONTRIBUTIONS

Years To Go	8%	10%	12%	15%	18%
5	5.9	6.1	6.4	6.7	7.2
10	14	16	18	20	24
15	27	32	37	48	61
20	46	57	72	102	147
25	73	98	133	213	343
30	113	164	241	435	791

SOURCE: ABCs of Investing Your Retirement Funds
C. Colburn Hardy

TABLE E

PROJECTING VALUE OF RETIREMENT PLAN

A.	Current value of fund	$20,000
B.	Years to retirement	20
C.	Annual rate of return	12%
D.	Growth factor (Table A)	9.6
E.	Value of current savings at retirement time (A x D)	$192,000
F.	Future annual contribution	S5,000
G.	Growth factor (Table B)	72
H.	Value of new additions at retirement time (F x G)	$360,000
I.	Value of total fund at retirement time (E + H)	$552,000

SOURCE: ABCs of Investing Your Retirement Funds
C. Colburn Hardy

CHAPTER 28

Stocks for Investment Portfolios

In investing, it is always best to stick with securities of well-managed, growing, profitable corporations that meet high standards of quality. Sure, some folks have made—and will make—quick gains with secondary stocks when their choices are sound, their timing right and their luck good. The trouble with marginal, untested corporations is that there is no way to make accurate projections. With quality companies, you can look at the record and use past performance as the logical base for future prospects. At times, you will have to be patient but you will *always* profit with stocks that continue to meet quality standards. By definition, that's true investing.

In the past year or so, the prices of stocks have edged up, and some have zoomed to record peaks. This is a prologue of what's ahead. Major investors have learned the hard way that, with high interest rates, outstanding fixed-income holdings can be disastrous. Now they are beginning to recognize that, in these years of tough competition and inflation, the best holdings are, and will be, shares of quality corporations. The risks are small and the potential large, even though the appreciation may be slower than can be obtained with volatile, speculative issues.

This trend to qualify will continue because, increasingly, thoughtful investors know that income alone can seldom outpace inflation. There must be growth as well. Right now, many investors, large and small, are buying shares of money market funds. They love the high yields and, too often, forget the true rate of return. This income is taxable at the highest rate: for those in the 50% tax bracket, that 15% interest nets 7.5%; for those in the 40% tax bracket, the net is 9.0%.

Both will do better with quality stocks that provide the same total returns: 5% dividends and 10% annual appreciation. Here the net is significantly greater: for the 50% taxpayer, 10.5%: 2.5% income and 8% after-tax capital gain; for the 40% taxpayer, it's 11.40%: 3% income plus 8.40% after paying the capital gain levy. *Remember:* these are average annual rates of appreciation and will not be achieved every year with every stock. The yields of liquid-asset investments are sure for a short period of time but not over the long term of investing. And, of course, stock selections have temporary fluctuations. But when you choose quality stocks, there is no long-term risk and they will also grow in value. This does not mean that one should always be fully invested in common stocks. It does mean that one should remain flexible and diversified.

At this time, the outlook for stocks is the best in years. When interest rates start to decline—and, basically, that's the goal of the Reagan program—people will move away from liquid assets into growth equities. This demand will boost the stock market and wise investors will make a lot of money! Don't be lured by the siren song of high yields if you really want to be a successful investor. With securities, the best investments to beat inflation are common stocks.

This is repetition but it's still sound advice.

You can select quality stocks mechanically: by buying shares of companies represented most frequently on lists in *Your Investments*. This will give you an excellent investment base: much like Sample Portfolio A.

Or you can take a more analytical approach by starting with the features you most desire and choosing securities only from lists which meet those specific investment objectives.

The Blue Chips: Sample Portfolio A

If you are very *conservative,* you might prefer to restrict yourself to stocks of companies which have never had an unprofitable year—"the stock market aristocrats."

If you are more concerned with *long-term growth,* concentrate on the lists of corporations which are well rated, have good records of fairly consistent, profitable growth, are in expanding markets and spend heavily for R & D.

Again, Sample Portfolio A is broken into two groups:
• *Those with comparatively low price/earnings ratios, high yields and slow steady growth* limited because of the huge size of the corporations. Even with higher prices, it's difficult to keep boosting revenues much faster than the Gross National Product.
• *Those that have almost unlimited potential . . .* for a while, at least. All of these companies have the capability of growing faster than the average business, either by expansion of their international markets or by new products, outlets or acquisitions domestically.

All Sample Portfolio A stocks are *solid blue chips.* Over the years these stocks have increased in value and there are sound reasons to anticipate that they will continue to do so in the future.

SAMPLE PORTFOLIO A
Quality Investment Grade, Backbone Stocks

Lower P/Es; Higher Yields; Slow, Steady Growth	*Growth Not Limited by Gross National Product*
American Home Products	Black & Decker
Beatrice Foods	Bristol-Myers
Coca-Cola	Emerson Electric
Dart & Kraft	Gannett Co.
Deere & Co.	General Mills
Eastman Kodak	Johnson & Johnson
Exxon Corp.	Melville Corp.
General Electric	Merck & Co.
General Foods	Phillips Petroleum
IBM	Reynolds (R.J.)
Koppers Company	Upjohn Co.
Mobil Corp.	Winn-Dixie

These are *great* corporations that play an essential role throughout the world. They are managed by tough-minded professionals who must produce or be replaced; generally they rank first or second in their industry. They may be slow to move, but they have tremendous resources in manpower, money, facilities, products, distribution and, in most cases, R & D. They all have long records of profitable growth and high returns on equity—over 10%

per year, and often 15% or more. These are the types of stocks which are in the portfolios of almost every institutional investor and should be part of the holdings of every *investor.*

The suggested changes involve about half of last year's listings: elimination of A.T.&T., Dana Corp., DuPont, General Motors and Gould, Inc. because of present or future problems. A.T.&T. faces law suits and must spend heavily to move into new areas of communications; Dana and GM are shaken by the debacle of the automotive industry; DuPont's prospects are mediocre; and Gould is plagued with management confusion.

Newcomers are all blue chips with better records and potential: American Home Products with its superb record of profitable growth; Beatrice Foods with its slow, steady progress and bent for acquisitions; Coca-Cola with a new management team and expanding wine business; General Foods with a solid base and a more aggressive program.

(Dart & Kraft is Kraft, Inc. after its merger with the more promotionally minded Dart Industries.)

In Column 2, the deletions reflect temporary aberrations in corporate profitability or growth: Briggs & Stratton, Burroughs Corp, K-Mart and MMM. Watch these stocks as they will bounce back.

The additions have better prospects for the year a head. They have dominant positions in their fields and are able to cope with the changing economic and product/service conditions: Bristol-Myers, Emerson Electric, Gannett Co. and Upjohn.

Again, the holdovers are recommended for the long term. Black & Decker has stumbled a bit and Phillips Petroleum has dropped with other energy equities. But both will come back, hopefully by the end of 1982.

Repeat: broadly speaking, there is nothing wrong with any of the stocks which were dropped, but the substitutes appear more rewarding because of current undervaluation and potential appreciation.

All these stocks are the kind which are of interest to institutional investors who account for two thirds of all NYSE transactions. In a broad sense the wisest investment philosophy is to *follow the leaders:* buy when they buy; sell when they unload. Your broker can keep you up to date on such activities or you can watch the Most-Active List.

These are the types of stocks that should be the base of all substantial portfolios. Their prices will fluctuate, but over the long term they will provide annual average total returns of close to 16%: 4% to 5% in dividends and the balance in appreciation. With such results, you will be able to bear inflation, keep building capital and, with prompt reinvestment (through dividend reinvestment plans), double your portfolio value every 4½ years.

Once you have acquired stocks like these, *do not lock them in a safe-deposit box.* Review them frequently, compare the returns with your investment goals and do not hesitate to sell when the company appears to be living on its reputation rather than its profits. And when a stock reaches your target price, sell unless there are very strong reasons to hang on for a while. Even solid blue chips can become overpriced.

Stocks for High Income: Sample Portfolio B

This has been an ever-changing mixture: REITs, bank stocks, utilities, convertibles and, for the past two years, utilities and more industrials.

This year, utilities are still important but the emphasis is on industrial/service companies that have consistently raised dividends and, in all probability, will continue to do so. Convertibles are not included as they are covered in greater detail elsewhere. But in some cases they can provide high income.

SAMPLE PORTFOLIO B
Quality Stocks with High Income

UTILITIES

10% or Higher Dividends

Central & Southwest
Florida Power & Light
Florida Power
Houston Industries

Public Service, Indiana
Southwestern Public Service
Texas Utilities
Tucson Electric

6% to 10% Dividends

A. T. & T.
Central Telephone
Columbia Gas
Nicor, Inc.

Peoples Energy
Rochester Telephone
Tampa Electric
United Telecommunications

INDUSTRIALS/BANKS

8% or Higher Dividends

American Brands
Avon Products
Bank of New York
Champion Spark Plug
Lucky Stores

Manufacturers Hanover
Maytag Co.
Purex Industries
Safeway Stores

7% to 8%

Anchor Hocking
Ashland Oil
Beatrice Foods
Clorox Co.
Colgate-Palmolive
Consolidated Foods
Dart & Kraft
Emhart Corp.

Exxon Corp.
National Detroit Bank
Norton Simon
Scott & Fetzer
Sybron Corp.
Transway International
V. F. Corp.

6% to 7% Dividends

American Home Products
Briggs & Stratton
Campbell Soup
Clark Equipment
Coca-Cola
Dana Corp.
Dennison Manufacturing
Dr. Pepper
Emery Air Freight
General Foods
Gerber Products

Gould, Inc.
Heublein, Inc.
Kellogg Co.
Morgan (J.P.)
National Service Industries
Norris Industries
RCA Corp.
Square D Co.
Textron, Inc.
Winn-Dixie Stores

SOURCE: Wright Investors' Service

With ever-lower yields of Treasury bills, CDs and, probably soon, money market funds, these securities offer a chance for both income and appreciation. As the cost of money drops, their values, based on yields, will rise. And, because most of these companies will boost their payouts, the gains should be even greater.

Do not take this progress for granted. Check the quarterly reports to see if profits are rising enough to warrant higher dividends. If there is one poor or flat

quarter, watch out; if there are two in succession, sell. Always keep that 10%-to-15% decline in mind. Unless you plan to hold the stocks for a long time, don't argue with the market. When the stock price drops, professionals are worried and no longer want to own these shares. If you are not satisfied with the income, sell and look for other opportunities where you can get what you want.

For High Total Returns: Sample Portfolio C

This portfolio is my idea of a real investment program: high total returns from income and popularity. These companies make a lot of money and keep raising their dividends. In three years, by 1985, their average compound annual rates of return can be a minimum of 30%. There's no guarantee that such results will be attained but these goals are logical and realistic, especially with the stronger market that many analysts predict. These companies are all BIG money makers and their stocks will command higher prices in the future.

SAMPLE PORTFOLIO C
Projected Total Returns by 1985

COMPANY	Div. Growth	Earn. Growth	Divs. Rein.	Earned Return	Change P/E	Total Return
Avon Prods.	+ 9.7%	+11.3%	+8.1%	+19.4%	+13.0%	+32.4%
Bank of NY	+ 9.7	+ 6.9	+8.8	+15.7	+14.7	+30.4
Beatrice Fds	+11.1	+11.6	+6.7	+18.3	+13.4	+31.7
Blue Bell	+13.5	+12.0	+7.1	+19.1	+13.3	+32.4
Dana Corp.	+11.7	+33.8	−4.3	+38.1	− 1.1	+37.0
Dr. Pepper	+12.4	+12.7	+6.4	+19.1	+11.4	+30.5
Mfr. Hanover	+10.7	+ 8.5	+8.4	+16.9	+15.2	+32.1
NCH Corp.	+11.5	+13.2	+3.6	+16.8	+17.6	+34.4
Pepsico, Inc.	+11.4	+11.3	+4.6	+15.9	+14.3	+30.2
Ralston Purina	+ 8.7	+12.2	+5.6	+17.8	+13.9	+31.7
Scott & Fetzer	+ 8.7	+15.3	+6.4	+21.7	+ 8.6	+30.3
Sears, Roebuck	+ 6.1	+16.2	+6.8	+23.0	+13.4	+36.4
Snap-On Tools	+14.0	+17.0	+4.0	+21.0	+ 9.2	+30.2
Transway Inter.	+15.4	+12.1	+7.3	+19.4	+11.2	+30.6

SOURCE: Wright Investors' Service

To varying degrees, these stocks are selling at bargain prices, well below their historic multiples. The greatest gains should come from an improved price/earnings ratio as more investors recognize their worth. But the dividends, reinvested, are significant, too.

The stocks in Sample Portfolio C are the type which should be included in the holdings of every investor who wants real growth plus steadily higher income. These are excellent stocks to buy in planning retirement and for gifts to children and grandchildren. They should be among the leaders in a bull market because they have the financial strength, investment acceptance and profitability and growth which attract institutional money managers.

The projections are based mathematically on the past performance of the corporation. Their annual rate of earnings growth is the product of internal management; the change in the P/E ratio is external and psychological, reflecting investor attitude toward common stocks in general and the company's stock in particular. These data are valuable for comparative analytical judgments; they are not to be assumed to be predictions of the future results of the company or the value of the stocks.

Long-Term Growth: Sample Portfolio D

Sample Portfolio D contains stocks selected from other tables. They are quality companies with excellent growth records and outstanding potential. Their managements are top-notch; their products/services are widely accepted; and they are all in growing industries. Their finances are not quite as strong, nor are their past records quite as good as those of the corporations in Sample Portfolio A. They are slightly pale blue chips which are suitable for both personal and fiduciary portfolios.

$5.63; Big Three Industries, from 52¢ to $3.97; Rite Aid, from 55¢ to $3.25.

Generally, dividends increased at a slower rate as managements preferred to reinvest a large portion of profits for expansion and research for the future benefit of stockholders. But even the payouts of some companies rose at an annual average rate well above that of inflation: Fort Howard, +14%; Gannett Company, +18%; and Times Mirror, +13.9%.

In a few cases, the stock market has recognized such sparkling records, but not in the majority of these suggestions. At their present prices, many of these stocks are undervalued. And all of these companies are worthwhile *investments*.

SAMPLE PORTFOLIO D
Some Very Profitable Companies

Company	Earned Growth Rate 1980	Earned Growth Rate 1971-80	Profit Rate 1980	Profit Rate 1971-80
American Standard	18.6%	10.3%	28.6%	16.0%
AMP, Inc.	19.8	18.3	27.3	24.6
Archer-Daniels.Mid.	21.8	14.1	23.1	16.2
Baker International	19.9	18.6	25.0	22.5
Conoco, Inc.	21.1	11.6	27.2	17.0
Data General	19.1	24.9	19.1	24.9
Dresser Industries	21.5	17.3	28.0	23.0
Helmerich Payne	23.5	17.1	25.9	18.8
Hewlett-Packard	19.5	16.0	21.4	17.9
Houston Nat. Gas	21.4	18.2	28.3	24.3
Lubrizol Corp.	20.9	16.3	30.4	25.4
Medtronic, Inc.	22.3	18.1	28.6	16.0
Mobil Corp.	19.8	19.3	26.8	14.9
Nat. Medical Care	21.2	19.3	30.6	22.7
Petrolane, Inc.	20.8	19.0	26.6	24.3
Phillips Petroleum	18.9	11.3	25.4	17.0
Schlumberger, Ltd.	33.9	22.4	41.4	28.2
Smith International	19.7	17.4	23.6	20.6
SmithKline	24.9	16.9	39.7	29.0
Sundstrand Corp.	18.0	15.2	26.9	22.1
Super Valu Stores	21.4	17.0	29.2	24.1
Texas Oil & Gas	32.5	25.4	36.1	27.2
Dow Jones Industrial	9.4	8.4	16.1	14.5

SOURCE: Wright Investors' Service

Every one of these stocks could be selling at double its present price in the next three years. To be on the safe side, let's cut that potential gain to 50%. Add annual dividends of about 4%, and the total returns could be 62%: an average annual rate of return of 20.6%.

Many of the previous suggestions in this group have been moved to other portfolios and almost all of them have advanced substantially in value since they were first listed. As long as these companies keep up their winning ways, they will be worthwhile holdings. There will be temporary periods of unpopularity but these are profitable *investments*.

Beating Inflation with Higher Earnings/Dividends: Sample Portfolio E

This portfolio is designed to show why quality stocks can outpace inflation with both income and growth. Despite the erratic economic conditions of the 1970s, almost all of the companies reported *average* annual growth in earnings of 20% per share: Blue Bell, from $1.23 to

SAMPLE PORTFOLIO E
Higher Earnings   Higher Dividends

Company	Between 1971 and 1980 Earnings		Dividends	
AMP, Inc.	$ .65	$3.65	$ .21	$1.00
American Standard	.12	5.69	.28	2.10
Amsted Industries	.97	6.16	.40	2.41
Baker International	.23	2.36	.09	.40
Baxter-Travenol	.68	3.72	.11	.67
Big Three Industries	.26	2.05	.07	.46
Blue Bell, Inc.	1.23	5.09	.30	1.80
Colt Industries	.85	7.38	.53	2.90
Cooper Industries	.28	4.26	.35	1.08
Crouse-Hinds	.49	2.50	.23	.96
Dennison Mfg.	.94	2.42	.23	1.16
Dexter Corp.	.54	2.80	.16	1.00
Disney Productions	.90	4.17	.09	.79
Dover Corporation	.72	4.10	.19	.95
Eckerd (Jack)	.67	3.13	.14	1.05
Edison Brothers	.80	3.68	.33	1.32
Engelhard Minerals	.52	7.85	.19	1.11
Fort Howard Paper	.44	2.55	.13	.78
Gannett Company	.67	2.81	.16	1.38
Halliburton Co.	.54	4.25	.17	1.05
Helmerich & Payne	.24	2.05	.02	.19
Houston Nat. Gas	.59	5.56	.17	1.30
Inter. Flavors	.47	1.73	.19	.89
Johnson & Johnson	1.82	6.50	.43	2.22
K Mart	.85	2.07	.16	.90
Knight-Ridder	.77	2.87	.13	.75
Loctite Corp.	.35	1.74	.14	.56
Lubrizol Corp.	1.16	5.74	.37	1.80
Malone & Hyde	1.00	3.47	.27	1.20
Masco Corporation	.48	3.03	.08	.49
Nalco Chemical	.86	3.61	.39	1.60
NCH Corporation	.63	2.67	.15	.72
Petrolane, Inc.	.32	1.60	.08	.38
Pioneer Corp.	.25	2.44	.17	.75
Revco, D.S.	.63	3.08	.14	.90
Rite Aid	.42	2.56	.06	.54
Rollins, Inc.	.44	1.42	.07	.42
Schlumberger, Ltd.	.31	5.21	.09	.94
Smith International	.36	3.73	.10	.62
Thiokol Corp.	.58	2.80	.20	1.00
Times Mirror	1.04	4.08	.25	1.51

SOURCE: Wright Investors' Service

Discount Bonds: Sample Portfolio F

For those who want to be sure of getting back their money (and more) with reasonable income while they wait, discount bonds can be excellent investments. Sample Portfolio F lists typical corporate and government bonds that are selling below their par value, are not likely to be called and will be redeemed in a relatively few years.

There may be temporary price declines if the cost of money rises but, as the maturity date nears, the values will move up to par. These bonds are ideal for investors who want steady income and a sure payoff at a time when they will need extra cash: to pay for college bills, the initial expenses of retirement or that long-dreamed-of trip around the world.

SAMPLE PORTFOLIO F
Discount Bonds for Income/Gains

Bond	S&P Rating	Recent Price	Recent Yield	Yield to Maturity
Am. Exp. Credit 8.5, '86	AA	82	10.4%	13.4%
Anaconda 6 5/8, '93	AA	64 1/2	10.3	12.2
Citicorp. 8 1/8, '07	AAA	60 1/2	13.4	13.7
Combust. Eng. 7.45, '96	A	58 3/4	12.7	14.0
Com. Edison 6 3/8, '98	A	52 1/8	12.2	13.6
Duke Power 7 3/4, '03	A+	56	13.8	14.4
DuPont 8, '86	AAA	83	9.6	12.6
Duquesne Light 7, '99	A	54 5/8	12.8	14.0
Ford Mt. Credit 9 1/2, '95	A	66	14.4	15.5
Indianap. P&L 7 1/8, '98	AA	59 1/2	12.0	13.1

SOURCE: New York Stock Exchange. Money Reporter

For Speculators: Sample Portfolio G

The dream of every speculator (and many investors) is to find another Xerox: a small company (*a*) with unique products or services and competent management; (*b*) whose stock will soar in value and be split again and again until there are sufficient shares for listing on the NYSE; and, presto, (*c*) which becomes an institutional favorite so that the original $1,000 will be worth $100,000 or more.

Only rarely does this work out, and then success takes many years. For every successful small, publicly owned company, there are six failures.

Yet there are a number of financially strong and well-managed small companies whose stocks are traded over-the-counter. Some are new, bright-eyed and bushy-tailed, scientifically oriented organizations; others are old-time, family-controlled firms. To most brokers, OTC stocks are "opportunities"; to realists, they are risks.

Sample Portfolio G lists some OTC stocks with strong growth records. They have all been around a while and have reported high returns on capital investment and excellent increases in profits. Prices are not shown because, in most cases, they have moved erratically: up 15% one week, down 20% the next. Such volatility goes with the territory. Most shareholders are shooting for quick profits, not long-term investments. Still, their long-term prospects are favorable if you are willing to pay the relatively high price/earnings ratios: from 11 for Charming Shoppes, 14 for Brooks Fashion Stores, to 30 for Sensormatic Electronics and 37 for U.S. Surgical.

OTC stocks have a place in an aggressive portfolio, with money you can afford to lose or tie up for several years.

In making your selections, follow these steps:

1. Look for companies with superior long-term records: five years if you want to gamble, ten if you are willing to accept a "businessman's risk."

SAMPLE PORTFOLIO G
OTC Stocks with Strong Growth Records

COMPANY	5 Year Growth Earnings Per Share	Consecutive Years Earnings Growth
Pic'n Save	60%	12
Sensormatic Electronics	58	8
Charming Shoppes, Inc.	44	5
U.S. Surgical	43	11
Hechinger Co.	43	11
Color Tile, Inc.	43	7
National Computer Systems	42	9
Food Town Stores	42	12
Postal Instant Press	38	8
Brooks Fashion Stores	37	0

SOURCE: The Johnson Survey

2. Find out which and how many major brokerage firms "make a market" in the stock, that is, hold shares in inventory and maintain active trading. With such support, there are not likely to be erratic price swings.

3. Learn how interested corporate management is in having the stock listed on the American or New York Stock Exchange. A good indication is the frequency of stock splits or stock dividends which boost the number of outstanding shares so that the public ownership will meet the necessary listing requirements.

Low Price, Low P/E Ratio: Sample Portfolio H

One way to find bargains is to locate stocks that are selling at low prices, low price/earnings ratios and well below book value. In theory, they have no place to go but UP. But there's no way to know how soon this move may come. These can be good speculations if only because your losses will be small and, with such low multiples, upswings can be substantial.

Portfolio H lists nine stocks, all major corporations, that come close to the "Magic Sixes" formula: priced at less than six times earnings, yielding around 6% and trading at less than 60% of book value. (Prices swing sharply, so when you read this may not be quite the same, but basically these securities are undervalued.) An improvement in any category should mean welcome gains.

In much the same way, low-priced stocks can be

SAMPLE PORTFOLIO H
LOW PRICE   LOW P/E RATIO   GOOD GROWTH

COMPANY	Recent Price	Dividend	Recent P/E Ratio	Book Value	Recent Yield
Avondale Mills	17 7/8	$1.20	5	$42.53	6.7%
Cone Mills	33 5/8	2.20	6	56.42	6.5
Continental Group	37 1/8	2.40	7	41.93	8.7
Crompton Co.	21 1/2	1.80	6	47.88	8.4
Man. Hanover	34 1/8	2.72	5	51.38	8.0
Movie Star	10 5/8	.60	4	20.22	5.6
National Detroit	26 3/4	2.00	4	54.08	7.5
Oxford Industries	13 1/4	.84	6	23.23	6.3
Springs Mills	20 1/2	1.36	6.6	38.60	6.6

SOURCE: Wright Investors' Service; New York Stock Exchange; American Stock Exchange; Forbes Magazine

profitable because studies show that, in a new bull market, the lower the stock price, the greater the percentage gain: Stocks selling at $5 outperformed those selling at $10 which, in turn, did better than those selling at $20 a share.

Yale Hirsch, publisher of *Smart Money,* uses the Square Root (SR) rule to set targets. The key to this formula is the Bull Market Increment (BMI) which varies according to the duration and slope of the market rise. When the upturn is modest, the factor is 1; when it's sustained, it's 3.

Take the SR of the stock's present price, add the BMI, then square the sum to predict the area the stock will reach. Thus, the SR of a stock at 4 is 2, to which 1 is added (to be conservative), and the answer is 3. Square this to get a goal of 9, a 125% gain. On the same basis, a $25 stock will rise only 44%!

When you try this formula, start with about $5,000; add $2,500 every few months—in the same stocks until their prices rise 25%; otherwise, in other opportunities.

With all types of speculations: (1) Use funds you can afford to lose. (2) Take risks only if you are lion-hearted enough to forget failure. (3) Set aside time to investigate first—and frequently. The odds are that 40% of speculative investments will be worthwhile and that only 10% will become really profitable!

CHAPTER 29

Portfolios for Times of Your Life

Once again, these suggestions outperformed the stock market. The total returns for the four portfolios averaged +43%, more than double those of the 30 stocks that make up the DJIA, which were up 14.9% and paid dividends of 5.7% for a gross of 20.6%.

The current prices are as of mid spring 1981. To be conservative, the dividends/interest were calculated on an 18-month basis: *actual* for the June 30, 1980 through June 30, 1981 year and *estimated,* without changes, for the last six months of 1981. So, if there were added payouts recently, the income would be slightly greater.

Portfolios for	Start	Total Value/End	Gain	% Return
30s	$27,625	$39,732	$12,107	+44%
40s	42,806	69,663	26,857	+63
50s	51,460	73,927	22,287	+43
60s	32,100	39,378	7,278	+23

The results would have been better if sales had been made when the price of some securities dropped 10% to 15% below cost, as recommended, and others sold at peaks so that the proceeds could be reinvested more profitably.

Keep in mind that these selections were made in the spring of 1980 but *Your Investments* was not available to the public until early the following year. *Anyone who follows the principles and practices outlined should have done better and easily outpaced the target average annual rate of return of 16%.*

This brings up the question: Why do so many professionals fail to perform as well? The individual does have the advantage of flexibility but he does not have access to as much information. From questions to these "experts," I gather that there are three reasons for mediocre results: (1) with large holdings, it is difficult to make choices; (2) investments must be made soon after the funds are received, often at a time when the stock market is falling; (3) the reluctance to unload what are considered quality holdings.

I never cease to be amazed at how many mutual fund managers hold on even though the prices of their holdings plummet. One major fund has reported some 50,000 shares of Avon Products for over ten years. Yet the stock price has fallen from 140 to 20, bounced up to over 60 and then dropped again, to around 40. If management had sold at the high and bought near the low, shareholders would have had some $6 million more profits!

Two significant comments: (1) The losses were minimal: only IBM, from a cost of 75 to a recent 60. In successful investing, it is just as important not to lose money as to make substantial profits. (2) The big gains came from a few winners: Petrolane, from an original cost of $3,000 to $9,600; Engelhard Minerals, whose per share value, adjusted for splits, zoomed from 6⅛ to 44¾; Texas Oil & Gas, from 9 to 28; and income-oriented Norfolk & Western, from $8,025 to $13,800 plus dividends of $1,050 in the last 18 months alone.

These portfolios point up the importance of wise selection, constant supervision and patience.

Selection. The key is QUALITY. With these stocks, you can make logical projections. The companies are financially strong, large enough to interest major investors and with long, fairly consistent records of strong growth and profitability.

With few exceptions, all of these corporations have an earned growth rate (EGR) of over 12% and a profit rate (PR) of more than 19%. These compare with 7.9% and 16.1% for the DJIA companies. The suggested companies have made, are making and can be expected to make lots of money. Their managements are skilled and experienced.

These are the *types* of securities to buy and, usually,

to hold. None of these are specific recommendations that will be good for everyone every time. Before you buy any stock, always review the company's recent financial performance and prospects. Then decide whether the returns meet your objectives of income or growth. Finally, check the charts: if the trend is down, *do not buy*. If it's flat, go back over the past 12 years to find the pattern to see if similar plateaus were reached before a strong upmove. If the trend is up and earnings strong enough to anticipate a 25% gain, *buy*.

Constant supervision. This is more important in trading than with long-term investing. By selling when the price drops 10% to 15% below cost or recent high, you will take small, usually quick losses. This is wiser than hanging on with hope . . . unless you are willing to wait two or three years. Unless your savings are in a pension plan or trust, never lock up securities for long: seldom more than one year, and often less.

Patience. Investing is a long-term commitment. Over the years, the returns on quality stocks such as those listed here may not come as fast as anticipated, but as long as the corporation deserves a quality rating, its value will move up. On the average, it takes 24 months for an investment to bring worthwhile total returns in stable or rising markets. Feel lucky if the gains come sooner.

Background of Portfolios

Perhaps the best way to describe these portfolios is to think of them as pension-plan investments: holdings designed for three years or more on the basis of fundamental quality and value, with timing a secondary factor.

Keep in mind that:

1. Some of the changes were made for illustration rather than for profit. In almost every case, securities that had small paper losses should have been held. They were, and are, sound investments that will be worth more, probably as the superior corporate performance continues; certainly with a better stock market.

2. Some of the changes were made to provide money to buy special securities for special investment techniques.

These portfolios are flexible. Generally speaking, all securities are suitable for all portfolios. Conservative investors, at any age, may prefer to concentrate on high yielders; aggressive individuals may want to put more of their savings into low-dividend, high-growth companies. Always look for stocks that will help you achieve your financial goals and that will enable you, and your spouse, to sleep well. Profits are pleasant, but peace of mind is always more important.

For Those in Their 30s

This portfolio was designed for long-term growth with modest income. It has grown from $20,000 in 1976 to $39,732 at this time. The total would have been substantially greater if some stocks had been sold when their prices started to fall from their peaks: last year, CBS at 65 instead of 55½; Snap-On Tools at about 27 instead of 24¾. And if those proceeds could have been reinvested promptly, you could have bought Chesebrough-Pond's at 27 instead of 34.

Hold

Heublein, Inc. (HBL). At long last, this stock appears to be moving up with the momentum its improved profits deserve. The stock has gone from 29 to 34 and the dividend was raised 10%. With the Kentucky Fried Chicken division in the black and liquor sales rising with the addition of new brands, the target price can be upped to 43 from 40. In a strong market, the stock can do even better. HBL is a good illustration of how long it takes for a stock that has fallen from Wall Street's grace to become popular again. Still, there's nothing wrong in doubling your money in three years—as seems possible.

Petrolane, Inc. (PTO). Once again, this was a winner, not as sensational as before but, after a 2 for 1 split, a welcome 9½ point gain. With its expanding interests in petroleum services, the company keeps making more money. For the last fiscal year, +23% on +25% higher revenues. Last year's target price of 25 (adjusted) was breached, so set a new goal of 35 soon and 50 for the longer term. There are few stocks that offer greater potential.

PORTFOLIO FOR THE 30s

Shares/Company	Cost	Value 1980	1981	Income 1980-81	Total Returns
HOLD					
200 Heublein, Inc.	26½*	29	34	$500	$2,000
400 Petrolane, Inc.	7½	14½	24	512**	7,112
100 Nabisco, Inc.	23	23	32	252**	1,152
100 Warner-Lambert	19	19	22	198	498
SELL					
100 CBS, Inc.	44	44	55½	420	1,520
100 Melville Corp.	19	29¼	44	250**	1,750
225 Snap-On	20¾	20	24¾	281**	681

With the proceeds: CBS, $5,500; Melville, $4,400; Snap-On Tools, $5,569 and dividends of $2,413, the total is $17,882.

BUY	Price	Anticipated Dividend
100 Avon Products	38	$ 300
150 Chesebrough-Pond's	34	228
100 Long's Drug Stores	32	82
100 Sperry Corp.	56	170

* 100 bought at 24; 100 at 29.   ** Increased dividend

Nabisco, Inc. (NAB). This stock moved up from 23 to 32 and the trend is favorable. This is a new high, so a breakout could be very profitable. Earnings are not likely to roar up 25% as they did in 1980 but, at an annual average rise of +12%, the stock could double in price before too long. Best of all, the EGR is up to 11.9% and PR to 21%. If management meets its goal of maintaining or surpassing these margins, a target price of 50 is justified. (N.B.: Since this was written, NAB has merged with Standard Brands. This new corporation appears to be an even better investment.)

Warner-Lambert (WLA). This stock was repurchased last year after performing below expectations in 1978 and 1979. It started to move up, from 19 to 22, hesitated when earnings were cut by unusual charges for a plant closing and, recently, was holding steady. Profits are expected to rise by +11% in 1981 as the result of consolidation of plants, higher earnings from the Entenmann division now that most expansion costs and acquisition good will have now been written off, and the approval of the sale of the money-losing American Optical division. Target: 30 but watch carefully for unexpected problems.

Sell

CBS, Inc. (CBS). This stock has risen steadily from 44 and should have been sold at its peak of 65: well above the recent 55½. Corporate earnings are still improving and chances are good that the high will be broken. But by selling, there will be a total return of +34% and, for illustrative purposes, the proceeds can be invested for equal or better rewards. When you're in your 30s, it's more fun to take your profits when you can.

Melville Corp. (MES). A fundamentalist might have sold in June 1980 at about 32. *Reason:* two apparel divisions reported slackening sales, and the unfavorable outlook for consumer spending. But a technician would have held because the chart pattern was favorable. The rising market did boost the stock to 44. At this point, there was a hefty total return of $1,750 on the original $1,900 investment. Sell and put the proceeds to work in undervalued situations.

Snap-On Tools (SNA). Last year, despite a price drop, I suggested holding the stock of this manufacturer of tools. The company had a long record of high returns on stockholders' equity (almost 25%). I was wrong. The economic downturn cut profits and forced down the stock price. SNA is still OK for the long term for a young investor but a sale is profitable and another investment has better prospects.

Buy

Avon Products (AVP). This is the kind of stock that is like the little girl with a curl. When it's popular, it's very, very good; when it's out of favor, it's very, very bad. In the early 1970s, AVP soared to 140, then dove to 19. This was Wall Street at its worst because corporate profits, per share, rose, with one interruption, from $2.16 to $4.01. At the same average growth rate, they will be $5.08 in 1982 and $7.20 by 1985. At a modest ten times earnings, that means a market value of 51 to 72, from the current cost of 38. Add the 4% dividend and that's a better-than-average return. And there's always the possibility that AVP will become a favorite again.

Chesebrough-Pond's (CBM). This company has diversified from drugs to cosmetics to apparel, yet still maintains a high rate of return: averaging over 20% a year. In the next five years, its stock price should double and with dividends provide total average annual returns of 25%. A proven money maker with a growth-oriented management.

Long's Drug Stores (LDG). This chain, whose stores are concentrated in the fast-growing West and Hawaii, continues to earn over 21¢ on every invested dollar and to increase dividends—from 15¢ per share to 82¢ in the past decade. Profits have been slowed by the recession but, based on its long record of profitable growth, this stock could almost triple in the next five years.

Sperry Corp. (SY). This a good example of a stock whose timing is favorable. The company ended fiscal 1980 with fourth-quarter income up 26%, year-end backlog +17% and a dividend hike. At 56, the stock is priced at book value and its price earnings ratio a low 7 compared to a ten-year range of 13–8. Management is shooting for a +15% average annual growth in profits. Historically, the stock has traded at a +30% premium over its equity value, so set a target of 100.

For Those in Their 40s

This portfolio was selected for stability and growth. In the first few years, there was more stability than growth, but last year most of the stocks did well and some were BIG winners: Engelhard Minerals, from a cost of $2,550 to total returns, after the sale, of $19,123; Johnson & Johnson, from 77 to 102 before the 3–1 stock split; and Reynolds Industries, from a cost of 29 to over 47. Overall, the portfolio's value increased +63%: from $42,806 last year to $69,663 this year. Sound selections paid off but you have to be lucky, too . . . at least in the timing.

Only one stock, Oklahoma Gas & Electric, bought for income, failed to keep pace. Its price dropped half a point but this decline was offset by the high dividends.

With these holdings, all sales reflect the opportunity to cash in for high total returns. Some of these stocks probably moved up with the stronger spring market, but by fundamental standards they should be sold or, for those who have time to check daily, watched carefully. It is always better to sell a little too soon than to hold for a few more points.

Hold

Chesebrough-Pond's (CBM). The prospects for this diversified company are outlined above. The stock is still undervalued if only because, in 1980, management was able to boost the EGR to 13.4% from 12.2% and its PR to 22.8% from 21.1%. With a billion-dollar company, this is not easy. The other key factors for its purchase are the strong basic growth per share in the past decade: book value from $4.65 to $15.39; earnings, from 97¢ to $4.65; and dividends, from 52¢ to $1.52.

Coca-Cola (KO). With a new management team, this solid blue chip is starting to move and its stock could double in value before long. Because of its huge size—$5 billion revenues—the percentage gains will be modest but they will be steady. The outlook is for continuing higher profits from worldwide sales, lower costs from the substitution of corn sweetener for sugar, the expansion of the wine division and the acquisition of major bottlers. Projected investment returns for the next five years: +26% average annual compound rate.

Johnson & Johnson (JNJ). This has been a big winner, moving from 77 to 103 after the announcement of a 3–1 stock split. If this were in the portfolio for the 60s, I'd suggest selling and putting the big profit into higher-income holdings. Once the enthusiasm of the split is over, chances are that the stock price will sag for a while but, for the long term, JNJ should be very profitable. New target: 50 in the next couple of years; 70 by 1985.

Oklahoma Gas & Electric (OGE). As stated before, this stock was recommended for income, close to 13%. A slight slip in corporate quality has held down its price but

PORTFOLIO FOR THE 40s

Shares/Company	Cost	1980	1981	Income 1980-81	Total Returns
HOLD					
100 Chesebrough-Pond's	32	27	34	$204*	$ 404
100 Coca-Cola	34	34	37	273*	573
100 Johnson & Johnson**	77	77	103	234	2,834
250 Oklahoma G&E	16	14	13½	610*	360
200 Ralston Purina	11	11	13	200*	600
150 V.F. Corp.	21	21	37	405*	2,005
SELL					
100 AMP, Inc.	32	36	55	160*	2,360
412 Englehard Min.***	6 1/8	13	44¾	696*	19,123
200 Reynolds Indus.***	29	35	47½	437*	4,137
100 Thomas & Betts	41	42	57½	258*	1,908

With the proceeds: AMP, $5,500; Englehard, $18,347; Reynolds, $9,500 and Thomas & Betts, $5,750 plus $3,477 dividends, the total is $42,574.

BUY	Price	Anticipated Dividend
100 Coca-Cola	37	$ 232
200 E.G. & G.	40	100
200 Emhart Corp.	37	480
100 Exxon Corp.	68	600
150 Square D	35	255
300 United Telecommunications	18	480
200 Upjohn	62	400
50 V.F. Corp.	37	100

*Increased dividend; ** 3-1 split coming; *** adjusted for split.

profits have been edging up and with readily available, and inexpensive, fuel sources, the downside risk is small and the potential appreciation modest to good, especially with the prospect of lower interest rates. Target is still 20.

Ralston Purina (RAL). This stock has moved up from 11 to 13, not as fast as expected, but the corporate comeback has been strong enough to justify a substantially higher price. The problem areas, in their restaurant and floriculture businesses, have been corrected and management expects to achieve a +12% average annual rate of profit growth. The stock is selling at just about book value and at only 8 times earnings. With better profits and higher multiple, this stock can reach 20 soon and 30 within the next four years for an average annual rate of total returns of over 16%.

V.F. Corporation (VFC). The stock of this apparel manufacturer surged from 21 to 37 as the result of ever-increasing profits: for 1981, an anticipated $5.81 per share vs. $5.15 the year before. Even if profits slow a bit, they should rise to $6.84 by 1983. With a higher multiple (9 vs. the current 7), this would mean a price of 62, almost triple the purchase value. And by 1986, not long for the middle-aged investor, such continued progress would justify a price of 90 and, probably, a stock split.

Sell

AMP, Inc. (AMP). Last year, I urged retention of this blue chip on the basis that "this is a good example of the frustration of long-term investing. The corporate record is superb . . . average annual growth rate of 17.3%. But Wall Street, intrigued with secondary issues, is just beginning to shift its money to quality securities." I set a target price of 50. This was breached and the stock should have been sold at 55 for a total return of $2,360

on the original $3,200 investment. *Reason:* a temporary slowdown in profits, up only +9% in 1980. Probably this will be improved, but at this time the prospects do not justify holding. Wait for confirmation of a comeback and get ready to repurchase when there's a sure return—two successive quarters—to the historically high growth and profitability.

Engelhard Minerals (ENG). You have to be lucky to pick a super-soarer such as this metals, trading, natural-resource company. The stock was bought at an adjusted price of 6⅛ and last year, when it was priced at 27, the advice was: "If it gets above 45, be cautious and set stop-loss orders." The biggest profits would have come in late 1980 when the stock twice peaked at around 65. But if you still hold, get out at about 45 for a gross profit of $16,573. ENG's glamour is gone: the company is splitting into two corporations: one for manufacturing and the other for trading. Maybe one, or both, will be profitable holdings but make management prove its money-making ability first.

Reynolds Industries (RJR). Basically, last year's advice was the same as with Engelhard: be wary when the stock price breaks into a new high, in this case 38. RJR did jump to 49 in early 1981 but has been moving down since. Be glad you can still get 47½. The company is highly profitable but primarily because of its tobacco business, not the result of diversification into the food/beverage fields. The prospects are not bright enough to warrant holding.

Thomas & Betts (TNB). As usually happens with these "early selections," this stock was slow to take off, dawdling around 40 for months. But when it started up, the rise was steady and strong and a sale, at 57½, brought a total return of about 50% in two years. After four years of earnings growth averaging +22%, TNB's 1980 profits slowed to +8%. Put this stock on your "future watch" list.

Buy

Coca-Cola (KO). This is such a basic stock that another 100 shares can provide stability and growth to the portfolio. With all holdings, you want some stocks that can be counted on to edge up, in price and dividends, over the years. Whenever you have extra savings, check the stocks you own first.

E.G. & G. (EGG). This electronics company specializes in items for energy, instruments and environmental control devices. In 1970, it was one of the hottest equities and sold at a price/earnings ratio of 100. But the company failed to fulfill its promise and, by 1978, was trading at a multiple of about 7. In 1979, however, management got things under control and since then, its PR has been over 31% and its EGR about 25%. Financially, the company is strong and paying ever-higher dividends. Its stock has doubled in value but prospects are good enough to look for a comparable gain in the next 24–36 months. Target: 55.

Emhart Industries (EMH). This diversified manufacturer of hardware, heavy equipment and indistrial components ran into trouble in 1979 but able management has made the necessary changes and profits are expected to be back to the +9% annual average rate reported over the past decade. The stock has moved up from 28 to 37 and could break 50 soon and 75 by 1985. Within the next three years, total returns, compounded, could be over 30% annually. But watch carefully because EMH operates in highly competitive areas.

Exxon Corporation (XON). This is a basic portfolio stock. One of the world's largest corporations, its stock is never going to jump ahead because of its huge capitalization. But XON has tremendous resources in oil, gas and coal and is slowly diversifying (through not always successfully) into word processing, electrical equipment and chemicals. Over the past decade, its book value has more than doubled, its earnings quadrupled and its dividends tripled. With its high yield, the total returns can average that 16% that the conservative investor seeks. Target: 100 when, if the past is repeated, there will be a stock split.

Square D (SQD). For this electrical-equipment manufacturer, earnings growth averaged +18% in the 1971–80 period despite a weak construction industry in recent years. With greater emphasis on foreign business and strong leadership, the company should outperform its industry and the stock market. Its ever-higher profits should boost the stock price from a recent 35 to a target of 70.

United Telecommunications (UT). Basically, as the third largest telephone company, this is an income stock but, flush with cash from the sale of a computer division, UT plans to move deeper into the telecommunications field. The yield is a good 7.1% and dividends have been raised consistently for more than a decade. Target: 30 in two years; 40 by 1985.

Upjohn Company (UPJ). This drug/pharmaceutical/agricultural manufacturer has been boosting its growth and profitability steadily and while the stock price has soared, from 32 in 1978 to 68 before it dipped back to 62, the prospects are still excellent. *Target:* 100 when, chances are, the stock will be split. Its per share book value has risen from $9.49 in 1971 to $28.80 in 1981, and by 1985 can be projected to be close to 50. Most drug stocks sell at twice book value.

V.F. Corporation (VFC). Buy 50 more shares to round out the holdings. Commissions, on sale, will be a bit less.

For Those in Their 50s

These securities were chosen for good income and intermediate-term growth with an eye to retirement. The results point out the importance of diversification, patience and managing for maximum returns. The greatest gains were from further appreciation of Texas Oil & Gas, the slow rise of Norfolk & Western and the ample income from Xerox and from premiums of calls written against the RCA convertible preferred. The total returns were $22,287 on a 1980 base of $51,640. Of this, 8.6% represented dividends including the tiny .6% yield of Texas O&G.

Both the retentions and the changes are made for illustration: to emphasize the need to maintain perspective and to recognize that, over the long term, the most profitable companies will make the most money for shareholders; to be willing to shift when income becomes more important than capital gains; and to take advantage of

special investment techniques. These days, when stock prices jump up and down with little reason, most investors in their 50s tend to prefer in-hand income over potential appreciation.

Hold

International Business Machines (IBM). This is a good example of the need for patience in investing. Two years ago, I suggested buying IBM at 75 with the warning to sell if its price dropped to 68. That was good advice as the stock plopped to 52. But last year, I assumed that most people were reluctant to sell such a legend and advised to "Hold the stock and keep the faith."

PORTFOLIO FOR THE 50s

		Value		Income	Total
Shares/Company	Cost	1980	1981	1980-81	Returns
HOLD					
50 IBM	75	56	60	$258	($1,242)
480 Texas Oil & Gas**	9	21	38	110*	14,750
125 Phillips Petroleum		40	47	350*	1,225
145 RCA $4 CV Pref.		48	57	1,170***	2,475
SELL					
300 Norfolk & Western	26¾	28	46	1,050*	6,825
100 Winn Dixie		25	29	264	664
300 Xerox Corp.	54	53	58	1,245*	2,445

With the proceeds of the sales: N&W, $13,800; Winn-Dixie, $2,900; Xerox, $17,400 plus $4,447 in dividends, the total is $38,547.

					****
BUY					
10 Continental Oil 7.5%, '99			62½		750
100 Dart & Kraft			49		340
10 Florida P&L 8, '99			62½		800
200 Manufacturers Hanover			32		544
10 SmithKline 8.15, '84			85		815
100 Square D			35		170

* Increased dividend; ** After stock dividends and splits;
*** Includes income from calls; ****Anticipated income

IBM's profits have edged up but not as far as many analysts predicted. Still, there are positives: strong finances of 88% equity and only 12% debt (in a period when cash counts); a 1980 PR of 23.8%; expenditures of nearly $1.5 *billion* for R&D and potential benefits from the newly accelerated depreciation schedules that are expected to be enacted in 1981. Again: "Hold the stock and keep the faith." Target: 100.

Texas Oil & Gas (TXO). Don't you wish every investment turned out so well? With a stock dividend and stock split, there are now 480 shares. The hefty 17 point (adjusted) rise, from 21 to 38, brought the stock above the 30 target price set last year. If you heeded the rules, you sold, but it's often wise (and certainly more enjoyable) to let your profits run . . . in this case to 50. Unlike most oil stocks, TXO's price has held rather well and the chart pattern shows a definite uptrend. Star this holding for close scrutiny and set a stop-loss order at about 10% below TXO's high. At 25 times earnings, it's trading at a dangerous level.

Phillips Petroleum (P). As with almost all energy stocks, P bounced way up into the 60s, then belly-flopped to the low 40s. This was the result of investor pessimism, not corporate failure. P still makes a bundle: EGR over

18% and PR about 24%. If you paid over 50 you should have sold, but with a cost of 40 you can afford to hold on. The future is bright if only because of oil reserves in the North Sea, in the U.S. and off Africa's Ivory Coast. Be patient until the stock breaks 70 and then hope for a stock split as has occurred in the past.

RCA Corp. (RCA) $4.00 preferred convertible to 2.14 shares of common stock. The company has had problems but, with a new CEO, things should improve as it's still a quality corporation. RCA is retained because of the opportunity for extra income from writing calls. With 145 preferred shares, you control 310 shares of common so can write three calls. With the stock at 26, the 30 calls, with a 7-month expiration date, carry a premium of 2⅛ ($637.50 not counting commissions). If the stock does not reach 30, you can write new calls to get, roughly, net extra income of $1,000 a year on the investment currently valued at $8,266.

If RCA common stock does reach 30 in seven months, you will get a gross gain of $1,200 (30 call price vs. 26 currently). At that point, you can buy back the calls (and cut your returns but expand your potential) or can convert the shares and deliver the common stock. *This is a good example of how to manage your portfolio for maximum returns.*

Sell

Norfolk & Western (NFK). This stock was bought for income but has moved up briskly since last year, to 46 from 28. Take the $6,825 profits because the corporate prospects are marginal due to problems over which management has little control: the probable reorganization of Conrail; the lower exports due to the industrial slowdown in Europe; and the continued unrest in the coal industry.

Winn-Dixie Stores (WIN). Last year this was suggested as a defensive stock. It worked out that way with a 6.8% dividend yield and a slow, steady rise from 25 to 29. But, together with most retailers, WIN ran into trouble and for two consecutive quarters its profits were below those of the year before. This was a sell signal. Even if WIN's able management gets the company back in line, the stock is not likely to do much for at least a year.

Xerox Corp. (XRX). This stock has been a disappointment although its total returns averaged about 15% a year. As I said last year, "Apparently, Wall Street is upset about competition." XRX is still a good long-term holding—an EGR of 12% and PR about 19%—but, to provide funds for other types of investments, sell.

Buy

Continental Oil 7.5%, '99; Florida Power & Light 8, '99; and SmithKline 8.15, '84. All of these quality bonds are selling at substantial discounts with current yields of 12%, 12.8% and 9.6% respectively. There's no danger of default or call and if and when interest rates decline, their prices will rise. Finally, you are sure of a sizable capital gain because you will get $1,000 each at maturity: in 1984 for SKF and 1999 for Conoco and Florida P&L. Safety, income, appreciation—just what's needed to provide a solid base for this portfolio for the middle-aged investor.

Dart & Kraft (DKI). This stock is included for three reasons: (1) diversification into the food industry; (2) the remarkable stability of the stock of its predecessor, Kraft, Inc. Despite the fact that between 1970 and 1981 per share book value rose from $18.83 to $48.00 and earnings from $2.30 to $6.86, the stock price was virtually unchanged. (3) The stock appears likely to break into a new high as the result of greater investor interest and, remember, volume precedes price.

At 49, DKI is selling at a low 7 times profits. If the demand continues, the stock could move up over 70 and, ere too long, to 100. Meantime, you'll get about 6% while waiting.

Manufacturers Hanover (MHC). In the coming shakeout of the financial industry, strong, profitable banks should stand out. With few retail branches, MHC has concentrated on commercial business here and abroad and has steadily boosted earnings and book value. Its stock, at 32, is at a bargain level, less than 5 times earnings, and with ever-higher dividends, yields over 8%. If interest rates drop and investors look more favorably on bank stocks, MHC could break 40 soon and double in value in 24 to 36 months. That means total returns averaging over 20% annually.

Square D (SQD). This was reviewed in the Portfolio for the 30s but there are some additional reasons for inclusion here. Despite the construction slump, SDQ's fourth quarter, 1980, was excellent: earnings +51% on a +28% sales advance. This was due to a strong performance by the utility/industrial division.

With SDQ, do not be worried if there is a temporary decline in the per share profits because, in September 1980, the company issued 1.6 shares of common stock to acquire Yates Industries, a supplier of copper foil for printed circuit boards, and to add to working capital. Since 1971, SDQ has reported an average EGR of 9.7% and a PR of 23%, and in 1980 bested both of these percentages. The rise in the price of the stock may be slow but, unless there are unforeseen developments, it will be sure.

For Those in Their 60s

This portfolio was chosen for people preparing for retirement, so the focus has always been on income and safety rather than growth. These securities did what they were supposed to do: an average annual yield of 10.9%. This was not as high as could have been obtained with money market funds but there was a $3,750 capital appreciation so total returns were +22.7%—half again as much as that of fixed-income holdings. And that gain was attained despite a 1½ point decline in the value of the shares of Texas Utilities.

In the original suggestions, in 1976, there were a number of convertibles. These were sold as market conditions changed, but last year several CVs were added, and this year even more.

CVs can be useful investments when their yields are ample and corporate prospects good. And, as outlined in the Portfolio for the 50s, they can often be used to write calls for extra income.

For older folks, they have an added appeal: as gifts or bequests to heirs. The older investor can count on income and the younger beneficiary can look for appreciation.

Note how the emphasis shifts toward income because

of the probability that interest-sensitive securities, such as CVs and utility stocks, will be worth more when the cost of money drops. Ideally, this portfolio should include some discount bonds but CVs achieve the same goal with greater flexibility.

Hold

Lucky Stores (LKS). This stock has moved within a narrow range for a couple of years, primarily because of the unpopularity of retail stocks. LKS profits were down to $1.80 from $2.01 in 1980 but are expected to be up to $2.10 in the fiscal year ending January 1982. The company continues to earn over 21¢ on every invested dollar and, if this comeback pace can be maintained, LKS's record will outpace that of the average industrial corporation. At only 8 times projected profits—compared to a ten-year low of 10—the stock could double in value in the next 24 months, and with acquisitions, do even better. Added attraction: a pleasant 6.7% dividend.

PORTFOLIO FOR THE 60s

Shares/Company	Cost	Value 1980	1981	Income 1980-81	Total Returns
HOLD					
200 Lucky Stores	15½	15½	16½	$336	$ 536
200 Rochester Telephone	18½	19½	21½	520*	1,120
150 Standard Brands		27	29	445	745
300 Texas Utilities	20	19	17½	792*	42
SELL					
100 American Home	26	28	34	260*	1,060
5 Becton Dick. 5, '89	830	710	850	375	475
100 Kidde $4 CV pref.			44	56	400	1,600
SWAP					
100 I. T. & T. #4 CV pref. for			46	54	400	1,200
165 I. T. & T.				33	429**	

With the proceeds of the sales: Becton Dickinson, $4,250; American Home, $3,400; Kidde, $5,600 plus $3,528 from dividends/interest, the total available is $16,778.

BUY		**
200 Continental Gr. $2 CV pref.	18	400
100 Houston Industries	27	296
50 Standard Brands	29	82
250 Tucson Electric	15	344
100 Champion Inter. $4.60 CV pref.	53	460

* Increased dividend   ** Anticipated dividend

Rochester Telephone (RTC). This regional utility keeps moving ahead with 22 years of ever-higher dividends. The target price of 30 still stands. Add the 8+% yield and you'll make more (and be taxed less) than if you invested the same sum in money market funds.

Standard Brands, Inc. (SB). This stock has started to move up to a more realistic value but there's plenty of room for more. The upmove has been delayed by the peanut shortage, but overall the company's food and liquor divisions are boosting profits by over +13% a year. These prospects justify retention of the current 150 shares and the purchase of 50 more. And if management makes a major acquisition—as indicated by past attempts—SB stock could be a real winner (*Note:* SB is an even better

buy as the result of its merger with Nabisco, Inc.)

Texas Utilities (TXL). As stated last year, you gotta be patient. This stock has moved within a narrow range but you were paid well (over 10%) while waiting. Because of its location in one of the fastest-growing areas and its access to natural gas, TXL offers an unusual opportunity for profitable growth. It is one of the better income stocks in that its dividend growth is forecast at a +5% average annual compound rate over the next five years. Thus, the yield on the current cost of each share should increase to 14% annually. And, again, if interest rates decline, the value of this stock will move up automatically. Target for 1983: 31; for 1986: 40.

Sell

American Home Products (AHP). This stock is coming out of Wall Street's doghouse and probably will hit 40 soon. But for illustration, let's sell at 34 for a nifty profit. By fundamental standards, AHP ranks high: almost no debt, a ten-year average PR over 30% and EGR of 13.2% and a current dividend yield of 5.4%. Wall Street has not been happy about the long-term president but, with his retirement, will be skeptical until his successor proves his mettle.

Becton Dickinson 5, '89. These bonds moved up above their cost price to provide a small profit. They are still worthwhile holdings but the total returns are less than can be obtained with other investments.

Kidde (Walter) & Co., Inc. (KDE). $4.00 convertible preferred. As the price of this stock moved up, its yield dropped to 7.1%. Now it is trading primarily on its conversion value: 1.16 shares of common stock, selling at 46 compared to a conversion value of 38. Take the profit now. KDE is not a quality company ... yet.

Swap

International Telephone & Telegraph (ITT) $4.00 preferred convertible into 1.65 shares of common stock. It is selling at just about the swap price. Incomewise, it would pay to make the exchange because the stock, with its $2.60 dividend, would pay $4.29 compared to the current $4.00. ITT is not a quality company but it's doing well and, with the higher defense budget, greater volume in communications equipment and higher coal prices, the stock is worth holding to a target price of 40.

Buy

Continental Group $2.00 convertible preferred. This is the old Continental Can Co., which has diversified into energy and insurance. In 1980, its big gains—$6.11 per share vs. $5.27 the year before—resulted from favorable currency exchange more than operations. But overall prospects are good. The preferred represents an income hedge: a 11.1% yield and the potential of appreciation by conversion into ⅓ of a share of common stock now trading at 36. This is below the book value of $42.80 and at a low 6 times the last 12-months earnings. That's a good combination for anyone in their 60s.

Houston Industries (HOU). This is an excellent conservative investment that yields over 9% and seems likely to keep raising its payout. As interest rates decline, the stock price will move up and, at 40, should be reviewed.

This utility serves a fast-growing industrial area, earns 15¢ on every invested dollar and should benefit from its relatively low-priced gas reserves.

Tucson Gas & Electric (TGE). This was sold last year but seems a good buy at this time. The sale was made more for illustration than for a valid reason. But this is one of the better utilities. It is financially strong, growing at about 6% a year (better than the average for the Dow Jones Utilities) and keeps boosting its payout: more than double in the past decade. With an 11% yield, the stock is undervalued and could double in price in the next two years. Buy for income; hold for growth.

Champion International (CHA) $4.60 preferred convertible into 1.7 shares of common now selling at 30. With the CV at 53, the premium is a modest 10%. CHA is no longer a top quality company but its stock has moved up sharply in recent months: from 22 to 29. Profits were down in 1980 but are improving and, with greater investor interest in natural-resource companies, could bring a more realistic market value. With the 8.7% yield, you can afford to wait.

Summary

Keep in mind that almost all of these securities are interchangeable—suitable for portfolios of any age. If you're 31 and conservative, take a look at the 60s; if you're 66 and have extra savings, buy some of the growth stocks listed in the Portfolio for the 30s. Set your objectives and buy the securities that will help you realize your goals.

CHAPTER 30

How to Profit from Forecasting and Patterns

The stock market always fluctuates in response to real or imagined facts, fears or hopes. The short, interim shifts are impossible to predict because they are influenced by temporary news: international tension, a change in the value of the dollar or the prime interest rate, the balance of trade, Washington action or inaction, news articles, etc. The broad trends are not always clear until they are well underway but there are established patterns of seasonal activity that can add a bit to profits and help avoid small losses. For the long-term investor, they are most beneficial in buying, as a delay may save a few points. For the trader, however, they can be very useful if only because they provide the pressure to make or postpone a decision.

Patterns are not always repeated so should never be taken as gospel. Traditionally, November has been an *up* month, but in 1979 the market was *down* as the result of the sharp rise in interest rates. In 1980, the pattern was back on track and the market rose a sizeable +7.5%.

Keep these monthly actions in mind when you have time to make investments. You may save a few dollars per share in buying and profit even more when selling.

From 1897 through 1980, the DJIA rose in 566 months and fell in 426. That's a favorable 57% on the upside. It points out that, roughly, the market goes up two-thirds of the time and down one-third. But monthly figures can be deceiving as one day can make a major difference in the month-end average.

Obviously, the same forces do not apply at all times but the shifts appear to be the results of: (1) a heavy flow of year-end dividends and bonuses into the market at the start of the new year; (2) the drain of income-tax payments reflected in the poor performance in May; (3) the summertime optimism often engendered by the normally

MONTHLY HIGHS AND LOWS
Since 1897

Month	Number Highs	Number Lows
January	13	17
February	4	10
March	4	8
April	4	5
May	1	4
June	3	6
July	4	5
August	4	1
September	7	3
October	3	6
November	11	6
December	28	11

Source: Dow Jones; New York Stock Exchange

anticipated pickup in business in the fall; (4) the frequent tax selling and switching in November and December; (5) the efforts by mutual funds and other institutional investors to dress up their performance by buying additional shares of profitable holdings just before the end of the reporting period: March 31, June 30, September 30 and December 31.

Monthly patterns. Based on advances and declines, the best months for selling are January, July and December; for buying, February and September—if you wait for the low points.

This pattern is more or less repeated by the number of highs and lows. Based on the past performance of the Dow, December and November are the periods of the greatest market rises but they are also leaders in declines. The odds for gains are least with May and for losses,

MONTHLY ADVANCES AND DECLINES IN THE DJIA SINCE 1897

| Month | Number of Times | | % Up |
	Up	Down	
January	52	31	63%
February	38	45	46
March	49	34	59
April	45	38	54
May	42	41	51
June	41	42	49
July	53	30	64
August*	56	26	68
September*	38	44	46
October*	43	39	52
November*	49	33	60
December	60	23	72

* Market closed in 1914

SOURCE: Dow Jones & Co.

August. Keep those months in mind when you are considering taking long-term capital gains.

Another interesting statistic: Since World War II, the odds have been about 3-1 that the June opening prices will be lower than the December close. On the average, the DJIA will gain about 50 points. This did not happen in 1979, but in 1980 the seven-months gain was 146 points.

SUMMER RALLY

YEAR	% Change June-August
1959	+ 3.4%
1960	− 0.3
1961	+ 4.9
1962	+ 8.0
1963	+ 4.6
1964	+ 1.3
1965	+ 3.7
1966	− 9.1
1967	+ 3.5
1968	− 0.6
1969	− 2.4
1970	+11.3
1971	+ 3.5
1972	+ 2.6
1973	− 4.7
1974	+ 0.1
1975	+ 0.1
1976	−17.4
1977	− 6.4
1978	+ 5.9
1979	+ 5.4
1980	+ 9.5

SOURCE: Dow Jones & Co.

Summer rally. One of the most dependable seasonal movements is the midsummer rally: between early June and late August. In the past 29 years, there were only four significant declines: 1966, 1969, 1973 and 1977. But the gains, while not always as strong, have been more or less steady: a hefty +11.3% in 1970, +8.0% in 1962, and for the last three years, +5.9%, +5.4% and +7.5% respectively. For quick profits, buy in late May and sell in late August.

Year-end surge. December is almost always a *good*

month. Since 1897, the market has risen in 60 years and declined in only 23. In most cases, the high has occurred around the middle of the month as year-end tax selling often depresses prices temporarily.

THE JANUARY FORECAST

| YEAR | S&P 500 STOCK COMPOSITE | |
	January	Year
1959	+ 0.4%	+ 8.5%
1960	− 7.1	− 3.0
1961	+ 6.3	+23.1
1962	− 3.8	−11.8
1963	+ 4.9	+18.9
1964	+ 2.7	+13.0
1965	+ 3.3	+ 9.1
1966	+ 0.5	−13.1
1967	+ 7.8	+20.1
1968	− 4.4	+ 7.7
1969	− 0.8	−11.4
1970	− 7.6	+ 0.1
1971	+ 4.0	+10.8
1972	+ 1.8	+15.6
1973	− 1.7	−17.4
1974	− 1.0	−29.7
1975	+12.3	+31.5
1976	+11.8	+19.1
1977	− 5.1	−11.5
1978	− 6.2	+ 1.1
1979	+ 4.0	+12.0
1980	+ 7.0	+26.0
1981	− 4.6	

SOURCE: The Stock Trader's Almanac; Wright Investors' Service

January indicator. January is *always* a key month. Many fundamentalists place considerable faith in its forecasting ability. In over three decades, what happened in the first month has predicted the full year's action 80% of the time. There were exceptions, so it's a good idea to wait until late January before making major commitments. If the trend is strongly upward, pick quality stocks that are in the spotlight. If there's little change, be selective. If there's a drop, buy for the long term, consider fixed income holdings or maintain a reserve in T-bills or liquid-asset funds.

In January 1980, the Dow was up 7.0% and the year ended with a handsome 26% gain. But in 1981, January's action was unfavorable: −4.6%, indicating that the market would probably end at a lower level. *But remember that these forecasts are based on a limited average: 30 stocks only.*

Special Price Patterns

The heavy institutional activity has confused the daily market pattern, but you may be able to pick up a few extra dollars by timing your purchases or sales in line with these not-so-well documented interim market actions:

Within any month, the stock market is often a bit stronger just before the end of a month and just after the start of the new month. *Sell around the end of the month.* Institutional investors frequently place orders in anticipation of their inflow of funds on the first of the month. With increasing redemptions of mutual fund shares, this is not as regular an occurrence as in years past, but especially in active markets, this still appears to be a time to gain an extra ⅛ or ¼ of a point.

Within any week, you will do better to buy Monday morning and to sell Friday afternoon. Here again, there's been some change due to the heightened role of institutions, but over a 42-year period, Merrill Analysis, Inc. found that the DJIA went up 63% of the time on the closing day of the trading week and went down 54% of the Mondays. In bear markets, there is often a long stream of blue Mondays.

One study shows that the average investment was 0.12% higher at the close on Friday than at the close on Thursday and about 0.22% lower at the close on Monday than at the close on Friday.

Within any day, the first and last hours are likely to be the most active. The opening hour volume is boosted by overnight decisions and, it appears, many investors review the market about 2 P.M. and make their moves before closing.

On the other hand, the 11 A.M. to noon, and 1 P.M. to 2 P.M. periods tend to show less price movement, regardless of which way the overall market is moving.

Another pattern that is repeated is a strong close followed by a strong opening the next day; then come buying opportunities.

And the studies show that stock prices decline in the last hour of trading as the professionals take their day's profits—or losses.

Before holidays, the market tends to rise. According to Arthur A. Merrill in *Behavior of Prices on Wall Street,* the DJIA rose almost two-thirds of the time before a one-day holiday and about three-quarters of the time before a three-day weekend.

Before the end of the quarters (March 31, June 30, etc.), buy one of the institution-favored stocks which have had a big move in the last two months. These are the securities which are likely to be purchased by aggressive funds seeking to add to their reported gains. This demand may push the shares to new highs.

But do not hang on after the end of the quarter. When orders dwindle, lower prices are almost certain.

Before the ex-dividend date, sell at the slightly higher price and buy back afterwards *if* you feel confident of the company's future and want to shift profits from high-taxed dividends to low-taxed capital gains.

Bright Fridays. Over almost two decades, the market rose on 62.2% of Fridays.

Blue Mondays. Historically, the market has gone down more often than up on Mondays: 60.5% of the time, down; 39.5%, up.

Therefore, if you are in doubt about carrying a long position over the weekend, don't. Sell on Friday and consider buying on Monday.

The Best Day of the Month

The stock market rises more often (66.7%) on the second trading day of the month than on any other. A period of four consecutive trading days (the first, second, third and last) of each month outperforms all others in price rises.

According to Yale Hirsch, these "good" days occur because people operate on a monthly fiscal basis. The majority of systematic investment programs (mutual fund contractual plans, union pension funds, etc.) all tend to act at the same time.

Stock Market Forecasting

According to John C. Touhey, in his book *Stock Market Forecasting for Alert Investors,* the stock market can be forecast 80% of the time. His comments do not fully qualify as forecasts but they are close enough to be summarized here. Here are some of the checkpoints he recommends:

• **Brokers' cash accounts.** When these increase for two consecutive months, *buy.* When they decline for the same period, *sell.*

• **Call loan interest rate.** When this declines by more than 3% in any one month, *buy.* When there are three consecutive monthly increases, *sell.*

• **Brokers' margin credit.** *Buy* when the monthly totals for the past 60 days are greater than those of the previous two months. *Sell* (or sell short) when they are less for two months.

• **Prime interest rate.** When this is lower than the yield of AAA corporate bonds, *buy.* When it is higher, be cautious and, generally, *sell* or do not buy.

CHAPTER 31

Making Money with Real Estate Investments

Real estate investments can provide good-to-high yields, excellent tax shelters and long-term capital appreciation. Historically, the leverage has been high but with soaring interest rates, this advantage has been reduced. If you are smart and lucky, you can score quick, speculative gains but, usually, profits require patience. Do not be conned by headlines, sales talks or unverified "success" stories. Real estate is always easier to get into than out of.

The great attraction of all real estate is *growth:* in recent years, from 10% to 20% annually. But only rarely does this continue over the life-span of true investments.

Selections must be carefully made; management must be able and cost-conscious; financing must be adequate; and there must always be a willingness to take profits when justified. Tax benefits are appealing but all real estate should be judged like any other investment: on the return on equity and the profit potential. *If it's not a good investment, it is not a good tax shelter.* Tax write-offs should be a plus, not the major reason for acquiring property.

Always be cautious and realistic. Do not be taken in by the "fantastic" returns that start with $1,000 down and by pyramiding (using one holding as collateral to buy another), build multi-million-dollar portfolios. The examples touted in most books and lectures are the exceptions, not the rule. The get-rich-quick formula succeeded only because of comparatively low interest rates and overly high, inflation-boosted appreciation. It's easy to make a bundle with an 8% interest rate and 15% annual rise in value but it's almost impossible to profit when money costs 15% and appreciation is 8% a year. With few exceptions, the authors of these books make more money with royalties and lecture fees than with their real estate investments.

Look for Skillful Guidance

If you plan to become seriously involved in real estate, it is essential to work with knowledgeable real estate and tax advisers and, whenever possible, to be willing to do your own personal research. Unfortunately, the real estate business is not noted for integrity or skilled management. Too many real estate "experts" are promoters who operate with too little capital. When there's a bind, they cop out! *More than in any other form of investing, it is imperative to deal only with reputable, competent, experienced individuals and organizations.*

Finding the right adviser is difficult. In small communities you can do well with a local broker. When you move into broader areas, always get references and check reputations and results with banks and professional investors.

Success takes time, patience and research. You should have a thorough knowledge of the area, the growth pattern, transportation and highway plans, and present and potential competition. Always double the number of years for the payoff claimed by the promoter-developer. And never (well, hardly ever) invest money that you will need in the next five years. *The single greatest danger in real estate investing is the lack of liquidity.* If you have to sell in a hurry, you are almost sure to take a loss, or, at best, receive less than the real value. *Exception:* shares of REITs listed on major stock exchanges are liquid but not always profitable investments. If you buy low and hold, you will win if corporate management is honest, reasonably competent and is involved with properties in growing or stable areas.

If you are making a sizable investment, inspect the property personally and retain competent local counsel to make sure that the location, price, yield and depreciation schedules and tax shelters of present and potential properties conform to expectations. *As tax rules change, so does your position. Most real estate investments have*

LONG-TERM payouts. Always project for 10 to 20 years.

You do not have to be a millionaire to make money in real estate. There are many excellent local investments: gas stations; small shopping centers; commercial buildings such as medical centers, office complexes, and free-standing stores used for franchised operations (convenience stores, fast-food outlets).

In most cases, the investor builds or renovates the property and then leases it to an operator. Leases can be flexible so that the tenant pays rent plus real estate taxes, insurance and maintenance. When a major corporation such as Exxon, McDonald's or 7-11 is involved, its reputation will make it possible to secure a higher mortgage and thus reduce the amount of cash required, but the lease will probably net a little less.

As owner, you can use some of the tax-free cash from depreciation to pay the mortgage, interest and amortization. Rapid obsolescence permits substantial deductions on the building, furniture and equipment. *IF there was proper advance planning.*

For opportunities, see your local banker or a large, commercially oriented real estate firm. They are always looking for investors and are often in a position to help you obtain the best mortgage terms.

Mortgage Investments

First mortgages are a traditional way to secure steady yields of 15% or more; second mortgages, with greater risk, can yield up to 20% for a short period; and if you are a real gambler, third mortgages provide even higher returns.

Each investor must decide whether the inherent risk is worth the income premium over good-grade bonds or stocks. With a mortgage, you are almost always assured of getting back your money. But you are locked in, often for 20 years or more. *Remember: Interest rates in the 1960s were less than half what they are today! As with all long-term commitments, the value of your income dollar depreciates with inflation.* And, as those old enough to remember the Great Depression know, there can be years when it is impossible to sell, or rent, property.

First mortgages can be a worthwhile investment if you can afford to tie up your money for a long time and want steady income. These days, if you sell your home, you may have to take back a mortgage. It's fine to count on a 15% return plus amortization every month BUT there could be a real problem if you need the money in a hurry. Your best hope will be that, as interest rates drop, the homeowner will find it profitable to refinance the loan.

For retirees, a first mortgage can be an excellent annuity if the borrower is able to keep up the payments and maintains the property. But foreclosure can be tragic and costly.

Second mortgages are usually for a short period, seldom more than five years. Their returns can be 3% to 5% above the current interest rate. With sound collateral and a reliable borrower, they can be one of the best fixed-income investments. But, by definition, they are not quality holdings. To minimize risks and avoid legal hassles, arrange for:

• **A penalty clause for late payments.** If the interest rates rise, the borrower has an incentive to pay on time. Without such an arrangement, you may have to foreclose. That's not easy if you are dealing with a local family.

• **An acceleration clause.** This gives you the option, in the event of a resale, of continuing the second mortgage with the new buyer or demanding that the note be paid off in full before the property can be sold.

• **A priority clause.** This provides that there can be no increase in the first mortgage without the second mortgage being paid off. Without such a clause, the borrower can refinance the first mortgage, get his down payment back, abandon the property and lose nothing. You would have to assume the first mortgage or lose your entire stake.

• **A notification clause.** This puts you on record that, in the event of a default on the first mortgage, you are willing to continue the payment on it. In return, you must be notified in advance of any forthcoming foreclosure. If the borrower kept up his payment on the first mortgage and defaulted on the second, the property might have to be auctioned off to satisfy the primary lender. This would leave no funds for you to claim.

Recently, some brokers, primarily on the West Coast, have offered shares in pools of second mortgages. These are risky. If the promoter promises yields of 25%, do not buy. There's no way such a high return can be maintained as too many of the borrowers will default. If the company is large, established and reputable, it may be able to pay 20%. But too often the mortgages will be based on the value of the property and not on the ability of the home buyer to meet the high payments. Foreclosures are costly and can tie up your money for years.

Real Estate Investments

Historically, the yields of real estate have been 2% to 3% above those available from fixed-income securities. This return reflects both the cash flow and the tax benefits.

With housing and commercial properties, it's best to split the deal into two parts: (1) *The underlying land* to be owned by an investor who wants income but not depreciation—a pension fund or trust. Usually, the lease calls for a percentage of gross income with a minimum payment. Thus, the investor wins as the rents rise. (2) *The buildings* to be held by an individual or group who want modest income plus the tax benefits. Keep this breakdown in mind when you make a deal. Developers always need money, so use this to make an agreement best for your purposes.

There are excellent real estate investments in every community. Among the best are: small apartment houses in an accessible location; strip shopping centers with a cluster of small stores anchored by a banking office: packaged deals for free-standing buildings for franchised fast-food restaurants, convenience food stores and, occasionally, service stations.

As a rule of thumb, the cash outlay should not be more than 20% of the first $1 million and 15% thereafter.

But in these days of super-high interest rates, more cash may be required or the lender will demand a piece of the action: an equity position in warrants for the stock, in a percentage of profits or a share of the proceeds of a profitable sale.

If you can find an honest, energetic, reputable promoter-developer, local real estate can be a worthwhile investment. But you must check frequently and be willing to wait for five years to achieve your target profits.

Syndicates and Partnerships

While it is possible to make money with real estate that you own alone or with a member of your family, most people do not have cash, credit or time to do it themselves. Major real estate investments are usually made through syndicates or partnerships.

Syndicates are limited partnerships that sell shares for as little as $3,000 each. They may be formed by local real estate agents or, more likely, by divisions of major brokerage firms. The offerings are for a specified sum so once the purchase is made, you are locked in. With larger syndicates, there may be a secondary market but, generally speaking, resales can be made only to other participants. That's why it's a good idea to work with friends or business associates who are able, and willing, to bail you out. Or vice versa.

Private partnerships attract the high-tax-bracket investor. Shares cost a minimum of $25,000 but can be paid over a three-year period. Usually, each deal involves a single project.

Broadly speaking, both syndicates and partnerships have two classes of investors: (1) general partners who put up a little money, assume full responsibility for operations (including liability for some debts), and take most of the profits; (2) limited partners who provide most of the money but who are liable only to the extent of agreed-upon contributions.

Under partnerships, all losses, depreciation, income and capital appreciation are passed through to the investors. These individuals pay taxes at regular income-tax rates on their returns and get the full benefit of any tax losses. This escapes the double taxation of corporations. The investors can use ordinary losses to offset ordinary income and carry them back or forward. Limited partners have the right to withdraw or assign interests, and death does not necessarily dissolve the partnership.

Limited partnerships are still used in many local situations, but real estate syndicates (often promotions) have taken over on major projects. They differ from the usual partnerships of professional real estate operators or buyers because of the participation of many nonprofessional investors. They are useful in deals involving ownership of office buildings, factories, apartment houses, bowling alleys, shopping centers and motels.

For small investors, syndicates have these advantages:

1. Basic yields that are about 3% greater than those of securities and are paid monthly.

When these appear to be overly high, they may be padded. They cannot be maintained without burdening the property's upkeep.

DO YOUR RESEARCH FIRST
Analysis of Benefits of Tax-Sheltered Limited Partnership

What the salesman said:

Year	Depreciation	Interest	Expenses Operations	Rental Income	Net Deductions	Tax Savings 50% Bracket
1	$3,669	$3,064	$5,244	$4,023	$7,954	$3,977
2	2,969	5,367	4,966	7,654	5,918	2,959
3	2,478	5,966	4,930	8,526	4,484	2,424
4	2,120	5,596	5,020	8,856	3,890	1,945
5	2,082	4,217	5,026	9,137	2,188	1,094

The Way It Really Was:

Year	Rental Income	LESS Depreciation	Interest	Expenses Operations	= Taxable Income	= Tax Savings	Net Income	PLUS Depreciation	Net Cash Flow
1	$4,023	−3,669	−3,064	−5,244	−7,954	3,977	−3,977	3,669	−308
2	7,654	−2,969	−5,637	−4,966	−5,918	2,959	−2,959	2,969	10
3	8,526	−2,478	−5,966	−4,930	−4,848	2,424	−2,424	2,478	54
4	8,856	−2,120	−5,596	−5,030	−3,890	1,945	−1,945	2,120	175
5	9,137	−2,062	−4,217	−5,026	−2,168	1,084	−1,084	2,062	978

SOURCE: Managing Your Money. Paul A. Randle & Philip R. Swensen

Example: to make cash-flow projections for an apartment house more attractive, the promoter-developer may eliminate the reserve for replacing kitchen appliances and shave estimates for maintenance, etc. Usually, 45% of rental income goes to operating costs. If the prospectus sets them at less, be careful.

Similarly, the projections may not be accurate, as shown by this proposal made to me by a local promoter. Fortunately, my neighbor, who is a retired property manager, took time to check the data.

2. Depreciation cuts taxes. The big plus, for wealthy investors, is that about half of syndication yields come from depreciation. These are considered return on capital so not taxable as income.

Attractive returns can be obtained from well-managed apartment houses. You can take advantage of *accelerated depreciation* (double the straight-line allowance), which is no longer available for commercial or industrial property. *There's no free ride.* Double depreciation takes away most of the profits when you sell.

Example: Dr. Hernia, who is in the 50% tax bracket, puts $20,000 into Moonglow Apartments on a syndicated basis. For the first four years he takes tax losses of $10,000 a year. This enables him to get back his investment as he deducts half of the total loss each year (four times $5,000).

During the next ten to twelve years, he continues to get some smaller tax losses and a modest cash income from the property. Over fifteen years, Dr. Hernia should end up with a 16% to 19% annual return on his money *if* there are no critical problems.

He gets the tax loss because the total deductions (for depreciation, mortgage interest and building operations) exceed the apartment rental income.

But there are negatives: (a) if Dr. Hernia has to sell in the early years, all his profits will be taxable, and if the sale is at a loss, the total losses are very likely to be far greater than the possible tax benefits; *(b)* rental income may dip and building expenses rise unless there is a strong, experienced management; *(c)* delays may eat up most of the capital or so increase the cost of the building that more capital will be needed (on the average it takes about three years between the original proposal and occupancy of the apartment); *(d)* there's plenty of paperwork, especially when you are dealing with Government-insured mortgages. Be sure to retain or include a reliable, experienced real estate law firm in the deal.

3. Long-term capital gains are probable—though not guaranteed. If the value of the real estate rises with population growth, inflation or the attractiveness of the property, there should be a good profit. Many syndication managers are adept at refinancing with new, larger mortgages. This makes it possible to withdraw large capital gains after the property has been sold. When you include partially income-tax-free monthly or quarterly payouts, the total returns can be rewarding, even better than those of growth stocks.

Check Those Costs

Compared to securities, real estate investments require huge sums off the top for: research, location and acquisition, printing the prospectus, accounting and legal fees, management, working capital and, often, special compensation for the current owner.

Here's an example of a $1.1 million apartment. Note that only 44.5% of the investors' money went for the building. The majority of the proceeds were used by the promoters: $160,000 to the general partner ($60,000 initial management fee, $40,000 general partners' fee and $60,000 to guarantee a letter of credit or to meet any negative partnership cash flow).

The big bite, $250,000 ($150,000 consultant's fee plus $100,000 non-competition fee), was paid to the former owner. Of course, if you were the seller, this would be gravy!

These costs are startling to the uninitiated but if the ultimate deal proves profitable, they are not significant. Still, they point up the extra risks of real estate invest-

HOW SYNDICATE FEES MOUNT UP

$1.25 Million Apartment House

Spent for	Amount	Percentage
Cash closing costs	$500,000	44.5%
Consulting fees	150,000	13.3
Noncompetition fee	100,000	8.9
Selling commissions	88,000	7.8
Legal/accounting/printing/ administrative	62,000	5.5
Initial management fee	60,000	5.3
General partner's fee	40,000	3.6
Working capital	20,000	1.8
Mortgage interest*	45,000	4.0
Guarantee fee	60,000	5.3
	$1,125,000	100.0%

* comparatively low as the commitment was made before interest rates skyrocketed.

SOURCE: Executive Wealth Advisory

Type of Property	Depreciation Permitted
Apartments	Choice between straight-line depreciation; 200% declining balance; or the sum of the digits
Old residential housing with useful life of twenty years	Straight-line or 125% declining balance
Office buildings, nonresidential properties	Straight-line or 150% declining balance (with some minor exceptions)
Rehabilitation units for low/ moderate-income housing	Straight-line depreciation over five years
All other used property	Straight-line depreciation over the remaining useful life

Ask your broker/agent to spell out the differences and then double-check this table for a $3 million building that has a useful life of 30 years.

CALCULATING DEPRECIATION:
$3,000,000 for 30 Years

Year	Straight-Line Total	10% Share	Double-Declining Total	10% Share
1	$100,000	$10,000	$200,000	$20,000
2	100,000	10,000	186,667	18,667
3	100,000	10,000	174,222	17,422
5	100,000	10,000	151,767	15,177
8	100,000	10,000	123,392	12,339
10	100,000	10,000	107,488	10,749
15	100,000	10,000	76,128	7,613

ments, especially if the projections are inaccurate or fail to work out.

To make that point again, let's check a typical limited partnership. There are 30,000 $1,000 units. The $30 million will be used to buy residential and commercial properties. The minimum purchase is $5,000.

In compliance with SEC regulations, the front of the prospectus bears this warning: "This offering involves a high degree of risk and substantial fees to the general partners and affiliates." Later, the text will get specific. In that $30 million deal, the general partners are to receive 16.25% of the gross proceeds: $502,000—off the top!

As with all third-party investments, the key is management. A properly structured deal, with the money invested in prime income-producing properties, can result in steady cash flow, excellent depreciation and, eventually, capital appreciation. But once that money is in the hands of the promoters, they tend to want to put it to work, and too often they will take unnecessary risks. *With all real estate, it is more important to know how to get out than how to get in.*

Added caveat: As always happens when some investment area becomes profitable, fast-buck operators move in. With one Florida real estate syndicate, investors put up 90% of the capital for 30% of the company—which has never declared a dividend, pays $1.5 million in salaries to its officers plus $60,000 to the promoter's father and never reveals the purchased properties until long after the sucker's check has cleared (and not always then).

Complex Accounting

Real estate accounting is complex and, to most people, baffling. Depreciation, for example, can be figured in a number of ways. The trick is to choose the schedule which will provide the greatest benefits on your investment. To give you an idea of the alternatives available, here's a schedule of depreciation possibilities:

With straight-line depreciation, you can deduct 1/30 of the cost each year: $100,000. Thus, if you invested $30,000 of a $300,000 down payment to get a 10% share of the building, you can deduct $10,000 a year from your tax return.

With double-declining depreciation, the rate is doubled and, in each succeeding year, that rate is applied against the remaining undepreciated cost of the building—e.g., *in Year 1,* the depreciation is 1/15th or $200,000, with your share at $20,000; *in Year 2,* the cost basis is $2.8 million, so the 1/15 deduction is $186,667 with $18,667 your share. Your total deductions are 25% more than the original investment; *in Year 3,* the cost basis is $2,613,334 and depreciation is $174,222, with $17,422 your share, etc. Note that the big write-off comes early so the deductions soon dwindle. And, as noted earlier with Moonglow Apartments, a sale can be very costly.

Guidelines for Real Estate Syndicates

1. Deal only with reliable, capable, reputable syndicators. Check bank references, standing with the local Chamber of Commerce, real estate board and past clients. Beware of anyone who tells you he's never had a loser. An average of 80% success is tops.

2. Review the agreement with an experienced real estate lawyer and/or accountant, not your faithful family retainer.

Many syndicates are headed by shrewd, aggressive operators who take advantage of every legal loophole and tax dodge. There may be clauses in the contract and related documents of which you are unaware or which you do not fully understand. In the end, these may cost you money or tie up your funds. Part ownership of a lease is worth much less than equivalent ownership in the leased property.

3. Never judge any syndication on its tax shelter potential. If there are no profits, you will be shelling out hard-earned dollars for little or no gain. You are making an investment. The tax benefits should be secondary.

4. Worry about what you will make, not how much the syndicator will take out. You are buying brains, so you will have to pay well for top results.

For your own profits, a rule of thumb is to try to make cash flow, tax shelter and equity buildup add up to 3% more than the current mortgage loan rate: 18% for residential and office properties and 20% for motels, bowling alleys, etc.

5. The more of his own money the syndicator puts up, the better the project. He is likely to work harder when he stands to gain.

6. The higher the percentage of the first mortgage, the better the operation. Some financial firm must have confidence in the project to put up so much money. Besides, the leverage is higher.

7. The longer the mortgage, the greater the leverage. You want a mortgage that runs well beyond the time you expect to put the property on the market—at least ten years, with no earlier call.

8. Never invest cash you may need in the next five to ten years. If you take out your money before that time, you may have to accept a loss and miss some tax benefits. Real estate is always a long-term proposition for investors.

9. Be skeptical of all appraisals. As one veteran SEC official comments, "Appraisers are independent only if they're not getting paid by those asking for the appraisal." If you are making the investment on your own, arrange for two separate appraisals.

On the average, a fair purchase price will be four times annual rent for office buildings, ten times annual cash production for apartments and nine times rent for a shopping center. But these figures assume solid, regularly-paying tenants, so always allow leeway for delinquency and for lower rentals if there's a chance of competition or overbuilding.

10. Be wary of projections of future value. If you buy at the right price and manage the property well, the ultimate value will be greater if there is no deterioration of the neighborhood or no unusual developments such as new highways, devastating fires, etc.

11. Check the track record of the promoter/builder with banks and mortgage lenders. If possible, get audited statements of operations of apartment houses and commercial buildings. Prospectuses may distort occupancy rates or fudge on gross profits.

12. Beware of promoters who call themselves investment advisers. These are the types who run a computerized analysis of your financial condition and then recommend that you "put some of your money in stocks, bonds and insurance and 50% in tax-sheltered holdings such as real estate"—and then casually mention some deal they happen to know of.

In an effort to beat competition, some real estate syndicates have extended their scope of financing to include specific businesses. They offer a package deal to acquire the land, erect the building and operate the project (bowling alley, motel, parking garage, country club, marina, etc.). The yields may be higher but the risks are greater.

It takes expertise to manage most businesses successfully—not just money.

Making Money with Real Estate

Most real estate provides two sources of profit: appreciation and depreciation. In the right location, property becomes more valuable; with proper structuring of the financing, there are tax deductions for interest on the mortgage, depreciation, investment tax credits and operating expenses.

These have been summarized in past editions of *Your Investments* but I felt that there was need to spell out the profit potential and tax consequences in greater detail. Here's an example based on a single-family house built in 1980, *before* the revised tax law. The projections were made by Gary Sellari, CPA. If you understand this, you can analyze proposals of limited partnerships and syndicates in all types of real estate.

Basic data: Dr. Pill, in the 50% tax bracket. Properly zoned lot in stable residential area. *House:* 3 bedrooms, 2 baths, with landscaping. *Mortgage:* 80% at 13% for 29 years. *Anticipated rate of appreciation:* 10% annually.

Table A shows the rounded-out figures. In other parts of the country, the costs and profits would have been similar but the gains probably not as rapid as in fast-growing south Florida.

The land cost $20,000: $10,000 cash plus a non-interest-bearing note to be paid from the proceeds of the mortgage. The house and landscaping cost $65,000. Add $2,000 for the sales commission on the land purchase and $3,000 for closing costs for a total of $90,000. But the property was appraised at $100,000, so the mortgage, at 80%, totaled $80,000. In effect, the good doctor had an immediate paper profit of $10,000.

The house was built for profit so, to qualify for favorable tax treatment on the capital gains from the sale, had to be held for 12 months. It was rented, unfurnished, for $700. The monthly outgo, for taxes and mortgage payments, was about $1,000, so the annual cash deficit was $3,600, fully tax deductible.

There were also tax deductions of $14,520: interest of $10,400; real estate taxes of about $1,320 and depreciation of $2,800. In Dr. Pill's 50% tax bracket, this meant net "savings" of $7,260 on that $10,000 investment. These are deductible from his earned income. At the sale, the depreciation must be recouped for tax purposes. In effect, this represents a tax-free loan from Uncle Sam.

The depreciation is conservative: $2,800 a year based on a straight-line calculation of 4%, for 25 years, of the $70,000 building value. The land is not depreciable.

TABLE A
BREAKDOWN OF BUILDING SINGLE FAMILY HOME

Land		$20,000*
House & Landscaping		65,000
Sales commission on land:	10%	2,000
Closing costs		3,000
Total tax cost basis		$90,000
Mark-up		10,000
Valuation base		$100,000
LESS:		
Mortgage		80,000
Repayment*		10,000
Original investment		10,000

* $10,000 cash and $10,000 non-interest-bearing note repaid from the mortgage proceeds.

TABLE B
BUILDING SINGLE FAMILY HOUSE: APPRECIATION + TAX BENEFITS

Single family house: valuation, $100,000; cost basis for tax purposes, $90,000. Annual appreciation: +10%; monthly rental, $700. Mortgage: $80,000; 29 years @ 13%.

When Sale is Made	After 1 year	After 5 years
Sales price	$110,000	$161,000
Less: commission	7,700	11,200
Gross receipts	102,300	149,800
Less: Mortgage repayment	79,718	78,240
Cash proceeds	22,582	71,560
LESS: Operating loss	3,600	18,000
Original investment	10,000	10,000
Net return before tax consequences	8,982	43,560

TAX CONSEQUENCES (Schedule D):
Capital Gains portion. TAXABLE

	After 1 year	After 5 years
Gross receipts	102,300	149,800
Less: cost basis	90,000	90,000
Depreciation: straight line at 4% a year	2,800	14,000
Tax basis	87,200	76,000
Gain on sale	15,100	73,300
Less: capital gains tax-20%	3,020	14,760
Net cash gain	$11,980	$58,540

TAX CONSEQUENCES (Schedule E):
Ordinary Tax portion. Deductible from earned income

	After 1 year	After 5 years
Depreciation: straight line @ 4% a year	2,800	14,000
Operating loss	3,600	18,000
Total	6,400	32,000
Tax savings @ 50% rate	3,200	16,000

RECAPTURE OF RETURN

	After 1 year	After 5 years
Cash before tax consequences	8,982	43,560
Less: capital gains tax	(3,030)	(14,760)
Net cash receipts	5,962	28,800
Plus tax savings	3,200	16,000
Dollar return on investment	$9,162	$44,800
Annual rate of return	91.6%	89.6%

SOURCE: Gary Sellari of Divine, Blalock & Martin, West Palm Beach, Fla.

It's also possible to use other methods to get higher depreciation benefits:

• *200% declining balance* where the annual rate is 8% of the undepreciated value: $5,600 in Year I, $5,112 in Year II because the value would be reduced to $64,400. And so on.

• *Component depreciation.* The house, with a 25-year life, would be depreciated at 4%; but the roof, appliances, air conditioner, etc., which can be expected to wear out in, say, ten years, at 10% annually.

Now we get into the complicated-to-the-amateur area: tax consequences. To calculate these for rental properties, the IRS has two forms: Schedule D for the capital gains portion; Schedule E for the items deductible from earned income. The return on investment is the sum of these: Table B.

At the end of the first year, a sale will bring $110,000. From this, deduct the $7,700 sales commission and the mortgage repayment of $79,718 for cash proceeds of $22,582. The operating loss was $3,600 and the cash investment $10,000 so the net return, before tax consequences, is $8,982.

Under Schedule D, the net price is $102,300: the cost basis is $90,000 (Table A); the annual depreciation, $2,800; so the tax basis is $87,200 and the profit is $15,100. The capital gains tax at 20% (40% of the profits at the 50% tax rate) is $3,020 so the net dollar proceeds are $11,980.

Schedule E shows the deductions against ordinary income: $2,800 depreciation plus operating loss of $3,600 for a total of $6,400. Taxwise, this reduces the tax base by $3,200.

In summary: from the $8,982 net return before tax consequences, a capital gains tax of $3,020 was paid to bring the net cash proceeds to $5,962. But the tax savings were $3,200 so the dollar return on investment was $9,162: an annual rate of return of 91.6%.

If the property is held for five years, it may be sold for $161,000, assuming that 10% annual rate of appreciation. Now the dollar return is $44,800 or an average annual rate of 89.6%. These are minimal in that they do not project a higher rental or interest on deposits for the first and last months' rent and clean-up costs.

These conditions do not provide for delays, cost overruns, delinquent payments or unexpected expenses but they provide the framework for judging, and profiting from, income-producing real estate.

For Mortgages: Income, Not Cost

With mortgaged property, forget about the cost of building. Lenders are more interested in income. For loan purposes, property is capitalized on the basis of assured income of $1,000 divided by the yield and then multiplied by the total income. A few years ago, when interest rates were not so high, a friend of mine got a $1.25 million loan on a property that yielded 8% a year: $1,000 divided by 8 equals $1,250 times $100,000 income equals $1.25 million.

Once in a while, with a successful project, the investor can mortgage out—get a new loan that will cover total cost.

Example: Mr. Burns built an apartment house for $185,000 (with the help of a construction loan from the local bank). Because of its design, location, and rental rates, the apartment house was an instant success and showed an annual income of $45,000. This was enough to get a $193,000 loan from an insurance company. Mr.

Burns "mortgaged out" (although he did not recover the $27,000 cost of the land, which by now was worth much more).

Two years later, the rents were raised and the mortgage refinanced for $278,000. *Result:* Mr. Burns had an income of $8,000 a year to infinity.

Rate of Appreciation

To compute the annual compound rate of appreciation of your real estate investment, start with the years column, estimate the appreciation factor with the help of your agent or, if it's a major holding, a professional appraiser, and then locate the potential return: for example, a 12-year-old property with an appreciation factor of 3.1% means an annual rate of return of 16%. Or to put it another way, if you want a 10% return on a 12-year-old property, look for a 5.9% rate of appreciation.

| Years | | | | | | |
| 4 | 6 | 8 | 10 | 12 | 15 | Rate of |
		Appreciation Factor				Return
1.3	1.4	1.6	1.8	2.0	2.4	6%
1.4	1.6	1.9	2.2	2.5	3.2	8
1.5	1.8	2.1	2.6	3.1	4.2	10
1.6	2.0	2.5	3.1	3.9	5.5	12
1.7	2.2	2.9	3.7	4.8	7.1	14
1.8	2.4	3.3	4.4	5.9	9.3	16

New Rules for Installment Sales

Under the old law, when a property was sold for 30% or less down, the balance could be deferred until the principal payments were received over the life of the contract. Now, the seller can receive as much as he wants as a down payment in the year of the sale and defer the balance. Other changes *(a)* eliminate the requirement that there must be two or more payments spread out over two years; *(b)* approve contingency sales (selling a shopping center on the base of future earnings); and *(c)* OK a third-party guarantee of payment.

Investing in Raw Land

This is one of the best investments for long-term capital gains, but to a greater degree than with most real estate, it is more important to know how to get *out* than to get *in*. For the land to become more valuable, someone must be willing and ready to make use of it. Always think ahead 3, 5, or even 10 years (if you're wealthy and patient) to project the possible future for the property.

Typically, a raw land purchase is financed by a commercial bank. But you should always try to get the owner to carry the mortgage. Do not assume that the seller wants only cash; many older farmers prefer to have an assured lifetime income and may even settle for a specific monthly payment with little heed to the interest rate.

Be slow to improve the land in a way which will make it easier to sell or develop. The IRS may consider you a developer, and then the ultimate profit could be taxed as ordinary income.

Raw land, whether pasture, forest, field or farm, should:

• *Be in the path of progress:* near highways, not far from other housing or commercial developments or recreation areas.

• *Be available with considerable leverage:* not more than 30% down payment and, hopefully, with a mortgage whereby only interest is due for a few years and there's no penalty for prepayment.

• *Have a potential of a minimum rise in value of 50% in 3 years, 100% in 5 years.* A somewhat lower target may be acceptable if there is assured income from rentals to a farmer, an outdoor group or a camping club.

• *Have annual carrying charges (taxes, interest and maintenance) of no more than 15% of your cost.* Inflation will help but you cannot wait too long as taxes will rise.

• *Be developable at a reasonable price.* It may sound exciting to join with friends in buying 100 acres of woodland with the idea of splitting the land into homesites, but unless you build your dream cabin, be cautious. You will tie up cash, can seldom get a bank loan, will have to pay a high commission when you sell and land values may not rise as rapidly as you anticipate.

Working farms are excellent investments if you do not pay too much and you have a competent tenant or manager. Be prepared to become personally involved if only to understand what must be done to operate profitably.

Unless you are experienced and have ample time, do not try to run an investment farm yourself. Uncle Sam insists that, to permit tax deductions, there must be a profit in at least two of the first five years. Otherwise, the IRS may classify the operation as a hobby and thus eliminate tax benefits.

Real Estate Investment Trusts (REITs)

These are similar to closed-end investment companies in that their shares are not redeemable upon request but are traded like regular stocks so that their prices reflect supply and demand. These trusts sell shares to the public and invest the proceeds in real estate, usually in mortgages and construction loans and, occasionally, raw land.

Until 1974 REITs were among the most rewarding investments. They provided a means for the small investor to participate in the ownership of real estate. Many REITs yielded 10% or more and were backed by prestigious bank holding companies and insurance firms.

But as so often happens with Wall Street's new darlings, the bright rewards of REITs were tarnished by the realities of a competitive world: high interest rate, slumping construction, loan defaults, fraud, and poor management.

Starting around 1977, REITs, as a group, became a disaster. Most of them were reorganized with horrendous losses to investors and sponsors: Loans were written off or stretched out (often without interest); properties were auctioned off at a fraction of cost; buildings were turned over to anyone who could finish them; and banks made swaps that enabled the funds to continue to operate. The worst is past and, for a while when the market was rising, the value of some shares went up. But not for long. When the market fell, REITs led the parade.

At long last, *some* REITS are becoming worthwhile investments. They own, or are involved in, properties that are increasing in value and new commitments are being made at high interest rates and with participation in profits.

Always check: (1) The underlying properties as to location, type, terms of loans, record of payments by the debtors and, if possible, realistic valuation. If 20% of the portfolio is in default or paying low interest rates, skip it. (2) The amount of money that goes for equity. These days, long-term debt is seldom profitable for the lender. What you want is a trust that puts your money into equity positions and uses OPM for leverage. One of the best-managed REITs, Koger Partnership, puts 90% of receipts into equity; McNeil IX, only 64%.

Common Mistakes in Real Estate Investing

Successful real estate investments depend a great deal on the cost of borrowed money. If you have, or can get, a low-interest loan, you are always sure to profit. But if you have to pay over 16%, there must be substantial appreciation to make the deal worthwhile. More than almost any other type of investment, real estate requires skill, experience, knowledge and patience.

But good properties, of all types, can be excellent hedges against inflation and, when properly financed and managed, can assure high total returns with the tax benefits. Perhaps the best counsel for those who want to make money with real estate is negative: to list some *Don'ts* as digested from the experience of a working-in-the-business author, George Bockl. He has never found a way to pyramid $1,000 into $1 million!

Don't buy problems, such as buildings in need of repair or tenanted by eccentric or unreasonable people.

Don't get into any deal that you cannot control. You can get fleeced as a small partner in a big deal. Start with property that you can manage or monitor yourself.

Don't invest in commercial property at the outset. Apartments are safer and steadier. You can understand what's happening and will not have to contend with the volatility of business/professional tenants.

Don't pay all cash. Leverage is the key to successful real estate. Borrow judiciously and, when possible, for the long term.

Don't let ambition override common sense. When you listen to applause instead of costs, you get into trouble.

Don't overpay. Investing in real estate is a cautious game. Stop, look and listen and re-examine the facts, figures and projections. When you fall in love with a property, you may be buying luxury rather than profits.

Don't accept unreasonable terms. Make sure that every investment can show a profit, after expenses and taxes, of at least 15% and can have reasonable expectations of annual appreciation of 10%.

Don't invest outside your community in the beginning. Chances of success decreases with distance.

Don't invest in downtown property unless it's cheap, you have an unusual idea or there is confirmed redevelopment. When property is run down, it can take years for a comeback—no matter what you may read in magazines or "How I Made $20 Million in Real Estate" books.

CHAPTER 32

Taxes Are Not *That* Important in Investing

Tax savings are the most profitable kind of income available to investors because they are *net after taxes*. But it is seldom wise to sell a stock solely for tax purposes, nor is it sensible to postpone a sale in order to postpone a tax unless you expect to die within a year or two.

There are few areas of investment on which advice is so abundant, so confusing and so inaccurate as tax selling. Yet, all that's needed is some common sense and the ability to make simple arithmetic calculations.

Tax benefits, for most individuals, are limited. Broadly speaking, the tax savings of losses are greater than those of gains. But the objective of investing is to *make,* not *lose,* money.

Too many people worry too much about taxes. They try to minimize their capital gains tax payments by:

1. Letting assets decline in value so that they can reduce or eliminate taxability when the eventual sale is made. NOTHING COULD BE MORE FOOLISH. Why should any intelligent investor deliberately strive to lose $1,000 in gains to save $100 or so in taxes?

2. Waiting until death so that their estate gets the stocks at their current values and the heirs can use these prices as a base for future taxes. Once in a while, this approach makes sense, but to be truly beneficial, the security holdings must be substantial.

3. Giving away securities and the tax burden with them. The wisdom of such action depends on the financial affluence and needs of the present owner. Usually, this is most beneficial when the owner is still working and in a high tax bracket. Unfortunately, however, most people do not consider such action until they are retired—when their taxes, and benefits, are far less.

If you have sufficient assets to make a sizable gift but you still need income, find out about trusts set up by hospitals, universities and other tax-exempt and ever-needy institutions. You can arrange for lifetime income to yourself and your spouse, for the principal to be used by the institution after your death—and you still take tax deductions while you live.

Don't Wait Until Year End

Tax selling and switching should *not* be solely a year-end affair. Action should be taken whenever advantageous and should *always* be secondary to investment considerations. Unfortunately, most people delay thinking about taxes until near the end of the year because they are not sure of their net capital position or whether their gains, or losses, are long- or short-term. It is wiser, easier and more rewarding to keep running records that will enable you to approximate your tax position.

Losses on securities transactions are always tax deductible with the amount determined by the length of the holding period and your tax bracket. Short-term losses are fully deductible (to a maximum of $3,000 a year under present laws) and any surplus can be carried over to future years. *But you cannot skip a year and still use the tax loss.* Long-term losses get only one-half the benefit. In all situations, the higher your tax rate, the greater the benefit of tax losses. But do not get carried away with tax-loss selling. Its real results are often less than anticipated.

When you review your portfolio quarterly, make marginal notes on the taxes due on gains or credits possible with losses. If you are planning to upgrade your holdings, weigh the desirability of taking some short-term gains and losses simultaneously so that you can realize some of the gains without taxes.

When you check your portfolio toward year-end, preferably with your tax adviser, watch the timing in selling to take gains or losses. To establish a gain, you must have the proceeds in hand on the last business day of the year. It takes five days to clear, so in 1982 the deadline is Friday, December 24. To establish a loss, you can trade through Friday, December 31.

You can nail down a gain as late as December 30 with a "next day" sale that is settled on the following business day, December 31. Or you can get in under the wire with a "cash" sale on December 31 as settlement will be made the same day.

It's also important to be aware of state tax laws and how they affect your investment decisions. In Connecticut, for example, the capital-gains tax does not allow for carry-forward losses. The investor who lives in Hartford might find it worthwhile to delay year-end selling, for a loss, until January.

Watch Out for Wash Sales

Losses from wash sales or exchanges of securities are not deductible on your federal income tax. Gains are taxable.

A *wash sale* is a sale for a capital loss where you buy the "same or substantially identical" securities within 30 days *before* or *after* the loss sale. That means a span of 61 days. The rules do not apply to securities acquired through gift, inheritance or tax-free exchange.

"Substantially identical" means just that: a common

stock, option or voting certificate representing that stock are considered the same. Voting stock and nonvoting stock paying the same dividend and selling at about the same price are *not* the same. Nor are two or more series of bonds of the same corporation with different coupon rates or maturity dates, nor a stock and a related warrant nor a call on a security.

These are the tax consequences of a *wash sale:*

1. The disallowed loss is *added* to your purchase price for the new securities to establish the base for determining a gain or loss on the future sale of these securities.

2. The holding period (over 12 months for long-term tax benefits) for the repurchased securities is extended to include that for the original securities.

Example: You buy 100 shares of International Eye Chart (IEC) at 40 on July 1. By October 15, the stock has dropped to 30, so you sell for what you believe is a tax loss of $1,000, as an offset against realized capital gains.

By November 1 (less than 30 days after the October sale), the price of IEC is down to 25. You feel that the stock is a good buy and likely to move up again soon. If you buy, your anticipated tax loss of $1,000 will be disallowed.

Warning: The wash-sale rule applies to call options, too. You cannot take a tax loss in a security and maintain your position in the stock by buying calls. The IRS will clamp down and disallow the tax loss if an option on that stock is bought within 30 days before or after the date of the stock sale.

To avoid wash-sale penalties: (1) Buy the stock of an equally good company in the same industry. (2) Buy an equivalent number of shares of the same security, then hold both blocks for 31 days to establish a loss on your original holdings. This requires additional capital and there's no way to know whether the future price will mean an even greater loss.

When a Wash-Sale Repurchase May Be Advantageous

Sometimes, it pays to accept the penalties of a disallowed wash sale. This happens when a security drops appreciably in price between the date of sale and the date of repurchase and then moves up sharply.

If IEC bounced up to 40 after you bought it at 25, your $1,500 paper profit would more than outweigh the loss of the $1,000 tax benefit.

Similarly, the longer holding period for the new purchase (including the original holding period) could also be favorable. It might enable your profit to qualify for the lower long-term capital gains tax rate. In the previous example, had you delayed your repurchase until November 16 (31 days after your sale on October 15), your new purchase would not become long term until mid May the next year. But by making a wash sale repurchase on November 1, you throw back the start of the holding period to July 1, so you can take your long-term profit (if any) in January.

The IRS frowns on losses between related parties:

members of the same family, controlled corporations, trusts, etc. However, if the property is later sold by the original transferee, the amount of any gain will be taxed only on the amount this exceeds the loss previously disallowed. *Example:* if you sold stock that cost $10,000 to your brother for $7,600, the $2,400 loss is not deductible. But if your brother sold the stock for $10,500, his taxable gain is only $500 because the $2,400 loss offsets the $2,900 gain. If your brother sold the stock at a loss, he could deduct only his own loss.

The IRS wants no trick deals, such as the husband making the sale and the wife buying the same stock within 30 days. *The only solace:* when the securities or property are subsequently sold for a capital gain by the family member who acquired them, only that portion of the gain in excess of the disallowed loss will be taxable.

Tax Treatment of Commissions/Costs

The commissions paid your broker and the fees and taxes on securities transactions can be used to cut your taxes. IRS considers the buying commission a part of your original cost and the selling expenses a deduction from the net proceeds.

Example: You bought 100 shares of a stock at 20 and sold them at 19¼: a dollar loss of $75. But, for income tax purposes, the loss would be considerably greater.

Assuming a buying commission of $45.14 and 80¢ in fees, your cost would be $2,045.94, not $2,000. Your selling proceeds would not be $1,925 but $1,876.42 because of the deductions for $43.99 in commissions, state tax of $3.75 and transfer fee of 84¢. Thus, on your tax return you could deduct $169.52, not just $75.

Tax Treatment of Gains and Losses

Under current law, *long-term* applies to property held over 12 months; *short-term* involves property sold within one year of purchase.

• Short-term gains are subject to the full income tax rate.

• Short-term losses can be deducted, dollar for dollar, against ordinary income which includes short-term gains. *Example:* At year-end you have a paper loss of $4,000 on one holding and an already realized short-term gain of $2,000 on another. If you sell the loss stock before the 12-month date, you can use $2,000 of that loss to offset the short-term gain. This results in a net short-term loss of $2,000, fully deductible against ordinary income.

• With long-term capital gains, only 60% of the profits are taxed. Thus the maximum tax rate for those in the highest (50%) tax bracket is 20%: 40% of 50%. For most people, the tax rate is much lower: 16% for those in the 40% tax bracket: 40% of 40%.

• Long-term losses are always deductible: *against ordinary income* on a 2 for 1 basis (i.e. every $2 loss offsets $1 of income to an annual limit of $3,000, and excess can be carried over); *against long-term gains* on a dollar-for-dollar basis.

Always separate your results into short-term and long-term categories and then offset them for the greatest tax benefits.

Try to Shift Gains from Short to Long Term

When your investments turn from losses to gains, a basic rule is to let short-term gains ride to become favorably taxed long-term ones *if* they cannot be used to offset short-term losses. In such cases, the tax advantages of holding beyond 12 months must be carefully weighed against the chance that your gains may disappear while you wait.

Each situation is specific and different. Taxwise, the higher your tax bracket, the greater the spread between the ordinary income tax rate and the capital gains tax rate and thus the larger the savings from letting short-term gains become long term.

Conversely, the potential gain can be considered the cost of eliminating the market risk in holding on to the security for more than one year. If you take your short-term gain, you are sure of a profit. But you also have to review the tax considerations.

Timing is also important. If you have a week or less to wait for the 12 months' limit, hang on unless it's an extremely erratic market. But a lot can happen in a couple of months. Just be sure the potential tax savings are worth the added risk!

New Tax Breaks

Recently, Uncle Sam added new tax benefits:

Exclusion of interest/dividends. Starting in 1982, this applies only to dividends, not interest, and is $100 per individual, $200 per couple.

But watch out. There are limits. The excluded amount of taxable interest may be treated by the IRS like exempt interest, under the rule that bars deductions on interest on loans used to invest in tax-exempt securities.

Example: Art May holds a taxable corporate bond in a margin account. The interest paid on that bond qualifies for the exclusion. But if Art takes the exclusion, he will not be able to deduct the interest paid on his margin account.

And when borrowed money is used to buy a CD, the tax consequences can be complex and disappointing.

Example: Marge Noppel buys a $10,000, 6-month CD with $5,000 cash and a $5,000 loan from her neighborhood savings bank. The CD rate is 12%; the loan rate 13%. At maturity, the return on the $5,000 cash investment is $275.

Under IRS rules, Marge will have to report interest income of $600 on the full CD. She can exclude $400 (assuming a joint tax return and no other interest/dividends). She will pay $325 interest to the bank but is allowed to deduct only one-third of that amount: $108. This is because the other two-thirds of the interest was paid for the production of excludable interest income. And if she fails to itemize that $108, she won't be able to deduct any portion of the $325 interest before the new law!

Inherited property. Here the tax base is the value at

date of death, not the original cost. This is important for property that has appreciated substantially since acquisition, often many years ago when records were not kept. Now the heirs pay a tax only on the increased value of the assets between the date of death and the final settlement of the estate.

Example: Uncle Fred paid $10,000 for stock that was worth $150,000 at his death. His will gives the shares to Nephew Ned who sells the shares for $200,000. Ned pays a capital gains tax on only $50,000.

Deciding to Sell to Increase Yield

If you want to decide whether to sell a stock to increase your yield with another holding, use this formula. It takes into consideration the tax to be paid.

$$SY = \frac{HY}{1 - TP}$$

SY = Switch Yield (on new security)
HY = Hold Yield (on present security)
TP = Tax-bite Percentage

Example: You purchased a stock at 20 and it is now selling at 100 and paying a $5 annual dividend. On the $80 profit, the tax, at the long-term capital-gains rate, might be 20% or $16 per share. To justify a switch for income only, you would have to get a stock paying 6% or more:

$$SY = \frac{5}{1 - .16} = \frac{5}{.84} = 5.95\%$$

Tax Savings with Gifts and Trusts

Tax savings are possible by having income on investments go to individuals who pay no or low taxes: typically, young children or older relatives.

Usually, these involve gifts under a trust, custodian account or the Uniform Gifts to Minors. This is a complex subject so consult a tax-wise lawyer first.

To give you an idea of the possible benefits, here's what happens when Bill McCormick gives $10,000 to his seven-year-old daughter (as there will be a gift tax when the annual gift exceeds $10,000). The money is invested to yield 12%: $1,200 a year. The daughter pays no tax because of a $1,000 personal exemption and the $200 dividend/interest exclusion ($100 starting in 1982).

Be careful: If the income is reinvested, the compounding will soon boost the income so that the daughter will have to pay income taxes, starting at a low 14% rate.

Note, too, that starting in 1982, the law that required that gifts made within three years be automatically included in the gross estate has been rescinded. Now, this provision applies only to certain types of gifts—namely, insurance policies going to the children or their trust. Be sure to consult your attorney for latest interpretations.

Basic Tax Factors in Deciding When and What to Sell, Switch or Rebuy

The two big questions on tax selling are *always:*

Am I using my investment funds to maximum advantage today?

Will my plans bring maximum returns from my investments tomorrow?

The price you pay for the security has little to do with the answers to these questions. The important thing in successful investing is TOMORROW.

It is discouraging when you have a severe loss in the price of a stock, but this gloom can be dispelled if the stock has the ability to recover its previous value and, hopefully, move up even more. If there is no realistic probability for a worthwhile advance, stop dreaming and *sell.*

Suppose you paid $1,000 for 100 shares of Sexy Electronics. It is now quoted at 5, might possibly get up to 7 in a bull market, but has little hope of hitting 10 for a long time. You will be better off to take your $500 loss as a tax offset and reinvest the balance (with some added savings) in a stock that has higher quality and greater promise.

Always take losses promptly when the prospects of the company are not good. As is stressed throughout this guide, the first loss is almost always the cheapest. More investors lose more money more often by holding stocks in an effort to justify their original judgment than in any other way. Forget about pride. Sell and put the proceeds into more rewarding situations.

The Case Against Frequent Profit-taking

Never be in a hurry to take profits. The stocks most likely to continue to move up are those which have been rising for some time. This does not mean that you should hold a stock when it becomes vastly overpriced. It does mean that you should not be too anxious to sell and reinvest. People who sell frequently usually lose money in the long run because:

1. Selling and switching to "salt down" profits takes attention away from investment objectives.

If you take profits on your successful holdings and retain the less profitable ones, your portfolio is sure to show quality deterioration. In the long run, this will hinder your ability to reach your investment goals.

2. The capital-gains tax on realized profits leads to erosion of capital.

When you buy any security/property, you have a silent partner, Uncle Sam. He wants a cut of your profits. As a result, your after-sales assets will be less.

Example: You bought Tailwagger, Inc., for $8,000 and, a year later, sold it for a net-after-commission $10,000. You are pleased· with the $2,000 profit but you will have to pay a capital-gains tax of, say, $200 plus a commission of about $200 on the new investment. This leaves a net of $9,600, 4% less than the worth of the shares before the sale.

Furthermore, you now have to find a new investment

that will appreciate at least $400 more than the sold securities.

Some people avoid such decisions by buying growth stocks and never selling. This will prove profitable if you live long enough. But far greater profits can be made by timing your investments: buying when a quality stock is undervalued, and selling when it becomes fully priced.

The Case for Periodic Profit-taking

Proponents of this view argue that you will come out ahead in the long run by taking profits periodically rather than by holding on indefinitely. Here is the reasoning:

1. You usually cannot achieve your investment objectives without periodic selling. This includes taking both profits and losses.

When you buy stocks, you are seeking maximum profits on your money. You should not be concerned with maintaining any particular portfolio of securities no matter how carefully selected. The performance, the profits and the prospects of all companies change. To achieve maximum investment results, your portfolio must be changed frequently, eliminating weaker securities (hopefully at a profit) and adding stronger equities.

By setting a specific time period (preferably 12 months to take advantage of the lower taxes on capital gains, but more frequently if you are a trader), you force yourself to make decisions.

2. Periodic profit-taking benefits from stock market swings.

You can take advantage of both the wide bull/bear market swings of 50% or more and the smaller, intermediate shifts of 20% to 30%. Periodic profit-taking forces you to study how you can gain from these gyrations. When you hold good growth stocks through a long bear market, you will miss the best buying opportunities. *Successful investing, unless for the long term, is never a static process.*

3. New buying opportunities when you take a profit.

At all times, there are some stocks that are relatively undervalued or some groups that are performing better than the averages, especially in rising markets and, often, in bear markets.

By periodic changes in your portfolio, you will catch some of these winners. Usually, of course, it's best to go slow and hold your savings in liquid assets such as Treasury bills, high-quality bonds or money market funds until you spot real bargains.

4. Once a stock reaches a target range, its advance is likely to slow. Postponing capital gains taxes at this point may cost you more than you save because your profits on other investments could be greater. When a stock becomes overpriced by your standards, *sell.* The risk of decline is greater than the potential gain.

5. Normal price swings can offset gains.

On the average, a stock will fluctuate 20%–25% a year. It's true that the higher the price of the stock sold, the greater the depletion of savings due to tax and commission costs. But too many people pay too much attention to the tax bite and neglect the gain. They hold stocks with ample profits too long. When a decline sets in—and this is almost inevitable in the stock market—their profits are reduced.

Repeat: Only for the wealthy should taxes ever be the major factor in the retention of any stock which has increased in value.

6. You never escape capital gains tax erosion by holding a stock indefinitely—unless you hold an appreciated asset until death or give it to an approved charitable, educational or other nonprofit organization. You merely postpone it.

The younger you are, the less likely you are to hold any stock until death. Only when you are old and/or retired is there any logical possibility of passing the tax burden to someone else. *Do not let tax considerations influence your investment decisions until you are over 75,* says one tax authority! Well, maybe he is exaggerating a bit.

7. Payment of a capital gains tax on the sale of securities results in a higher tax basis on your new securities. As a result, your *future* tax liability is correspondingly reduced. From a tax standpoint, it is often better to pay a relatively small capital gains tax frequently rather than a larger tax at one time—you will have a lower average rate.

Summary: Possible price erosion is more of a danger than the certain tax erosion. In borderline cases where it is difficult to make an accurate future projection, you will generally fare better by paying rather than by postponing the taxes or avoiding them while watching gains disappear.

One rote solution: When you review your portfolio, plan to weed out at least one weak holding, and over the year expect to sell 20% of your securities and reinvest the proceeds in stocks which are doing well or in new growth/income opportunities.

Deductible Investment-related Expenses

Subscriptions to investment advisory services, financial publications and investment books

Stock transfer taxes

Custodian fees to banks, mutual funds, and investment managers of income-producing property

Accounting and auditing expenses for income-producing property

Investment counsel and management fees

Legal fees in connection with investments

Fees for preparing tax returns

Interest on margin accounts

Office expenses in connection with investments: clerical salaries and home office if used exclusively for money management

With short sales: dividends paid to buyers, and premiums for borrowed stock

Trustees' fees

Rental of a safe-deposit box used for investment records

Commissions to brokers on the sale of property

No deductions for interest to buy or carry tax-exempt securities

Keeping Records

Record-keeping is an all-year chore. Always file the information slips of security transactions or receipts of real estate deals. This will make it easier to compile your annual tax returns and, more important, you will have proof if you should receive an audit notice from the IRS questioning purchases or sales made two or three years ago.

The burden of proof is on the taxpayer. You may be lucky enough to have a broker who retains records, but it's almost impossible for a brokerage firm to locate old confirmation slips.

Lack of documentation can also be costly if a company has to make payments to stockholders of a certain date as the result of legal decisions. Even if you have sold the securities since, you are entitled to payment if you can prove ownership.

To minimize trouble at tax time because your securities sales and purchases aren't in one place:

• Keep all purchase slips in one pile, bound by a rubber band.

• When you sell, pull out the corresponding purchase slip, staple the two together and place in a separate file.

• With stock splits/dividends, record data on the original slip.

• When you sell less than the block of shares you bought—say, 200 shares of a 500 share purchase—leave the original sales slip in the purchase file but mark it with data on the sale: date, receipts and whether gain or loss was short or long term.

• Keep a running log of all transactions with date, price, cost, etc. Your broker will give you a printed form.

CHAPTER 33

Swinging Speculations: Commodities/Collectibles

There is nothing wrong in speculation. In most cases it is risky and should involve only money that you can afford to lose. But it offers opportunities to build capital quickly and, under certain conditions, can be used conservatively to hedge and sell short. Everyone who invests in anything should understand speculative holdings and, on occasion, make use of these special situations.

Success with speculations requires the same research and projections as are the key to profitable investments. You must be able to spot situations where the rewards are greater than the risks. With the odds in your favor, and the use of leverage, you can achieve excellent profits, usually quickly. With investments, patience is essential. The longer you wait, the more probable, and ample, your gains. With speculations, profits should come fast because in most cases your money is not providing income and probably is diminishing due to costs of interest and commissions.

This chapter concentrates on "swinging" investments such as commodities, metals and foreign currencies, and reviews "collectibles"—which, in my view, are better for pleasure than profit. Because of their special conditions, financial futures are discussed separately.

Basically, these speculations are dominated by professionals. But the techniques are easily grasped and can be utilized by anyone who will take time to learn the ground rules, understand what's happening and do his or her homework. To be successful, it is important to keep abreast of developments, act only when the opportunities for gains are substantially greater than the possibility of losses and to seek and heed expert counsel.

Speculating in Commodities

Commodity trading is for speculators who are tough-skinned, strong-minded and willing to take risks. This is one of the few remaining areas where an individual with small capital can strike it rich, but, according to one study, 75% of commodities speculators lose money. Moreover, their aggregate losses were six times as great as their gains! Even the best speculators lose more often than they win, but by keeping their losses small and piling up their profits, they make out very well.

Profits in the commodities markets can be quick and large. In eight months, one speculator made a $28,300 profit on a $1,500 investment when the price of soybeans soared from $4.54 to $12.90 per bushel. That $1,500 was all that was needed to buy a 5,000-bushel, $12,500 contract for future delivery.

The cash requirements for all commodities trading are low: 5% to 10%, varying according to the commodity and to the broker's standards. But when there is extreme speculation, those margins can be raised far and fast. There are no interest payments on the balance. Roughly, commissions average about $35 per round trip.

The lures of fast action, minimal capital and high potential profits are enticing but before you start trading corn, wheat, soybeans, silver or any other commodity, heed these warnings from professionals:

• The odds are against making a profit on any one trade. You have to make a hit big enough to offset the losses. Only a handful of amateurs last more than three years. The rest are broke.

• Emotional stability is essential. You have to be able to control your sense of fear and greed and train yourself to accept losses without too great a strain. Until a few years ago, some brokerage firms refused to accept female customers!

• Be ready to risk at least $10,000: $5,000 at once, the rest to back up margin calls.

Commodity trading is different from investing in stocks. When you buy a common stock, you own part of the corporation and share in its profits, if any. If you pick a profitable company, the price of your stock will eventually move up.

With commodities there is no equity. You buy only hope. Once the futures contract has expired, there's no tomorrow. If your trade turned out badly, you must take the full loss.

The economic reason for a futures market is hedging (that is, removing or reducing the risk of a commitment by taking an offsetting one). A farmer who borrows money to plant a 10,000-bushel soybean crop may be asked by his banker to sell two futures contracts (5,000 bushels each) for December delivery. This contract calls for a fixed price, say $5.30 per bushel. If the December price is $5.00, the farmer loses 30¢ per bushel in the cash market, but makes up the loss by buying back his futures contracts for less than he paid. The opposite happens when the December price rises. Either way, the farmer is assured of a return of $5.30 per bushel so that he can repay his bank loan and probably turn a profit, too.

On the other hand, a food processor who sells his products throughout the year wants a predetermined cost for his soybean purchases. He buys futures in the appropriate forward month. If the price rises, he pays more in the cash market but profits when he sells the futures contract.

In both cases there must be someone to take the opposite side of the transaction. That's the role of the speculator. He assumes the risk because he thinks he can buy or sell the contract at a profit before the delivery date.

Here's what might happen: the hedger, who needs soybeans for processing in December, buys (goes long on) one 5,000-bushel soybean contract:

June 4: Buy one December soybean contract $5.30		$26,500
Dec. 6: Sell one December soybean contract $5.00		25,000
	Loss	$ 1,500
	Commission	45
	Total Loss	$ 1,545

The farmer who owns soybeans will sell short:

June 4: Sell one December soybean contract $5.30		$26,500
Dec. 6: Buy one December soybean contract $5.00		25,000
	Profit	$ 1,500
	Commission	45
	Total Profit	$ 1,455

Note: In the spring, January soybeans moved from about $5.10 a bushel to $6.90 in less than six weeks. For some speculators this was very profitable because that $1.80 move was worth $9,000 per contract on a margin of about $2,000!

Because the buyers and sellers seldom match, the speculator moves in to take the opposite side of the contract. He holds the long contract as long as prices are rising (up to delivery date) and cuts his losses by selling fast when the market declines. Vice versa for the short sale. In almost every case, he takes action long before the contract becomes due. That's the excitement and profit opportunity of trading in commodities!

Advice for the Novice

1. Read a good book about commodity trading. Your broker can provide you with a folder from his firm or the commodity exchanges. Or study the books listed in the Bibliography. Then decide if you have the stomach and the funds to start speculating.

2. Get current information. There is no inside information about commodities. All statistics are available in Government reports, business publications and newsletters. Study several of these and then review your conclusions with your broker. You will have to become something of an expert in both the fundamental and technical aspects of a few commodities.

3. Choose an experienced broker. Deal only with a reputable firm that *(a)* has extensive commodities trading services, and *(b)* includes a broker who knows speculation and can guide you.

4. Zero in on a few commodities, preferably those in the news. Staples such as corn, wheat and hogs always have strong markets, but the best speculative profits can be made in the active groups, recently natural resources such as metals and petroleum.

5. Avoid thin markets. You can score when such a commodity takes off but the swings can be too fast and may send prices soaring, or plummeting, so that the amateur can get caught with no chance of closing a position.

6. Look for a ratio of net profit to net loss of 2:1. Since the percentage of losses will always be greater than that of profits, choose commodities where the potential gains (based on confirmed trends) can be more than double the possible losses. When you make such projections, include commission costs as they can be a major factor when dealing in small units and small price shifts.

7. Prepare an operational plan. Before you turn over any cash, test your hypotheses on paper until you feel confident. Set up a game plan like this:

On that soybean contract, a 3% rise will mean about a 16¢-per-bushel gain: from $5.30 to $5.46. If you are right and the contract can be sold at that target price, your profit will be $1,500 minus $45 commission for a net profit of $1,455 on a $1,500 margin.

Now assume that you are wrong and the market drops 3% to $5.14 per bushel. With every 5¢ decline, you will have to increase your margin by $150, so your invested capital will jump to $1,650. At $5.14 per bushel, your loss will be $800 plus the commission, and you will have to come up with even more margin.

Most traders prefer to let their profits run: up when long, down when short. They also set real (not mental) stop-loss prices and take a small loss, then shoot for big profits later.

8. Never meet a margin call. When your original

margin is impaired by 25%, your broker will call for more money. Except in the most unusual circumstances, do not send in more money. Liquidate your position and accept your loss.

This is a form of stop-loss safeguard. When a declining trend has been established, further losses can be expected.

9. If you are not sure, don't. Never get carried away by the unreal world of paper. You may be watching tapes, reading reports or plotting charts, but you are doing business with *real money*. If there is *any* question in your mind about the future of the price of a commodity, do not buy or maintain a position. It is far better to miss a few profit opportunities through caution than to throw away money in reckless speculations. To be a successful commodities trader, *you gotta believe.*

10. Be alert to special situations. Information is the key to profitable speculation. As you become more knowledgeable, you will pick up many pointers, such as:

• If there's heavy spring-summer rain in Maine, buy long on potatoes. They need ideal weather.

• If there's a bad tornado over large portions of the Great Plains, buy wheat contracts. Chances are the wheat crop will be damaged, thus changing the supply/demand.

There are, of course, many other factors to analyze before reaching any final decision. As with everything involving the profit potential of money, knowledge plus luck are important.

11. Devote time to learning how the markets work and why prices move as they do. You should know why economic recovery in Europe means higher soybean prices in Chicago and why higher soybean prices can pick up the price of silver in New York.

12. Trade with the major trend, against the minor trend. With copper, for example, if you project a worldwide shortage of the metal and the market is in an uptrend, buy futures when the market suffers temporary weak spells. As long as prices keep moving up, you want to accumulate a meaningful position.

Corollary to this, never average down. Adding to your loss position increases the number of contracts that are returning a loss. By buying more, you put yourself in a stance where you can lose on more contracts if the price continues to drop.

Generally, if the trend is down, either sell short or stay out of the market. And never (well, hardly ever) buy a commodity after it has passed its seasonal high or sell a commodity after it has passed its seasonal low.

13. Watch the spreads between different delivery dates. In the strong summer market, the premium for January soybeans is 8¢ per bushel above the November contract. Buy November and sell January.

If the bull market persists, the premium should disappear and you will have a pleasant, limited profit. Carrying charges on soybeans run about 6½¢ per month, so it is not likely that the spread will widen to more than 13¢ per bushel. Thus, with that 8¢ spread, the real risk is not more than 5¢ per bushel.

14. Do not take a position unless your profit objective is at least 8 to 10 times your commissions. Newcomers are intrigued with the idea that every day they will skillfully dip into the market and remove money. To do this, they must be right 60% of the time in order to cover the loss trades and hefty commissions. That means DO NOT DAY TRADE.

15. If you cannot afford to lose, you cannot afford to win. If you are not in a position to accept losses, either psychologically or financially, you have no business speculating.

16. Margin requirements are irrelevant to profit and loss objectives. Margin is not a cost, a purchase price, a measure of value or of available capital. It's a security deposit and nothing more.

N.B.: Some of these comments are repetitive . . . on purpose.

Commodities Mutual Funds

These are the latest Wall Street "pitch" to let the little man gain the profits hitherto possible only for the wealthy. For as little as $5,000, you can buy participations in a diversified portfolio managed by professionals that have tripled client assets over the past decade.

The pitch proclaims: "Smart money goes where the profits are. In the past decade, a $100,000 portfolio in a conservatively managed commodities trading account has risen to over $500,000. Every active investor should have a portion of his assets in commodities. The rewards are high and, by tested techniques, losses are limited and profits can run."

Maybe so—but let's examine how these new funds operate.

These funds are an outgrowth of "managed accounts" for wealthy individuals. They are similar to mutual funds in that brokerage firms sell "shares" (actually limited partnership interests) to the public, generally in five $1,000 units. The proceeds are pooled to buy, or sell, futures contracts in some 15–18 of the most active, most profit-promising contracts.

Management is handled by a team of professionals who operate under proven-successful systems that automatically trigger sales and signal buying points. They are speculations and, usually, the fund is structured so that it will be closed out when 50% of the original capital is wiped out.

Participations can be bought and sold (with 15 days' notice) at the end of each reporting period, monthly or quarterly. If you need money in a hurry, you will have to sell at a loss if the market is down at the time. There are no dividends, only capital gains or losses. These are short-term and taxable, to the individual, at regular Federal income tax rates.

While the exact terms will vary, the proposals appear likely to call for:

• Limitation of sales to individuals who have a net worth (exclusive of home, furnishings, and automobiles) of: *(a)* $50,000 or *(b)* $20,000 and an annual income of $20,000.

• No sales load. All of your dollars are used to trade in commodities.

• Commissions 20% to 25% below the regular rates charged to most individual customers.

• Payments to the registered representative of 15% to 25% of total commission on a proportionate basis—e.g., for a $5 million fund, the broker who sells 5 units ($5,000) will get 1/10 of 1%. This sounds small but, over a year, will be substantial. An extreme example is one fund that reported adjusted brokerage fees of $203,385 on fund assets of $7.2 million in three months!

That was just a starter. In addition (and this is typical), the management group receives 20% of net profits plus 1% of net monthly assets if the net assets exceed 3.2% of fund assets *plus* interest on the investment of cash reserves in Treasury bills.

The single biggest advantage of commodities funds is their staying power. They have sufficient resources to keep going despite interim losses . . . usually. But they can go broke, too—as did two funds managed by ContiCommodity, a subsidiary of Continental Grain.

Never forget that these are speculations. The managers are trading against each other in a series of paper transactions. *By no stretch of the definition can they be considered investors!*

Fund Management

Here's the approach to management outlined by a veteran trader/adviser, Richard D. Donchian of Shearson/American Express:

"I'm a trend follower. I believe that a trend, in either direction, once established, has a strong tendency to persist. With commodities trading, one of the best indicators is a Moving Average (MA). This is a progressive average in which the closing price of a commodity is added and then divided by the time span. Each day the price of the last sale is added to the accumulated total and the earliest figure dropped. Thus, with a 20-day MA, you total the closing prices for the past 20 days and divide it by 20 to get the base data. On Day 21, you drop Day 1 price and add that of Day 21.

"The value of the MA is that, experience shows, no commodity can stage an uptrend without its price moving above the MA as the result of more buying than selling. Vice versa on the downside.

"When the closing price of a commodity crosses the MA by an amount exceeding a predetermined amount of the maximum penetration in the same direction in any one day, no matter how long ago this occurred, we act: buying when the breakthrough is up, selling when it's down. Unlike the stock market where stocks tend to move in a group, each commodity develops its own pattern."

Donchian also considers fundamentals such as the outlook for crops, damage due to drought or storms, unusual demands for metals, shifts in government support policies, changes in the interest rate, and so on. This managed approach accomplishes two essential goals:

Limited losses because positions must be closed out at definite points. Over the years, this has kept losses low.

Unlimited profits. Whenever there's a sustained move, this method captures, as profit, a large slice of the middle of the move. As long as the move continues without a valid crossing of the MA in the opposite direction, positions are maintained. Purchases are not made at the bottom nor sales at the top.

Adds Donchian, "This system has worked well for two decades, with, of course, improvements based on experience. Only rarely has it been necessary to cover margin calls and, on confirmed upswings, we can make additions quickly for extra gains."

One of his proforma portfolios started with $16,000 and grew to over $500,000 rather quickly. In most cases, the profits were in a few positions: one year, over $25,000 each in soybeans and soybean meal; in coffee in another, etc.

But in the last year or so, losses have outpaced gains and total assets have fluctuated within a narrow range. But, as with all speculations, hope springs eternal . . . especially with the registered representatives.

Caveat: Watch the tax angle. These funds are limited partnerships, so your share of realized gains and losses will be passed along directly to your tax return. Most gains and losses are short-term so taxed at ordinary rates or with limited deductibility. For the individual, the important factor is the period of holding. One fund finished the year with $1.8 million in unrealized profits (so no benefits) and $1 million in realized losses (tax deductible). And there are changes under the 1981 tax law.

Commodities Options

These are agreements to purchase the commodity at a specified price on a specified date. As with stock options, the buyer pays a premium to the party granting the option. There's no margin, so the most the buyer can lose is the premium. The seller accepts a modest gain rather than a possibly higher profit and takes the risk that the value of the contract will not drop too far.

Agricultural commodity options are illegal in the U.S. Metal options can be sold only by a handful of recognized dealers.

Since the major market for commodities options is London, there are extra problems in currency conversion and profit retrieval. When an American buys a London option, the broker must convert dollars into British pounds, and back again into dollars if there's a profit. That's expensive.

Anyone who buys commodities options is dealing in pipe dreams. Unlike stock options, there is no actual delivery. The risks are very high and the rewards may be great on rare occasions, but 90% of the deals fail.

According to government estimates, con men take $100 million a year with commodities scams. When contracts come due, the company vanishes or files for alleged bankruptcy. In most cases, the operators walk away when the commodity price drops and fail to pay when it rises. *Never buy any commodities option over the phone; never send any money without a signed contract; and always make sure you are dealing with a representative of an established British firm.*

Speculating in Foreign Currency

The fluctuations of foreign currency and the opening of the International Monetary Market Division (IMM) of the Chicago Mercantile Exchange provide unusual speculative opportunities. Just as with commodities futures, speculators perform an essential function by taking opposite sides of contracts bought or sold by corporations and financial institutions to hedge their monetary-risk exposure around the world. Unlike other types of commodity trading, currency futures reflect reactions to what has already happened rather than anticipation of what's ahead.

For small margins of 1.5% to 4.2%, roughly $1,500 to $2,500, you can control large sums of money: 100,000 Canadian dollars; 125,000 deutsche marks; 12.5 million Japanese yen, etc.

The attraction is leverage. You can speculate that at a fixed date in the future the value of your contract will be greater (if you buy long) or less (if you sell short).

The daily fluctuations of each currency futures contract are limited by IMM rules. A rise of $750 per day provides a 37.5% profit on a $2,000 investment. That's a net gain of $705 ($750 less $45 in commissions). If the value declines, you are faced with a wipe-out or, if you set a stop order, the loss of part of your security deposit. Vice versa when you sell short.

The IMM provides a formal marketplace for hedging currencies of other nations as they relate to U.S. dollars. Importers, exporters and multinational firms rely on forward contracts to protect their profits. They are willing to pay to reduce their foreign exchange risks.

The speculator takes the opposite side of the deal or he can use spreads between the values of major currencies. Stanley W. Angrist gives this example in *Forbes:*

The deutsche mark is quoted at $.5016 and the British pound at $1.9045. Each mark contract calls for 125,000 marks, the pound contract for 25,000 pounds. To get the dollar difference, multiply and subtract: (125,000 × $.5016) minus (25,000 × $1.9045) gives $15,087. Since the trader believes that the mark is more stable than the pound, he buys the mark and sells the pound.

In a few months, when the spread widens to $18,000, he closes out the deal, pays a round-trip commission of $150 and takes his profit.

Warning: The IMM is a thin market. The speculator may not be able to get out when he wants at the price he expects. On a one-day trade (and there have been many), the value of the currency can still fluctuate. All the speculator can do is watch helplessly and *hope.*

Rules for Successful Currency Speculation

Maintain a reserve. If the market moves against you, you may have to cover as much as your original margin deposit. If you set aside $5,000 for speculation, keep $1,500 in reserve. Better yet, set stop-loss orders and keep your capital.

Become familiar with the world economic scene. You should understand and follow regularly export-import imbalances, tariff changes, fluctuating interest rates, inflation interest rates, inflation, etc., in the U.S. and in the nations whose currencies you hold.

Don't "day-trade." This means getting in and out of a position in one trading day. That's second-guessing and no game for the amateur. Chances are you will always be one step ahead or one step behind. *Exception:* if the price moves adversely, get out fast.

Don't sit on losses. Sour trades seldom sweeten. A drop of a few cents (or a rise if you're short) in this highly leveraged market can be costly. Set stop limits and hope you can get out in time.

Don't open a discretionary account. Your broker may know more than you do about currency, but it's unfair to put pressure on him to make all the decisions. You can heed his suggestions *but it's your money!*

Concentrate on limited supply currencies, such as the Swiss franc. There are only $50 billion available compared to $500 billion Eurodollars. It takes little to move the Swiss currency up or down.

For information, send $15 for IMM's home-study course on foreign exchange: International Monetary Market, 444 West Jackson Boulevard, Chicago, Ill. 60606.

Gold: Poor Investment; Great Speculation

To millions of people, gold is the finest form of tangible wealth. It is a symbol of security that protects the individual against inflation, confiscation of income through taxes, and worldwide threats of war and revolution. They enjoy the thrill and comfort of owning the precious metal as bullion or coins and boast of the profits from its ever-rising value. In the six years since January 1975 when it could first be bought by Americans, gold rose from $197.50 to over $870 per ounce.

That's a huge gain, far above that of the stock market average or of fixed-income holdings. But there was no income and many quality stocks did better . . . with far fewer risks and fluctuations.

By definition, gold is not an investment but it can be an excellent speculation. If you bought at the low and sold at the high, you might have stayed a step ahead of inflation. You would always have done better by owning shares of high-dividend-paying gold mining stocks or with shares of American and Canadian gold mining companies.

Figure it out for yourself. In early 1975, gold was selling at $197.50 per ounce. This was the peak for almost three years. Gold did not reach $243 until October 1978. After a year of seesawing it skyrocketed to over $800 per ounce. Then, as had happened before, the price fell sharply and, with short spurts, stayed around $580 per ounce. At best, the investor tripled his money.

With gold-mining stocks, he could have counted on steady income from dividends of from 10% to 20% a year. With compounding, that meant average annual rates of return of 12% to 30% plus capital gains from 25% to 50% depending on the stocks selected.

Over the same six years, the investor in Petrolane, Inc., a diversified oil/gas/retail firm, watched his money grow more than 18-fold. If he bought 100 shares in January 1975, he paid $800. By reinvesting the dividends in additional shares and after two 2–1 splits, he owned some 596 shares worth over $12,000!

The best profits with gold come from speculating: buying low and selling high; selling short and buying back at the next low; and so on. The trader made a lot of money: selling short in January 1975 at $197, covering his position in August 1976 at $104, holding until January 1977 to sell at $174; buying in 1978 to benefit from the surge from about $200 to $800; selling short and covering at around $500. Over the six years, he might have made 30 trades and increased his capital 25 times IF he was smart and lucky.

If you do succumb to gold fever, here are the general choices:

1. Companies listed on major stock exchanges. Most of these are large, relatively stable U.S. and Canadian corporations with other mineral assets. They provide full, detailed reports to stockholders and their shares can be bought and sold easily.

2. Holding companies. *ASA Limited,* a closed-end investment company with some 70% of its assets in South African gold mining shares; *Anglo-American Corporation,* the largest mining finance firm and the number one producer of both gold and diamonds; *Anglo-American Investment Company,* with holdings in a number of gold mines. With all of these, you are buying the equivalent of shares in a mutual fund.

3. Gold certificates. These are certificates which represent ownership of a specific portion of bullion stores in a Swiss bank. There's no U.S. bank account, no sales tax and no report to IRS.

The sales price includes fees for insurance and storage plus commissions, which run from 3% to 1% depending on quantity. The certificates are not negotiable or assignable, so they must be sold back to the dealer.

4. Gold futures contracts. These give the speculator the biggest bang for the buck. Similar to contracts for commodities, they can be handled by most brokers and are actively traded on the New York Commodity Exchange and the International Monetary Market in Chicago.

You can buy and sell 100-ounce contracts with different future delivery dates on margins of 5% to 15%. Thus, with gold at $500 an ounce, each contract is worth $50,000 and can be leveraged with about $5,000. Be sure that you have ample collateral; gold prices can move fast, and when they go down, you must come up with more cash or securities or your position will be sold out at the end of the day. Most brokers ask for a minimum balance of $10,000.

It's wise to set target prices. You can let your profits run, but, to protect your holdings, give the broker a stop-loss price: either at the price at which additional margin will be needed or at the average price of the last 30 trading days. Thus, if you bought a contract when gold was $500 an ounce and used a 10% margin, the sell price would be $450 if you are conservative. As the price of the metal moves up, boost the stop-loss accordingly.

Even stops may not protect you. Commodity traders try to knock off those stops late in the afternoon—e.g., when the price of gold drops below $455, the professionals, knowing that amateurs have set stops at $450, will go short. This will drop the price again so that the trader may be able to buy back his contracts at about $440. He makes a quick profit and you're out of luck ... and money.

In bull markets, trading in gold futures can be very profitable. A 5-point move is not unusual, and with a little patience you can pick up a 10-point move.

5. Gold coins (non-numismatic). These are special coins minted only to take advantage of the gold craze. The major forms are:

Krugerrands: South African coins in four sizes ac-
cording to the gold content: 1 oz., ½ oz., ¼ oz. and ¹⁄₁₀ oz. The sales pitch is that you can check the daily value of your holdings in the press or from radio/TV reports.

Because of coinage and distribution costs, Krugerrands sell at a 5% to 8% premium over gold. Local sales taxes can add another 8%. Before you buy these "golden opportunities," do your homework and calculate how much you can lose. The loss will be tax deductible but as Barnum proved ...

U.S. Medallions: in ½ and 1 oz. units. There's no sales tax and you can buy only three units of each kind per year. It takes five weeks for delivery; the weight and fineness are not marked; the cost is about 2% above the New York "spot" price; and there's no major market for resale.

Franklin Mint Medallions: similar to the U.S. ones with a price that is about 30% above the gold value.

Foreign coins: such as Canadian Maple Leafs, Mexican pesos, Austrian coronas. You will pay a modest premium but there's an active after-market.

With all but U.S. medallions, transactions can be anonymous. Sellers rarely put down the buyer's name on the sales slip and if the transaction is for less than $10,000, there are no reports to the IRS.

6. Gold Options. These give you the right to buy gold at a set price before a set date. They are speculations that involve leverage. If you guess right, you can do well.

Example: In January 1981, gold was selling at $562 an ounce and the trend was up. Charlie Davis puts up $4,000 to buy 10 options (at $400 each) to buy gold at $600 an ounce at any time through March. He controls 1,000 ounces of gold.

Charlie is right. By March, the price of gold jumps to $610 an ounce. Each option is now worth $1,000 so he owns $10,000 for a gross profit of $6,000: a 150% return on his investment.

But if the price of gold had risen only slightly, Charlie would have lost a little. If it had declined, he could have lost the full $4,000.

7. Installment Buying. These are billed as "sure-fire" systems. They require consistent investing with the goal of building substantial holdings. You buy bullion on the installment plan. It is stored abroad or in a state where there are no taxes.

New York's Citibank sets an initial minimum of $1,000 with additions in units of $100. There's a 3% load and a 1% fee on the sale.

Merrill Lynch's Sharebuilder Gold Plan requires a basic $100 with additions in units of $50. The gold is purchased at $1 an ounce above the London price.

Usually, there are two types of contracts:

Unit price averaging: where the investor agrees to buy a fixed amount of gold regularly: paying less when the price is low; more when high.

Cost averaging: investing a fixed sum at periodic intervals: buying more when the price is low, less when high.

Rules for Buying Gold

Here are some caveats suggested by Paul Sarnoff, Director of Research, Rudolf Wolff Commodity Brokers:

• Never commit more than half your money at risk. If you have $50,000, use only $25,000. Put the balance in money market funds for quick retrieval.

• Limit the possible loss to 25% of the total account.

• In trading, stay flexible and alert.

• Paper trade for at least one month before you commit any dollars. Make decisions, calculate margins, set stop-loss prices, etc.

• Check three commodities firms and read all their bulletins and reports.

• Use charts to check price movements and trends.

• Never give discretionary powers to anyone.

Petroleum Futures

These have been around for some time but, with ever-rising prices and temporary shortages, have become one of the most popular trading vehicles. They meet an essential need by establishing a mechanism to be used by professional sellers and buyers to be sure of firm future prices through hedging.

As with all futures contracts, the original margins are low: 10% with a $1,500 minimum. That means that if the price of the contract rises 20%, the speculator (who takes the opposite side of what may be a professional's contract) will double his money. But if the price falls 30%, the speculator may be wiped out. Trading is on the New York Mercantile Exchange.

The base contract for petroleum futures is 42,000 U.S. gallons (1,000 U.S. barrels) of No. 2 heating oil or No. 6 industrial fuel oil with delivery at the Port of New York. (To get the dollar equivalent, multiply 42 by the quoted-in-the-press price: at 75¢ per gallon, it's $31.50 per barrel.) Contracts are sold for delivery in the months of January, February, March, May, July, September, November, and December.

Under exchange rules, the minimum daily price fluctuation is .01¢ per gallon ($4.20 per contract) to a maximum of 1¢ per gallon ($420 per contract). The margin can be put up in cash or collateral such as a letter of credit or Treasury bills (up to 90% of market value). When you use bills, you can apply the interest against the cost.

In the market itself, the moving force is the professional. Let's say that, in June, the purchasing agent of Smith Manufacturing Co. (SMC) is asked to order 10,000 barrels of No. 2 heating oil for December delivery at the current market price of 75¢ per gallon. If he buys now, he will have to put up $75,000 (the normal 10% margin), arrange for storage of the heating oil that was purchased and pay interest on the money.

Instead, SMC buys 10 December futures contracts at 87.25¢ per gallon (the 25¢ is added for all futures and the 12¢ reflects the costs of storage and financing). This requires a cash outlay of $8,725.

In December, with another price boost by OPEC, the cash price of No. 2 oil is 85¢ per gallon. The purchasing agent buys 10,000 gallons for $85,000. This is $10,000 more than budgeted but he sells his futures contracts for the same price. The small loss, $2,250, represents his insurance premium.

Role of Speculator

The speculator gets into the act in June when he thinks that, before December, there will be an oversupply so that the price of the oil will drop a bit. He sells short 10 Decembers futures contracts at $75.25 each. That means he does not own the oil but merely agrees to make delivery in December. That's no fee, no interest.

The speculator is right. In October, the price of the oil dips, so he buys back his contracts at 70.25¢ per gallon and chalks up a $5,000 gross profit on a margin of $7,250—in five months.

If he guesses wrong and the price of oil goes up, he will have to cover his position at a loss and hope for a bigger profit on his next deal.

When he becomes experienced and has the aid of a knowledgeable, computer-savvy broker, the venturesome speculator can use hedges of his own to protect some of his holdings. Or he can take advantage of unusual spreads between current and future prices: as much as 33¢ per gallon: 65¢ in the cash market and 98¢ in the six-months futures market. If he sells the 98¢ contract short and the spread narrows, he can buy back at a lower price for a profit. Or when the spread is narrow, he can buy long on one contract and sell short on the other.

But he should always remember that 80% of all futures contracts end up with a loss! You must make a big hit to win.

Collectibles

Many people, alarmed at inflation, prefer to own something tangible: diamonds, art, antiques, stamps and so forth. If you enjoy these, great, but *never consider them as worthwhile investments.* The costs are high: 15% or more on each side of a transaction. That means 30% plus taxes if you sell for a profit. It is true that the values of many of these items have risen sharply in recent years but you get no income and if you have to sell in a hurry, you will never get a fair price.

To illustrate the potential profits and real perils, let's discuss diamonds. Their values have soared: for a one-carat quality stone in 1976: $6,700; 1977: $7,700; 1978: $18,000; 1979: $22,000; 1980: $50,000; 1981: down to $44,000.

Diamonds may be forever but there's no money until they are sold. Then, your profit depends on the size of the dealer's commission. You are always buying at retail and selling at wholesale.

The best bet is to buy several small stones rather than one big one. You can sell one gem easily. But remember that the sale price will be far less than the quoted value!

As with all collectibles bought for "investment," make sure that you deal with a reliable organization, insist on double certification (by the dealer and, with diamonds, the Gemological Institute of America, 580 Fifth Avenue, New York, N.Y. 10036) and when you buy or sell, make certain that the certificate matches the stone.

As is to be expected, Wall Street has not let this fad pass by. Thomson McKinnon has a Diamond Trust. This is similar to a Municipal Bond Fund in that it has a fixed capitalization. The professional manager puts 95% of the proceeds in diamonds and the balance in gold. He buys only the top 25 grades. The entry fee is $1,000 minus an 8% sales load. There is a market for resale and, according to the prospectus, the trust will be liquidated: 25% each in 1984, 1986 and 1988 and terminated in 1990.

CHAPTER 34

Financial Futures: Playing the Interest Rate Game

In the past few years, the unprecedented swings in interest rates have exposed businesses and financial institutions to severe risks. To protect themselves from these hard-to-predict fluctuations, professional money managers, with strong support from Wall Street, have developed the financial futures market. Its growth has been explosive: from a handful of contracts in Ginnie Mae passthroughs in 1975 to over 90 million contracts dealing in Treasury bills, notes and bonds; commercial paper; certificates of deposit; bankers' acceptances, etc. Contracts are traded on half a dozen exchanges and are a major force in the financial world.

Basically, these financial futures are a new form of the commodities contracts widely used with wheat, corn, copper and other foods and metals. They are standardized packages of debt securities whose prices move with interest rates: up when the cost of money falls; down when it rises.

In familiar-to-the-investor terms, here's the situation: A bank buys a 20-year, 8% Treasury bond at issue, for $1,000. When the interest rate rises to 12%, the value of the bond drops to about 66 ($660). Similarly, if the cost of money should decline to 7%, that bond would sell at around 112 ($1,120). At maturity, the bond would be worth 100 ($1,000) again. But, meantime, the banker has problems. If he needs extra funds in a hurry, he must sell at a loss. As a businessman, he would prefer to have stable, predictable assets. That's where hedging—and the financial futures market—comes in. It enables the money manager to take positions in the futures market to protect positions in the cash market. When the cost of money changes, the loss in the cash market is offset by a profit in the futures market. And vice versa.

In each position, someone has to take the opposite side of the contract. This may be a speculator seeking a quick profit by buying or selling short according to his view of the cost of money in the days or months ahead.

For full comments, read the chapter on swinging speculations. Repetition is worthwhile because, for the individual investor/speculator, all types of futures markets are little more than gambling. It's a professional "game" where only 20% of all transactions are profitable. True, the profits can be big and fast but the losses can be bigger and faster. As one conscientious commodity trader warns, "You can make enough money in a morning to send your kids to college. But, in the afternoon, you can lose enough to have to sell your house."

When you guess right (and don't let anyone kid you that success is based solely on skill), you can do well, but all futures are a zero-sum game: for every winner there's a loser. In the stock market, at least, you will usually be moving with the majority. If the market goes up, nearly everyone wins. If it goes down, nearly everyone loses.

As the table shows, all contracts are pretty much the same but there are variations in the value, daily price limits and margin requirements. Here are two examples of how financial futures have been used for hedging:

Long hedge. In the spring, a portfolio manager expected an inflow of $1 million later in the year. He planned to invest the money in 5-year, 8% Treasury notes to yield 9.01% but he feared a drop in the rate of return.

To lock in his position, he bought 10 futures contracts at $100,000 each for 95 16/32nds ($95,500). He put up $10,000 in margin: $1,000 per contract.

By September, interest rates dropped, as he expected, so the price of the notes rose to 99 16/32nds ($99,500). He chalked up a $40,000 profit ($4,000 per contract).

In October, when the $1 million in cash came in, the price of the notes was up to 100. Now he had to pay $1 million but his actual cost was $960,000 since he had a $40,000 gain in the futures market. Thus, the yield on the 8% notes was the targeted 9.01%.

Short hedge. In mid fall, a bond dealer contracted to sell bonds held in his inventory to a permanent investor. The interest rates would rise so that his holding would be worth less than their current 99 8/32nds for a yield of 8.18%. He sold 10 futures contracts at 98 24/32nds ($980,750).

Three weeks later, interest rates were up so the dealer bought back the contracts at 93 24/32nds ($930,750) for a $50,000 profit, enough to offset the loss in the value of the inventory bonds.

Mr. Speculator could also profit. In the first example, if he bought in anticipation of a drop in the cost of money, he would make the $40,000 profit. In the second example, if he looked for a rise in interest rates, he sold short and covered his position for a $50,000 gain.

In both cases, if interest rates moved opposite to his guess, Mr. Speculator would have lost money. But he would not have waited until the expiration of the con-

FINANCIAL FUTURES

Type/Description	Maturities	Trading Unit	How Quoted	Price Limits	Typical Margin
U.S. Treasury Bills	3 months 6 months	$1,000,000	100 minus annualized discount	1/100 of 1% or $25 per contract	$1,000
	12 months	350,000	i.e. at 12%, 1 year contract at 88; 3 months: 25% below face value		600
Commercial Paper	30 days	3,000,000	Indexed basis; same as T-Bills	1/100th of 1% or $25 per contract	1,500
	90 days	1,000,000	Same	Same	1,500
Ginnie Maes	Vary	100,000	As % of par based on interest rate: i.e. on 8% coupon	1/32 or $31.25 per contract	1,500
U.S. Treasury Notes	4-6 years	100,000	As % of par	1/32 or $31.25 per contract	900
U.S. Treasury Bonds	Long-Term	100,000	As % of par	1/32 or $31.25 per contract	2,000

N.B. Terms vary according to exchange on which futures are traded

SOURCE: Chicago Board of Trade

---

tracts. Knowing that 75% of all trades result in a loss, he would have taken a quick, small loss, probably by means of a stop order.

There are similar opportunities with Ginnie Mae (Government National Mortgage Association) certificates representing a portfolio of FHA and VA mortgages and commercial paper.

With all of these financial futures, don't let the daily price limits fool you. They do set the maximum change, up or down, at $625 to $2,000 per contract, but in an active market, those small shifts can add up. Here's how margins work:

On Monday, you buy a $1 million, 90-day Treasury bill futures contract yielding 15% with a $1,000 margin (more than required by the exchange but probably the minimum set by your broker). Since these are quoted at a discount, the contract cost is 85 (100% minus 15%). Each rise or fall of 1 basis point equals $25: 1/100th of 1% times $1 million divided by 4 (¼-year maturity, since these are 90-day bills).

In a week or so, the yield on T-bills rises 10 basis points to 15.10% so the price of the contract falls to 84.85. The loss is $250: 10 basis points times $25. Immediately, you must add $250 to your margin.

Next day, the yield goes back to 15% so the price of the contract is the original 85. Now your margin account is $1,000 and the extra $250 goes into your reserve.

After the Saturday Night Special (October 6, 1979) when the Federal Reserve Board boosted the discount rate a full point (from 11% to 12%), the value of government securities alone fell $50 billion. Speculators had to come up with millions of dollars almost overnight or be sold out. This was a dramatic move but it points up the risks of trading in financial futures.

Usually, trading involves going long or short but it's possible to use spreads: buying one contract month and selling another. This technique is used when there's an abnormal relationship between the yields and, thus, the prices of two contracts with different maturities. The speculator hopes to profit when a normal relationship is

restored. Here's an example cited by a physician friend:

In January, Dr. Smart notices that futures of Treasury bonds, for June delivery, are selling at 80 11/32nds (each 1/32nd of 1% equals $31.25 of a standard

---

HOW FINANCIAL FUTURES ARE QUOTED

GNMA 8% (CBT)—$100,000 prncpl; pts., 32nds of 100%

	Open	High	Low	Settle	Chg	Yield Settle	Chg	Open Interest
Mar	67-25	68-00	67-21	67-28	+ 16	13.632	− .118	1,558
June	68-07	68-16	68-01	68-10	+ 16	13.530	− .117	11,313
Sept	68-18	68-24	68-08	68-18	+ 15	13.472	− .109	8,706
Dec	68-22	68-30	68-17	68-23	+ 14	13.436	− .101	8,309
Mar82	68-29	68-29	68-18	68-26	+ 14	13.415	− .101	11,959
June	68-25	68-30	68-18	68-25	+ 14	13.422	− .101	15,680
Sept	68-15	68-26	68-15	68-23	+ 14	13.436	− .101	15,898
Dec	68-20	68-20	68-15	68-20	+ 14	13.458	− .101	9,821
Mar83	68-20	68-23	68-12	68-17	+ 14	13.479	− .102	4,873
June	68-16	69-14	68-09	68-14	+ 14	13.501	− .102	3,270
Sept	68-08	68-11	68-06	68-11	+ 14	13.523	− .102	2,651

Est vol 7,500; vol Thu 4,662; open int 94,307, −105.

TREASURY BONDS (CBT)—$100,000; pts. 32nds of 100%

	Open	High	Low	Settle	Chg	Yield Settle	Chg	Open Interest
Mar	67-21	68-03	67-18	68-02	+ 30	12.335	− .176	5,877
June	68-14	68-30	68-11	68-28	+ 28	12.186	− .161	52,191
Sept	69-01	69-16	68-28	69-14	+ 27	12.084	− .153	23,834
Dec	69-05	69-25	69-05	69-22	+ 26	12.039	− .147	21,875
Mar82	69-19	69-27	69-14	69-27	+ 25	12.011	− .141	22,801
June	69-24	69-31	69-19	69-31	+ 25	11.989	− .140	27,515
Sept	69-26	70-01	69-22	70-01	+ 25	11.978	− .140	23,655
Dec	69-31	70-03	69-21	70-03	+ 25	11.967	− .139	23,026
Mar83	70-01	70-05	69-26	70-05	+ 25	11.956	− .139	13,862
June	70-01	70-07	69-29	70-07	+ 25	11.945	− .139	7,430
Sept	70-03	70-09	69-31	70-09	+ 25	11.934	− .139	3,683
Dec	70-07	70-11	70-01	70-11	+ 25	11.923	− .139	80

Est vol 45,000; vol Thu 37,589; open int 225,829, +2,022.

TREASURY BONDS (NYFE)—$100,000; pts. 32nds of 100

	Open	High	Low	Settle	Chg	Yield Settle	Chg	Open Interest
May	75-05	75-21	75-05	75-21	+ 31	12.302	− .167	769
Aug	75-31	76-03	75-27	76-03	+ 29	12.222	− .155	247
Nov	76-08	76-08	76-04	76-11	+ 28	12.180	− .149	330
Fb82	....	....	....	76-17	+ 28	12.149	− .143	437
May	....	....	....	76-19	+ 27	12.138	− .143	812
Aug	....	....	....	76-21	+ 26	12.128	− .137	602
Nov	....	....	....	76-23	+ 25	12.118	− .131	315
Fb83	....	....	....	76-25	+ 24	12.107	− .126	1

Est vol 890; vol Thu 1,232; open int 3,513, +24.

TREASURY BILLS (IMM)—$1 mil.; pts. of 100%

	Open	High	Low	Settle	Chg	Discount Settle	Chg	Open Interest
Mar	86.71	86.84	86.63	86.81	+ .39	13.19	− .39	5,181
June	88.68	88.87	88.63	88.84	+ .38	11.16	− .38	19,943
Sept	89.35	89.40	89.21	89.38	+ .26	10.62	− .26	6,123
Dec	89.47	89.50	89.35	89.47	+ .20	10.53	− .20	4,321
Mr82	89.35	89.43	89.29	89.37	+ .15	10.63	− .15	2,206
June	89.29	89.30	89.21	89.25	+ .20	10.75	− .20	900
Sept	89.16	89.17	89.13	89.13	+ .08	10.87	− .08	480
Dec	89.09	89.10	89.05	89.05	+ .05	10.95	− .05	84

Est vol 18,223; vol Thu 17,203; open int 39,238, +771.

CBT: Chicago Board of Trade
NYFE: New York Stock Exchange Futures Market
IMM: International Monetary Market
SOURCE: Wall Street Journal

$100,000 contract). From past experience, he decides this 26/32nds difference is out of line and will narrow. He sells September and buys June.

He's right: Three weeks later, the price of the September contract is 81 8/32nds but the June contract is way up to 80 24/32nds. At this point, the September contract (which he sold and must deliver at 81 5/32nds) shows a loss of 3/32nds ($93.75) and the June contract (which he bought at 80 11/32nds) has a profit of 13/32nds ($406.25). He closes out both positions for a gain of $312.50, not counting commissions ($406.25 minus $93.75).

For Ginnie Maes and U.S. Treasury bonds, the quotations are in 32nds of 100. For the September Ginnie Maes, the opening price of 68–08 means $680.25 for each $1,000 face value contract with an 8% yield.

For Treasury bills, the quotations are in points of 100%. The December bills closed at 89.05 or $890.50.

The yields are yields to maturity. Thus, the September 1983 Ginnie Maes, with an opening price of 68–08, had a current yield of 11.76% (8% divided by $680.25) but, when appreciation is added, the yield to maturity, at the slightly higher settlement price, is 13.523%.

T-bills are sold at a discount representing the yield at issue. Thus, for the June bills, last sold at 88.84, the yield/discount is 11.16%.

"Open-High-Low" are self-explanatory. "Settlement" is the last price at which the last transaction took place. It includes the price plus accrued interest.

The "change" columns show the differences from the previous trading day's close: in the 5th column, the price; in the 7th, the yield.

"Open interest" reports the number of outstanding contracts at the end of the day.

Lack of Safeguards

At the risk of being boring, let me re-emphasize some of the dangers of trading financial futures (and, of course, all commodities). For the amateur, as pointed out in *Forbes* magazine, these markets lack many of the safeguards of stocks and bonds:

• **No ban on inside information.** With stocks, executives and brokers who use inside information to anticipate or cause stock movements are subject to severe penalties and even jail. Futures traders have no such restraints.

• **Limited public disclosure.** Investors who own 5% or more of a company's stock must publicly disclose their holdings. Large commodity traders do have to inform the Commodity Futures Trading Commission and the exchanges but that's of little use to small speculators.

• **Stock orders must be processed when received.** Futures traders can place orders for their own accounts and the public at the same time. This can create a conflict of interest and, possibly, force amateurs to pay too much or receive too little.

• **The pooled funds, sponsored by brokerage firms, can influence the market.** For small investors, the big advantage is a negative one: that they can lose no more than the money actually put into the funds.

• **No screening of customers.** With the tiny margins, anyone can get into the game and, with minimal governmental regulation, can be persuaded by commission-hungry brokers to get in over his/her head.

But not everything is stacked against the individual: the New York Futures Exchange offers SPRINT, a computer simulation that uses actual trading data and prices for a theoretical $250,000 paper account. Each day, it shows what your decisions have netted or lost.

Competing with Professionals in Hedging

Too few amateurs understand all of the risks of speculating in financial futures. There are important variables which are utilized by professionals. Here are some cited by Ben Weberman in *Forbes*:

• *Basis.* This is the difference in price or yield between the closest delivery month of a Treasury bill, Treasury bond or Ginnie Mae futures contract and the present cash market price of that same instrument.

Let's say that you want to hedge a position in T-bonds. What could happen is that the cash market drops 1½ points while the futures market falls only one point. That's a half a point against you. With a hedge where you bought $100,000 in bonds and sold a $100,000 futures contract, you would have lost $15,000 on the bonds you owned and earned back $10,000 on the short sale of the futures contract.

• *Cheapest to deliver.* All sellers have the right to deliver those securities that are "cheapest to deliver" from a pool of securities. For bonds, the maturity must be at least 15 years. Usually, the highest-interest-rate, longest-maturity Treasury bond is the cheapest to deliver. By the same token, the highest coupon rate on outstanding GNMA pools should be the cheapest to deliver. Here's what this means:

On August 28, 1980, the September 1980 GNMA futures contract closed at 70 6/32nds with a yield equivalent of 13.104%. At the same time, the 8% GNMA certificates in the cash market closed at 75, a yield of 12.08%.

Why should the 8% futures trade at a higher yield than the cash contract? Because the price of the futures market was not set by the 8% pool but by the 12½% pool.

• *Cost of financing a cash position.* When the annual cost of carrying an 11% Treasury note (assuming almost full value loan) is 10%, there's a positive carry of 1%. But at a 12% cost, there would be a negative carry of 1%. That can make a big difference in the ultimate profit. The professional understands these extra risks and trades accordingly. Too often, however, the amateur does not know, or understand, such important variables.

Follow Strict Rules

If you have money you can afford to lose, time enough to keep abreast of developments, strong nerves and a trustworthy, knowledgeable broker, trading in financial futures may be rewarding, and surely will be exciting. But follow these rules:

• Make dry runs on paper for several months. Pick different types of futures contracts each week and keep practicing until you get a feel of the market and risk and can chalk up more winners than losers.

• Buy long when you look for a drop in interest rates. With lower yields, the prices of the contracts will rise.

• Sell short when you expect a higher cost of money. This will force down the value of the contracts and you can cover your position at a profit.

• Set a strategy and stick to it. Don't try to mix contracts until you feel comfortable and are making money.

• Set stop and limits orders, not market orders. A market order is executed immediately at the best possible price. A stop order, to buy or sell at a given price, becomes a market order when that price is touched. A limit order is the maximum price at which to buy and the minimum at which to sell.

• Buy a rabbit's foot. Even the best traders guess wrong. No matter how intense your research, there will always be unexpected changes resulting from political or economic decisions or actions in the U.S. and abroad.

CHAPTER 35

Abbreviations, Averages and Glossary

In keeping with the Wall Street custom, initials are used frequently in *Your Investments*. Here are some of the more important:

Exchanges

NYSE: New York Stock Exchange. This is the major auction market for common stocks and corporate bonds.

AMEX: American Stock Exchange. This lists stocks of companies with fewer shareholders and smaller capital than those on the NYSE. Generally, the stocks are more speculative.

BOS: Boston Stock Exchange.
MID: Midwest Stock Exchange.
MSE: Montreal Stock Exchange.
PE: Philadelphia Stock Exchange. Formerly the Philadelphia-Baltimore-Washington Exchange. This lists a number of common stocks and a limited number of options.
TSE: Toronto Stock Exchange.
PSE: Pacific Stock Exchange: stocks and options.

OTC: Over-the-counter. This is the market for securities that are not listed on major exchanges. The trading is conducted by dealers who are members of the NASD and who may or may not be members of securities exchanges. Trading is bid and asked. Many firms make markets in certain stocks.

NASD: National Association of Securities Dealers. An association of brokers and dealers in OTC securities.

CBOE: Chicago Board of Options Exchange. The first auction market for calls and puts, primarily on NYSE stocks.

AMEX: Options Exchange. The division of AMEX which trades options, almost entirely on NYSE-listed stocks.

CBT: Chicago Board of Trade. A major market for futures contracts: commodities, interest-rate-sensitive securities, commercial paper, etc.

CME: Chicago Mercantile Exchange. Futures contracts in a wide list of commodities and, through IMM (International Monetary Market), of futures in T-bills,

gold, silver, copper and foreign currencies.

COMEX (formerly New York Commodity Exchange). Futures in a limited number of commodities and futures.

New York Cotton Exchange. Trading in futures in cotton, liquefied propane, citrus, etc.

Federal Agencies

SEC: Securities and Exchange Commission. A Federal agency established to help protect investors. It is responsible for administering Congressional acts regarding securities, stock exchanges, corporate reporting, investment companies, investment advisers and public utility holding companies.

FRB: Federal Reserve Board. The Federal agency responsible for control of such important investment items as the discount rate, money supply, margin requirements.

FDIC: Federal Deposit Insurance Corporation. An agency which provides insurance of bank deposits.

FSLIC: Federal Savings and Loan Insurance Corporation. A similar insurance-of-deposits agency for savings and loan associations.

CFTC: Commodity Futures Trading Commission. This is a watchdog for the commodities futures trading industry.

Stock-Market Averages

DJIA: Dow Jones Industrial Average. The oldest and most widely used stock-market average. This shows the market action of the stocks of 30 major corporations on a weighted basis: i.e., American Brands, at 75, carries three times as much impact as Woolworth at 25.

In recent years, the composition of the stocks has been changed to reflect the growing scientific and international thrust of American business. In 1976, Minnesota Mining & Manufacturing replaced Anaconda Co., which was acquired by Atlantic-Richfield, and in June 1979, International Business Machines and Merck & Co., Inc., were substituted for Chrysler Corp. and Esmark Inc.

As a result, the DJIA is slightly more indicative of what's happening in the overall stock market, but in recent years, with emphasis on energy-related stocks, it has not fully reflected investor sentiment.

The average is determined by dividing the closing prices of the 30 stocks by a divisor that compensates for past stock splits and stock dividends. In mid 1981, it was 1.388.

Dow Jones Transportation Average. This is made up of the stocks of 18 major transportation companies: airlines, railroads, trucking firms, and a freight forwarder. In recent years, changes have been made to make the average more relevant: Missouri Pacific Corporation has replaced the bankrupt Penn-Central, and Transway International is the new name for U.S. Freight. The recent divisor was 2.062.

Dow Jones Utilities Average. This consists of 15 major utilities to provide geographic representation. With more utilities forming holding companies to engage in oil and gas exploration and production, its value is greatest as a point of reference. The recent divisor was 3.427.

STOCKS IN DOW JONES AVERAGES

INDUSTRIALS (DJIA)

Allied Chemical	International Harvester
Aluminum Company	International Paper
American Brands	Johns-Manville
American Can	Merck & Co.
American Tel. & Tel.	Minnesota, Mining & Mfg.
Bethlehem Steel	Owens-Illinois
Dupont, E.I.	Procter & Gamble
Eastman Kodak	Sears, Roebuck
Exxon Corporation	Standard Oil (Calif.)
General Electric	Texaco, Inc.
General Foods	Union Carbide
General Motors	United Technologies
Goodyear Tire	U.S. Steel
Inco, Ltd.	Westinghouse Electric
International Business Machine	Woolworth (F.W.)

TRANSPORTATION (DJTA)

American Airlines	Northwest Airlines
Burlington Northern	Overnite Transportation
Canadian Pacific	Pan-American World Airways
Consolidated Freightways	Santa Fe Industries
CSX Corporation	Southern Pacific
Delta Airlines	Southern Railway
Eastern Airlines	Transway International
McLean Trucking Co.	Trans-World
MoPac Corporation	UAL, Inc.
Norfolk & Western	Union Pacific

UTILITIES (DJUA)

American Electric Power	Niagara Mohawk Power
Cleveland Electric	Pacific Gas & Electric
Columbia Gas System	Panhandle Eastern Pipe
Commonwealth Edison	Peoples Energy
Consolidated Edison	Philadelphia Electric
Consolidated Natural Gas	Public Service E & G
Detroit Edison	So. California Edison
Houston Industries	

S & P Index: Standard & Poor's Stock Price Index. This is made up of the stock-market action of 500 major corporations: 425 industrials; 20 railroads; 55 utilities. All are NYSE-listed companies. The S & P 425 industrials are also used as an index.

NYSE Common Stock Index. A composite index covering price movements of all common stocks listed on the Big Board. It is based on the close of the market December 31, 1965, and is weighted according to the number of shares listed for each issue. Point changes are converted to dollars and cents to provide a meaningful measure of price action.

Dow Jones Bond Average. This consists of bonds of 10 public utilities and 10 industrial corporations.

Dow Jones Municipal Bond Yield Average. This is a changing average but, basically, shows the yields of low-coupon bonds in five states and 15 major cities.

Glossary

Accrued Interest. The amount accumulated since the last payment. It is included in the sale price of a bond.

Amortize. To provide for the gradual reduction of an obligation. With debt, to pay part of the principal semi-annually; with a mortgage, monthly.

Bearer Certificate. A security not registered in the owner's name. It can be sold without endorsement, so it should be kept in a safe place.

BV: book value. An accounting term; the net worth (assets minus liabilities) of a corporation with respect to common stockholders. To obtain the BV per common share, divide the net assets by the number of common shares outstanding.

Call. (1) The date on which all or part of a bond issue may be redeemed by the issuing corporation, under definite conditions, before maturity; (2) an option to buy a specific stock at a specific price within a fixed period of time.

Capital Gain. The profit from the sale of a capital asset, such as a security or real estate. A capital gain acquired in less than 12 months is short-term and taxed at the full Federal income tax rate. A long-term capital gain, on property held for more than one year, is subject to a lower tax rate. Currently, the tax applies to only 40% of the long-term profit but this may be changed by Congress.

Capital Loss. The loss from the sale of a capital asset, such as a security or real estate. All capital losses are tax-deductible to some degree.

Commodity Future. A contract for the delivery of a commodity in a stated future month—unless the contract is liquidated earlier. It is the basis for trading in many farm products, metals, and money market instruments.

CV: convertible. A bond (debenture) or preferred stock which may be exchanged, by the owner, for common stock or another security, usually of the same company, in accordance with terms set forth at issue.

Depreciation. Normally, an amount charged against earnings to write off the cost, less salvage value, of an asset over its estimated useful life. It is a bookkeeping entry and does not represent any cash outlay or any funds earmarked for that purpose.

Discount. The amount by which a preferred stock or bond may sell below its par value. Used as a verb, *to discount* means *to take into account:* for example, the price of the stock *has discounted* the expected dividend cut.

Earned Growth Rate (EGR). The compound annual rate at which the company has been increasing its per share equity capital through reinvested earnings after the dividend payout.

Earned Surplus. A company's net income after it pays dividends; the profits plowed back into the business. It is shown as a cumulative figure on the corporate balance sheet.

Employee Retirement Income Security Act (ERISA). The law that controls all private retirement plans. It sets rules and regulations for prudent investing, the vesting of benefits, and reporting to IRS and the Department of Labor.

Equity. The ownership interest of common and preferred stockholders in a company. It also refers to the excess of the value of securities over the debit balance in a margin account.

Ex-Dividend. "Without dividend." The owner of a stock so listed does not receive the recently declared but not-yet-distributed dividend.

Face Value. The value that appears on the face of a bond, unless the value is otherwise specified by the issuing company. Face value is ordinarily the amount the issuing company promises to pay at maturity. It is not an indication of market value.

Fiscal Year. The accounting period of 12 months that usually differs from the calendar year.

Futures Contract. A transferable agreement to make or take delivery of a standardized amount of a commodity/certificate/security at a specified future price: on a certain day or within a month. It is traded under standardized terms with prices determined by open bidding. The trade may be offset by an opposite trade.

Hedge. The technique used to protect oneself against financial loss, e.g. counterbalancing the purchase of one security/certificate/commodity future by buying another that is likely to move in the opposite direction or fluctuate to a different degree.

Index. A measure or average of prices of stocks or bonds traded on an exchange or of securities in a group or industry.

Investment Company. The term applies to organizations that sell shares to the public and invest the proceeds in securities. In Wall Street jargon, these are called "mutual funds," although actually this applies only to open-end funds.

Load. The portion of the purchasing price of shares of mutual funds that covers sales commissions. It is deducted from the amount of the investment so that not all of the savings are invested.

Long. Ownership of securities/commodities/contracts. Being long 100 shares means that you own 100 shares of stock. With futures contracts, it is the market position of the buyer whose purchase obligates him to accept and pay for the contract.

Margin. The amount paid by the customer when he uses his broker's credit to buy a security. Under Federal Reserve regulations, the initial margin required in the past 25 years has ranged from 100% to 50% of the purchase price of the security.

Market Maker. A broker or dealer who is ready to buy or sell securities of a certain company that, usually, is not listed on a stock exchange.

Municipal Bond. A bond issued by a state or a political subdivision (such as a county, city, town or village). The term also designates bonds issued by governmental agencies and authorities. In general, the interest paid on municipal bonds is exempt from federal income taxes and state and local income taxes within the state of issue.

Negotiable Security. A security whose title is transferable upon delivery.

Net Asset Value. The net worth, based on the closing market prices, of all securities owned by an investment company when divided by the number of fund shares outstanding. With mutual funds, this is the price you pay when you buy (without commission) and that which you receive when you sell.

Net Change. The price difference of a security from its closing price on the previous trading day. In the daily listing of stock transactions, this is usually the last figure on the right side of the table. The figure −½ means that the value of each share dropped 50¢.

Odd Lot. An amount of stock less than the established 100-share unit. Odd-lot prices may be 12½¢ a share more.

Par. On a common stock, the dollar amount assigned to the share by the company's charter.

Par value may be used to compute the dollar amount of the common shares on the balance sheet. It has little relation to the market value of a stock. Many corporations issue no-par stock, then assign a stated per share value on the balance sheet.

Par value is important on preferred stocks and bonds: it often signifies the dollar value upon which dividends or interest is figured. Thus, an 8% bond will pay 8% of the par value (normally $1,000).

Point. For a stock, $1 a share. For a bond, $10 per unit, since the price of a bond is quoted as a percentage of each $1,000 of face value. With a market average, it is one unit of change. On a mortgage, it is an extra charge, to the borrower, equal to 1% of the loan.

P/D: price/dividend ratio. The price of a share of common stock divided by the dividend per share for a 12-month period. *Example:* a stock selling at 20 and paying a dividend of $1 would have a P/D of 20.

P/E: price/earnings ratio. The price of a share of common stock divided by earnings per share for a 12-month period. *Example:* a stock selling for $50 per share, with earnings of $5 per share, has a P/E ratio of 10.

Profit Rate (PR). This is the percentage profit returned on stockholders' equity. It is usually cited on an annual basis and per share book value.

Prudent-Man Rule. A retirement plan investment standard that must be followed under ERISA. Generally, it refers to securities/property that would be purchased by a prudent person of discretion and intelligence who is seeking reasonable income and preservation of capital.

Put. An option to sell a specific stock at a specific price within a fixed period of time. The opposite of a call.

Record Date. The date on which you must be registered as a shareholder on a company's books in order to receive a declared dividend or, among other things, to vote on company affairs.

Redemption Price. The price at which a bond may be redeemed before maturity, at the option of the issuing company. Redemption value also applies to the price the company must pay to call in certain types of preferred stock.

Registered Bond. A bond registered on the books of the issuing corporation in the name of the owner. It is safer than a bearer bond because it can be transferred only when endorsed by the registered owner or his/her representative.

Regulation T. The federal regulation governing the amount of credit which may be advanced by brokers and dealers to customers for the purchase of securities.

Regulation U. The federal regulation governing the amount of credit which may be advanced by a bank to its customers for the purchase of listed stocks.

REIT: real estate investment trust. An organization similar to an investment company in some respects in that its funds are the result of purchase of shares by investors. Monies are concentrated in real estate investments.

Reward/Risk Ratio. Possible gain versus possible loss. If an investor/speculator thinks a stock, now at 10, can either rise to 20 or fall to 5, the reward/risk ratio is up 10, down 5, or 2:1.

Right. Allows shareholders to buy new securities below market price in proportion to the number of shares owned. Rights have a market value separate from that of the stock and, in some issues, are actively traded.

Round Lot. A unit of trading or a multiple thereof. On the NYSE, the unit of trading is generally 100 shares for stocks, and $1,000 par value for bonds. In some inactive stocks, the unit of trading is 10 shares.

Serial Bonds. Debt securities with the same issue date but different maturities extended over many years.

Short. When you sell securities/contracts you do not own in anticipation of purchasing them at a lower price in the near future. Opposite of long.

Sinking Fund. Money regularly set aside by a corporation or government to redeem its bonds, debentures, or preferred stocks. The mark of a superior debt issue.

Spread. The purchase of one security/option/contract against the sale of another in the same or related market. The speculator anticipates that the difference in prices will change sufficiently to make the trade profitable.

Stockholder of Record. A shareholder whose name is registered on the books of the issuing corporation.

Tax Shelter. An investment vehicle in which certain expenses can be offset against regular income or in which the taxes on income normally subject to taxation are deferred.

Tender. An offer to buy stock to gain control of a corporation. Usually, the bid is higher than the current market price and often leads to competitive bidding by others also interested in acquiring the company.

Turnover. (1) The volume of business in a security or of the entire market. If daily turnover on the NYSE is reported at 40 million, it means that 40 million shares changed hands. (2) When used with portfolios, it indicates the percent of holdings that were bought and sold during a year. Anything over a 50% turnover is considered high and, generally, speculative.

Underwriter. A broker or investment banker who acts as middleman between the corporation seeking funds and investors.

Yield. The dividends/interest paid by a company expressed as a percentage of the current price. A stock selling at 12 with a dividend of $1.20 per share would yield 10%.

Bibliography

Basic Background

Amling, Frederick. *Investments.* Englewood Cliffs, N.J.: Prentice-Hall, 1978.

Andersen, Ian. *Making Money.* New York: Vanguard, 1978.

Anderson, Frank R. *Quality Controlled Investing.* New York: Wiley, 1978.

Appel, Gerald and Hitscher, Fred. *Stock Market Trading Systems.* Homewood, Ill.: Dow Jones–Irwin, 1980.

Barnes, Leo and Feldman, Stephen. *Handbook of Wealth Management.* New York: McGraw-Hill, 1977.

Bellemore, Douglas H. and Ritchie, John C. *Investments: Principles, Practice and Analysis.* Cincinnati: SW Publishing, 1974.

Blackman, Richard. *Follow the Leaders.* New York: Cornerstone Press, 1979.

Blotnick, Srully. *Winning: The Psychology of Successful Investing.* New York: McGraw-Hill, 1978.

Branch, Ben. *Fundamentals of Investing.* New York: Wiley, 1976.

Bridwell, Rodger W. *The Battle for Financial Security.* New York: Times Books, 1980.

Casey, Douglas R. *Crisis Investing.* New York: Harper & Row, 1981.

Christy, George A. et al. *Introduction to Investments.* New York: McGraw-Hill, 1977.

Clasing, Henry K. and Rudd, Andrew. *Modern Portfolio Theory.* Homewood, Ill.: Dow Jones–Irwin, 1981.

Cobleigh, Ira. *Double Your Dollars.* New York: Crown, 1979.

Cobleigh, Ira and Dorfman, Bruce. *The Dowbeaters.* New York: Macmillan, 1979.

Cohen, Jerome B. et al. *Guide to Intelligent Investing.* Homewood, Ill.: Dow Jones–Irwin, 1977.

Craig, Gary H. *Unscrewing the Small Investor.* New York: Van Nostrand Reinhold, 1976.

Crane, Burton. *The Sophisticated Investor.* New York: Simon & Schuster, 1964.

Crowell, Richard A. *Stock Market Strategy*. New York: McGraw-Hill, 1977.

Curley, Anthony J. and Bear, Robert M. *Investment Analysis and Management*. New York: Harper & Row, 1979.

D'Ambrosio, Charles D. *Principles of Modern Investments*. Princeton, N.J.: Science Press, 1976.

Dirks, Ray. *Heads You Win; Tails You Win*. New York: Bantam Books, 1980.

Dougall, Herbert E. and Corrigan, Francis J. *Investments*. Englewood Cliffs, N.J.: Prentice-Hall, 1978.

Dreman, David N. *Contrarian Investment Strategy*. New York: Random House, 1980.

Eder, George J. *What's Behind Inflation and How to Beat It*. Englewood Cliffs, N.J.: Prentice-Hall, 1979.

Elton, E. J. and Gruber, M. J. *Modern Portfolio Theory*. New York: Wiley, 1981.

Emory, Eric S. *When to Sell Stocks*. New York: Exposition Press, 1980.

Engel, Louis. *How to Buy Stocks*. New York: Bantam Books, 1977.

Farrell, M. L. et al. *Dow Jones Investors' Handbook*. Homewood, Ill.: Dow Jones–Irwin, 1980.

Findlay, M. C. and Williams, Edward E. *Investment Analysis*. Englewood Cliffs, N.J.: Prentice-Hall, 1974.

Fischer, Donald E. and Jordan, Ronald J. *Security Analysis and Portfolio Management*. Englewood Cliffs, N.J.: Prentice-Hall, 1979.

Fisher, Philip A. *Conservative Investors Sleep Well*. New York: Harper & Row, 1975.

Francis, Clark and Archer, Stephen H. *Portfolio Analysis*. Englewood Cliffs, N.J.: Prentice-Hall, 1979.

Goldberg, Richard H. *Planting Your Money Tree*. New York: Chatham Square, 1977.

Graham, Benjamin. *The Intelligent Investor*. New York: Harper & Row, 1973.

———— et al. *Security Analysis*. New York: McGraw-Hill, 1962.

Hagin, Robert. *The Dow Jones–Irwin Guide to Modern Portfolio Theory*. Homewood, Ill.: Dow Jones–Irwin, 1980.

Heller, Robert. *The Naked Investor*. New York: Delacorte, 1977.

Johnson, Timothy E. *Investment Principles*. Englewood Cliffs, N.J.: Prentice-Hall, 1978.

Jones, Charles P. et al. *Essentials of Modern Investments*. New York: Wiley, 1977.

King, David and Levine, Karen. *The Best Way in the World for a Woman to Make Money*. New York: Rawson, Wade, 1980.

Lasry, George. *Valuing Common Stock*. New York: AMACOM, 1980.

Latane, Henry A. et al. *Security Analysis and Portfolio Management*. New York: Wiley, 1975.

LeBaron, Dean. *The Ins and Outs of Institutional Investing*. Chicago: Nelson-Hall, 1976.

Levine, Sumner N. et al. *Investment Manager's Handbook*. Homewood, Ill.: Dow Jones–Irwin, 1980.

————. *Financial Analyst's Handbook*. Homewood, Ill.: Dow Jones–Irwin, 1980.

Levitt, Arthur, Jr. *How to Make Your Money Make Money*. Homewood, Ill. Dow Jones–Irwin, 1981.

Loeb, Gerald M. *The Battle for Investment Survival*. New York: Simon & Schuster, 1965.

————. *The Battle for Stock Market Profits*. New York: Simon & Schuster, 1971.

Love, Richard S. and Husted, Darnell. *Superperformance Stocks*. Englewood Cliffs, N.J.: Prentice-Hall, 1977.

Mader, Chris and Hagin, Robert. *Dow Jones–Irwin Guide to Common Stocks*. Homewood, Ill.: Dow Jones–Irwin, 1980.

Malkiel, Burton G. *A Random Walk Down Wall Street*. New York: Norton, 1973.

————. *The Inflation Beater's Investment Guide*. New York: Norton, 1980.

Mamis, Justin and Robert. *When to Sell*. New York: Farrar, Straus & Giroux, 1977.

Meltzer, Yale. *Putting Money to Work*. Englewood Cliffs, N.J.: Prentice-Hall, 1976.

Mendelson, Morris and Robbins, Sidney. *Investment Analysis and Securities Markets*. New York: Basic Books, 1976.

Nauheim, Fred. *Move Your Assets to Beat Inflation*. Englewood Cliffs, N.J.: Prentice-Hall, 1980.

Nelson, Paula. *The Joy of Money*. New York: Bantam Books, 1977.

Noddings, Thomas C. *Advanced Investment Strategies*. Homewood, Ill.: Dow Jones–Irwin, 1978.

Randle, Paul A. and Swensen, Philip R. *Managing Your Money*. Belmont, Calif.: Wadsworth, Inc., 1979.

Righetti, Raymond R. *Stock Market Strategy*. Chicago: Nelson-Hall, 1980.

Rogers, Mary, Joyce and Nancy. *Women and Money*. New York: McGraw-Hill, 1978.

Rosenberg, Claude N. *The Common Sense Way to Stock Market Profits*. New York: New American Library, 1978.

Rukeyser, Louis. *How to Make Money in Wall Street*. Garden City, N.Y.: Doubleday, 1974.

Rush, Richard H. *Investments You Can Live with and Enjoy*. Washington, D.C.: U.S. News & World Report, 1976.

Rutberg, Sidney. *The Money Balloon*. New York: Simon & Schuster, 1975.

Sargent, David R. *Stock Market Profits and Higher Income for You*. New York: Simon & Schuster, 1978.

Schneider, Bernard. *Your Money—Going or Growing?* Minneapolis: Finney Publishing, 1978.

Sharpe, William F. *Investments*. Englewood Cliffs, N.J.: Prentice-Hall, 1978.

Shulman, Morton. *How to Invest Your Money and Profit from Inflation*. New York: Random House, 1980.

Smith, Adam. *Paper Money*. New York: Summit Books, 1981.

Smith, Thurman L. *Investors Can Beat Inflation*. New York: Liberty Publishing, 1980.

Sokoloff, Kiril. *The Thinking Investor's Guide to the Stock Market*. New York: McGraw-Hill, 1978.

————. *Paine Webber Handbook of Stock and Bond Analysis*. New York: McGraw-Hill, 1979.

Sprinkel, Beryl W. and Genetski, Robert J. *Winning with Money*. Homewood, Ill.: Dow Jones–Irwin, 1977.

Stein, Ben and Herbert. *Moneypower: How to Profit from Inflation*. New York: Harper & Row, 1980.

Stigum, Marcia. *The Money Market.* Homewood, Ill.: Dow Jones–Irwin, 1978.

Tobias, Andrew. *The Funny Money Game.* Chicago: Playboy Press, 1978.

_____. *The Only Investment Guide You'll Ever Need.* New York: Bantam Books, 1979.

Tracy, John A. *How to Read a Financial Report.* New York: Wiley, 1979.

Train, John. *The Dance of the Money Bees.* New York: Harper & Row, 1974.

_____. *The Money Masters.* New York: Harper & Row, 1980.

Tucille, Jerome. *Everything the Beginner Needs to Know to Invest Shrewdly.* New Rochelle, N.Y.: Arlington House, 1978.

_____. *The Optimist's Guide to Making Money in the 1980s.* New Rochelle, N.Y.: Arlington House, 1979.

_____. *Mind Over Money.* New York: Morrow, 1980.

Van Caspel, Venita. *The New Money Dynamics.* Englewood Cliffs, N.J.: Reston, 1980.

Whitman, Martin and Shubik, Martin. *The Aggressive Conservative Investor.* New York: Random House, 1979.

Widicus, Wilbur W. and Stitzel, Thomas E. *Personal Investing.* Homewood, Ill.: Dow Jones–Irwin, 1980.

Williams, Arthur. *Managing Your Investments.* Homewood, Ill.: Dow Jones–Irwin, 1980.

Wuliger, Betty S. *Dollars and Sense.* New York: Random House, 1976.

Zahorchak, Michael G. *The Art of Low Risk Investing.* New York: Van Nostrand Reinhold, 1977.

Zarb, Frank G. and Kerkes, Gabriel T. et al. *The Stock Market Handbook.* Homewood, Ill.: Dow Jones–Irwin, 1976.

_____, and Fabozzi, Frank J. *Handbook of Financial Markets.* Homewood, Ill.: Dow Jones–Irwin, 1981.

Technical Analysis

Abrams, Don. *The Profit Taker.* New York: Wiley, 1980.

Edwards, Robert D. and Magee, John. *Technical Analysis of Stock Trends.* Springfield, Mass.: John Magee & Associates, 1976.

Fosback, Norman G. *Stock Market Logic.* Fort Lauderdale, Fla.: Institute for Econometric Research, 1976.

Frost, A. J. and Prechter, Robert. *Elliott Wave Principle.* New York: New Classics, 1980.

George, Wilfred R. *The Profit Box System of Forecasting Stock Prices.* Homewood, Ill.: Dow Jones–Irwin, 1978.

Granville, Joseph E. *New Strategy of Daily Stock Market Timing for Maximum Profits.* Englewood Cliffs, N.J.: Prentice-Hall, 1976.

Hayes, Michael. *Dow Jones–Irwin Guide to Stock Market Cycles.* Homewood, Ill.: Dow Jones–Irwin, 1977.

_____. *Money: How to Get It and Keep It.* New York: AMACOM, 1979.

_____. *Stock Market Forecasting.* New York: AMACOM, 1980.

Holt, Thomas J. *Total Investing.* New Rochelle, N.Y.: Arlington House, 1978.

Jiler, William. *How Charts Can Help You in the Stock Market.* New York: Trendline (Standard & Poor's), 1976.

Pring, Martin J. *Technical Analysis Explained.* New York: McGraw-Hill, 1980.

Thomas, Conrad. *How to Sell Short and Perform Other Wondrous Feats.* Homewood, Ill.: Dow Jones–Irwin, 1976.

Touhey, John C. *Stock Market Forecasting for Alert Investors.* New York: AMACOM, 1980.

Special Securities/Speculations

Ansbacher, Max G. *The New Options Market.* New York: Walker, 1978.

Beckhardt, Israel. *The Small Investor's Guide to Gold.* New York: Manor Books, 1979.

Beckner, Steven K. *The Hard Money Book.* New York: Dutton, 1980.

Bernstein, Jacob. *The Investor's Quotient: Psychology of Successful Investing.* New York: Wiley, 1980.

Bookbinder, Albert. *Security Options Strategy.* Houston: Progressive Publishing, 1976.

Browne, Harry. *You Can Profit from the Monetary Crisis.* New York: Macmillan, 1979.

_____. *Inflation-Proofing Your Investments.* New York: Morrow, 1980.

Clasing, Henry F. *The Dow Jones–Irwin Guide to Put and Call Options.* Homewood, Ill.: Dow Jones–Irwin, 1980.

Dames, Ralph. *The Winning Option.* Chicago: Nelson-Hall, 1980.

Darst, David M. *The Complete Bond Book.* New York: McGraw-Hill, 1980.

Dickson, David T. *Tax Shelters for the Not-So-Rich.* New York: Contemporary, 1980.

Drollinger, William C. *Tax Shelters and Tax-Free Income.* Orchard Lake, Mich.: Epic Press, 1979.

Fischer, Robert. *Stock or Options?* New York: Wiley, 1980.

Freedman, Michael. *The Diamond Book.* Homewood, Ill.: Dow Jones–Irwin, 1981.

Fried, Sidney. *Investing and Speculating with Convertibles.* New York: Crown, 1976.

_____. *Speculating with Warrants.* New York: Crown, 1972.

Gastineau, Gary L. *The Stock Options Manual.* New York: McGraw-Hill, 1979.

Gaylord, Sherwood B. *Sensible Speculating with Put and Call Options.* New York: Simon & Schuster, 1976.

Grushcow, Jack and Smith, Courtney. *Profits Through Seasonal Trading.* New York: Wiley, 1980.

Hamilton, Harper. *Tax Shelters for Everybody.* New York: Stein & Day, 1978.

Hardy, C. Colburn. *ABCs of Investing Your Retirement Funds.* Oradell, N.J.: Medical Economics, 1982.

Herzfeld, Thomas J. *The Herzfeld Hedge.* New York: McGraw-Hill, 1979.

Homer, Sidney. *The Great American Bond Market.* Homewood, Ill.: Dow Jones–Irwin, 1978.

Kinsman, Robert. *Guide to Tax Havens.* Homewood, Ill.: Dow Jones–Irwin, 1979.

Klein, Howard J. *Fad Money: Fads, Crazes and Trends.* New York: Watts Press, 1979.

Lamb, Robert and Rappaport, Stephen P. *Municipal Bonds.* New York: McGraw-Hill, 1980.

Loosigian, Allan N. *Interest Rate Futures.* Homewood, Ill.: Dow Jones–Irwin, 1981.

McMillan, Lawrence G. *Options as a Strategic Investment.* Englewood Cliffs, N.J.: Prentice-Hall, 1980.

McQuown, Judith. *Tax Shelters That Work.* New York: McGraw-Hill, 1979.

Noddings, Thomas C. *Guide to Convertible Securities.* Homewood, Ill.: Dow Jones–Irwin, 1976.

————. and Zagore, Earl. *CBOE Options.* Homewood, Ill.: Dow Jones–Irwin, 1976.

Ober, Stuart A. *Everybody's Guide to Tax Shelters.* New York: Wyden Books, 1980.

Powers, Mark J. and Vogel, David J. *Inside the Financial Futures Market.* New York: Wiley, 1981.

Prendergast, Lawrence S. *Uncommon Profits Through Stock Purchase Warrants.* Homewood, Ill.: Dow Jones–Irwin, 1973.

Rodolakis, Anthony and Tetrick, Nicholas. *Buying Opportunities: Wall Street on a Shoestring.* New York: McGraw-Hill, 1979.

Rosen, Lawrence R. *When and How to Profit from Buying and Selling Gold.* Homewood, Ill.: Dow Jones–Irwin, 1975.

Rubenstein, Mark and Cox, John C. *Options Markets.* Englewood Cliffs, N.J.: Prentice-Hall, 1980.

Ruff, Howard J. *How to Prosper During Coming Bad Years.* New York: Times Books, 1979.

Schwarz, Edward W. *How to Use Interest Rate Futures Contracts.* Homewood, Ill.: Dow Jones–Irwin, 1980.

Sherwood, Hugh. *How to Invest in Bonds.* New York: McGraw-Hill, 1976.

Simon, Arthur C. *How to Invest in Diamonds, Metals and Collectibles.* New York: Future Press, 1980.

Tannenhauser, Robert and Carol. *Tax Shelters.* New York: New American Library, 1980.

Tso, Lin. *Complete Investor's Guide to Listed Options.* Englewood Cliffs, N.J.: Prentice-Hall, 1980.

Commodities

Angell, George. *Winning in the Commodities Markets.* Garden City, N.Y.: Doubleday, 1979.

Angrist, Stanley W. *Sensible Speculating in Commodities.* New York: Simon & Schuster, 1975.

Gould, Bruce. *Guide to Commodities Trading.* Homewood, Ill.: Dow Jones–Irwin, 1981.

Kaufman, P. J. *Commodity Trading Systems and Methods.* New York: Wiley, 1980.

Prestbo, John A. et al. *The Dow Jones–Irwin Commodities Handbook.* Homewood, Ill.: Dow Jones–Irwin, 1977.

Trend Research Ltd. *New Concepts in Technical Trading Systems.* P.O. Box 450, Greensboro, N.C. 27402

Zieg, Kermit C. and Nix, William E. *The Commodities Options Market.* Homewood, Ill.: Dow Jones–Irwin, 1978.

Information on Investment Companies

Investment Company Institute, 1775 K Street, N.W., Washington, D.C. 20006.

Lipper Analytical Distributors, 74 Trinity Place, New York, NY 10006.

Mutual Funds Almanac, 6 Deer Trail, Old Tappan, NJ 07675.

United Business Services, 210 Newbury Street, Boston MA 02116.

Vickers Associates, 226 New York Avenue, Huntington, NY 11746.

Wiesenberger Services, 870 Seventh Avenue, New York, NY 10019.

Chart Services

Chartcraft, Inc., One West Avenue, Larchmont, NY 10538.

Commodity Research Bureau, 1 Liberty Plaza, New York, NY 10006.

Daily Graphics, William O'Neil & Co., Box 24933, Los Angeles, CA 90024.

M. C. Horsey & Co., 120 South Boulevard, Salisbury, MD 21801.

Harry Lankford, Box 213, Wichita, KS 67201.

R. W. Mansfield Co., 26 Journal Square, Jersey City, NJ 07306.

Securities Research Company, 208 Newbury Street, Boston, MA 02116.

Trendline, Inc., 25 Broadway, New York, NY 10004.

Real Estate

Bagby, Joseph. *Real Estate Financial Desk Book.* Scranton, Pa.: International Business Planning, 1977.

Beaton, William R. *Real Estate Finance.* Englewood Cliffs, N.J.: Prentice-Hall, 1975.

Case, Fred E. *Investing in Real Estate.* Englewood Cliffs, N.J.: Prentice-Hall, 1978.

Goodkin, Sanford R. *Guide to Winning in Real Estate.* New York: David McKay, 1977.

Harney, Kenneth R. *Beating Inflation with Real Estate.* New York: Random House, 1979.

Mader, Chris. *The Dow Jones–Irwin Guide to Real Estate Investing.* Homewood, Ill.: Dow Jones–Irwin, 1978.

Miller, Daniel A. *How to Invest in Real Estate Syndicates.* Homewood, Ill.: Dow Jones–Irwin, 1978.

Nicely, Glen. *How to Reap Riches from Raw Land.* Englewood Cliffs, N.J.: Prentice-Hall, 1974.

Seldin, Maury et al. *The Real Estate Handbook.* Homewood, Ill.: Dow Jones–Irwin, 1980.

Walters, David W. *The Intelligent Investor's Guide to Real Estate.* New York: Wiley, 1981.

Sources of Investment Information

Barron's, 22 Cortlandt Street, New York, NY 10007.

Better Investing, Box 220, Royal Oak, MI 48068.

The Chronicle, 120 Broadway, New York, NY 10005.

Donoghue's MONEYLETTER, Box 416, Holliston, MA 01746.

Executive Wealth Advisory, 589 Fifth Avenue, New York, NY 10017.

Finance, 8 West 40th Street, New York, NY 10018.

Financial Weekly, P.O. Box 26565, Richmond, VA 23261.

Financial World, 919 Third Avenue, New York, NY 10022.

Forbes, 60 Fifth Avenue, New York, NY 10011.

Fortune, Time-Life Building, New York, NY 10020.

Institutional Investor, 488 Madison Avenue, New York, NY 10022.

Investment Dealers' Digest, 150 Broadway, New York, NY 10038.

ML Market Letter, P.O. Box 60, Church Street Station, New York, NY 10008.

Money, 1271 Avenue of the Americas, New York, NY 10020.

The Money Manager, 77 Water Street, New York, NY 10007.

Money Reporter, 509 Madison Avenue, New York, NY 10022.

Value Line, 711 Third Avenue, New York, NY 10017.

The Wall Street Journal, 22 Cortlandt Street, New York, NY 10007.

Wall Street Transcript, 120 Wall Street, New York, NY 10005.

Investment Services and Advisory Reports

Anametrics, Inc., 30 Rockefeller Plaza, New York, NY 10020.

Babson's Reports, Wellesley Hills, MA 02181.

Burns-Kirkpatrick Letter, 49 Riverside Avenue, Westport, CT 06880.

The Cabot Market Letter, Box 1012, Salem, MA 01970.

Commodities, 219 Parkade 506 B, Cedar Falls, IA 50613.

Commodity Research Bureau, 1 Liberty Plaza, New York, NY 10006.

Dines Letter, Box 22, Belvedere, CA 94920.

Dow Forecasts, Box 4550, Grand Central Station, New York, NY 10017.

Dow Theory Letters, Box 1759, La Jolla, CA 92038.

Dunn & Hargitt, Box 620, Lafayette, IN 47902.

Granville Market Letter, Box 58, Holly Hills, FL 32017.

Growth Fund Research, Inc., Ureka, CA 96067.

Growth Stock Outlook, Box 9911, Chevy Chase, MD 20015.

Holt Investory Advisory, 290 Post Road West, Westport, CT 06880.

Indicator Digest, 451 Grand Avenue, Palisades Park, NJ 07650.

International Diamond Corporation, 39 San Pablo Avenue, San Rafael, CA 94903.

International Investor's Viewpoint, 9450 S.W. Commerce Circle, Wilsonville, OR 97070.

Investors' Intelligence, 2 East Avenue, Larchmont, NY 10538.

Janeway Letter, P.O. Box 2121, Memphis, TN 38159.

Johnson Survey (formerly *America's Fastest Growing Companies*), 35 Mason Street, Greenwich, CT 06830.

Lowry's Reports, 350 Royal Palm Way, Palm Beach, FL 33480.

Lynch International Investment Survey, 120 Broadway, New York, NY 10271.

Maratta Advisory Service, 1220 Post Road, Fairfield, CT 06430.

Powell Monetary Analyst, 50 Broad Street, New York, NY 10004.

Professional Tape Reader, Box 2407, Hollywood, FL 33022.

Profitquest, Box 2700, Huntington, CA 92647.

R.H.M. Associates, 417 Northern Blvd., Great Neck, NY 11021.

Silver & Gold Report, P.O. Box 325, Newtown, CT 06470

Smart Money, 6 Deer Trail, Old Tappan, NJ 07675.

Speculative Investor, 120 Wall Street, New York, NY 10005.

Stock Market Timer, P.O. Box 3712, Nashua, NH 03061.

Stock Research Corporation, 50 Broadway, New York, NY 10004.

Switch Fund Advisory, P.O. Box 1454, Rockville, MD 20850.

Trendex Research, 300 Maverick Bldg., San Antonio, TX 73805.

Trendway Advisory Service, P.O. Box 7184, Louisville, KY 40207.

United Business Service, 210 Newbury Street, Boston, MA 02116.

United Philatelics, 355 Lexington Avenue, New York, NY 10017.

Value Line, 711 Third Avenue, New York, NY 10017.

Worden & Worden, Inc., 1915 Floranada Road, Fort Lauderdale, FL 33308.

Zweig Forecast, 747 Third Avenue, New York, NY 10017.

Investment Trading Information

American Stock Exchange, 86 Trinity Place, New York, NY 10006.

Canadian Business Service, Suite 700, 133 Richmond Street, West, Toronto, M5H 3M8 Canada.

Chicago Board Options Exchange, LaSalle at Jackson, Chicago, IL 60604.

Chicago Board of Trade, LaSalle at Jackson, Chicago, IL 60604.

COMEX (Commodity Exchange, Inc.), 4 World Trade Center, New York, NY 10048.

International Monetary Market, 444 West Jackson Boulevard, Chicago, IL 60606.

Moody's Investors Service, 99 Church Street, New York, NY 10005.

NASDAQ (National Association of Securities Dealers), Inc., 1735 K Street N.W., Washington, D.C. 20006.

New York Stock Exchange (NYSE), 11 Wall Street, New York, NY 10005.

Securities and Exchange Commission, 500 North Capitol N.W., Washington, D.C. 20549.

Standard & Poor's, 25 Broadway, New York, NY 10004.

Index

Index of Securities